Entrepreneurial Finance
FOR NEW AND EMERGING BUSINESSES

James McNeill Stancill
University of Southern California

THOMSON
——*——™
SOUTH-WESTERN

Australia · Canada · Mexico · Singapore · Spain · United Kingdom · United States

THOMSON
✳
SOUTH-WESTERN

Entrepreneurial Finance
for New and Emerging Businesses

James McNeill Stancill

Vice President/Editorial Director
Jack Calhoun

Vice President/Editor-in-Chief:
Mike Roche

Executive Editor:
Mike Reynolds

Developmental Editor:
Andy McGuire

Senior Marketing Manager:
Charlie Stutesman

Production Editor:
Cliff Kallemeyn

Media Developmental Editor:
John Barans

Media Production Editor:
Mark Sears

Manufacturing Coordinator:
Sandee Milewski

Designer:
Rik Moore

Project Management/ Composition:
Pre-Press Company, Inc.

Printer:
Phoenix Color Corp.
   Hagerstown, MD

Library of Congress Control Number: 2003104172

ISBN: 0-324-13475-4

Brief Contents

INTRODUCTION *xxvii*

Part 1   **GETTING STARTED, MANAGING PROFIT, AND CASH FLOW** *1*

Chapter 1   **DOING A START-UP** *2*

Chapter 2   **PACKAGING AND FINANCING A START-UP** *21*

Chapter 3   **MANAGING PROFIT AND FINANCIAL STATEMENTS** *50*

Chapter 4   **CASH FLOW ANALYSIS** *76*

Part 2   **GROWING A FIRM—INTERNALLY** *115*

Chapter 5   **GROWING A FIRM: A REVIEW OF FUNDAMENTALS** *116*

Chapter 6   **AN ENTREPRENEURIAL CAPITAL BUDGETING MODEL** *141*

Chapter 7   **CAPITAL STRUCTURE AND LEVERAGE** *163*

Part 3   **FINANCING TOOLS** *183*

Chapter 8   **RAISING FUNDS EXTERNALLY: AN OVERVIEW OF INVESTMENT BANKING** *184*

Chapter 9   **LONG-TERM FINANCING: SWEETENED ISSUES AND INNOVATIONS** *205*

Chapter 10   **INTERMEDIATE-TERM FINANCING: TERM LOANS AND PRIVATE PLACEMENTS** *235*

Chapter 11   **SHORT-TERM FINANCING—INCLUDING EQUIPMENT FINANCING** *252*

Part 4   **L/Cs AND WORKING CAPITAL MANAGEMENT** *277*

Chapter 12   **LETTERS OF CREDIT** *278*

Chapter 13   **CASH MANAGEMENT AND MONEY MARKET SECURITIES** *299*

Chapter 14   **MANAGEMENT OF ACCOUNTS RECEIVABLE** *317*

Part 5   **EXTERNAL EXPANSION: MERGERS AND ACQUISITIONS, INCLUDING DOING A LBO** *335*

Chapter 15   **EXTERNAL EXPANSION: SEARCHING FOR AN ACQUISITION** *336*

Chapter 16   **EXTERNAL EXPANSION: TECHNICAL ASPECTS OF ACQUIRING A FIRM** *362*

Chapter 17   **THE ABLE CASE: DOING A LEVERAGED BUYOUT** *382*

Part 6   **DRESSING UP YOUR COMPANY FOR A BETTER MULTIPLE** *409*

Chapter 18   **MANAGING THE MULTIPLIER AND YOUR COMPANY'S IMAGE** *410*

Epilogue   **VALUATION AND WHAT WE LEARNED FROM THE DOT.COM BUST** *430*

Index   *433*

Contents

PREFACE *xxiii*

INTRODUCTION *xxvii*

Part 1   **GETTING STARTED, MANAGING PROFIT, AND CASH FLOW** *1*

Chapter 1   **DOING A START-UP** *2*

Why Do a Start-Up? *2*

    The Ingredients for Doing a Start-Up *3*

    The Order of Things *3*

Criteria for the Basic Idea *4*

    Form of the Organization *4*

    Basic Profitability *6*

    Market Size: Too Big, Too Little *7*

    Capital Intensity *9*

    A One-Product Firm *11*

    Repeat Orders *vs.* Single Sale *11*

    Capable of an "Out" *12*

    Product Too Simple *13*

    Out of Vogue *14*

    An Understandable Deal *14*

    Recapping the Criteria *15*

Key Person or Management Team *15*

    Evaluating a Key Person *15*

       Conditioning *15*

       Confidence *16*

       Courage *17*

       Competitiveness *17*

Charisma 17

Character 17

The Management Team *19*

Summary *20*

Questions for Discussion *20*

Chapter 2   **PACKAGING AND FINANCING A START-UP** *21*

The Private Placement Memorandum *21*

The Outline *22*

Introduction and Summary 22

The Product 22

Marketing 24

Key Person/Management Team 24

The Financial Summary 26

Sales and Profit Forecast *26*

Implications of the Profitability Statement: How Much Equity to Offer? 26

Dividing the Stock in a High-Tech Deal—Valuation 28

How Much Money Do You Need for a Start-Up? *30*

Sequencing the Financing 31

Running Out of Money 34

The Pro-Forma Financials *35*

Financing with Venture Capital *36*

Types of Venture Capital *37*

Strategies for Finding Start-Up Capital *38*

The Investor Confidence Scale 38

The Role of the Intermediary 39

Summary *42*

Questions for Discussion *43*

Appendix 1: Reflections on the Dot.com Bubble *44*

Appendix 2: Exit Strategies and "Harvesting" *47*

Appendix 3: Illustrative Valuation Model *48*

Chapter 3 **MANAGING PROFIT AND FINANCIAL STATEMENTS** *50*

The Concept of Profit *50*

The Measures of Profitability *51*

Using the DuPont Formula *53*

Managing the Income Statement *54*

Ways to Report Sales *54*

Cost of Goods Sold and Gross Profit *56*

Unethical Aspects of Inventory Valuation *58*

The Practice of Revenue Enhancement *59*

Depreciation Expense *59*

Accelerated Depreciation *59*

Unit Depreciation *60*

Decelerated Depreciation *61*

The Balance Sheet *61*

First Impressions: The Cash Account *62*

Money Market Securities *63*

The Current Portion of Long-Term Debt *63*

The Current Ratio and Liquidation *63*

Priorities of Assets *64*

The General Creditor Ratio *65*

The Debt/Equity Ratio *66*

Two Types of Subordination *67*

Appraisal Surplus *67*

Financial Statements vs. Tax Statements *68*

Types of Financial Statements *68*

The Compiled Statement *68*

The Reviewed Statement *69*

The (Audited) Certified Statement *69*

The Accounting System *70*

Financial Baths and Other Write-offs *70*

A Change of Management *71*

When a Firm Is Reporting a Loss Anyway *71*

When Your Stock Price Is Really Down 72

When the Stock Market Is Strongly Bullish 72

The "Me Too" Circumstance 72

Who Should Prepare Financial Statements? 73

Summary 74

Questions for Discussion 74

Chapter 4 **CASH FLOW ANALYSIS** 76

Why Cash Flow? 76

A Generic Cash Flow Statement 77

Operating Cash Inflows 79

Operating Cash Outflows 79

Priority Outflows 80

Discretionary Outflows 80

Financial Flows 81

Net Change in Cash and Marketable Securities Accounts 81

Evaluating Our Cash Flow Measurement 82

Measures of Cash Flow Under Different Scenarios 82

The Steady Sales Scenario 83

A Manufacturing Company 84

A Wholesale Company 84

A Service Company 84

The Growth Scenario 88

A Manufacturing Company 88

The Hot Buttons: Testing Sensitivities 88

A Wholesale Company 92

Pushing Hot Buttons 92

A Service Company 92

The Recession Scenario *92*

   A Manufacturing Company 96

   A Wholesale and a Service Company 99

Forecasting Cash Flow Components *99*

   Ratio Approach *102*

     Accounts Receivable 102

     Other Income 102

     Cost of Goods Sold 102

     General and Administrative Expense and Selling Expense 103

     Taxes and Accrued Taxes 103

     Inventory 103

     Accounts Payable 104

     Prepaid Expense 104

     The Remaining Items 104

   Forecasting with Regression Analysis *104*

     Accounts Receivable 104

     Cost of Goods Sold 104

     General and Administrative Expense 105

     Selling Expense 106

     Taxes and Accrued Taxes 106

     Inventory 106

     Accounts Payable 106

     Prepaid Expense and Other Items Below NOCF 107

   A Comparison Between the Ratio Approach and Regression Analysis *107*

   Items That Are Not Used *108*

Chapter Summary *109*

Questions for Discussion *110*

Problems *111*

Part 2   **GROWING A FIRM—INTERNALLY** *115*

Chapter 5   **GROWING A FIRM: A REVIEW OF FUNDAMENTALS** *116*

What Is Meant by "Growth"? *116*

Why Grow a Firm? *117*

Desired Growth versus Expected Growth *118*

"More of the Same" *118*

Share Repurchase *119*

Capital Budgeting *120*

The Meaning of Capital Budgeting *120*

Money Available for Capital Budgeting *120*

Criteria for Capital Budgeting *122*

Time Value of Money *122*

Time Shape of Cash Flow *123*

Four Basic Methods of Rationing Capital Budgeting Money *124*

Payback *124*

Average Rate of Return *125*

Net Present Value *126*

Profitability Index *127*

Internal Rate of Return *127*

Calculating the Internal Rate of Return *129*

Summarizing the Four Commonly Used Discriminants *129*

Summary *130*

Questions for Discussion *130*

Appendix: Illustrations of Present Value Formulations *133*

Chapter 6   **AN ENTREPRENEURIAL CAPITAL BUDGETING MODEL** *141*

What Makes an "Entrepreneurial" Model Different? *141*

Getting Started: Format for Comparison *142*

Calculating a Proposal's Internal Rate of Return *143*

Deriving the IRR *144*

Steps in the Computer Model *145*

    Step 1 *145*

      Weighting the Proposals' ERR 145

      The Second Part of the Objective Function 146

    Step 2 *146*

    Step 3 *146*

    Step 4 *148*

    Step 5 *149*

      Deriving the Index of Diffusion 149

      Plotting the Sets 151

      Accuracy of the Estimate 152

Using the Model Without a Computer *152*

    Step 1 *152*

    Step 2 *152*

    Step 3 *153*

    Step 4 *153*

    Step 5 *153*

The Practical Importance of the Model *154*

Decisions in Evaluating Proposals *154*

    The Lease-Buy Decision *155*

    Abandonment Value *155*

    Technological Obsolescence and Development *156*

Summary *157*

Questions for Discussion *157*

Appendix: Alternative Capital Budgeting Models *158*

    The Hertz Model *158*

      The First Stage 158

      The Second Stage 159

      The Third Stage 160

    Weston's CAPM Model *161*

Chapter 7   **CAPITAL STRUCTURE AND LEVERAGE** *163*

What Is Leverage? *163*

Financial Leverage *164*

The Traditional Approach *164*

The Debt/Equity Ratio and the Modigliani and Miller Approach *166*

Cash Flow Approach *168*

Heterogeneity of Debt *168*

   Net Operating Cash Flow Double Prime *169*

Debt-Servicing Capacity Through Simulation *170*

Is There an Optimal Capital Structure? *172*

Operating Leverage *172*

Traditional Cost-Volume-Profit Analysis *172*

Certain Sales vs. Probabilistic Sales *174*

Leverage and Cash Flow *177*

NOCF″ and the Assumed Probability Density Function *178*

Summary *181*

Questions for Discussion *182*

Part 3   **FINANCING TOOLS** *183*

Chapter 8   **RAISING FUNDS EXTERNALLY: AN OVERVIEW OF INVESTMENT BANKING** *184*

Public Offerings vs. Private Offerings *184*

Regulations on Selling Securities *184*

SEC vs. the State Corporations Commission *185*

Private Placement *187*

Public Offerings *188*

Registration of Private Placements *189*

Public Registration of Securities *190*

   The S-1 Registration *190*

   The S-18 Registration *191*

Selecting an Underwriter *192*

    The Organization of the Investment Banking Industry *193*

      Classification by Size 193

      Structure 194

      The Importance of Quality in the Underwriter 195

    The Letter of Commitment *196*

    Firm Commitment vs. Best Offering *196*

    Selling Preparations *197*

Going Public via the Back Door *198*

Summary *202*

Questions for Discussion *203*

Appendix: Types of Exemption *204*

Chapter 9   **LONG-TERM FINANCING: SWEETENED ISSUES AND INNOVATIONS** *205*

Historical Perspective *205*

Convertible Debentures *208*

    The Exercise Price for the Stock in the Convertible *209*

    Convertible Bonds and Arbitrage *210*

Bonds with Warrants *210*

    What Is a Warrant? *210*

    Bonds with Warrants "in the Money" *211*

    Number of Warrants to Place with the Bond *212*

    The Interest Rate Question *213*

    Subordination Feature *214*

Earnings Per Share *215*

Variations in Convertibles and Bonds with Warrants *216*

    Exchangeable Warrants *217*

    Zero Coupon Convertibles *217*

    Claw Back Provisions *218*

    Shadow Warrants *219*

    Calculating the Number of Warrants *220*

Putting Sweeteners and Other Tools in Perspective 221

Securities Innovation 222

    Historical Perspective and Common Stock 222

Modifying Common Stock 225

    A Brief Digression: "Piggy-Back Financing" 225

Preferred Stock 226

    Dichotomizing Preferred Stock 227

    Money Market Preferred 228

    Creating Classes of Stock 228

    Other Uses for Classified Stock 229

    Warning About Terminology 230

Innovative Debt Securities 231

    "Payment in Kind" Securities 231

    Several Other Debt Innovations 232

Chapter Summary 233

Questions for Discussion 233

Chapter 10   **INTERMEDIATE-TERM FINANCING: TERM LOANS AND PRIVATE PLACEMENTS** 235

The Factor of Firm Size 236

Credit Market Characteristics 237

The Evolution of the Credit Market 239

    The Changing Position of Life Insurance Companies 239

    Other Sources of Private Placement 241

Loan Covenants 243

    Affirmative Covenants 243

    Representations and Warranties 243

    Negative Covenants 244

        Cash Flow Control 244

        Control Over Strategy 245

        Balance Sheet Preservation 245

Asset Preservation 246
The Trigger 247

Negotiating a Strategy *248*
Putting Yourself in the Head of the Lender *248*
Devising a Strategy to Confront the Lender *248*

Summary *251*

Questions for Discussion *251*

Chapter 11   **SHORT-TERM FINANCING—INCLUDING EQUIPMENT FINANCING** *252*

The Uniform Commercial Code *252*
The UCC Forms *253*

Bank Loans *254*
The Psychology of Being a Bank's Customer *254*
Retail Banks 254
Wholesale-Oriented Banks 255
Combination Banks 255
Choosing the Right Bankers 256
Building Rapport with Your Banker 257
Signature Loans *258*

Accounts Receivable Pledging *259*
Eligible Receivables *259*
The Case of Service Companies 260
Government Accounts Receivable 260
The Concentration Factor 261
The Diffusion Factor 261
Accounts Receivable Plans *262*

Inventory Financing *263*
Criteria for Borrowing *264*
Other Ways of Financing Inventory *265*

Equipment Financing *265*
Types of Appraisers *266*
Factors That Influence an Appraisal *266*

Borrowing Percentage on Equipment *267*

Cost of Equipment Appraisals *267*

Borrowing from Financing Companies 268

Accounts Receivable Pledging *268*

Accounts Receivable Factoring *269*

Predominant Use in the Garment Industry *269*

Other Features of Factoring *270*

Inventory Pledging *271*

Differences in the Priorities of Finance Companies and Banks *272*

Government Sources of Short-Term Financing *273*

Small Business Administration Financing *273*

The Rural Business-Cooperative Service *274*

The Export-Import Bank *274*

Summary *275*

Questions for Discussion 276

Part 4   L/Cs AND WORKING CAPITAL MANAGEMENT 277

Chapter 12   LETTERS OF CREDIT 278

What Is a Letter of Credit? 279

Types of Letters of Credit 279

The Use of a L/C: An Example from International Trading *280*

Revocable vs. Irrevocable *281*

Documented vs. Clean *282*

Actual vs. Standby *282*

Confirmed vs. Unconfirmed *282*

General Features of the Application for a Letter of Credit 238

General Features of a Letter of Credit 287

Costs of Letters of Credit 289

Domestic Letters of Credit 289

Examples of the Use of Domestic Letters of Credit *289*

Standby Letters of Credit *290*

Advantages of L/Cs *291*

Three Ways to Do Business Without a Substantial
Balance Sheet *291*

"Back-to-Back" Letters of Credit 291

A Transferable Letter of Credit 292

An Assignment of Proceeds 292

Using Letters of Credit with a Revolving Line of Credit *292*

Clean Letters of Credit *293*

Additional Bank Services *295*

Documents on Payment *295*

Documents on Approval *296*

Summary *297*

Questions for Discussion *298*

Chapter 13   **CASH MANAGEMENT AND MONEY MARKET
SECURITIES** *299*

Cash Management *299*

Determining Management's Willingness to Be Overdrawn *300*

Determining the Optimal Amount of Cash *301*

Random Variables 301

Including the Controllable Variables 302

A Picture of Dissynchronization 303

Other Ways of Reducing Undesirable Dissynchronization *304*

Utilizing a Lock Box 304

Playing the Federal Reserve Float 305

Payment with Drafts *306*

Backing Up the Cash Account *306*

Securities Appropriate for the M_o and M_c Account *307*

Commercial Paper *308*

The Development of Commercial Paper 308

An Example for a Developing Firm 310

CDs and Bank Deposit Notes *311*

Banker's Acceptances *311*

Repurchase Agreements *312*

Short-Term Municipal Notes *313*

Money Market Preferreds *314*

Where to Procure Money Market Securities *314*

Summary *316*

Questions for Discussion *316*

Chapter 14   **MANAGEMENT OF ACCOUNTS RECEIVABLE** *317*

Analysis of the Cash Discount *318*

Determinants of Elasticity *318*

Elasticity of the Cash Discount versus Pre-tax Income 320

Elasticity of the Cash Discount versus the Volume of Receivables 321

Elasticity of NOCF versus the Cash Discount 321

A Reduction in the Cash Discount versus Bad Debt Expense 321

The Cash Discount Period *323*

The Role of the Computer *323*

Taking a Discount and Paying Later *323*

The Credit Period *324*

Effect on the Volume of Receivables *326*

Credit Period versus Bad Debt Expense *326*

The Collection Effort *327*

The Variables *327*

Collection Effort versus Sales 327

Collection Effort versus Net Income 328

Collection Effort versus ROA and Rate of Return on Sales 328

Collection Effort versus Bad Debt Expense 329

The Credit-Granting Decision Rule *329*

An Example 330

An Abbreviated Decision Rule 330

Implications of the Model 331

Summary *333*

Questions for Discussion *334*

Part 5   **EXTERNAL EXPANSION: MERGERS AND ACQUISITIONS, INCLUDING DOING A LBO** *335*

Chapter 15   **EXTERNAL EXPANSION: SEARCHING FOR AN ACQUISITION** *336*

How Conglomerates Were Created—A Slight Digression *337*

The Magic of the "Pop in Earnings" *337*

The Key to the Game *338*

Criteria for a LBO *339*

"Hockable Assets" *340*

Low or No Long-Term Debt *341*

Status as an Old Firm *341*

Good, Dependable Cash Flow *342*

Size *343*

Type of Company *344*

Compelling Reason to Sell *344*

No Insurmountable Pollution Problems *345*

Long-Term Future *346*

A Quiet Deal *347*

What Other Criteria Are There? *348*

Finding a LBO Target *348*

Personal Knowledge *348*

Ads in the *Wall Street Journal* and Other City Papers *349*

Business Brokers *349*

  Business Opportunity Brokers *349*

  Merger and Acquisition Brokers *350*

Corporate Finance/M & A Departments of Banks and Major Accounting Firms *351*

Trust Companies *351*

Manufacturers' Directory *352*

What to Look For *353*

The Approach Letter *355*

    The Letter Itself *355*

    The Telephone Call Follow-up *355*

The Due Diligence Process *356*

    Verifying Financial Statements *356*

    Asset Verification and Appraisal *357*

    Customer Satisfaction *358*

    Due Diligence "Cook Books" *358*

    To Summarize the Due Diligence Process *359*

Summary *360*

Questions for Discussion *361*

Chapter 16   **EXTERNAL EXPANSION: TECHNICAL ASPECTS OF ACQUIRING A FIRM** *362*

Valuing a Closely Held Company *362*

Calculating the Floor Price *363*

    Accounting Book Value *363*

    Market Value *363*

    Replacement Value *364*

    Liquidation Value *364*

Adjusted Book Value—The Suggested Method *365*

    Inventory and Equipment *365*

    Liabilities *366*

Determining the Ceiling *367*

Negotiating Between the Floor and the Ceiling *368*

Forms of Transaction *369*

    Purchase/Sale of Assets *370*

    Depreciation Recapture *370*

    Advantages and Disadvantages of an Asset Purchase *371*

        Taxes 372

Contingent Liability 372

The Right of Offset Clause 373

Fraudulent Conveyance 373

Purchase/Sale of Stock 374

Soft Dollars 375

Summary 378

Questions for Discussion 379

Appendix: Summary of Rappaport's Alcar Model 380

Chapter 17   **THE ABLE CASE: DOING A LEVERAGED BUYOUT** 382

Background of the Able Company 382

Review and Comments on the Information Provided in the Case 384

Addressing the Questions Asked in the Case 387

Determining the Floor Price 388

Calculating the Ceiling Value 389

Raising Money on the Assets of the Company 391

Syndicating the Equity 394

Structuring the Deal 395

Soft Dollars 396

Other Expenses 397

Putting Value on the Soft-Dollar Contracts 397

The Subordinated Note 398

Summary of the Financing 399

The Offer Letter 401

Checking the Bank's Requirements 404

Ability to Service These Commitments 405

Concluding Details 406

An Alternate Way of Financing the Deal 407

Part 6   **DRESSING UP YOUR COMPANY FOR A BETTER MULTIPLE** *409*

Chapter 18   **MANAGING THE MULTIPLIER AND YOUR COMPANY'S IMAGE** *410*

The Company's Industry *411*

The Pattern of Earnings *412*

  The "Where Are You Going?" Pattern *412*

  The "We Never Pay Taxes" Syndrome *413*

  The "Big Bath" Pattern of Earnings *414*

  The "Hockey Stick" Pattern *414*

  The Ideal Pattern *415*

Absolute Earnings Per Share *416*

Management *417*

State of the Stock Market *417*

Dividends *420*

The Debt/Equity Ratio *420*

What's in a Name? *421*

Graphic Image *423*

  Corporate Logo *423*

  Corporate Stationery *424*

  Annual Report *424*

Financial Analysts Meetings *425*

  Beating the Analyst's Estimates *425*

Financial Public Relations *426*

Corporate Uniqueness *427*

Summary *428*

Questions for Discussion *429*

Epilogue *430*

Index *433*

Preface

Are you interested in learning about managing a new or emerging business firm from a financial point of view? *Entrepreneurial Finance for New and Emerging Businesses* is for entrepreneurs who either already own their own company or wish to own an emerging firm in the near future. By "emerging firm" we mean a company that is trying to grow from an embryonic stage into a larger firm. This term includes what are popularly called "middle-market" firms.

COVERAGE AND APPROACH

Entrepreneurial Finance for New and Emerging Businesses uses a "life-cycle" approach to cover everything from starting a business to eventually cashing out. Using the growth cycle of a typical firm as a way to organize the text, the book begins with a discussion of doing a start-up. This is followed by an explanation of the two basic ways to grow a company: by internal means and by external means. From there the text covers financing methods, working capital management, external expansion, and finally preparing the company to be sold. The book gives students real-world experiences and approaches rather than theories that often fail in practice.

To this author, entrepreneurial finance is mostly strategy, which does not involve lots of "number crunching." Students who have had an introductory course in corporate finance, and perhaps an introductory course in accounting, would have the vocabulary and background knowledge that this book assumes. It is assumed that the reader can handle basic statistics and a little mathematical presentation, but there is very little mathematics or statistics in the text itself. Nevertheless, just because a textbook does not rely heavily on mathematics does not mean it isn't challenging. In fact, this book relies on sophisticated decision making that goes well beyond simple number-crunching.

Entrepreneurial Finance for New and Emerging Businesses is the culmination of years of working with real firms making real decisions about the directions they were taking. As the environment (such as the recent fluctuations in the financial markets) in which these firms operate and grow changes, it has become necessary to revisit textbook coverage to help entrepreneurs make better decisions. This text was built to do a better job of it. The decisions have changed, the environment is different, and the requirements are evolving. This text addresses those issues. Take a look. I think you will appreciate the new strategic approach and design.

KEY FEATURES

1. **Technology boxes**: Boxed features supplement the text by giving examples of entrepreneurial approaches from the world of technology and e-commerce.

Although this textbook does not focus primarily on the tech industry, a very large percentage of start-ups are still tech companies, in spite of recent industry downturns. These examples include such high-profile companies as Amazon.com and Netscape, as well as smaller, lesser-known firms. Through these boxes, students will be able to learn from the experiences of other entrepreneurs.

2. **Part openers:** Each part begins with an explanation of the general flow of the firm's life-cycle. This frames the presentation so students can follow the decisions managers and owners will face as their firms grow.

3. **Questions for Discussion**: At the end of each chapter, questions coming out of actual consulting and working with real firms help students review, reinforce, and apply the concepts learned throughout the chapters. The questions help to focus learners on decisions they will have to make.

4. **Summary**: Each chapter contains a summary that helps students organize and review the concepts of the chapter.

SUPPLEMENTS

Instructor's Manual: Written by the text author, this supplement provides guidelines for those teaching this course, as well as answers to end-of-chapter questions. Instructors can order a printed instructor's manual, or it can be downloaded from the book's Web site at <http://stancill.swlearning.com>.

PowerPoint Lecture Slides: Lecture outline slides in Microsoft PowerPoint are downloadable from the Stancill Web site, <http://stancill.swlearning.com>. The slides include outlines of the chapters and highlights of key concepts and examples.

Cash FlowCast® Spreadsheet: Excel spreadsheets are downloadable from the Stancill website at http://stancill.swlearning.com. These spreadsheets will help the entrepreneur estimate cashflows.

Web site: Visit the Web site for Stancill's *Entrepreneurial Finance for New and Emerging Businesses* at <http://stancill.swlearning.com>. This site contains helpful tools for students and instructors including PowerPoint slides, "Newswire: Finance in the News" current articles, and an Investment Analysis Calculator.

ACKNOWLEDGEMENTS

It is with sincere gratitude that I wish to acknowledge the help provided by the following people. Jim Morris helped early in the process with Chapters 1 and 2 and generally encouraged me throughout the preparation of the book. William R. Zimmerman was particularly helpful with Chapters 16, 17, and 18 concerning LBOs. He is a master at this, and his comments were particularly helpful. I am also grateful to the staff of the USC Marshall School Computer Center for their help over the years that it has taken to write this book. Richard Bergen helped materially in the preparation of the PowerPoint slides. Paulina Chang and Sidney Nguyen assisted with the graphics in Chapter 4.

Professor Dolores Conway of the Marshall School provided invaluable assistance in the development of the Entrepreneurial Capital Budgeting model. Her suggestion for the Coefficient of Diffusion was most helpful. Joseph Sherwood, Managing Director for Investment Banking, Seidler Companies was extremely helpful with Chapter 9, Long Term Financing: Sweetened Issues and Innovations. Duke K. Bristow of the Corporate Governance Program at UCLA also offered valuable assistance with this project.

Helpful suggestions and often detailed reviews were provided by:

Richard Bliss
Babson College

Carol Boyer
Clarkson University

Cynthia Brown
University of Texas, Pan-American

Karen Chambliss
Florida Institute of Technology

Susan Coleman
University of Hartford

Suzanne Erickson
Seattle University

Jim Hatch
University of Western Ontario

Evan Jones
Duke University

Jan Klein
Fairleigh Dickinson University

Michael Mino
Clemson University

Charles Ruscher
University of Arizona

Thanks also go to the editorial staff of South-Western College Publishers and to Rassoul Yazdipour, president of California Technology Entrepreneurship Center, for providing the technology boxes. The helpful comments of the staff of Silicon Valley Bank were also most useful. John Morris, president of the Tech Coast Angels, was particularly helpful with the chapters on doing a start-up.

And last but not least, I wish to express my sincerest thanks to Terry Lichvar, of the Department of Finance and Business Economics of the Marshall School of Business, for her splendid help with computer software. Were it not for her help, I would still be struggling with the graphics included in the book, not to mention the other problems she solved for me with regard to the computer.

For the remaining mistakes and typos I, alone, am to blame.

James McNeill Stancill, Ph.D.
Professor of Finance
Marshall School of Business
University of Southern California

Dedicated to my wife Catherine for her love and support and especially, for her never-ending patience with me while I chased after another deal.

Introduction

This book is all about managing a new or emerging business firm from a finance point of view. It is for entrepreneurs who either already own a company or intend to own an emerging firm. By "emerging firm" we mean a business that is trying to grow from an embryonic stage into a larger firm. Many emerging firms fit into the category of what are popularly called "middle-market" firms. Emerging firms and middle-market firms are not always one and the same, however. Some owners of middle-market firms are not interested in "growing" their companies. There are, however, many who *are* interested in growth, and it is to these individuals, and to students who would like to be one of these business owners, that this book is addressed.

This text is not about "small business finance," which may be an oxymoron. In a very small firm, what is needed is a good bookkeeper or accountant. The types of decisions discussed in this book are not to be found, for the most part, in small companies that do not have growth potential.

On the other hand, this book is also not about what might be called "General Motors finance"—the type of finance that is the basis of most textbooks in corporate finance. In the typical corporate finance textbook, the company is assumed to be public with a broad and deep market so that "perfect market" assumptions can take place. Nowhere in this book is there a reference to a "perfect capital market"; in fact, there is *no* assumption that the company is publicly owned. There are over two million so-called middle-market companies in America that could be included in what are here called "emerging business firms." Contrast that with the less than twenty-five thousand publicly held companies in the United States. Admittedly these publicly held firms account for a major share of the nation's Gross Domestic Product, but there is another world of businesses that exists, and this is the world that is addressed here.

CONTENTS OF THE BOOK

Following the general idea of the growth cycle of a firm, the book begins with a discussion of doing a start-up. It is this author's opinion that the only time you attempt to do a start-up is when you *have* to do a start-up. It is probably far easier and less traumatic to buy out an existing company than it is to start one. (This process of buying a company with mostly other people's money, called a leveraged buy out, is discussed in the book.) The days of some bright—and possibly very young—"computer-nik" starting an Internet or "dot.com" company in his or her dining room, with a computer and little else, may be gone. At least, for while, if not forever. The wounds of the spring of 2000 run pretty deep!

PART ONE: GETTING STARTED, MANAGING PROFIT, AND CASH FLOW

The first two chapters are devoted to doing a start-up and this discussion follows four themes: the "basic idea"; the key person/management team; the "private placement memorandum"; and, finally, the venture capital needed.

In the "basic idea" section there are presented a number of factors that one should consider when thinking about doing a start-up. Because there are times when a start-up should be attempted, we go into some detail about the things that one needs to think about to make a viable—and saleable—company from a start-up. *It is very important to note that this discussion may also be useful when thinking about* expanding *an existing business.* The importance of having an idea that is a "pain killer" instead of a "vitamin" is discussed. Chapter 1 also deals with the characteristics of the person doing the start-up and the management team that is going to run the company.

Chapter 2 deals first with how to write the "private placement memorandum" or, as it is called in the vernacular, the "Package" or "business plan." Every sophisticated source of venture capital is constantly on the lookout for what might be called the "tip of the iceberg"—some slight flaw that tells the venture capitalist or "angel" that there is something wrong with the idea or the person presenting the idea. When writing the Package one cannot be too careful; keep from revealing some flaw in the basic idea. If there is some little thing that strikes the source of venture capital as being out of place, this would be taken much as one would view the tip of an iceberg: there is a whole lot more under the water than can be seen above it. So beware! The days of having an "idea" that sounded enticing—but no plan—have disappeared along with the large chunks of money that were "thrown" at dot.com ideas.

The second section of this chapter deals with how to raise venture capital. In this context it is necessary to draw a sharp distinction between a "plain vanilla" start-up and a high-tech start-up. In the latter case there is still venture capital out in the "market" today for the "right" idea. Well, perhaps this is an exaggeration, but it is not too much of a stretch to say that the "right deal" will find funding. Most of the venture capitalists' money today is going toward shoring up investments *already made*. A so-called "plain vanilla" start-up will require much more effort (and luck!) to raise the venture capital, whether from an "angel" or a professional venture capital source, primarily because of the absence of an exciting "exit strategy." In fact it may seem downright impossible. In this case there is one caveat to remember: *"A shopped deal is no deal."* This means that sending a Package to a number of sources decreases your chance of getting the company funded in an almost exponential manner. The way to approach the funding for either type of start-up is to use an "intermediary," someone who can take you and your idea to a source of money. Who these intermediaries are and how to find one is also discussed in this chapter. The process of "staging the financing" of a New Economy business puts more perspective on the fund-raising process.

The next chapter deals with a discussion of "managing" the company's financial statement and profit. This is the kind of subject that many accountants object to as being "unethical" or simply undesired. To entrepreneurial owners/managers of developing firms, this is ridiculous. Using accurate information, it is management's job to present their best face to their bankers and other interested parties. Unfortunately, many business owners seldom pay attention to their financial statements, delegating this task to their internal or external accountants. There is no need to be a trained accountant to know the basics of "statement management." Furthermore, "managing" the company's *profit* is not the job of an outside accountant. The profit the company makes is like a trail that is laid to the future. Once laid, it is difficult to change. This does *not* mean that I am advocating "hyping" the company's profit. Far from this! Rather I mean that the entrepreneurial owner/manager should think about this trail of profits and realize the impact this will have on outside interested parties, such as bankers, investors, and even possible buyers of the company. There are ways of managing profit that are known to "street smart" business owners that are never mentioned in conventional textbooks on corporate finance, but they are mentioned in this book. These are the lessons learned from being on the "street." In fact, most of what is mentioned and discussed in this book does not appear in conventional textbooks on corporate finance. For example, tricks used by street-smart business owners regarding their financial statements are discussed to keep aspiring business owners from making some bad mistakes. Some of these are simple things, to be sure, but they are important nevertheless.

The next subject covered in Part One is cash flow analysis. For the entrepreneurial manager of a developing or emerging firm, no subject is more important. Business runs on *cash*, not "profits." In Chapter 4, three measures of "cash flow" are discussed: Earnings Before Interest and Taxes (EBIT), Net Income Plus Depreciation (NIPD), and a new measure called Net Operating Cash Flow (NOCF). When is there "cash" in cash flow? To answer this question, assumptions are made about three different kinds of companies: a manufacturing company, a distribution company, and a service company. Additionally, these three types of companies are cast in three scenarios: a steady sales scenario, a growth scenario, and a recession simulation. We follow the way these three measures of "cash flow" behave in these scenarios. By seeing how these measures interact, the reader will gain an understanding of what consumes cash and when cash is thrown off from operations. Also, questions like which statement—Income Statement or Balance Sheet—is more important to "manage" in a recession will be addressed. *It is important for the reader to fully understand this chapter on cash flow because many of the succeeding topics assume an understanding of NOCF and everything that goes into managing it.* It is imperative for an entrepreneurial owner/manger to thoroughly understand every aspect of the management of cash flow.

PART TWO: GROWING A FIRM—INTERNALLY

Here attention is turned to the idea of "growing" a company. Perhaps this is a slight misuse of this term, but it rather clearly says what we are trying to do. In this regard there are two basic ways to grow a company: by internal means and by external means. *Internal means* refers to three things: "more of the same" (including cost savings), share repurchase (for publicly held firms only), and capital budgeting. Doing "more of the same" refers to increasing the business up to capacity—if there is such a thing. A chain of stores like Kinko's can expand by doing more of what it already does (just open more stores). A manufacturing firm can increase production up to some practical level that is referred to as "full capacity," then it has to increase capacity, which is a capital budgeting problem. "Growing" a company through *external means* is the process that is commonly referred to as "mergers and acquisitions." Do you know that it is possible to "grow" the company by *buying* earnings and/or by "*marrying*" earnings—meaning merging with another company? This external means of expansion is dealt with later in the book.

After exploring what is meant by "growing" a company—that is growth in *earnings*—we review common methods of discriminating between capital budgeting proposals (i.e., the usual "textbook" way of doing capital budgeting). Exception is taken with the conventional way of doing capital budgeting (i.e., by investing down to your "cost of capital" or investing as long as you have a positive net present value). What is "wrong" with either method is that if you had the best Internal Rate of Return proposal or highest Net Present Value proposal you had ever seen, and that proposal "bankrupts" the company, what have you accomplished? To some theorists in corporate finance, this is "no problem" really because all that happens is the changing of places in the ranking of the stakeholders of the company. But if *you* owned the company and had all of your wealth tied up in that company, would you feel that bankruptcy was "no problem"? Hardly!

Even if a proposal has a good rate of return, there are other factors that define a proposal. What is called the "time shape of the cash flow" may be critical in considering a certain proposal. Considering just one more discriminant in the selection process, other than rate of return, may mean that you would suboptimize the set of proposals by simply ranking them according to their rate of return. To answer these problems, an "entrepreneurial capital budgeting model" is presented. In this model, a case is made for considering proposals *in sets*, not individually. In addition to rate of return and the "time shape of the cash flow" another discriminant is used—earnings—and, finally, a new method of measuring the risk of getting the rate of return for a set of proposals is presented. This latter discriminant, called the "coefficient of diffusion," has some interesting implications. For example, a proposal may be definitely acceptable when put into a particular set, whereas it would otherwise be rejected as not having a high enough rate of return or as having too high a risk of getting that rate of return. Also, firms that feel they adequately take account of risk by screening *individual* proposals may be actually taking on more "risk" of getting the rate of return than they ever thought.

After dealing with capital budgeting, the highly important topic of the firm's *capital structure* is addressed. Probably the most important single ratio that anyone could ever apply to any company is the company's Debt/Equity ratio. If you need money and the banker says "Sorry, you are over your limit," no amount of persuasion will diminish the importance of this statement to you. All students of business should know that there are two types of leverage: *operating* and *financial*. Operating leverage includes such things as depreciation or rent. Financial leverage includes such things as interest (or debt repayment on a cash flow statement.) In either case, *leverage means the inclusion of a "fixed charge" on the Income Statement (or Cash Flow Statement)*.

On an Income Statement, use of leverage causes a *more than* proportional *change in Net Income for a given change in Sales*, or a more than proportional change in the company's cash flow. How to decide how much leverage to accept is a question of great magnitude to an entrepreneurial owner/manager of a developing firm. The way to solve this conundrum is to take a hard look at the prospects for the company's sales. How sure are you that the estimated sales will be realized? What is the expected probability density function of sales? If the expected distribution is reasonably peaked, one can enter into leverage with more assurance that there will not be a "cash insufficiency" in the near future; if the expected sales distribution is spread out considerably (uncertain), then management should approach leverage very cautiously.

PART THREE: FINANCING TOOLS

Raising funds externally is the subject of Chapter 8. There are two methods by which a company can raise funds externally: through a private placement or through a public offering. The private "route" has a number of advantages, including privacy and speed. These private offerings are made through what is called a "Reg. D Exemption." Probably more money is raised through private placements than through public offerings of debt and, possibly, stock. The public offerings, whether they be stock or debt issues are usually made under one of two SEC regulations: an S-1 offering or the newer S-18 offering. Under S-1 there are a number of factors for management to remember, but the important thing is to be sure not to spend the money before you actually have the funds in the bank. Many a firm has been disappointed when their underwriter exercised its "market out clause" and refused to do the deal. The importance of selecting an underwriter of integrity is stressed. Someone once said that "if you lie down with dogs, you get up with fleas."

Following this introduction of publicly issued securities—there are two chapters having to do with long-term securities and intermediate-term debt. Because this is a book regarding entrepreneurial finance, the first part of the first chapter deals with "sweetened" securities—convertibles and bonds with warrants. Attractive developing firms might wish to issue straight debt, but investors are usually more interested in a "stock play." (Institutional) investors can do this, while still holding "debt" in their portfolio by buying convertibles. For a company issuing convertibles, it is considered a "cheap" way to issue stock. And the nice thing about convertibles is that when the company calls the bonds and forces conversion to stock, it will be increasing its equity and thus be in a position to issue more debt. (An emerging company grows on its equity.) Bonds with warrants became popular about 1970 when there was a credit crunch and a recession. When the Federal Reserve decided to place margin requirements on convertible debt, the market merely responded by issuing bonds with detachable or nondetachable warrants in numbers not seen before.

What is different about this discussion of "sweetened" securities is that it is probably the only one written from the point of view of determining the terms *before* they are placed on the bond. In short, this discussion deals with what the entrepreneurial owner/manager should think about before he or she goes "downtown" to talk to the investment bankers. In addition to the publicly issued sweetened securities, Chapter 9 deals with what are called "shadow warrants." When trying to do an acquisition of a private company, for example, an entrepreneur-to-be might find a lender who wants a "piece of the action." Because this is a middle-market deal and the acquiring company (or you!) is not publicly held, conventional warrants are not possible. But there is a rather simple way to reward the lender with a sweetener by issuing shadow warrants. Because these are not very familiar to most people attempting to do a deal, the secret is trying to figure out how many shadow warrants to give the lender. This topic and the related subject of success fees that were used when finance conditions tightened (as in 1991 and 2002) are also discussed.

The second part of the chapter deals with what might be called variations on long-term securities. In short, these, like the sweetened securities are, the tools of finance. It is these securities that an entrepreneur will use when attempting to "do a deal" or to raise money for an existing business. Securities such as "classified common stock" (which is seldom if ever mentioned in conventional books on corporate finance) and hybrid securities are particularly useful. Admittedly these securities represent a good deal of memorizing, but when the time comes to reach down in your bag and pull out a security designed to accomplish a particular purpose, you will be glad you committed to memory these securities. Indeed, this is the whole point in discussing these securities. You will learn how to *tailor a security to accomplish a particular goal*. For example, when doing a start-up, the person providing the money might insist on being "ahead" of the entrepreneur in case the venture turns out badly. This is easily accomplished by classifying the common stock to give preference to the money source in liquidation. Or, there might be two classes with different voting rights. Or, in the course of doing an acquisition, it might be useful to make some of the debt securities "PIK," meaning that if the company cannot pay the interest or dividend, then the company can pay in kind, with a payment including more of the same security in lieu of cash.

There is a decided prejudice by many professors of finance against teaching "descriptive finance," which was the hallmark of finance textbooks before Modgliani and Miller happened on the scene and it became unpopular to teach something as mundane as types of securities. But for an entrepreneur there are two ways to learn about these different tools: by experience or by reading about them. Even with experience, there are securities that may happen to escape one's notice. This chapter attempts to correct that.

Chapter 10 deals with what is termed "intermediate-term" debt—or, more simply, "term loans." Not just what the entrepreneur needs to know about the different types of term loans, but with special attention given to the changing market for intermediate- and long-term securities. Banks are no longer the primary source of term loans. Instead, banks are becoming intermediaries to other institutional lenders such as pension funds and life insurance companies. It is estimated that banks loan only about 25 percent of the bank's own money; the rest is institutional money. In this chapter there is also a discussion of the strategy of obtaining a term (or really any type) of loan. Such things as putting yourself in the head of the banker are mentioned. Also discussed are the types of things that a manager should think about *before* meeting with the banker.

Following this there is a chapter on short-term sources of financing from both banks and finance companies. There is no single source of financing more popular (or necessary) for the emerging firm than Accounts Receivable and Inventory financing. These are discussed from the point of view of borrowing from both banks and finance companies. What makes good collateral and how much is loaned against this collateral is discussed. Also, term loans made against equipment is discussed, since these loans are made by both banks and finance companies. When a manager of an emerging firm needs short-term financing, he or she will learn the mechanics of Accounts Receivable and/or Inventory financing quickly enough. But when attempting to do a LBO knowing the criteria banks and finance companies use to make such loans will greatly simplify a search and acquisition.

Also of importance to the entrepreneur is a discussion of the three types of appraisal companies and the different types of appraisals they can make—and what difference this makes in getting a loan on equipment. Equipment can be a main source of financing in doing an asset-based LBO.

PART FOUR: L/Cs AND WORKING CAPITAL MANAGEMENT

Because business today is really "world business," the next chapter is a discussion of Letters of Credit. If a businessperson today doesn't think "internationally," he or she is about twenty to forty years behind times. And international—and even some domestic—business involves the use of Letters of Credit. The treatment of this subject is one that is not all-encompassing or designed to be the last source of authority to the businessperson. Personally, I have fallen asleep every time I have attempted to read a manual on Letters of Credit. This is because the *detail* is stifling. Instead, the emphasis in this chapter is on the *use* of Letters of Credit. The aim is to get the reader to recognize situations where they can use a Letter of Credit to their own advantage. Letters of Credit can be "beautiful" if you are getting them but painful if you are giving a Letter of Credit, at least with most banks in the United States.

One section of this chapter deals with "doing business without a Balance Sheet." By this is meant the ability to do a trading business, by receiving a "transferable" Letter of Credit, when you do not have a sizeable Balance Sheet to impress a vendor.

Until recent years, "Clean Letters of Credit" were rarely used by firms in the United States. But with CPA review courses discussing them, they no longer are ignored. "Clean Letters of Credit" mean that they are clean of documentation, meaning that no merchandise (documentation) is involved. These clean L/Cs are extremely useful for effecting "guarantees" and making payments. (For those who are used to using L/Cs only with merchandise, this information may be news.) Every businessperson of today should be familiar with L/Cs, both clean and documented. And domestic L/Cs are coming into their own, as well.

The next two chapters deal with what is generally called "working capital" management. First, the question of cash management and the different types of money market securities are discussed. It is easy to know when your company is carrying too little cash; your bank will let you know quite quickly! But how do you determine if you are carrying too much cash and (near cash) money market securities? Simple statistical models are presented which help to determine if you are carrying too much cash. Fortunately, with most big banks offering "sweep accounts" or, alternatively, "zero balance" accounts, managing cash has never been easier. But it is important to realize what causes *dissynchronization* in the company's cash inflows and outflows, because this is what causes the firm to carry more cash rather than less. And since cash is one of the *least* most "profitable" assets to carry, it is advantageous to know what makes the company carry more cash than it might otherwise do.

The management of Accounts Receivable is the next subject discussed, in Chapter 14. This is undoubtedly one of the most important topics of managerial concern for entrepreneurial business firms. Often, the very success of the company rides on making the right decisions regarding the granting of trade credit—Accounts Receivable. This subject is discussed from the point of view of what are called the four *parameters*: the cash discount, the cash discount period, the credit period, and the collection effort. Then these parameters are shown interacting with what are called the firm's *variables*: Sales, Net Income, the volume of Accounts Receivable, Net Operating Cash Flow, and Bad Debt Expense. Here the point of interest is the *elasticity of demand* of these parameters with the variables. It is important for management to recognize when the parameters affect the variables and when they don't. Much can be gained from analyzing these parameters against the variables, including possibly a large increase in Net Profits. The chapter concludes with the presentation of a credit-granting decision rule: If the customer's probability of paying is estimated to be greater than the critical probability of collection, then grant credit. The definition of the "critical probability of collection" is given.

PART FIVE: EXTERNAL EXPANSION: MERGERS AND ACQUISITIONS, INCLUDING DOING A LBO

Earlier in the book the distinction was made between two ways to "grow" a firm, internally and externally. In the earlier discussion, capital budgeting was discussed as possibly the main way to effect this type of growth. In this part of the book, *external* expansion is discussed. It is possible to "buy" earnings. But instead of taking the position of acquiring another company when you already own one, the discussion here (one which is possibly more widely relevant) is directed to the individual who wants to *acquire* one. And instead of assuming that the person has all the money needed to "pay cash" for the new company, the assumption is made that the individual has to do what is called a "Leveraged Buyout" or LBO. In this case, the acquisition is made with generous amounts of borrowed money—other people's money. All of the important technical and legal factors that need to be considered in *any* type of acquisition are covered. But by casting the discussion in terms of a LBO, it is felt that more entrepreneurs and wannabe entrepreneurs will be served.

To begin this series of chapters, there is a discussion of the criteria for a LBO. These are the factors that make for a good LBO candidate; they include such obvious factors as good assets on which you can borrow, good cash flow (no "turn arounds") and, not so obvious, a "compelling reason to sell." Essentially these criteria add up to the conclusion that the "best" candidate for a LBO is a manufacturing company with a lot of good, "hockable" assets—assets that have a high borrowing rate. Companies that are in the distribution industry do not have the kinds of assets that make for good collateral nor do service companies. Inventory, for example, is poor collateral for a loan. With service companies, their principal assets are their people—and people do not make "good" collateral. Once these criteria are understood, finding a LBO candidate may not be too hard. Essentially it is a process of *deductive reasoning*. But in the second half of this chapter, there is a formal discussion of the various sources of finding a LBO candidate. Some promising ways are mentioned—as well as some that may not be promising. The discussion ends with a suggestion that possibly the best place to look for a LBO candidate—as well as any "good" company for sale—is in the Manufacturer's Directory. Every year good middle-market firms that are solely owned are put up for sale because the owner wants to retire. In this Manufacturer's Directory, which may be online in many states, you are able to spot many companies that could be owned by individuals who may want to retire. Suggestions for spotting these potential candidates are given.

The technical aspects of acquiring a company are next discussed. After a brief discussion of how the conglomerates were formed, the critical distinctions between tax-free mergers and acquisitions made by what is known as "purchase accounting" are made. In the latter, there is a big difference between a "purchase/sale of assets" and a "purchase/sale of stock." The former is highly desirable from the point of view of the buyer and the latter is most desirable from the point of view of the seller. But the name of the game in doing a LBO is *terms*. By knowing in general detail what the advantages of each method are to the respective parties (buyer and seller), the buyer may be able to get the seller to concede on an important point—like the form of transaction—and get in return concessions that make the whole deal possible. The form of transaction—purchase/sale of assets or purchase/sale of stock—also affects the transaction depending on whether or not a bank is used for financing or a finance company is used. This is because of something called "fraudulent conveyance"—laws that remove secured creditors in favor of the unsecured creditors. Understanding these laws may help in securing financing for a LBO.

Another important aspect of acquiring a firm via any means, not just via the LBO route, is understanding how to *price* a middle-market firm. In this book an argument will be made for setting a "floor" price and a "ceiling" price and then negotiating between these two values. It is important to set a floor price, even though you are the buyer, in order to know what the seller might be thinking. Also, you may want to brag to your banker about what a good deal you are getting by having a price so close to the floor. In setting the ceiling price, the usual way taught in most conventional textbooks teaching "General Motors finance," is contrasted with the way most middle-market firms are usually valued, that is by using a multiple of what I call "Adjusted EBITDA." Instead of taking the cash flows and discounting them to the present, the way middle-market firms are usually valued is by somehow "adjusting" the target's earnings before interest, taxes, depreciation, and amortization of intangibles. Just figuring out what the EBIT is for many a middle-market firm is something of a chore because many owners typically "load" as much personal expense into their privately owned company as they can. For the new owner, these "expenses" would disappear with the change in ownership, so this money can be used as though it were "profit." How one "adjusts" these "expenses" is also a good trick for the aspiring business owner, however. This fairly simplistic method of valuing these middle-market firms contrasts dramatically with the exotic valuation methods employed during the dot.com bubble.

With the groundwork laid, the last chapter of Part Five deals with the actual process of acquiring a company via the LBO route: The Abel Case. This is a company that is doing $26 million in sales and is owned by a 68-year-old man who wishes to retire. The Background Information yields considerable information about the company and the situation as it affects doing a LBO. Following the presentation of "background information," there is an interpretation of the various points in the "Background." Then there is a step-by-step discussion of just how this company might be bought for only $500,000 in equity when the asking price is $23 million. And if the wannabe owner does not have $500,000 to put forward as equity in the deal, there is a discussion of how he or she might raise most of the $500,000 through a process of what is known as *syndication*. The various steps such as the raising of the money on the assets, the use of what is known as "soft dollars," and the drafting of the subordinated note are all discussed. Without a "subordinated note" there is no deal. By accepting a subordinated note the seller unwittingly is supplying *de facto* equity for the buyer. (How and why this happens is explained in the chapter.) Then the "deal" is compared to what the bank is expected to approve. Finally, a test is made to see if the company's cash flow will support the new fixed charges that will be incurred by the LBO.

PART SIX: DRESSING UP THE COMPANY FOR A BETTER MULTIPLE

And finally there is a chapter on "Managing the Multiplier," the Price/Earnings multiplier. It has always been interesting to see one company sell for, say, four times Adjusted EBIT and another sell for some higher multiple, say, six or eight. Since these are privately held companies, there are not good "comparable" companies such as you might have in widely traded publicly held firms. Or instead of a privately held firm, what can be done to improve the P/E multiple of a lightly traded publicly held "emerging" firm? In short, how can management make their company more attractive to a buyer or get a higher P/E in the public market? To those finance experts who assume that the market is "perfect," or some variation of it, this type of discussion is anathema. But there are a number of common sense things that can be done to make a firm more attractive to buyers or shareholders, and these are discussed.

In Conclusion

Managing a developing firm is not the same as "rocket science." There are many things that are nothing much more than intuition or common sense, but *organized* common sense, or "common sense" things once someone has pointed them out. In this book you will find both things that one might call simply common sense and some that are not so intuitive. Collectively they are the things that an entrepreneurial manager might find useful when managing an emerging firm.

Instead of trying to make "conventional" financial theory fit the case of these privately held or lightly traded publicly held firms, the "theory" that is espoused in this book is theory that actually works. There is none of this "good in theory but not in practice" hypothesizing in this book. If it does not work, then it should not be taught. This does not mean that the analysis should not be as rigorous as possible. It simply means that what is suggested or put forward as theory should be applicable and capable of working. For some this will be upsetting: The "theory" herein presented may not be consistent with what they learned as doctrine in other courses in finance. It is not my contention that the other theories are not valid; it is that *they are not valid for the types of companies assumed in this book*. Virtually everything contained in this book is the result of personal experience or observation of the management of emerging firms as they actually are.

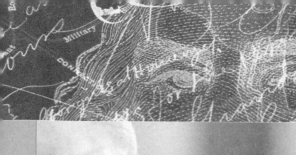

Part 1

Getting Started, Managing Profit, and Cash Flow

Chapter 1: Doing a Start-Up

Chapter 2: Packaging and Financing a Start-Up

Chapter 3: Managing Profit and Financial Statements

Chapter 4: Cash Flow Analysis

1

Doing a Start-Up

WHY DO A START-UP?

To paraphrase a former president of the University of Chicago, when you get the desire to do a start-up, you should lie down until the feeling goes away. Attempting a start-up should not be taken lightly. That being said, there is a good chance that anyone with an entrepreneurial bone in his or her body will be involved in a start-up sometime in the not-too-distant future, in either its creation, acquisition, financing, and/or management. This chapter and all that follow will explore the information, techniques, documents, and skills you will need at each level of entrepreneurship.

You should only do a start-up when it doesn't make sense not to. Doing a start-up is an extremely difficult and trying task. This is particularly true for the entrepreneur new to being a chief executive. There will be the tensions of making many significant decisions, working with people perhaps not well known to you, and the strain on your personal finances. After you have reviewed your personal capacities, you should consider one additional factor: the complete support of your spouse or significant other. The attention that a start-up demands—if you are to be successful—can rupture even reasonably sound relationships. Unless you are thinking of a high-technology start-up, it is usually easier to buy an existing business, since you are stepping into an established organization.

Acquisition is not always practical or wise, however. There are times when it makes good sense to do a start-up rather than attempt to buy an existing firm. A number of exceptions come to mind: if you want to own a very high-tech company, a software company, an Internet company, or a cosmetics company. If you were to attempt to buy any one of these types of companies, you would find that you are buying a lot of goodwill, and while that goodwill may be worth the asking price, it would be difficult to borrow on this asset—something needed in a leveraged buyout. In these cases, if you have all the necessary ingredients to do a start-up, you would probably be well advised to make that your goal.

THE INGREDIENTS FOR DOING A START-UP

There are four ingredients necessary for doing a start-up—any kind of start-up, high-tech, or **Old Economy**:

1. **The basic idea.** This is the *raison d'être* of the whole operation. It is the product you want to make or sell or the service you want to provide.
2. **The key person or management team.** This is the entrepreneur or, in the case of certain start-ups, a management team.
3. **The private placement memorandum**—or, as it is known in the vernacular, "the **Package**." This is the business plan, and today it is more important than ever if looking for outside funds.
4. **The venture capital.** This is the capital needed to start and grow the new venture. Later the various sources of this capital will be discussed.

This chapter discusses the first two factors; Chapter 2 covers the last two.

THE ORDER OF THINGS

The usual sequence in which these "ingredients" come about is as listed above, but it can certainly vary. The first start-up I worked on as a planning consultant originated in a conversation my client, the entrepreneur, had with his next-door neighbor. The neighbor said, "Why don't you start up your own firm and let me put some money behind you for financing. You can get some of your other friends to put up money, and with the people you know in the business, you can assemble a staff with no trouble." In this case, the would-be entrepreneur had chosen the industry in which he was employed—the manufacture of small pumps—(and in which the profits were already razor-thin, not the kind of thing you like to see in a start-up situation). It will provide us with useful illustrations, mostly of "Don't do's." (Fortunately, it has developed into an industry leader.)

As we will see, if the sequence of ingredients starts from the idea, proceeds carefully to the management team, then to the package, and finally to the venture capital, the idea may never get off the ground. One should have a notion of where the venture capital is coming from before the basic idea gets too far along, as it may be impossible to raise the venture capital after time has passed.

We have to start somewhere, of course. Let us assume you have a Basic Idea, and see what criteria must be applied to test its feasibility. In applying these criteria, keep in mind that they are designed to help you formulate a better idea—not necessarily to reject your idea. You can alter your idea to accommodate the criteria.

CRITERIA FOR THE BASIC IDEA

- Form of the organization

- Basic profitability

- Market size

- Capital intensity

- A one-product firm

- Repeat orders vs. single sale

- Capable of an "out"

- Product too simple

- Out of vogue

- An understandable deal

FORM OF THE ORGANIZATION

The first criterion to be addressed is the type of firm that is being envisaged to deliver your product or service. Is it going to be a mom-and-pop type of organization or a functional management structure?

A **mom-and-pop organization** is one that is thoroughly dependent on one or two people: Mom and Pop. If this person (persons) has to make all the important decisions, this may be the strength of the organization, but it will also be the principal weakness. We will take a closer look at personal traits that best contribute to start-up success later in this chapter. The problem with this organization type lies in the expression bankers have for it. They say "When the owner goes home, the business goes home." To a banker, this means that the business and the individual owning it are one and the same. What is so important here is that the business will not get any more credit than the individual would by himself or herself. There are, then, two things wrong with the mom-and-pop organization:

It is difficult to finance—both from a bank lending and an investment point of view.

It is difficult to sell the business when the entrepreneur wishes to exit the company.

If a potential buyer perceives that most—sometimes all—of the business sales are generated because of the owner/manager's personality, drive, connections, or whatever, then what is there to buy? Without the individual in question, where would the business come from? It is tragic to see business owners wanting to retire and faced with the prospect that the only way they can get their money out is to put the assets on the sidewalk for sale, in a manner of speaking.

The alternative, of course, is to found a business that will itself grow and prosper—one which could be sold for a substantial amount of money when the owner wishes to retire, say in 10 to 30 years. Or a whole lot sooner, if the new company is an exciting New Economy company. Another way of looking at this is to imagine a company's **Balance Sheet** and visualize the **Net Worth** section growing over time. Even if this business is sold for only book value, it would be a substantial amount. And all the time that the business is growing, the owner/manager may be receiving a substantial salary and bonus. The exception to this scenario is the kind of "business" that is represented by individuals such as actors, professional athletes, and other professions, such as lawyers and doctors in private practice: When they stop working, their income stops. This is called a lifestyle form of business. Therefore what they need to do is invest wisely the money they make while they are in business because they may have nothing to sell when they leave it.

Functional management, in comparison to the mom-and-pop structure, is the kind of organization that can keep going indefinitely, at least in theory. It has "replaceable parts" that allow the continued existence of the firm. In other words, the organization takes on a character all its own. The bankers will look to the *company* when making the credit decision, rather than just loaning against the personal Balance Sheet of the owner and whatever it will support. And when someone buys the business, he or she can feel confident that the business will continue uninterrupted.

The main advantage of the functional management type of firm is the ability to sell the business for a larger multiple of earnings than is possible with the mom-and-pop firm. (For a while, New Economy firms of all types sold on bases other than earnings. Some of them sold for extraordinary dollar amounts even though they had never even had a sale or made a profit! With the shakeout of the spring of 2000, this phenomenom lost power, but this sort of thing may still happen. Large firms may buy relatively new firms—high-tech firms—because it is cheaper or quicker than doing for themselves what this new firm is already doing.)

At this juncture it may be well to make a point regarding these "criteria" that may not be apparent. All the various criteria offered here are not intended to preempt a certain start-up; rather they are intended to be factors that a wannabe entrepreneur should think about when designing the firm. If you know, for example, that it is important to form an organization that is functional in nature, then you can do so and avoid a mom-and-pop organization that might otherwise be selected—perhaps by default! In short, these criteria should help the entrepreneur *design* a firm that will be superior to others.

BASIC PROFITABILITY

After deciding on the form of organization, it behooves the entrepreneur to take a hard look at the **Gross Profit** potential of the new firm, its "**Basic Profitability.**" When someone gets an idea for a new company, enthusiasm often is likely to take over where judgment should prevail. (Clearly this was never so apparent as with the dot.com wave!) And when someone is terribly enthusiastic, it is easy to excuse "a few little problems" such as whether the company will be profitable or not. The problem, of course, stems from pricing the product and estimating the size of the market. This is particularly true of dot.com or New Economy start-ups.

How much will people pay for this product or service, in these quantities?

There are two types of products that might be sold: one for which there is a demand (a demand-driven product) and the type of product that people have to be induced to buy. For my money, I'll take a product that is "demand-driven" anytime over a product the world doesn't know it needs. One "angel"—an early stage investor—refers to this as a product that is a pain killer rather than a vitamin.▲ For a pain killer, people will pay what is asked to get the product—reluctantly perhaps—but they *will pay*! With a vitamin, they may rationalize not buying the product by saying that they "will get these vitamins later, perhaps at a saving," even though they recognize that the vitamin "is good for them." There is a fundamental difference: immediate need vs. discretionary purchase. The old expression "Build a better mousetrap, and the world will beat a path to your door" expresses the sentiment entirely. If people really want the product, then profitability should be no problem.

Inventors are particularly prone to making mistakes in pricing. Typically inventors get rather upset when they ask how much the product should sell for and are given a figure that is close to or less than the cost. "Don't you realize that it costs $34 to make this product?" "How can you say you would only pay about $30 for it?" Well, the world could care less what something costs when it comes to evaluating the product and its price. If people think that the price should be $30 (for the quantity in question), then that's what they would be willing to pay.▲▲ And, of course, the fatal mistake in this regard is to start to try to rationalize a *higher* price once you realize that the Basic Profitability is not there. "Oh well," you say, "I am sure that people will pay a little more." Of course. But if they don't?

Pricing the product by marking up the cost is a sign of an amateur entrepreneur. This could result in leaving a large profit on the table, in a manner of

▲ Special thanks go to John Morris, president of Tech Coast Angels and partner in GKM Ventures, for this thought and some others in this chapter.

▲▲ One example that comes to mind was a plastic "saucer" that one uses to raise and keep potted plants off a good wood floor. I purchased one recently for $5.97 fully realizing that it probably cost the manufacturer no more than a few **cents** to make this simple product. I bought it because to me it was **worth $5.97!**

speaking. This may be the way that some products get priced in very large organizations, but it is not good business in innovative start-up situations.

What kind of profitability should one expect from a start-up? To answer this it is necessary to differentiate between a start-up for a new, innovative product and a start-up for a product that is like others already in the market. In the former case, a Gross Profit of 75–90 percent is not too unusual—at least to begin. In the latter case, the new company will have to squeeze into the market and understand what the market will allow. In the example of the small pump manufacturer, the Gross Profit was only about 25 percent—hardly enough to get excited about!

In the case of an innovative product, it is important to have a large Gross Profit for several reasons, not the least important of which is competition. If you have a skinny Gross Profit to begin with, what are you going to do when a competitive challenge is made? If someone finds a cheaper way to produce or obtain whatever it is you are trying to sell, where does that leave you if you already have a *low* Gross Profit? When you cite an example it is usually possible to think of exceptions. One that comes to mind here is a rather small company that makes specialized parts for automobile engines. The company keeps its price rather low—relative to cost and absolutely—in the hopes that some competitor will not enter the field. The company's sales are "only" about $3 million, hardly enough for a big firm to get interested. But the Pre-Tax Profit is about $1 million! What about the pricing strategy of a company like buy.com, where they apparently were trying to sell (initially, at least) for a **negative Gross Profit?** This is an anomaly and will be discussed below. Apparently, they were trying to *buy* market share, assuming that if they had market share, profits would not be far behind once they could raise prices. This idea would not fly today.

The other principal reason for having a large Gross Profit in an innovative start-up has to do with the percentage of the company that the entrepreneur will have to give up if he or she goes outside looking for financing. This subject will be treated in a later section dealing with the raising of venture capital.

MARKET SIZE: TOO BIG, TOO LITTLE

Intertwined with profitability, as we have just seen, is market share. Once an aspiring entrepreneur came to me with what he thought was an outstanding idea for a new product that would be used by "one-telephone companies." When we started to discuss how many one-telephone businesses there were, and then factored in the *percentage* of such firms that could buy the product, the entrepreneur's enthusiasm sank in a puddle of dismay. The market he had assumed just wasn't there.

But the bigger mistake regarding projections of market size has to do with what is called the "1 percent syndrome." To illustrate: consider the case of the wannabe entrepreneur who wanted to sell a magazine at all the National Football League stadiums. He knew the *total* number of people who attended *all* the football games at these stadiums, and he reasoned that "If only 1 percent

TRADING STRATEGY

HOW COULD ETOYS.COM FAIL?

eToys.com was started back in 1997 by a well-qualified and well-connected entrepreneur, Toby Lenks. Having recognized a very unusual market niche, Lenks put together a dream team, acquired **initial start-up financing**, and, soon after, **growth financing** to make his dream come true. Lenks also took the company public in May 1999. Within a few months, the company's market value had reached the mercurial $10 billion level. Somewhere along the line, the team had figured out they needed to capture less than 1 percent of the $100 billion toy market in order to break even and become profitable.

Unfortunately, such a meteoric success did not last long enough to turn Lenks's plans into reality. Bur-

dened with a debt of $274 million—with no prospects for new financing—along with a worthless stock (9 cents at the time), eToys.com called it quits on February 26, 2001 and filed for bankruptcy. Shortly thereafter, in May 2001, the company sold its heart and soul of the business—the logos, trademark, Web address and some software—to the Pittsburgh-based KB Toys for $3.35 million.

Apparently the culprits here were a combination of logistics-related problems and costly infrastructure building, leading to unrealistic sales expectations by the company, and an increasingly skeptical stock market. Insistence on being an "Internet pure player" may also be added to the list.

of the people buy my magazine, it will be a big success." But how do you know that 1 percent of the people actually will buy your magazine? Have you done any market research to try to ascertain whether at least 1 percent would buy the product? Or, is someone supposed to rely on your statement of "Trust me!"

Another example of this was supplied by one of my students. His parents, who had a business in the Lake Tahoe area, were impressed with the amount of traffic carried by the highway leading up to the Lake. Based upon a traffic count, they decided to build a new restaurant on this highway and said to themselves, "If only 2 percent of the cars using this highway stop, the restaurant will be a huge success." They did no market research of any kind to back up their supposition. Well, you know how this story turned out. The couple stood by their brand-new restaurant and watched the traffic speed by—and never stop. More will be said about market research in Chapter 2, where we examine the Package, or business proposal, but the importance of doing adequate market research cannot be overstressed.

While the problem of a market that is too small is rather easy to imagine, the problem of a market that is too big may not occur to many entrepreneurs. (Again, New Economy firms were thought to be the exception to this point. Here, the bigger the better. But look what happened!) This was first brought to my attention when I saw a product—I had better not identify it—in the office of a venture capital firm. It seemed to me that this product would have lots of potential. Indeed, the people in the venture capital firm thought so, too. When I asked if they were going to back this new product they said no, because they thought that if they did—and were successful—competition from big, well-established firms in the market would be able to overwhelm this start-up operation. They would *prove out* the market for someone else.

Reaching the retail market is another aspect of the criterion of market size. How is the product to be sold? By squeezing onto shelf space in a supermarket? This kind of effort would take potentially a very large marketing/selling budget that may be well beyond the resources of the start-up operation.

One of the most outstanding start-up operations I have ever seen is John Paul Mitchell Systems Inc., a distributor of Paul Mitchell Shampoo products, started with only $700 in the late 1970s. The entrepreneurs overcame the marketing problem by selling only to prescreened beauty salons, at first, and then, when they had a sufficient number of such salons in a given geographic area, appointing a distributor to service the salons in that area. In this way it was possible to distribute Paul Mitchell products with *very* little marketing expense. It fact, it was some time before the company even had to advertise, instead using trade shows to get its message home to the salons (retailers). Having very limited capital, the owners of this start-up company would have been overwhelmed if they had attempted to "go retail" on their own. In fact, the company made a big point of saying they would *never* sell directly to retailers. This assuaged the fears of the salon owners, who feared the big stores would undercut their prices, and made them feel special in the sale of the products. In this way, the entrepreneur (who was the CEO), John Paul DeJoria, took what could have been a major problem and turned it into an advantage.

CAPITAL INTENSITY

Capital intensity means the amount of **sunk** or capital invested in the start-up. Does the basic idea involve a large amount of invested capital that would be lost or severely impaired if the new company does not succeed? Or is there some way of reducing or eliminating the sunk costs without hurting the product?

If the product is a chemical formulation, for example, the product can be produced and bottled by specialized firms that do this for all kinds of different products. Furthermore, you don't even have to have a formula of your own in some cases. All you have to do is specify what you want the product to do and the bottler will produce the product. Imagine what this saves in the way of capital. None of the expensive equipment required for chemical blending has to be purchased. Instead, that capital can be used for such things as **working capital** (**Accounts Receivable** and **Inventory**) that will facilitate greater sales. The John Paul Mitchell Systems company never has had its own bottling facility. Instead, it has a "captive" bottling company next door—as well as other specialized ones—so that all it has to do is send a truck or forklift to the next-door plant and bring back another load of product in the quantity desired.

There is the case of another firm that has a line of household cleaners—none of which are bottled by the company. This company has the bottler ship the desired amounts to the customers designated. (Some people do not prefer to do this, since they fear that the customer's list would be stolen or misappropriated.) If the product is a software program, perhaps the product can be outsourced to a contract software provider. Or the product may be something that could be formed by an injection-molding machine or some other mechanical means.

One wannabe entrepreneur/inventor, who had a line of plastic parts that would be used by a homeowner for gardening purposes, dismissed such a saving opportunity. His product had never been sold, but nevertheless the inventor wanted a venture capitalist to put up the money to build a building—and put his name on it, perhaps. He wanted the VC to buy all the injection-molding equipment needed, as well as all the other capital equipment. Only then would production begin. When it was suggested that a custom shop could be found that would make these products for a new start-up company, the entrepreneur/inventor was incensed. "What and give up all that profit to someone else?" This is Income-Statement thinking; it ignores the Balance Sheet. This individual was forgetting that all that equipment and building represented **capital investment**—capital that has an **opportunity cost**! If, instead of investing in the equipment and building, the same money had been invested in working capital, much more business could be done, with more profit.

Another example of ways to save capital investment lies in the experience of a start-up manufacturer of cosmetics and related supplies. The entrepreneur started out, as many entrepreneurs do, by attempting to manufacture everything he sold. Because of a problem with insurance, he decided to subcontract the production of several items. Almost immediately he realized how much better off his business would be if he subcontracted more, across the board. In short order, he found he was subcontracting almost everything; the only thing he did in his factory was storing and packaging the individual items. By giving up the production of the individual items, he found that he could actually lower his cost by not manufacturing the product, but, equally important, he found that he was dramatically reducing his break-even point. If he didn't need very much of an item, he simply didn't order it. If he were producing it himself, he may have been forced to make the parts—even though he didn't need them—or he could have paid for the machines and labor to stand idle.

Through a quirk of fate, this entrepreneur learned a valuable lesson. *You don't have to make what you sell!* The benefit of learning this lesson was the large amount of money that he freed up for working capital purposes. With the same amount of capital he was able to do many times more sales than he could previously. Although this example is in the manufacturing sector, the principle might be applied to service and distribution companies as well. With China now in the WTO, a lot of firms are beginning to ask themselves why they should make something they can have made in China—for a whole lot less, and just as high in quality. Software firms, too, are learning that they can have their computer programs written in Bangalore or Beijing.

Finally, there is one more type of sunk investment that should be reckoned with: advertising. What is more sunk than an ad in last month's magazine? If the start-up is going to depend on heavy advertising in the early stages, this start-up will be much riskier and require more capital than another start-up that somehow avoids this investment in sunk capital. This has proved to be a major problem with many dot.com companies, especially the ones that were heavily reliant on advertising revenues for themselves. If they did not advertise, then how would someone pay them for their readers' attention?

A ONE-PRODUCT FIRM

Many, if not all, firms start out as one-product firms and there is nothing wrong with that. But does the company *remain* a one-product firm well after it is started? The problem with one-product firms is twofold: on the one hand it is subject to the product life cycle—up and down—and on the other it does not take advantage of the opportunity to sell more product to an established customer. Amazon.com started out selling books, but all too soon it realized the opportunity—and need—to sell items other than books. By analogy, view the firm as having a kind of pipeline to a customer. A one-product firm may have only a very small pipeline to the market. This of course applies to service and distribution companies as well as manufacturers.

REPEAT ORDERS VS. SINGLE SALE

This criterion follows from the preceding one. Ideally, a firm would like to have many repeat orders. The reason for this is that *the most expensive sale is the first sale,* and it is expensive in two ways: money and human effort.

One start-up had a product that would be sold to hospitals. Unlike some products that cost thousands or even hundreds of thousands of dollars, this rather simple device sold for less than $400. The problem with this is that the expense of selling the device to a hospital was such that there was not enough money in the selling price to pay for the **selling expense**. Unfortunately there are many wonderful products invented that simply do not have a selling price high enough to warrant the sales effort. They were vitamins instead of pain killers. When computers were new on the market they were, indeed, a single-sale item. The difference then was that the price was high enough to provide for a hefty selling expense. Today, the price of computers, especially personal computers, is so low that there is no longer the money in the selling price to pay for personal selling effort. Competition has squeezed all the slack out of the selling price.

The other problem with a single-sale product is that it wears out the sales force, which would *always* be making cold calls. If the product were really expensive—as many computers were in the 1960s, for example—the sales staff might not mind being turned down frequently or having to spend a lot of time on a sales call. But anything less than this would be trying on the sales staff, leading to the need to replace them frequently. This in itself is expensive and time-consuming, not to mention distasteful.

Focus on Technology

COMPUTERS FROM IOWA? . . . COOL!

"We have to be successful in the "box business" (the simple business of selling PCs in the famous cow-skin-designed boxes) if we are going to go "beyond the box" (selling so many bundled non-PC products)."

Ted Waitt, Founder, Gateway 2000

These are the niche-renewing and strategy-setting words that Ted Waitt used recently when he returned "back to the saddle" at the declining Gateway. Gateway's profits had plummeted 26 percent the last year and its stock nose dived—of course partly due to the general slowdown in the computer market. A year earlier, Waitt had switched his role to a nonexecutive Chairman so that he could follow his other interests. He had apparently done this reluctantly and under some pressure from Wall Street.

The thinking at the company was that they needed "professional, big company management," so they hired a top AT&T executive as the new CEO. As it turned out, that was not a sound decision. Waitt's heroic return was triggered by the fact that the company he had founded at the age of 22 had lost sight of its core market niche, its core strategies, and its vital entrepreneurial spirit. One strategic misstep was the flap over the "box strategy."

Waitt, with partner Mike Hammond, founded Gateway back in 1985 on his family's farm in Iowa, and with almost no start-up capital. He found his niche of direct selling PCs when he worked in a computer store as a sales clerk in Sioux City, Iowa. Gateway actually started as a Texas Instrument user's club, charging an annual fee of $20 for club membership and a companion newsletter that would catalogue add-on products for TI computers. At that time, TI did not have any after-market business activity for the computers it sold; it had no add-on products or services. And this is the niche that Gateway discovered early on, building a giant manufacturing and service firm around it.

Waitt and Hammond generated $100,000 revenue just in their first four months of operation in 1985. Later in 1987 they started selling fully configured PCs through direct mail and made $1.5 million in that year. Finding an unserved niche was Gateway's entry to selling PCs directly to the customers. The folksy company grew at an annual rate of 20 percent in the 1990s and become the second-largest direct seller of PCs, with sales of close to $10 billion in year 2000, and 20,000 employees.

Supplied by Rassoul Yazdipour, Ph.D. California State University and California Technology Entrepreneurship Center-CTEC

CAPABLE OF AN "OUT"

This criterion, which probably deserves higher ranking, may make or break a start-up deal. (This is extremely important with many New Economy firms, such as e-tailers.) If investors do not see a way to get their investment out of a deal—with their required profit—then they will naturally be reluctant to invest in the first place. The price for many investors, at least professional investors, for non–New Economy deals is five to ten times their money in 3 to 5 years. (The price for the Internet type of deals will be discussed below.) To get this kind of return, it is usually necessary that the firm be sold or that it "**go public,**" meaning that it sells its stock to the public. *Note: This is true for ALL types of firms!* This means that merely promising to pay dividends—money that may be taxed twice, once to the company and then to the recipient—is not going to excite many investors, unless the dividends are really big relative to the investment.

With just a moment's reflection one can see that this criterion involves several of the foregoing criteria. If the firm is perceived to be a mom-and-pop operation, who would want to buy the company or take it public? Profitability may also be an issue. As will be explained later, these profitless wonders that are so beautiful in the inventor's/entrepreneur's eyes may require that an inordinate amount of the company is given up when securing the necessary venture capital, or there just may be no interest in such an unprofitable type of firm. (See the discussion of "Staging Financing" in Chapter 2.)

The importance of "self-financing" a start-up cannot be overstated. If the new company can be financed with the resources that the entrepreneur can muster—and then grow through financial internal means—the entrepreneur can avoid many difficult problems. When outside investors get involved in a deal, the whole situation changes for the entrepreneur. He or she is no longer master of the ship! Unfortunately, some wannabe entrepreneurs associate raising a lot of "outside" money as being a measure of success (sounds like the go-go 1990s?).

PRODUCT TOO SIMPLE

Some time ago someone called and said that he had a product that he wished to promote in a company. When I asked him what the product was, he said that he couldn't tell me because if he did everyone would know what it was. This, then, is what I mean by a product that is too simple. If your idea can be easily copied by someone—without much expense—then it appears that it would be rather hard to turn such a product into a business. Many entrepreneurs of New Economy firms felt they could be the "First Mover" and by so doing preempt others. A goodly number of them found out that it might be better to be the second or third company rather than the trail blazer.

Again, an example opens the door to all sorts of exceptions. One of them is the successful retail branch operation Kinko's Graphics. This chain of stores started out as one copying store and has expanded to become an international chain. Why? Because there is something proprietary in this operation? I do not think so. What made these stores different initially was their location near campuses; now it is their package of services. Remaining open 24 hours a day was another innovation that made the store different. Mail Boxes Etc. is another example of an exception to this criterion, which is more clearly illustrated by a computer software program written with standard software to do a certain job—for example, to find new cars in California. Anyone who knows a little about computers and their software could create such a program if told to do so. So how could this program—maybe more like a spread sheet—be the basis for a company in which people would invest?

OUT OF VOGUE

It does not matter if a product is not yet in vogue to be a successful new venture, but it is extremely difficult to find financing for an idea that was in vogue *last year*, like business-to-consumers dot.com companies were in the late 1990s. Experience shows that investors are reluctant to invest in such ventures. Some potential entrepreneurs seem to be behind the times, however, and are seen persisting in trying to find financing for out-of-vogue ideas.

AN UNDERSTANDABLE DEAL

This criterion refers to the type and explanation of the *deal* that is being presented. It does not refer to the complexity of the product itself. This criterion first became apparent when I was asked to work on a start-up venture involving a very complicated real estate deal. After two hours of explaining the intricacies of the deal to someone who was quite an expert in real estate deals, we popped the question: "Are you interested?" "Great idea," this man said, "but how would you ever explain this to a group of physicians or other wealthy people who would make up a syndicate, when it took you 2 hours to explain it to me?"

The entrepreneur simply must find a way to tell someone in a very brief and terse way exactly what it is that he or she is trying to do. John Morris calls this the "elevator pitch." You must be able to tell someone what it is that you are doing "while the elevator is still moving." Another Tech Coast Angel, George Kenney of the Shepherd Fund, refers to this criterion as the "Rule of 16." He says that an entrepreneur has to be able to present his or her idea in 16 words, in 16 seconds with words that are appropriate for someone with an IQ of an average 16-year-old. This may not be very complimentary, but it makes a lot of sense! Another example of this exercise in brevity is a story told about David Bonnett, founder of GEO Cities. After pitching his idea many times to potential investors, he finally met one who told him he only had 30 seconds, since he was leaving, and asked what it was he was trying to do. Because of the terseness of his answer, the VC was so impressed that he said "Tell me more." It is hard to minimize the importance of a simple, direct explanation of what the idea is all about.

The criteria presented here are supposed to help make a start-up more doable. This one amounts to keeping a deal simple. Deals have their own way of getting complicated as they go along, so starting off with a simple model seems to make good sense.

This criterion also involves a measure of ego for a number of potential entrepreneurs. For example, a man once came to me with an idea to start a car wash. This was a reasonable thing if the location was right, but the thing this man had on his mind was doing a big deal. He wanted to set up a **Master Limited Partnership** that just seemed unreasonable for what should have been a rather simple corporation, partnership, or (today) **Limited Liability Company**. Instead of worrying about the business details of such a venture, this man kept returning to "deal aspects" of the idea.

RECAPPING THE CRITERIA

The criteria just presented are intended to be checkpoints against which a new idea can be evaluated or screened. In each instance, an effort was made to offer an alternative that, if taken, would improve the new company itself or, perhaps more importantly, improve the chances of getting the new idea funded. The one exception to this is the criterion of basic profitability. Many ideas seem like good ideas until scrutinized for the inherent profitability of the company set up to manufacture or otherwise deliver the product or service. Here, mental and emotional discipline is needed. No matter how intriguing the product may be, if people do not want to pay enough to allow you to produce a satisfactory profit, then the idea should be dropped. For many inventors, this is a difficult pill to swallow. One of the mistakes made during the dot.com era was following the notion that profitability was not really important—market share was!

KEY PERSON OR MANAGEMENT TEAM

Now we come to the second of the four basic ingredients for a start-up: the individual or team behind it.

EVALUATING A KEY PERSON

What makes a good entrepreneur? Who knows! Although there are numerous studies that profile the personality of entrepreneurs, until an individual is thrust into that position, you can only conjecture how this person will perform. Yet there are techniques of use to people who may be asked to finance a start-up or otherwise work on a start-up. Some years ago, an individual was asked to give a talk on this subject to our students. Paraphrasing an article he had read, he titled his talk "$C^{12} D^2$." He explained that one can describe an entrepreneur by using twelve words that begin with a "C" and two terms that begin with a "D" (Driving Force and Direction Finder). Since this has been found useful in discussing the relevant characteristics of entrepreneurs or, better, wannabe entrepreneurs, let's discuss some of these "C" words as criteria for the start-up management.

Conditioning

Attempting to do a start-up is extremely taxing, both mentally and physically. Does this person have the stamina to put in long hours? What is the physical condition of the potential entrepreneur? In doing a start-up for an ophthalmic lab once, it was noted that the General Manager who would run the shop was a heavy smoker and noticeably overweight. The person who was backing the deal

Focus on Technology

"JUST DO IT"!

Business ideas and opportunities coming even from the most visionary people are worth nothing if one cannot develop appropriate strategies to put them in the form of a product or service. One of the great "idea men" and innovators of our time was William Von Meister, the founder of Control Video Corporation in the early 1980s. He died unknown and broke in 1995 at the age of 53. I am sure very few of you have heard of him. However, among his many credits is the following: "Without Bill Von Meister, there would have been no America Online"!

The point, and this is true for all successful ventures, is this: Implementation is everything, ideas are nothing! One more thing: If you study the history of all great products, you will see without exception that all such products and services had a clumsy start. Why? The answer may lie in the saying "Someone had to do it"! Here are two quotes from the people who should know:

"I did not . . . create the perfect mousetrap. Some companies spend so long developing their mousetraps that by the time they hit the market, there are whole new kinds of mice to trap . . . The trick is to be in the marketplace just as the demand is accelerating. Too early is sometimes as bad as too late."
Sandra Kurtzig, Founder of ASK, Inc.

"Success in the post–start-up stage is a matter of holding the line, moving forward through calculated risk, and solving hundreds of small problems every month, instead of coming up with big ideas every day and risking everything."
Jim Clark, Founder of Netscape

Supplied by Rassool Yazdipour, Ph.D. California State University and California Technology Entrepreneurship Center-CTEC

dismissed concerns that were expressed regarding these factors and pointed out what a good manager he was. Well, about 6 weeks after opening, the General Manager had to take sick leave and within 6 months he was dead from throat cancer. Perhaps this is an extreme example, but it is a real case in point. Furthermore, it should be remembered that subordinates in the new organization derive their strength from the person in charge. If that person is tired, this will be reflected in how others feel and act.

Confidence

When you ask someone whether he or she can run the new company, what kind of answer do you receive? "Oh, I guess I can run the company." Is that the kind of answer that generates enthusiasm and confidence in the potential entrepreneur? Hardly. Something bordering on overconfidence would be more reassuring. Someone who says "You bet I can run this new company!" would provide the kind of confidence needed to motivate the entire organization. *The most contagious thing in the world is enthusiasm!*

Courage

Has this potential entrepreneur ever met an obstacle and overcome it? Some people have never been in a position where they were faced with adversity in business—or otherwise. Does this person have enough courage to survive a start-up attempt? One manager confided that he liked to hire pilots because it takes a certain amount of courage just to land an airplane.

Competitiveness

Anyone who says "after you" is probably going to have a difficult time surviving in a new business environment. This criterion is similar to the preceding one. Has this person ever competed against someone? Once a woman graduate student came to me after class and said that she had a disability which prevented her from competing in sports. So how could she be expected to be competitive? I answered by asking who said anything about sports? A competitive sense applies to more than sports! A woman who was a sales manager for a firm for which I was consulting was about the most competitive person I have ever met, and she was no athlete. When she shook your hand it was a real handshake, not just a polite one. If you went to a cocktail lounge for a drink, she would ask what it is that you wanted and then she would say "I'll have one, too, only make mine double!" I thought at the time what a terrific entrepreneur this woman would make.

Charisma

Some people think that charisma is the major factor to look for in a potential entrepreneur. True, charisma will help a lot in getting the deal done, but what about after the company is founded? Indeed, just how far will charisma carry the CEO of the new firm, if that is all he or she has to offer? No, charisma is great to have, for it helps to get the deal funded, but it is still second to the next factor. Once the company is up and running, it takes more than charisma to manage and guide it.

Character

Having unwittingly worked with some out-and-out crooks in attempting to do a start-up, I am convinced that character is the one absolutely indispensable ingredient in the potential entrepreneur. There are many people running around in pursuit of someone to help them do a start-up who are either phonies or basically dishonest. This is why in the first half-hour of my conversation with a potential entrepreneur I ask two questions: Have you ever been in jail? and Have you ever been bankrupt? This is not to say that I am passing judgment on *all* persons who have served time in jail or declared bankruptcy, but these are such large impediments to raising money for a start-up that I want to know these facts up front. Some swindlers can be quite clever. I remember one instance in which the potential entrepreneur was asked for a list of twenty-five people who could be a reference. On hearing this, this individual went into a sort of rage and said, "I don't even know twenty-five people I could ask for a

SHIFTING FOR GROWTH

"The best thing that I learned at Sun (Microsystems) was to never accept today as good enough. It was always critical to bring out new products that improved on ourselves. . . . I've tried to instill that aggressiveness and sense of urgency here."
Carol Bartz, CEO of Autodesk

From its founding in 1982 by a group of "cowboy coders" bent on bringing computer-aided-design (CAD) solutions for PCs, and working at their own eccentric pace and schedules, Autodesk has come a long way. Autodesk was founded by John Walker and his friends to manufacture exciting products without much regard for profitability or even marketability. But, given its novelty and huge market potentials, the "lifestyle" venture had its IPO 3 years after its inception, and by 1987 it had already shipped its one hundred thousandth copy of PC AutoCAD to its clients.

However, as is common at many new ventures—including the Internet commerce giant eBay—an outside professional manager had to be brought in to manage the CAD company's vast potentials. For Autodesk in 1992, this was Carol Bartz—a Sun veteran. Upon her arrival, Bartz introduced a set of carefully thought-out initiatives within the company and positioned Autodesk for expansion and high growth. Such house-rearranging helped Autodesk to ship its one millionth copy of Auto-CAD by 1994 and its two millionth by 1999. Autodesk's sales figure for fiscal year 2001 has grown to the vicinity of $1 billion.

Although not a company founder, Bartz continues to keep her innovating and risk-taking edge at Autodesk. She takes risks that very few traditional managers would take. "As a business leader," she says, "I've learned that, to keep up with the quick pace of change, you have to constantly challenge yourself. Take risks—I preach that to employees, to colleagues, to everyone, really. Jump out of your comfort zone. That is what makes being a CEO fun."

Autodesk and eBay are among the many examples of new companies where transition from start-up to high growth calls for bringing in a team of professional managers to help the original entrepreneurs in their quest for growth. Of course, eBay's Pierre Omidyar actually helped the transition process and reaped the huge benefits as a result. However, Autodesk's founder Walker had to be eased out. Regarding these pioneers, you could also make your own judgment as to who did the right thing.

reference." But he did produce a short list of references—a list that contained the names of some prominent or important people. Unfortunately, this man "owned" everyone on the list, including a municipal judge and a CPA who was head of his own firm. This short list all gave good references, but they were false or misleading. If you are going to get involved in a start-up with someone, it behooves you to check out this person in any way you can. There are services that provide complete background checks on individuals, and if you are thinking of investing money in a person's deal, it might be well to retain such a service.

THE MANAGEMENT TEAM

Is it better to have one individual or a management team? This depends on the type of firm and the background and **track record**▲ of the potential entrepreneur. For scientific/high-tech start-ups, it may be quite necessary to have a *team* of individuals forming the nucleus of the new firm. For a nontechnical, plain-vanilla-start-up, the most important person always is the prospective CEO. If this person is the right person for this challenge, he or she should be able to reach out among his or her acquaintances in the industry and recruit competent people to fill the important positions in the new company. Adding these other names at the outset is really adding nothing and may indicate a lack of confidence on the part of the potential entrepreneur.

A subset of this point is the case of the "Co-CEO." Once I was in a meeting with two individuals who were making a pitch for money to back their proposed new venture. When asked which of the two would be the CEO, one of the individuals answered, "Oh, it doesn't matter. George can be the CEO or I can do the job." Well, this may have seemed like a modest thing to say, but I knew at that moment that we would not get financing from this source. Most venture capitalists want to invest in take-charge people and these two individuals did not demonstrate this attribute. It would have been much better if this individual had said, "George will be the boss and I'll do everything I can to support him." (Subsequently they became real estate development partners and are now very successful.)

▲ "Track record," in the vernacular of finance, refers to whether or not someone has had "profit-and-loss" responsibility. Has this person ever done a job that resulted in making a profit?

SUMMARY

In this chapter it was noted that it takes four "ingredients" to start a company: the basic idea, the key person, the "Package" or private placement memoradum, and the venture capital. The first two were the subject of this chapter; the other two are treated in the next chapter. "Criteria" were examined as things that the budding entrepreneur should keep in mind when evaluating an idea for a start-up. Taking these factors into account should make the idea more feasible. It was stressed that the idea had to be a *pain killer* and not a vitamin. Occasionally, these criteria may show that an idea is not a *good* idea and the whole thing should be scrapped. The discussion of the key person and management team was intended to alert the entrepreneur-to-be of the main thing that investors look for: a track record. If the wannabe entrepreneur does not have any sort of track record ("Have you ever managed an Income Statement and made any money with it?"), he or she should do something to get this track record before seeking outside capital, especially professional funds. This is explored in Chapter 2.

QUESTIONS FOR DISCUSSION

Using all the criteria that are articulated in this chapter, evaluate the following proposed start-ups:

a. A snowboard manufacturing company.
b. A company to design, develop, and distribute systems software for distribution companies.
c. A company to manufacture components for broadband telecommunications.
d. A chain of retail dry cleaning stores.

1

CHAPTER REVIEW

2

Packaging and Financing a Start-Up

THE PRIVATE PLACEMENT MEMORANDUM

We have acquired, in Chapter 1, an understanding of how the idea and the individual(s) behind a start-up interact. In turning to the other two ingredients, we start with the format of the Private Placement Memorandum—or, as it is known colloquially, "the Package" or the "business plan." Before proceeding to the outline or contents of the Package, however, we might consider what the Package should look like.

The best approach is knowing what a Package should *not* look like. It should not look like a request for government funding or some other equally voluminous document. The package should be no more than about 20 to 25 pages double-spaced plus the financials as an appendix.▲ The people who read these documents, whether they be professional venture capitalists or wealthy individuals, do not wish to wade through a thick volume. This means that the writer—and the writer had better be the wannabe entrepreneur, as most venture capitalists will not discuss a Package that has been written by someone else—has to be extremely careful in preparing this document and not waste any

▲ One wealthy individual I know insists that the "Package" be no more than **one** page! Obviously, this is really hard to do. This really needs to be an elevator pitch!

words. The document should be perfect, meaning that it should not have any typographical errors. This lack of mistakes should not be a problem with computers and spelling checks, but it behooves the entrepreneur to be careful and make sure the document does not have any typographical or other mistakes, however small. Remember, too, spelling checkers do not alert you to a missing word or a word that is correctly spelled but not the one intended. Nothing replaces proofreading.

The importance of having a business plan for high-tech start-ups is even more important today. It may be that it is next to impossible to do an adequate forecast that is inherent in such a business plan. At the height of the dot.com bubble, many angel investors and VCs went ahead with little or no business plan. I wonder, if the situation were repeated with the experience we now have, what would happen. Today, surely they would require one—a good one—even if this seems extraordinarily difficult.

THE OUTLINE

What should be included in any business plan? Briefly, the Package should contain the following:

1. Introduction and summary (evaluation summary)
2. The product—what it is you are going to sell
3. Marketing
4. Key person—management team
5. Financial summary, including the pro-forma project statements

Introduction and Summary

This section, which is usually written last, should be no more than about one-and-a-half pages (double-spaced). This is the selling point for the whole Package. If the reader does not get turned on here, he or she may never go beyond this section. This is much like the "elevator" pitch. Each of the subsequent sections is summarized in one or two sentences.

The Product

In this section there is a discussion of what it is that the company will make or distribute, or the service to be supplied. But how much detail do you tell about the product in this section? To answer this question, you need to realize *who* will be reading this Package. There are sometimes—especially if the reader is a professional venture capitalist—three people who might read your business plan: in addition to the principal, an accounting type and a technical person. If the product is quite technical, a professional source of financing may go to an expert in the field for an opinion of this product, assuming that this type of expertise is not available in-house. What this technical person will be looking for is the general idea presented, not all the minute details. If there are trade secrets involved, the way to handle this is by use of a nondisclosure agreement that can be drafted by an attorney, especially one who is expert with patents. Such an agreement states the secret details of the product, and the venture capital source signs in acknowledgment that the entrepreneur is divulging this trade secret for the exclusive purpose of raising funds for the start-up. Later, if the entrepreneur feels that the other party has stolen the idea, there is a basis for a lawsuit. Many venture capitalists and big corporate investors simply will not sign such documents feeling that they expose themselves to too much litigation. When this happens it presents a dilemma for the wannabe entrepreneur. Generally speaking, professional sources are not interested in stealing ideas, since an idea without the person behind the idea is usually not worth very much. Besides, start-up backers don't really want deals that they can invest in; they want *people* who can make money for them.

In discussion of the product, the question of whether or not to obtain a patent on the product arises. It is difficult to give a definitive answer to this question, but, in general, it is *not* a good idea to take out a patent on the product before getting the new company funded. The main reason has to do with time. If you wait to get the patent, which can easily take two years or more, you present this question to the person reading your Package: "What have you been doing with this product for the past two years? Have you been showing this product around town?" No amount of denial is likely to convince someone that you have not been showing your deal to others—that you have not been shopping your deal. And remember, with a few exceptions, mostly high-tech type deals, *a shopped deal is no deal!*

The other reason involves protection of your idea. The patent process involves first the filing and then the issuance of the patent. The patent applies from the moment the application is presented to the Patent Office, not when the patent is issued.▲ Some people put in many irrelevant and superfluous factors in their application in order to delay the actual issuance of the patent—which is probably a good idea. Once the patent is issued, the whole world can see what the secret is. However, until that time, no one can see the details.

There is another disadvantage to taking out a patent. Once you patent the product, you tell everyone what it is that you have that is special. If it can be shown that this particular claim was in the public domain, say, through the publication of an article sometime in the past, then your claim can be overthrown. If nothing else, you may not have the necessary capital needed to defend your claim.▲▲ Instead of patenting a product, many managers/entrepre-

---

▲ It is reported that Alexander Graham Bell beat another individual to the patent office by a scant 20 minutes when patenting the telephone.

▲▲ This recalls a deal where a client of mine purchased a division of a major manufacturer and shipped it to California. Included in this purchase was a consumer product that had a unique feature. We immediately recognized that a major (big!) competitor had a similar product with this feature. "Ah," we said "this looks like a patent infringement suit to us!" At least we said this until we talked to a patent attorney and were told how much it would take as a *down payment* just to start such a case, not to mention what the subsequent costs might be.

neurs elect to keep the *process* of manufacturing the product secret. In this way they believe they can keep their competitive advantage. Certain very technical products might be an exception to the general rule of avoiding patents before obtaining funding. It might be necessary to have a patent on the product and it is the presence of this patent that the wannabe entrepreneur is seeking backing for. It obviously depends on the product and the circumstances as to whether or not you even apply for a patent, not to mention having the patent issued. But the point that should be kept in mind is the timing problem associated with the patent process and the implications this would have on the shopped-deal problem.

Marketing

This section discusses (1) how you are going to sell the product and, most importantly, (2) your substantiation of your sales forecast. *There is no part of this whole package more important than this justification for the sales forecast.* If the reader of the business plan agrees with you when you state your assumptions, then the conclusion (sales) naturally follows. But if you have to convince the reader that you can make the sales you forecast, then all the rest of the effort is uphill. Again, this is true with all sorts of deals, "plain-vanilla," high-tech, dot.com, whatever!

How, then, does one convince the reader that the sales projections are realistic and doable? Again, this is a very difficult question to answer. For many products, the answer lies in some sort of **marketing research**. Whether you undertake test marketing in a small city, as is usual in conventional test marketing, or you do it some other way, you have to squarely face the issue raised in Chapter 1: "Will people buy this product or service in the quantities indicated for this price?" Have you ever sold this product or service, or are you just saying "Trust me, people will buy this product." This is what happened in a lot of dot.com start-ups. If the reader is convinced that the product will sell—to whomever—then the numbers take on a credence they would not otherwise have. If the product is a nonconsumer product, do you have letters from business firms expressing interest in buying this product? Whatever it takes to produce a feeling of belief on the part of the reader is the job that must be done. In today's VC climate, actual sales may be required.

Key Person/Management Team

This section presents the qualifications and background of the entrepreneur/ CEO for the new firm, plus the qualifications for the key positions—if that is advisable. If the new company is going to be the kind of firm that is not dependent on one or more individuals, e.g., scientists that are members of a team or, perhaps, specialized computer specialists, then it is not really necessary to include the résumés of second-level executives. As mentioned above, the assumption should be that if the CEO is the right person, then he or she should know capable people to bring in for the other jobs, such as the marketing director or the production manager.

Putting someone's résumé in the Package may not be the helpful act that at first it might appear. There was one instance in which an individual's résumé was included as the Vice President of Marketing for the proposed new firm. A presentation was made downtown, and before everyone could get back to their respective offices, a phone call was made to the marketing individual's president, who summoned him as soon as he arrived back at his office. "What do you mean trying to bail out of here? Haven't we treated you well?" He was then fired. In this case, the marketing expert went on to sign with another start-up, sold out his share for millions of dollars, and retired when he was about 40. So it eventually worked out well for him but had a negative impact on the original start-up.

The résumé that is included in this section is not the kind that you might use for getting a job. Things that represent the individual's track record must be emphasized. This is typically the first thing that an experienced venture capitalist or investor will look for. The track record provides the individual's success rate of managing an Income Statement and making money with it. It is not enough to be well educated or witty or in a responsible staff position; what is needed is a record of making money—for yourself or someone else. It is so easy to say that surely this person would make a good manager, but experience suggests that it is wise to be suspicious if someone has not actually had the responsibility for profit on an Income Statement. Ideally, the wannabe entrepreneur could point to his or her record and say: "I took this division/company/product, whatever, and made money with it." This means line responsibility and not a staff position, no matter how good a staff position it is. Of course, there are exceptions, but saying that you were head of an engineering section with a budget of $10 million a year is not the same as saying that you took a product or company and made money.▲

Including the résumés of professionals at the accounting or legal firm that the new company will retain is not a good idea. This indicates a weakness on the part of the entrepreneur and an attempt to "beef up" the management. Including the name (but not the résumé) of some individual who is much respected as a manager may have a halo effect, however. If this person has agreed to be on the Board of Directors, it may be construed as a vote of confidence in the entrepreneur by those individuals that are contemplating investing in the firm.

It is possible to save some space and minimize the page length of your Package by single-spacing the résumés that are included. Furthermore, it is quite unwise to include in an individual's résumé such things as memberships in clubs and nonbusiness activities. Being a Boy Scout leader may be

---

▲ For students and other young entrepreneurs-to-be just getting started, this should mean that you should be selective in choosing your jobs. If you want to develop your own "track record," you won't be able to do this by taking some nice soft staff job just because it pays more than a line position. You have to find a job that will give you the ability to point and say "I did this." It is not enough to say "Oh, I am sure I can do it."

highly commendable in the community, but it does not belong in the résumé *for this purpose.* Likewise, a wannabe entrepreneur may be extremely proud of his or her record of patents, but including examples of these patents would be quite unwise. Remember, sources of venture capital are looking for any slip-up on the part of the entrepreneur in the Package, no matter how small. They look for the proverbial "tip of the iceberg." Everything that goes into the résumés should reflect one thing: success in business. Anything else should be avoided.

The Financial Summary

There are three parts to the Financial Summary:

1. A summary of the sales and profits forecast for the firm
2. A critique of how much money will be needed to finance the start-up
3. The pro-forma financials—the forecast Income Statement, the Balance Sheet, and the Cash Flow Statement, plus the footnotes needed to explain each item

Each of these will be discussed separately and at length.

SALES AND PROFIT FORECAST

The Package must contain discussion both of the sales that are forecast—and the justification for these sales forecasts—and of the profits that would result when that sales forecast materializes. It is usually necessary to forecast sales and profits for 5 years—even though this might seem a bit ambitious—in order to be able to arrive at an estimate of profits for purposes of allocating ownership interests. If venture capitalists want to see what profits will be in 5 years, it behooves the wannabe entrepreneur to supply these data. The high-tech exceptions will be detailed below.

Implications of the Profitability Statement: How Much Equity to Offer?

A group of angel investors might tell you what they want—and "Take it or leave it." But if you are dealing with someone other than an angel, or professional venture capitalists, very often the source of capital will ask "What percentage are you willing to give me for this money?" When this question is presented to you, you need a reasonable reply. How do you decide how much of the company—what percentage of the stock—to give up for the venture capital that is invested?

The decision rule for the percentage of the company to offer, called **PR**, is as follows:

$$PR = \frac{\text{Desired multiple of investment} \times \text{amount invested}}{\text{Value of company in 5 years [fifth-year earnings} \times \text{some multiple]}}$$

The usual multiple for firms (other than very high tech) that is desired by professional sources of venture capital is five to ten times the investment in 3 to 5 years.▲ So if we are talking about needing $500,000 as the amount invested, then the numerator would be, say, $5 million. The denominator would be the fifth-year earnings times some multiple. An example follows:

$$\text{Percentage of Company to Offer} = \frac{\$5,000,000 \ (=\$500,000 \times 10)}{\$15,000,000 \ (=\$1,000,000 \times 15)}$$
$$= 33.3\,\%$$

Here the investor gets 33 percent and the entrepreneur gets 67 percent. Now it should be clear why the basic profitability of the proposed business (first discussed in Chapter 1) is so important. If the firm's projected earnings are rather anemic, then the denominator will be smaller and the percentage that you will need to give up will be larger.

The size of the cut may go up quite quickly. If the firm projected only $400,000 in earnings and the multiple held steady at 15, then the denominator would be only $6,000,000 and the amount needed to give up would jump to 83+ percent. Would you as an aspiring entrepreneur want to risk all for a share of the company of only 16+ percent—assuming you do not have to give up any stock to management members or to seed-money suppliers? Of course the size of the deal would have to be considered in this context. If the proposal is a gigantic deal, the entrepreneur may be more than willing to get only 16 percent.

All this should point up the importance of proposing a firm that has unusual profitability. Incidentally, you do not show this calculation in the Package. This is for *you*, the wannabe entrepreneur, to have when the time comes when the venture capital source asks "How much of the company are you willing to give up?"

Another factor that is exceedingly important is the multiple of **after-tax earnings** that is suggested. It may be quite appropriate to suggest in the Financial Summary section of your plan what the *multiple* might be. You can do so by implication and association. If you can cite several examples of firms that have gone public recently, and you give the multiples at which they were sold, then you may be able to support the multiple that you use when the discussion comes around to the percentage of ownership shares.

The timing of a start-up is important. If you attempt to do a start-up when the stock market is dramatically down, you may find yourself using very low multiples in your ratio. Attempting a start-up when the market is in a full-blown bull market has the advantage of letting you suggest rather large multiples. Also,

---

▲Idealab, the California Internet "incubator," supposedly used the rule of thumb of 100 times their investment. This will be covered in more detail in a subsequent section (currently, Idealab is fighting for its life).

venture capital is easier to get when people are making money in the stock market—during a bull market. Conversely, if the general stock market is in a decided bear market situation, which usually means that the **IPO** (initial public offering market) is really down, it is hard to get anyone interested, even if you use an otherwise relatively low multiple. If you get your idea for a start-up in the midst of a real down market, you may have to wait (if the idea will wait). Fortunately, bear markets do not last for too many years.

Trying to raise external funds in a "down" market is akin to swimming against the tide. Whether it be raising money for a start-up or for other corporate purposes, timing is extraordinarily important.

Dividing the Stock in a High-Tech Deal—Valuation

While the approach just outlined illustrates the way to divide the stock of a "plain-vanilla" start-up, it can be applied to other situations. First, the professional investors make a "guess" as to what the company will be worth in the market, say, 5 years hence. They do this by estimating the company's profit at that time and then "guessing" at a multiple—an imprecise exercise at best. Then they look for a certain **rate of return** (or a multiple of investment, which results in the same thing), depending on the economic times and their perception of the risk involved. Consider the following example.

Time zero: A group of friends form a company to do something that is considered "high tech." They form a corporation and own all 100 percent of the stock. Their initial financing includes their credit cards, personal savings, and money from family and friends. Hopefully they do not have to give up any stock to "outsiders"—including family and friends—at this stage. If they do, a potential problem comes up if they value the company highly—whatever that means—because if in subsequent **rounds** of financing the angels and venture capitalists use a *lower value*, many hard feelings might result among uncles, grandmothers, and friends.

Year one: Sometime in the first year or so the founders decide that they need more money to continue. They make a "game plan" and go to angels for $1 million in risk financing. At this point the angels will set a value that would allow them to achieve their expected rates of return based on a projected value of the company at the time of exit.▲ Presumably the company is not far enough along in its business that it can make a reasonable forecast of its fifth-year revenues and earnings. Often the angels would ask for 25 percent of the company for their $1 million. This values the company at $4 million. But before investing, the angels try to appraise just how big the company might be—in market value—at the end of, say, 5 years. If the angels were very early investors and were looking for twenty times their money in 5 years, they are looking to have their investment valued at $20 million at exit after allowing for future **dilutions** from additional future rounds of venture capitalization and perhaps a public offering. At that point, the angels then have to ask if this budding company could

---

▲ Since so many angels were "burned" in 2000, today the angels will probably only come in if they can induce a venture capitalist or two to join them in this early-round financing.

have a market capitalization of $80 million or more in 5 years. This means that their 25 percent of $80 million will be the $20 million they require. If the answer is "no," the idea isn't big enough to warrant an $80 million market value, then the angels might ask for more than 25 percent. But this could get them into dangerous waters, as there might not be enough left, after all the subsequent dilution, to incentivize the entrepreneurs.

Investors often want pre-conditions as part of their investment. For example, they would ask the founders to reserve 15–25 percent of the stock for future key employees. Fifteen to 25 percent would be an acceptable range assuming the team needs some key people in its planned development. As a result of the stock options and the anticipated angel investment, the founders would be diluted to approximately 50 percent, assuming 25 percent dilution for the stock options and 25 percent dilution for the angel investment. Appendix 3 is a numerical example of this process.

Year two or three: Depending on the **"burn rate"** of the cash in the company, the management and angels (and their venture capitalist partners) now may decide that they need to get more cash invested. This is where the venture capitalists come in, probably the same ones who invested a "small" amount along with the angels at the very "early stage." (It is precisely for this reason that angels want the VCs to join them in the early stage investment, even if they invest but a modest amount; this increases the probability that they will be there when the next round of financing is needed.) Presumably, at this point in time, the company has developed enough so that a reasonable forecast can be made of fifth-year performance and—highly important today—profits.

Let's suppose that the consensus is that there will be about $9 million in **Net Income** in year 5. If you were to value those earnings at a multiple of 20,▲ the company would have a market value of about $180 million. If there were an IPO at that time, the usual assumption is that about 25 percent of the company would be sold to the public. This would leave a value of about $135 million ($180/75=$135) for the "old" stockholders—founders, key employees, angels, and VCs. Now at this point the VCs will indicate what rate of return (or multiple) they want, given the prospects of the company, the perceived risk of getting this rate of return, and—most importantly—the economic climate at the time. Suppose they feel that they want five times their money in that fifth year of forecast. If the VCs put in $5 million, this would mean that they want $25 million "in market value," out of the $135 million that would be left outside of the "public's" 25 percent. Twenty-five million dollars would be about 19 percent of the value of the company at year 5, but we must take into account the fact that a 25 percent dilution of the stock will ensue with the IPO. So if they have about 25 percent of the stock **outstanding** when they invest their money, they could end up with their desired 19 percent *after* the IPO (25% × 75% = 19%). Of course, if they ask for something like ten times their money—because of the

▲ This is a function of the times. Remember the point made earlier about trying to raise money when the stock market is really down? If there were a robust bull market, maybe, a larger multiple would be used.

apparent risk of getting their rate of return—this percentage would rise substantially. (This again points up the necessity of having good profitability to begin with, otherwise what stock that would be left for the founders would not be worth very much.) At this point the original founders would own about 23 percent of the company. But of course this is not the really relevant number. The relevant number is "How much is their 23 percent worth in dollars in 5 years?" If it were 23 percent of $180 million, this would mean that the founder's stock would be worth about $41 million. Some would consider this a good return for their effort over the 5 years.

If—and this is a big "if"—the company had to go back to the venture capitalists for more money after their $5 million was spent, this founder's percentage would go down, along with the dollar value most likely. How far down would be a function of how much the VCs wanted in the way of return at that point. Has the risk of getting their rate of return gone up or down since their last investment? (See Appendix 3.)

HOW MUCH MONEY DO YOU NEED FOR A START-UP?

How much money does the new venture need to get started and run successfully? This is a good question and one for which we have an answer, thanks to the Cash Flowcast© program to be discussed in Chapter 4. To use this approach, you make *three scenarios* for sales and all the associated costs and Balance Sheet items. You would consider the most likely scenario, the most pessimistic scenario, and the most optimistic scenario. Next you calculate the **maximum negative cash balance** for the most likely scenario and call it M. To understand why we are doing this, consider what a maximum negative cash balance of, for example, $854,500 means. It we were to put exactly that amount in the corporate checking account, then we could go as long as that balance would take us: for ten months, for example, or whenever the balance falls to zero. Then, if we were to start *adding* in the eleventh month to the cash balance through internal means, the firm would not need additional cash until some time in the future, if ever.

Next we take the maximum negative cash balance for the pessimistic scenario and call it A. Then we do the same thing for the maximum negative cash balance for the optimistic scenario and call that B.

The amount of cash the new venture will require is the amount needed for the most likely scenario, M, plus a **contingency amount.** The contingency amount is found by taking the *larger* of the difference between the A and the M, and the B and the M and then rounding that number for cosmetic purposes.▲ We round off this difference so that the *total* amount is a reasonable amount and not some apparently precise amount that is specious.

▲ You do not always know which of these two differences will be the larger because of the idiosyncrasies of each proposal. It may be that slow sales will result in a larger difference, but then perhaps rapid sales will require a larger difference.

For example,

if M = $850,000, A = $925,000 and B = $1,050,000 then:

Amount of money needed	$850,000
Plus: Contingency	200,000
Equals: Total amount needed	$1,050,000

Wouldn't it look peculiar if we put the contingency as $217,535? Maybe this **is** correct according to the computer printout, but does it make sense to be so precise? Wouldn't the reader of your Package question the intelligence—if not the wisdom—of whomever wrote a number with such apparent precision?

Saying you need $1,050,000 would also look specious. Remember, professional sources of venture capital are constantly on the lookout for any chink in the armor of the wannabe entrepreneur. Any little mistake may be one too many.

A surprisingly large number of people put down some "rule of thumb" contingency such as 10 percent. Where did they get this number? Did it come down from above? A contingency should have some basis in fact, such as pro-forma (projected) financials, and not just what somebody "feels."

Once the amount of the necessary venture capital has been determined, the wannabe entrepreneur should step back and ask "Is this too much money to request in view of my track record?" If the answer is yes, what then do you do? In fact, you can do quite a lot. You can go back to the pro-forma financials cited on page 26 and basically redesign the whole approach that you have taken. For example, do you need new equipment? Or used equipment? Or do you really need to buy the equipment at all? Maybe you can subcontract the whole production. Or how about sales? Are you trying to grow too fast? Or not fast enough? How about your overhead? Can you get along in less expensive quarters? What are your Accounts Receivable policies? Your inventory policies, if any? The list can go on. You may want to scale *back* your capital requirements, but there is also the (somewhat unlikely) possibility that you may need to *expand* your capital requirements to get the attention of some source of venture capital. Being able to play the "what if" game is what makes computer applications, such as the computerized Cash Flowcast© program, worthwhile. Many changes can be made with little effort.

Sequencing the Financing

Almost all sources of venture capital, once they agree to fund the project, suggest that you do not need *all* of the money up front: They can **stage** the investment. For some start-up deals—especially high-tech and New Economy ones, this seems perfectly appropriate. On the other hand, for many deals, this may result in a serious problem after you start. Let's review the difficulties that spreading out financing would present for a start-up.

What happens, when you make a request for additional money, if—for any one of a number of reasons—your source of venture capital declines or simply says that he or she does not have the money presently, that in the near future he or she will invest more money. What are you supposed to do now? Ask your employees to hold their breath until you can pay them? Or your suppliers? What are you going to tell them?

This happened on the very first start-up I worked on and I have seen this problem repeated several times since. On the small pump start-up introduced in Chapter 1, my client agreed to defer some of the venture capital because we were confident that my client's investor was good for the money. When my client did make the call, the investor asked that the other investors put up their money first, and as soon as he could sell some property, he would put up his share. Well, you can imagine what happened. Being suspicious, the other investors declined to put up *any* more money until the main investor put up his share.▲ This small pump business almost failed until sufficient money could be raised.▲▲ The problem, of course, is that if the new start-up is not doing as well as expected, the source of venture capital may simply decide not to put up additional funds. This dilemma leads me to offer this rule of venture capital that was coined by one of my former students who happened to be an Air Force officer: *"If you want to fly to financial paradise, have enough gas to make the trip as there are no good service stations on the way."* A major exception to this rule is the practice of "staging financing," to which we now turn.

While the suggested rule of getting the money up front applies to plain-vanilla start-ups, the major exception to the rule is a high-tech start-up, such as a computer or biotech start-up. Here the usual practice is to **sequence** the financing with clear milestones indicated for more financing. If these milestones are met, then additional financing will be forthcoming. Of course, this assumes that there is no question of whether the financing will be available when needed. If there is any doubt, then the "get it while it's hot" rule applies.

With a high-tech or similar start-up, the usual way to fund such a business is as follows. (See also Exhibit 2.1.)

In the *first stage,* the wannabe entrepreneur has to rely on his or her own resources (savings, credit cards) and/or on his or her family and friends. *This is far and away the chief source of initial funds for high tech or any other start-up.* Most start-ups are *never* funded by professional venture capital firms—either initially or second stage financing—but rather by *ad hoc* sources of finance. This includes credit from suppliers, something not to be overlooked.

The concept of **"bootstrapping"** a start-up is relevant. An example might help one to understand the possibilities. When John Paul DeJoria and Paul Mitchell started John Paul Mitchell Systems, the haircare company mentioned in Chapter 1, they had a combined total of $700. To **leverage** this, they went to

---

▲ This reminds me of a horse race in which you ask if you can wait until the race is well under way before you place your bet. In this way you can see if it looks wise to bet. Wouldn't this be a strange state of affairs?

▲▲ Now, however, this struggling start-up is an industry leader, FloTech.

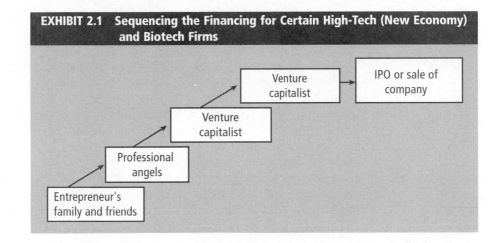

EXHIBIT 2.1   Sequencing the Financing for Certain High-Tech (New Economy) and Biotech Firms

a "bottler," a company that makes chemical formulations to order, and told them what they wanted. They then went to a company that made bottles for packaging the product and, because black-and-white printing was the cheapest, chose that color combination (which persists as a distinctive feature today), and made a deal for the bottle maker to make some product and get paid "later." With product in hand, they were off and running.

If a start up can be successful without external funding, the rewards to the original entrepreneur(s) will be dramatically greater, not to mention the headaches saved by not having outside investors involved in your management and/or direction of the company. The outsiders might be beneficial because of their technical or managerial skill, but if not, they are a force to be reckoned with.

At this point, when considering outside money beyond the initial stage, the value of a firm might be quite up in the air. But a common mistake is to value the firm too highly. As pointed out previously, if in subsequent financing rounds a *lower* valuation is attached to the firm, the original investors of family and friends might be quite upset.

Once the company is at least organized, the angels might get involved. These angels are individuals acting alone, or more usually, in organized groups and now, with venture capitalists. Such a group is the Tech Coast Angels of Southern California, the Band of Angels operating in the San Francisco/Silicon Valley area, the Alliance of Angels in Seattle, or similar local groups. The Tech Coast Angels consist of about 120 individuals with high net worth, who are divided into three groups for the Los Angeles, Orange County, and San Diego areas. They meet regularly and invite certain prospective wannabe entrepreneurs to meet and present their stories. If some of the members like the presentation—and the individual presenting the idea—some money is invested in the new company. The value they set on this brand-new company will usually be in the $1–5 million range. This does not mean that these angels expect the new firm to be worth *only* this amount when it matures, but at this point in the life of the new company they are saying that this is what they think the new company will be worth in the immediate future. The amount of money that each of these angels might invest may be about $100,000 (or less) to more than half a million. Collectively, they might invest $1–2 million at this stage.

These angels are really looking for only some high-technology firm that has a very bright future. The plain-vanilla start-up has little promise for them. However, these individuals might also consider buy-outs of another firm if it looks like a deal where other financing might be available. (This is particularly true since the dot.com bubble burst in the spring of 2000.)

To invest in a new company angels must believe that professional venture capital money can't be far behind. If it appears that the angels would be the *only* investors, they would probably *not* do the deal. Since the dot.com bubble burst, angels are currently looking for venture capitalists to *join* them in their early-stage financing. As mentioned above, this raises the possibility of VCs coming in with second-stage financing.

In the *next stage* of financing, the professional venture capitalists get involved. (It is also quite possible that there might be more than one financing from angels.)▲ At this second stage VCs might invest from as low as $1–2 million to many times that amount, depending on the deal. At this point the VCs will set their own **valuation** on the new company. It will be, usually, substantially more than the valuation set by the angels. And as with the financing from angels, there might be more than one round of financing. This is particularly true of Internet start-ups and certain other high-tech start-ups.

There is another source of financing not to be overlooked. Just prior to this stage or after the first round, it might be possible to obtain financing from an unusual bank, such as Silicon Valley Bank. If it appears certain that a professional venture capitalist will be getting involved in the new company, or already has, and the new firm will need more money than the VC is looking to invest *in that round*, Silicon Valley Bank might get involved by putting in the difference between what the VCs put in and the cash flow break-even point. The bank is looking to be taken out of their loan by the VC money, however. The only conditions that must be present are that there be what they call "intellectual property" and the aforementioned certainty of a VC take-out. Intellectual property is the thing that was the reason for starting the firm such as a proprietary process, technical innovation, or some proprietary software. It is something that could be sold, if need be.▲▲

Running Out of Money

With plain vanilla start-ups, a formidable problem occurs when the asked for amount of capital is invested but the firm runs out of cash before it gets to the

---

▲ At this point, Garage Technology Ventures (garage.com) might get involved. This is a boutique investment banking house doing early-stage financing of new high-tech companies.

▲▲ Curiously enough, conventional banks will not loan on intellectual property, only on real assets.

break-even point. In this case, when you attempt to go back to your source of venture capital, what do you have to show for your progress up to that time? Very often it is a trail of red ink that is not very attractive. In this case, the price you have to pay for this additional money may be *much* more expensive than the first round. *Deliberately* going into a start-up with the idea of getting venture capital at different dates in the future is called staging, as discussed above. It is when this is *not* the intention that problems arise. In one instance, a delay was experienced because the chief financial officer became ill. And when the new company went out belatedly to obtain additional financing it *really needed* the additional funds. Sensing that the firm was in trouble, investors were reluctant to invest more money in the company. (And when is the worst time to ask for money?)

THE PRO-FORMA FINANCIALS

The **pro-forma financials** consist of the forecast Income Statement, Balance Sheet, and the Cash Flow Statement, plus the footnotes of explanation for each item In projecting "high, low, most likely" scenerios, you will want to make three versions of each of these statements, this does *not mean* that you should put all three of these statements in the Package. This would make the Package unnecessarily large. Instead, you put the *most likely* statement in the Package and retain the other two statements as supporting documents.

It is a good idea to have the format of the statements be *monthly* for two years and *quarterly* for the next three. This is so for management's own use, but not necessarily for prospective investors. In this way you can show expenses in more detail, something that is more important in the beginning than when the company is well under way. Quarterly statements maybe acceptable for prospective investors, however.

The most important suggestion regarding these pro-forma financials is that *each item on all three statements should be footnoted*—with an explanation for that item—even if it is the same number on the Income Statement or Balance Sheet or Cash Flow Statement. This footnote may say something like "See Schedule Three" in which you detail the items included, for example, in the General and Administrative Expenses. Remember that there are likely to be three sets of eyes that will review the Package, and one of them belongs to an accounting type. If you can explain *all* the items that you include, you will preempt discussions beginning with "Where did you get this number?" Even if you are just guessing about a particular number, state "We do not know the exact amount for this item. We think this will be the order of magnitude for the actual expense." You will preclude detailed probing into the number. Having someone constantly probe the rationale behind the forecasts is not a desirable way to get started. It behooves the wannabe entrepreneur to avoid prolonged discussions or outright disagreements in the preliminary stage of the company. Problems enough loom down the road without providing the grist for an unnecessary one.

FINANCING WITH VENTURE CAPITAL

Of all the activities in business few are as frustrating as the process of finding venture capital, even though some people had incredible success in 1998 and 1999 getting money for dot.coms. As outlined at the beginning of this book, for most aspiring entrepreneurs, the typical process begins in this way:

1. The development of the idea, or what has been called "the basic idea"
2. The putting together of the management team
3. The writing of the business plan—or what is called "the Package."

When this is all done the next logical step is the raising of the required capital. It is precisely at this point that many people make what may be a fatal mistake: They then try to shop the deal with known sources of venture capital. If this is the process followed, failure to raise the requisite venture capital will almost certainly result. This is true for many types of start-up firms, although it may not be true for *all* start-ups. As mentioned, certain types of high-tech start-ups may be funded through presentations at forums sponsored by such organizations as the Tech Coast Angels or The Band of Angels in Palo Alto. While these may turn out to be the really spectacular start-ups, there are very few of these compared to the thousands of non–high-tech start-ups elsewhere in the country.

Some years ago there was a cartoon that showed a "Package" being thrown over the transom of a door. This cartoon illustrated the text of an article in which a senior officer of one of the largest venture capital funds made the statement that his company had never funded a proposal that came "in over the transom," meaning a Package coming unsolicited or without referral. The problem here is not too different from the situation that prevails in the London merchant-banking community. To do any business in London, one must be properly introduced. Likewise, to get one's proposal funded it is necessary to have one's proposal also properly introduced, in a manner of speaking. Deal proposals that simply arrive in the mail are not the ones that get funded, or even seriously considered. For a while, in the halcyon days of 1998, 1999, and early 2000, it seemed to many that this was Old Economy thinking and thus obsolete. Wannabe entrepreneurs were e-mailing their ideas in to sources. Since the dot.com bubble burst, however, the importance of a proper introduction has reasserted itself. Even if you are approaching an angel, it really helps to have someone respected by the source of capital to introduce you. This is another old rule that potential entrepreneurs are rediscovering!

While appearing before a Congressional Hearings panel, the president of a venture capital fund was asked how many proposals he received in a year. He replied about 500 a month, or about 6,000 a year. Asked how many he had funded in the past year, he replied, "Three." More recently, this experience has been repeated with angel investors and most definitely, with VCs. Sending in a "cold proposal" today will most likely result in no action, as before! Even the groups of angels fund only a very small portion of the deals they see.

In an article on raising venture capital some years ago, the authors, reporting on a survey of venture capital sources, state that they discovered that it was perfectly good practice to send a proposal to a number of logical sources for funding.▲ However, if you do that, you are putting your proposal in that group of 6,000. Do you really like the odds of 3 in 6,000? Do not feel that because this is the twenty-first century we can do things differently.

A shopped deal is no deal! Sending unsolicited packages to venture capital sources is a sure way to get rejected—and that includes sending it to a great many venture capital sources. In fact, the odds of success are inversely proportional to the number of potential sources contacted.

TYPES OF VENTURE CAPITAL

Since different types of venture capital require different strategies for acquisition, it will be useful to review the four types of venture capital:

    seed money

    angel round money

    venture capital

    second-stage financing

The typical sources of **seed money** are personal resources, family resources, and friends. Obviously, if big money—perhaps hundreds of thousands or millions of dollars—is needed, then these sources may be inadequate. The reason for not going outside your own personal circle to obtain seed money is a matter of equity in the deal. If you give up a share of equity in your deal in the course of obtaining this seed money, there will be that much less when the expensive start-up money is raised. As mentioned previously, the trick in raising this seed money is not to value the company too highly.

The angel round of financing was mentioned in the discussion of staging of financing, and little needs to be added here. Before the debacle of the high-tech "bubble," angels would go into a deal at a very early stage, but currently, as mentioned, they want to go into a deal *along with a VC*, thus enhancing the chances that the VC will be there for the next round of financing.

As discussed earlier, second-stage financing comes about when the firm has been running for some time and reaches a plateau of sorts. If it receives a new infusion of capital, it can progress to another stage (or just continue growing). The thing that makes second-stage financing different from start-up capital is the question of *necessity*. If the firm has to have the money to continue in

▲ Jeffrey A. Timmons and David E. Gumpert, "Discard many old rules about getting venture capital," *Harvard Business Review*, Jan./Feb. 1982.

business, it is *not* second-stage financing; it is *start-up capital*, which is much more expensive. If, in fact, the company can get along without that money, it will have to pay substantially *less* for this additional financing. Finding this type of second-stage money involves all the usual sources of financing such as banks, finance companies, investment banking sources and certain types of venture capital firms. An exploration of these sources is beyond the scope of this discussion and will be treated in Chapter 10.

The secrecy needed for the start-up money, which is a large part of the strategy for finding start-up capital, is not necessary at this point. If the money is second-stage money, meaning the company can exist without it, it may be reasonable to advertise, in a manner of speaking, for this money—something one should never do for start-up money.

STRATEGIES FOR FINDING START-UP CAPITAL

Perhaps the overriding rule in raising venture capital is to recognize the fact that to a VC a proposal must appear to be fresh; that is, no one is supposed to have seen the deal before. Note that I said that the deal must *appear* fresh, not that it *is*, in fact, fresh. The problem here is that if it is known that a deal has been reviewed by another venture capital source, then there are questions: "Why didn't that source see fit to fund the deal? Do they know something that we don't know? They are a pretty smart outfit, there must be something wrong with this deal or they would have grabbed this deal." These thoughts necessarily run through the mind of a prospective source of funding. The chances of getting venture capital for a non–high-tech deal are slim enough. Do nothing to minimize them.

What do you do if a prospective source turns you down? How then do you take your fresh deal to some one else? The answer is a little like saying "How do I get an 850-pound gorilla to do something?" The answer is "Very carefully." If you have to admit that so-and-so saw the proposal and turned it down (unless there is a very good reason for the turn down), the odds of the party you are talking to doing the deal are extremely low.

The Investor Confidence Scale
Assuming that you have the secrecy problem under control, and that you have not shopped your deal with venture capital sources, let us turn our attention to the problem of getting a venture capital source to say yes once they do get to see the Package. Perhaps the best way to illustrate this is by analogy. In Exhibit 2.2, there is a scale that runs from 0 to 100. This is the **confidence scale** that a venture capital source has before you present the deal to him or her.

Somewhere on this scale is a point, a bell line if you will. If your total proposal gets to this confidence level, the source will say "Yes, we have a deal" and the bell will sound. This confidence level is not permanently fixed and independent of time and circumstances; rather it is moving up or down with the demand and availability of venture capital. Way back in the 1960s, it appeared that

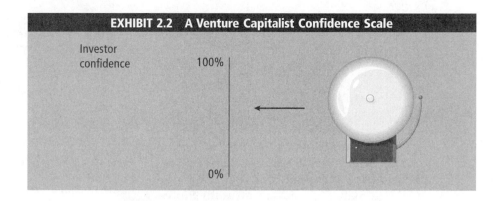

EXHIBIT 2.2   A Venture Capitalist Confidence Scale

the bell line was set to go off about at the 60 level. In the 1970s, it seemed that the level was set somewhere near body temperature, about 98.6. With the onset of the 1980s, because venture capital was more abundant, the confidence line dropped down substantially. And with the bull market in stocks in the 1990s, the confidence line dropped even more. Since the burst of the technology and Internet stocks in the spring of 2000, availability of venture capital for high-tech deals has dropped markedly. Now, what capital is available is usually reserved for supporting successful ventures in which the VC has already invested. It is very difficult to get a new idea funded currently.

While this is an admittedly debatable argument (for example, there are those who would point to the 1986 Tax Act as a main contributor), it appears that many sources of venture capital are affected by the stock market. If investors are winning in the stock market, they are more inclined to invest in venture capital deals, and the reverse is also true. This is particularly true for periods when there is a robust new issues market—an IPO bull market.   Another apparent reason for this willingness to invest in venture capital deals is the strange phenomenon that if the market is doing well *now,* the tendency is to assume that it will do well for an indeterminate future. This means that venture capitalists see—or imagine they see—a bright exit strategy if they invest in a start-up deal. Conversely, when the stock market bears are running wild, there is a pessimism that fosters reluctance to invest in anything but conservative investments. For whatever reason, the confidence level of individuals managing venture capital seems to move up and down. This is another example of the psychology of finance. Hopefully, when you want to raise venture capital the bell line won't be set too close to the top.

The Role of the Intermediary

Your problem is how to get your deal over the confidence line, to set off the bell, so to speak. Your basic idea may be worth 40 points, your track record of management accomplishment may be worth 30 points, and your package may be worth 10 points. While this adds up to 80 points, the bar may be set at 85. In

Focus on Technology

TURNING $2,000 INTO $450,000,000—ANNUALLY!

One of the great success stories in Silicon Valley belongs to a woman entrepreneur who grew her fledgling venture out of her bedroom and turned it into a publicly traded company with annual sales reaching half a billion dollars. The entrepreneur: 24-year-old Sandra L. Kurtzig. The company: ASK, Inc. The niche: Automating the management functions, such as inventory control and production tasks at small to medium size manufacturing companies.

ASK was started by Sandra Kurtzig back in 1971. Originally, Kurtzig started the company to support her family when she left her secure but non-satisfying sales job at GE's computer division. Bringing in one small account at a time and doing all the work herself, Kurtzig soon managed to build strategic partnerships with such giants as Hewlett Packard and Digital Equipment Corporation. As a matter of fact, Kurtzig created a whole new industry that not only served her well, but also facilitated the advent and expansion of mini and micro-computers everywhere.

KEY TO GROWTH: FOCUS ON YOUR CHOSEN NICHE

One of the main reasons behind ASK's phenomenal growth in just a few years after its start was Kurtzig's determination to stay sharply focused on her new business. This meant she had to turn down new orders if such orders did not fit the overall vision of her company—even if those orders came from well-monied companies like Boeing!

Of course there are times that you can afford to be selective and there are times that you cannot. It took ASK four years to get to that level. Before that time, she had to be flexible so that she could make some sales and keep the business afloat. That meant contract work and consulting. "Once a business concentrates on a finite market and becomes the expert in that market, it is an ideal position—as ASK soon was—to use its reputation to broaden its focus and move into other areas (if needed)."

" . . . new kinds of mice to trap. . . The trick is to be in the marketplace just as the demand is accelerating. Too early is sometimes as bad as too late."

Sandra Kurtzig, Founder of ASK, Inc.

this case, you wind up with the standard reply: "Thanks very much for showing us your deal, but we think we'll pass this time."

How do you overcome this problem? To me the answer to this question is simple. And this answer applies to *any type of deal!* Come to the venture capitalist at a level that is already *over* the bar! The best way to do this is to be introduced to the venture capital source by an **intermediary** who has the confidence of the source of venture capital. Not just any intermediary, but one that is so respected by the venture capitalist that he or she is saying "Bring us another good deal." This is a sure way to get a warm reception; if you are not already over the bar, you will be very close to it. If the intermediary has taken a successful deal to the venture capital source, then this source will be all too willing to take a hard look at another deal that this person brings to them. This person has provided not only the proper introduction but has lent his or her reputation to the deal.

But who are these intermediaries? Who are they *not*? And how does one find such individuals?

They most likely are not paid middlemen, someone who stands to gain in a pecuniary way from bringing the deal to the venture capitalist. Rather, these intermediaries are highly respected accountants, senior-level bankers, investment bankers, senior corporate executives (perhaps from a company that was funded by this venture capital source), certain senior attorneys or certain stock brokers who have very substantial clients. For example, there is a senior partner of an accounting firm that caters to a clientele from Beverly Hills and Newport Beach, California. If this man sees a deal that he likes, all he has to do is make one or two phone calls and the funding is assured. Or a Florida stock broker who has a clientele on both coasts. Each of these could be an intermediary. For a high-tech deal it is someone who is really into such deals, like entrepreneurs who have been funded recently. Or, perhaps, a prominent tech scientist in the field.

True, if you do not know anyone who might serve as an intermediary, you have a problem. But meeting or finding such a person may be less of an obstacle than finding a source of venture capital that will look at a deal that "comes in over the transom." If you know that you will want to raise venture capital *sometime* in the future, then pursuing a strategy that will get you introduced to prospective intermediaries may be quite fruitful. Getting out to meet people of all types is certainly a step in the right direction. Remember, it's a "people world": The more people you know, the better off you are in the world of business. If you have what it takes to successfully start and run a business, finding an intermediary should not be an insurmountable obstacle. Knowing that this is the key to success will prevent getting a proposal rejected out of hand. Having the right intermediary will make short work of those 3 in 6,000 odds.

SUMMARY

With the shortage of venture capital and the need to present even better deals than ever before, the importance of writing a good business plan has increased immeasurably. This document must present the proposal in a way that is clear and convincing. But paying a professional person or, for example, hiring an accounting firm to write a proposal, is not a good idea. In fact, it may ruin your chances of getting the deal financed. Generally speaking, sources of venture capital want the entrepreneur to write the deal personally. This does not mean that some help may be received, say, in the financial forecasting and accounting, but the entrepreneur had better know what each and every number means.

The "Package," as it is called in the vernacular, should be well written and concise, and certainly not overly long or exceedingly technical. It should be written with the thought in mind that there might be three sets of eyes reading it: the VC, a technical person (if that is not the VC), and an accounting type.▲

The outline of the Package is simple: the Introduction and Summary, the information about the product (or whatever you are selling), the marketing of the product, and the financial summary. The Introduction is done last. If this doesn't "sell," the reader may not go beyond this section.

The section about what the product is should be written in a way that the idea is clearly presented, but without great detail. If the proposal is to be presented to professional angels or VCs, the chances are they know what you are doing all too well. Putting in lots of detail is neither necessary nor wanted. The question of patenting a product depends on the individual deal. Usually it is not a good idea to patent the product and *then* look for venture capital financing. This is because of the several years it takes to patent an invention. How would you explain the lapse of time to a source of venture capital? It implies that you have been shopping the deal.

The marketing section is possibly the most important. If the reader is convinced that the product will sell in the quantities indicated, then the rest should be "details." If the reader questions whether you can sell the product in the amounts indicated, you have a real problem getting that person to say "Yes." This is why, today, you have to virtually *show* sales and profits to get a professional source interested. Saying "Trust me, it will sell" may have worked in the halcyon days of the late 1990s, but it won't work today.

The financial summary contains three parts: a recap of sales and profits, with a suggestion of the price/earnings ratios of recent IPOs; how much money the new company will need; and the pro-forma financials.

The idea that there is safety in numbers is certainly not the appropriate axiom in the strategy for raising venture capital. Getting a

---

▲ At one presentation in the late 1990s, I heard one individual from an accounting firm brag that they did a Package for a new venture that cost the new firm $250,000. The professional sources that were present all agreed that if some entrepreneur was so foolish as to pay this much for a Package, they would not invest in the deal.

Package ready and then sending it to many sources of venture capital is surely a great way *not* to get a proposal funded. Would you invest in a deal that was turned down by someone you respect as a worthy competitor in the world of venture capital? You would have to be thinking that there must be something wrong with this deal, otherwise the other party would have funded it. And remember, the world of venture capitalists is very small. I vividly remember trying to get a proposal funded with a group of investors in a neighboring town. Prior to the meeting, I had lunch with a trusted friend of mine—at least I thought he was trustworthy—and discussed the deal with this man who was a senior banker, in confidence, I

thought. Well when I got to the meeting of the investor group, the lead person said "I have heard about this deal!" Well, in that instant I knew that I was not going to get this group to fund the deal, and they didn't. A shopped deal is no deal.

An argument has been made for the use of an intermediary who has the confidence of a source of venture capital, even of angel money. With the right intermediary, the venture capital source may have his or her confidence up to a point where they are ready to accept the deal if everything else looks all right. Of course it is difficult to find such an intermediary, but would you rather throw your proposal over the transom?

QUESTIONS FOR DISCUSSION

1. Using the companies mentioned in the "Question for Discussion" section of Chapter 1, discuss how you would advise someone to gain financing for **each** of these types of companies.
2. In your own personal life, think of whom you might use as an "intermediary" in your search for funds to finance a project. If you don't have one, how would you go about trying to obtain one for when you really need this person? Why would this person be a good intermediary?
3. Is today's economy good for raising money? Why or why not?

CHAPTER REVIEW

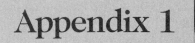

Appendix 1

REFLECTIONS ON THE DOT.COM BUBBLE

The Internet, the Information Age, and all the technology that goes along with them, are here to stay, thank heavens. But what about all the dot.com companies that were started in the late 1990s and which started going belly up in 2000 or 2001? It is unfortunate that so many aspiring entrepreneurs are finding out that the world did not beat a path to their door, so to speak. Nevertheless, there are lessons that can be learned from this debacle. Here then are some of the principal mistakes—if it is proper to call them that—that were made during this bubble, which saw some enormous fortunes made and lost.

First, there was excessive exuberance about the size of the market for whatever it was that someone was trying to capture. Because there was so much ignorance concerning a market that had never been tapped, people incorrectly assumed that it would be huge, whatever that meant. And while scoping out the new market, the participants in this New Economy "revolution" started to invent new terms to rationalize their activity. You had to be the **"first mover"** in any new market, they argued, and if you were, success would surely follow. Well, some firms found that they were, in fact, the *first mover* in a new market which subsequently turned out to be surprisingly small. In some cases it turned out that the "first mover" *proved out a market*, only to have a better financed company come in and take the market away—something mentioned in the criteria discussion (page 7). So, even though they got there first, the reward was not to be had.

Others got there first, only to find that even though there appeared to be no competition, as soon as they "proved out" the new market there was a surprising amount of competition!

Companies like buy.com argued that it did not make any difference that that they were selling below cost because they were building market share and, sooner or later, the loyal customers would start buying from them at reasonable prices. In short, the criterion stated in Chapter 1 dealing with profitability was, at least, temporarily forgotten—conveniently so. Venture capitalists poured money into these companies, betting that they were right, that making a profit was only a matter of time.

Then another new term was invented: "burn rate." This meant the amount of money that the new company would burn, that is "use," each month. Investors were supposed to look upon this as a necessary evil—the price one had to pay for getting into the game. And the success stories that were evolving with new firms going public were so spectacular that investors were afraid to offer any counterarguments. One angel investor invested about $100,000 in a dot.com firm in the spring of 1998. By October the company had a chance to sell for $10 million, making a tidy profit for all the investors. They declined and by November, the firm went public. By the spring of 1999 the stock that these early investors had in the company was worth $70 per share, compared to their basis of $1! Stories like these continued to fuel the investors' appetite for deals. As in any bull market, the players were afraid of getting left behind.

It appears that another major mistake was the fact that some of these computer-based companies were being managed by clever "computernicks," who had what seemed like a good idea for a market, but who had absolutely no business experience. They had a clever solution to a problem. The problem, however, was elusive. You don't want a solution looking for a problem!

The story is told of one such company in New England. When they had the celebratory dinner to commemorate the funding of the deal, the only persons at the table able to order a drink were the venture capitalists. The new management of the firm was, to the last one, too young to be served alcohol. This is not to say that young persons cannot be good managers; it is just to imply that they lacked management experience and knowledge of the topics covered in this book, for example.

Another example of the so-called mistakes was the mistaken impression that knowing the technology that would solve the problem was, in and of itself, sufficient. As Tech Angel Gene Miller has said, "Where once only a handful of individuals could design and produce semiconductor chips for a specific application now many can. Where once only a few could stitch DNA and reconfigure genes now many can. The consequence of these shifts has meant that the skills now more highly prized are those of the market entry strategy, customer relationships, and consummating sales."▲ Expressed somewhat differently, the cleverness of the idea—the *raison d'être* of the wannabe entrepreneur—is now seen to be not as important as the management skills and, perhaps more importantly, the plan for marketing the new idea. This of course does not apply just to Internet dot.com companies. As Miller points out this happened with biotech firms before the dot.coms, and before that, computers. (He also points out the similar situation with optical character recognition and speech recognition.)

Miller also points out that the dot.com era brought with it the development in the 1990s of a new type of investor: the professional *angel*. It simply was not feasible for the important venture capital firms to invest in small deals, because they did not just invest money and leave it at that: They sought to monitor their investments, and there was only so much time in the day. Thus the VCs needed to limit their investments to larger deals, leaving the smaller deals to the high-tech angels (known by other names in different parts of the country). With venture capitalists needing to invest *bigger sums of money* in a single deal—because of the availability of huge amounts of venture capital— there was created a need for smaller investors.

▲ Gene Miller, Tech Coast Angels and Clinical Professor of Entrepreneurial Studies, Greif Center for Entrepreneurial Studies, Marshall School of Business, USC.

Additionally Miller points out that specific criteria for judging investments change over time. But the criteria mentioned in Chapter 1 are of such a general nature that they will be relevant whether applied to the current situation or to a time in the future. Ignoring these criteria by stating that this is a new age and we now have "a new paradigm" is to delude oneself. New products and new markets yes, but there is no difference in substance. As mentioned, the criteria examined in Chapter 1 are not intended to be deal breakers, but rather factors to consider when designing a new company. They are supposed to be something, that when considered, will give the new firm a better chance of success.

Appendix 2

EXIT STRATEGIES AND "HARVESTING"

The New Economy bubble brought with it some interesting new financial terms. One such term is **harvesting**. This was a term that applied to the entrepreneur who started one high-tech firm, and then sold it or took it public. He is said to have "harvested" the investment. It was simple! Having once done a successful start-up, the entrepreneur had established his or her track record and the same venture capitalists or others would gladly back a new venture. If one was really good at this harvesting technique, one might do it every year or two. Well, the days of harvesting are over, at least for a while. Major complications have arisen in the process which are giving food for thought to many VCs, or other investors.

The automatic assumption that one can go public (meaning do an initial public offering of stock, or IPO) is seriously in doubt now. The psychology of the situation is such that with the disappearance of the IPO market as of this writing, it is common to believe that it may a *very long time* before the IPO market will open up for new companies. And if this is not bad enough, the possibility of being acquired by another company, possibly for synergistic reasons, has also been diminished by the serious decline in the stock price of many high-tech firms. The "Chinese money"—meaning high P/E stock that was abundant in the late 1990s—is gone. Now, if another high-tech firm acquires another firm, it is with stock that is much more conservatively priced—or with cash. With new accounting standards dictating that when an acquisition declines in value, the acquiring firm must take a write-off on its Income Statement is another limiting factor.

GETTING AN "OUT"

In Chapter 1, one of the criteria mentioned for a start-up was "capable of an out." When the market is in a serious bear market stage, as it has been in 2001 and 2002, the likelihood of getting an "out"—in which investors will be able to get a multiple of their investment out of the deal—is in doubt. If the IPO market appears to be closed and other companies are reluctant to buy new firms, where is the "out" going to come from? To be sure, it is possible to sell a fairly new firm to, say, a strategic buyer, but the main business of the new company better be a good one! True, many more new companies are sold than go public—by a big factor—but bear market conditions do not make the job of getting an "out" any easier. When the stock market is in a bull market condition, money is not only easier to raise for new, start-up firms, but the anticipation for a really good "out" is present, thus providing the incentive to make start-up investments. If it is unusually difficult to do a start-up in bear market conditions, it is also true that except for a few years in the late 1990s, it has never been easy to do a start-up. If it were . . .

Appendix 3

ILLUSTRATIVE VALUATION MODEL
(DOLLARS IN THOUSANDS)

FUTURE YEARS	2002	2003	2004	2005	2006
ANNUAL GROWTH RATES OF SALES		390.7%	174.1%	69.5%	0.0%
SALES	$ 3,020.0	$ 14,820.0	$ 40,621.0	$ 68,846.0	$ 68,846.0
GROSS PROFIT MARGIN	34.3%	47.9%	52.4%	62.9%	62.9%
GROSS PROFIT	$ 1,035.0	$ 7,106.0	$ 21,279.0	$ 43,320.0	$ 43,320.0
OPERATING EXPENSES	$ 3,543.0	$ 5,799.0	$ 13,158.0	$ 17,790.0	$ 17,790.0
OPER. EXPENSE % OF SALES	117.3%	39.1%	32.4%	25.8%	25.8%
S&M					
G&A					
FACILITIES					
LESS: OPERATING EXPENSES	$ 3,543.0	$ 5,799.0	$ 13,158.0	$ 17,790.0	$ 17,790.0
EQUALS: OPERATING PROFIT	$ (2,508.0)	$ 1,307.0	$ 8,121.0	$ 25,530.0	$ 25,530.0
OPERATING PROFIT MARGIN		8.8%	20.0%	37.1%	37.1%
TAX RATE	40.0%	40%	40%	40%	40%
INCOME TAXES	$ (1,003.2)	$ 522.8	$ 3,248.4	$ 10,212.0	$ 10,212.0
NET INCOME	$ (1,504.8)	$ 784.2	$ 4,872.6	$ 15,318.0	$ 15,318.0

Ownership at closing:

		2002	2003	2004	2005	2006
FOUNDERS	66.7%	29.7%	20.8%	20.8%	20.8%	14.0%
MANAGEMENT	1.0%	0.9%	0.6%	0.6%	0.6%	0.4%
GRANTED OPTIONS	3.8%	2.0%	1.4%	1.4%	1.4%	1.0%
RESERVED OPTIONS	6.4%	10.0%	7.0%	7.0%	7.0%	4.7%
NEW OPTIONS			5.0%	5.0%	5.0%	3.4%
PRIOR INVESTORS	22.2%	12.1%	8.5%	8.5%	8.5%	5.7%
SERIES A INVESTOR		45.5%	31.8%	31.8%	31.8%	21.4%
SERIES B INVESTOR			25.0%	25.0%	25.0%	16.8%
PUBLIC INVESTORS						32.6%
TOTAL	100.0%	100.2%	100.1%	100.1%	100.1%	100.1%

Projected Fundings:

	2002	2003	2006
SERIES A INVESTOR	$ 5,000.0		
SERIES B INVESTOR		$ 10,000.0	
IPO GROSS PROCEEDS			$ 75,000.0

Appendix 3

ILLUSTRATIVE VALUATION MODEL
(DOLLARS IN THOUSANDS)

Exit IPO valuation:

Exit PE Multiple	15x
Confidence factor	100.0%
Exit value	$ 229,770.0
IPO shares sold	32.6%
Offering size	$ 75,000.0
Premoney value for IPO	$ 154,770.0
	$ 229,770.0

Exit value returns to investors:

Prior investors	$ 13,136.6
Series A	$ 49,245.0
Series B	$ 38,692.5
Founders, Management and options	$ 53,915.5
Public	$ 75,000.0
Total value of offering at time of issue	$ 229,989.6

Series A Investment returns:

Equity investment	$ 5,000.0		$ 10,000.0
Required ROI multiple	10.0x		4.0x
Required exit value	$50,000.0		$40,000.0
Required equity for Series A	43.1%		25.0%
Projected exit value	$ 49,245.0		$ 38,692.5
Premoney	$ 6,000.0		$ 30,000.0
Post money	$ 11,000.0		$ 40,000.0
Proposed equity for Series A	45.5%		25.0%
IRR	58.0%		40.3%

Special thanks to John Morris & GKM Ventures who uses this model and for permission to reproduce this.

3

Managing Profit and Financial Statements

THE CONCEPT OF PROFIT

The term profit is one of the most ambiguous in the lexicon of business. But when the word *profit* is coupled with the word *management*, the next word many people think of is *hype*, or artificial inflation of profit. In this book we are going to be talking a lot about profit—and the attendant wealth of a company's stockholders—as well as how to increase it. But you will not see instruction in "hyping profits". Rather we will be talking about *managing profits*—or more specifically, profitability. When a firm creates an Income (or Profit and Loss) Statement, it is tracing the path of its financial success—or lack thereof. Once this trail is laid down, there is little if anything a firm can do about it. It is therefore incumbent upon management to concern themselves with issues that affect their firm's profitability as they go along—that is, well before the bottom line.

We will begin by discussing profit from a conceptual point of view and conclude by asking such questions as

What kind of profitability do you want to see in a company?

Do you want less sales but a larger percentage of those sales going to profit; or do you want more sales even though those sales result in lower profits as a percent of sales?

And what difference does it make just as long as the *amount* of dollars is good enough?

50

With the financial scandals involving Enron, WorldCom, and others, the subject of this chapter could easily be misunderstood. With emerging middle-market companies, there is a *legitimate* need to "manage profits." Within the purview of accounting standards, this is completely proper. What those very large, and sometimes not so large *publicly owned*, headline-making firms did recently was an attempt to mislead the investing public and others into thinking that their companies had operating results that were different from what they should have shown, or a Balance Sheet that had less debt than was the case. With regard to the Income Statement, the two types of offences were either inflated revenue or concealed costs.

Each of these techniques is mentioned for one reason: In the course of owning and/or managing an emerging or middle-market firm, there will be occasions when the financial statements of *other* companies will be examined. Ignorance of some of these techniques may place the entrepreneur in a difficult position. Also, the very common practice of inventory manipulation may not be understood by students of entrepreneurial finance. This chapter deals with unethical or illegal accounting practices *only* in an attempt to correct for any lack of understanding. The intention is to help entrepreneurial managers spot "cooked books" when they see them.

But first let's discuss the popular use of the word *profit* versus the technical use of the term—that is, actual **measures of profitability**.

In everyday discussion of business, "profit" can be used to connote many different things. To convey praise, one might say "You must be really profitable!" Or in a denigrating use of the term, one might say "You're nothing but a grubby profit seeker!" And then there are the several denotative uses of the word, such as in **ROI** (Return on Investment) or Return on Sales.

THE MEASURES OF PROFITABILITY

We opened this chapter by mentioning the ambiguity found in the word *profit*. To illustrate, the example of the various measures of profitability associated with a grocery store may be useful. In Exhibit 3.1 the Income Statement and Balance Sheet of Jim's Grocery Store are expressed in a common size manner—as though sales were $1 million.

Would you invest in such an enterprise if you were told that the *profitability* was only 4 percent? Hardly. But expressing the profitability in a different manner may completely change the implication associated with the term.

Consider the three following measures of profitability:

Return on Sales: $40,000/$1,000,000 = 4%
Return on Assets: $40,000/$400,000 = 10%
Return on Equity: $40,000/$100,000 = 40%

EXHIBIT 3.1	Financial Statements of a Grocery Store		

JIM'S GROCERY STORE

INCOME STATEMENT

SALES	$1,000,000
MINUS ALL COSTS	940,000
EQUALS PRE-TAX PROFIT	60,000
TAX	20,000
NET PROFIT	40,000

BALANCE SHEET

CASH	$100,000	ACCOUNTS PAYABLE	$150,000
ACCOUNTS RECEIVABLE	20,000	DUE BANK	50,000
INVENTORY	100,000	LONG-TERM DEBT	100,000
FURNITURE AND FIXTURES	180,000	EQUITY	100,000
TOTAL ASSETS	$400,000	TOTAL LIABILITIES AND CAPITAL	$400,000

By saying that the store makes only 4 percent profit, one would depict the investment as being less than attractive; by saying that one could make 40 percent, the impression is entirely different.

Putting impression aside, what do these measures of profitability really mean? Rate of Return on Sales is simply the amount left over—the *profit*—from sales after all expenses are deducted. ROI, a favorite measure of economists, means Return on Investment or Invested Capital. Return on Assets (ROA) is how much the company made on the assets the business owns. This measure says nothing about *who* supplied the money. But the measure that means the most to an investor is the Return on Equity—what is made on what you put into the company initially.

The industry a company is in affects the profitability of that company. Some companies have a very narrow Return on Sales, but excellent Return on Assets or Equity, such as our grocery company. The problem with a narrow Return on Sales is that if there is even a slight business hiccup, the bottom line is suddenly red instead of black. Grocery stores can live with a narrow Return on Sales because they have very little fluctuation in sales. More volatile companies—technology-oriented companies, or cosmetics companies—do not typically have this kind of sales consistency and therefore could not exist in a world of razor-thin Rates of Return on Sales. Of course, the ideal kind of company to own would be one that had

Large Gross Profits

Rather small expenses

Sizable Net Incomes relative to Sales

In this case, even if there were business downturns, the company would probably not be in any jeopardy.

Discussion of profitability was introduced in the first two chapters of this book because it is a basic criterion for anyone doing a start-up or becoming involved in entrepreneurial management. If you have any choice in selecting the kinds of firms that you might get involved in, it would be wise to think first about profitability. Are you trying to get into a company that is in an industry so competitive that "abnormal profits"—as the economists would say—have been beaten out of the picture? Some people do get into profitless firms because that sector is the only one they know. But most of us can change and learn new businesses. Naturally, you should not dive into something for which you are totally unprepared or ill-suited. But if you do have a choice, considering the appropriate profitability would be in your best interest.

USING THE DUPONT FORMULA

In considering measures of profitability, note one ratio that epitomizes the entire art of financial management of a developing firm: the DuPont formula for Rate of Return on Investment (see Exhibit 3.2).

By showing this ratio in two parts instead of a single ratio (which would be Net Income / Total Assets), one can see the *balance* that is needed in financial management. On the left side, one can see the firm's asset efficiency. This means how well the firm is utilizing the assets that were employed. On the right side, one can see the so-called "operating efficiency"—or, how profitably the firm is producing whatever it is supposed to produce. Now it is plain to see that if management concentrates on increasing its operating efficiency at the expense of its asset efficiency, it may *lower* its ROI. It could do this by, for example, stocking too much inventory or having unnecessary machinery or even automating its production process when it is economically unwise to do so. Conversely, if management is trying too hard to minimize assets—such as having low inventory—it may actually cost sales and thus lower Net Income and ROI!

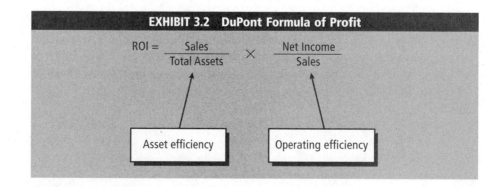

EXHIBIT 3.2   DuPont Formula of Profit

$$ROI = \frac{Sales}{Total\ Assets} \times \frac{Net\ Income}{Sales}$$

Asset efficiency   Operating efficiency

Only by thinking of this **optimization process** will management find the appropriate balance between these two measures of financial fitness that collectively we call ROI.

Having talked about profit, we will now turn our attention to the *reporting* of a firm's profit.

MANAGING THE INCOME STATEMENT

Let's pretend that you have been asked by your superior to prepare the company's financial statement. (In order to avoid distraction, only the published Financial Statement is discussed here; the company's tax return will be covered later in this chapter, under Types of Financial Statements, page 68.) Because accounting is not your strength, you are a bit peeved, but you go ahead and produce the Income Statement as shown in Exhibit 3.3.

The company had sales of $5,000,000 and a Net Profit After Tax of $300,000, according to your calculations. Pleased with your work, you report to your boss (the owner of the company) that the company had a Profit After Tax of $300,000. "What do you mean 'After Tax,'" your boss inquires. "Well," you reply, "the company made $500,000 before tax and, after a tax of $200,000, the company had a Net Profit of $300,000." Quite upset, your boss says "Did you say a tax of $200,000? Are you out of your mind? Get rid of that tax!"

With this admonishment, you retreat to your office to try to address this problem. Let's start from the top and work down through the Income Statement. You begin with a look at Sales.

WAYS TO REPORT SALES

There are several ways to report Sales. The simplest way is the way this hypothetical company does it. When you make a shipment, you invoice the customer, and create a sale. Pretty simple. But another way your company might report Sales is called the **"Percentage of Completion" Method**. In this method, you

EXHIBIT 3.3 Sample Income Statement	
TROJAN CO.	
SALES	$5,000,000
− COST OF GOODS	3,500,000
GROSS PROFIT	1,500,000
⎧ GENERAL AND ADMINISTRATIVE EXPENSE	250,000
−⎨ SELLING EXPENSE	250,000
⎩ DEPRECIATION EXPENSE	500,000
PRE-TAX PROFIT	500,000
− TAX	200,000
NET INCOME	$ 300,000

take the Sales to date and to that amount you add the percentage of the **Work In Process** that is finished. This involves observing production and actually checking the jobs that are being manufactured—or otherwise produced, such as custom computer software. This involves quite a bit of subjective estimation, which is surprising for someone who thought that accounting was such a hard and cold factual matter. But if you overestimate a job now, you will have lower Sales for the next period. In general, the process tends to balance itself out.

It used to be, before the 1986 Tax Reform Act, that business firms had a choice between the **Completed Contract Method** of reporting Sales and the Percentage of Completion Method. Because Completed Contract had the effect of *postponing* Sales—and thus the taxable Income on these Sales—the U.S. government prohibited the use of the Completed Contract Method for most business firms for tax return purposes. This is, of course, to avoid the *postponement* of taxes.

There is still another way of reporting Sales that should be used in certain circumstances: the **Installment Method.** There are essentially two instances in which a firm should use the Installment Method.

The first is when a firm receives all—or almost all—of the total payment at the outset but contracts to deliver a service over a period of time. For example, if a firm sells a franchise and receives $100,000 up front for this franchise but promises to deliver certain services over 7 years. The proper reporting of this transaction would be to report as Sales only one-seventh of the $100,000 in the year it is received and then in each subsequent year another one-seventh. If a firm did not do this, it would dramatically *overstate* Sales and Net Income for the subject year. Years ago there was a notorious bankruptcy of a firm called Minnie Pearl's Chicken which was *not* using the Installment Method. The company had spectacular growth in Sales—as long as these sales of new franchises were growing—but as soon as this growth in Sales declined, Sales and Net Income dropped dramatically.▴

The second use of the Installment Method comes about when a company sells something for a down payment and receives the balance over time. For example, if a firm sold a piece of land for $100,000 and received $10,000 as a down payment and the balance over the next 10 years, it should show Sales in the initial period of only $10,000, not $100,000. About 1970, the lid was blown off the real estate development industry when it was reported that many (most?) of the real estate development firms at the time were *not* using the Installment Method and were thus greatly overreporting Sales and Net Income. This revelation shook the industry in such a profound way that publicly traded real estate firms saw their Price/Earnings multiple shrink to unbelievable levels—four, five, and six times Earnings, when they had been substantially higher. This trauma continues even today, although in a somewhat reduced form, attesting to the fact that once you lose the creditability of the market—or anyone, for that matter—it is hard, if not impossible to get it back! If you ever see a Financial Statement from a company that *should* use the Installment Method of

---

▴ Enron used a variation of this with their subsidiaries, resulting in a dramatically different impression.

reporting Sales, but does not, you should look for the nearest exit! That's a company to leave alone.

COST OF GOODS SOLD AND GROSS PROFIT

Undoubtedly, the most common way to manage a firm's Net Income is through the Cost of Goods Sold section and, in particular, the Cost of Materials. Recall that the Cost of Goods Sold from the Income Statement includes the following:

Direct Labor	$1,500,000
+ Cost of Materials	$1,500,000
+ Factory Overhead	$ 500,000

There is nothing that can be done with the Direct Labor item, because this is money that has been spent, and that is that. Factory Overhead includes a number of items, some of which allow management discretion, such as Depreciation, but for the most part this section is not very manageable. Cost of Materials, however, is another matter.

Cost of materials is defined as follows:

Beginning Inventory	$1,500,000
+ Purchases	$1,500,000
− Ending Inventory	$1,500,000
Equals: Cost of Materials	$1,500,000

Now the question is "How do you record Ending Inventory?" This gets us into the whole question of Inventory valuation—and then some. If we use the **FIFO (First-In First-Out) Method** of valuing Inventory, we would be valuing the Ending Inventory at current prices, and if the cost of the Inventory has been rising, this valuation method will result in a *higher* Ending Inventory, and thus a higher Gross Profit. (Remember, the price of *this* Inventory has to be rising; it makes no difference what is happening to prices *in general!*)

Or the Inventory can be valued at the **LIFO (Last-In, First-Out) Method.** In this case, the Inventory will be valued at some historical cost—sometimes a very historical cost. The Ending Inventory, under this method, will thus be shown at a relatively *low* amount and, accordingly, the Cost of Goods Sold will be higher and the Gross profit will be correspondingly lower.

Simply stated, when you take the physical inventory, how do you value the Ending Inventory? If you use the current prices, you are using FIFO; when you use the "old" prices, you are using LIFO. But there are other ways of affecting the Ending Inventory, ways that are frequently employed. The most common way to affect the Ending Inventory is through the declaration of some of the Inventory as **obsolete Inventory**. In this case, management evaluates the Inventory in terms of its economic value and not its usefulness or appearance. Inventory may be perfectly good in every sense of the word, but because the company has too much of this particular Inventory, it is deemed to be superfluous—or obsolete. Or the Inventory may be designated for a discontinued product line. Another instance of obsolescence would be where the parts—perfectly good mechanically and otherwise—are not turning over rapidly enough in the course of trade. For example, it may be determined that a particular part turns over only once in 5 years.▲ In these cases, therefore, management declares the Inventory to be obsolete and writes it off the books. In the illustration of Trojan Co., let's assume that management has decided that $500,000 of Inventory is now obsolete. The resulting Cost of Materials would thus be:

	OLD	NEW
Beginning Inventory	$1,500,000	$1,500,000
+ Purchases	$1,500,000	$1,500,000
− Ending Inventory	($1,500,000)	($1,000,000)
Equals: Cost of Materials	$1,500,000	$2,000,000

Now if we take this new Cost of Materials and insert it in the Cost of Goods Sold calculation, we have the following:

	OLD	NEW
Direct Labor	$1,500,000	$1,500,000
+ Cost of Materials	$1,500,000	$2,000,000
+ Factory Overhead	$ 500,000	$ 500,000
Equals: Cost of Goods Sold	$3,500,000	$4,000,000

Now let's insert this new Cost of Goods Sold into the company's Income Statement:

ADJUSTED INCOME STATEMENT

	OLD	NEW
Sales	$5,000,000	$5,000,000
− Cost of Goods Sold	3,500,000	4,000,000
Equals: Gross Profit	$1,500,000	$1,000,000
− General & Administrative Expense	(500,000)	(500,000)
− Selling Expense	(500,000)	(500,000)
Equals: Net Income Before Tax	$500,000	0
− Tax	(200,000)	0
Net Income	$300,000	0

So how did Trojan Company's profit of $300,000—and a Tax of $200,000—go to *nothing*? Simple! Inventory was declared to be obsolete.

To recap what happens when Inventory is adjusted, remember the following rule about Inventory:

▲ When Henry Ford had a downturn, he kept his workers busy by making parts. When a new management team went into Ford Motor Company in the 1950s they found that the company had about 1,200 years supply of some parts.

The higher the Ending Inventory, the higher the Gross Profit; the lower the Ending Inventory, the lower the Gross Profit—if sales levels remain consistent!

"How much will the Gross Profit change for a given change in the Inventory level?" The answer is *dollar for dollar*. In our example we **wrote down** the Inventory by $500,000, and by doing so we reduced the Gross Profit by an equal amount, $500,000.

UNETHICAL ASPECTS OF INVENTORY VALUATION

Before continuing with our discussion of managing the Income Statement, it may be well to review certain other aspects of Inventory valuation that you may encounter in looking at the Income Statements of other firms. Some of these methods may be subsumed under the label "Cheating with Inventory."

Some managers, desperate for additional Net Income—and thus greater Net Worth on their Balance Sheet—fall prey to the temptation to produce more Income than they can legitimately account for. Knowing the rule stated above, regarding Inventory, they decide to value Ending Inventory at a somewhat higher price because "We all know that this inventory is going to go up in price, so what's wrong with anticipating this increase?" The only thing wrong with this is that it is cheating—pure and simple *cheating*!

Another way some unethical managers try to boost their Net Income and Balance Sheet Net Worth may be illustrated by Exhibit 3.4, which shows the Net Income for a mail order distribution house.

The numbers shown in the bar graph were presented to me by the president of a company he was trying to sell. The 5-year record of Net Income is beautiful. And the fact that the Net Income dropped a little in the fifth year makes it all the more believable!

Unfortunately, the entire record is a fabrication; the numbers were created using an accounting technique that is expressly *prohibited* by **Generally Accepted Accounting Practice (GAAP)**. The owner of this business used the *higher* figure of cost or market price instead of the *lower* of cost or market. By using this tech-

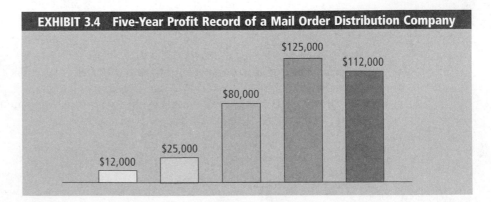

EXHIBIT 3.4   Five-Year Profit Record of a Mail Order Distribution Company

$12,000 $25,000 $80,000 $125,000 $112,000

nique—illegal because it is not approved by GAAP—he created a *higher* Ending Inventory and, as the rule says, the higher the Ending Inventory, the higher the Gross Profit. Wanting to sell his company, this owner not only desired a handsome trail of Earnings but he also wanted a larger Net Worth on his Balance Sheet. He got both of these wishes by cheating.▲ If the Inventory had been properly presented, with the "Lower of Cost or Market" used as a basis, I think the 5-year results would have shown *zero* profits each of the 5 years! Hardly the kind of company someone would like to buy.

THE PRACTICE OF REVENUE ENHANCEMENT

Since many new high-tech companies, especially the dot.com companies, have little or no inventory with which to play the "inventory game" just described, they have resorted to other methods to boost income or sales. In fabricating their Income Statements, they use tricks to enhance the revenue stream to the company. For example, if the new company is selling something for which it is entitled to a commission and nothing else, it might try to show Sales as the whole amount of the sale instead of only *their* commission. This can result in spectacular numbers for Sales, even if they do not show much of a profit. In an effort to stop this practice of **revenue enhancement**, the SEC has issued new guidelines for revenue reporting. As reported in the *Wall Street Journal* the new guidelines say that if the Internet companies "merely act as an 'agent' for a sale, they must book only the commission fee as revenue." They go on to specify the following criteria: "They have an agreement to deliver goods or services; they have actually delivered the products or services; they have fixed a price for the products or services; and they can collect the specified price."▲▲

The financial press has reported on a continuing array of firms—lately, usually high-tech firms—that have resorted to improper means of reporting revenue. **Revenue recognition** is the new term. Some use fairly obvious methods such as advancing sales that should be booked in future periods; some use more arcane methods. The upshot of each is the reporting of more sales now than is the case resulting in an increase in profit.

DEPRECIATION EXPENSE

Accelerated Depreciation

Referring again to our model, Trojan Co., the next significant item that needs to be managed on the Income Statement is Depreciation. Since 1986, firms have had to use **MACRS (*Modified* Accelerated Cost Recovery System)** for their tax return statement and **Straight Line** for financial reporting purposes. It used to

---

▲ Before I went out to look at this company, I was told that the seller was getting an "audited" statement. When I arrived I asked the seller why this statement was not audited. He then said to me "Listen, when I say something is worth $10, it's worth $10. The fact that I can buy it for less is a tribute to my skill. I'm not trying to deceive you." No, not much!

▲▲ *Wall Street Journal,* December 6, 1999, p. C17.

be that firms would use Accelerated Depreciation for tax purposes and Straight Line for financial reporting purposes but since MACRS is, in effect, an *accelerated* method there is little to gain even if the earlier ACRS were permitted—which it is not. MACRS is required for taxation, so there is no option there.

The question management has to decide with respect to Straight Line is how long the depreciable life will be. One could say that the depreciable life should be the economic and/or useful life of the asset. This is indeed reasonable, but very often unwise. For example, many machine tools have useful lives, if properly maintained, of 20 to 40 years. If a firm were to select such an extraordinarily long period, it would undoubtedly raise questions of concern from the reader of the Income Statement. Charges of hyping the Net Income would surely be made or at least occur to the reader.▲

And any thought in the mind of the reader that questions the creditability of the financial statement is to be avoided at all cost.

If a reader does not accept the creditability of the Statement at face, then all you have is a piece of worthless paper. The proper depreciable life for depreciable property is what would normally be taken by firms in that industry. If it is *usual* for firms to depreciate machine tools of a certain type over 7 or 8 years—even though they last for 30 or more years—then the proper depreciable life would be 7 or 8 years.

Unit Depreciation

Another method of depreciation that may be used and which may be appropriate in certain situations is **Unit Depreciation.** In this method, a depreciable machine is determined to be capable of producing a certain number of units—or parts. Then the depreciable amount—cost less any salvage—is divided by this number to arrive at a per-unit amount of depreciation. Remember, it is a rule of accounting that you may not switch back and forth in your methods of depreciation from year to year except by restating prior year's statements. But you can use this method, for example, when a firm is purchased▲▲ or when it begins as a start-up. The main advantage of this method is that it converts a **fixed cost** into a **variable cost.** When a manufacturing firm is just starting its corporate life, production is usually low and the Unit Depreciation method may keep the firm from showing a loss, which would of course impair its Net Worth. Another example would be when a firm is taken over in a **turnaround state** (meaning that the firm is showing a loss on its Income Statement but has the potential to

---

▲ By using a longer depreciable life than "normal," you raise the reported Net Income. I once had a client company in which I recommended using an 18-year life for its printing equipment. I thought they could defend that time period when questioned—by saying that the machines could last for 30 or more years—because the company so desperately needed any boost it could get to its Net Income and, thus, its Net Worth section of its Balance Sheet. I realized we were taking a bit of a gamble, but in this case circumstances dictated the gamble with creditability.

▲▲ This statement assumes a "purchase of assets" form of transaction, something which will be dealt with in Chapter 16.

become profitable). The tried-and-true rule for what to do in a turnaround is to convert a fixed cost into a variable cost, if the problem is inadequate Sales and/or underproduction. By using Unit Depreciation, this aim would be achieved.

Decelerated Depreciation

Another form of depreciation that is technically correct is **Decelerated Depreciation.** This is the opposite of Accelerated Depreciation and the same obsolete methods that are used for Accelerated Depreciation, namely, **Sum-of-the-Years-Digits** (SOYD, also known as sum-of-digits method) or Double Declining Balance can be used except in reverse. In sum-of- the-year's-digits method, if an asset is being depreciated over 8 years, the amount of depreciation taken in the first year is 8/36ths, the amount in the second is 7/36ths, etc. The sum of the digits from 1 to 8 is 36. This is a thoroughly logical method of depreciating an asset in that usually the greatest wear and tear on a machine, for example, is in the latter years of the useful life of the asset, and the lowest wear and tear is found in the early years. This, then, would be consistent with Decelerated Depreciation as the lowest amount of depreciation is taken in the early years. Unfortunately, this method is so rarely used▲ that its use would be tantamount to a red flag to the reader of an Income Statement. He or she undoubtedly would think that the use of this extremely rare depreciation method was for the purpose of hyping the company's Net Income—which is certainly *not* what management would want. The principal reason for even mentioning this method is to point out once again the necessity of avoiding *any* action that would take away creditability from the financial statement.

THE BALANCE SHEET

The **Balance Sheet**, also known as a statement of condition or financial position, provides a statement of a firm's assets and liabilities, as well as its owners equity—as of a specific date. It's called a *balance* sheet because it shows the relation of assets to the other two. Management of the Balance Sheet involves a combination of psychology and the utilization of legitimate accounting options. Too many managers treat the Balance Sheet as a "poor relation" to the Income Statement. But this is definitely a mistake. For lenders, the Balance Sheet is far and away more significant—if it is proper to say such a thing—than the Income Statement. Very important decisions can be made, positively or negatively, on the basis of the Balance Sheet that may not be made on the basis of the Income Statement.

Just one example is the **Debt/Equity Ratio** (for further discussion, see page 65). Many banks have rather arbitrary rules about the D/E ratio that are

---

▲ When regulated public utilities have their review for a rate increase, in California before deregulation, at least, there is usually a suggestion put forward to force the utility to use Decelerated Depreciation as this would lower the near-term depreciation expense—perhaps even permanently—which must be included in the utility charge that consumers pay.

virtually inviolable: For example, they might have a 4/1 maximum on this ratio. Exceed it and you will find that you are being asked to leave the bank.

FIRST IMPRESSIONS: THE CASH ACCOUNT

If it is true that first impressions are lasting impressions, what is the first impression you get from looking at a Balance Sheet? Since we read from left to right, top to bottom, you are most likely to notice the Cash account at first glance. What do you see?

A strong, rather large Cash account probably conveys to the reader the idea that the company is in rather good financial position. Conversely, a *negative* Cash balance will probably convey the impression that the firm is "broke." How do the accountants derive the Cash balance that is shown? The way they are *supposed* to compile the Cash account is to take the end-of-period cash balance on the company's checking account register—the company's checkbook. It matters not whether the company has a large balance in the bank at the closing date; the only thing that matters is the company's checkbook.

Now then, how can a company improve its Cash account? Perhaps the most expedient way is to stop writing checks for several days, or a week or more, *before the end* of the accounting period. This should be done, of course, with an eye on supplier relations, but if done only at year end, or at most quarter end, this should not upset any good vendor/supplier relations the company might have developed.

Another technical aspect of this matter is the fact that lumping *all* Cash accounts makes a better impression than showing several Cash accounts. For example, the Cash account might be shown (unwisely) as follows:

Petty cash	$124.35
Cash in Union Bank	1,450.54
Cash in CitiBank	215,505.90

This presentation may state the information accurately, but what if the reader hurriedly glances at the Statement and remembers the $124, instead of adding all three accounts together and thinking of that *total* as the company's Cash position? Most good accounting firms would do this summarization without having to be asked, but some smaller accounting practitioners may have computer programs that print out all items on the firm's Chart of Accounts and if the firm has three Cash accounts, that's what will be printed on the Balance Sheet.

Another way to boost the Cash account is to include the company's money market securities in the same account as cash so that the account would read "Cash and Money Market Securities." With many large city banks utilizing **sweep accounts** for their corporate customers, money moves between the company's cash account (its checking account at the bank) and money market securities electronically.

In summary, it is well to remember the psychological effects of seeing a large Cash account. As a successful businessman once told me, "Always put your gold in the window if you want people to see it." If people are impressed with a large Cash account, provide it if you can. There are those who would say that a large Cash account bespeaks poor asset management. There is a lot to say for that position, but there is also more to say about a healthy liquidity position, too.

MONEY MARKET SECURITIES

Under the provisions of Statement of Financial Accounting Standards Board No. 115, management is required to classify their investment into three categories: held-to-maturity securities, available-for-sale securities, and trading securities. Held-to-maturity securities are listed at amortized cost, and can be listed in the Other Assets section. Available-for-sale securities are recorded at market value with unrealized gains and losses reported as a separate item in the Stockholder's Equity section. Trading securities, on the other hand, are recorded at market value with unrealized gains and losses reported as part of Earnings. This is somewhat of a change from the old method of recording money market securities, but the conclusion one reaches from this new SFAS 115 is that almost all developing firms should record their money market securities in the Current Assets section.

THE CURRENT PORTION OF LONG-TERM DEBT

Using GAAP (Generally Accepted Accounting Practice), it is possible to relocate the current portion of long-term debt from the Current Liabilities section to the Long-term Debt section if the accountant is convinced (usually by checking with the banker) that the lender—usually the bank or finance company—is going to roll over the loan if the company's financial condition continues in a satisfactory condition. This is possible even if the loan is evidenced by a 90-day note, for example. Removing an item usually as large as the current portion of Long-term Debt from the denominator of the **Current Ratio** (current assets divided by current liabilities) can have a terrific impact on the financial picture.

Despite having been used for many years, the Current Ratio suffers from major problems. A major one stems from the fact that there are two intended meanings for Current Ratio.

The Current Ratio and Liquidation

The first thing Current Ratio is supposed to denote is what one of my colleagues in accounting once called "pounce value," meaning that if the assets shrunk to half their value, then any Current Liability holders could "pounce" on the assets and still realize what is owed to them. This may not be true at all: One or more of the Current Liability holders—for example, the bank from which the company is borrowing—may have a **secured interest** in the Accounts Receivable and/or the Inventory. Coupled with a **Right of Offset**—meaning that the bank can seize any cash the company has as partial payment for a loan—the bank would be able to seize these assets and satisfy its own indebtedness *before* any other creditors could receive anything from the liquidation of these **Current Assets.** So even if there is a Current Ratio greater than the traditional 2/1, there is no assurance that all Current Liability holders would be repaid merely from observing the Current Ratio.

Priorities of Assets

Related to the subject of the secured position of creditors is the matter of the **priorities of assets** in bankruptcy.▴ The general categories that are established for the claims against a firm in bankruptcy are:

1. *Priority Claims,* such as court costs, accounting and legal claims, Receiver's Notes and wages and salaries up to some specified amount, and certain taxes, such as payroll taxes.

2. *Secured Creditors' Claims.* Later in the book there will be discussed the Uniform Commercial Code, which provides a way of perfecting a secured interest in what is called Personalty—items such as Inventory, Accounts Receivable, Equipment, and other non–real estate assets. Also in this section would be the secured Real Estate (real property) claims. If some claim goes unsatisfied after the sale of these secured assets, that party would become a General Creditor for the balance.

3. *General Creditors.* This category includes a rather long list of claimants. Such things as trade creditors, debenture bondholders, unsecured creditors, claims in excess of what the secured assets produced if sold, wages and salaries over the minimum amount specified above, and certain taxes. (Trade creditors are those creditors who sold to the company on "open book account"; that is, on a company's promise to pay.) We will look closer at their claimant potential below.

4. *Subordinated Creditors.* This topic also will be discussed separately; suffice it to say here that these creditors—and there can be multiple categories of Subordinated Creditors, such as Senior Subordinated, Subordinated, and Junior Subordinated—come *after* the general creditors.

5. *Equity holders.* These are the stockholders and they may be classed as Preferred and Common Stockholders.

There are two general approaches that a court may take in a bankruptcy and they are called **absolute priority** and **relative priority**. Under absolute priority, the court would go down the list as it is stated above until the money is exhausted. In relative priority, the court may allow certain claimants to maintain some position (but of lower rank), and thus they may allow stockholders, who otherwise would get nothing, to maintain some position, perhaps after they pay some money to the corporation. There are two particularly relevant "Chapters"

▴ It is well beyond the purpose of this chapter to deal in any detail with all the items in all the categories in bankruptcy. Instead only a rough outline will be attempted.

(or sections of the code) in bankruptcy: Chapter 7, dealing with the liquidation of a firm, and Chapter 11, which gives the firm time to reorganize its affairs, and in so doing keep the creditors at bay. The list of five categories of claimants given above particularly applies to the case where the firm is liquidated; it is generally the order of asset liquidation in bankruptcy. You will also note that none of these categories is labeled "short-term" creditor or "long-term" creditor. These are terms that the accountants have invented for financial reporting; the terms used in our list are legal terms.

When the Current Ratio was invented, probably well before 1900, the United States did not even have a bankruptcy code similar to what we have today. So the suggestion that Current Assets could be used to pay off Current Liabilities (most likely, trade creditors) was not too unreasonable. Unfortunately, while the laws and circumstances have changed materially over time, this keystone of financial analysis has survived to this day. No one will admit that they place great importance in the Current Ratio, but it is still used extensively, at least as one of several ratios for testing the financial condition of a company.

As the foregoing discussion shows, however, the *denotative* meaning of the Current Ratio may be incorrect and the *connotative* meaning—namely that the company is in good shape financially—can be determined much better through analysis of the Cash Flow Statement, which is discussed in the next chapter. And the person who says that the **Acid Test Ratio**—(similar to the Current Ratio, but from which the inventory has been removed from the numerator)—is reliable may be just as misled. If one creditor has a secured interest in an asset, then that asset is not available for any General Creditor. So even if the removal of inventory makes it appear that the Current Liability holders are safe, this assertion may be quite incorrect: The remaining assets may be unavailable.

THE GENERAL CREDITOR RATIO

As stated, one of the meanings of the Current Ratio is that, in liquidation proceedings, there will be enough value in assets to pay off the liability. Since we have seen that this cannot actually be determined by the Current Ratio, the following **General Creditor Ratio** is presented—for those people who like ratios:

$$\text{GCR} = \frac{\text{Assets available for General Creditors}}{\text{General Creditor Claims}}$$

While this ratio may help a creditor of a business firm determine whether or not it feels secure in its General Creditor position, there is serious doubt whether this ratio will ever be popularly adopted, primarily because it would require the auditing accountant to make a determination of which assets are *available* for General Creditors. This may not be as easy as it may seem at first; it also may involve checking with the Secretary of State's Office to determine if there is a claim on certain assets. For people who *believe* in the Current Ratio, however, *this* GCR ratio may be a significant revelation. The GCR uses legal concepts instead of just accounting concepts.

THE DEBT/EQUITY RATIO

Probably no ratio is as important as the Debt/Equity Ratio. Variously defined as Total Debt / (Total Debt + Equity) *or,* more usually, as (Short-term + Long-term Debt) / Equity, this ratio is the "dividing line" for many banks. For example, many banks have a limit of 4/1 on this ratio for bank lending.▲ If a firm is over this limit, the bank will either not accept the firm as a customer or the bank will tell the customer—perhaps in a polite way, perhaps not—to leave the bank. Is there anything a company can do to improve this ratio? Perhaps. It may be worth trying: Excessive debt can lead to financial distress or bankruptcy—neither a desirable event!

After General Creditors in the prioritized list (see page 64) come Subordinated Creditors. If a firm has **Subordinated Debt** outstanding, it probably has this debt included in its Long-term Debt category. But this does not have to be. If the firm listed the Subordinated Debt as a *separate* line item *under the Long-term Debt and directly above the Equity section,* it would point out to the reader of the statement that this debt is ***de facto*** equity—that is, it is debt that serves as equity. When the Subordinated Debt is figured in with the Equity, the Debt/Equity Ratio will improve, perhaps dramatically.

The reason the Subordinated Debt is included with the Equity in computing the D/E Ratio is that if the Subordinated Debt is paid off *after* the (bank or General Creditors) debt the debtor is just as protected *as if* the Subordinated Debt were Equity. True, it is not "Equity" but it serves the same as Equity when computing the ratio. Understanding this is a mark of an experienced financial manager/deal person.

This is illustrated in the dilemma once faced by the president of a chain of home furnishing stores. Shortly after he and his brother purchased the store from their retiring parents, mostly for a note, the company's banker appeared and informed the president that the bank would like their company to find another bank. This after the company had been dealing with that bank for over 30 years! A little investigation quickly revealed the problem. When the two sons bought the business, they gave their parents a note for most of the purchase price. The company's Chief Financial Officer, an accountant who had been with the company for over 25 years, did what he thought was proper. He listed the note to the parents with the other Long-term Debt—thus creating a horrendous Debt/Equity Ratio!

If the parents had subordinated the note to the bank, however, the whole ratio would have been reversed; instead of a terrible ratio, the com-

---

▲ But the number varies by bank and industry. For example, some banks might allow a 6/1 D/E Ratio for some customers. If possible, ask your bank what number they consider to be the "dividing line" and then keep this in mind.

pany would have had a very good one—*if* the bank had counted the Subordinated Debt as Equity in calculating the ratio. True, the Subordinated Debt is, in fact, debt and because of this, some people think that it belongs with the other Long-term Debt. But *if* the bank counts Subordinated Debt as Equity—or *de facto* equity—then it is the equivalent of equity and should not be listed with the Long-term Debt. Including Subordinated Debt with the regular Long-term Debt is fairly common. In our example of the home furnishing store, the problem might have been eased if the accountant or the bank officer had suggested to the two sons that they get the parents to subordinate their note to the bank, but neither did so. Perhaps the accountant did not think about the problem with the Debt/Equity Ratio and perhaps the banker was reluctant to interfere in the internal financial affairs of the company. Banks have to be extraordinarily careful not to interfere in the internal financial affairs of a customer company as the bank might be sued by the customer if financial difficulty ever occurs. This is not a trivial problem to banks.

Two Types of Subordination

There are two types of subordination that may be used: General and Specific. **General Subordination** is when the debt is placed *after* General Creditors and **Specific Subordination** is when the debt is placed after some specific debt, such as a loan from a bank. In privately owned firms, it is not unusual for the owners to loan money to their own companies. But if that same owner/manager wishes to have the company borrow money from the company's bank, the bank will almost surely insist that the owner of the business subordinate his/her claim to the bank's claim. In this way, as the figure of speech goes, the owner is "not in the same room" as the bank in the event of financial difficulty.

From the point of view of the financial manager or a "deal person,"

Subordinated Debt is like manna from heaven: It is debt that serves as Equity when calculating the all-important Debt/Equity Ratio.

Appraisal Surplus

If a firm needs to improve its Equity section, in order to improve its D/E Ratio, it might resort—if all else fails—to a technique called **Appraisal Surplus**. To do this, a firm would list its equipment and/or its real estate at *market value* on the Assets side of the Balance Sheet and the resulting increase over the old value on the Liabilities and Capital side in the Equity section as a separate line item labeled "Appraisal Surplus." This may be sufficient to turn a *negative* Net Worth section into a *positive* amount. But you should be aware that whenever you see Appraisal Surplus on a Balance Sheet, it is immediately clear the firm was trying to improve its Net Worth section any way it could legitimately. (And of course, a positive Net Worth certainly looks better than a negative Net Worth.)

FINANCIAL STATEMENTS VS. TAX STATEMENTS

Earlier in this chapter, in discussing published Financial Statements, we noted that there is a separate reporting for tax purposes. In the United States it is usual and proper to have *two* and only two financial statements for a business: a Tax Statement and a Financial Statement.▲ Any third *internal* financial statement—for monitoring the operations of the firm—is usually just plain cheating. Yet for some managers, there may be a question of ethics in preparing even the two statements. Statements like "I have nothing to hide" are offered when only one statement is prepared—the required tax return. But this suggests that having two statements is in some way immoral. Nothing could be farther from the truth!

Out of ignorance or because they are just too cheap to hire an accountant to prepare a Financial Statement, some managers use just their tax return to convey the financial condition of the company to its stakeholders.▲▲ This is usually a mistake. The **Tax Statement** is prepared according to the tax laws of the country and may have little resemblance to the appropriate financial condition of the company. For example, in the extractive industries (coal, oil), depletion allowances may make it seem that the company is not making any money, when in fact it may be highly profitable. It is in these statements, which we collectively call the Financial Statement, that management communicates the company's financial condition to its stakeholders—stockholders, creditors, employees, suppliers.

But not all Financial Statements are created equal. There are three types of Financial Statements that might be prepared, and they can be vastly different.

TYPES OF FINANCIAL STATEMENTS

The three types of Financial Statements that can be prepared are as follows:

The Compiled Statement

Whether prepared by the company's accounting department or prepared by an outside independent Certified Public Accountant (CPA), the Compiled Statement is far and away the most common statement prepared in the United States. It merely says what management wants to say, and this may be completely independent of accounting rules—the so-called Generally Accepted Ac-

---

▲ In some countries (Germany, for example) it is possible to have only one statement, a combination of the Tax Statement and the Financial Statement. In some countries (e.g., Latin American countries), the Tax Statement is prepared by government tax auditors.

▲▲ The height of absurdity occurred once when looking at a middle-market manufacturer of ice cream products. I was shown the "Financial Statement"—in rough draft form *in pencil!* When I asked for the finished copy, the President of the company said that what I was looking at was the finished copy— ". . . I save money by not getting it typed."

counting Practice. Management may make a statement—that is, give a number—on something for which there is no factual basis whatsoever! For example, if management wishes to have a larger Net Worth section, it may value one of its patents—or even an unpatented product—at whatever it wishes! Yes, whatever it thinks the patent is worth—independent of what some outsider might think the value is. And it can get an independent CPA to prepare such a statement, even though the CPA states that he or she is only recording the numbers that management supplies and not passing on the correctness or appropriateness of the item. What, then, is the control over the reasonableness of the statement? Only the integrity of the management.

The Reviewed Statement

In order to answer the needs of the many middle-market firms in the United Sates, the Financial Accounting Standards Board developed, in the 1980s, the Reviewed Statement, which is somewhere between the "anything goes" Compiled Statement and the Certified Statement, common with large and publicly held firms. Basically the Reviewed Statement states that the external, independent CPA has prepared the statement according to Generally Accepted Accounting Practice, meaning that all the rules of accounting have been followed in preparing the statement. Also, while the opinion of the independent CPA states that this Review merely means that the statement is prepared according to GAAP, it is usually assumed that the independent CPA has approved the Accounting System employed by the firm. (This last condition is one of the requirements of the Certified Statement, discussed below.) This has been a widely used type of statement, particularly among middle-market firms who are borrowing from banks or finance companies.

The (Audited) Certified Statement

Prepared by an independent CPA, the Certified Statement is the ultimate in accounting assurance in the United States, at least. True, there are those who can point out irregularities that may be found even in Certified Statements, and the quality and reputation of the CPA firm preparing the statement must be considered, but far and away this statement commands the respect of virtually everyone.

   Trying to tell this to the stockholders or stakeholders of Enron would be an interesting exercise in futility. On a smaller scale, the author was examining the financial statements of a middle-market company that was a relatively small subsidiary of a large public firm. When I asked for a Certified Statement, I was told that would be no problem. After reviewing the actual condition of the company with the "certified" statement I received, it appeared to be at great variance with what I saw. Why did the national accounting firm "certify" to something they should not have done—they should have done some checking on the company's books? The answer I received was that this subsidiary was not "significant" in the overall condition of the parent.

For additional caveats on the veracity of certified statements all one has to do is talk with those management consultants who deal in corporate rescues and turnarounds.

But the point remains the same. For better or worse, the Certified Statement is the best we have at present.

In this statement, the CPA does three things of note. First a verification of Accounts Receivable (A/Rs), Accounts Payable (A/Ps), and Inventory is made. Letters are sent to customers and suppliers asking the customer or supplier to verify that they owe the company money on a certain invoice or that the company owes it money on a certain invoice. Also, a physical count is made of inventory at the start of the year and at the end of the year. It is this procedure that leads to much of the disagreement that might ensue between the company and the independent CPA. If the CPA thinks that certain inventory is obsolete, or that it is turning over too slowly, or for other reasons, it may insist on writing down this inventory with the attendant result on Net Income and, of course, the Net Worth section of the Balance Sheet. Verification is also made of all the covenants attached to the firm's debt instruments outstanding to see that the company is not in violation of any of these covenants.

The Accounting System

This is of vital importance. If the accounting system is unreliable, all manner of mistakes might slip through and go undetected, resulting in major changes on the financial statements. In one case, the entire year's Net Income was wiped out because of a glitch in the accounting system involving the counting of the work-in-process inventory that was discovered only after the year was over. When engaging a new independent CPA firm, one of the first areas of concern—and expense to the employing firm—is the accounting system in use by the company. Incidentally, if the management of the firm thinks that it will want to go public at a future date and will need a Certified Statement by a major accounting firm (a point discussed in Chapter 8), it would do well to hire an outside small accounting firm that uses the same accounting system as the desired large accounting firm that will be later employed when doing the IPO. In this case, the large accounting firm may review the work of the former accounting associate in the preparation of its Certified Statement and for a reasonable price provide a so-called "white paper" that could be used when a certification is required for the IPO.

The statements are prepared according to GAAP. This means that all the accounting rules—whether they be called APBs or FASBs or SFASBs—have been followed in the preparation of such statements. Exhibit 3.5 summarizes the three types of statements and what is involved in each.

FINANCIAL BATHS AND OTHER WRITE-OFFS

First started in the early years of the twentieth century, the **financial bath**—or, as it is sometimes called, "Wall Street Arithmetic"—is the practice of taking a write-off on the Income Statement in the current period in order to relieve a fu-

EXHIBIT 3.5 Three Types of Financial Statements			
	VERIFY A/R, INVENTORY, A/P	APPROVE ACCOUNTING SYSTEM	STATEMENTS ACCORDING TO GAAP
COMPILED	NO	NO	NO
REVIEWED	NO	?	YES
AUDITED	YES	YES	YES

ture income statement of a charge that would reduce income. Assets which are old or obsolete may have to be written off to the income statement in future periods. By writing off these assets in the current period, the future is spared. Old receivables, obsolete inventory, obsolete equipment and, quite importantly, goodwill may be likely candidates for such write-offs. Goodwill can result from a number of things. For example, when a company purchases another company in a "purchase of assets" form of transaction and pays more than the asset value, goodwill is created. Under the new FASB 141, a company cannot "amortize" goodwill; instead, the auditor performs a test and compares the "fair value" of the asset with the goodwill amount. If the fair value is *less* than the goodwill amount, then an adjustment has to be made. This is another extremely complicated accounting ruling.

The origins of the financial bath are probably lost in time, but when first used, the idea behind the strategy was quite clear: If you are going to have a loss, the stock price of publicly held firms would fall. But how far could the price fall? Obviously, there is a floor on how far the price can fall—but there is no floor on the amount of the loss that can be reported! So if you are going to have a loss, why not have a *big* loss?

Since its origin, this practice has been used by management for a variety of reasons. Occasions for the use of this technique are as follows:

A Change of Management

This appears to be probably the most logical of all reasons. When new management takes over the direction of a publicly held firm from a prior management that is not part of the current management's entourage, then taking a large write-off and blaming it on prior management's lack of discipline—or whatever term you want to use—is one of the most common uses of this technique.

When a Firm Is Reporting a Loss Anyway

This is the idea behind the "Wall Street Arithmetic." But the reader should not read into this strategy that if profits are going to be *lower*, then you might as well show a loss. There is a big difference between a *reduction* in earnings that are still *positive* and a *loss* on the Income Statement. It is unwise to show a loss if it is *elective* by taking a financial bath. The exception to this might be the current practice of writing off goodwill associated with an acquisition of a firm with relatively small assets—for example, a software company.

When Your Stock Price Is Really Down

Why your stock is down may have a bearing on this circumstance, but if it is because the market is down, or your industry segment is down, then this might be a good time to take a financial bath. Why not? This bath may push down the stock a bit more, but trying to fight a really down market is not unlike trying to swim against the current. Parenthetically, a down market is also not a good time to come out with really good news, such as greatly improved earnings. It won't have its desired impact. Better to wait until the tide has turned, and *then* bring out the good news!

In the spring of 2001, a number of high-tech manufacturing firms took write-offs of unneeded inventory. This resulted in some sizeable losses. (Whether this would have been in conjunction with a loss, anyway, is conjectural.) What is interesting is the fact that when the economy turns up *for them*, these companies will find the "written-off" inventory and sell it with surprisingly good profits as a result. This is because the cost of the inventory was written off in a prior period!

This is not unlike the company that "finds" inventory—to boost the level of inventory—in the several years prior to when the owner wishes to retire and sell the company.

When the Stock Market Is Strongly Bullish

This is a rather new phenomenon that was particularly noticeable in the 1980s. The risk is that if the bullish market really reacts negatively to such a move, it may hurt the stock for some time to come.

The "Me Too" Circumstance

This was first noticed in the early 1980s when Citicorp announced that it was going to take a large write-off on its South American loans. The market was relieved to see such a move on the part of Citicorp's management—and the stock went up! Playing copycat, many of the other major banks which also had questionable loans in South America decided that this was a good time for them to write off their loans as well.

Although it is not quite the same thing as a financial bath, the practice of companies taking a large write-off to account for major reorganizations or pension fund matters seems to go unnoticed in the stock market. In any event, these are matters that affect mostly rather large firms and therefore are not really relevant to our middle-market firms.

One of the most interesting tricks employed by some publicly held firms is the practice of going *back* to the prior year and amending that statement by taking a big hit to the *prior year's* Income Statement. This is *history* and the market attempts to look to the future! So the usual result of such a maneuver is that the market for the company's stock is unaffected.

WHO SHOULD PREPARE FINANCIAL STATEMENTS?

Many managers feel that preparing the company's financial statements is a matter that should be handled strictly by the firm's independent CPA firm. They follow the mantra: "They know best." This is *not* always the best course, but for many managers, ignorance of even the basics of accounting leads them to this unwise decision. It is my opinion that the overall story and appearance of the firm's financial statements should be the responsibility of management.▲ I am sure most CPAs would agree with this statement, too. It is simply unfair to place all decisions attendant to the presentation of the financial results of the firm on the shoulders of the independent CPA. These statements tell a story and it behooves management to guide the story that is told. Even if management does not know all the accounting rules, they can ask if something is possible. In this way they can get the results—using *proper* accounting rules—that they desire. Understanding these basics of accounting and finance is mandatory for good management, and is, in fact, a hallmark of good management.

▲ This captures the spirit behind the new Sarbanes-Oxley law.

SUMMARY

Managers who say—or claim—that they leave the accounting to the accountants probably never managed an emerging or middle-market company. It behooves such a manager to be reasonably cognizant of basic accounting rules. This chapter first explained the way in which managers have "managed their profits" for generations: through inventory manipulation. This extremely basic maneuver is usually not taught in formal business school classes.

The second purpose of this chapter was to show how some companies "cook their books." This was not intended to give entrepreneurs undesirable ideas, but rather how to spot the nefarious practice when they see it. In the course of "growing the company" or acquiring a company, it is important for the entrepreneur to be able to detect statements that are bloated. It is simply not realistic to say "I leave that to my experts."

The third purpose of this chapter was to get the reader to realize that the way the company presents its Balance Sheet may make a big difference. For example, the reason behind listing the Subordinated Debt on a separate line is not to mislead a reader, but rather to point out to bankers and others that this debt is "special." It is debt, but because of priorities in bankruptcy, it may be counted as *de facto* Equity when calculating the all important Debt/Equity Ratio. Many managers have no idea of the importance of this *Subordinated Debt*; it may make the difference in doing a deal and not doing it. In the Able case (Chapter 17), the reader can see just how this LBO deal is possible through the use of Subordinated Debt.

QUESTIONS FOR DISCUSSION

1. Suppose that you were looking at a company with the intention of buying it. In the course of reviewing the company, you are presented with a set of financials that show a rising Net Income. Would you take these financials on their face value, or would you check on items within the statements? What items would you look for to enhance sales and revenue? And how about the Balance Sheet? What questions would you pose regarding the Balance Sheet?

2. Using a company in the current headlines—or in recent past news, such as Enron—try to see what "sins" might have been committed on these companies' statements.

3. If you were managing your own company, how would you "manage" Net Income and what would be your objective? Assume different types of companies: a manufacturing company, a distribution company, and a service company. Be sure to explicitly state your objectives in each case.

3

CHAPTER REVIEW

Focus on Technology

"BUILD IT AND THEY WILL COME"!

"Build it and they will come!" This is exactly what Jim Clark did when he brought cofounder Marc Andreessen and his team to launch Netscape back in 1984. "My attitude was that we'd generate such a ground swell that we'd figure out later how to make money. . . . With so many people on the Internet, I thought: How can I avoid making money?" Clark once said. Of course, there is one caveat in here. If you are Jim Clark—who had been a Stanford professor, had already launched and taken public Silicon Graphics (a multi-billion dollar company), and could write a $4 M check to start a company—it may make a little bit of difference!

However, aside from the rather exceptional record of Clark and his team, as well as what the pioneering Internet company brought us afterwards, Clark's systemic method of searching for and starting a company is not an exception at all. Most of such "methodical" ventures—where an entrepreneur launches a well-orchestrated, and at times prefunded, search for viable opportunities—stay private and do not become as high profile as Netscape. Furthermore, in the field of entrepreneurial finance, there is a venture investment vehicle called "the Search Fund" Model specifically used for such a mode of investing.

Another entrepreneur that followed the same mentality is Amazon.com's Jeff Bezos. Back in 1994, Jeff Bezos, then a 30-year-old investment banker with a more than comfortable salary, developed the passion to start a company in the then fuzzy world of electronic commerce. The passion came from his early familiarity with the World Wide Web as he worked for his employer, the investment banking firm of D.E. Shaw.

Bezos however had no idea as to what line of product or service he wanted to promote over the Net. So, he put on a piece of paper a list of twenty potential retail ideas that could be pursued over the still developing World Wide Web. His main thought: Marry the traditional mail order business and the Internet and make money in the process. His value proposition for customers: Convenience! With this niche in mind, he embarked on a search process and soon figured out selling books over the Net was the smart thing to do. With that in mind, he packed and left New York for Seattle—a place also close to the distribution center of a major book wholesaler, the Ingram Group.

Now, what do you do if you want to sell books and don't know much about that business? Well, you learn about it! Where can one learn about an industry and its inner working? Industry's trade associations! That is exactly what Bezos did the next day by attending the annual meeting of the American Booksellers Association in Los Angeles. "So I went to their booths (the wholesalers) and told them I was thinking of doing this." (Talk about not being afraid that someone may steal your idea!) Well, you know the rest of the story!

CHAPTER REVIEW

4

Cash Flow Analysis▴

WHY CASH FLOW?

In the preceding chapter we examined the Income Statement and the Balance Sheet and we discussed managing profit. As important as *profit* is, one must realize that it is *cash*, not profit, on which firms run. You pay bills and meet payroll with cash.

To understand what creates cash and what uses cash in an operating firm, it is useful to examine the two popular measures of cash flow: (1) **Net Income Plus Depreciation (NIPD)** and (2) **Earnings Before Interest and Taxes (EBIT)** along with a new measure of cash flow that really measures the *change* in cash, called "NOCF," or Net Operating Cash Flow Double Prime. As we will see, everything starts with NOCF, which becomes prime and double prime according to cash flow priorities. This chapter will show that serious mistakes can be made by using Net Income Plus Depreciation or EBIT in certain scenarios—that is, in growth or recession scenarios.

Above all, this chapter will foster a better appreciation of the importance of the Balance Sheet. *Balance Sheet changes markedly affect cash flow* and many man-

▴ This chapter is based largely on my article "When is there cash in cash flow," *Harvard Business Review,* March/April, 1987.

agers fail to realize these causal factors. Too many managers focus on Income Statement items but fail to appreciate the Balance Sheet factors that cause change in the cash flow.

A GENERIC CASH FLOW STATEMENT

The format for cash flow used in this book divides the cash flow into four *main* groupings (and seven overall):

- Operations

- Priority Outflows

- Discretionary Outflows

- Financial Flows

This system has an important advantage over the format assumed by **FASB (Financial Accounting Standards Board)** 95 because FASB 95 includes interest and dividends in one category (they are separate in the format used here) and divides cash flow into three groupings: operations, financial flows, and investment. Using the three divisions of FASB 95 confuses the issue and prevents the modeling that will be discussed shortly. I believe that a statement should "talk" to its reader; the reader should be able to see clearly relationships that are meaningful. You can do this with the format I use here; I have not found a way to do this with FASB 95.

Of great significance is the fact that the Cash Flow Statement should be a tool for forecasting; it is not a rear-view mirror. One of the main reasons I started using this Cash Flow Statement was the fact that I was having trouble *forecasting* a **Sources and Applications of Funds Statement.** This statement, also known as the "Where from, where go statement," is, in my opinion, about the most little used—and therefore, worthless—statement that the accounting profession has ever invented. It does tell the manager where the cash came from and on what it was spent, but it is otherwise useless. Note the past tense: spent. For some few purposes this information is important but what is really useful for management decision purposes is a forecasting tool that would answer questions like "Will we have enough cash?" or "Will we be able to service this amount of debt?" or "How much will we have for capital expenditures or bonuses?" The Cash Flow Statement we use can answer questions like this.

See Exhibit 4.1. What follows is an examination of each of its components. While there are four *main* sections of the Cash Flow Statement, the first one, dealing with Operations, is divided into two sections: Inflows and Outflows.

EXHIBIT 4.1   Cash Flow Statement

CASH FLOW STATEMENT for the period _____ to _____

DATE - PERIOD			
OPERATING CASH INFLOWS			
+ NET SALES	$	$	$
+ OTHER INCOME			
− Δ ACCOUNTS RECEIVABLE			
(1) NET OPERATING CASH INFLOWS	$	$	$
OPERATING CASH OUTFLOWS			
+ COST OF GOODS SOLD			
(LESS DEPRECIATION)	$	$	$
+ GENERAL & ADMINISTRATIVE EXPENSES			
+ SELLING EXPENSES			
+ TAXES			
− Δ ACCRUED TAXES			
+ Δ INVENTORY			
+ Δ PREPAID EXPENSES			
− Δ ACCOUNTS PAYABLE			
(2) TOTAL OPERATING CASH OUTFLOWS	$	$	$
(3) NET OPERATING CASH FLOW			
* (ITEM 1 LESS ITEM 2)*	$	$	$
PRIORITY OUTFLOWS			
+ INTEREST EXPENSE	$	$	$
+ CURRENT DEBT REPAYMENT			
(4) TOTAL PRIORITY OUTFLOWS	$	$	$
DISCRETIONARY OUTFLOWS			
+ CAPITAL EXPENDITURES	$	$	$
+ RESEARCH & DEVELOPMENT EXPENSE			
+ PREFERRED STOCK DIVIDENDS			
+ COMMON STOCK DIVIDENDS			
+ BONUS			
(5) TOTAL DISCRETIONARY OUTFLOWS	$	$	$
FINANCIAL FLOWS			
+ Δ DEBT INSTRUMENTS (BORROWINGS)	$	$	$
+ Δ STOCK SECURITIES (EQUITY)			
+ Δ TERM LOANS			
(6) TOTAL FINANCIAL FLOWS	$	$	$
NET CHANGE IN CASH AND			
** MARKETABLE SECURITIES ACCOUNTS**			
+ NET OPERATING CASH FLOW	$	$	$
− PRIORITY OUTFLOWS			
− DISCRETIONARY OUTFLOWS			
+ FINANCIAL FLOWS			
(7) NET CHANGE IN CASH AND			
* MARKETABLE SECURITIES*	$	$	$
END OF PERIOD CASH BALANCE	$	$	$

Δ = PERIOD-TO-PERIOD CHANGE IN TOTAL DOLLAR AMOUNT

OPERATING CASH INFLOWS

In this first section, the first item is Net Sales, that is, gross sales net of any returns and allowances. This item is, of course, from the Income Statement, and like the next item, you take the amount for the period in question. Next there is an item, Other Income, that has nothing to do with Operations, but we do not know a better place to put it. Also, it is either not included on many Income Statements (especially, for middle-market firms), or it is immaterial. The next item is quite material, however, and it is Accounts Receivable. Note that on the statement there is a + sign in front of the Other Income item, because it is an Income Statement item. Before the Accounts Receivable item there is a *minus delta* sign—meaning minus a positive change. This is because this item is a Balance Sheet item, and with Balance Sheet items we must include the **period-to-period change** in that item, not the value of the item *per se*. To understand the meaning of "minus a positive change," refer to Exhibit 4.2, where t_0 represents the start, or time zero. Note that when sales were going up—and the firm was building up Accounts Receivable, which takes cash—the Net Operating Cash Inflow was positive but less than that period's Sales. But in the fourth period, however, Sales went down but Net Operating Cash Flow went up! Why? You can also see that it is because of the arithmetic of the format: Minus a minus in algebra is a *plus*, and therefore we add the change in the Accounts Receivable balance. In short, when Accounts Receivable go up, it takes cash; when Accounts Receivable go down, it generates cash.

> **Understanding that for Balance Sheet items we must include the *change* in that item, is central to understanding the mechanics of cash flow.**

We must train ourselves to realize this in the course of general management or financial management: We must get to the point of "feeling the Balance Sheet."

OPERATING CASH OUTFLOWS

The first item in this section, Operating Cash Outflows, is Cost of Goods Sold, less any Depreciation that may be imbedded in this item. The reason we take out depreciation, of course, is that this item is a **noncash** item, and we only

EXHIBIT 4.2	**Illustration of "Minus a Positive Change"**				
CHANGES IN ACCOUNTS RECEIVABLE (A/R)					
PERIODS	t_0	1	2	3	4
SALES		$10	$15	$25	$10
− CHANGE IN A/R		(10)	(5)	(10)	15
A/R BALANCE	0	10	15	25	10
CHANGE IN A/R BALANCE		+10	+5	+10	−15
(1) NET OPERATING CASH INFLOW		$0	$10	$15	$25

include cash items in the Cash Flow Statement. Other noncash items would be, for example, Depletion Allowances, Amortization of Goodwill, nonfunded Reserves, such as Reserve for Bad Debts, and earned surplus.

The next items are General and Administrative Expenses and Selling Expenses. Naturally these items must be shown less any Depreciation or other noncash expense that might be included in these items as well. Next, Taxes from the Income Statement is shown followed by minus a positive change in Accrued Taxes from the Balance Sheet. We next add a positive change in the Inventory account from the Balance Sheet as well as a positive change in Prepaid Expenses from the Balance Sheet. Finally, we subtract a positive change in Accounts Payable, also from the Balance Sheet. When Inventory increases, it takes cash. When Accounts Payable increase, it generates cash. The reserve is true.

Naturally, you should realize that this generic listing of items may be tailored to fit any individual company's requirements. If your company has an item that is not included in this listing, add it; if your company does not use one of these items, delete it. For example, in the former case, your company might have Engineering Expense as an item—perhaps, a rather large item.

Algebraically add these items and we have Item 2, Net Operating Cash Outflows. Subtract Item 2 from Item 1, Net Operating Cash Inflows and we get Item 3, **Net Operating Cash Flow,** called **NOCF.**

PRIORITY OUTFLOWS

NOCF is the amount of cash that a firm generates from **operations**—which may be construed as the basic operation of the firm, its *raison d'être. This is the amount of cash that a firm has with which to do things.* The first thing that a firm needs to do is to pay its Interest and Debt Repayments. Thus the next section is called Priority Outflows. Doing the pro-forma forecasts for a leveraged buyout, for example, might involve several separate Interest Payment lines and several Debt Repayment lines. It is best not to combine these items.

DISCRETIONARY OUTFLOWS

Following the Priority Outflows section is Discretionary Outflows. In this section we put such items as Capital Expenditures, Research and Development Expenses, Bonuses, and/or Common and Preferred Dividends. The ordering shown on the sample Cash Flow Statement is purely arbitrary; if your company has different priorities, then rearrange the items or substitute others. For example, most emerging or middle-market firms do not pay dividends, but they may pay bonuses. So substitute Bonuses for Dividends. For a manufacturing firm that makes such items as toys, Advertising Expenses might be quite substantial, perhaps 10 percent of Sales. Also, management might want to "back into" this amount, meaning that it might want to know what its cash flow is expected to be before settling upon its Advertising Expenses—a sort of simultaneous solution. This same process might be used for dividends. A firm might want to balance its investment in Capital Expenditures with its Dividend; again, a simultaneous solution.

The amount of cash that a firm has to make Discretionary Expenditures may be seen from the following model:

$$NOCF' = NOCF - \text{Priority Outflows}$$

NOCF' answers one of the most important questions management can ask: "How much money will we have for Discretionary Outflows?" Or: "How much money will we have for Capital Expenditures and Bonuses?" Capital Expenditures are a way for a firm to plow cash back into the firm; Bonuses are a way for a firm to pay out cash. So another way of looking at NOCF' is to say that this is the amount of cash a firm has to "plow back or pay out." Deciding how to allocate amounts between these two items is what the art of financial management is all about.

FINANCIAL FLOWS

The next section, Financial Flows, includes such large items as the sale of stock or the placement of debt. It does *not* include the *periodic* payment of debt under a loan arrangement in which the firm makes a monthly or periodic payment to a bank or financial institution; these payments are shown in the Priority Outflows section. If a firm wished to call a bond issue, however, it would show this (big) item as a *negative* Financial Flow. Similarly, if a firm wished to repurchase the stock of one of its shareholders, it would show that expenditure as a *negative* Financial Flow. It may be helpful to think of this section as containing the really large items that might be called "financial items."

NET CHANGE IN CASH AND MARKETABLE SECURITIES ACCOUNTS

The concluding section is the sum total of the above sections. Thus:

$$\text{Net Change in Cash} =$$
$$NOCF - (\text{Priority} + \text{Discretionary Outflows}) + \text{Financial Flows}$$

Numerically, this section would be defined as:

$$7 = 3 - (4 + 5) + 6$$

The reason Item 7 is called the Net Change in Cash and Money Market Securities is that most firms combine (or should combine) their Cash Account with their Money Market Securities Account. This is usually facilitated by an arrangement with the firm's bank called a "Sweep Account." If a firm chooses not to combine these two accounts, however, it should show this item as Net Change in Cash and then show separate line items, Net Change in Cash and Net Change in Money Market Securities.

EVALUATING OUR CASH FLOW MEASUREMENT

Now that we have reviewed the separate line items in the Cash Flow Statement, we can now turn our attention to comparing our measure of cash flow with two popular notions of cash flow: (1) Net Income Plus Depreciation (NIPD) and Earnings Before Interest and Taxes (EBIT). The measure we use is simply a variation of NOCF which is called NOCF". NOCF" is defined as:

$$NOCF'' = NOCF - \text{Nec Discretionary}$$

Nec **Discretionary**, means "necessary discretionary." At first this term might seem like an oxymoron, but it really is not a contradiction in terms. It says that in the section, called "Discretionary" there might be some minor items that are deemed to be "necessary," however defined. Nec Discretionary is defined as that amount of cash which the firm wishes to have available in a worst case scenario for Discretionary Outflows. For example, a firm may regularly spend $1 million to $1.5 million on Capital Expenditure but in a really bad year it would want to have perhaps $300,000 available for Capital Expenditures—or more correctly, Discretionary Expenditures. But whatever it puts in this "Nec Discretionary" section, it will have that much less to service its debt in a worst case scenario. In words, NOCF" means the *amount of cash that a firm has to service its debt*.

The reason "Double Prime" is used to modify NOCF should be obvious to the reader. *Everything starts with NOCF.* The more of NOCF a firm allocates to Debt Service (Priority Outflows), the less it has for Discretionary Outflows—and vice versa. The more a firm allocates to Discretionary Outflows, the less it has for Debt Service (Priority Outflows). NOCF" is rather like another popular measure of cash flow called **Free Cash Flow**—different from NOCF" in that it does not include Taxes, which might be quite important. One must be careful to understand the definition that is being used for "Free Cash Flow." It may be that the user intends for it to mean NOCF', not NOCF" We now have three measures of cash flow that we can compare under different scenarios and with three different types of companies.

MEASURES OF CASH FLOW UNDER DIFFERENT SCENARIOS

Some time ago, a banker had a visit from one of his best corporate accounts—a small but rapidly growing high-tech subsidiary of a large mature company. In this visit the president, the vice president, and the controller explained that there had been considerable friction with top management of the parent company—so much so that the parent's management told the subsidiary's management that if they could raise the money, they would sell them the subsidiary. To this end, they proposed borrowing a certain amount of money with the understanding that they would repay the loan at so much per quarter—because they had great cash flow.

The banker knew that the subsidiary had been quite profitable and had excellent prospects for continued growth. His initial thought was that this was a slam dunk, and he started to reach for the loan application when he paused and said, "Maybe we'd better work out a Cash Flow Statement on you." They did, and to the surprise of all, the cash flow available to service the debt was woefully low compared to the proposed quarterly payments of principal and interest. But how could this be? It was plainly evident that Net Income Plus Depreciation—the measure of cash flow that they were using—was more than adequate to meet the payments. Why, then, did the Cash Flow Statement that the banker used show a cash insufficiency? The reason, of course, is that the measure of cash flow that was used, NIPD, did not take into account the working capital items—principally, the Accounts Receivable, Inventory, and net of the Accounts Payable.

Fortunately, there is a happy ending to this story because the subsidiary was financially very viable. All that was necessary was to tailor the payments so that they started out low enough to be covered by the real cash flow that the company was generating and gradually increase it over time. Of course, they could have reduced the growth in sales, which would have produced a higher cash flow, but that was clearly an undesirable solution for the firm. Since it was detrimental to the company, the bank didn't really want that alternative either.

Undoubtedly, this story has been repeated many times, especially when people forget that the two most popular measures of cash flow—NIPD and EBIT, or EBITDA, meaning Earnings Before Interest and Taxes plus Depreciation and Amortization—are only Income Statement concepts and do not include Balance Sheet working capital items. The Cash Flow Statement shown as Exhibit 4.1 (p. 78) does take account of *both* the Income Statement and the Balance Sheet items; furthermore, as stated, the format of this statement permits modeling.

To get an answer to the query of how NOCF" differs from two other common measures of cash flow, we took three different kinds of companies, a manufacturing company, a wholesale company, and a service company, stylized▲ their Income Statements and Balance Sheets and then simulated these companies in three different scenarios:

- Steady sales

- Growth in sales

- Recession

THE STEADY SALES SCENARIO

The three simulations showing steady sales (with debt) provide graphic evidence that there is at least one situation in which NIPD and EBIT approximates cash flow. To show this, a simulation is made for each type of company under a

▲ The manufacturing company was a middle-market machine tool manufacturer, the distribution company was a paper merchant (wholesaler), and the service company was a wholesale laundry. "Stylizing" means that "typical" ratios for these types of companies were taken from the Robert Morris Associates *Statement Studies*.

steady sales situation, meaning that sales were allowed to vary up or down by no more than 5 percent. The graphics in Exhibit 4.3 show the assumptions for each simulation:

> The progression of sales over the 6-year period (in 6-month intervals—because bond interest is paid this way).
>
> The three measures of cash flow—EBIT, NIPD, and NOCF".
>
> The cash balance that would result if the scenario evolved and there were no other uses of cash other than that assumed for capital expenditures.

A Manufacturing Company

In this first scenario (Exhibit 4.3) the difference between NIPD and NOCF" is, mostly, the amount "necessary Discretionary Outflows." But, most importantly, with the exception of the amount for minimum Capital Expenditures, NIPD is approximately the same as NOCF" because the *net change* in the Balance Sheet working capital items—Accounts Receivable, Inventory, Accounts Payable, and Accrued Taxes—*is close to zero*. With reference to the Cash Flow Statement, (Exhibit 4.1), it can be seen that if these Balance Sheet items were removed from Items 1 and 2, what is left would be *only* Income Statement items. When sales are neither declining nor rising, there should be no reason for the working capital items to increase or decrease on balance. Or expressed differently, the net change in the (Balance Sheet) working capital items is approximately zero. Thus, in this scenario, NOCF" is essentially only an Income Statement concept—but *only* in this scenario!

Whenever NOCF" exceeds Priority Outflows, because of the assumptions made in these simulations, the cash balance will increase over time. And because the difference (between NOCF" and Priority Outflows) is more or less *constant* over time, the increase in the cash balance is virtually monotonic.

In a real-life situation, it is quite doubtful that a firm would allow its Cash (and Marketable Securities) balance to increase constantly over time, but that is beside the point here. The only point of this exercise is to show what would happen if the assumptions held.

A Wholesale Company

This similarity of NIPD and NOCF" is all the more apparent in the simulation for the wholesale company, Exhibit 4.4. Here, NOCF" crosses over NIPD for a period of time (when sales were declining a little) but generally the two measures of cash flow are roughly equivalent because the "necessary Discretionary" is quite small in this kind of company (wholesale paper companies are not very capital-intensive) and, of course, the changes in the working capital Balance Sheet items also net out to approximately zero.

A Service Company

This situation is repeated in the simulation for the service company (Exhibit 4.5).

To summarize the cash flow situation in the assumed steady sales situation, NIPD is a fair estimation of NOCF"—and thus cash flow—*because the Balance*

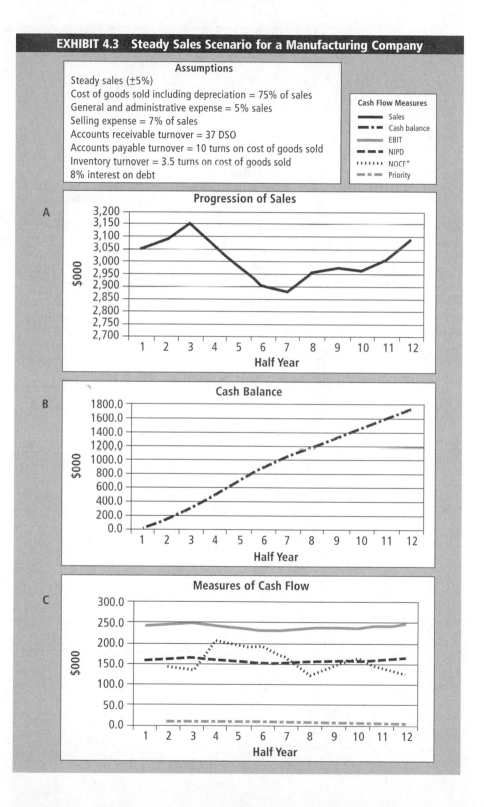

EXHIBIT 4.3   Steady Sales Scenario for a Manufacturing Company

Assumptions
Steady sales (±5%)
Cost of goods sold including depreciation = 75% of sales
General and administrative expense = 5% sales
Selling expense = 7% of sales
Accounts receivable turnover = 37 DSO
Accounts payable turnover = 10 turns on cost of goods sold
Inventory turnover = 3.5 turns on cost of goods sold
8% interest on debt

Cash Flow Measures
——— Sales
—·—· Cash balance
——— EBIT
— — NIPD
······· NOCF"
— — Priority

A

Progression of Sales

B

Cash Balance

C

Measures of Cash Flow

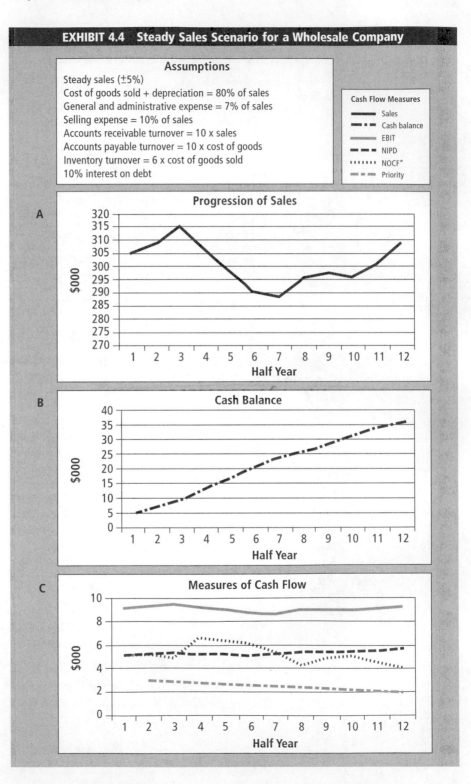

EXHIBIT 4.4   Steady Sales Scenario for a Wholesale Company

Assumptions

Steady sales (±5%)
Cost of goods sold + depreciation = 80% of sales
General and administrative expense = 7% of sales
Selling expense = 10% of sales
Accounts receivable turnover = 10 x sales
Accounts payable turnover = 10 x cost of goods
Inventory turnover = 6 x cost of goods sold
10% interest on debt

Cash Flow Measures

— Sales
—·—· Cash balance
— EBIT
– – – NIPD
········· NOCF"
—··— Priority

A   **Progression of Sales**

B   **Cash Balance**

C   **Measures of Cash Flow**

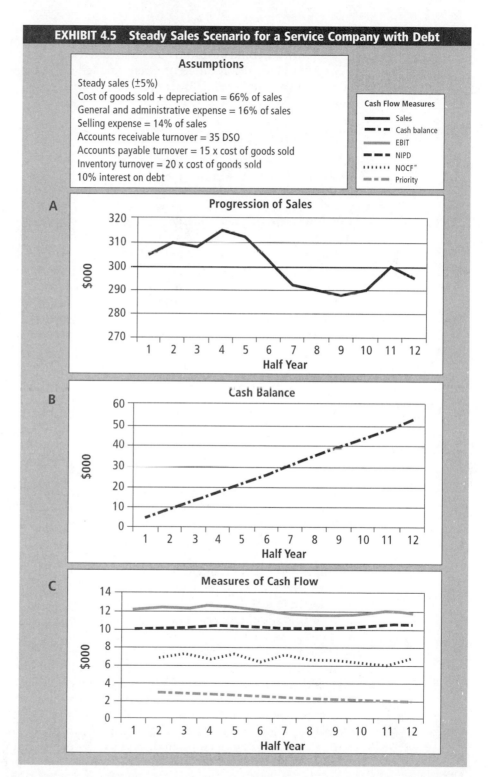

Sheet working capital item changes netted out to approximately zero. The amount of the cash increase could be directly traced to differences between NOCF" and the Priority Outflows. If this difference were smaller, indicating, for example, that the companies had larger debt service, then the cash balance would have risen slower, and vice versa.

THE GROWTH SCENARIO

Now that we have established the situation in which NIPD and EBIT are fair estimators of cash flow, just the opposite can be shown quite dramatically in the three growth scenarios.

A Manufacturing Company

In the case of the manufacturing company (Exhibit 4.6), we let sales increase over the 6-year period at the rate of 30 percent per year. EBIT and NIPD rise accordingly, and the apparent cash flow looks great, unless you observe what is happening to NOCF" and the cash balance.

NOCF" does not increase nearly as rapidly as do EBIT and NIPD. And in this case, the cash balance increases over the 7-year period. But if the *growth rate* with this company (we assumed a 30 percent growth rate) were to increase to 48 percent or more, the cash balance would turn negative because NOCF" would be declining. If the growth is so severe as to put the cash balance into a negative position, management could ask this question: *How much cash would it take for this firm to finance growth in Sales equal to the assumed growth rate per annum?* In this scenario, it is assumed there is no **debt service** at all. If there were Priority Outflows, the situation would have been exacerbated and the cash balance would have risen less, or even might fall to a negative, if the firm had debt service, depending on the growth and other assumptions.

The Hot Buttons: Testing Sensitivities

To get the results of this simulation, certain assumptions had to be made, especially regarding what I call the company's "hot buttons": Cost of Goods Sold, Accounts Receivable management, Inventory management, and Accounts Payable management. While not directly related to the question of NOCF" versus NIPD and EBIT, it is interesting to observe what would happen to these hot buttons over the planning period if they were changed. Exhibit 4.7 illustrates variation in one of these hot buttons.

For this simulation we assumed different values for the Cost of Goods Sold of 70, 73, 75, and 78 percent. Instead of the 75 percent that was assumed in Exhibit 4.6, if the company could take just two percentage points out of its Cost of Goods Sold, it could accumulate about $1 million more over the planning period; if it could improve its Cost of Goods Sold to 70 percent, it could generate over $3 million more. Conversely, if it became careless and let Cost of Goods Sold slip to 78 percent, it would have about $2 million less over this planning period. Notice that if the company, through some sort of breakthrough (perhaps by outsourcing) were to reduce its Cost of Goods Sold to something less than 70 percent, the rather imposing 30 percent growth rate

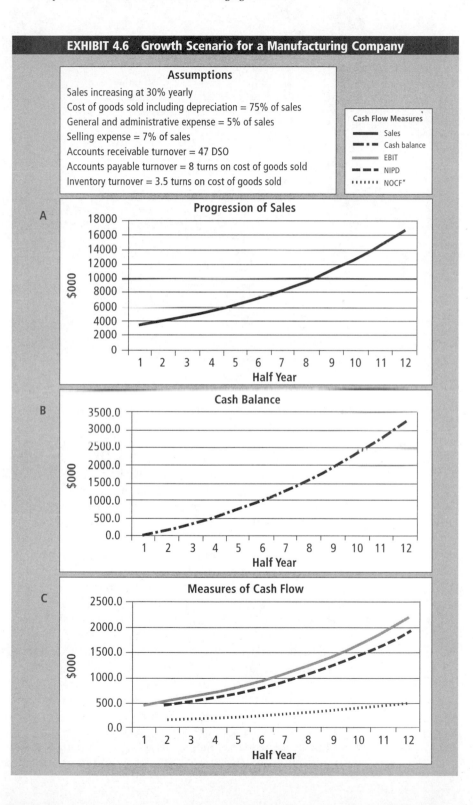

EXHIBIT 4.6   Growth Scenario for a Manufacturing Company

Assumptions

Sales increasing at 30% yearly
Cost of goods sold including depreciation = 75% of sales
General and administrative expense = 5% of sales
Selling expense = 7% of sales
Accounts receivable turnover = 47 DSO
Accounts payable turnover = 8 turns on cost of goods sold
Inventory turnover = 3.5 turns on cost of goods sold

Cash Flow Measures
——— Sales
—·—· Cash balance
——— EBIT
— — NIPD
······· NOCF"

A   **Progression of Sales**

B   **Cash Balance**

C   **Measures of Cash Flow**

EXHIBIT 4.7   Cost of Goods Sold Sensitivity for a Manufacturing Company

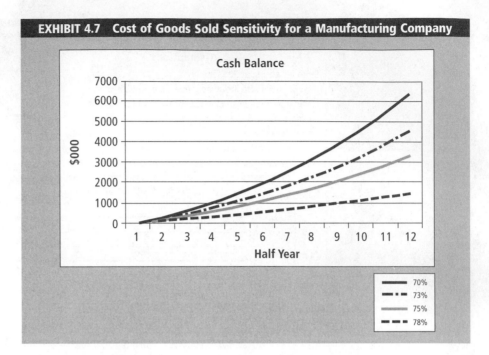

could be self-financed entirely and generate a million more over this planning period, other things being unchanged.

In the basic scenario (Exhibit 4.6), we assumed an Accounts Receivable turnover rate of 47 Days Sales Outstanding (DSO). In Exhibit 4.8, in order to test the Accounts Receivable sensitivity, we let the A/R turnover slow down to 60 DSO and then we speeded up collections so that the Accounts Receivable turnover was 36 DSO. The cumulative effect—for this company—was not terribly significant for the 6-year period. (Being a devoted "cash flownic," this result surprised me. I would have thought that variation in the Accounts Receivable turnover would have had more impact.) You must remember that generalizing on the basis of *this* scenario for *this* manufacturing firm could be quite misleading. In individual cases it is necessary to actually simulate the cash flow to see what effect a certain change would have on a given case.

The variation in the inventory assumption—another "hot button"—proved much more exciting, however. Notice that in the basic scenario (Exhibit 4.6) we assumed a rather anemic 3.5 inventory turns a year. (Remember this represented the average inventory turnover for this kind of company according to Robert Morris Associates; it wasn't just assumed.) But, if through better inventory management—perhaps the introduction of some just-in-time practices—the inventory turnover could be increased to 4.5 times a year (which doesn't seem Herculean at all) then over the 6-year planning period almost $2 million more would be generated (Exhibit 4.9). And if the company turns up the growth meter significantly, this increased efficiency would make the difference between a

EXHIBIT 4.8 Accounts Receivable Sensitivity for a Manufacturing Company

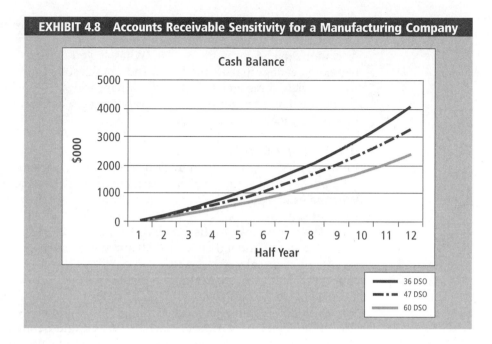

EXHIBIT 4.9 Inventory Sensitivity for a Manufacturing Company

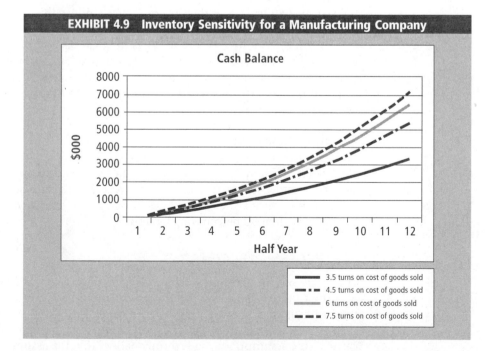

positive cash balance and a negative one. For many people working in a manufacturing environment—especially in the production process—this may be a revelation. You hear statements like, "What do you mean cash? These are just a few extra bearings that are produced, and can sell sometime." From a cash flow point of view, these aren't "just a few more bearings." If the inventory goes up $1, the cash balance goes down $1, everything else remaining equal. This is a lesson every manager *must* learn.

A Wholesale Company

In the wholesale company simulation (Exhibit 4.10) we let sales stay steady for 4 half-year periods, then we let sales increase at 30 percent a year thereafter. When sales were steady, NIPD and NOCF" were rather close, but as soon as we let sales start climbing, NIPD went up and NOCF" leveled off and declined. Why? What happened to the cash balance was quite predictable: It rose when sales were steady, and it then leveled off and started falling as soon as this rather robust growth in sales was effected.

At this point you should be able to observe that from a planning point of view, this model—particularly in the computerized version—permits the effective testing of just how much growth in sales could be effected and still self-finance. Or, alternatively, how much growth should be attempted, given the amount of external financing available—whether it be working capital financing or other financing.

Pushing Hot Buttons

We assumed 80 percent as the Cost of Goods Sold for this wholesale firm in the basic scenario (Exhibit 4.4), but when we sensitized this variable (Exhibit 4.11), we got some very interesting results. As long as this company kept its Cost of Goods sold at 80 percent or better, it could self-finance growth of 30 percent a year. But if it got careless and let its Cost of Goods Sold slip to 82 or 84 percent, it would find that its cash balance would drop into the red at the end of the 6-year planning period.

A Service Company

The growth simulation for the service company (Exhibit 4.12), produced results somewhat different from those in the wholesale company simulation. While sales were rather steady, the cash balance rose, but as soon as growth of 30 percent was introduced, the cash balance nosedived. Obviously, for this company, annual growth of 30 percent was too much.

THE RECESSION SCENARIO

The recession simulations present a marked contrast to the growth simulations and the intuitive belief about recessions. Instead of running out of cash, all three simulations showed that the firm came out of the recession with more cash than when it entered the recession. Remember, however, that this was because of the assumptions made. I truly believe that the assumptions made were

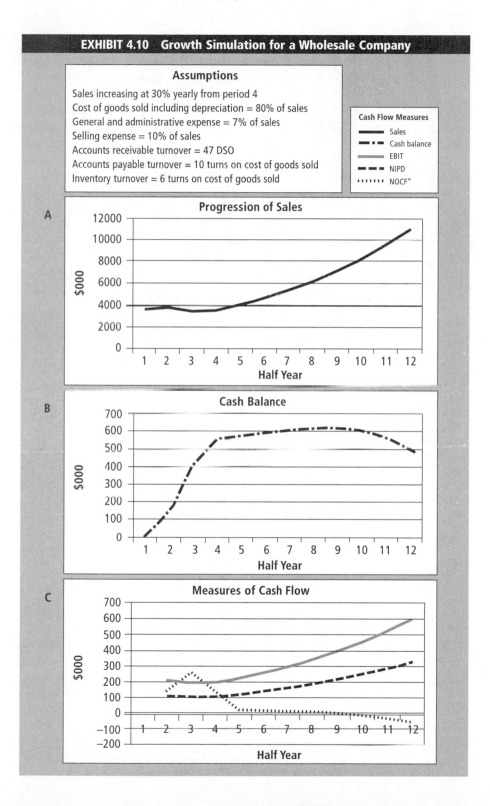

EXHIBIT 4.11   Cost Of Goods Sold Sensitivity in a Wholesale Company

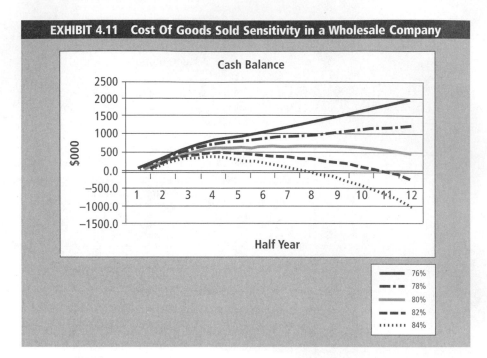

plausible assumptions—and, in fact, the sign of a well-managed firm—but if you vary the assumptions, you will vary the results. In giving a talk once on cash flow to an industry trade group association, I let the sample firm run out of cash and crash, so to speak. When the talk was finished, the very first respondent from the audience commented that he had never had as much cash as he had at the end of the last recession. Let's find out how this happened.

In the basic simulation for all three types of firms, it was assumed that the full decrease in sales (25 percent for the manufacturing and service companies and 30 percent for the wholesale company) during the recession occurred during the fifth and sixth periods, or over 1 year. The recovery, however, was assumed to take place over 1.5 years.

In all three basic simulations, the Cost of Goods Sold percentage was allowed to increase (relative to Sales) as sales decreased, but not in equal proportion. This was done to attempt to simulate observed practice resulting from management's desire to hold certain key production personnel despite falling sales. It would be questionable, if not foolhardy, to lay off employees without regard to their potential importance once sales rebound. Also, the indirect overhead component of Cost of Goods Sold (because it contains rent and/or Depreciation) tends to be rather fixed and results in upward pressure on the Cost of Goods Sold percentage as sales decrease during a recession.

Additionally, the Accounts Receivable turnover ratio slowed, as did the Accounts Payable turnover. The Inventory turnover was held constant for the manufacturing firm in its simulation, but it was allowed to decrease for the whole-

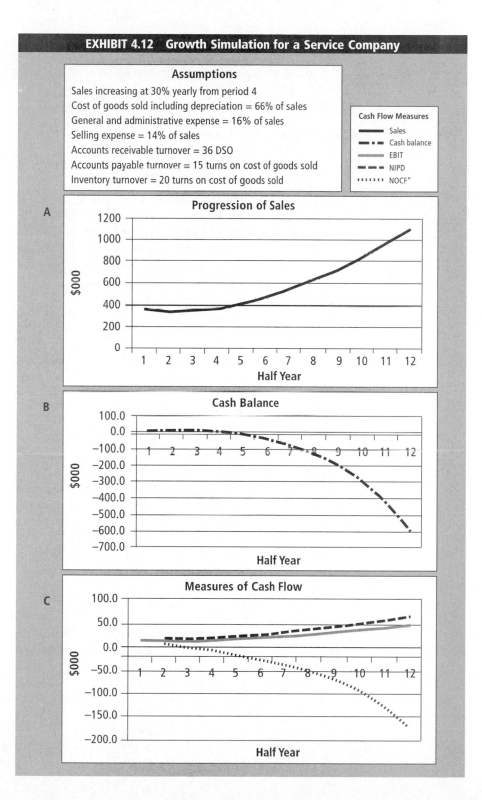

EXHIBIT 4.12   Growth Simulation for a Service Company

Assumptions

Sales increasing at 30% yearly from period 4
Cost of goods sold including depreciation = 66% of sales
General and administrative expense = 16% of sales
Selling expense = 14% of sales
Accounts receivable turnover = 36 DSO
Accounts payable turnover = 15 turns on cost of goods sold
Inventory turnover = 20 turns on cost of goods sold

Cash Flow Measures
— Sales
—·— Cash balance
— EBIT
– – NIPD
······· NOCF"

sale and service companies. (To check the effect of Inventory turnover on cash flow, we sensitized this variable separately—as discussed below.)

General and Administrative Expenses, as well as Selling Expenses, were allowed to decrease as the recession approached its trough, but not at the same rate as sales. This, too, was an attempt to simulate reality.

A Manufacturing Company

In the manufacturing company simulation (Exhibit 4.13), we allowed sales to start dropping after the fourth (half-year) period. *Since NOCF" exceeded the Priority Outflows during these first four periods, the cash balance went up*. As Sales started to decline, EBIT and NIPD also declined, but at a faster rate because of the leverage—both financial and operating—employed. Now as Sales start up in period 6, EBIT and NIPD also rise briskly and start to level out in the 9th period. This is expected because EBIT and NIPD are both solely Income Statement concepts. As such, these measures are tied to Sales; there is no lag in the downward or upward movement.

NOCF", on the other hand, does not move in concert with the two Income Statement measures of cash flow. In fact, when Sales decline in the fifth period, NOCF" actually *increases*, then it decreases but at a slower rate than either EBIT or NIPD. This occurs, of course, because of the "running off" of Receivables and Inventory. (Remember the construction of the Cash Flow Statement; when Accounts Receivable, for example, are down, the *change* is negative, so you *add* it to the cash inflow. See Exhibit 4.2.) The result of this is that *at the trough of the recession, NOCF" is actually greater than EBIT or NIPD!* This is because of the runoff of Inventory and the reduction of Accounts Receivable. For those who are used to thinking of NIPD as cash flow, this is, perhaps, an unexpected situation. For operating managers who have observed this phenomenon, however, this should come as no surprise.

Another contrast in the comparison of these three measures of cash flow comes when Sales starts its upward movement. As Exhibit 4.13 shows, NOCF" moves down a little in period 6, but subsequently turns down rather markedly. In fact, NOCF" does not hit its trough until period 7—or 6 months after the popular measures of cash flow have bottomed out. The apparent reason for this lag effect is the need to *rebuild* the depleted Inventory and Accounts Receivable accounts.

In all other simulations or actual cash flow analyses done on firms where inventory was of significance, this general pattern of NOCF" relative to the movement in Sales was observed. In some cases, the upswing in NOCF" as Sales decreased initially was even more pronounced than shown in Exhibit 4.13.

The cash balance is generally upward over the whole period except for the one period when NOCF" dropped below Priority Outflows. But while this is the "good" reason to explain why the cash balance was higher at the end of the recession than it was at the beginning, the "real" reason for this phenomenon is that Cost of Goods Sold (and General and Administrative Expenses and Selling Expenses) *was cut back decisively and punctually*. If management is slow in

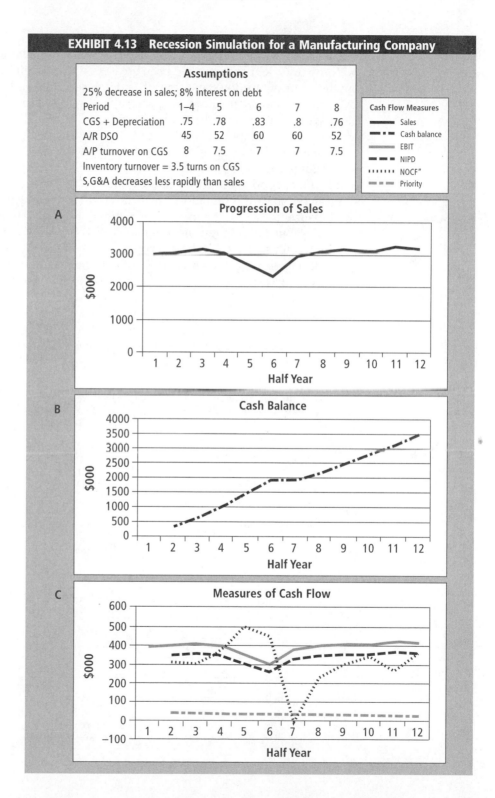

EXHIBIT 4.13   Recession Simulation for a Manufacturing Company

Assumptions

25% decrease in sales; 8% interest on debt

Period	1–4	5	6	7	8
CGS + Depreciation	.75	.78	.83	.8	.76
A/R DSO	45	52	60	60	52
A/P turnover on CGS	8	7.5	7	7	7.5

Inventory turnover = 3.5 turns on CGS

S,G&A decreases less rapidly than sales

Cash Flow Measures
- Sales
- Cash balance
- EBIT
- NIPD
- NOCF″
- Priority

A — Progression of Sales

B — Cash Balance

C — Measures of Cash Flow

reacting to a major sales slowdown, the cash expended will quickly push down NOCF"—and with it the cash balance. Note also that if the Priority Outflows—the company's debt service—had been greater, NOCF" might have dipped below the Priority Outflows and, thus, the decrease in the cash balance would have occurred sooner and been more severe. So severe, in fact, that the company may have had a major cash insufficiency, to use Gordon Donaldson's term. (More on this in Chapter 7, Leverage and Capital Structure.)

To see the effect of variation in the Accounts Receivable turnover, a simulation (Exhibit 4.14) was performed on this one variable. Note that as Sales start to drop after period 4, the Cash Balance is affected due to the three different Accounts Receivable turnover ratios. But what is most interesting is the fact that the cash balance in each of the three cases returns to the *same* amount when the Days Sales Outstanding returns to equality. If you ever wondered if there is *Cash* in Accounts Receivable, here is your proof. Yes, there is cash and it is dollar for dollar with the Accounts Receivable. If the Accounts Receivable are up $100,000, the Cash Balance will be down $100,000. A similar result was obtained when the Inventory was sensitized.

Before proceeding with the next simulations, it may be worthwhile to review a conclusion one might draw from our discussion so far. *Is it better to watch the Income Statement items more during a recession or the Balance Sheet items?* The

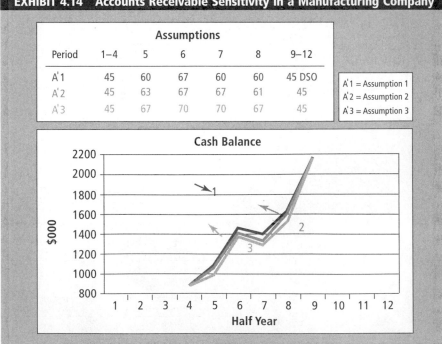

EXHIBIT 4.14   Accounts Receivable Sensitivity in a Manufacturing Company

Assumptions

Period	1–4	5	6	7	8	9–12	
A'1	45	60	67	60	60	45 DSO	A'1 = Assumption 1
A'2	45	63	67	67	61	45	A'2 = Assumption 2
A'3	45	67	70	70	67	45	A'3 = Assumption 3

Cash Balance

answer, of course, is that if Income Statement expenses are not watched carefully as a recession hits, *those dollars that might have been saved are gone forever!* Balance Sheet items, on the other hand, can be recovered even if it takes a while, as Exhibit 4.14 shows. This is not to say that the increase in the Balance Sheet items should go unattended as they will have an effect on the cash balance; but, given time, these Receivables and Inventory can be converted into Cash. *If you pay dollars for salaries of redundant personnel—even though you think it is wise to do so—this cash will never be recovered.*

A Wholesale and a Service Company

The simulations on the wholesale company (Exhibit 4.15) produced results that were quite similar to the manufacturing company. In this simulation, when sales dipped down, NOCF" actually went up for one period, reflecting the runoff in Receivables and Inventory. Afterward, NOCF" dropped dramatically.

When NOCF" broke below the Priority Outflows, the Cash Balance *declined* for several periods and then started back up again. At the end of the planning period, the cash balance was higher than it had ever been. In this simulation, the company survived a drop in sales of 30 percent and survived beautifully. But this was because of the assumptions made: that General and Administrative Expenses decreased with the decrease in Sales, even though at a lesser rate.

In the recession simulation for the service company (Exhibit 4.16) we see the usual pattern emerge, but in this case, because of the lack of importance of Accounts Receivable and Inventory, the drop in NOCF" is more closely aligned to the EBIT and NIPD functions. The cash balance increases as the sales are steady during the first four periods. When the recession sets in, however, EBIT and NIPD start down, mirroring what is happening to sales. NOCF" goes down simultaneously with EBIT and NIPD. The cash balance reflects the fact that NOCF" dropped below Priority Outflows for several periods.

FORECASTING CASH FLOW COMPONENTS

There are, generally speaking, two approaches to forecasting the component items of the Cash Flow Statement:

- A ratio approach

- Regression analysis

Although each of these approaches will be discussed, the latter will be only generally covered, as it applies to financial forecasting; the discussion will not involve the technical aspects of regression analysis which would, obviously, be beyond the scope of this chapter. In both cases Sales will be assumed to be a given.

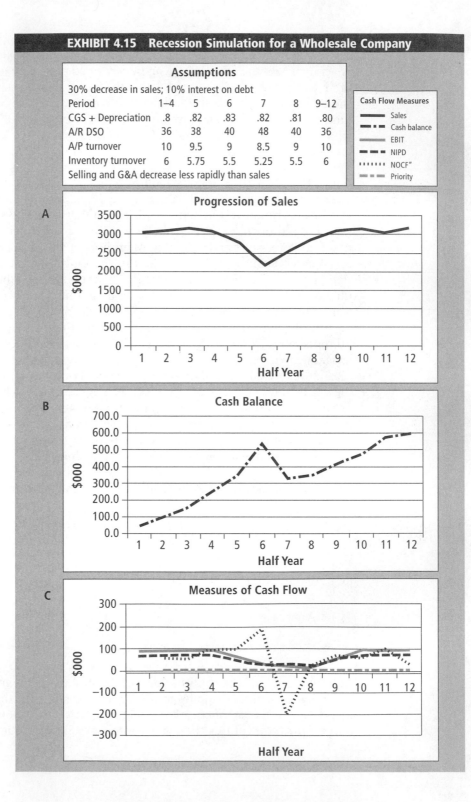

EXHIBIT 4.15   Recession Simulation for a Wholesale Company

Assumptions

30% decrease in sales; 10% interest on debt

Period	1–4	5	6	7	8	9–12
CGS + Depreciation	.8	.82	.83	.82	.81	.80
A/R DSO	36	38	40	48	40	36
A/P turnover	10	9.5	9	8.5	9	10
Inventory turnover	6	5.75	5.5	5.25	5.5	6

Selling and G&A decrease less rapidly than sales

Cash Flow Measures

- ——— Sales
- —·—·— Cash balance
- ——— EBIT
- – – – NIPD
- ········ NOCF"
- –·–·– Priority

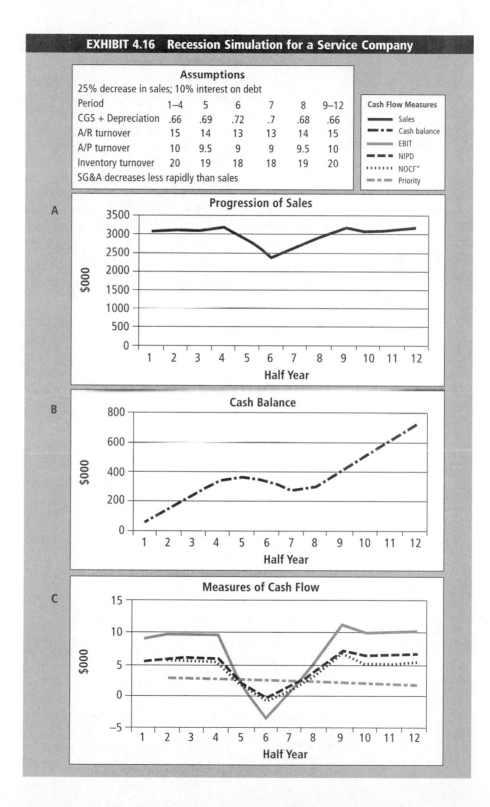

EXHIBIT 4.16   Recession Simulation for a Service Company

Assumptions

25% decrease in sales; 10% interest on debt

Period	1–4	5	6	7	8	9–12
CGS + Depreciation	.66	.69	.72	.7	.68	.66
A/R turnover	15	14	13	13	14	15
A/P turnover	10	9.5	9	9	9.5	10
Inventory turnover	20	19	18	18	19	20

SG&A decreases less rapidly than sales

Cash Flow Measures
- Sales
- Cash balance
- EBIT
- NIPD
- NOCF"
- Priority

A   **Progression of Sales**

B   **Cash Balance**

C   **Measures of Cash Flow**

RATIO APPROACH

Accounts Receivable

Following the Cash Flow Statement format (see page 77), the first item to be forecast is the Accounts Receivable. There are two ways to approach this ratio.

Perhaps the more informative of the two approaches is the ratio Days Sales Outstanding (DSO). This ratio is derived as follows:

$$DSO = \text{Accounts Receivable Balance}/(\text{Yearly Sales}/365)$$

For example, if a firm had \$800,000 of Accounts Receivable at the end of its fiscal year and Sales for the year of \$5,400,000, it would have Days Sales Outstanding of 54.1 days. Thus:

$$54.1 \text{ DSO} = \$800,000/(\$5,400,000/365)$$

The second approach is to use the ratio Accounts Receivable Turnover, thus:

$$\text{A/R Turnover} = \frac{\text{Sales}}{\text{Accounts Receivable Balance}}$$

For our data the ratio would be: 6.75 Turns = \$5,400,000/\$800,000

Either approach will yield the same forecast amount (except for a rounding error) of Accounts Receivable. For example, if we are trying to forecast what the Accounts Receivable Balance would be for forecast Sales of \$6,000,000, the arithmetic would be:

$$\text{For Days Sales Outstanding, } \$6,000,000/365 =$$
$$\$16,438.36 \text{ times } 54.1 \text{ DSO} = \$889,315$$

$$\text{For Accounts Receivable Turnover, } \$6,000,000/6.75 \text{ turns} = \$888,889$$

The difference of \$426 is due to rounding. Generally speaking, DSO conveys more meaning and is the recommended way.

Other Income

Since this item has very little to do with sales, the best way to forecast this item is just to estimate it. For middle-market firms it will usually be insignificant—if it is included at all.

Cost of Goods Sold

There is only one commonly used way using ratios to estimate this important item, and that is to take this item as a percentage of sales. This will yield a percentage that will usually be rather stable. Most firms seem to go along with little if any change in this variable. Changing the underlying assumptions could change this forecast quite a bit, however. For example, if the firm uses a bidding approach to pricing its product and it changed the formula used in this bidding—for example, it might change its hourly charge for a particular machine or it might change its overhead factor or even its profit factor—this might result in significantly different forecasts. Or, the market might change significantly and force the firm into an entirely different pricing structure. Without changes such as these, however, the Percentage of Sales technique will generally hold rather well. In fact this item, of all the items, is the closest thing most firms have to a purely *variable* item.

General and Administrative Expense and Selling Expense

Both General and Administrative Expense and Selling Expense are forecast as a Percentage of Sales. On the face of it, this approach makes more sense for Selling Expense than for General and Administrative Expense because it would seem to be more variable. After all, isn't General and Administrative Expense supposed to be the firm's fixed cost? If it is fixed, why would it vary (even somewhat) proportional to sales? Indeed, as will be pointed out in the discussion of this variable with regression analysis, this item is not really "fixed"—meaning perfectly flat—in most business firms, but it is not a *perfectly proportionate* variable either. Realizing this, it behooves anyone forecasting General and Administrative Expense to realize that the forecasting error will *increase* the farther the forecast gets from the base period.

Taxes and Accrued Taxes

The only two items in the Operating Inflows and Outflows sections that are *not* forecast using ratios (or regression analysis) are Taxes and Accrued Taxes. These two items are forecast using a pro-forma Income Statement. The pro-forma Income Statement will indicate what the forecast Pre-Tax Income will be, and then all you do is apply the tax rules to this figure to arrive at the tax due.▲ The Accrued Tax is arrived at by applying the tax rules to the forecast tax. For Federal tax purposes, taxes are due, technically at least, on the fifteenth day of the fourth, sixth, ninth, and twelfth months. This means that, for quarterly forecasts, the only period that would have any accrued tax would be the first quarter. The tax would be paid (at least it is *supposed* to be paid) before the end of these next three quarters and the Accrued Tax would be, therefore, zero.

Inventory

Inventory is forecast, usually, as a function of "forecast Cost of Goods Sold." Sometimes it is forecast by relating it to Sales, but because it is closer to Cost of Goods Sold, it is usually related to Cost of Goods Sold. Similarly to Accounts Receivable, Inventory can be forecast as a turnover of Cost of Goods Sold *or*

▲ While forecasting for "middle-market" firms, I usually use 38 percent as the tax figure, if there is a state tax. This takes account of Federal tax of 34 percent and a State tax. If the numbers are particularly small, use a smaller rate for the tax that is less for the first $100,000 of taxable income.

Days Inventory On Hand (DIOH). In the former case, the ratio is simply: Cost of Goods Sold/Inventory. In the latter, the formula is

$$DIOH = Inventory/(Costs of Goods Sold/365)$$

Accounts Payable
The second item that is related to Cost of Goods Sold is Accounts Payable. The usual ratio for forecasting this item is simply Accounts Payable turnover, and then this figure is derived by dividing Cost of Goods Sold by Accounts Payable. Then, using this number, divide the *forecast* Cost of Goods Sold by this turnover number to get the forecast Accounts Payable.

Prepaid Expense
This item, which is usually minor, is forecast by straight estimation or extrapolation of prior numbers.

The Remaining Items
The above items represent the most commonly used items to forecast the first two sections of the Cash Flow Statement, Items 1 and 2. Subtracting Item 2 from Item 1 yields Item 3, NOCF. Forecasting the items in the next three sections, Priority Outflows, Discretionary Outflows, and Financial Flows, is merely a matter of plugging in the numbers associated with the respective items. For example, in the Priorities Section, the Interest Payment would be simply the interest on whatever debt that is assumed. It is similar with the periodic debt repayments. In the Discretionary Outflows section, the forecast of such items as Capital Expenditures and Bonuses would be supplied by whoever is making the forecast. The Financial Flows section is handled similarly. The concluding section, Net Change in Cash and Marketable Securities, is simply the arithmetic sum of the preceding items.

FORECASTING WITH REGRESSION ANALYSIS

The functional relationships that apply to the various items to be forecast are the same, of course, for regression analysis as they are for the ratio approach. But there are certain aspects of the regression approach that make separate discussion advisable.▲

Accounts Receivable
To forecast Accounts Receivable, regress Accounts Receivable on Sales. This is usually a good fit and is generally clear cut.

Cost of Goods Sold
Because Cost of Goods Sold is such a high percentage of Sales—for most companies—you would expect that there would be a good correlation, and there is.

▲ Regression packages are rather easy to obtain today. These packages include SAS, SPSS, Minitab, and even Excel.

If you regressed Sales on Sales, you get a "perfect" correlation; if you regress something that is 70 or 80 percent of Sales on Sales, you are going to get a good fit, too. For certain high-tech firms or software companies which might have a Cost of Goods Sold of only about 50 percent, the relationship might not be as clear.

General and Administrative Expense

While this is supposed to be the fixed expense for firms, experience indicates that it is not as "fixed" as most managements would like. This is not to say that it is impossible to keep this item fixed, it is just that most managements— American managements, at least—decline to keep this function level to Sales. The reason for this is quite apparent: This is the account where management puts all its generous perquisites—the expensive cars and fancy dinners and lunches; the conferences held at expensive resorts; and, of course, the hefty salaries. If you observe firms as they grow from $5 million to $10 million to $50 million and beyond, the rate of return on Sales tends to remain quite constant. But why should this be? Aren't there economies of scale operating here? There should be, but all too often other expenses—in particular, General and Administrative Expense—increase in proportion to the increase in Sales, thus obviating any economy of scale. What to do about this tendency? Discipline in this overhead expense should begin at the top. If top management is frugal with their expense, others below them will be, too. If management is liberal with their G & A Expense, others will be as well. To paraphrase a popular cliché, "fun and games" will expand to fill the money allocated to it.

Another problem with General and Administrative Expense is what is known as the "irreversibility problem." Observe Exhibit 4.17, where G & A Expense is plotted against Sales.

Note that as sales increase, General and Administrative Expense increases. But at some point, when sales decline—for instance, during a recession—General and Administrative Expense declines *but on a less sloped function*. The G & A Expense declines but less than it would if it were declining *proportionally* to the decrease in sales. The reason this happens so frequently is that most people in management positions are not as quick to *cut* G & A Expense as they are to add it! Take presidents' salaries, for example. Do you think they would give themselves a *decrease* in pay at the same point in sales they gave themselves an increase in salary? Or the Accounting Department supervisor; do you think this person is going to lay off that good new accountant he or she hired recently (before sales turned down) at the same sales volume at which this new person was hired? *Any delay in adjusting this General and Administrative Expense to a decrease in Sales will result in a less sloped function.*

This is not the worst of the problem, however. Once Sales start back up after having been in a contracting mode, what happens to the General and Administrative Expense from that point on? Will it retrace the same functional line on which it retreated? Usually it will not. It tends to go up on another function. And this is how firms get fat. The General and Administrative Expense will now be a larger percentage of Sales than it was when the recession started. *Knowing this*

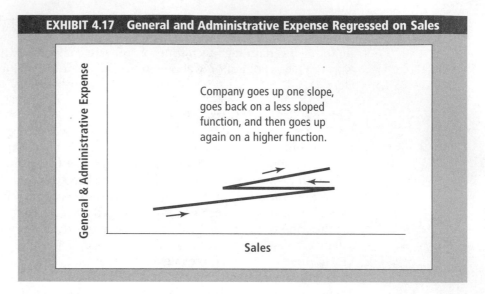

EXHIBIT 4.17   General and Administrative Expense Regressed on Sales

tendency may help top management avoid this pitfall. This kind of excess is certainly not going to help a developing firm, which needs all the cash it can get!

Selling Expense
Selling expense is forecast by regressing on Sales.

Taxes and Accrued Taxes
As with the ratio approach, you do *not* regress taxes on anything. You forecast Taxes and Accrued Taxes in the same way as with ratios: Calculate a pro-forma Income Statement and apply the taxes rates and tax rules.

Inventory
Inventory is forecast by regressing on Cost of Goods Sold. You must be careful when doing this regression to make sure that some fundamental change is not taking place. In Exhibit 4.18 there is shown a regression of Inventory on Cost of Goods Sold. The data points are quarterly for a period of years. Note that there are two sets of data points, the ones on the lower left and the ones to the upper right of the other data points. The dashed line traces a false regression line—one that includes *all* the data points. This would be a natural thing to do—except that in this case the data points in the lower left are from an earlier time period, and the ones in the upper right are from a later time period. These data points are from a machine tool manufacturer and what actually happened was that there was a change in the product manufactured. The machines were computerized and the complexity of the machines was changed with the addition of many more parts—parts that had to be inventoried. *There was a* shift *in the function.*

Accounts Payable

Accounts Payable is regressed on Cost of Goods Sold.

Prepaid Expense and Other Items Below NOCF

As with the ratio approach, Prepaid Expenses are merely estimated; do not attempt a regression. As for the other items below NOCF, they must be calculated as with the ratio approach. There are no other useful regression relationships that may be employed, at least for middle-market firms.

A COMPARISON BETWEEN THE RATIO APPROACH AND REGRESSION ANALYSIS

Clearly, regression analysis is superior to a ratio approach for financial forecasting. The reason for this is the fact that all functions do not have a functional slope of 1. A "slope of 1" means that for any given change in the independent variable (horizontal) there is an equally proportional change in the dependent variable (vertical). If you regressed Sales on Sales, the slope would be 1. But some variables—for example, General and Administrative Expense—have functional slopes a lot different from 1. Therefore, as one goes out in time with a ratio approach forecast, the forecast will become more and more inaccurate and, in general, will *overstate* items. If these are expense items, such as G & A, the error will be on the side of needing more cash than the situation should, in fact, require.

Unfortunately, the data points needed are not always available for a correct regression approach. This leaves us with the much more common ratio approach. In fact, when doing a cash flow forecast for a Leveraged Buyout candidate, I have never had the data—nor, truthfully, the determination to get the

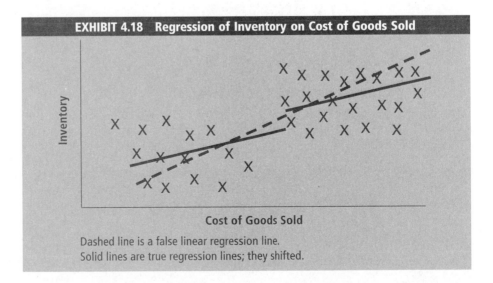

EXHIBIT 4.18   Regression of Inventory on Cost of Goods Sold

Dashed line is a false linear regression line.
Solid lines are true regression lines; they shifted.

data—to use regression analysis. The Cash Flowcast program that is included with this book is done in a ratio approach. Knowing the possibility of error—and being able to estimate the extent of the error—from using the ratio approach should cushion the conclusions based on this forecast, however.

ITEMS THAT ARE NOT USED

While it is now clear that in order to produce a Cash Flow Statement it is necessary to put together the items from the Income Statement and the Balance Sheet, there are several items that are *not* included, because they do not represent *cash*. The principal one is the **Retained Earnings** (or whatever it is called) section of the Balance Sheet. There is *no cash* in Retained Earnings, only profit that is cleared over from the Income Statement. Other Balance Sheet items that are not used are such things as the Reserve for Depreciation and similar other *nonfunded* reserves such as **Reserve for Deferred Tax Liability**. On the Income Statement none of the *summary* items—for example, Net Income or Gross Profit—are used.

SUMMARY

Businesses run on cash—not profits. Understanding what affects cash is surely one of the most important pieces of information a manager could have. And although most managers think about Income Statements, it behooves one to think about Balance Sheets, too, for it is the change in Balance Sheet items that can affect the firm's cash flow in such a significant way. Laxity in collecting Accounts Receivable, for example, or making a few extra parts may seem to those employees on the firing line to be innocuous enough (in fact, it may seem like the thing to do), but the effect of their actions on the firm's cash flow may not be perceived. What would production workers do if, instead of producing bearings, for example, they produced $20 bills? And if they took $20 bills to the storeroom, would it make any difference to them whether they stored them in drawers? And yet from a cash flow point of view, it is exactly the same. It's the same thing for managers who cannot fully understand that there is *cash* in Accounts Receivable. Would they not be more alert to send out invoices as soon as they can if this would help to get the cash? For some managers, however, taking care of everything else seems to be more important than attention to the Accounts Receivable. Those innocent-looking pieces of paper in the Accounts Receivable file amount to real dollar bills—but do all managers realize that?

This chapter, in addition to covering the mechanics of the Cash Flow Statement, intro-duced two models concerning NOCF, Net Operating Cash Flow. These models were NOCF' and NOCF". As explained, the reason for using the suffix prime and double prime was to place importance on NOCF.

Everything starts with Sales and from the basic operations of the firm there results NOCF. NOCF is the amount of money that a firm has with which to do "things."

The first "thing" that has to be taken care of is the Priority Payments—the Interest and Debt Repayment. This leaves an amount of money for Discretionary Outflows. The model for this is NOCF', defined as

$$NOCF' = NOCF - Priority\ Outflows$$

Since Discretionary Outflows are of two general types, *NOCF' is the amount of money a firm will have to "plow back or pay out."*

The second model, NOCF", will be expanded upon in Chapter 7, which discusses the firm's capital structure and its debt capacity. The basic ideas of the Cash Flow Statement permeate virtually every succeeding chapter and, of course, the concept of NOCF is of central importance. Mastery of the Cash Flow Statement will help materially in understanding so much of what follows in this book and the practice of financial management, in general.

SUMMARIZING THE FORECAST TECHNIQUES

FORECASTING CASH FLOWS

	RATIO	*REGRESSION*
Sales	Given	Given
+ Other Income	Estimate	Estimate
− Change in A/R	Days Sales Outstanding	Regress/Sales
Cost of Goods Sold		
− Depreciation Expense	Percentage of Sales	Regress/Sales
+ General & Administrative	Percentage of Sales	Regress/Sales
+ Selling Expense	Percentage of Sales	Regress/Sales
+ Taxes	Pro-Forma I/S	Pro-Forma I/S
− Change in Accrued Taxes	Apply Tax Rules	Apply Tax Rules
+ Change in Inventory	Turnover to CGS	Regress/CGS
− Change in Accounts Payable	Turnover to CGS	Regress/CGS
+ Change in Prepaid Expense	Estimate	Estimate

QUESTIONS FOR DISCUSSION

1. If you were a management consultant and you were advising a company that was growing significantly, what would you say to the president who complained that "Even though I am growing rapidly, I still don't have any cash"? What suggestions would you make to improve this situation? What if the situation is desperate and there is no chance of securing outside funding anytime soon? What then would you recommend?

2. Is it more important for you as a manager to "manage" your Income Statement during a recession or your Balance Sheet? Why? And if you say "both," discuss what you could do with both statements in the way of "managing" them.

3. In what sales "situation" could you estimate a company's NOCF if all you saw were the Income Statement and Balance Sheet? How would you do this? (Hint: Compare the three popular measures of "cash flow.")

PROBLEMS

1. Do a Cash Flow Statement for 2002, using the following Balance Sheets and Income Statement:

SC COMPANY
BALANCE SHEET

	2001	2002		2001	2002
CASH	$ 10	$ 17	ACCOUNTS PAYABLE	$ 20	$ 25
ACCOUNTS RECEIVABLE	$ 40	$ 45	CURRENT DEBT PAYABLE	$ 10	$ 10
INVENTORY	$ 20	$ 25			
			LONG-TERM DEBT	$ 30	$ 20
PLANT, PROPERTY					
AND EQUIPMENT	$ 50	$ 55			
LESS: RESERVE					
FOR DEPRECIATION	$ 25	$ 25	EQUITY:		
NET PLANT AND EQUIPMENT	$ 25	$ 30			
			COMMON STOCK	$ 20	$ 20
PREPAID EXPENSE	$ 5	$ 3	RETAINED EARNINGS	$ 20	$ 45
			TOTAL LIABILITIES		
TOTAL ASSETS	$100	$120	AND CAPITAL	$100	$120

INCOME STATEMENT

	2000
SALES	$ 200
COST OF GOODS SOLD	$ 140
GROSS PROFIT	$ 60
GENERAL & ADMINISTRATIVE EXPENSE	$ 10
SELLING EXPENSE	$ 10
INTEREST EXPENSE	$ 3
PRE-TAX INCOME	$ 37
TAX	$ 12
NET INCOME	$ 25

INCLUDED IN THE COST OF GOODS SOLD FOR 2002 IS $10 OF DEPRECIATION.
CAPITAL EXPENDITURES WERE $10 FOR 2001 AND $15 FOR 2002.
AMOUNTS ARE IN MILLIONS.

4

CHAPTER REVIEW

EXHIBIT 4.19   Solution to Cash Flow Problem 1

Sales	$	200
− Change in A/R		(5)
(1) Net operating cash inflow	$	195
Cost of goods sold − depreciation	$	130
+ General and administrative expense		10
+ Selling expense		10
+ Taxes		12
− Change in accrued taxes		0
+ Change in inventory		5
− Change in accounts payable		(5)
+ Change in prepaid expense		(2)
(2) Net operating cash outflow	$	160
(3) Net operating cash flow	$	35
Priority outflows		
Interest		3
Current debt repaid		10
(4) Total	$	13
Discretionary outflows		
Capital expenditures		15
(5) Total	$	15
(6) Financial flows		0
(7) Net change in cash	$	7

2. Using the same Balance Sheets and Income Statement as above, do a **forecast** Cash Flow Statement for 2003, assuming Sales to be $250. Use the ratio approach.

Solution to Cash Flow Problem 2

Sales	$ 250.00	45/(200/365) = 82.26 DSO
− Change in A/R	$ (11.30) ◄—	250/365 × 82.26 = $56.3
(1) Operating Cash Inflow	$ 238.70	$56.30 − 45.00 = 11.3
Cost of Goods Sold		
− Depreciation	$ 162.50 ◄—	(140 − 10)/200 = .65 × 250 = 162.50)
+ General and Administrative		
Expense	$ 12.50	.05 × 250 = $12.50
+ Selling Expense	$ 12.50	
+ Taxes	$ 20.10	
− Change in Accrued Taxes	$ —	See Pro-forma Income Statement
+ Change in Inventory	$ 6.30	130/25 = 5.2; 162.5/5.2 = $31.3
− Change in Accounts Payable	$ (6.30)	Chg = 31.3 − 25 = $6.3
+ Change in Prepaid Expense	$ 2.00	
(2) Operating Cash Outflows	$ 209.60	Assume Decrease of $2.00
(3) Net Operating Cash Flow	$ 29.10 ◄—	Item 1 − Item 2

Priority Outflows		
+ Interest	$ 2.25 ◄—	$25 × .09
+ Debt Repayment	$ 10.00 ◄—	$30 to $20
(4) Total Priority Outflows	$ 12.25	
Discretionary Outflows		
+ Capital Expenditures	$ 15.00 ◄—	We will assume this.
(5) Total Discretionary	$ 15.00	
Financial Flows		
+ Debt	$ -	The decrease in long-term debt is accounted for in Priority Outflows.
+ Stock	$ -	
(6) Total Financial Flows	$ -	
(7) Net Change in Cash	$ 1.85 ◄—	= NOCF − Priority − Discretionary

4

CHAPTER REVIEW

PRO-FORMA INCOME STATEMENT

SALES	$ 250.00
— COST OF GOODS SOLD	$ 172.50
GROSS PROFIT	$ 77.50
— GENERAL & ADMINISTRATIVE EXPENSE	$ 12.50
— SELLING EXPENSE	$ 12.50
— INTEREST	$ 2.25
PRE-TAX PROFIT	$ 50.25
— TAXES	$ 20.10
NET PROFIT	$ 30.15

← $162.5 + $10 DEP. = $172.5

← $50.25 × .40(TAX RATE) = $20.10

CALCULATION OF INTEREST

	'01	'02	'03
CURRENT DEBT	$ 10.00	$ 10.00	$ 10.00
LONG-TERM DEBT	$ 30.00	$ 20.00	$ 10.00
AVERAGE		$ 35.00	$ 25.00

$3/35 = .09$ $25 × 0.09 = 2.25$

4

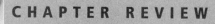

CHAPTER REVIEW

Part 2

Growing a
Firm—Internally

Chapter 5: Growing a Firm: A Review of Fundamentals

Chapter 6: An Entrepreneurial Capital Budgeting Model

Chapter 7: Capital Structure and Leverage

5

Growing a Firm: A Review of Fundamentals

WHAT IS MEANT BY "GROWTH"?

Like *profit, growth* is an ambiguous word in the world of business. To different people it means different things. To some owner/managers, growth means an increase in plant and equipment; to others it means an increase in sales. To a car dealer growth might be an increase in the cars he has for sale—as when it takes a helicopter to photograph the acres of cars on his lot. But for most managers, growth means growth in *earnings.* If you don't have growth in earnings—and/or cash flow—how can you say the business is growing? Is the value of the business—meaning its market price—increasing? As will be observed throughout this book, the assumption made is not necessarily that the firm is publicly owned, and therefore references to "market value" could mean the value of a closely held company if sold, *or* the market value of a publicly held company. While there are possibly some 25,000 publicly owned firms in the United States, there are at least several million privately owned firms in the United States. These latter firms are the focus of this book. (This does not mean that no reference will be made to publicly owned firms, but when this is the intention, the reference will be explicit.)

There are those who at this point would argue, with considerable merit, that *real* growth means an increase in **market share**. And to get this increase in market share it may be necessary to forgo profits—or at least to lower profits—while the process of increasing market share is taking place. This is true, but the purpose of increasing market share is, of course, to increase profits, albeit at a later date. *Growing a firm* means closing the **earnings gap** between what the firm expects to earn (if the status quo is maintained) and what the firm wants to earn. In general, there are two ways to fill the earnings gap: through *internal* means and through *external* means. This part explores the former; Part Three covers outside financing, and Part Five discusses external expansion and acquisition.

The **internal** means consists of the following:

- "More of the same"

- (Share repurchase)

- Capital budgeting

The **external** means consists of:

- Mergers and acquisitions

For firms that have pursued their customary sales efforts and still cannot dramatically increase their earnings, corporate acquisition may be the most expeditious way to fill the earnings gap.

WHY GROW A FIRM?▲

There seem to be two reasons for wanting to grow a firm: economic and personal. Economically based reasons include economics of scale, power and position in the marketplace, reduction in resource dependencies (**vertical integration**), expansion of a horizontal nature, more efficient utilization of resources, and survival in general. Recently, the owner of a profitable business, with sales of about $27 million, tried to sell the company but without success. He was convinced that the profitability was not impressive enough to command the price that he thought the business was worth. It then occurred to this owner that if he expanded the business—and in so doing increased the profits more than proportionately—he would be able to sell the business at a later time. This is another rational or "economic" reason for growing a firm: priming it for future sale.

Another reason may be to provide greater opportunities to present employees and, thus, give them an incentive to work hard and to stay with the business.

▲ This section has benefited from an article entitled "A Qualitative Study of Managerial Challenges Facing Small Business Geographic Expansion" by Daniel W. Greening, Bruce R. Baringer, and Granger Macy, *Journal of Business Venturing* 11, no. 4 (July 1996) 233–56.

Would you like to work for a firm that was *not* growing? This would hardly be what is meant by an "emerging firm."

A reason part economic, part emotional for growing a firm might be to increase the value of the business so that it would provide a better retirement vehicle. In addition to the rational reasons, there are purely subjective ones. For some business owners the business is an extension of their own psyche. And being ambitious people, they want to see the business grow as a way of seeing themselves grow. Or, an owner may want to grow the business in order to provide room for a relative or other loved one to be able to join the business. Subjective reasons may be the dominant reasons why some firms grow.

Taking this point a bit further, why is it some firms get to a certain size after their founding, but grow no more? Many owner/managers simply do not *wish* to make the effort to grow and are content with what they have. So why grow? For some owners a reason such as employee retention is, however, sufficient to virtually *force* them to grow—whether or not they really want to. Or the market may simply take off and grow in a most unexpected manner, pulling the business with it.

Assuming that a business owner does want to grow, before embarking on any aggressive growth plan it is necessary to ask some rather pointed questions:

Are you willing to make the effort required to grow?

Are your key people capable enough to handle growth in responsibilities? Perhaps it will be necessary to replace certain key people in the organization if growth is to occur. Are you willing to do this?

It is the lack of personal desire to grow that is the main limiting constraint to growing a firm. One should not offer reasons such as "I don't have the money to grow." Money is only a challenge; it should not be a limiting factor to growth.

DESIRED GROWTH VERSUS EXPECTED GROWTH

Let us look more closely at the internal means of growing a firm.

"MORE OF THE SAME"

Exhibit 5.1 projects a firm's financial forecast for 5 years—*assuming it will go along as it has in the past.* This forecast is predicated on "realistic" assumptions and a willingness to undertake expansion. The higher the Desired Earnings relative to Expected Earnings, the less realistic the whole model becomes. But this sort of thing is exactly what some publicly owned firms do when they "promise," say, 20-percent growth in earnings to their shareholders.

"More of the same" seems like such a perfectly natural way to grow the firm that it hardly seems necessary to list it as a separate *way* to grow the firm. But it is also the way most overlooked in textbooks dealing with capital budgeting.

For many firms with unused capacity in production facilities, doing more of the same may be the most direct and likely way to fill the earnings gap. To do

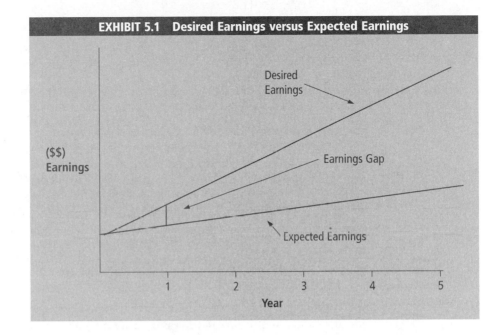

EXHIBIT 5.1   Desired Earnings versus Expected Earnings

this may require more marketing—perhaps, salesmanship may be the better word—and *no* additional capital requirements. But for many other firms, this may be the most difficult. The firm may be doing the best it can to secure additional sales and, thus, utilize its productive capacity.

In still other companies, doing more of the same may mean expansion of more branch outlets or additional facilities. For example, H & R Block is a chain of stores that provide assistance to individuals and others in the preparation of their taxes. To open additional stores requires very little, if any, real capital investment. Furthermore, working capital is not really a requirement of additional stores, either. True, they must train more new employees, but this is not what is usually included in the term **capital budgeting** (to be discussed shortly).

SHARE REPURCHASE

Share repurchase is put in parentheses in the list on page 112 because, although it technically is a way to fill the earnings gap if you mean **Earnings Per Share**, this method of filling the earnings gap does not usually apply to the privately owned, middle-market firms assumed in this book. But for some publicly owned firms, expecially during a bear market, using money to reacquire their shares in the market may be the most prudent way to increase the firm's value and, thus, shareholder wealth. Indeed this practice may be seen in the financial press frequently. This is especially true of cash-rich firms. In these cases it is quite common for stockholders to vociferously express their desire for management to do a share repurchase.

CAPITAL BUDGETING

The really significant method to *internally* fill the earnings gap is, of course, capital budgeting. This we will now study in considerable detail.

THE MEANING OF CAPITAL BUDGETING

For many students of introductory finance, *capital budgeting* is the process of **discounting the cash flows**. But the question of *which* cash flows is usually a major concern—so major in fact, that many students fail to realize what they are actually doing in the process of discounting the cash flows. They fail to realize that they are working on a problem to grow the firm.▲

To many introductory students, capital budgeting involves *only* a piece of equipment, and the whole process is finding out the present value or rate of return for that piece of equipment. If that is the case, then much of what is subsumed in the term capital budgeting would be missed. Capital budgeting needs to be thought of as the process of developing useful, profitable proposals of a capital, or major, item.

Too often, textbooks seem to imply that there are always *more* proposals (or specific capital requirements) than there are resources with which to fund the proposals. This may be conventional wisdom when it comes to "General Motors (or megacorporate) finance" but for many, or perhaps most, of the middle-market firms assumed in this book, this may not be the case. Experience shows that for many firms, there is a real dearth of *good* capital budgeting proposals. True, if you tell employees that there is money available to purchase some capital assets, most employees will find a need that just cannot wait, (sort of a variation of Parkinson's law), but are these "needs" such that by filling them, the company will fill its earnings gap?

For many companies, there may be a need to develop profit-making proposals that will truly fill the earnings gap. This may require that someone in this middle-market, emerging firm be appointed to assist production, marketing, and other personnel in conceiving of and developing really worthwhile capital budgeting proposals. By "worthwhile" we mean high-rate-of-return proposals—proposals that will produce earnings which can be used to fill the earnings gap. But, assuming that the firm *does* have *enough* good proposals, the next question is: How much money is available to finance these proposals?

MONEY AVAILABLE FOR CAPITAL BUDGETING

Forecasting the money available for capital budgeting is relatively easy when using the Cash Flow Statement. You will recall the model for NOCF' from our discussion in Chapter 4 (see p. 81).

$$\text{NOCF}' = \text{NOCF} - \text{Priority Outflows}$$

▲ Adopting a capital budgeting strategy to keep a firm's earnings from *declining* is, really, quite the same thing as "growing" earnings.

NOCF' is the amount available for discretionary outflows. Since there are two general types of Discretionary Outflows (Capital Expenditures and Dividends, or bonuses), this leads us to say that NOCF' is the amount of money to "plow back or pay out." But after you subtract the amount reserved for bonuses (or dividends), is all the remaining amount available for capital budgeting—in the sense of proposals to fill the earnings gap? No one who has ever handled the requests for capital expenditures in the real world would answer this question in the affirmative. Instead, requests for capital expenditure funds seem to fall into these categories:

- "Necessary" capital expenditures

  Health and safety
  Other "necessary" expenditures (*e.g.,* construction of a new office for someone)
  "Hanky panky"

- Profit producing expenditures

Under the dubious term "Necessary," there are three categories, only two of which appear to be really necessary: "Health and safety" and "Other necessary." For example, if the wind blows the roof off the company's building, what are you going to do, call a meeting of the Capital Budgeting Committee and try to calculate what the rate of return is for a new roof? Or if the health inspector walks into the company's cafeteria and says that unless you install a new $5,000 dishwasher they will close down the cafeteria? In both of these cases the only reasonable thing to do is to dip into an account and make the expenditure. (Now if the whole building is destroyed, that is another question. Perhaps management will decide not to replace the building!) Or in the case of the "Other necessary" budgetary category, if someone is appointed head of Purchasing and it is decided that he or she needs to have a private office, from where will the money come for this expenditure?

These two categories are not the real problem, however. No, the real problem is what the slang of the day calls "hanky panky." This comes about when the president calls into his or her office the chief financial officer and starts to talk about how much time he or she is wasting by ". . . standing around the drafty airports." You know what is coming next. Or, the sales manager who calls up with an urgent request for a new computer for her secretary. Seems that the production manager's secretary has gotten a new computer and if ". . . my secretary doesn't get a new computer he will quit! And if he quits, I'm quitting, too!" So how do you handle this request? Or, the quality control manager says that if he does not have a new $8,000 platen (marble table), he will quit—after 10 years on the job.

These and a plethora of similar requests are commonplace in most organizations. How do you handle these requests for limited capital budgeting funds? Who knows! But here is a suggestion. If you allocate only a limited amount of money to this "Necessary" category, you can queue up the requests with a statement like "We're out of Category 1C money at this time, but we'll put this request in the queue and as soon as we get more money in this account, we'll accede to this request." (Sometimes, if a big desire is postponed, the urge will go away by the time the money is available.) Whatever trick is tried, however, some control over these types of expenditures *must* be initiated, or else much less will be left for the really important profit producing proposals.

CRITERIA FOR CAPITAL BUDGETING

In an earlier section, capital budgeting was described as the selection of attractive investment proposals. In the next chapter, an argument will be made that this selection process should be made with **sets** of proposals, rather than examining proposals individually. Combining proposals into sets, each with their own characteristics, can result in a better total set of proposals. To prepare for that discussion, a review is needed of the basic discriminants used in capital budgeting as it is currently being taught in basic textbooks. This will be only a limited review; this book puts forth the advice that *no one* discriminant should be used exclusively. Doing so may result in suboptimizing a *set* of proposals. You might jeopardize the very existence of the firm by taking a high-rate-of-return proposal if you ignore other features of that proposal such as its "time shape of the cash flow." Before reviewing the four commonly used methods of discriminating between proposals—or what is called here the "four naïve methods" of discriminating between proposals because they compose only *one* discriminant model—it is well to establish criteria against which these discriminants can be judged. While there may be more, the three that seem to be most important are:

- Does the proposal measure profitability?

- Does the discriminant take account accurately of the "time value of money?"

- Does the discriminant take account of the "time shape of the cash flow?"

Time Value of Money

This is an extremely important criterion, because it is the basis for so much of the rationale of finance: A dollar today is worth more than a dollar a year from now. This is, of course, because of the concept of interest. But people are not born with knowledge of that concept. It is something that all good business people must *learn*. For example, when negotiating with a seller for the sale of his or her business, it may be necessary to add to the purchase price. If you add $400,000 to the price but do so by tacking it onto the fifth year's payment, have you really increased the price by $400,000 in present value terms? One cannot deny the fact that the price has risen by $400,000, but it would not take $400,000 today to pay $400,000 in 5 years. A lesser amount could be invested and, with interest added, the amount would be $400,000 in 5 years. Anyone reading this book should be very familiar with the time value of money but how often do we forget this learning? This idea—and the concept of **opportunity cost** are two concepts that an alert businessperson should have at the ready at *all* times.

Time Shape of Cash Flow

This is a new concept that first occurred to me when a friend of mine, after having taken over a struggling American Stock Exchange company, decided to survey the projects the company had in its pipeline. One particular project looked particularly promising and had a very healthy rate of return. Without a sensitivity to the project's cash flow, this manager ordered all-out production of the product involved. Well it was not long before that project was gobbling up large amounts of cash. When the CEO went back to the bank, which had placed him in the position of CEO, and asked for more money, he was told not too politely that he was placed in this position to pay back the money owing the bank—not the other way around! In short, if a project has a very negative cash flow pattern it does not matter how good a return the proposal has *if* sufficient money cannot be found to support the proposal.

In a text on "General Motors" finance the problem of the scarcity of cash is assumed away on the theory that if the rate of return exceeds the cost of capital the project should be accepted. Anyone who has ever had hands-on management experience, however, knows that theory does not pay bills: Cash pays bills! Middle-market managers had better pay attention to cash flow or they will find their ship hard aground. Incidentally, this CEO in the example above had to find another job   mostly because of his failure to be sensitive to his company's cash flow needs.

There appear to be three types of cash flow patterns that an individual proposal might have. Exhibit 5.2 identifies these.

The first pattern of cash flow, "Smoothie," is probably the most common one. For example, a cost-saving device, such as a new conveyor system, would

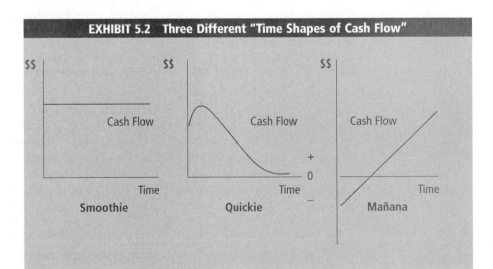

EXHIBIT 5.2   Three Different "Time Shapes of Cash Flow"

tend to have rather constant cash flows over time. The second pattern, the "Quickie," might be the pattern for some project that has an initial surge but rapidly drops off. The third pattern, using the Spanish word for tomorrow, "Mañana," is the pattern for proposals such as a start-up factory or a product that requires substantial research and development. These are the types of proposals in which you expect to find very high rates of return but in which you could find serious cash flow distress in your business. It is these types of proposals that have the "good news, bad news" implications: They have wonderful rates of return (the good news) but if you take them without offsetting their very negative pattern of cash flows, you might bankrupt the company—or, at least, cause a major cash shortage (the bad news).

Chapter 6 shows how these cash flow patterns come into play in forming *sets*. Most importantly, it will point out ways a firm can guard against being hurt by severely adverse patterns.

Now that criteria have been specified for the four commonly used discriminants, a brief discussion follows of each of them:

- Payback

- Average rate of return

- Net present value

- Internal rate of return

FOUR BASIC METHODS OF RATIONING CAPITAL BUDGETING MONEY

PAYBACK

Probably the oldest test of a capital budgeting proposal is its "payback." **Payback** is defined as:

Payback period = Length of time it takes to recover the investment

Who in business has not said "What is its payback?" But when this term is put under a microscope, it fails to meet any of the criteria. It does not use the time value of money concept, nor does it really measure profitability. About all it really says is how long it takes to recover the investment. And what happens after the investment is recovered? Payback says nothing about that, either. The whole proposal can wither and die for all the payback says about a proposal.

Why, then, do so many people still refer to a project's payback? The answer lies in the following ratio, which is called "Relative Payback":

$$\text{Relative Payback} = \frac{\text{Economic life of the asset}}{\text{Payback period}}$$

People may not overtly calculate this ratio when talking about payback, but they are most likely *thinking* this when they use the term. Obviously no rational person would want a proposal that has a short payback period if the economic life is no longer than the payback period. What makes a proposal interesting is if it has a very large ratio of economic life to payback. For example, when asked about a particular machine tool, with an economic life of at least 20 or 30 years, a manager remarked that it was a great investment because it had a payback of less than 2 years. In this case citing the payback connoted useful information, even though payback *per se* is so limited. As a formal discriminant, however, payback leaves a lot to be desired. Furthermore, it is not even a good discriminant when used together with another method. If you want to limit the life of a proposal because of any of the possible reasons, such as political risk, just delete the cash flows after a certain date. It's that simple.

AVERAGE RATE OF RETURN

Another discriminant that dates back over 50 years is a measure called **Average Rate of Return**. This measure, which has numerous variations and names (it is sometimes called the "Accountants method") is defined as:

$$\text{Average Rate of Return} = \frac{\text{Average yearly net income}}{\text{Average investment}}$$

"Average investment" is defined as "Cost plus salvage divided by 2." Note that it is cost *plus* salvage, not cost minus salvage. One may see this by noting an investment that costs $1000 and has a salvage of $200. The "average" investment in the asset was $600 over the period of time, not $400. Let's look at this discriminant and see how it measures up to our criteria. Does this discriminant measure profitability? It does, to some extent. You get an answer that looks like a percentage rate of return—and, in fact, is a rate of return—but it is *not* a rate of return that takes into account the time value of money. This rate of return may be likened to a *simple* interest rate of return. This is a *higher* rate of return than a rate of return that utilizes the time value of money, such as the **Internal Rate of Return** or IRR—if put on the same basis as a rate of return that utilizes the time value of money. Unfortunately the fact that it appears to be *larger* than an IRR makes it all the more dangerous. Once when waiting to show a deal to a prospective investor, we were asked what "rate of return" our deal had. We replied, "25 percent." "Oh," said the investor, "this other deal has yours beat by 10 points." When he was pressed to reveal details, it came out that the other proposal's rate of return was calculated using the Average Rate of Return method. If that proposal's rate of return had been calculated "correctly," using the time value of money, it would have been much less than 25 percent! Whenever one gets into a "battle of rates of return," it is well to check to see if the "rates" being compared are comparable.

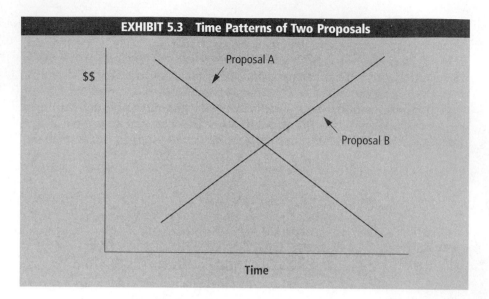

The fact that Average Rate of Return uses "average investment" is also a problem. Consider Exhibit 5.3. Note that both Proposal A and B have the *same* average investment but that that of Proposal A is declining over time while B's is increasing over time. Does this make these two proposals comparable? Hardly, if you appreciate the notion of the time value of money.

The numerator also has its problems. Net income takes into account such *noncash* charges as depreciation and, in fact, is lessened to this extent. A building, for example, may, in fact, be *appreciating*, but because depreciation is allowed for tax purposes—and is the usual way of calculating Net Income—the Net Income figure is shown *after* depreciation. When calculating cash flow for purposes of calculating a rate of return, such accounting conventions as depreciation are taken into account only through their effect on taxes, not in their absolute form.

For our purposes, Average Rate of Return is not very valuable. It does not take into account the time value of money, nor does it measure profitability accurately according to conventional financial practice.

NET PRESENT VALUE

Developed into a popular discriminant since World War II, **Net Present Value** (**NPV**) is defined as *the net present value of the cash flows, given the discount rate.*

The discount rate in this instance is what most people trained in finance call the **Cost of Capital**. In this model, a proposal is thought to be acceptable if it has a *positive* Net Present Value. Using this model, it is reasoned, the proposal is yielding a return greater than its cost, and therefore it is increasing the wealth of the shareholders. On the surface it seems hard to quarrel with this reasoning.

Only when this model is placed in an operational mode do the problems reveal themselves.

For example, what if a proposal has a "Mañana" time shape of cash flow? If the firm takes the proposal and experiences severe—and perhaps fatal—cash shortages, would it look like it was increasing the wealth of the shareholders? (This applies to all four of these discriminants.) The problem with Net Present Value is that it should be used *only* when comparing *mutually exclusive proposals*. How are you going to compare two proposals, one with a NPV of $100,000 and the other with a NPV of $1,450,000? Which do you want? Obviously, the bigger of the two. But the second one is a *much* larger proposal and has an Internal Rate of Return (discussed below) of less than the smaller NPV.

So: When using Net Present Value as a discriminant, it *must* be kept in mind that this discriminant assumes that all proposals are the *same size* and have the *same time horizon*. The latter assumption is necessary because of the notion of the time value of money. If you generate your cash flow in 2 years, it is quite different from getting it in 5 years.

Profitability Index

There are a number of variations to Net Present Value, one of which is the **Profitability Index.** This little-used discriminant is defined as:

$$\text{Profitability Index} = \frac{\text{Present Value of Cash Inflows}}{\text{Present Value of Cash Outflows}}$$

If this index is greater than 1.0, you presumably would take the proposal because it is earning more than its cost of capital. By using this relative measure, it is hoped that Net Present Value could be used for mutually inclusive proposals. In surveys of financial officers in large companies, this Profitability Index has never been very popular; it has been declining in popularity in recent years. One of the objections to this discriminant is that you have to refer to a proposal's profitability in terms of an abstract index number, for example, "a 1.34 proposal." Compare this to a proposal with "a 42 percent rate of return." Whatever the reason, the popularity of the next discriminant, Internal Rate of Return, is increasing and the popularity of Net Present Value (and its subset, Profitability Index) is decreasing.

Internal Rate of Return

The **Internal Rate of Return (IRR)** is defined as *that rate of discount (interest) that makes the net present value of the cash flows equal to zero*. Even though the IRR will be used in the model that follows in the next chapter, this does not mean that the IRR is without fault. Specifically, any change in "sign" (plus or minus) of a cash flow item in the string of items will result in a mathematical condition (called *multiple roots*) such that more than one rate of return will make the Net Present Value of the cash flows equal zero. For example, 14 percent, 195 percent, and 1,367 percent may make the Net Present Value of a series of cash flows

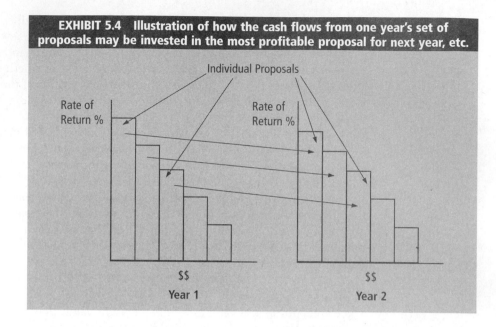

EXHIBIT 5.4   Illustration of how the cash flows from one year's set of proposals may be invested in the most profitable proposal for next year, etc.

equal to zero. This does not seem to be a debilitating problem, however, as the model will be instructed to select the *lowest* rate of return and let it go at that.

Another assumption of the IRR is that the *ex post* (realized) rate of return is equal to the *ex ante* (expected) rate of return. This means that the *reinvestment rate* must equal the *ex ante* rate of return. While this is true, this condition does not represent a debilitating condition either, as it may be argued that in capital budgeting (as opposed to portfolio analysis) who is to say that the cash flow of the most profitable proposal does not go to fund the most profitable proposal next year? Consider Exhibit 5.4. Presumably, the cash flow from the first year's most profitable proposal is invested in the most profitable proposal for the following year. If this were to happen, then the requirement that the reinvestment rate be equal to the *ex ante* rate would be fulfilled— if not precisely, then practically.

Among the many variations of IRR is a method that is variously known but is generally called the **Financial Management Rate of Return**. In this variation, which seems quite useful for analyzing a real estate proposal in isolation, cash flows are pushed forward to fill in the holes created by any negative cash flows. In this way, the multiplicity of rates of return is avoided. Then the model sets dollar limits for reinvestment of cash flows, such as $5,000. Until that amount is reached, the cash flows are assumed to earn either no interest or a low rate.

The next chapter argues that no *one* discriminant should be used, no matter how correct that method is. Although IRR is used in the multiple discriminant model in Chapter 6, it is used as just one of several discriminants, and not the *only* discriminant.

Calculating the Internal Rate of Return

With all types of computers in such widespread use today, it is no longer necessary to calculate the IRR manually. While extremely useful, this advancement has, for some, completely clouded the process of calculating the IRR and, more specifically, the *significance* of the numbers involved. Every businessperson, especially managers of middle-market firms who often have to "shoot from the hip," so to speak, should have a sense of what compound interest is all about. Compound interest differs from simple interest in that compound interest earns interest on the interest at the same rate of interest as the principal earns interest. With simple interest, only the principal earns interest. This is why there is the assumption in the IRR that the reinvestment rate has to be the same as the calculated rate. For example, how long does it take for a dollar amount to double in size if it is compounding at 15 percent interest? (Answer: About 5 years.) In order to know this, it is necessary to be able to read and interpret a table of compound interest rates. In the Appendix to this chapter there is such a table and a brief note explaining how to calculate an IRR—as well as some problems using compound interest (using the old fashioned "iteration" method). While I do not expect anyone to really use this method to calculate the IRR today, it would be useful if the reader would refresh himself or herself on the methodology in order to have a better feel for compound interest. When making decisions on the spot, one does not have the resources of a computer to calculate—or even estimate—the IRR.

SUMMARIZING THE FOUR COMMONLY USED DISCRIMINANTS

Exhibit 5.5 summarizes the way the four commonly used discriminants relate to the three criteria that were posited earlier. The term "sort of" for the Average Rate of Return refers to the fact that the model does produce a "Rate of Return" calculation, but that it is only a *simple interest* calculation and is *not* comparable to an IRR, which uses compound interest to obtain its result. This Average Rate of Return can be quite misleading when compared to IRRs, however.

EXHIBIT 5.5   The Four Commonly Used Discriminants and Their Comparison to the Three Criteria

	PROFITABILITY	TIME VALUE OF MONEY	TIME SHAPE OF CF
■ PAYBACK	No	No	No
■ AVERAGE RATE OF RETURN	"SORT OF"	No	No
■ NET PRESENT VALUE	YES	YES	No
■ INTERNAL RATE OF RETURN	YES	YES	No

SUMMARY

In this chapter growth was defined as growth in earnings. True, cash flow is extremely important, but most companies are evaluated on the basis of their earnings. How much to grow is an utterly subjective matter for the majority of companies. The question then is "How do you fill the earnings gap?" This gap is the difference between what earnings will be if no capital budgeting takes place and what is desired. In case this seems too academic, remember that most "growth" companies do *exactly* this. They may "promise" some certain growth in earnings and then they set about trying to fulfill their promise.

The two general ways of "filling the earnings gap" are internal ways (doing more of the same, for public companies share repurchase, and capital budgeting) and externally by mergers and acquisitions. With the virtual elimination of "pooling of interest accounting," it is getting to be redundant to say "mergers" any more. Now, nearly all business combinations are going to be accounted for by "purchase accounting." The old "pooling of interests" method of combining Balance Sheets is no longer used.

Next, the four basic ways to evaluate a proposal currently were examined and placed against criteria. The argument was made that no one method of discrimination is good in an entrepreneurial company because of what is called the "time shape of the cash flow." In the next chapter this point will be elaborated upon and an "entrepreneurial capital budgeting model" will be presented. The chapter closes with a reminder that for many people, computers have obscured the meaning of *discounting and present valuing*. Reviewing the simple numbers may help to fix present value in a better perspective.

QUESTIONS FOR DISCUSSION

1. If you were the CEO for a company, discuss your *thought process* for "growing the company." What factors would you have to take into consideration? What type of company do you have?

2. If you were the CEO of a company, and it looked like there was no real chance for "growth" in your industry because you already have a very large share of the potential market, is there anything that could be done to still "grow earnings"? Should you be content to have the lion's share of your industry if it is not a huge industry segment?

5

CHAPTER REVIEW

THE TECHNOLOGY ADOPTION LIFE CYCLE
A POWERFUL MODEL FOR STARTING AND GROWING A VENTURE

If there is one powerful tool that can explain why some start-ups succeed so brilliantly while others fail so miserably, it has to be the Technology Adoption Life Cycle (TALC)—as extended and brought to life by one of Silicon Valley's most prominent gurus, Geoffrey Moore. TALC is so powerful, and yet so intuitive, it should be part of the curriculum at every business school. Although the model has been mainly positioned as a marketing apparatus it is as helpful in analyzing and evaluating ventures from a financial point of view. Here is what the model is, and how it can help you in your field.

Technology Adoption Life Cycle posits that in order for a start-up to make it completely and grow to reach its highest possible potential, it has to successfully pass through four levels of acceptance as commanded by :

- Innovators—"The Techies"
- Early Adopters—"Market Openers"
- Early Majority—"King Makers"
- Late Majority—"Followers"

Innovators ("the techies"). These are the people who buy a new product for the fun of it and the excitement that it creates for them. It does not matter if the product functions at all; because it is something new and technologically advanced they buy it (think of those people who purchased early Apples, early Palms, etc.). I cannot even imagine if we did not have these types of joy-seeking customers. Who would buy so many scrappy products that might later turn out to be something of value? So, there is hope for even the clumsiest entrepreneurs—at least in the initial phase!

Early Adopters ("market openers"). These nontechnologists could just be your "market openers" and your next best chance to succeed in the marketplace. What they need to see in the product/service is some functionality, some envisioned benefit.

Early Majority ("king makers"). This relatively large group (estimated to be one third of the whole cycle) is your "king maker." These are the people who do not mind to wait until the product gets some general acceptability. For them, the product/service has to work and work well. This is exactly where so many products will never gain public recognition and the venture has to either fold or be taken over by others that may have a chance at improving the product or service. From the operational point of view, making it to this stage is equivalent to going IPO.

Late Majority ("followers"). If a company comes this long and especially can afford to do an IPO—as is common for many technology firms—then there is a good chance the venture will make it. This group is also large and is estimated to be one third of the cycle.

GROWTH BY IMPROVISATION! NO "STRATEGISTS" WANTED HERE!

Focus on Technology

Did you ever think that when AOL got rolling, it had a plan and a strategy to acquire the giant Time Warner? How about AOL acquiring Netscape? What about the early growth plans between Microsoft and Intel (the "Wintell" alliance)? About Amazon.com going into the distribution of medicine; and—among other things—joining hands with Toys 'R' Us to create "Babies 'R' Us"? About eBay acquiring the famous offline auction house Sotheby's?

Strategic planning and formal planning for growth are necessities for larger established companies. For such companies, major studies and research have to be carried out and approved within the corporate hierarchy; goals for growth have to be negotiated and set; strategies to be designed; resources to be allocated; teams to be put in place; and finally, the well-thought-out tasks to be carried out.

However, such an expensive and time-consuming process cannot work for many start-ups for the following reasons. First, many new ventures do not even know if they will be in business by the following month, let alone next year; and even worse, 3 years down the road. Second, resources for new businesses are extremely limited; so forget about any sophisticated and expensive market research along with detailed planning and strategizing. Third,

start-ups by nature are innovators and niche players. As such, they know—or at least they think they know—where to attack and how! Fourth, especially in the technology sector, windows of opportunities open and close very fast. Therefore, there is not much time for the entrepreneur to formally design, evaluate, and strategize growth options.

It may then be asked: How do start-ups grow? The answer is simple: They "just do it!" You can actually say that entrepreneurs improvise as they grow! However, not all start-ups grow into larger entities. The major difference between the winners and losers lies in what we said right at the beginning: Laser-like focus! Focus on the identified niche! The niche could be lower prices, more convenience for customers, faster service, better quality, a whole new product or service, etc., etc.

As more customers are served and as the niche is verified, the knowledgeable entrepreneur finds ways to bring in more customers, and at the same time he/she finds ways to meet the increased demand—the growth. This is done by outsourcing, in-house expansion, strategic partnership, etc. If you look carefully, this is the type of growth model that you see in all technology boxes, as well as in chapters of this book.

Appendix: Illustrations of Present Value Formulations

There are two kinds of illustrations.

1. An annuity—defined as a continuous constant dollar amount for a definite period of time. If the annuity goes on forever it is called a perpetuity.

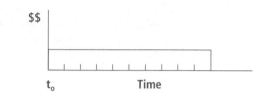

2. A future dollar amount to be received or paid.

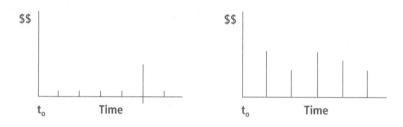

Because there are two kinds of problems we have two tables (see pages 137–138): "Present Worth (or Value) of $1," Table 5.1; and "Present Worth (or Value) of an Annuity of $1," Table 5.2.

VARIABLES

In all "present value" problems, there are *four* factors, *three* of which must be given in order to solve for the fourth. These factors are:

P = present value (of $1 in the future) or (of an "annuity due," the buzzword for the present value of an annuity).

A = the future dollar amount or the constant periodic (annual, monthly?) payment if an annuity.

i = the compound interest rate factor. (Note: this rate is alternately called the "interest rate," the "interest factor," or the "discount rate".)

n = the period of time—the period of the annuity, e.g., 10 years, or the future time period if the dollar amount is not an annuity. Most tables in textbooks are expressed in *years*. Other tables have monthly figures.

"*PV Factor*" = this is a combination of i and n and is a *cell value* in a table.

133

OBJECTIVE

The object, therefore, of present value problems is to find (1) the present value of the cash flows A; or (2) to find the interest rate, i. The "present value" method requires the former; the Internal Rate of Return requires the computation of the latter.

METHODOLOGY FOR SOLUTION OF A PROBLEM

1. Decide whether you are dealing with an annuity or a simple future dollar amount (or a series of dollar amounts). Note: If you have a constant dollar amount beginning sometime in the future and ending in the future, you have *both* types of problems.

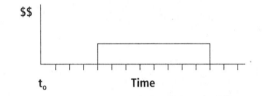

To get a present value at t_0 find the present value of the annuity and then discount that present value back to t_0.

2. Write down which of the four factors you have, thereby indicating what it is you don't have.

3. All formulas work from this basic formula:

$$P = A \times PV \text{ factor}$$

Variations are:

$$A = \frac{P}{PV \text{ factor}} \quad \text{or} \quad PV \text{ factor} = \frac{P}{A}$$

4. Pick the appropriate formula and use the proper table (or tables).

SAMPLE PROBLEM 1

If a Savings and Loan pays 6 percent (compound) interest, how much would I have to deposit in a Savings and Loan today in order to have $5000 10 years from now? (Hint: This is another way of saying "what is the *present value* today of $5000 10 years hence?")

Given:

$$A = \$5000$$
$$i = 6\%$$
$$n = 10$$
$$P = ?$$

$$PV \text{ factor} = .558$$

Formula:

$$P = A \times PV \text{ factor}$$
$$P = 5000 \times .558$$
$$P = \$2790$$

Answer:

$2790 has to be deposited today (at 6% interest) to have $5000 on deposit 10 years hence. *Note*: $5000 will be *both* principal and interest.

SAMPLE PROBLEM 2

If $5000 were invested in a Savings and Loan at 6 percent interest, how much would be available for withdrawal 5 years hence? *Note*: This means the total sum available, not just the interest. Also, remember that *compound* interest, which is what you are dealing with in present value problems, implies that *interest earns interest at the same rate of interest as the principal earns interest*.

Given:

$$P = \$5000$$
$$i = 6\%$$
$$n = 5$$
$$A = ?$$

$$PV \text{ factor} = .747 \text{ from Table 5.1}$$

Formula:

$$A = \frac{P}{PV \text{ factor}}$$

Answer:

$$P = \frac{\$5000}{.747} = \$6{,}693.44$$

$6,693.44 can be withdrawn at the end of 5 years.

SAMPLE PROBLEM 3

How much will have to be deposited in a Savings account, paying 6 percent interest, such that a person can withdraw $5000 a year (for school expenses) for 4 years? *Note:* The last withdrawal will take all the money out of the account.

Given:

$P = ?$

$i = 6\%$ *PV factor 3.465 from Table 5.2*

$n = 4$

$A = \$5000/\text{yr}$

Formula: $P = A \times PV \text{ factor}$

Answer:

$P = 5000 \times 3.465$

$P = 17{,}325$

$17,325 will have to be deposited such that $5000 can be withdrawn each year for 4 years if the account earns 6 percent interest.

SAMPLE PROBLEM 4

A man dies and leaves $100,000 insurance to his widow. She has an expected life of 12 more years (at her age at that time). The insurance company figures interest at 8 percent. If she elects to take a yearly annuity instead of the $100,000 in one sum, how much will she receive each year?

Given:

$P = \$100{,}000$

$i = 8\%$ *PV factor = 7.536 from Table 5.2*

$n = 12$

$A = ?$

Formula: $A = \dfrac{P}{PV \text{ factor}}$

Answer:

$A = \dfrac{\$100{,}000}{7.536}$

$A = \$13{,}269.64$

The widow could receive $13,269.64 for the rest of her life if she elects to take the proceeds of the insurance as an annuity instead of one payment. *Note:* Insurance companies know that this 12-year figure is an *average*; it doesn't matter to them whether the widow lives 30 more years or only 1 year for purposes of the annuity computation.

SAMPLE PROBLEM 5

A businessperson is offered a capital investment that will cost $10,000 but will save $3,000 a year (after tax) for the economic life of the assets—which is 5 years. What is the *Internal Rate of Return* on this proposal?

Given:

$$P = \$10,000$$
$$A = \$3,000$$
$$n = 5$$
$$i = ?$$

PV factor $= ? = 3.333$

Formula:

$$PV \text{ factor} = \frac{P}{A}$$

Answer:

Since this is an annuity, consult Table 5.2, "Present Worth of an Annuity of $1." Look across the row $n = 5$ until you come to a cell value of or about 3.33. Note that at 14 percent, the cell value is 3.433 which is very close to 3.33. The answer, therefore, is approximately 14 percent, which will be the *Internal Rate of Return* of this proposal. *Note:* If a more precise answer is desired, interpolation between 14 and 16 percent can be performed (or better yet, put in on your computer).

SAMPLE PROBLEM 6

Calculate the Internal Rate of Return for this proposal: A piece of land is available for $100,000 cash. First-year improvements will cost $20,000; the second year sewers will have to be added costing $30,000; the third year property can be sold as a subdivision for $255,000 total. *Note:* Ignore taxes for purposes of this simple problem.

Given:

$$P = \$100,000$$
$$A = \text{Year } 1 = \$20,000$$
$$\text{Year } 2 = 30,000$$
$$\text{Year } 3 = 225,000$$
$$n = 3$$
$$i = ?$$

PV factor $= ?$

Formula: $$PV \text{ factor} = \frac{P}{A}$$

Answer:

A trial and error, interactive process is indicated. (*Note:* the problem is not an annuity.)

Which rate to choose initially is rather difficult, but with experience one develops a feel for it. For a start, however, choose 10 percent. Thus,

Trial 1:

$$\begin{aligned}
\text{Year } 1 &= (20,000) \times .909 \text{ (PV factor)} = (\$\ 18,180) \\
\text{Year } 2 &= (30,000) \times .826 & = (\$\ 24,780) \\
\text{Year } 3 &= 225,900) \times .751 & = \underline{\$168,975} \\
& \text{Total Present Value} & = \$126,015 \\
& \text{Cost} & = \$100,000 \\
& \text{Excess} & = \underline{\$\ \ 26,015}
\end{aligned}$$

If we had chosen the exact interest rate—or *Internal Rate of Return*—there would be no *excess* as the definition of the Internal Rate of Return is *that rate of interest that makes the net present value equal to zero.* Therefore, we used a rate that was *too low* and we must try a rate that is higher.

Note: If our first try was with an interest rate that was *too high*, our present value difference would be *negative*.

Trial 2 (assume 18 percent):

$$\begin{aligned}
\text{Year } 1 &= (20,000) \times .847 = (\$\ 16,940) \\
\text{Year } 2 &= (30,000) \times .718 = (\$\ 21,540) \\
\text{Year } 3 &= 225,900 \times .609 = \underline{\$137,025} \\
& \text{Total Present Value} = \$\ 98,545 \\
& \text{Cost} \qquad\qquad\quad = \underline{\$100,000} \\
& \text{Excess} \qquad\qquad = \$\ \ \ 1,455
\end{aligned}$$

Since the difference is *slightly* negative, we know that the answer is approximately 18 percent. If a more precise answer is needed, we would make another iteration at 16 percent and this would yield an answer that was slightly positive. Then interpolation would yield the answer.

					TABLE 5.1		Present Worth (Value) of $1						
YEAR	1%	2%	3%	4%	5%	6%	7%	8%	9%	10%	12%	14%	15%
1	.990	.980	.971	.962	.952	.943	.935	.926	.917	.909	.893	.877	.870
2	.980	.961	.943	.925	.907	.890	.873	.857	.842	.828	.797	.769	.756
3	.971	.942	.915	.889	.864	.840	.816	.794	.772	.751	.712	.675	.658
4	.961	.924	.889	.855	.823	.792	.763	.735	.708	.683	.636	.592	.572
5	.951	.906	.863	.822	.784	.747	.713	.681	.650	.621	.567	.519	.497
6	.942	.888	.838	.790	.746	.705	.666	.630	.596	.564	.507	.456	.432
7	.933	.871	.813	.760	.711	.665	.623	.583	.547	.513	.452	.400	.376
8	.923	.853	.789	.731	.677	.627	.582	.540	.502	.467	.404	.351	.327
9	.914	.837	.766	.703	.645	.592	.544	.500	.460	.424	.361	.308	.284
10	.905	.820	.744	.676	.614	.558	.508	.463	.422	.386	.322	.270	.247
11	.896	.804	.722	.650	.585	.527	.475	.429	.388	.350	.287	.237	.215
12	.887	.788	.701	.625	.557	.497	.444	.397	.356	.319	.257	.208	.187
13	.879	.773	.681	.601	.530	.469	.415	.368	.326	.290	.229	.182	.163
14	.870	.758	.661	.577	.505	.442	.388	.340	.299	.263	.205	.160	.141
15	.861	.743	.642	.555	.481	.417	.362	.315	.275	.239	.183	.140	.123
16	.853	.728	.623	.534	.458	.394	.339	.291	.252	.218	.163	.123	.107
17	.844	.714	.605	.513	.436	.371	.317	.270	.231	.198	.146	.108	.093
18	.836	.700	.587	.494	.416	.350	.296	.250	.212	.180	.130	.095	.081
19	.828	.686	.570	.475	.398	.331	.276	.232	.194	.164	.116	.083	.070
20	.820	.673	.554	.456	.377	.319	.258	.215	.178	.149	.104	.073	.061
25	.780	.610	.478	.375	.295	.233	.184	.146	.116	.092	.059	.038	.030
30	.742	.552	.412	.308	.231	.174	.131	.099	.075	.057	.033	.020	.015

YEAR	16%	18%	20%	24%	28%	32%	36%	40%	50%	60%	70%	80%	90%
1	.862	.847	.833	.806	.781	.758	.735	.714	.667	.625	.588	.556	.526
2	.743	.718	.694	.650	.610	.574	.541	.510	.444	.391	.346	.309	.277
3	.641	.601	.579	.524	.477	.435	.398	.364	.296	.241	.204	.171	.146
4	.552	.516	.482	.423	.373	.321	.292	.260	.198	.153	.120	.095	.077
5	.476	.437	.402	.341	.291	.250	.215	.186	.132	.095	.170	.053	.040
6	.410	.370	.335	.275	.227	.189	.158	.133	.088	.060	.041	.029	.021
7	.354	.314	.279	.222	.178	.143	.116	.015	.059	.037	.024	.016	.011
8	.305	.266	.233	.179	.139	.108	.085	.068	.031	.023	.014	.019	.006
9	.263	.228	.194	.144	.108	.182	.063	.048	.026	.015	.008	.005	.003
10	.227	.111	.162	.116	.085	.062	.046	.035	.017	.009	.005	.003	.002
11	.115	.162	.135	.014	.066	.047	.034	.125	.012	.016	.003	.002	.001
12	.168	.137	.112	.076	.052	.036	.025	.018	.008	.014	.002	.001	.001
13	.145	.116	.093	.061	.040	.027	.018	.013	.005	.002	.901	.001	.000
14	.125	.099	.078	.049	.032	.021	.014	.009	.003	.001	.001	.001	.000
15	.108	.084	.065	.040	.025	.016	.010	.006	.002	.001	.000	.000	
16	.093	.071	.054	.032	.019	.012	.007	.005	.002	.001	.000	.000	
17	.011	.060	.045	.026	.015	.009	.005	.003	.001	.000	.000		
18	.039	.051	.038	.021	.012	.007	.004	.002	.001	.000			
19	.030	.043	.031	.017	.009	.005	.003	.002	.000	.000			
20	.051	.037	.026	.014	.007	.004	.002	.001	.000	.000			
25	.024	.016	.010	.005	.002	.001	.000	.000					
30	.012	.007	.004	.002	.001	.000	.000						

YEAR	1%	2%	3%	4%	5%	6%	7%	8%	9%	10%
				TABLE 5.2 Present Worth (Value) of an Annuity of $1						
1	0.990	0.980	0.971	0.962	0.952	0.943	0.935	0.926	0.917	0.909
2	1.970	1.942	1.913	1.886	1.859	1.833	1.808	1.783	1.759	1.736
3	2.941	2.884	2.829	2.775	2.723	2.673	2.624	2.577	2.531	2.487
4	3.902	3.808	3.717	3.630	3.546	3.465	3.387	3.312	3.240	3.170
5	4.853	4.713	4.580	4.452	4.329	4.212	4.100	3.993	3.890	3.791
6	5.795	5.601	5.417	5.242	5.076	4.917	4.766	4.623	4.486	4.355
7	6.728	6.472	6.230	6.002	5.786	5.582	5.389	5.206	5.033	4.868
8	7.652	7.325	7.020	6.733	6.463	6.210	6.971	5.747	5.535	5.335
9	8.566	8.162	7.786	7.435	7.108	6.802	6.515	6.247	5.985	5.759
10	9.471	8.983	8.530	8.111	7.722	7.360	7.024	6.710	6.418	6.145
11	10.368	9.787	9.253	8.760	8.306	7.887	7.499	7.139	6.805	6.495
12	11.255	10.575	9.954	9.385	8.863	8.384	7.943	7.536	7.161	6.814
13	12.134	11.348	16.635	9.986	9.394	8.853	8.358	7.904	7.487	7.103
14	13.004	12.106	11.296	10.563	9.899	9.295	8.745	8.244	7.786	7.367
15	13.865	12.849	11.938	11.118	10.380	9.712	9.108	8.559	8.060	7.606
16	14.718	13.578	12.561	11.652	10.838	10.106	9.447	8.851	8.312	7.824
17	15.562	14.292	13.166	12.166	11.274	10.477	9.763	9.122	8.544	8.022
18	16.318	14.992	13.754	12.659	11.690	10.828	10.059	9.372	8.756	8.201
19	17.226	15.678	14.324	13.134	12.085	11.158	10.336	9.604	8.950	8.365
20	18.046	16.351	14.877	13.590	12.462	11.470	10.594	9.818	9.128	8.514
25	22.023	19.523	17.413	15.622	14.094	12.783	11.654	10.675	9.823	9.077
30	25.808	22.397	19.600	17.292	15.373	13.765	12.409	11.258	10.274	9.427

YEAR	12%	14%	16%	18%	20%	24%	28%	32%	36%	40%	45%	50%
1	0.893	0.877	0.862	0.847	0.833	0.806	0.781	0.758	11.735	0.714	0.690	0.667
2	1.690	1.647	1.605	1.566	1.528	1.457	1.392	1.332	1.276	1.224	1.165	1.111
3	2.402	2.322	2.246	2.174	2.106	1.981	1.868	1.766	1.674	1.589	1.493	1.407
4	3.037	2.914	2.798	2.690	2.589	2.404	2.241	2.096	1.966	1.849	1.720	1.605
5	3.605	3.433	3.274	3.127	2.991	2.745	2.532	2.345	2.181	2.035	1.876	1.737
6	4 111	3.881	3.685	3.498	3.326	3.020	2.759	2.534	2.339	2.168	1.983	1.824
7	4.564	4.288	4.031	3.812	3.605	3.242	2.937	2.678	2.455	2.263	2.057	1.663
8	4.968	4.631	4.344	4.078	3.837	3.421	3.076	2.786	2.540	2.331	2.108	1.922
9	5.328	4.146	4.617	4.303	4.031	3.566	3.184	2.868	2.603	2.379	2.144	1.948
10	5.651	5.216	4.833	4.414	4.193	3.682	3.269	2.930	2.650	2.414	2.368	1.965
11	5.988	5.453	5.020	4.656	4.327	3.776	3.335	2.978	2.683	2.438	2.185	1.977
12	6.194	5.660	5.197	4.793	4.439	3.851	3.387	3.013	2.708	2.456	2.196	1.985
13	6.424	5.842	5.342	4.910	4.533	3.912	3.427	3.041	2.727	2.468	2.204	1.990
14	6.628	6.002	5.468	5.008	4.611	3.962	3.459	3.061	2.740	2.470	2.210	1.093
15	6.811	6.142	5.575	5.092	4.675	4.011	3.483	3.076	2.750	2.484	2.214	1.995
16	6.974	6.265	5.669	5.162	4.730	4.033	3.503	3.088	2.758	2.489	2.216	1.997
17	7.120	5.373	5.749	5.222	4.775	4.051	3.518	3.097	2.763	2.492	2.218	1.998
18	7.250	6.467	5.818	5.273	4.812	4.080	3.529	3.104	2.767	2.494	2.219	1.999
19	7.366	6.550	5.877	5.316	4.844	4.097	3.539	3.161	2.770	2.496	2.220	1.999
20	7.461	6.623	5.929	5.353	4.870	4.110	3.546	3.113	2.772	2.497	2.221	1.999
25	7.840	6.873	6.097	5.467	4.948	4.147	3.564	3.122	2.776	2.499	2.222	2.000
30	8.055	7.003	6.177	5.517	4.979	4.160	3.569	3.124	2.778	2.500	2.222	2.000

6

An Entrepreneurial Capital Budgeting Model

In the previous chapter we discussed growing the firm. One of the main ways of growing by internal means is capital budgeting. As a review, we discussed the traditional capital budgeting approach and noted that while it may be quite appropriate for large companies, it could be a disaster for new and emerging companies like the ones we deal with. In this chapter we expand the model to take into account more than one discriminant—rate of return—and develop an entrepreneurial capital budgeting model.

WHAT MAKES AN "ENTREPRENEURIAL" MODEL DIFFERENT?

Conventional financial wisdom takes the approach that all one has to do to select a capital budgeting proposal is to make sure that the proposal has a positive net present value or, alternatively, that the proposal has an Internal Rate of Return greater than the firm's cost of capital.

Some years ago, a friend of mine took over a fairly high-tech firm that was struggling. The first thing he did was to get an evaluation of the proposals the company had in its research pipeline. One particular proposal, a piece of computer peripheral equipment, had an unusually attractive Internal Rate of Return. "Let's do it!" the new chief executive exclaimed. Here indeed was a proposal that had a better rate of return than the firm's cost of capital, however calculated. The only trouble with this proposal was that it had a time shape of the cash flow that was the quintessence of a "Mañana" deal. It had a very heavy *negative cash flow* in the early periods, and only after a considerable investment of money and time would it have a positive cash flow. And cash flow was the major problem the company faced.

When management asked their bank for more money, they were rather emphatically declined. The company tried to generate the funds internally and, later, with an issue of convertible bonds, but it was not enough. Some time thereafter the company filed for bankruptcy. How could this happen? Didn't management do as they were supposed to do? They invested in a proposal that had a great rate of return—much greater than its cost of capital.

With General Motors it wouldn't matter that the proposal took quite a bit of cash, but with this company it made a great deal of difference. Management forgot about the time shape of the cash flow. This incident had a major impact on the way I look at capital budgeting; it brought the realization that there are more things to examine in a proposal than just its rate of return. The time shape of the cash flow must be included in the analysis for a middle-market or entrepreneurial firm. The implicit assumption that enough money would be available—assumed with usual capital budgeting models for major companies—simply is not correct.

Remembering the lesson that Harry Markowitz taught us over 40 years ago: What about the risk of getting a rate of return for a *set* of proposals? Would considering proposals in a set or group rather than individually make any difference in the proposals selected? In order to answer these queries, it is necessary to consider more than just one discriminant; it is necessary to consider multiple discriminants.

If one were doing the capital budgeting in order to fill the earnings gap, as discussed in Chapter 5, why not explicitly consider the expected earnings that a set of proposals would produce? Obviously, making earnings is not as important to a developing firm as its cash flow; you run on cash, not *earnings.* It would still be useful to see if a set of proposals could fill the earnings gap as management would hope. If we can add the time shape of the cash flow to the model, we can also add earnings.

GETTING STARTED: FORMAT FOR COMPARISON

Before describing the mathematical/computer model, let me reassure the non-mathematical/computer person that it is necessary to develop this model formally and then we can talk about the lessons that can be learned from the model and how we can use it even if we don't computerize it.

In order to use this model (consideration of a set of proposals) it is necessary to present all proposals in exactly the same format. This is done in order to be able to add column totals; this process also makes it easier to organize the data needed for a proposal. Each proposal should be presented with an Income

Statement, a Balance Sheet, and a Cash Flow Statement. Each statement should have a high, a low, and a most likely estimate. Furthermore, each statement should have the same time periods: a "time zero" column (t_0), with the first year expressed quarterly and yearly after that for however long the project will last.▲ Additionally, each proposal will have both a very brief write-up describing the proposal and then a longer description. The brief description could be, preferably, a one-sentence statement. Once the proposals are presented in this format, the next step would be to obtain the Internal Rate of Return (IRR) for *each version* of a proposal.

CALCULATING A PROPOSAL'S INTERNAL RATE OF RETURN

One of the most confusing aspects of capital budgeting for many people is the question "What cash flow do you discount?" Fortunately, we have an answer for that in that we have Cash Flow Statements, for all proposals. Refer to Item 7, the Net Change in Cash and Money Market Securities, which is the cash flow that is discounted to time zero (t_0), in order to get the IRR for each version of a proposal. When doing this, however, you may feel that you are violating one of the tenets of finance: Separate the financing from the investing decision. But this premise is not valid when a proposal brings along its own financing.

For example, if a firm is contemplating the construction of a new building for expansion, and it fully intends to secure long-term financing for the project, why not calculate that proposal's IRR *with the financing in place*? Or, a proposal may involve buying a piece of machinery on which the manufacturer offers financing of two-thirds of the purchase price, and the firm intends to accept that financing. It doesn't make sense to view the rate of return on either proposal as though the firm were going to use all equity financing. Admittedly, in any large organization, it might make sense to separate the financing from the investment as the firm may have access to unlimited funds at rates lower than subordinate divisions can get, but a developing firm cannot make this assumption.

Similarly, if a proposal involves receivables and inventory and the firm intends to borrow against these assets, the proposal should reflect this and not pretend that this type of financing would not be used. In most cases, it would seem like the inclusion of "bring-along financing" would result in a *higher* rate of return than if all equity financing were assumed. But this is beside the point. *If* the proposal's IRR is greater because of this inclusion—and this is the way the firm intends to act—why would it want to evaluate the proposal as though it did *not* intend to accept the financing offered? By including this "bring-along financing," I am not, however, suggesting that *all* financing—for example, the working capital financing needed over and above this "bring-along financing"— should be likewise included.

▲ Later, there will be a discussion of how to compute the optimal tenure for a proposal.

DERIVING THE IRR

Once the IRRs for the three versions of the proposal are derived what results is a low IRR, a high IRR, and a **modal IRR**—because the "most likely" version is really a mode. And indeed it should be a modal estimate. People do not think in terms of *means* but rather modes when the distribution is skewed. When the distribution is "normal," the mean and the mode are equal, so it does not matter. But it would be foolhardy to assume that *all* capital budgeting cash flow distributions are normal. In fact, it would seem that most proposals would have a skewed distribution, either right or left. We do need a *mean* value in order to work with most probability tables, but we can define the mean if we know the range and modal value. To do this, we employ a Beta distribution to calculate the mean value, e_i, of the IRR of the ith proposal. Thus the "mean IRR" (or the Expected Rate of Return, ERR, or e_i) can be approximated by the following:

$$e_i = (a_i + 4m_i + b_i)/6$$

a_i = the IRR for the "low" version

b_i = the IRR for the "high" version

m_i = the IRR for the "most likely version"

The Standard Deviation is given by:

$$\sigma_i = \sqrt{\frac{(b_i - a_i)^2}{3}}$$

For example, if a proposal had an a_i of 10 percent, a b_i of 40 percent, and a m_i of 15 percent, then its *mean* IRR would be:

$$[10 + 4(15) + 40]/6 = 18.3\%$$

Since this distribution is skewed to the right, the mean is *greater* than the mode. People who derive the financial data that goes into a proposal do not have to *estimate* the mean in this situation, thanks to this handy formula. The standard deviation for this mean would be:

$$\sigma_i = \sqrt{\frac{(40 - 10)^2}{36}} = 5\%$$

Now that we have the ERR, (e_i) for a single proposal and its standard deviation, σ_i, we can proceed to the next step.

STEPS IN THE COMPUTER MODEL

STEP 1

Once we have the ERR for each proposal, we can start to form sets and begin the model. The model will take all permutations and combinations of all the proposals and calculate the "Expected Rate of Return for a Set of Proposals" or what we will call $\overline{R}$. Thus:

$$\text{Opt. } \overline{R} = \sum_{i=1}^{n}\left(e_i\frac{w_i}{K}\right) + \left(\frac{K - \sum_{i=1}^{n} w_i}{K}\right)\rho$$

$\overline{R}$ = the rate of return for a *set* of proposals

e_i = the ERR for a single proposal, i

w_i = the "Time Zero" (t_0) value of Item 7, Net Change in Cash, for the ith proposal

K = the amount of capital available for capital budgeting

ρ (rho) = An "Opportunity Cost" for money not invested in proposals

Now for an explanation of the model. The first part of the equation above merely says that you want to get the weighted ERR for a set of proposals. The present computer model for this simply calculates all permutations and combinations; it would seem that this problem is a natural for an integer (linear) programming (IP) model, but considering the relatively small number of proposals that a firm would have and considering the speed of today's computers, it hardly seems necessary to use an IP technique.

Weighting the Proposals' ERR

It would not make any sense to simply take an *unweighted* mean of a set of proposal's ERRs, because proposals come in all sorts of sizes. How to weight these proposals when combining them is an open question. I have chosen to weight these proposals by the percentage of the firm's capital budget (K) that a proposal requires initially. For example, if a firm had $1 million for its capital budgeting, and a proposal used $100,000 as its initial or going-in cost, then that proposal would be weighted at 10 percent. Naturally, the initial or "going-in cost" may be only the tip of the iceberg, so to speak. A proposal may require large amounts of additional capital once it is started. This is true, but it is something that will be accounted for in a third discriminant—the time shape of the cash flow. Admittedly, this confuses the weighting process, but until a better way comes along, the weighting will be done according to the amount of initial capital a proposal uses.

The Second Part of the Objective Function

It is entirely likely that when a set is formed, that set might require more *initial capital* than the firm has available ($\Sigma w_i > K$). This is accounted for in the second *step* of the model, but what if the set takes *less* than K ? This entirely possible eventuality is accounted for in the second part of the objective function. In this expression, the sum of the w_i's ("going-in costs") is subtracted from K and this amount is divided by K in order to get it weighted properly. This amount is then invested at a rate of ρ. This is the "opportunity cost" of money in the developing firm.

For example, if a firm has redundant money market securities—money that it does not need in the business at the moment—then its *rho* would be the rate of return it is making on those money market securities. Or, suppose that the firm does not have any such money market securities and is, instead, borrowing from a bank at 12 percent. For this firm, it appears that its opportunity cost of money is at least 12 percent. And if the firm feels that it is "loaned up" at its bank, but if it had more money available, it could expand sales and profitably invest in more receivables or inventory. In this case, the firm may feel that it has an opportunity cost of something like 30 or more percent! Whatever percentage the firm uses, this will be its *rho*. And keep in mind that one *set* of investment proposals would be to invest *all* of K at this rate of *rho*. So, this rate of *rho* is a kind of cut-off rate of return; if a *set* of proposals does not earn at least this rate, then it would not be acceptable.▲ Its rate of return would have more risk than *rho* and less return. Remember, this admonition applies to the rate of return for a *set* of proposals $(\overline{R})$, *not* for any individual proposal. So, to summarize the first equation, $\overline{R}$ is the rate of return for a set of proposals which includes the weighted rate of return for the individual proposals in the set, $e_i \dfrac{w_i}{K}$, *plus* the weighted rate of return for the money left over.

STEP 2

The next step is simply a constraint that you do not spend more money than you have. This is shown in the equation:

$$\Sigma w_i \leq K, \text{ your capital budget}$$

The w_i's are readily available from Item 7 (Net Change in Cash), Time Zero (t_0) column of the Cash Flow Statement for each proposal.

STEP 3

In this step we take account of the time shape of the cash flows of the *set* of proposals. Because we have as input for each proposal a Cash Flow Statement with

---

▲ Some might like to call this rate the firm's "cost of capital." I prefer to simply call it an "opportunity cost" since it is just that, and this avoids the troublesome problem of trying to calculate a "cost of capital" for the firm in question, especially if the firm is privately held.

the first year expressed quarterly, we can algebraically add the amounts in Item 7 of the Cash Flow Statement to see, in each quarter, what the implications would be to the firm's cash account *if* that set of proposals were accepted. If the amount in a given quarter is *positive*, there is no worry. But if the amount in a quarter is *negative*, this could have serious implications for the company's cash position. Fortunately, there is a rather simple way of testing to see if a negative amount for any one quarter would exceed the amount of money the firm would have available to service a set of capital budgeting proposals in a manner of speaking. But just comparing the mean cash balance for a set of proposals $(\overline{X})$ to A (the amount of cash available for the quarter) would be statistically inappropriate because $\overline{X}$ is merely the *mean* dollar amount of a distribution with a positive standard distribution.▲ We can check to see if $\overline{X}$ is statistically significantly different from A, however, with a simple one tail *mean difference test.* Thus:

$$\left(\frac{A_{1-4} - \overline{X}_{1-4}}{S_{1-4}}\right) \leq Y_p$$

Where A_{1-4} is a subjectively set dollar amount (actually a negative dollar amount) that management feels could be devoted to servicing the negative cash requirements of a set of proposals for each quarter, 1–4.

X_{1-4} is the *mean* cash balance for a set of proposals for each quarter, 1 to 4, derived by adding the mean cash balance for each proposal in a set.

S_{1-4} is the standard deviation of this cash balance mean.

Y_p is the number of standard deviations that $\overline{X}$ is below the available amount of money. We can then use this number Y_p to find the area in the tail of a normal distribution as shown in Exhibit 6.1.

If, for example $\overline{X}_1$ were $400,000, A_1 were $600,000, and the standard deviation were $200,000, there would be approximately a 15 percent chance that the *actual* cash balance for that set of proposals for the first quarter would be greater than minus $600,000. In this case Y_p would be equal to 1 and from Exhibit 6.1, a standard deviation (Y) of 1 means that there is a probability of 0.1587 that the actual change in the cash balance would be greater than A_1. In short, it is necessary to check to see if $\overline{X}$ is *statistically significantly different* from A with a certain probability. In this example, if management specified that they were willing to take a 15 percent chance of going below A (hurting the company's cash balance) in any one quarter, then that set would pass this "cash insufficiency" test for the quarter in question. Obviously, management is in a position to specify the chance they are willing to take of hurting or killing the

▲ If $\overline{X}$ were a straight line projecting upward, it would have a standard deviation of zero. This would be, indeed, a strange distribution. One should not make the mistake of assuming that just because X is less than A, there is *no* probability of the *actual* amount being greater than A.

EXHIBIT 6.1   "Right Tail" Area under the Normal Probability Distribution

(Y REFERS TO THE NUMBER OF STANDARD DEVIATIONS FROM THE MEAN OF A NORMAL DISTRIBUTION WITH A MEAN OF ZERO AND A STANDARD DEVIATION OF ONE.)

Y	0.00	0.05
0.1	0.4602	0.4404
0.2	0.4207	0.4013
0.3	0.3821	0.3632
0.4	0.3446	0.3264
0.5	0.3085	0.2912
0.6	0.2743	0.2578
0.7	0.2420	0.2266
0.8	0.2119	0.1977
0.9	0.1841	0.1711
1.0	0.1587	0.1469
1.5	0.0668	0.0606
2.0	0.0228	0.0202

company's cash balance based on what resources the company has available *if A* is broached. For example, if the firm has an unused line of credit at its bank, the company's management might be willing to take a larger chance of exceeding *A* than if the company's management felt strapped for cash or, simply had no outside means of obtaining more cash quickly.

STEP 4

Step 4 deals with the question of why we are doing this capital budgeting in the first place. You will remember from the last chapter that we are talking about *growing the firm.* By this we mean "filling the earnings gap." But up to this point this model has not even touched on the matter of earnings. True, we do not want to calculate a proposal's rate of return using earnings, but it would be quite informative to know whether or not a set of proposals is providing the earnings necessary to fill the earnings gap. Do we have that information? Indeed we do.

All we have to do is to calculate a **mean earnings** for each proposal and then *add* these mean earnings when we make up a set. The sum of these mean earnings would then be the mean earnings for a set, which is precisely what we want when we are looking to see if a set of proposals fills the earnings gap. Once we get this mean earnings $(\overline{X}')$ and the standard deviation of the mean $(\overline{S}')$, we can then compare this mean to that amount of earnings that we need to fill the earnings gap, called E. Then we can use a **mean difference** test similar to what we did in Step 3. Thus:

$$\left(\frac{\overline{X}' - E}{S'}\right) \geq Y_p$$

In this equation we can calculate Y and then by referring to Exhibit 6.1, we can see if the *mean earnings* $(\overline{X}')$ are statistically significantly greater than E, the amount of earnings that we specified as being needed to fill the earnings gap.

Note that we are treating earnings for the year instead of quarterly, as we did for the cash balance. While we might not want to use yearly data for cash (you need to know your situation sooner or more often), it does not seem prudent to use quarterly data for earnings. Why throw out an otherwise good set of proposals just because the set has insufficient earnings for a particular quarter, yet has sufficient earnings for the year as a whole. On the other hand, if some management wants to check *quarterly* earnings the data is available and the technique is the same as for the Step 2.

STEP 5

Up to this point we have not mentioned the risk of getting the rate of return for a set $(\overline{R})$. For a number of years, I, like most academics in finance, was thinking that we needed to calculate the risk of getting the rate of return for *each* proposal and compare this to some standard. It was then that I remembered the point that Harry Markowitz made in his famous work on portfolio management.[•] This was the fact that in a portfolio of securities, it was possible to have *less* risk of getting the rate of return on a *set* of securities than one might have on any one security in that portfolio. The reason for this was simply the concept of **covariance**, defined as equaling the Coefficient Correlation)(the standard deviation of the rates of return $_{i...n}$. This concept of covariance is often forgotten.

In a set of capital budgeting proposals we do not care if we minimize the risk of getting the rate of return, as in a portfolio of securities, because we would like for *all* the proposals in a set to go up if they can. Thus we do not want the coefficient of multiple correlation to be used where it runs from 1 to -1. What we want is a measure of dependence/independence that runs from 1 to zero.[••] We will call this the **Index of Diffusion** (d) and we will then multiply this coefficient by the risk of getting the rates of return, weighted, for the proposals in the set to get what is called the **Coefficient of Diffusion** (D) for a set. Thus:

$$D = d \sum_{i=1}^{n}\left(\sigma_i \frac{w_i}{K}\right)$$

Deriving the Index of Diffusion

To derive d, the Index of Diffusion, it is necessary to look at the proposals in a set and subjectively estimate d. If the proposals in the set seem to be quite tied into one another, the d would be given a number close to 1, perhaps .9 or .85 or .95. Or, if the proposals seem to be quite independent of each other, then d would be close to zero: .1 or .15 or .05. If the proposals seem to be somewhat

---

[•] The source of my remembering was an article by James VanHorne, "Capital Budgeting Decisions Involving Combinations of Risky Investments," *Management Science* (October 1966) B84–91.

[••] I wish to thank my colleague Professor Dolores Conway for suggesting this approach.

dependent to each other, perhaps a *d* of .5 or .6 or .4 would seem appropriate. The way the computer model is written currently, when all the permutations and combinations are calculated, the sets that pass through the first four screens are then presented in a way that gives the analyst a one-sentence statement about each proposal in the set. This is the reason that two explanatory statements are presented with each proposal: a reasonably complete explanation of the proposal and then the short, possibly one sentence, description sufficient for the analyst to recognize the proposals in the set. The analyst is then able to make an assessment of the *combined* risk of getting the rate of return for the proposals in a set.

For example, if a firm had a fairly flat organization and had four branches in cities in the four corners of the country—say Los Angeles, Seattle, New York, and Atlanta—and if a set came up with five proposals, four of which were from the Seattle branch, this would seem to mean that there was a high degree of *dependence* between proposals, or a *d* of, say, .90. If something happens to the Seattle market, all four of the proposals would be in trouble. Contrast that with the situation of five proposals in a set, one each in New York, Atlanta, and Los Angeles, and two proposals in Seattle. Or, in a one-plant situation, all the proposals in the possible set are such that they are quite independent from one another. Of course, one might logically argue that because all the proposals were in the one company, that all sets had a high degree of risk. While this is conceptually true, it might be argued that there are *shades* of dependence/independence that are relevant here.▲

Thus, *D* is now the risk of getting the rate of return for a set of proposals. This concept has very interesting implications for a set of proposals. For example, suppose that a firm has a host of really low-risk proposals, all quite interrelated. Management might think that by carefully screening each proposal they are actually *reducing* the risk to the company. But if these proposals are interdependent, the *d* for that **set** would be quite high, possibly .9 or .95. This means that the *product* of *d* and the sum of the σ's would result in a Coefficient of Diffusion that could be quite high—even though the component proposals are quite low in risk of getting the rate of return.

Another example would be the case where the firm has a set of proposals that, individually, are really high risk. That is, the proposals have a high risk of getting the rate of return for each proposal. At first blush, one would think that that *set* would be a risky set, but suppose these proposals are quite *independent* of each other. Because of this variation of the concept of covariance, which we are calling Coefficient of Diffusion, the *d* in this case would be actually quite small, .1 or .15 or .05. Therefore, when you multiply the rather large sum of the (large) σ's by a rather *low* Index of Diffusion (d), the Coefficient of Diffusion is now quite small, or at least reasonable. Understanding this principal can be

---

▲ I think it would be a mistake to try to refine the process of obtaining the *d* by mathematical means. We are dealing with something that is quite subjective and to try to make it more "scientific" would be specious.

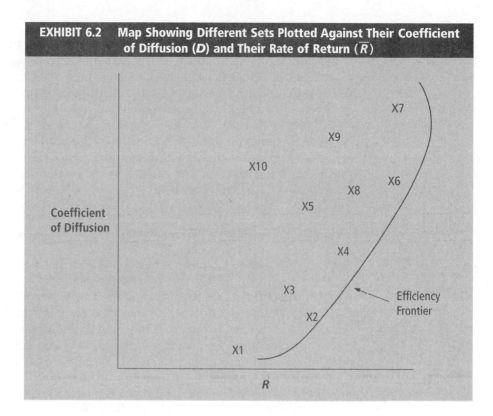

EXHIBIT 6.2   **Map Showing Different Sets Plotted Against Their Coefficient of Diffusion (*D*) and Their Rate of Return ($\overline{R}$)**

most useful in the real world of financial management for it tends to be somewhat counterintuitive.

Plotting the Sets

Once the *d* of each proposal in the sets is determined, and the Coefficient of Diffusion is calculated for each set that screens through the first four steps, the surviving sets can then be plotted on a map the relates the Coefficient of Diffusion of a set (*D*) with the expected rate of return for a set ($\overline{R}$). See Exhibit 6.2

In this figure we see the various possible sets, *X1. . . X10*, sets that passed through the first four steps, plotted against their Coefficient of Diffusion and their $\overline{R}$. The line that envelopes the outside sets is called the **Efficiency Frontier**. The only sets that should be selected lie on or close to this Efficiency Frontier. For example, *X3* would not be selected because *X2* has *a higher* rate of return and a *lower* risk. Similarly, *X4* and *X9* have approximately the same $\overline{R}$ but *X9* has much higher risk of getting this rate of return. Which set should management select? This depends on their preference for risk and return—which , of course, depends on the condition of the firm and management's desires. Offhand, it appears that *X4* or *X6* would be the most likely sets selected. *X4* has less $\overline{R}$ than *X6*, but it also has less risk of getting that rate of return. *X6* has more $\overline{R}$ than *X4*, but it has *proportionately* more risk. So take your choice!

Accuracy of the Estimate

While it might seem to some that *subjectively* estimating d, the Index of Diffusion, would be quite questionable, in practice the effect is not particularly bad. For example, if *X2* had an estimated d that was more than it should have been, the locus of *X2* would have been somewhat higher than it is shown. But it would not be a lot higher if the d were only .25 instead of .15. *X2* would still be relatively better than *X3*, for example, and in the overall map its relative position would be about the same. Remember, even though d is estimated in the calculation of the Coefficient of Diffusion, nothing happens to $\overline{R}$. Therefore, any error in estimating d will only be reflected in an *upward* or *downward* movement in the position of the set on the map.

USING THE MODEL WITHOUT A COMPUTER

Up to this point, the discussion of the entrepreneurial multiple-discriminant model has presumed the use of a computer model to select sets of proposals and then place them on a map relating the Coefficient of Diffusion and $\overline{R}$. While it is true that computers have pervaded every aspect of the workplace, the lesson that can be learned from this model can be applied even *without* a computer—even if the firm utilizes *ad hoc* capital budgeting procedures. The complete explanation of the model was necessary to establish the theoretical foundation for the model, but the commonsense aspects of the model can—and should—be used by any manager who is passing judgment on capital budgeting proposals. To illustrate this, let's walk through the model.

Ideally, the company should do its capital budgeting at periodic times so that a number of proposals would be available for selection. But life being what it is in new or emerging firms, there may be a practice of *ad hoc* capital budgeting, or examining individual proposals as they come up. Remember, however, that even if we have only one proposal for consideration, the "other" proposal is the firm itself.

STEP 1

When examining a proposal the first question that presumably would be asked is, What is the expected rate of return? Whatever the answer, this proposal would be judged by the ERRs of other proposals submitted recently. For example, if someone said that the ERR was only 12 percent, the logical reply might be "Why even present it? If it were, for instance, 45 percent this would be a different matter."

STEP 2

Next, the question to ask is, What is the "going-in cost"? How much will it cost to get started with this proposal? If the amount is within the budget of the company, then proceed to the next step.

STEP 3

If the firm can afford the "going-in cost" (equal to Item 7, Net Change in Cash, for the t_0 time period or the firm's cash balance that could be utilized), then the next question is whether or not the proposal will hurt the firm's cash position in the upcoming year—and beyond, if need be—if it were accepted. What is the *time shape of the cash flow* for this proposal? Is it a real *Mañana* type of deal (see page 124), such as a research and development type of proposal, or is it something like the "smooth and steady" cash flow pattern that is characteristic of a cost-saving proposal such as a new conveyor system. Would the firm's cash balance be able to absorb a real negative cash balance for the proposal for the first few quarters—or beyond?

Doing *ad hoc* capital budgeting is not the best approach although it is extremely pragmatic. And this third step is a good illustration as to why it is useful—and important—to consider a number of proposals at one time. If two or more proposals were presented at the same time, the negative *time shape of the cash flow* of one proposal might be offset by the good cash flow of another proposal(s). This may be thought of as the **Portfolio Effect** of the model. So, in the vernacular, this third step asks the question, Are we going to kill the company's cash flow if we accept this proposal?

STEP 4

Next it is useful to ask, If we accept this proposal, will we be helping to reach our earnings goal necessary to fill the earnings gap? How much importance is placed on this criterion depends on the company itself. Is the company privately owned or is it publicly owned? What are the earnings of the other proposals we have accepted in this period? Although earnings are important—and ultimately the *raison d'être* for the whole capital budgeting process—they are not the same as cash flow in that without cash the firm could be forced into a grave position. If a proposal has a really good ERR, and an *acceptable time shape of the cash flow*, it may be that the firm can take it, knowing that the earnings will come sometime—assuming that is not too distant.

STEP 5

Doing *ad hoc* capital budgeting would seem to negate the important fifth step, the notion of the risk of getting the rate of return. We called this the Coefficient of Diffusion for a set of proposals. But what does one do if there is only one proposal to consider? As mentioned above, the answer to this conundrum is that there is *always a second proposal: the firm itself*. In fact, it is wise to consider the firm itself when estimating d in the Coefficient of Diffusion. So it is possible to ask questions like "Is this proposal like the last few proposals we have accepted? And if we take this proposal will we exacerbate or help the overall risk for the company?" If the proposal under consideration is quite like the last four or five proposals accepted, it does not take much imagination to realize that taking another similar proposal would be rather like putting all of one's eggs in the same basket. What if something happens to that division? Or that product line? Or . . .

THE PRACTICAL IMPORTANCE OF THE MODEL

While the use of a (somewhat) mathematical, entrepreneurial capital budgeting model might seem incongruous relative to the rest of the book, I hope that I have succeeded in showing the importance of *each* step in the model. It would be a lot easier to say, as practically all the textbooks do, that all you have to do with respect to capital budgeting is to accept all proposals that have a rate of return greater than the firm's cost of capital. But to do so would be to forget such important considerations as the *time shape of the cash flow* of a proposal. If the firm takes on a proposal that has such a negative time shape of cash flow that it will put the firm's very existence into question, would it console the manager to say "but the proposal has a return greater than the firm's cost of capital"? What difference does it make if the proposal has an excellent ERR if, by taking it, the firm faces a grave cash insufficiency? Perhaps in General Motors it would not be necessary to worry about such things, but in the real world of managing a developing firm, if management forgets its cash flow, it will most likely be in dire straits.

Likewise, the Coefficient of Diffusion, introduced in this chapter, is an extremely important notion for all capital budgeting decision makers.

**The risk of getting the rate of return of individual proposals
should not be considered individually.**

The covariance principal that Harry Markowitz wrote about 40 years ago should not be forgotten. When the risk of an individual proposal is considered by itself, this notion is violated. A *portfolio* of securities may include securities that have way too much risk in and of themselves, but when placed in the context of a portfolio, the risk is quite acceptable. Only by considering *sets* of capital budgeting proposals together are we able to take advantage of this covariance idea. And trying to manipulate a cost of capital by using higher rates for certain situations, such as cost-saving proposals or, new, creative proposals, still does not do the same thing as considering the proposals in a *set* and considering that set's Coefficient of Diffusion.

DECISIONS IN EVALUATING PROPOSALS

It would be absurd to say that *all* situations are covered in this Entrepreneurial Capital Budgeting model. There will always be cases that do not fit the model. For example, there may be situations in which the company can lease the capital asset rather than buy it. Let's consider that possibility.

THE LEASE-BUY DECISION

For many capital budgeting decisions, management has the option of leasing some asset—a piece of equipment or, perhaps, a building—instead of buying the asset that is part of the proposal. How should this decision be made? And should the decision be made before submitting the proposal to the model? The best way to handle this decision is to submit the proposal in *two* versions, one as a "buy decision" and one as a "lease decision." But these versions must be submitted as *mutually exclusive proposals*. If one version is accepted in a set, then it would not be possible to accept the *other* version of the proposal in the same set. In this way the portfolio effect is brought into play. For example, in the *buy* version, let's say the ERR of the proposal is better than it is for the *lease* version. But the time shape of the cash flow for the buy version is distinctly inferior (meaning that it has a larger cash drain) than the lease version. So, in some sets (ones with a cash problem), it would be better to include the proposal as a *lease* version rather than as a *buy* version. Or, the opposite might be true. This points out again the desirability of considering proposals in *sets* and not individually. For example, the buy version might be quite superior in terms of ERR, to the lease version. But if considered in isolation, this version of the proposal might be rejected because of the adverse *time shape of the cash flow* or, possibly, because it takes excessive "going-in cost" (w_i). Coupled with other proposals, however, the higher ERR proposal version might be acceptable. This would be the same situation as a proposal with a poor ERR but with other favorable characteristics: low "going-in cost," favorable *time shape of the cash flow*, or impressive positive earnings. Again the importance of the "portfolio" effect is emphasized.

ABANDONMENT VALUE

Another factor is the optimal length of time that a proposal should run. Is there a way to calculate when a proposal should be terminated? And if so, would this calculation make a difference in the rate of return for that proposal?

Fortunately, there is a relatively simple way to do this. It is called the **calculation of abandonment value**. (See Exhibit 6.3.) All one has to do is to estimate for each proposal at the end of each year a value that could be recovered *if* that proposal were terminated. This means that all receivables would be collected,

EXHIBIT 6.3	Illustration of IRR without Abandonment Value							
CASH FLOWS FOR A PROPOSAL								
TIME IN YEARS								
	t_0	1	2	3	4	5	6	7
IRR = 55%	($45)	$20	25	35	30	40	25	20
ABANDONMENT VALUE =		$40	45	50	65	70	60	30

THE IRR FOR THE PROPOSAL IS 55% WITHOUT INCLUDING ABANDONMENT VALUE.

EXHIBIT 6.4   Illustration of IRR if Abandonment Value Is Considered at End of First Year

CASH FLOWS FOR A PROPOSAL

TIME IN YEARS

	t_0	1	2	3	4	5	6	7
IRR = 55% W/O AV	($45)	$20	25	35	30	40	25	20
ABANDONMENT VALUE =		$40	45	50	65	70	60	30
IRR IF ABANDONED =		33	49	57	60	61	59	57%

all inventory sold, any machinery disposed of in the most profitable way, and all liabilities paid. If this value were then placed beneath Item 7 (Net Change in Cash), on the Cash Flow Statement, then it is possible to calculate an IRR using this value as a type of "scrap value," in the traditional sense. Merely taking the cash flows at the end of each time period results in an IRR of 55 percent. But if the project were terminated after the first year, and the abandonment value at the end of the first year was taken into consideration the IRR is 33 percent. Exhibit 6.4 illustrates this.

If this process is continued, each year dropping down and including the abandonment value at the end of that year, and excluding the remaining years, it is possible to derive the IRR for that strategy. Exhibit 6.4 also illustrates this.

By going beyond the fifth year, the abandonment value decreases, as does the IRR with abandonment value included. Note that by including abandonment value it is possible to get a larger IRR. Five years is the optimal time.

TECHNOLOGICAL OBSOLESCENCE AND DEVELOPMENT

In some industries—computers and bio-science, for example—technology moves so fast that any proposal that promises cash flows beyond some time (3 or 4 years, perhaps) would seem quite impractical. What to do in this case? Simply delete any cash flows beyond the arbitrary cut-off date. This puts a heavier burden on the early years' cash flow, but this is consistent with reality.

The opposite of this situation exists in industries such as the pharmaceutical industry, in which projects may take years to come to fruition. In this case, considering only the first years' cash flow seems quite inadequate. In this case, it is imperative that future years' cash flows be taken into account in using the model. The model does not do this in the present form; to do so would involve modeling the firm in the second year (and, if necessary, still another year or two.) This is necessary because of the cash flow and earnings assumptions. The reason it is necessary to model the performance of the firm is because in the second year another set of proposals would be undertaken and these proposals would influence the firm's cash flow, just as this year's set of proposals would influence this year's cash flow.

SUMMARY

In Chapter 5, it was suggested that there is a need for more than one discriminant in capital budgeting. The three discriminants that were offered in this chapter are the "time shape of the cash flow," the projected earnings, and a measure of risk of getting the rate of return called the "Coefficient of Diffusion."

In contrast to the situation with large corporations, an entrepreneurial company presents special circumstances. For one thing, the time shape of the cash flow, if significant in a negative way, may actually lead to a **cash insufficiency** or worse. This may happen to large companies, but there is much more likelihood of it in smaller, developing firms. The estimate of a set's earnings is useful to see if they can help close the company's "earnings gap."

The other significant addition to the usual capital budgeting model is the risk of getting the rate of return, which we called the Coefficient of Diffusion. This has implications for many managerial decisions. Basically it says that if you add all the risks of getting the rate of return for individual proposals, you can multiply this sum by something called the Index of Diffusion. This index ($1.0 < d < 0$) indicates the relationship of the proposals in the set to each other—and the firm itself. If the proposals are independent, then this Index is close to (but not equal to) zero; if they are highly related, the Index is closer to one. (This is a variation of covariance that Markowitz reminded us to use.) This means that a company can accept proposals involving greater risk of getting the rate of return if the proposals are independent.

Even if the reader never uses a computer to get the optimum set, the model is useful for allowing a manager to ask significant questions about a proposal if the capital budgeting is done on an *ad hoc* basis.

The appendix reviews classic models that a manager is likely to encounter in the course of time—and asks the question "What's wrong with this model?"

QUESTIONS FOR DISCUSSION

1. Take a hypothetical capital budgeting proposal and submit it to the five steps involved in the model.

2. Why doesn't the Entrepreneurial Capital Budgeting model use "cost of capital" to evaluate proposals?

6

CHAPTER REVIEW

Appendix:
Alternative Capital
Budgeting Models

There are many other capital budgeting models in existence, too many to recap here. But there are two classic models that illustrate what I believe to be errors in logic.

THE HERTZ MODEL

This model was developed in the heyday of academic interest in capital budgeting, the 1960s and 1970s. This model, developed by David Hertz, is actually a three stage model developed in two papers.▲

THE FIRST STAGE

In the first stage, a proposal is submitted such that there are nine probability density functions which collectively describe the project. These nine variables are shown in Exhibit 6.5.

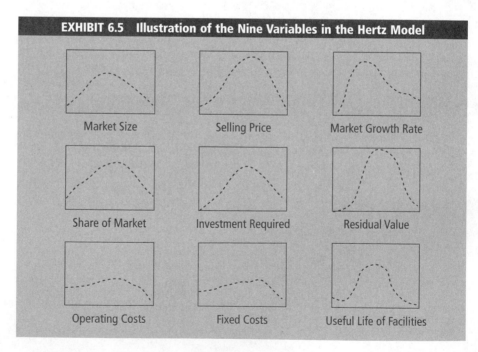

EXHIBIT 6.5   Illustration of the Nine Variables in the Hertz Model

Market Size   Selling Price   Market Growth Rate

Share of Market   Investment Required   Residual Value

Operating Costs   Fixed Costs   Useful Life of Facilities

▲ David B. Hertz, "Investment policies that pay off," *Harvard Business Review* January–February 1968, 96 ff. and David B. Hertz, "Risk analysis in capital investment," *Harvard Business Review* September–October 1979, 169 ff.

Note that the first four variables really represent Sales, which we entered directly in the entrepreneurial multiple discriminant model. Other variables also are interesting. For example, Hertz has the capital investment as a distribution where we use a point estimate of this for each scenario of a proposal. If one were to consider the investment as the *total* capital investment needed for a proposal, then, in fact, it would be a "distribution." Of course, a "point estimate," that is a straight line projecting upward, is *per se* a distribution. But by "distribution" I mean of the kind shown in Exhibit 6.5. Also, note that Hertz has two variables for what we are calling the "abandonment value." And where we are using point estimates of this "abandonment value," he considers this a variable.

Using a random number generator, a point is picked on each distribution. This, then, defines a *version* of the proposal. By discounting the cash flows associated with the respective versions, one obtains an IRR for that version. If this is done many times it is possible to plot a distribution of these IRRs. This is the process called "Monte Carlo Simulation." By taking the mean of this distribution of IRRs, the mean or Expected Rate of Return (ERR) is found.

THE SECOND STAGE

Once the distribution of IRRs is accomplished, it is possible to make a "cumulative probability distribution" for *each* proposal (Exhibit 6.6).

Then "risk screens" are formed for low-risk proposals, medium-risk proposals, and high-risk proposals. For example, a "low-risk" *screen* might be a 90 percent chance of making at least a 12 percent IRR and a ten percent chance of making at least 20 percent IRR. Once these profiles are derived, and assuming capital rationing, sets are formed from the proposals in each risk pile. Once these sets are formed, they are now plotted on a map that relates the Coefficient of Variation (the *relative* standard deviation to whatever is the independent

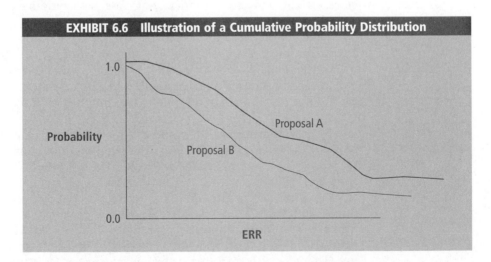

EXHIBIT 6.6   Illustration of a Cumulative Probability Distribution

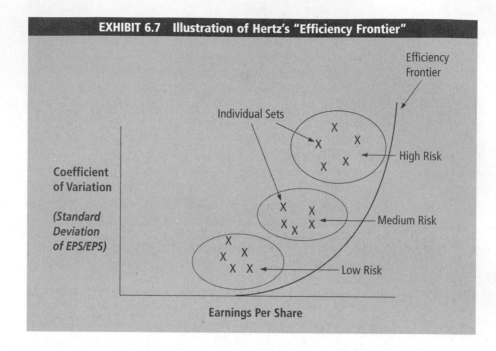

EXHIBIT 6.7   Illustration of Hertz's "Efficiency Frontier"

variable) to expected Earnings Per Share. In this case, the risk coefficient, called the Coefficient of Variation is: Standard Deviation of EPS/Earnings Per Share.

THE THIRD STAGE

In Exhibit 6.7, there are shown sets of low-risk, medium-risk, and high-risk proposals. The only set that should be chosen in each grouping is the set that lies closest to the "efficiency frontier." Any other set would have more risk or less earnings per share.

What's wrong with this approach? By placing the proposals in individual piles according to their risk (of getting their rate of return), you are denying the Markowitz portfolio effect that comes with considering *all proposals in a set*. This is a denial of the idea behind covariance and with reference to the entrepreneurial multiple discriminant model it is a denial of the Coefficient of Diffusion.

> **By accepting *any* and *all* proposals in a set, it may be possible to get a better return with less risk of getting that return than if proposals were screened for risk first.**

This is the reason that I do not use the concept of cost of capital. In conventional models, if a proposal does not have a return equal to or greater than the firm's cost of capital—however measured—it is rejected. But in the Entrepreneurial Capital Budgeting model, a proposal may be accepted because it has a time shape of cash flows that is beneficial to a set, or it may have unusually good earnings, or, by inclusion, the overall Coefficient of Diffusion might become acceptable where it otherwise would not be—*even if it had an ERR less than the cost of capital.*

WESTON'S CAPM MODEL

Among many financial economists there is a feeling that "financial laws"—that is, principles—that are valid in the investments field are equally valid in any other field of finance, such as corporate finance. When the Capital Asset Pricing Model came onto the screen, a prominent finance professor, J. Fred Weston, tried to show how the CAPM could be used in capital budgeting. This model is a one-stage model.[▲]

The central idea behind the model is this: If the ERR for a proposal is equal or greater than the required rate of return (RRR) for that proposal, then the proposal should be accepted. The trick is how to get the ERR and the RRR. To get the ERR you make four forecasts of the proposal. Then, he says, you ask the economics department of the firm to determine the probability of the four versions (or scenarios). If you then take the IRR for each version and multiply by the probability of achieving that version and then adding the products you get the ERR for the proposal.

The RRR is determined from using the CAPM:

$$E(R_j) = R_f + [E(R_m) - R_f]\beta_i$$

Where $E(R_j)$ is the required expected return on a security or real investment[▲▲] and R_f is a risk-free interest rate. $E(R_m)$ is the expected return on a broad-based market index (a portfolio of securities or real assets.) Presumably, this "market index" is the Standard and Poor's 500 Index. The β_i is a measure of the volatility of the individual security relative to market returns. β_i is measured by the ratio of the covariance of the returns of the individual security with the market returns divided by the variance of market returns.

Thus:

$$\beta_i = \frac{Cov_{i,m}}{Var_m}$$

The effect of this model may be shown graphically in Exhibit 6.8. Weston has a rather ingenious way of deriving the covariance of the proposal to the market index[▲▲▲] but this means that if the proposal is a new conveyor system, for example, then the variance of this proposal would be compared to the

---

[▲] J. Fred Weston, "Investment Decisions Using the Capital Asset Model," *Financial Management* Spring 1973, 25–33.

[▲▲] *Ibid.* p. 25.

[▲▲▲] See the paper for details of the calculation.

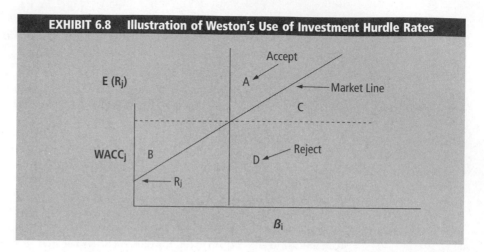

EXHIBIT 6.8   Illustration of Weston's Use of Investment Hurdle Rates

variance of, for instance, the Standard and Poor's Index. This seems bizarre to me, but this is not what I think is wrong with this model. In this depiction, Proposal A would be acceptable both because it has a better return than required from its β, and because it has a return better than its WACC. But if you use the firm's Weighted Average Cost of Capital, B would not be chosen. It would be chosen if you use the "Market Line." C would not be chosen because it has a lower rate of return than dictated by its β and D would be rejected because it fails on *both* criteria.

> By screening individual proposals for risk, however, you are denying the
> idea expressed in the Coefficient of Diffusion—and, of course, *covariance*
> which is the basis of the Coefficient of Diffusion.

Proposals B, C, and D might be perfectly acceptable if taken in a set, especially if more than one factor is used as a discriminant. In short, like Hertz's model, this model also fails to take account of the *portfolio effect*.

7

Capital Structure
and Leverage

Most textbooks treat the subject of financial leverage (also known as trading on the equity, because return on borrowed money exceeds costs) under the title of "Theory of the Capital Structure" or some such term. The chapter title was chosen to include the topic of financial leverage in the same chapter as operating leverage because they both have a similar effect on the firm's Income Statement. This is not to say that they themselves are similar.

It has sometimes been said that you grow a company on its equity. This means that in order to grow, a company has to have sufficient equity to support the debt that comes before it on the Balance Sheet. Taking on debt and contracts that resemble debt, such as lease contracts, is usually associated with, and sometimes needed for, the growth of a company. Internal growth through capital budgeting was discussed in Chapters 5 and 6. In this chapter we discuss the rationale for how much debt—or fixed charges—a firm can have relative to its equity (and cash flow). In short, we are discussing the company's Debt/Equity (D/E) ratio.

WHAT IS LEVERAGE?

Whenever a fixed charge is introduced into an Income Statement, **leverage** results. Leverage means that there will be a *more than proportional change* in the Net

Income (Loss) for a given change in Sales. For example, if Sales increase 10 percent, Net Income will increase *more* than 10 percent. And the greater the leverage, the greater the **magnification** of the change.

There are essentially two types of leverage that a firm may employ: *financial* and *operating*. Financial leverage results from the inclusion of debt in the firm's capital structure with its resulting interest charge. Operating leverage results from a number of things—the fixed costs a company bears—and the principal one is usually assumed to be the Depreciation charge on the firm's equipment and/or building. For some businesses, *rent* might be the surrogate for depreciation on a building. The more expensive or elaborate the building, or the more equipment the firm has, the more depreciation it has and the more leverage it will have in its Income Statement. In this chapter we will discuss both types of leverage, dealing with financial leverage first.

FINANCIAL LEVERAGE

To repeat, financial leverage involves the inclusion of debt or borrowed funds in a company's capital structure.

How much debt should a firm have? The answers to this age-old question will usually fall into three general types of explanations:

- The traditional approach

- The newer theoretical approach as extolled by Modigliani and Miller

- A cash flow approach

We will explore each of these approaches.

THE TRADITIONAL APPROACH

Before the turn of the twentieth century, the usual approach to determining a firm's capital structure—how much debt it could have—was derived from a model of **Earnings Coverage** or, as it is usually known, **Times Interest Earned.** This is defined as:

$$\text{Times Interest Earned} = \frac{\text{Earnings Before Interest and Taxes}}{\text{Interest}} = \frac{\text{EBIT}}{\text{INTEREST}}$$

Presumably, if the ratio is greater than 1/1, the firm could pay its interest and thus the debt would be secure. The higher the ratio, the safer the debt—which in those days was probably bonds. And since industries differ in their apparent risk, there developed various heuristics that analysts had for the Debt/ Equity ratios of various industries.▲

Before 1929, most bonds were simply interest-only bonds, meaning that no **sinking fund** was required. As we have learned, this is a fund into which the firm must put actual cash or the bond itself, in order to repay the debt at maturity. Since most of the firms that issued bonds before 1929 were mature, large firms, EBIT was a rather good estimate of the cash available to service debt—as was pointed out in Chapter 4. But after the Crash of '29, the interest-only bonds that were prevalent before the Great Depression began to be replaced by bonds that did require a sinking fund so that money would be accumulated in order to repay the bond when it became due. (Similarly, bank loans for all sorts of things, e.g., a home loan or a loan to buy a farm, were simply "interest-only" before the Crash of '29, but when homeowners and farm owners showed up at their banks and admitted that they did not have the money to repay the loan, *amortization* of principal was introduced and the loans became what we know today.) This meant that a firm could be thrown into bankruptcy if it did not make its periodic interest payment and/or its required sinking fund payment. This required some new sort of ratio for analyzing the safety of bonds, and the new ratio was called **Times Burden Earned**. This ratio was defined as:

$$\frac{\text{Times}}{\text{Burden Earned}} = \frac{\text{Earnings Before Interest and Taxes}}{\text{Interest Plus [Required Sinking Fund Payment/1} - \text{Tax]}}$$

In the 1950s, the concept of Accelerated Depreciation was introduced (see page 59). This meant that earnings, as they were traditionally thought of, were now not quite the same, because of this increase in depreciation that is deducted before net earnings. In an effort to rationalize *Price/Earnings* multiples that were considered high by Great Depression standards—which many people were still applying in the mid-1950s—the concept of Cash Flow was introduced. This was

▲ Graham and Dodd (and Cottle), in the last edition (1962) of their hugely successful book on Security Analysis, originally written in 1934, even stated what the Earnings Coverage should be for three industries:

Type	Before Taxes	After Taxes
Public Utilities	4X	2.4X
Railroads	5X	2.9X
Industrials	7X	3.8X

In the 1988 edition, authored by Sidney Cottle, Roger Murray, and Frank Block, this listing was dropped in favor of Z scores and Zeta ratings. It was interesting that Graham and Dodd in the earlier editions did not give any empirical justification for these coverage ratios; they merely said that they "recommend" them.

defined at the time, and still is for many people, as **Net Income Plus Depreciation**. Taking this concept and applying it to the concept of Times Interest Earned
or Times Burden Earned was accomplished by altering the numerator. To EBIT
was added *D*, for Depreciation. Thus EBIT became EBITD, and in more recent
times, with the requirement that a company write off goodwill, *A* (for Amortization) was added. This made it EBITDA. But if you were going to alter the numerator, why not do something to the denominator to make it more realistic?
Since most firms have to spend some of their Depreciation money for Capital
Expenditures, why not add Capital Expenditures to the denominator? The ratio
would then look like this:

$$\text{Times Debt Charges Earned} = \frac{\text{EBITDA}}{\text{Interest Plus Sinking Fund Payments Plus Capital Expenditures}}$$

And undoubtedly there are other variations on this familiar ratio.

Note the assumption that there is cash in earnings. This matter was dealt
with extensively in Chapter 4, so there is no need to repeat the discussion here.
The important thing to take note of at this time, however, is that this ratio,
Times Interest Earned, has been around for a long time and to this day still has
significance for some people—perhaps your banker! While we now know that
there is cash in Net Income or EBIT *only* under certain circumstances (a steady
sales scenario) this ratio should be used with care. But it would be foolish to disregard it because we "know better now." If people think it is important, then it
must be important, in a manner of speaking.

THE DEBT/EQUITY RATIO AND
THE MODIGLIANI AND MILLER APPROACH

As an apparent indication of financial health, every ratio pales in comparison to
the Debt/Equity ratio, defined usually as:

$$\text{Debt/Equity Ratio} = \frac{\text{Total Debt}}{\text{Equity}}$$

This ratio can also be defined so that the numerator includes only the firm's
long-term debt. While this may be the more common practice in security analysis, banks generally include *all* debt in the numerator. This concept is also
shown sometimes with *Total Liabilities and Capital* in the denominator instead
of just Equity.

Banks generally have had limits on the amount of debt a customer business
firm can have. (Currently, some of the more progressive banks have abandoned
their strict limit on Debt/Equity ratios and instead are going to the approach
that will be advocated in this chapter—a cash flow approach; and interestingly
enough, when competing with other banks for a particularly attractive loan, the

bank may only look to the firm's ability to *pay interest!*) With middle-market firms, 4/1 seems to be a common—but not the only—limit. This means that if a customer exceeds this (arbitrary) limit, the bank will notify the firm that it is over the bank's Debt/Equity limit and, if the firm does not bring the debt down to within the acceptable limit, then the bank will proceed to take more drastic measures to ensure compliance. If the firm still does not comply, the bank will, in all likelihood, ask the firm to find another bank. The reason banks get so upset with customers exceeding the bank's Debt/Equity limit is that when loans to customers exceed the stated limit, the bank's auditors will **classify the loan**, which means that the bank will have to create a reserve for the amount of the loan and deduct this amount from its capital section. This is cause for alarm to banks, since they have relatively little capital to support their liabilities, sometimes only 5 percent of total assets; if a customer had as little capital as the bank has, the bank would throw the customer out without a second thought.

An interesting aspect of this Debt/Equity limit for banks is the fact that bankers may be reluctant to tell the customer what to do about their violation of the bank's Debt/Equity limit. For example, in Chapter 3, we saw that if the firm would get the debt holder to subordinate the debt to the bank—either with specific subordination or general subordination—then the bank can count this debt as *de facto* Equity and reduce the Debt/Equity ratio, perhaps significantly. The reason most bankers are so reluctant to suggest that a firm do anything with their debt is the fear of being sued for interfering with the operation of the firm, especially if the customer firm subsequently defaults on the loan. So instead of pointing out how the firm might solve their dilemma, the bank takes a rather mute position and just says "Too much!"

When Franco Modigliani and Merton Miller wrote their seminal paper on corporate finance in 1958, they ushered in a new wave of thinking about the firm's capital structure.▲ Subsequent papers tried to tweak the theory or were written to respond to papers critical of their theory.▲▲

In the simplest possible terms, Modigliani and Miller (M & M) stated that the value of a firm, V, $= D + S$, where $D =$ the market value of the firm's debt and $S =$ the market value of the firm's stock. If the firm issues more debt—and thus increases its risk—the market value of the stock will decrease. Thus even if D goes up substantially, V will tend to stay steady because of the offsetting effects of S. Thus, the firm's capital structure will not really affect the firm's market value. *In short, it does not matter what Debt/Equity ratio the firm has.* Richard Roll, among others, pointed out that M & M were forgetting about taxes and that if they included taxes, their conclusions would have to be changed. Nevertheless,

▲ F. Modigliani and M.H. Miller, "The Cost of Capital, Corporate Finance and the Theory of Investment," *American Economic Review* June 1958, 261–97.

▲▲ See F. Modigliani and M.H. Miller, "Corporate Income Taxes and the Cost of Capital: A Correction," *American Economic Review* June 1958, 433–43. Also, M.H. Miller, "Debt and Taxes," *Journal of Finance* May 1977, 261–78.

these M & M papers ushered in a new era of thinking. Led by the Chicago School of thought, it is now assumed by many that there is a perfect capital market and that whatever the firm does is reflected in the market price of the firm's stock and that it is not possible to change this opinion by "cooking" the firm's books, as Ross and Westerfield noted.[▲] In a more recent paper, Stewart Myers joined in the parade and argued that there is an optimal structure, and that it is determined by observing the firm's Cost of Capital—essentially the firm's market price for its stock and the tax effects of leverage.[▲▲]

CASH FLOW APPROACH

Most simply expressed, the Cash Flow approach to the capital structure of a firm is *a firm can have only as much debt as it can support.* This statement implies that there is a way to measure the firm's ability to support debt. There is, and it's called NOCF". It also implies that the terms of the debt are known. To understand what is meant by this statement, it is necessary to discuss the **heterogeneity of debt**.

HETEROGENEITY OF DEBT

Debt as we now know it is not homogeneous; it is heterogeneous. This means that all debt does not have the same terms and conditions; interest rates *differ,* sometimes materially, and the term of the loan may differ also materially, with differing payoff periods. This is what makes the use of the Debt/Equity ratio so questionable.

Before the turn of the twentieth century, virtually all debt was of the same type—interest only—and the range of interest rates, especially for publicly traded bonds, was not particularly significant. In short, debt was reasonably *homogeneous.* It is doubtful that the term "amortization of principal" was ever used before World War II, or at least the Great Depression. Certainly, term loans were unknown. When corporations borrowed from lenders under bonded indebtedness, there was seldom, if ever, any *contractual* requirement that the firm meet sinking fund payments. But following the Depression, required sinking funds became the standard, at least for developing firms—and for the past 40 or 50 years, finance companies have been doing substantial business with developing firms. This meant the interest rates on loans to developing firms could *range* from prime (4 to 6 to 8 percent, for example) to 20 or 30 percent *routinely.* Factoring Accounts Receivable might even carry interest rates as high as 60 percent! And practically all debt required some sort of repayment. So debt no longer qualifies as being homogeneous. And yet we still point to the firm's Debt/Equity ratio as though debt were homogeneous.

[▲] Stephen Ross and Randolph Westerfield, *Corporate Finance.* Times Mirror/Mosby College Publishing, 1988, 299.

[▲▲] Stewart C. Myers, "The Search for Optimal Structure," *Midland Corporate Finance Journal 1*, no. 1 (Spring 1983), 6–16.

Net Operating Cash Flow Double Prime

In Chapter 4, we introduced the concept of NOCF. This is the amount of money a firm has to service its debt. NOCF" is defined as

$$\text{NOCF"} = \text{Net Operating Cash Flow} - {}_{\text{Nec}}\text{Discretionary}$$

"Nec Discretionary," meaning "necessary discretionary," is defined as the *minimum amount management desires to have for discretionary expenditures in a future year*—a purely subjective concept. Another way of defining this is to say: How much does management want to have for discretionary expenditures—capital expenditures and/or bonuses—in a really bad year? The more "Nec Discretionary" there is, the less money will be left for debt service, and vice versa. In doing the pro-forma financial projections for a leveraged buyout, for example, you may want to make "Nec Discretionary" equal zero if you feel that the company has enough equipment to last the next, say, 5 years. If anything adverse happens, you must have enough debt capacity remaining to borrow what is needed, assuming that this is not very much.

Using this model, it is now possible to illustrate the heterogeneity of debt and how this is reflected in the differing amounts of debt that a firm can service, given the terms of the debt. The maximum amount of debt a firm can service may thus be shown by the following amounts of debt for a *constant* amount of NOCF":

$$\text{Maximum amount of debt} = \text{NOCF"} / I + SF$$

I = the interest rate on the loan and SF = the required sinking fund amount expressed as a percentage of the principal. (This should be thought of as only the first approximation of the "amount of debt a firm can service," because once some principal has been paid, the interest payments may reduce.) To illustrate this, consider the following situations in which NOCF" is assumed to be a constant amount of $1,000,000 with differing amounts for interest and sinking fund payments (expressed as a percentage of principal). See Exhibit 7.1.

From the exhibit it can be seen that $1,000,000 of NOCF" can support four markedly different amounts of debt with four different terms on the debt. At the top, the firm could support $10 million in debt *if* the debt were interest only. At the other extreme, if the firm had a 3-year fully amortized term loan at 12 percent interest, it could only support $2,857,142. Now consider what conclusions

---

EXHIBIT 7.1   Illustration of Four Different Amounts of Debt That Can Be Serviced with the Same Amount of NOCF"

(1) $1,000,000 / .10 = $10,000,000
(2) $1,000,000 / .15 = $6,666,666
(3) $1,000,000 / .10 + .15 = $4,000,000
(4) $1,000,000 / .12 + .33 = $2,857,142

one might make if one only looked at this firm's Debt/Equity ratio. Assuming the firm had $1 million in equity, in situation (1), it would have a horrendous ratio of 10/1. In situation (2), the Debt/Equity ratio comes down to 6.6/1. In situation (3), the ratio comes down even more to 4/1, and in situation (4), the ratio is "only" 2.85/1. Yet in each instance the firm is having the same amount of trouble *servicing* the debt! Granted, in situation (1) the loan is an interest-only loan, and in the last instance (4) the loan is fully amortized, but if you are only looking at the firm's Debt/Equity ratio you would conclude that the firm was *overly* leveraged in situation (1) and very reasonably leveraged in situation (4). So much for the invincibility of the Debt/Equity ratio.

DEBT SERVICING CAPACITY THROUGH SIMULATION

Using the same approach that was utilized in the discussion of cash flow in Chapter 4, we may see what might happen in three different scenarios (steady sales, growth, and recession). See Exhibits 7.2 through 7.4.

In the "Steady Sales" scenario, NOCF" seems to be more than adequate to service the debt represented by the Priority Outflows shown for *this scenario*. If this firm were to embark on an expansion strategy, however, this cash sufficiency might turn into a serious *cash insufficiency* as Exhibit 7.3 shows. The need for working capital when the firm is in a growth mode severely restricts NOCF"—so much so that it might cause NOCF" to fall *below* Priority Outflows which, of course, causes the cash balance to fall. Whether there is enough cash to sustain this drain is moot; if the company has enough cash it is safe, but if it does not, then this firm will have a major cash insufficiency.

The usual, intuitive, way to measure debt tolerance is to observe the firm during a recession. Exhibit 7.4 shows what might happen to this firm during a recession. NOCF" drops and during the period it is below Priority Outflows the cash balance will decrease. But the amount of the decrease—the total dollar amount that the cash balance will shrink—may be tolerable, if the firm has a sufficient cash balance. On the other hand, it is conceivable that the amount of cash decrease would be sufficient to seriously impair the firm's cash position—and of course its ability to grow, or survive.

Note also that if NOCF" had been *closer* to Priority Outflows before the recession started, then the duration of decrease and the amount of the cash insufficiency would have been greater. Conversely, if NOCF" had been greater, or if Priority Outflows had been less, this company would have come through the recession in fine shape, financially speaking. Indeed, in Chapter 4, it was shown how it might be possible for a firm to come through a recession with more cash than it had at the start of the recession.

So while it is intuitive to worry about recessions for firms with financial leverage, the greater threat might be a growth scenario in which the firm grows too fast for it own good, cash flow–wise. Of course, this might be thought of as a "good" problem, meaning one that might be solved without disastrous consequences.

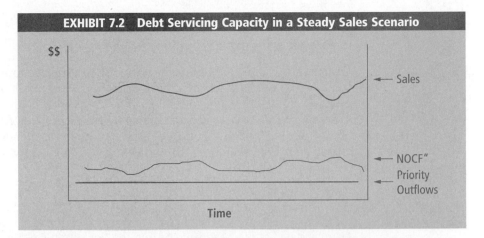

EXHIBIT 7.2 Debt Servicing Capacity in a Steady Sales Scenario

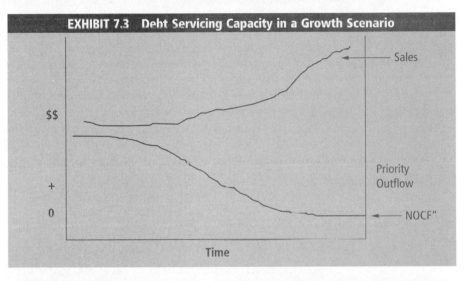

EXHIBIT 7.3 Debt Servicing Capacity in a Growth Scenario

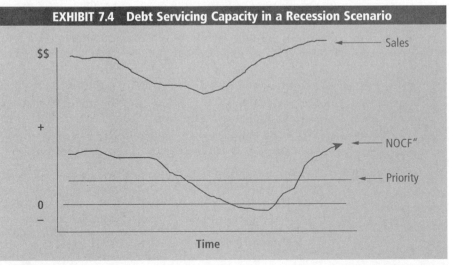

EXHIBIT 7.4 Debt Servicing Capacity in a Recession Scenario

IS THERE AN OPTIMAL CAPITAL STRUCTURE?

To answer this question, it appears that one would have to ask "under which scenario?" Clearly, under the growth scenario, the optimal amount of debt is probably *no debt*. It really could not service any debt.▲ With the recession scenario, one would have to postulate some degree of recession for a given amount of NOCF" and Priority Outflows. Presumably, if NOCF" does not go *below* Priority Outflows, then the firm would survive. But is this what one would call optimal?

OPERATING LEVERAGE

As mentioned at the beginning of this chapter, *operating leverage* includes such things as depreciation charges and rent, or any expense that is essentially *fixed*. True, because depreciation expense is not a cash charge, it is, in fact, quite different from financial leverage (an interest payment and/or a principal payment). But from an Income Statement point of view, interest and depreciation are indistinguishable; they *both can cause a magnification in the change in earnings* for a given change in sales. Since principal payments do not affect the Income Statement, there is no effect on earnings (loss).

The same questions that might be asked about financial leverage might also be asked about operating leverage. *Is there an optimal amount of operating leverage?* Or total leverage? To be quite accurate here, should one couch this question with regard to an Income Statement or a Cash Flow Statement? To approach an answer to this query, it may be useful to borrow some techniques from the literature on **Cost-Volume-Profit Analysis.**

TRADITIONAL COST-VOLUME-PROFIT ANALYSIS

Under traditional cost-volume-profit analysis, some heroic assumptions are made—for example that fixed costs are really fixed. From an operating point of view, some things that we think of as "fixed" might, in fact might not be so fixed. For example, rent is usually thought of as fixed, but the assumption in this type of traditional analysis is that the fixed charge is fixed over the *entire range* of sales assumptions. As a matter of fact, many a developing firm, faced with serious shortages of sales or just cash, might not pay their rent—even for a rather prolonged period of time, say 6 months. Under some circumstances, the landlord may simply forgive the business the accrued rent, realizing that by so doing the landlord retains a client. But with this caveat in mind, the traditional cost-volume-breakeven can be charted as shown in Exhibit 7.5.

▲ In Stewart Myers's paper, *ibid.*, he suggests that rapidly growing firms do not have very much debt. Of course they do not have very much debt; they cannot service much debt, if at all. If Myers had couched his approach to a firm's "optimal" capital structure in terms of a firm's ability to service its debt with cash flow, he could have explained this observation more clearly.

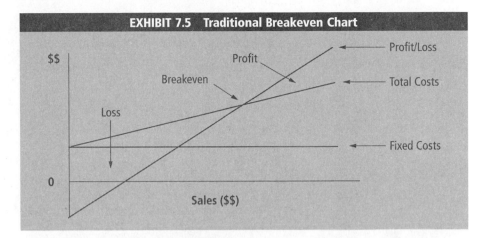

EXHIBIT 7.5   Traditional Breakeven Chart

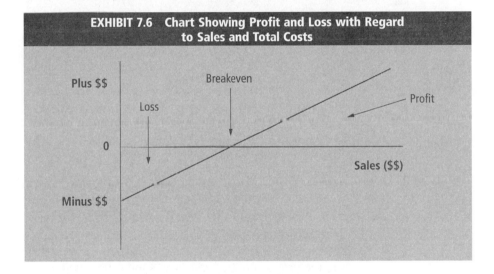

EXHIBIT 7.6   Chart Showing Profit and Loss with Regard to Sales and Total Costs

The chart shows at what level of sales the firm's breakeven occurs. Beyond that point, the firm shows profits and below that point losses. If we were to take the Total Costs line, and lay it horizontally, and the Sales line as it is, we have the chart shown in Exhibit 7.6.

For any given level of sales, shown on the horizontal line, the firm's profit or loss may be shown—given the firm's *fixed costs.* If the firm's fixed costs were to increase, that line, which we shall now call the "Profit/Loss" line, will *shift to the right* as shown in Exhibit 7.7.

In this chart the effect of increasing the firm's fixed charges (for example, interest or depreciation) may be seen, as can the effect of increasing the firm's variable costs (for example, an increase in labor rates). Because of the assumptions made, the increase in the fixed charges pushes out the firm's

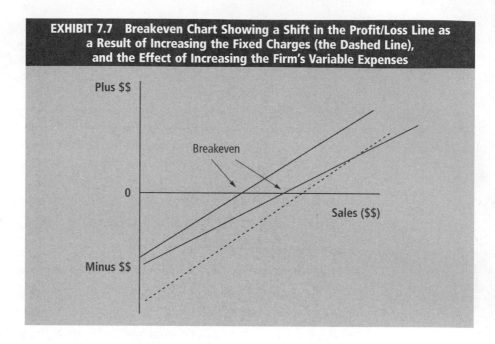

EXHIBIT 7.7   Breakeven Chart Showing a Shift in the Profit/Loss Line as a Result of Increasing the Fixed Charges (the Dashed Line), and the Effect of Increasing the Firm's Variable Expenses

breakeven point farther than an increase in the firm's variable costs—but this is only because of the assumptions made. One cannot conclude that this would be the case for all changes in fixed and variable costs. With an increase in variable costs, the breakeven point is increased—but at zero output, the loss is not increased.

CERTAIN SALES VS. PROBABILISTIC SALES

If sales were certain for a firm, it would have no problem choosing the amount of leverage to employ. As long as the "certain" sales were above the breakeven point, the firm could service its debt (and otherwise cover its fixed costs). Then, by varying the amount of leverage—the "Profit/Loss" line—up or down, it could find the profit amount for the chosen sales level that it wanted, presumably, the highest profit.

But the world is not made that way. Firms face a probabilistic, or uncertain, density function of sales. If—even in a rough sort of way—management could look to the future and define the probability density function that it is going to assume, it could materially improve its decision making with regard to the amount of leverage it undertakes. This will be shown in the Exhibit 7.8, where the area under the curve represents approximately 100 percent of the possible outcomes of sales.

Exhibit 7.8 shows that a firm can reasonably expect to service its debt for any range of sales assumed by the probability density function shown. Note that there is not even a small chance that the sales level would result in a loss. This is so because no part of the tail of the density function extends on the left *below*

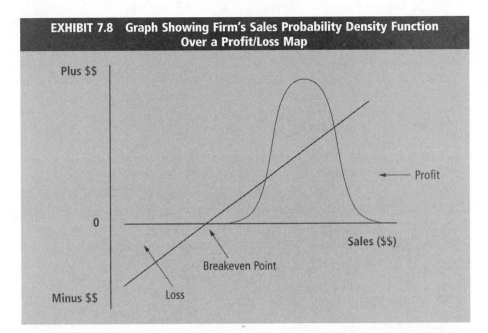

EXHIBIT 7.8   Graph Showing Firm's Sales Probability Density Function Over a Profit/Loss Map

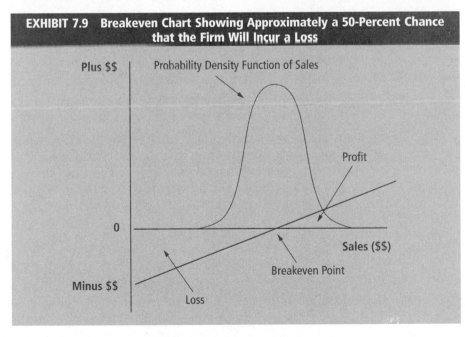

EXHIBIT 7.9   Breakeven Chart Showing Approximately a 50-Percent Chance that the Firm Will Incur a Loss

the breakeven point. (Statistically speaking this is a bit of an overstatement; there is *some* chance of not meeting the sales.)

In Exhibit 7.9 this is *not* the case. In this figure, it appears that the firm faces about a 50 percent chance that, because of the leverage assumed, it

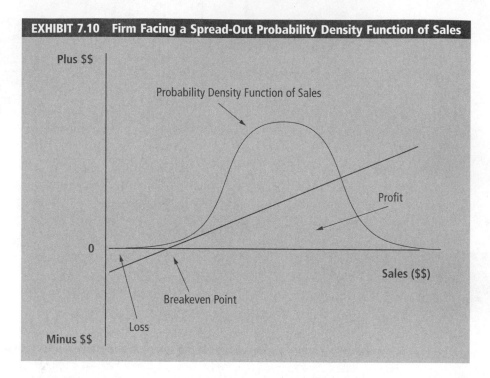

EXHIBIT 7.10   Firm Facing a Spread-Out Probability Density Function of Sales

would have a *loss* in the forecast period. If we try to generalize on this figure, it is apparent that:

> **The location and shape of the probability density of sales should be the *dominant factor* in determining the amount of leverage to undertake.**

Exhibit 7.10 shows a firm that faces a *very* uncertain future in sales; it faces a probability density function that is spread out considerably. In this example, the firm is facing a sales density function that is so spread out that the firm can incur only a small amount of leverage without facing a large chance of incurring a loss. With a real-growth, perhaps high-tech, company, this is precisely the situation the company faces. The probability density function of sales *is* spread out and quite uncertain. This is why strong growth companies must use leverage sparingly.

Conversely, if the firm were reasonably sure that sales would be within a rather narrow range, it could be more aggressive with its leverage. See Exhibit 7.11. An example of this was brought to our attention recently with a company whose income came from monthly fees for service—cable television.

In Exhibit 7.11, the firm can be quite aggressive incurring leverage as long as it keeps its breakeven point below the low end of the expected sales function and it does not greatly increase its variable expense. If it did increase its variable expense, the "Profit/Loss" line would rotate to the right as shown in an earlier figure. But by keeping its variable expense relatively low, this firm's "Profit/Loss" line rises quite steeply. As sales surpass the breakeven level, the profit rises quite sharply.

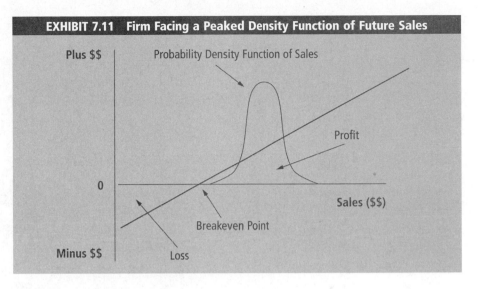

EXHIBIT 7.11   Firm Facing a Peaked Density Function of Future Sales

LEVERAGE AND CASH FLOW

Although the exhibits provided depict the situation that would occur with leverage and its effect on the Income Statement, for managers of developing firms the more important question becomes *How will leverage affect the firm's cash position?* Or, *Will we be able to service debt in the future?* The key to answering these questions again lies in the shape of the probability density function of sales the firm will be facing. To say that it is "impossible" to estimate the probability density of sales the firm faces is just not so. The density function may be extremely spread out, maybe even starting at zero, but because management feels uneasy in estimating the density function does not mean that it cannot be done. By not forecasting sales, the firm is actually "forecasting" sales; "no forecast" is actually a forecast.

The importance of the probability density function of sales was established in the preceding exhibits. When talking about whether or not the firm will have the cash to service its debt—which we have defined as NOCF"—all that is really needed is to utilize the same type of model and show the vertical axis as "Cash dollars" instead of profit dollars. In this way it can be seen that for any level of sales the firm's cash position will be positive or negative depending on the Priority Outflows that the firm undertakes—and, of course, what is happening to the NOCF" function. Doing this in a practical situation is not difficult at all. One only has to vary sales up or down using the Cash Flow Statement and observing the cash balance for each such level of sales. This is done graphically in Exhibit 7.12.

So, instead of showing the area between the "Profit/Loss" line as "Profit" or "Loss," the areas under the "Profit/Loss" line will now be labeled "Positive Cash" or "Negative Cash." What makes this depiction of the firm's cash balance a function of NOCF" is the fact that, unlike the Income Statement figure, NOCF" will

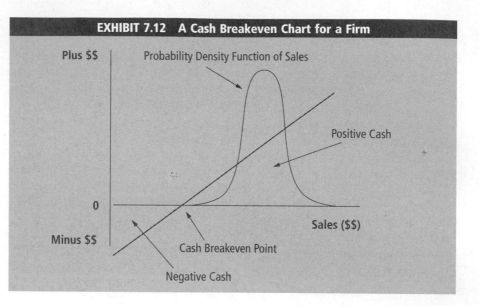

EXHIBIT 7.12   A Cash Breakeven Chart for a Firm

be affected by *both* variable costs *and working capital* items. In Exhibit 7.7, we noted that variable expenses have the effect of rotating the function to the right. Well, net increases to the three working capital items that are subsumed in NOCF" exacerbate the firm's cash position for a given amount of sales just the same way that increases in variable cost items do. This is shown in Exhibit 7.12.

Exhibit 7.12 shows the relationship between cash and the firm's probability density function *for a given amount of Priority Outflows*—financial leverage. Remember, increases in variable cost items and increases in net working capital items affect the function by rotating it outward (more variable costs and increases in working capital), or upward for less variable expense or lower increases in working capital. If the firm is facing a spread-out probability density function of expected sales, it would be taking a significant risk of a negative cash balance. If sales are expected to increase quite a bit, the probability density function of sales will shift outward as shown in the next exhibit.

In Exhibit 7.13, the firm is experiencing a dramatic shift in the probability density of expected sales from A to B (or, in plain English, it is expecting a sharp rise in sales). Instead of having a lot of cash, this figure shows the NOCF" line rotating significantly, so much so that there appears that there would be about a 50 percent chance of a cash insufficiency *at that advanced level of sales*. It wasn't an increase in variable costs that caused the problem; it was the increase in the **working capital** that caused the cash shortage.

NOCF" AND THE ASSUMED PROBABILITY DENSITY FUNCTION

In the NOCF" model we have been discussing, we must keep in mind that when calculating NOCF" one is necessarily assuming a particular probability density

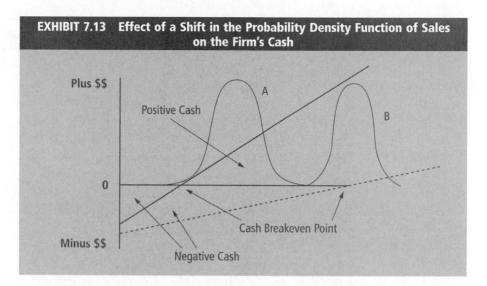

EXHIBIT 7.13   Effect of a Shift in the Probability Density Function of Sales on the Firm's Cash

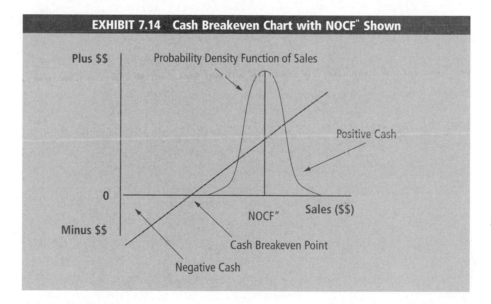

EXHIBIT 7.14   Cash Breakeven Chart with NOCF" Shown

function for sales. While the Cash Flow Statement might show that NOCF" exceeds Priority Outflows, saying that the firm can service its debt, when looked at probabilistically, the situation may be different. Let's take Exhibit 7.12 and show NOCF" on that graph.

In Exhibit 7.14, the mode of the distribution of sales is assumed to be NOCF". In this case, it is clear that there is no danger that the firm will not be able to service its debt. In fact, the cash breakeven point is about 4 or 5 standard

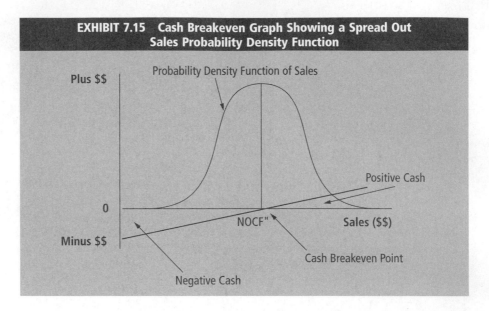

EXHIBIT 7.15   Cash Breakeven Graph Showing a Spread Out Sales Probability Density Function

deviations below the modal (and mean) sales assumption. But as discussed above in a prior section, if the probability density function of sales is spread out, indicating more uncertainty in the sales forecast, the firm would be quite foolish for undertaking the leverage indicated by the Cash breakeven line as Exhibit 7.15 shows.

SUMMARY

We began this chapter by noting that there are two types of leverage: Financial and Operating, and that they both affect the Income Statement in the same way. Leverage, meaning the inclusion of a fixed charge in the Income Statement, affects profitability in a way so as to *magnify* the change in profit (or loss) for a given change in sales. If sales are up a certain amount, then profit will be up more than proportionally; if sales are down, the decrease in profit will be more than proportional to the decrease in sales.

While most textbooks attempt to discuss the firm's capital structure, without regard to operating leverage, this chapter notes that since the two affect profit the same way, the two topics can be joined. From a practical, managerial point of view, if the firm incurs too much rent, for example, this may have the same effect on the firm's Income Statement as too much interest on debt. (Remember, there is no mention of debt repayment on an Income Statement.)

The more important question for the management of a developing firm is whether it can service the amount of debt—and other fixed charges—for the expected probability density function of sales that it is facing. When a firm is expecting great disparity in its potential sales it would be well advised to incur relatively low debt and possibly limit other fixed charges such as rent. Conversely, if the firm feels quite confident that it is facing a rather peaked density function of sales, and that this function is centered at a relatively high amount of sales, it can

be more aggressive in incurring debt (Priority Outflows), and other fixed charges.

As to whether or not there is an optimal capital structure, the discussion raised the question, optimal to what? In a steady sales scenario, the firm may be able to service an amount of debt that would not be possible in, for example, a growth scenario. And when discussing capital structure this implies discussion of the firm's Debt/Equity ratio.

It was mentioned that Debt/Equity ratios may be quite misleading today. Debt, it was pointed out, is *heterogeneous and not homogenous* as assumed in a Debt/Equity ratio. Debt may have quite different interest payments and widely different payment schedules, all of which are assumed in the Priority Outflows section of the Cash Flow Statement, if not the Income Statement. And certainly not in the Balance Sheet from which the Debt/Equity is constructed.

Finally, utilizing the model employed in Cost-Volume-Profit analysis, it was shown that when the firm's management is contemplating incurring debt—or fixed charges, in general—it would do well to construct a "Cash Breakeven" chart, such as is shown in Exhibits 7.12 to 7.15, and see what chance it is taking of not being able to service its debt. Very uncertain sales forecasts call for very little debt; with greater confidence in a relatively high sales forecast, the firm can be more aggressive in incurring debt—and/or fixed charges.

QUESTIONS FOR DISCUSSION

1. Suppose you were consulting for an emerging company and the question came up as to how much debt this company could have. How would you go about answering this question? What plan for action would you recommend?

2. Are banks acting "irrationally" by placing a lot of emphasis on the "Times Interest Earned" calculation on the debt a company has outstanding with the bank? Explain your reasoning. As CEO, how would you respond to the knowledge that the bank uses this "tried-and-true" method of evaluating bank loans?

3. Discuss Modigliani and Miller's approach to how much debt a company can have on its Balance Sheet. Is this approach helpful for our type of emerging and developing firms? Would this approach be helpful for very large, publicly traded companies? Would it be useful for privately owned companies? Or small, emerging, publicly owned companies?

7

CHAPTER REVIEW

Part 3

Financing Tools

Chapter 8: Raising Funds Externally: An Overview of Investment Banking

Chapter 9: Long-Term Financing: Sweetened Issues and Innovations

Chapter 10: Intermediate-Term Financing: Term Loans and Private Placements

Chapter 11: Short-Term Financing Including Equipment Financing

8

Raising Funds Externally: An Overview of Investment Banking

In this chapter and the three that follow, we discuss what I call financial tools: ways of securing financing outside the company. First we will review the legal framework for the sale of securities and the organization of the investment funding industry. This is intended as a guide for managers of emerging companies that need to raise capital externally.

PUBLIC OFFERINGS VS. PRIVATE OFFERINGS

When management is considering the raising of funds externally, a decision must be made as to whether or not the firm wishes to sell such securities to one or a limited number of parties, usually institutional investors—a process known as a **private offering**—or whether it wished to sell its securities to the public—a process known as **going public**. Let's explore the advantages and disadvantages of each, but first we will discuss the regulations related to the public and private sale of securities.

REGULATIONS ON SELLING SECURITIES

In the United States, in order to sell securities to the public, it is necessary to register the offering with the Securities and Exchange Commission for federal registration, and/or with the Department of Corporations (or some other such name) for the state(s) in which the securities are to be sold▲. This is a rather complicated process; to cover it completely would be well beyond the scope of this chapter. This chapter attempts to convey a general overview of the process of obtaining funds externally and the registration process normally undertaken to effect such a placement of securities necessary to obtain funds.

SEC VS. THE STATE CORPORATIONS COMMISSION

When Congress established the Securities and Exchange Commission (SEC) in 1933, it stipulated that the Commission's job was to ensure that there was full disclosure in the financial documents and operational information presented to the public. This registration statement, containing a document called a **Prospectus** which is circulated to the public, is examined by both accounting professionals and legal experts in the SEC. Presumably, if the filer were revealing everything, the buyer would be fully warned. This **Full Disclosure** dictum still exists today. Technically, the *quality* of the offering has nothing to do with whether or not the Commission approves the offering for sale to the public. It should be noted that there are different categories of "public" investor, as will be explained later in this chapter; "public" does not always mean the same thing in all situations.

If the offering appears to be too egregious, the Commission may take a considerable amount of time before it authorizes its release to the public—through the issuance of what are known as **deficiency letters**—but sooner or later, the offering will be permitted to reach the public. For example, when some bonds—now referred to as **junk bonds**—have been sold primarily to institutional lenders, the prospectus has stated explicitly that the company that was issuing the bonds could not service the interest required by the bond. As long as the issuing company *discloses* this fact, the Commission considers the offering as having complied with the (federal) law.

State law may emulate or differ materially from this Full Disclosure directive of the federal SEC. In California, for example, the State Department of Corporations was given the directive of "fairness." Were all parties to the transaction being "fair" (whatever that meant) to each other? For example, if two parties were forming a corporation to operate a gas filling station, the Department of Corporations would sit in judgment over the issue of whether these two parties were being fair to each other. That is, if one stockholder received more stock for a certain amount of money than the other stockholder received was that fair?

When a securities offering is registered with the SEC, state Corporation Commissions normally give the offering less scrutiny than if the offering were being offered exclusively in that state. But this does not mean that the state commission or department merely "rubber stamps" the SEC's approval. Listing with the New York Stock Exchange, the AMEX, or the NASDAQ allows the company to basically skip the state registration.

▲ An exception to this will be noted later when discussing listing on the New York Stock Exchange (NYSE) or NASDAQ.

When selling securities—stocks or bonds—in more than one state, approval must be obtained from the respective commission or department in *each and every* state. This means that a state commissioner might set restrictions on the offering that are unacceptable to the management of the issuing firm. For example, one state's Department of Corporations might attempt to restrict the amount of stock that the president of the company can sell in the offering, or the department may stipulate the time before which the president would be able to sell any of his or her stock. When these kind of restrictions are unacceptable to the management of the offering firm, it may elect to skip that state when the securities are sold. Naturally, if the state is important to the offering—such as New York, Texas, and California would be for most offerings—or because the company is domiciled in the state for which the department has unacceptable restrictions, then the company must attempt to work out a compromise or otherwise resolve the dispute with the Department of Corporations.

For the sale of securities in a single state, it is not necessary to register with the SEC, but this type of registration, known as an "Intra-State registration," can be an extraordinary problem. If any one of the stockholders were to sell his or her stock to a party in another state before a restriction period expires, the federal law would be violated. In one case stock was sold to a considerable number of physicians and dentists in California. The only way any stockholder could sell his or her stock was to call the corporate office and ask if they knew of anyone who wished to buy. Naturally, no respectable stock brokerage firm would want to get involved in an Intra-State registration.

In private placements of securities (usually stock) for a relatively small corporation—the kind of firm assumed in this book, where all the stockholders reside in the same state—registration of the securities is made with the Department of Corporations (or comparable department) and the securities are stamped with a statement that the securities may not be sold except under certain circumstances and/or with the prior approval of the Department of Corporations. Originally, a letter accompanied the securities to state that sale of the securities was restricted in some way, such as sale to another stockholder or with the approval of the Department of Corporations. The term used to refer to such restricted securities was **lettered stock**, a term that persists today even though a letter is no longer used to advise the holder of such securities that sale is restricted.▲ If the stockholder holds stock in a firm that is fully registered with the proper authorities, such as the SEC and the respective states, he or she may sell his or her shares only through the process specified in Rule 144 of the Securities Act of 1933, as amended. This is essentially what might be called a "dribble" rule. For example, if an individual sells his or her company for stock in a large publicly held corporation with millions of shares outstanding, then he or she may a sell a portion of the unregistered shares each month over a period of time, even if it is not registered.

▲ Interestingly enough, stock brokerage firms always have a few people who try to sell such restricted shares.

PRIVATE PLACEMENT

Perhaps the foremost advantage of a **private placement** is the speed with which this process may be completed. Typically, a firm may need only weeks or, more likely, only a month or two to complete the whole process and receive their money, as compared with several months minimum for an **initial public offering (IPO)**. This process is covered in more detail in Chapter 10.

This speed is not without its cost, however. Usually, a private placement will carry a higher interest rate, if the offering is debt, or a lower Price/Earnings ratio if the offering is stock. This is quite understandable as, by definition, there is no public market for the securities and, thus, there is less liquidity. Less liquidity means the offering is not as desirable as an offering of securities that could be sold on the open market at the election of the securities holder. Therefore, the higher price results.

While the firm will face higher interest costs or a lower P/E ratio, there will be a cost saving of another sort: the saving in the costs of registration and the commission paid to an underwriter for offering the securities to the public. These costs can be substantial, even for a rather small offering,▲ and can amount to hundreds of thousands of dollars for accounting, legal, and printing expenses attendant to the offering. True, there will be some costs incurred in a private placement, but these will be minor compared to a public registration, especially an IPO.

To the owners of middle-market firms that are not publicly held, the fact that the whole process of raising money through a private placement is *confidential* may be the most important criterion. Once the firm is public, life will never be the same for the principals of the company. The principals must be ever vigilant to make sure that nothing is said to anyone about the company's affairs which is not said to the whole market. There are strict federal and state laws that prohibit divulging so-called "insider" information.▲▲ Being public also exposes the directors and top management to a possible lawsuit in case anything is wrong with the original registration statement. Many firms, especially high-tech ones in recent years, get sued routinely by law firms whose specialty is such suits, for things such as not meeting financial forecasts. By doing a private placement, the firm largely avoids this legal exposure.

The preservation of the confidential nature of a private placement is not to be taken lightly. A company going public must divulge all sorts of information—such as officers' salaries—that are considered quite confidential when a firm is privately held. Perhaps of more pressing importance is the fact that profit margins have to be divulged; this is something many managements want to keep secret from the competition. Furthermore, management sometimes must

---

▲ Later an S-18 Registration will be discussed which is a registration for an offering under $7.5 million, a process that will save money in the registration process.

▲▲ In recent years this prohibition has been expanded to lower-ranking employees of the company, including secretaries.

submit to quite acrimonious questioning at the annual stockholders meeting. Having to report to someone may be a new—and an often undesirable—experience for entrepreneurial-owned firms.

Another advantage of a private placement if stock is involved is that the market may not be right for a public offering. By making a private placement with, for example, a venture capital group, the firm may sidestep an unattractive stock market. By so doing the firm is given some breathing room while waiting for a better market or, simply, for the firm to mature enough for a public offering.

PUBLIC OFFERINGS

For many owners of a privately owned firm, the ultimate goal is to create a firm that can go public one day. This opportunity to sell the company's stock to the public means for many the realization of a dream, a time when they get rich. Finally, the founders can get not only their investment back, but hopefully *many times* their original investment, and this for selling only a portion of the stock they own. When the firm is privately owned, there is no precise way to know what the firm's stock is worth; when the firm goes public, one can get instant quotes on the firm's stock price. The recent dot.com bubble was a classic example of taking a firm public and getting rich. Shortly after starting, a number of the dot.com firms went public at tremendous prices, not to mention an infinite P/E as there were no earnings. When this bubble burst, the whole process came back to earth, so to speak.

Another reason for going public is the fact that when the firm is privately owned, it is not possible for the owner(s) to borrow money on the stock. But once the firm is public, it may be possible for the owners to borrow from a bank with the stock as collateral.

If the management of the firm has any aspirations of growing the firm by acquisitions, it may be quite useful to have the firm's stock publicly owned. It is doubtful if the owner of a prospective target would welcome exchanging his or her stock for stock in a privately held firm—especially as a minority stockholder. So having a publicly traded stock is usually a prerequisite to acquiring other firms with stock.

If the firm is thinking of selling stock, a higher price can usually be gotten from selling the stock to the public than from selling a block of stock to an institutional investor through a private placement. Sometimes this is done as a "bridge" before a public offering—possibly a much larger offering—but the discount in price usually demanded by the investor of unregistered stock can be quite substantial. The institutional investor only has to ask what would happen if the firm didn't have the anticipated public offering.

The increased expense of making a public offering, *vis-à-vis* a private placement, has been mentioned as up-front costs. But there is another kind of expense incurred in going public: the cost of effecting the periodic reports that must be filed with the requisite government authorities, including the SEC. For even small firms, this can be a considerable expense in both time and per-

EXHIBIT 8.1 An Overview of Regulation D			
	TYPES OF EXEMPTION		
TERMS AND CONDITIONS	**RULE 504**	**RULE 505**	**RULE 506**
1 NATURE OF EXEMPTION PLACEMENT	SMALL OFFERINGS	SMALL OFFERINGS	PRIVATE
2 LIMITS ON SIZE	$1 MILLION	UP TO $5 MILLION	NONE
3 NUMBER AND TYPE OF INVESTORS	NO LIMITS ON NUMBER AND NO REQUIREMENT FOR TYPE	NO LIMIT ON NUMBER OF ACCREDITED; UP TO 35 UNACCREDITED; NO REQUIREMENTS FOR TYPE OF ACCREDITED.	NO LIMIT ON ACCREDITED; UP TO 35 UNACCREDITED; UNACCREDITED MUST BE SOPHISTICATED.

sonnel effort. These filings include the quarterly and annual reports as well as the incidental reports whenever something unusual happens. And these reports might have to be filed in each state in which the firm's offering is registered, not just the SEC.

Another obvious disadvantage of a public offering is that if the shares sold in a public stock offering are sufficient in number it could be that if one party bought these shares that party would control the company. In short, if a firm sells a majority of shares to the public, it may be subject to a raid and the former owners could lose control of the company. With a private placement this possibility is avoided.

REGISTRATION OF PRIVATE PLACEMENTS

If a firm elects to place its securities through a private placement offering, it is usually necessary to file with the SEC for what is known as a "Reg. D" exemption from full registration.▲ This allows the firm to cross state boundaries when placing the securities even though the placement is to one or only a few sources of financing. An abbreviated synopsis of the regulations is shown in Exhibit 8.1. (A fuller explanation is contained in the Appendix to this chapter.)

The term "accredited investors" is used in the exhibit to define a number of different types of investors, a partial listing of which includes institutional investors, tax-exempt organizations, executive officers and directors of the company, and wealthy individuals. The term "sophisticated investor" is also a technical term used in the document; basically it means an individual or party who is sufficiently wealthy to be able to afford experienced counsel when making financial decisions.

▲ This section is based largely on Jerry L. Arnold's article "Exempt offerings: going public privately," *Harvard Business Review* January–February 1985, Reprint number 85101. Exhibit 8.1 is reproduced from this article. Used by permission.

A word of caution about registering under Reg. D may be in order. Just because a firm registers for an exemption from registration does not mean that the firm can play loose with the rules. It is quite important for the firm to avoid breaching *any* of the rules that apply to a particular exemption (for example, advertising an offering when this is prohibited). (What does "advertising" mean? It could mean something much more subtle than running an advertisement in a paper. It may be a verbal form of advertising.) The reason for this attention to the rules is that if someone buys some of the securities and later feels that the investment is not what he or she thought it was, a lawyer could be retained; if the lawyer can find even one breach of the rules, the injured party may be able to sue or otherwise recover his or her investment.

PUBLIC REGISTRATION OF SECURITIES

There are a number of types of public registrations of securities, depending on the type of firm and/or the size of the issue. These options are denoted by the letter "S" (if domestic) followed by a numerical, for example, an S-1 offering. There are "S" registrations applying to such diverse situations as the registration of a bank or a savings and loan or a toll bridge or transactions such as the sale of the securities to an off-shore entity. For our purposes, there are really just two forms of registration of interest: the S-1 registration and the newer S-18 registration.

The S-1 Registration

The requirements for an S-1 registration may be summarized rather simply, although this should not be taken as being definitive. There is no dollar limit on the amount of the offering. The firm must register with the main office of the SEC in Washington, D.C. In the registration packet, which is a voluminous document containing such things as long-term contracts and details of the financial data, there must be contained 3 years of certified financial statements (not older than 90 days) using something called **S-X accounting** (as opposed to GAAP accounting).

Although there is no rule or law that dictates what accounting firm must certify the statements, most experienced underwriters handling an offering prefer to have a major accounting firm do the certification. For one thing, major firms are experienced in dealing with the SEC; for another, the accounting division of the SEC which reviews the registration statement will have confidence in a major firm. Furthermore, there is an implied threat that if the accounting firm were to make a serious mistake, the SEC accounting division could hold up subsequent filings for a considerable period of time.

The same thing applies to the law firm selected to do the legal work on a filing. If a major law firm is used, the SEC will have a great deal more confidence in the filing and the same latent threat is there for the law firms as for the accounting firms: Don't make a mistake, or the next group of offerings that come across the desk of the legal division's lawyers will undergo great scrutiny. Many offerings also have a prominent Washington-based law firm retained for the underwriting. If the offering is substantial, this may be money well spent! So, even though major accounting firms and major law firms are reasonably expensive—and one must realize that a lot of their fee goes toward the payment of liability insurance—they are really quite necessary for a sizable S-1 offering. Furthermore, in recent years, the major accounting firms, and apparently the major law firms, have been quite selective when accepting a new firm that wishes to apply for securities registration. The ZZZZ Best scandal in the 1980s did a lot to convince the accounting firms that they had better be extremely vigilant when agreeing to "certify" a firm's financial statements or they can be sued for hundreds of millions of dollars if fraud is later discovered.

The 3 years of certified financial statements may pose a problem for some firms. If the firm does not have 3 years of certified statements, what can it do? Well, for a price, an accounting firm can usually go back over the firm's books of record and *reconstruct* the data needed for a certification for each of those 3 years. Indeed, the price for this work may be substantial—huge might be a more appropriate description—but it can be done.

In order to save money, most developing firms do not have a major accounting firm prepare their financial statements. But some firms assume that sometime in the future they will need certified statements from a major accounting firm. For them the expense of hiring a major firm—even their so-called small-business practice—may seem high compared with the fees for a smaller, regional accounting firm. In this situation there is something a developing firm can do to accomplish its intention and save money as well. It can ask a major accounting firm to review the methods and paperwork generated by the regional accounting firm and issue, for a quite reasonable fee, what is called a "white paper" in which the major accounting firm says that if formal certified statements are needed in the future, they will step in and make such statements for a much more reasonable fee than if they had not observed the certification process of the regional accounting firm. Incidentally, the fact that most accountants train with a major accounting firm in order to qualify for their CPA status means that those accountants usually adopt the systems and working-paper procedures of their former employer. This means that that a major accounting firm who once employed the CPA would be a good accounting firm to ask to prepare this "white paper."

The S-18 Registration

Responding to the need to make access to the capital markets easier for smaller firms, the SEC introduced the S-18 registration procedure. In this registration process, only 2 years of certified financial statements are required—and, quite importantly, these statements only need to be certified using GAAP accounting procedures rather than S-X accounting (which is something only accountants experienced in filing with the SEC know). The company is then given a grace period in which to introduce S-X accounting. From a cost point of view, the S-18 registration is much less expensive in two ways: accounting fees and legal fees.

Furthermore, a firm may file the S-18 registration *regionally* rather than of necessity in Washington, D.C. What this means is that a regional accounting firm and a regional law firm can be employed instead of the major firm that is necessary for an S-1 registration. The SEC regional offices are instructed to assist these local or regional accounting or law firms should they have problems in completing the registration process. On the surface, this may not seem like an important advantage over the S-1, but there may be a difference of a total of several hundred thousand dollars in the combined fees charged by a smaller regional or local accounting or law firm. There is a *maximum dollar amount* that may be offered each year, however, of **$7.5 million**. (The S-18 Registration effectively replaces the old "short form" Reg. A registration that was capped at $1.5 million.)

Because of this dollar cap, many developing firms have decided, wisely, to avoid this "going public" route and do a private placement for the same or more money than permitted under this S-18.

Unless this maximum is raised substantially, this trend will likely continue.

SELECTING AN UNDERWRITER

Finding an underwriter, who is sometimes called an investment banker, for a public offering is usually not a problem: When a firm gets to such a size and maturity that management is thinking of going public, some appropriate underwriter has probably already made contact with the company to present its credentials. Hopefully the firm will have a choice between several underwriters and thus be better able to choose a firm that is right for them. By "right" we mean a firm that is neither too big for the aspiring firm nor too small, in terms of capital.

It is important for the aspiring firm to find an underwriter who will take an interest in the firm *after* the offering and not just during the romancing that goes on before the offering. It would be a mistake for a small firm, with, for instance, an offering of only about $10 million to sign on with one of the largest underwriters. That would be rather like a fly on an elephant's back. After the offering, it is important for the underwriter to **support** the stock in the market. If the firm is really small, compared to the underwriter, then the underwriter might well be too preoccupied with bigger deals or more important stocks, and not be able to "mother" a newly public stock.

Conversely, it is important for an underwriter to be financially viable enough to do the offering and to support the stock after the offering. By going too small, a firm may find that the underwriter *really* wants their business (a good sign), but if allowed to do the underwriting it may falter in their support of the stock. Or, even worse, the undercapitalized underwriter may bow out of the offering—at great expense to the aspiring firm—before the offering date.

It is traditional for the underwriter to support the stock price for a period of time following the offering. This is usually a month. During this period the underwriter will openly support the price by buying and, possibly, selling the stock. The buying action is to try to ensure that the stock price does not fall below the offering price during the support period. If the firm that is going public selects an underwriter who is financially weak, then it stands to reason that this underwriter will not be able to support the stock price in the event that there is selling pressure. This situation for the underwriter may come about because the underwriter is undercapitalized in general or it may come about because the underwriter had several unsuccessful offerings before it undertook the offering in question, by which time it simply ran out of ammunition.

There are other criteria as well. Until recently, who were the analysts for the prospective investment banking (IB) firm? This can be very important. With the current controversy over the role of analysts, however, this point may be moot in the future. Is this firm a boutique IB specializing in your type of company or industry? How does the IB propose selling your stock initially? Sometimes there are innovative marketing strategies that might set one IB firm ahead of the others vying for your business.

THE ORGANIZATION OF THE INVESTMENT BANKING INDUSTRY

The term "investment banking" is a curious one. The so-called investment bankers hope and pray that they are not "investing" in the firms they are underwriting *and* they certainly are not bankers in the "commercial banker" sense. But then they would not like to be called "New and used stock sellers." The more general term "investment banker" is much more flattering!

Classification by Size

The investment banking industry may be classified into various categories, depending on size, primarily. The major investment banking firms, called simply the "majors," consist of about twenty firms, mostly headquartered in New York. Of this number, there are a group of about five or six that are referred to as "bulge bracket" majors. Such names as Credit Suisse First Boston; Goldman, Sachs & Co.; Merrill Lynch; and Solomon Smith Barney are quite well known names in this grouping. Typically, these firms will only do substantial underwritings, for example, $50 million and up for firms with at least $1 million in after-tax earnings. Other major underwriters include such firms as A.G. Edwards; Bank of America Securities; Bear Stearns; Chase H & Q; CIBC World Markets; and First Union Securities.

Below the majors is what are called the "sub-majors." Some of the oldest and most respected names on Wall Street are represented in this group, including Allen & Co.; Needham & Co.; and Raymond James.

Below the sub-majors are the regional investment banking firms, of which there are many. Some of these are Adams, Harkness & Hill; Crowell Weedon;

and Seidler Companies. These firms will do underwritings that are too small for the majors and sub-majors, although there is some overlap with the sub-majors. To identify who these regional firms are, one only has to examine the front page of a prospectus or a "tombstone" ad▲ for an offering. There is a strict pecking order for the way the underwriters are listed. The group that subscribes to the largest number of shares, for example, 50,000 each, would be the majors, all listed alphabetically, then the next largest group of subscribers, for example 25,000 shares—and these will usually be the sub-majors and large regionals—and then, finally, the smallest group of underwriters who subscribe to only about 5,000 or 10,000 shares each. Sometimes, there may be only one or two underwriters. Also, If a small underwriter gets an offering that it feels is too big, it can bring in a larger "partner" who has the financial muscle to do the deal. Then the two underwriters will be listed beside each other with the larger of the two being listed in the left position.

Below the regionals, there are a group of underwriters who might be called "sub-regionals." These firms, some of which are quite old and well known locally, will usually be the firms that do the smaller S-1 offerings and, possibly, the S-18 offerings. In the selection of an underwriter it would be quite important to ascertain the experience of the underwriter in the particular industry and type of offering involved. These regional firms may be well known for some specialty, such as biotech companies or computer companies.▲▲ In other cases, the underwriter may offer a clever marketing plan which other underwriters do not offer. In one such case, a medical equipment leasing company with offices throughout the country wanted to go public. The underwriter offered to limit the sale of the share of stock to only medical customers of the underwriter and then only 200 shares to each buyer. In this way, the equipment leasing company could expect to attract new customers from among its list of stockholders.

Structure

Exhibit 8.2 is the organization chart of an investment banking firm; there are usually at least three divisions in a major investment banking firm. There may be additional departments, such as Consulting or Government Finance, in the United States and, possibly, a number more in other countries such as the United Kingdom.

The Retail/Institutional sales division is the one that has contact with the retail or institutional customer. (A few investment bankers deal only with institutional buyers or very wealthy individuals.) This "retail" business is the stock brokerage business that is familiar to anyone who purchases stocks through a non-online broker.

▲ So named because the ads are supposed to have no more spice than a "tombstone" has.
▲▲ For example, a number of underwriters in the San Francisco area with their close proximity to Silicon Valley. One such firm, Chase H & Q, has made so much money with computer and high-tech underwritings, that they are now considered a "major" in most offerings.

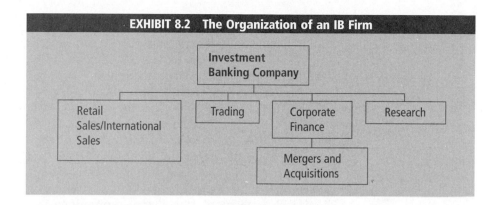

EXHIBIT 8.2   The Organization of an IB Firm

In the trading unit, the investment banker buys and sells securities and matches sale and buy orders for customers. If an investment banker takes a firm public it will usually "make a market" in that firm's stock for at least a month, and then may continue to trade in that firm's stock.

The third division shown in Exhibit 8.2 is Corporate Finance. It is this division with which the aspiring firm will deal when negotiating an underwriter agreement. A subset of this division may be the Mergers and Acquisitions division—the "shock troops" of the department that assist firms in buying another company or selling the firm. Not all IB firms have such departments, but the majors do and a large part of the firm's earnings each year come from this activity.

The Importance of Quality in the Underwriter

It is of the utmost importance to select an underwriter of the highest quality and reputation. There are more than enough underwriters of all descriptions out there in this cruel world, but the trick is to try to select an underwriter with impeccable credentials, not just the one who offers the highest price for the shares. If too high a price is received for the shares in an IPO, and there subsequently is a drop in price, this will result in a lot of very unhappy shareholders, something no intelligent management wants. It is important, therefore, to check on the reputation—and appropriateness—of the underwriter before signing up for its service. Be wary of the underwriter who attempts to "buy" a new offering by suggesting a too-high offering price.

In one instance, a firm was advised by a lawyer-turned-financial-advisor to "go public" with an unknown investment banker in New York even though the relatively small manufacturer was in Southern California. Just before the offering was to take place, the underwriter withdrew, leaving the manufacturer with several hundred thousand dollars worth of certified statements and legal documents it was unable to use.

In another instance, a particular company had a "Letter of Intent" from an investment banker who seemed impressive until someone knowledgeable about investment banking, and this IB in particular, commented "There is no way that this firm could do an offering this large."

THE LETTER OF COMMITMENT

Once the firm and the underwriter have reached an agreement on what is to be sold and the price range, if it is to be stock, the underwriter will prepare a **Letter of Commitment**, which sets forth what the underwriter proposes to do with the offering. Toward the end of this document is a clause that makes the name of this document seem particularly strange. Invariably, in the Letter of Commitment there is a clause that says something to the effect that if market conditions are not right, or for any other reason, the underwriter reserves the right to cancel the Letter of Commitment. This is called a **Market Out Clause**. What this means is that this Letter of Commitment is really a "Letter of *Non-Commitment.*"

Because it is apparent to all that market conditions may be such that the underwriter cannot go through with the public offering—for example, because the market crashed, as it did in 1987 or the spring of 2000—this clause is perfectly reasonable. But suppose the underwriter has had several unsuccessful offerings in a row, and because the underwriter had to commit so much of its capital to support these rather unsuccessful offerings, the underwriter may feel that he or she does not have the financial resources to do the upcoming stock offering. Here the *market* is not at fault; it is simply a problem peculiar to the underwriter. Or, for some other reason—such as the market for the firm's products has suddenly been clouded, or the underwriter discovers an adverse material fact that was not disclosed—the underwriter may decide to back out of the commitment. Where does this leave the company that is counting on this public offering for finance? Legally, the company would not have a very good complaint against the underwriter because the company agreed to the "market out clause" when it accepted the Letter of Commitment. True, backing out of on offering is quite unusual, and certainly not the norm, but the reason this much attention is being given to the possibility of an underwriter backing out of a deal and leaving the company, perhaps, in a precarious position is to alert the reader to this possibility and to reiterate the need for a firm to sign up with a very reputable underwriter. The reputation of the underwriter will have its effect on the company for a long time indeed.

FIRM COMMITMENT VS. BEST OFFERING

In a firm commitment, the underwriter states that it will purchase *all* of the securities and, in turn, it will resell the securities to its customers or to a syndicate of stockbrokers. This is the usual way of doing business today. But it wasn't always that way. Way back in the Great Depression, the stock market was so unstable that an underwriter could not take a chance on buying securities that it might not sell. So they used a form of a deal called a **best efforts** offering. In this arrangement, the underwriter says that it will attempt in all good faith to sell the securities in question, but that if it is unable to sell over some amount, such as 50 percent, it will return all the securities to the company and refund the money

An unusual example of an underwriter pulling a stock offering was reported in the *Wall Street Journal* on March 6, 1995, page A7C. In this story, the *WSJ* reported that the Palm Springs Golf Co. thought that they were a "public" company because they had an agreement with The Dillon-Gage Securities Inc. of Dallas, Texas for a $4 million stock offering. On Monday of the week in which the deal was supposed to close, the stock of the company started to trade on a "when issued basis," meaning that as soon as the deal closed and the shares were available, they would be delivered to the buyer. Instead the day the deal was supposed to close and the company would receive the check—money that the company was counting on to repay $2.7 million in debt and for money to expand its product line—the underwriter invoked its "Market out clause" and canceled the deal. The article says that the stock when first traded was at $12.50 but had declined during the week to $9.50. Presumably if the underwriter had much of the stock, it would have had a 24 percent loss. Possibly, the underwriter did not have the capital to "support" the stock. Reading this article makes one wonder why a company would want to go to a "stranger" as its investment banker.

paid for the securities. If the underwriter sold the agreed upon proportion of securities, all well and good. But if the underwriter did not sell the prescribed amount, the underwriter would not take a loss on the deal. But how would you like to be asked by your brokerage firm to buy a stock that the underwriter was offering on a best efforts basis? If it is all right for me to buy this stock, why isn't it all right for the underwriter to buy the issue from the issuing company? Does he know something we don't know?

Occasionally one comes across a best efforts offering such as one made by a regional investment banking company as a civic gesture to assist a Minority Enterprise Small Business Investment Co. This seemed like a perfectly reasonable thing at the time and was really quite unlike a company making a best efforts offering. Generally, no reputable underwriter today would even suggest a best efforts offering to a potential client for a public underwriting. At times this seems like a pity. Why not let the market decide if a company should be publicly owned? It comes down to: Who would want to buy the stock of a company if the underwriter does not believe enough in the company to buy the stock itself?

SELLING PREPARATIONS

Once the underwriter and the firm have made their agreement to offer securities publicly, and while the registration statements are being prepared, a concerted effort is undertaken by the underwriter to arrange buyers for the securities. Typically, especially for a fairly unknown, small firm with an IPO, the underwriter will attempt to put together a **syndicate** for the retail distribution of the securities. The ability to put together a good syndicate distinguishes one underwriter from another. During this time, when a **Red Herring prospectus** will be circulated, the underwriter will convene a meeting of the prospective retail distributors (stockbrokers) and the company's management will be asked to make a presentation on the company. (A "Red Herring" is a prospectus—or information document—that is similar to the finished Prospectus which is filed with the SEC, except that the offering price of the security is not given and there is a legend on the side of the front page, printed in red, that states that this is a *preliminary* registration statement.) This can be an extremely important meeting, as opinions will be formed that might be difficult to reverse. It is incumbent on management to put on a good show at this point. It would be smart to have a senior member of the management team—one who is articulate and used to speaking before a group—make the presentation for the company. One president of a company made a stumbling presentation to an assembled group of prospective dealers. He grew up in the construction industry and was not comfortable speaking before a group; he and everyone around him should have known this. But because of ego, the president said that he would make the presentation. What he should have done was to let the executive vice president, who was a trained lawyer and experienced public speaker, make the presentation while he stood in the background and acted like a senior statesman. Because he did not, the company suffered from a reputation of inept management from that point on. True, chief executives are not expected to be orators, but neither do people expect them to be stumbling and stammering in their presentation of the company's merits. Remember in business, like in life in general, one's reputation depends not so much what you are, but rather what people *think* you are!

Going Public via the Back Door

While the preceding discussion has dealt with the normal way to take a firm public, there is another way—*albeit I do not recommend it*. This is the process that in the vernacular is called "going public via the back door."

Assume that the owner of a privately held firm wishes to have a public market for his or her stock. The first thing this person has to do is find a **shell corporation**. This is a viable corporation, meaning that someone has paid the annual fees imposed by the Secretary of State in one of the various states. Nevada, Utah, and Arizona are quite popular for this purpose; such corporations often come about by starting out as a mining exploration company. When the funds raised are spent, and no more funds are forthcoming, the corporation becomes an effective *shell*. It has stockholders, but no assets.

Someone, however, pays the annual fees to keep the corporation alive. This may involve the payment of only a few hundred dollars. Whoever has paid this

Focus on Technology

NO REASON FOR DESPAIR! IF YOUR STOCK DID NOT DO WELL ON WALL STREET, IT MAY DO WELL ON "SCRIPOPHILY STREET"!

A visit to Scripophily.com tells us a lot about the history of entrepreneurial companies that changed the face of America forever. On that site, a worthless stock certificate for the now defunct eToys.com was being traded at a whopping price of $139.95! Remember, eToy's stock had last been traded at $.09 right before NASDAQ halted trading on that stock.

Scripophily is a leading provider of collectible stock and bond certificates and other old paper items. It bills itself as "the Internet's #1 Store for buying and selling Old Stock and Bond Certificates and our products are guaranteed to be 100% authentic or we will gladly refund your money!" At Scripophily.com, there is no section for "Technology Stocks," but one for "Telecom, Computers, and Media." The site is both entertaining and informative. For some of the companies listed and traded at the site, you could actually trace the history of that company to its founder(s). As an example, I found the information about the Atari Corporation at the site very interesting.

One more thing! In the media, we often run across analogies drawn between the present day's Internet and E-commerce industries on the one hand, and the automobile industry's early years, on the other hand. You may know that there were practically hundreds of automobile manufacturers when the automobile era started. Today, there are only a few large auto manufacturers in the United States. Well, you see where the comparison is going! By the way, you can check out the stocks, and the story, of all those players in the old automobile industry at Scripophily.com. This may also be a good exercise for the reader to gain new perspective on E-commerce and the Internet—and what it may hold for the future.

fee (and thus has the record books of the company) and the owner of the privately held firm, and the person who controls the shell, somehow get together, either through an ad in a paper such as the *Wall Street Journal*, or through a merger broker or an investment banking firm. The owner of the privately held firm then makes an offer to the person who controls the shell to exchange all of the shell's shares outstanding for some percentage of the privately held firm's shares—5 percent is typical. If the offer is accepted, the privately held firm has a stock split, if needed, so that 5 percent (or whatever the agreed-to percentage is) of the total is an appropriate number of shares to be outstanding, e.g., one million shares. Then there is effected a tax-free merger of the two companies, with the result that now the privately held firm has as its stockholders the stockholders of the old *shell* corporation and the stockholder(s) of the privately held firm.

The apparent advantage in this maneuver is getting the privately held firm public in as short a time as possible. Also, it may be that the privately held

Focus on Technology

NOTABLE QUOTES

◆ **ON LEARNING FROM FAILURE:**

". . . it occurred to me that my entire professional life had been built around resurrecting successes out of failures. My failed first experience with computers at the UCLA computer center led to my success at TRW. My failed experience at Bell Labs led to my success at Pulverizing Machinery. And now I saw that my failure at Powertec could still lead to a stronger, potentially more profitable connection with HP."

Sandra Kurtzig, founder of ASK, Inc.

◆ **ON BEING AHEAD OF YOUR TIME AND HEADING FOR FULL DEMISE:**

"I will give away the razors [meaning computers] to sell the razor blades [meaning information]."

William Von Meister, AOL pioneer, 1979

◆ **ON THE IMPORTANCE OF KEEPING YOUR FOCUS AND TURNING YOUR VISION INTO A MANTRA:**

"The Network is the Computer"!

(This referring to the vision that computer networks would someday take over the PC market and make all PCs obsolete—a mantra that drove Sun to stardom and has even made Bill Gates change his long-held beliefs in PCs and his computing strategies.)

Scott McNally, Sun CEO and co-founder

---

firm feels that it wants to be public but does not need additional funds at that time. Another reason might be that the privately held firm thinks that it can prove that it is worth more than some underwriters think it is worth. (How it is going to do that is a mystery to me.)

While the advantages of going public via the back door seem clear, the disadvantages may not be as apparent. The biggest problem with this maneuver is that once the private firm is publicly owned there is no **market maker** for the stock. When firms go public in the conventional manner, there is at least one "market maker"—an investment banking firm that has a reason for making a market in the stock. Remember in the organization chart of a typical investment banking firm (see page 195) there is a department labeled Trading. This is the unit that makes a market in the stock by buying when the sellers are many and selling when the buyers outnumber the sellers, and in so doing giving the stock a degree of *liquidity* that would otherwise be absent. If an investment banking firm has made a good-sized commission by underwriting the issue of stock, it would be inclined to see to it that it made a market for that stock—to help *its* customers as well as the firm. But this vital link is missing when the firm elects to go public via the back door. *If there is no market maker,* and the stock price lags badly after the firm is public, instead of impressing some investment banker with the real value of your company, *the opposite effect results.* Then it is many times more difficult to argue that your company is really worth a higher P/E ratio. It is not only the fact that by going public via conventional means you get an investment banker—market maker—involved, but this comes back to what was said about the *quality* of the investment banker. If you have the right investment banker for a public offering, then that investment banker will support your stock in an appropriate manner after the fact.

SUMMARY

When management decides to raise capital external to the company, it should not undertake this decision lightly. When the company is operating on its "own" money, it does not have responsibility to outsiders—stockholders, bondholders, institutional investors, etc. Management's life is much more simple. In this chapter, we have outlined the decision process of raising funds from the public, and briefly compared this process to raising funds through a private placement—a subject covered more extensively in Chapter 10.

In order to raise funds publicly, you must register with the Securities and Exchange Commission (SEC). In the course of doing this, there are several forms or procedures that must be followed. The principal form for doing an initial public offering (IPO) is the S-1 form. This requires 3 years of certified statements, according to something called S-X accounting, a variation of GAAP. Also, the filing company must realize that even though the law does not specify what law firms and accounting firms you are to employ, experience and common sense do. It is important that the filing company retain the most competent and experienced law and accounting firm it can find and afford. This will definitely expedite the passage of the filing statement with the SEC.

The exemptions to the general registration process, known as "Reg. D exemptions" were also covered. There are 3 basic types of exemptions: Rules 504, 505, and 506, each covering different situations. Before the filing takes place, it is necessary to secure the services of an investment banking firm, also called an underwriter. It was stressed that this is perhaps the most important part of the decision in deciding to raise funds outside the company. The reputation of the underwriter will follow the company long after the IPO is finished. In this regard the reader was cautioned to be wary of the investment banker who attempts to secure your company's business by promising the highest stock price. Ask how the underwriter arrived at this price and examine the reasoning underlying the price.

The chapter concluded with a brief discussion of the process of what is called "going public via the back door." In this procedure (which is definitely *not* recommended) the privately held company finds a shell corporation with a sufficient number of stockholders—and hopefully no liabilities—and merges with this shell company. The major problem with this short-cut method of going public is that no underwriter is involved. Instead of being a benefit—and a saving of money—it means that there is no *market maker* for the stock. With no market maker there is no investment banker to support the price of the stock, and this could be disastrous for the stock price after the merger.

QUESTIONS FOR DISCUSSION

1. As CEO or CFO of an emerging company, you find that you are in need of about $20–25 million in the near future. You are privately owned and have not used venture capitalists up to this point. Your sales prospects are excellent and you expect to be selling twice your current sales volume of $25 million in the next 2 to 3 years. You are currently profitable and have been almost since you started 4 years ago. You sell proprietary products to the hospital and nursing care field. What sort of strategy should you consider to obtain this financing? Discuss your reasoning.

2. How would you go about selecting an investment banker for your business? What factors would you consider?

3. What factors should you as CEO consider in making the decision to raise money via a public offering versus a private placement?

8

CHAPTER REVIEW

Appendix

TYPES OF EXEMPTION

TERMS AND CONDITIONS	RULE 504	RULE 505	RULE 506
1 NATURE OF EXEMPTION PLACEMENT	SMALL OFFERINGS	SMALL OFFERINGS	PRIVATE
2 LIMITS ON SIZE	$1 MILLION	UP TO $5 MILLION	NONE
3 NUMBER AND TYPE OF INVESTORS	NO LIMITS ON NUMBER AND NO REQUIREMENT FOR TYPE	NO LIMIT ON NUMBER OF ACCREDITED; UP TO 35 UNACCREDITED; NO REQUIREMENTS FOR TYPE OF ACCREDITED.	NO LIMIT ON ACCREDITED; UP TO 35 UNACCREDITED; UNACCREDITED MUST BE SOPHISTICATED.
4 ADVERTISING AND GENERAL SOLICITATION OF INVESTORS	PROHIBITED EXCEPT WHEN REGISTERED IN STATES REQUIRING DELIVERY OF DISCLOSURE DOCUMENTS; IF REGISTERED THERE, ADVERTISING AND/OR SOLICITING ALLOWABLE IN THOSE STATES ONLY	PROHIBITED	PROHIBITED
5 LIMITATIONS ON RESALE	RESALES RESTRICTED UNLESS REGISTERED AND SOLD ONLY IN STATES REQUIRING DELIVERY OF DISCLOSURE DOCUMENTS; THEN RESALE RESTRICTIONS REMOVED	RESALES RESTRICTED	RESALES RESTRICTED
6 LIMITATIONS ON AVAILABILITY	NONPUBLIC COMPANIES, PRINCIPALS WHO HAVE VIOLATED SECURITIES LAWS	NOT AVAILABLE IF ANY PRINCIPALS HAVE VIOLATED SECURITIES LAWS	NONE
7 REQUIRED DOCUMENT TO BE FILED WITH SEC	FORM D	FORM D	FORM D
8 INFORMATION THAT MUST BE SUPPLIED PURCHASERS	NONE SPECIFIED	NONE SPECIFIED IF ALL ARE ACCREDITED; IF ANY ARE UNACCREDITED ISSUER MUST FURNISH TO ALL INVESTORS INFORMATION SIMILIAR TO THAT IN THE SIMPLIFIED REGISTRATION. AVAILABLE FOR SMALL ISSUERS, INCLUDING FINANCIAL STATEMENTS; MIN. FINANCIAL STMT. REQUIREMENTS: TWO YEARS, MOST RECENT YEAR AUDITED; IF "UNDUE EFFORT OR EXPENSE" IS INVOLVED IN MEETING AUDIT REQUIREMENT, CORP. ISSUERS CAN SUBMIT ONLY AUDITED BALANCE SHEET FOR MOST RECENT YEAR, AND LIMITED PARTNERSHIPS CAN SUBMIT TAX BASIS FINANCIALS, REPORTED ON BY CPA FOR MOST RECENT YEAR	NONE SPECIFIED IF ALL ARE ACCREDITED; IF ANY ARE UNACCREDITED ISSUER MUST FURNISH TO ALL INVESTORS INFORMATION SIMILIAR TO THAT IN THE SIMPLIFIED REGISTRATION. AVAILABLE FORM OF REGISTRATION; MINIMUM FINANCIAL STATEMENT REQUIREMENTS: TWO OR THREE YEARS (DEPENDING ON OFFERING SIZE), ALL AUDITED; IF EFFORT OR EXPENSE IS INVOLVED, HOWEVER, SOME RELIEF AVAILABLE AS IN RULE 505 OFFERINGS.

9

Long-Term Securities: Sweetened Securities and Innovations

Today, when developing firms attempt to raise funds externally to the organization, they will most often be met with a request for some sort of "sweetener," such as the right to buy a share of stock at a certain price by a certain date. This chapter presents, first, discussions of the kinds of **sweetened securities** that are used with new and emerging business firms when they attempt to raise money through debt. Then there is presented a discussion about the other kinds of securities that are available for use by these emerging firms, including stock and a few other forms of debt. It would be well for any wannabe entrepreneur or business owner who is thinking of "doing a deal" to learn these types of securities as they represent the tools of the trade for deal makers. Saying "I will learn these when I need them" is not good enough. You will be expected to already know them when the time comes.

HISTORICAL PERSPECTIVE

As a prelude to our discussion of "sweetened" securities, we need a brief review of what preceded these types of securities. Sweeteners are a phenomenon that came about after World War II. Before this, there was a distinctly different attitude regarding debt securities. Before the crash of '29 bonds were issued mostly by large firms heavy on assets. It wasn't until 1928 that insurance companies in New York State were allowed to purchase **debentures**, or unsecured bonds. "Unsecured" is the popular term for these securities although it is a bit of a misnomer. What is meant by the term *unsecured* is that there is no specific security collateralizing the bonds. These bonds have "general creditor" claims on the company's assets. This priority will be explained in greater detail in Chapter 11. Prior to this, all types of bonds were backed by some sort of collateral, usually real estate, in the so-called "mortgage" bonds.

There was also something called a "collateral trust" bond, which had as its security stocks of another company. There were elaborate rules about what happened when the price of the underlying stock changed. These bonds could be used when a company might want to buy another company. They would borrow the money for the purchase and pledge the stock of the acquired company as collateral. (And we thought that leveraged buyouts were a strictly modern invention!) Incidentally, a modern bond that had its genesis in collateral trust bonds is **collateral mortgage obligation**, a security that was invented in the 1970s when the savings and loan industry wanted to gain some liquidity from its holdings of illiquid mortgages. Instead of stock in another company, mortgages were used as collateral for the bond. Later this type of bond was collateralized with such things as Accounts Receivable for a credit card company—or other types of financial assets.

Another bond used before the crash of '29 was the so-called **joint bond**, a bond that was guaranteed by two or more other companies. For example, if two railroads wished to cross a river at about the same point, they might form a jointly owned bridge company and finance the undertaking with joint bonds. Today a version of this is referred to simply as "guaranteed" bonds. For example, if the subsidiary of a large well-financed firm wishes to issue bonds, it could do so at a much better ranking—and thus a lower interest rate—if the parent guaranteed the bond.

After the crash of '29, the market for most securities all but disappeared. Stock offerings were seldom seen, and bond offerings were no different. In fact, in 1934 the sum total of new bond offerings for the entire United States totaled only $4 million! (Today, that much is issued, on average, in a matter of minutes.) As the country struggled out of the Great Depression, an interesting bond type was invented as a matter of necessity. In the late 1930s, almost every railroad in the United States went bankrupt. Not only once, but many times. Courts found that as soon as they fixed one bankrupt railroad with a reorganization the railroad was soon thereafter unable to service the interest attendant to that bond offering, and the railroad found itself back in bankruptcy again. So there was invented a type of bond called the **income bond**. The company issuing the bond paid interest if—and only if—it earned the interest. In this way, if the issuer failed to pay interest, normally an act of bankruptcy, the company continued on without having to declare bankruptcy again.

Unfortunately for the holders of these income bonds, this was not the best of all worlds. The holders of these bonds did not elect or choose to own them;

they were given to them in exchange for the senior securities they owned prior to a bankruptcy. Income bond became synonymous with "unwanted" but *high-risk* securities. After World War II, history repeated itself. With sky-high tax rates and extremely low interest rates, owners of middle-market firms used income bonds to try to get money out of their corporations as a tax-deductible expense instead of as dividend income. In this technique, business owners would loan their company money and receive in return "income notes," securities just like income bonds, but because the firm was privately held they were called "notes." Because of the bad connotation of income bonds, however, the owner/managers were able to say that because these were high-risk securities, they were able to charge and receive much higher interest rates than they would have been paid on some sort of regular debt instruments—for example, 15 percent instead of 3 percent.

Later, this type of debt instrument was used by unscrupulous deal makers who were trying to buy privately held firms from retiring (and usually rather old) entrepreneurs. These rascals would enter into negotiations to buy a person's company and when it came to terms, they would offer income notes. When a prospective seller objected, they would quickly snap back "What! Do you know something that we don't know? Are you trying to unload a sick company on us?" Often, this was enough to intimidate an older business owner, who acquiesced in accepting the infamous income note.

After World War II, the United States began a period of great growth and revitalization. New companies sprang up all over America. This meant a great demand for capital in the form of equity offerings as well as bonds. As the 1950s evolved, the stock market began to take on interesting growth patterns. Emerging firms found that there was a market for their debt issues if they sweetened the offering with some feature that permitted the holder to ultimately participate in the growth of the company—meaning growth in its stock price. With the bull market of the 1960s the use of **convertibles**—bonds converted into stock—soared. The dynamic bull market of the 1990s proved another heyday for convertible offerings.

At the close of the 1960s, when the market dropped so dramatically, everyone wanted to put the blame on someone or something. Even the Federal Reserve jumped on the bandwagon and said that no longer could individuals get around the **margin requirements** on bonds by buying convertibles; they put margin requirements on the large convertible bond issues that were outstanding. A "margin" requirement is imposed by the government to make the buyer of a security put up some percentage of the purchase price in cash. This meant that the buyer could not borrow 100 percent (hypothetically, as no one really ever borrowed *all* of the purchase price. By raising the "margin" requirement, the government could restrain excess speculation in securities. In the 1960s it was possible to put up as little as 10 percent of the purchase price and borrow 90 percent. If the security was a convertible bond, the holder may receive enough interest from the bond to pay the interest charge from a bank which loaned the buyer the money to buy the bond in the first place. The buyer of the convertible bond then had a **"call"** on the company's stock for a very small down payment.

Wall Street responded to the new Fed rules by simply turning to the use of **warrants**—options to buy a share of stock for a certain price before a certain date—instead of exclusively using the more popular convertible feature. Both convertibles and bonds with warrants give the buyer a chance to benefit by a rise in the price of the company's stock. Each of these stypes of "sweetened" securities will be explained below.

CONVERTIBLE DEBENTURES

A **convertible debenture** is a bond issued by a company to enable the bond-holder to turn in the bond in exchange for stock, either for so many shares or at some specified price per share. Additionally, the company could force the holder, after a stipulated **first call date**, to either exchange the bond for stock or be paid the face amount of the bond plus a **call premium**. This call premium might start out at 8 percent, for example, of the face amount of the bond and then decline as the bond approaches maturity. Typically, no rational person accepts the call price of the bond if the stock price is greater than the stock price stipulated in the bond. For example, if the bond is convertible into 50 shares of common stock, this implies that the stock is valued at $20 per share (because the typical and usual bond face amount is $1,000). If the market price at the time of the call is, for instance, $30 per share, then the holder could realize a gain of $10 per share by converting to the common stock (50 shares $\times$ $30 = $1500 − $1000, or $10 per share), less any expenses of selling the stock, of course.

Because many institutional investors—and institutional investors dominate the market for securities currently, especially bonds—have limits on the amount of equities and debt securities in their portfolio, they may feel that they have the best of both worlds when they buy a convertible debenture. In this security they have something they can count as debt, yet if the stock goes up in value, so does the bond. Thus, the "equity play." But it is very important to realize that institutional investors do not like to have a convertible bond called away from them soon after they purchased the bond, presumably after performing some research into the company. To restrain the company from calling the bond soon after issuance, most underwriters will insist that the first call date be some time in the future, for example, 3 to 5 years from the issue date. Even then, prudent management should exercise restraint in exercising the call feature on the bond.

One firm exercised the call option the moment it became available, 2 years from the issue date, much to the chagrin of the institutional bond holders. Co-incidentally, the company soon received an unwanted "tender offer" for its stock by another firm; the company was being "raided." Management needed the support of its shareholders but because the institutional shareholders were so miffed at management for calling the bond away from them, they let it be known quite quickly how they would vote regarding the unwanted tender offer. Realizing this, the company had to turn to a "White Knight," another company with whom the company had a favorable relationship to bail out the company and agree to a merger. Certainly, the "quick" call of the company's convertible bonds was not the sole cause of the company having to be sold, but it helped!

The first call date is also a function of interest rates at the time of issuance. When short-term rates peaked dramatically in the 1980s, many firms issuing convertible bonds put an extremely short first call date on their convertibles. This was understandable at the time, but if a company tried to do that in more normal interest rate periods, it would be considered a most undesirable feature of the bond and would certainly hurt the sale of such bonds even if an underwriter approved of such a strategy.

After World War II, there was almost a universal requirement that firms include a sinking fund provision so that there would be enough money when the bond matured to repay the bondholders. In recent years, this requirement has been modified somewhat by requiring the firm to have a sinking fund equal to only 75 percent, for example, of the amount of the offering. This sinking fund is actually a **funded reserve**, meaning that the reserve has to be actually funded with cash—or the bond itself, which takes cash to purchase it—as opposed to an "unfunded reserve" such as the reserve for Depreciation. Since this sinking fund is such a burden on the firm's cash flow—this reserve is not tax deductible as the reserve for Depreciation is—a growing firm would prefer to be relieved of this requirement, as reasonable as it is. (It should list this "funded reserve" in its Priority Outflows section of the Cash Flow Statement to show its effect on the company's cash flow.) If the issuer of the bond really is thought of as a high-growth firm, it is usual to defer the start of a sinking fund to the start of the first call date. In this case, the company will have had an "interest-only" loan for this period, assuming the company calls the bond at the first call date. If this is in 5 years, this would be a particularly advantageous situation for the company. It receives money in the form of debt, gets a tax deduction for the interest, and then is able to issue stock instead of paying off the principal. *Remember: Companies grow on their equity!*

THE EXERCISE PRICE FOR THE STOCK IN THE CONVERTIBLE

There is a Wall Street heuristic for the exercise price of the stock for which the bond is convertible. This heuristic is approximately 115 percent of the current stock price when the bonds are issued. There are some variations to this practice, such as 115 percent for the first 3 years and then 120 percent, but the psychology behind this heuristic is persuasive. If a growth company came to an underwriter and wanted to issue convertibles, they would probably be quite upset if they were told that the exercise price would have to be only 115 percent of the current price, especially if the first call date is 3 years hence. Why should the exercise price not be, for example, 150 percent? The stock has risen dramatically in the last year and it is anticipated by management that the 115 percent price would be broached within 6 months—at least! Unfortunately for the issuing firm, the underwriter would put itself in an untenable position if it acquiesced to management's request for a higher exercise price. If the underwriter went along with a request for a higher exercise price, it would, in effect, be promising its customers—or the customers of the selling syndicate that the price of the stock of this company was going up 50 percent, and then some! This is something no responsible underwriter would do. In short, the underwriter would be touting the stock price. What would you think of an underwriter who sold you a convertible bond with an abnormally high exercise price *if* the price of the stock did not rise to that level—for whatever reason? To say the underwriter would be embarrassed would be a gross understatement. There tends to be a relationship between the coupon rate and the premium price. The lower the coupon, the lower the exercise price.

CONVERTIBLE BONDS AND ARBITRAGE

Once convertible bonds are sold to the public, their market prices are determined by the **coupon rate** (the interest on the bond expressed as a percentage of the face amount of the bond), and the price of the underlying stock. Until the stock price gets to the exercise price stated in the bond, the price of the convertible bond is mostly determined by the coupon rate of interest—and, of course, by the *expectation* of what is going to happen to the stock price. But once the stock price *passes* the exercise price, the price of the bond will follow the price of the stock *pari passu*—that is, the price of the bond must be *in step* with the price of the stock. If the price of the bond falls proportionately behind the price of the stock, individuals in the market (who pay no fees to anyone because they own seats on an exchange or otherwise pay no brokerage fees) can simply buy a number of bonds. They then order that the bonds be converted to stock, and then order that the stock be sold—all this with just three snaps of the finger. In so doing there would be a guaranteed profit on the transaction. These individuals would be effecting what is known as **arbitrage**. And the individuals are known as *arbitrageurs*. (Arbitrage, in general terms, is the almost simultaneous buying and selling of a security in order to make a quick profit.) This is why a company will experience a continual "dribble" of conversions if it has an issue of convertible bonds outstanding.

BONDS WITH WARRANTS

WHAT IS A WARRANT?

Bonds may be issued with warrants. And this combination of securities—a bond with warrant—is sometimes referred to as a **synthetic convertible**. A convertible debenture, you will recall, allows the bondholder to turn in the bond in exchange for stock, either for so many shares or at some specified price per share. Warrants, on the other hand, may be either "detachable" or "nondetachable," the latter meaning the bond must be turned in when the warrant is exercised. In effect, this would make the bond with warrants somewhat similar to a convertible bond. Variations of the nondetachable mode might be where the company says that even though the warrants are detachable the bond may be presented at *face value* as consideration when purchasing stock with the warrants.

Most bonds with warrants are of the "detachable" type. When the warrants are detached they are sold as stand-alone warrants in the market. These warrants would normally be listed with the stock of the company in the newspapers or wherever stock listings and prices are to be found. When the warrants are detached from the bonds, the bond drops in price. By accepting the bond at *face value*, the issuing company would be putting a kind of floor under the price of the bond in the market if the stock is above the exercise price.

Warrants typically have a maturity of 5 to 7 years, with a range of about 3 to 10 years. A warrant differs from a "call" option in that the call option is for a maximum 270 days. A "long-term option," called "LEAPS," is limited to 2 years. The exercise price usually follows the same heuristic as the convertible bond—115 percent of the stock price at the time of issue. The logic behind this is the same as for the convertible bonds: the underwriter would be touting the stock if it used a much higher exercise price. Note also that a warrant is different from a convertible in that the warrant is not converted to stock; the warrant must be presented along with cash to *purchase* a share of stock. So when warrants are exercised, usually on the last day of the life of the warrant, and then by some investment banker/dealer, the firm receives an infusion of cash—unlike the situation when a firm calls a convertible bond. With this cash, the company can buy back the bonds in the market as far as the money received will permit, or it can use the money for corporate purposes—or even for retiring stock. But in the latter two cases, the bond remains outstanding.

It should also be noted that warrants can be exchanged for shares of the company. For example, if you had warrants to purchase 100,000 shares of XYZ and my cost was $5 each, but the market price of the warrant was $10, you have the option of receiving 50,000 shares of XYZ under the Net Exercise provision rather than utilizing cash to exercise the warrants. The calculation is as follows: $1,000,000 (total underlying value of the common stock) less $500,000 (total exercise price of the warrants) divided by $10 (current market price of the common stock) equals 50,000 shares. In short, instead of selling the warrant for $10—a profit of $5 each warrant—and then buying 50,000 shares of stock, you could just turn in the warrant to the company and receive 50,000 shares of stock.

BONDS WITH WARRANTS "IN THE MONEY"

When bonds are issued with warrants that have an exercise price *below* the current stock price, the warrant is said to be "in the money." This feature may be expressed two ways. The price may be stipulated as a certain dollar price *or* the price may be stated as, for example, 90 percent of the stock price, whatever the stock price is. An issuing firm might want to do this in order to make sure that stock is purchased through the warrants. An example of an issue that might have warrants "in the money" might be a Real Estate Investment Trust. In the case of a REIT, the managers receive two types of fees, one based on performance and the other based on the size of the fund managed. Obviously it is to the advantage of the fund management to make the fund as large as possible or feasible.

NUMBER OF WARRANTS TO PLACE WITH THE BOND

An interesting question arises when the *number* of warrants to place with the bond comes up. Underwriters may say that knowing how to answer this question is one of the reasons they are paid the big bucks. However, the process is not as much a mystery as investment bankers might want client firms to think. The formula for how many warrants to place with a bond is:

$$\text{Number of Warrants} = \frac{\text{Expected drop in the price of the bond}}{\text{Expected price of the warrant}}$$

The expected drop in the price of the bond is a function of the coupon rate of interest put on the bond, the maturity of the bond, and the rating of the bond. There are three services which "rate" or grade bonds by such classes as AAA, AA, or B–. These three rating services, Moody's, Standard and Poor's, and Fitch, all use a slightly different lettering system for the grading, but they all have the highest ratings shown as "A" or some variation of "A." If a bond is rated B, for example, it might be expected to carry an interest rate and yield to maturity of, say, 9 percent. But if there is a lower interest rate coupon on the bond, the bond will have to drop in price to a point where the buyer of the bond will receive a yield to maturity of 9 percent. Take the difference in the face amount of the bond—or the price at which the bond is issued—and the price to which the bond is expected to drop, and you have the numerator.

The denominator is another Wall Street heuristic: 40 percent of the current (time of issue) stock price. Now, there are no empirical studies to back up this heuristic that I know of, but consider this: The warrant would have to sell for *some* percentage of the stock price. By settling on 40 percent, Wall Street is using a price that seems reasonable and that can be supported during the "support period" after issuance of the bond. Once the warrants are past this support period, if there is one, then the movement of the stock price will determine what happens to the price of the warrant.▲

▲ Books on investments—and sometimes corporate finance texts—go into considerable detail in showing what happens to warrant prices *after* issuance of the bonds, but this is irrelevant to our discussion in this book. What is discussed here is what is relevant for management to know and understand *before* discussions with the investment banker.

With respect to warrants on such things as subordinated notes in a (currently) privately held company placed with institutional lenders, the number of warrants will be a function of the coupon rate of interest and the estimated market value of the company. If the coupon rate on the note is 10 percent, and the usual desired rate of return (IRR) is 20–25 percent—over a 5-year period, most frequently—then the number of warrants will be the based on the market value of the company in 5 years. What percentage of this "guessed at" market will produce a number such that when added at the end of 5 years to the periodic coupon rate of interest will produce the desired rate of interest (say, 20 percent)? This will be made clearer in the discussion of the number of shadow warrants to attach to a loan (pages 220–221).

THE INTEREST RATE QUESTION

It should come as no surprise that the heuristic used above for the exercise price of the warrant (see page 211) is the same as was used for the exercise price of convertible bonds, *viz.*, 115 percent of the stock price at the time of issuance. If the underwriter did not use this heuristic, it would be guilty of touting the stock.

Deciding on the interest rate to assign a convertible bond *vis-à-vis* a bond with warrants is a decidedly different process. With regard to convertibles, the interest rate will reflect the anticipated increase in the rise of the stock price. At least this approach would seem to be the rational one. If there seems to be a lot of buyer enthusiasm for the convertible bond, then why not place as low an interest rate on the bond as possible—and still sell the bond? Once the stock price goes beyond the conversion price in the convertible bond, the bond price will rise *pari passu* with the rise in the stock price—*completely independent of the interest rate on the bond*. Whether the bond has a relatively high rate or a low rate, the bond will move in concert with the stock price or the arbitrageurs will step in and make this price parity a reality.

Putting the interest rate on a bond with warrants is a completely different exercise, however. Remember, the formula for how many warrants to place on a bond involves the expected drop in the price of the bond *after* the warrants are detached. For example, if the bond's grade indicates that it should carry a 10 percent coupon rate *if it did not have any warrants*, and the interest rate assigned was only 5 percent, then the bond would drop in price after issuance from $1,000 to $543—a difference of $457. If a 7 percent coupon were attached to the same bond, the price of the bond would drop to $721, or a difference of $279. And if a coupon rate of 8.5 percent were assigned to the bond, the difference in price would be only $137. If the firm's stock were selling for $10 per share, then the heuristic would indicate that the warrants should be valued at about $4 each. Dividing $4 into the difference of $543, and rounding, yields the answer that about 135 warrants should be attached to that bond. For the difference of $457, approximately 115 warrants should be attached. For the difference of $137, one would expect that only about 35 warrants would be attached in order to compensate the buyer of the bond for the drop in the price of the bond when the warrants are detached.

This range for the three interest rates selected of between 135 and 35 is quite a difference! But which interest rate to choose? If the lower interest rate is chosen, management will have to sell 135 shares of stock when the warrants expire for each $1,000 worth of bonds outstanding, but only 35 if the higher rate were selected. Suppose the stock is selling for $20 or $30 or even $40. When the warrants expire in 5 to 10 years, would management think they were really smart when they set the interest rate—an interest rate that is tax-deductible—at 5 percent instead of, for example, 8.5 percent—when they had to sell 135 shares at $10 instead of 35 shares at $10 when they could otherwise sell stock for $20 or $30 a share? Perhaps this is overstating the possibilities: If you put an interest rate of 8.5 percent on the bond, a buyer might not be enticed to buy the bond because it did not appear to have enough of a "stock play." But at least you could put the 7 percent coupon on the bond and save some warrants. A cynic might observe at this point that if the firm's stock does not get to the point where the warrants are valuable—that is, they mature worthless—then *no* shares would have to be issued. But this is an *ex post* idea, and the decision has to be made *ex ante*. Furthermore, if an underwriter, acting in good faith, really believed that the firm's stock would *never* get above the exercise price, or, at least, was unlikely to get above the exercise price, he or she should never agree to issue a bond with warrants.

If interest rate is important in the decision between issuing convertibles and bonds with warrants, it appears that the nod should go to convertibles. If one places a relatively low interest rate on bonds with warrants, one would have to issue a relatively large number of warrants; if the same low interest rate were placed on the convertible bond, the number of shares of stock that would have to issued when the convertibles were converted would be the *same* as though a higher rate were used.

SUBORDINATION FEATURE

One potentially advantageous possibility of sweetening a bond offering is the chance to add a subordination feature to the bond, thereby creating *de facto* equity. By subordinating a regular debenture, the issuer will normally have to increase—usually substantially—the interest rate applied to the bond. But when adding a convertible feature to a bond or adding warrants, the buyer's attention is, presumably, directed to the "play" on the underlying stock and overlooks the fact that the bond has been subordinated to other general creditors, ranking it lower in the bankruptcy chain. In this way, the issuing company can obtain funds through tax-deductible debt and yet still not hurt its Debt/Equity ratio, in fact, it may even improve its Debt/Equity ratio. In Chapter 7, a lot was said about the worthlessness of the Debt/Equity ratio. But whether the Debt/Equity ratio is worthless or not, if people *think* it is important, it should be important to the firm's management.

EARNINGS PER SHARE

As one of the many repercussions of the excesses of the 1960s, the Accounting Principals Board, undoubtedly reacting to pressure from the Securities and Exchange Commission and other political pressure, decided to put an end to what some accountants called "funny money" (securities that were not really stock or debt; in fact, who knew what to call these unusual securities?) and passed Accounting Principals Board Ruling Number 15 (APB 15).▲ "What would earnings be if all this 'funny money' came back to the company?"

Subsequently amended, most recently on December 15, 1997, this FASB ruling was directed toward the reporting of earnings per share and requires that consideration be given to what are called **common stock equivalents**: warrants, stock options, and, under certain circumstances, convertible securities. The inclusion of these common stock equivalents results in what is called a "complex capital" structure and this means currently that the company has to report earnings two ways, "*basic*" and "*diluted*."▲▲ "Basic" earnings reflect the average number of common shares outstanding during the year, and "diluted" earnings reflect the addition of the outstanding common stock equivalents.

The calculations for Diluted Earnings Per Share are now rather easy. For *convertibles* they are:

$$\text{Diluted Earnings Per Share} = \frac{\text{Earnings plus interest saved}}{\text{Average number of outstanding shares} + \text{Number of new shares}}$$

For bonds with *warrants*, the calculation is a little different:

$$\text{Diluted Earnings Per Share} = \frac{\text{Earnings}}{\begin{array}{l}\text{Average number of outstanding shares} \\ + \text{ Number of new shares because of} \\ \quad \text{the exercise of the warrants} \\ - \text{ Number of shares that could be} \\ \quad \text{purchased with the proceeds of the} \\ \quad \text{sale of the stock through the warrants}\end{array}}$$

The part of the formula that says "the number of shares that could be repurchased with the proceeds of the sale of the stock through the warrants" is controversial. For example, if the exercise price in the warrant is $10 and stock is selling for $10, then it is reasonable that the warrants would not be exercised

---

▲ The APB of the American Institute of Certified Public Accountants existed from 1959 to 1973, when it was replaced by the independent Financial Accounting Standards Board (FASB).

▲▲ There used to be a requirement that the difference had to be 3 percent or more. In the most recent revision, this 3 percent rule has been dropped.

and, accordingly, no new shares would be issued to dilute the outstanding shares. If the stock is *lower priced* in the market than $10 this would be antidilutive and the FASB prohibits the inclusion of *less* shares than the exercise of the warrants would otherwise result. To illustrate:

$$\text{Diluted Earnings Per Share} = \frac{\$1,000,000}{\begin{array}{l}1,000,000 \text{ Shares outstanding} \\ + \ 100,000 \text{ New shares through warrants} \\ - \ 100,000 \text{ Shares that could be repurchased}\end{array}}$$

The interesting thing about the FASB is what happens when the stock *goes up* in price. Suppose the market price of the company's stock goes up to $20 or $30 or even $40? In this case the number of shares that are to be *subtracted* would be reduced, first to 50,000 then to 33,333 then to 25,000. The *denominator* would be *increased*. Because of this, the Diluted Earnings Per Share would be $0.95, $0.94 and $0.93, respectively. This is not much of a change, but in other circumstances the difference might be relatively more. And why? Because the market price has risen? It seems a pity that management would have to have *lower* diluted earnings just because the company's *stock* has risen in price.

Note Well: This explanation of basic and diluted earnings ignores the problem of stock options (as well as some other details), which for many developing firms is reasonably significant. But a more thorough explanation would be beyond the scope of this chapter.

VARIATIONS IN CONVERTIBLES AND BONDS WITH WARRANTS

It is possible, although rare, for the stock into which the bond is convertible to be the stock of *another* firm. This situation can come about from a circumstance similar to the following scenario. A firm acquires a large block of stock in another firm, perhaps as a prelude to acquiring that firm. For some reason, the acquiring firm changes its mind and decides not to pursue the acquisition. The question arises, therefore, as to how the firm can divest itself of the stock of this second firm. Of course, it could sell the stock on the open market, either piecemeal or, perhaps, in one large block to an institutional investor. But to do so, it would probably have to reduce the price, most likely 10 to 20 percent. An alternative way to dispose of this stock would be to issue convertible bonds with the stock of the second firm as the convertible stock. If it followed the usual heuristic of pricing the exercise price at 115 percent of the current stock price, and the stock were later converted through the call of the bond, the first company would have succeeded in divesting itself of this stock at a *gain* of 10 to 20 percent instead of a *loss* of 10 to 20 percent—a difference of 20 to 40 percent!

Another possibility is a situation where a large firm wishes to sell a division. A potential buyer appears but the buyer is short of cash. If the large firm wished—perhaps because it had no other offers—it could accept stock from the smaller firm, if the stock of the smaller firm were publicly traded. Then the large firm could turn around and issue convertible bonds with the bond convertible into the stock of the smaller firm. True it would have to pay interest—but tax-deductible interest—until the small firm's stock rose in value sufficiently to permit the call of the bond and the forced conversion to stock of the smaller firm. With a delayed call, this may be 2 or 3 years, but it still may be a worthwhile strategy.

EXCHANGEABLE WARRRANTS

If a firm can use the stock of another firm as the conversion stock in a convertible bond, why cannot stock of another firm be used with a warrant? Why not indeed! In fact this is also done occasionally, and for the same sort of reasons as for the convertibles. In fact, if a company has a large block of stock that it wishes to dispose of, but does not wish to dump it on the market, it can merely sell warrants to purchase the stock just as in the case of a warrant issued with a bond. This may be a rather short-term warrant, perhaps 3 or 4 years, but again, with an exercise price of approximately 115 percent of the stock price at the time of issuance, this may represent a swing of twenty five to thirty percent.

And then there are the circumstances in which the company sells warrants by themselves—without a bond. This is done rarely, but probably as often as warrants exercisable into stock of another company mentioned directly above.

ZERO COUPON CONVERTIBLES

Presumably invented in the merger/buyout boom years of the 1980s, **zero coupon convertibles** offer another interesting variation. While **zero coupon bonds** (also called **deep discount bonds**) are convertible into the company's stock, the issuing company realizes some potential advantages. Because the conversion feature is a "sweetener," and thus an enticement to the potential buyer, it would seem this feature should be good for *reducing* the interest rate that the bond would have to carry; actually, because the bond pays no cash interest as such, this feature could mean that the firm would sell the bond for a *smaller discount* (equivalent to a lower interest rate) from the face amount of the bond. This means a larger interest rate.

A second possible advantage of the zero coupon convertible would be the fact that when the bond matured, the company would pay off the bondholders by "merely" writing stock certificates. Obviously this is not the sort of thing that one would expect to be used in a closely held firm—not even, in fact, in a rather small publicly held emerging firm—but the possibility is there. For example, suppose that a growing privately held firm needed a cash infusion, but did not really have the cash flow to service a normal note. Suppose further that one of the investors of this privately held firm had a nontaxable IRA or other retirement account with sufficient funds therein to fund the company. If this investor wished, he or she could invest the needed capital by purchasing a zero coupon note from the company. Zero coupon bonds (or notes) have three advantages to the company issuing them:

1. They pay no interest.
2. The company is able to take a tax deduction for interest just as though it paid the interest in cash.
3. The company has no sinking fund payments to make, payments that are *not* tax deductible, thus hurting the firm's cash flow even more than taxable deductions.

Naturally, if these instruments are tax advantaged, there must be a tax *disadvantage* to someone. In this case, the buyer of the bonds (or notes) would have to pay tax on the *implicit* interest income they are receiving—even though they do not actually receive the interest! This is why it is suggested that the stockholder use his or her tax exempt IRA or other retirement fund to purchase the notes in this privately held company.

An interesting twist of the zero coupon bond or note is if it is made *convertible* into common stock. In this way the issuing company does not even have to pay off the security at its maturity—it simply issues more stock. Of course, for developing firms or privately held firms, this may not be a particularly attractive option. Invented by Merrill Lynch in 1985, zero coupon convertibles (called LYONs, for "liquid yield option notes") had a burst of activity in the early 1990s, when interest rates were relatively high, but when interest rates declined around 1993, a number of the large issuers found that they could issue regular bonds at lower rates of interest and therefore they exercised their call option on these LYONs. A number of buyers found to their dismay that the call price was *less* than the price they paid for the bond, even though it was purchased at a discount. Also, when first used by giant companies, the issuance of a few more shares more or less didn't matter. It might matter quite a lot in a closely held developing firm, however.▲

CLAW BACK PROVISIONS

While more popular with convertible preferred stock (see discussion on page 226) sometimes there is attached to the convertible note—not usually a publicly traded bond—a provision that if the company makes its forecast as projected, the lender will reduce the amount of stock into which the note is con-

▲ See "Are LYONs Becoming a Dying Breed?" *Wall Street Journal,* March 8, 1993, p. C1.

vertible. This way, if a company feels that the lender is being unduly harsh, it can reduce the resulting stock dilution by meeting its forecast. Sounds simple, and the logic of this from the lender's point of view is simple. If the company meets its forecast, the stock value will be more—maybe a lot more—and the lender can make its intended rate of return. If the company is overly optimistic in its forecast, which is not an uncommon occurrence, then the lender is protected and may make its hoped-for rate of return with more stock.

SHADOW WARRANTS

When the first real credit crunch that anyone could remember occurred in the late 1960s and early 1970s, banks and other financial institutions were besieged with requests for funding for various projects. Sensing that they were in a particularly strong position, these lenders invented something that has come to be known as **shadow warrants**. As one of my students once remarked, shadow warrants might be called "make believe" warrants. The lender may be willing to make a loan to buy another business but wants more than just a routine interest rate. Or, in some cases they want a higher return than the borrower can pay in the form of interest. If the potential borrower were a publicly held firm, the lender could ask for warrants on the company's stock. In this way the lender could participate in the success of the (borrowing) firm that is to receive the loan. But in many of these situations, the borrowing party was not a publicly held firm. And what lending institution would want to purchase stock—a minority interest at that!—in a closely held firm? To get the same, or almost the same, result with a privately held firm as with a publicly held firm, the lender would agree to take part of their remuneration for doing the deal in the form of shadow warrants. Here's how they work.

First, it is necessary to assume a Price/Earnings ratio for the stock of the privately held firm. It does not matter that this P/E ratio is *similar* to the P/E ratio of similar, publicly held firms (usually a rather low multiple is assumed, such as 5/1), but the *number* of shadow warrants must be reduced the higher the P/E multiple assumed. (Often this multiple is a pre-tax multiple as well.) Because the loan is requested to do a deal—acquire another firm—forecasts are made of the firm's earnings in the future—with the acquisition, for example, 5 years hence. By multiplying the current earnings per share by the assumed multiple the *assumed* current stock price is derived. Then, by doing the same thing to the future earnings per share, using the constant assumed P/E multiple, a future stock price is derived. By comparing the present stock price with the future stock price, a profit per warrant would thus be derived. This is shown in Exhibit 9.1.

In the exhibit, the shadow warrant is assumed to be worth $10 at the end of 5 years *if* the firm, in fact, earns $3 per share. If the firm earns more than $3, then the warrant will be worth more and accordingly the profit per warrant will be more. Conversely, the lender, by accepting this shadow warrant arrangement, would receive less if the firm earned less than the forecast earnings per share.

EXHIBIT 9.1	Calculation of the Expected Profit Per Warrant		
CURRENT EARNINGS	$1,000,000	FIFTH-YEAR EARNINGS	$3,000,000
SHARES OUTSTANDING	1,000,000	SHARES OUTSTANDING	1,000,000
EARNINGS PER SHARE	$1	EARNINGS PER SHARE	$3
ASSUMED MULTIPLE	5/1	ASSUMED MULTIPLE	5/1
ASSUMED STOCK PRICE	$5	ASSUMED STOCK PRICE	$15

PROFIT PER WARRANT = $15 − $5 = $10

CALCULATING THE NUMBER OF WARRANTS

While the above example is quite easy, the question of how many warrants to give to the lender presents a bit more of a problem. To rationally approach an answer to this question, one should ask what rate of return the lender expects on your loan. For many lenders, especially finance companies, working with individuals or companies wishing to buy another firm, for example, an annual return of 25 to 35 percent is usual if the amount of money needed is relatively small, say, under $5 million. A business that has just been bought cannot afford a coupon rate of interest of 25 or 35 percent because of the strain on its cash flow. To get around this, the parties to the deal can agree that they will set an interest rate that is affordable of, perhaps, 10 percent, with the balance represented by shadow warrant profits. In order to get the number of shadow warrants to place on the loan in this circumstance, it will be necessary to calculate what the bonus at the end of the forecast period will amount to in order to give the lender the desired rate of return. Simple trial and error, with interpolation, will quickly produce the amount in question. Exhibit 9.2 shows this process. The amount of the bonus calculated by the formulation in the exhibit could be substantial. How then could a firm hope to pay such a bonus? The answer is that the same lender who made the loan in the first place is the leading candidate to loan the firm the money it needs to pay this substantial bonus. But this time, presumably, the firm is a distinctly different credit risk, having reduced its debt to much more acceptable levels. Furthermore, in this case the loan is not for a speculative effort like buying a firm through a leveraged buyout. Now, the firm might be able to borrow at rates close to prime.

The "X" in the Exhibit 9.2 is the same sort of number that is sought in larger subordinated loan deals where there is a reasonable expectation of either going public or selling the company, referred to in a prior section. It would be the percentage of the company (measured by its market value) that would produce a number that results in the desired Internal Rate of Return for the time period.

When the credit crunch hit in 1991, the banks were told to analyze their portfolios of loans and declare those loans to firms in which there was a heavy debt to be "highly leveraged transactions."▲ As a result, the commercial banks

▲ Declaring a loan as a "HLT" was not in and of itself onerous. The problem was that the bank then had to take a reserve against its capital position—something the lightly leveraged banks are loath to do!

EXHIBIT 9.2   Calculation of the Number of Shadow Warrants to Assign to a Deal

$$\frac{\text{Amount of bonus needed to get "desired IRR"} = X}{\text{Estimated profit per warrant}}$$

TO OBTAIN THE BONUS, X, ASSUME A NUMBER AT THE END OF THE INTEREST PERIODS AND ADD THIS NUMBER TO THE LAST INTEREST PAYMENT. THEN DISCOUNT TO TIME ZERO ALL THE INTEREST PAYMENTS PLUS A TRIAL BONUS TO GET THE DESIRED IRR. (ASSUME DIFFERENT X'S UNTIL THE DESIRED IRR IS FOUND.) ONCE THIS BONUS IS FOUND, DIVIDE THIS AMOUNT BY THE EXPECTED PROFIT PER WARRANT TO GET THE *NUMBER OF WARRANTS* TO ATTACH. FOR EXAMPLE:

	YEARS				
	1	**2**	**3**	**4**	**5**
INTEREST PAYMENT $$	$Y	$Y	$Y	$Y	$Y
					$X

WITHOUT THE BONUS (X), THE IRR OF THE INTEREST PAYMENTS IS THE AGREED-UPON 10 PERCENT. BUT IF X IS ADDED, THE IRR FOR THE PERIOD BECOMES, SAY, 30 PERCENT. SOLVING FOR X PRODUCES THE BONUS REQUIRED. DIVIDING X BY THE EXPECTED PROFIT PER SHADOW WARRANT EQUALS THE NUMBER OF SHADOW WARRANTS TO PLACE ON THE LOAN.

---

virtually stopped lending to leveraged buyout proposals and similar requests. With the banks out of the market the commercial finance companies in the United States had a field day making the loans that the banks were spurning. In fact, if a deal had anything the least bit wrong with it,▲ the deal would probably be rejected by these finance companies. Also, these finance companies were in such a strong competitive position that they did not have to engage in the more sporting practice of using shadow warrants—where the amount of the bonus was based on a firm realizing a certain earnings, and thus was somewhat uncertain. Instead they would just name the amount of bonus they expected, including perhaps an "exit bonus" when the firm paid off the loan or refinanced the loan through an outside source. In short, if the finance company wanted to realize a certain rate of return on a loan (e.g., 30 percent), it would stipulate the amount of the bonus at the time the loan was taken out.

PUTTING SWEETENERS AND OTHER TOOLS IN PERSPECTIVE

When developing firms look today for debt financing they are likely to face a requirement to sweeten the offering in some way, either through a convertible feature of some sort or through the use of warrants, either negotiable for publicly owned firms or through shadow warrants if the firm is closely held. In this

---

▲ In the vernacular of finance, this was known as having "hair" or warts. If a deal had any "hair" on it, probably it was rejected as there were deals waiting in line that were "clean."

portion of the chapter, an attempt was made to familiarize the reader with the usual terms that might be expected to be included in these sweetened offerings. It behooves management to be prepared when negotiating a loan or a bond offering. (More on this point below when term loans will be discussed.) But it is also advantageous for management to know the rationale of the various aspects of sweetened offerings and not be at the mercy of the investment banker. The topics that were discussed above are the kinds of things that investment bankers would just as soon keep to themselves.

SECURITIES INNOVATION

The preceding discussion was about convertible securities and bonds and notes with warrants. While these are the typical securities that a developing firm can expect to issue, they are by no means the only types of securities that a new or emerging firm can expect to issue. Rather there are a number of types of securities, both debt and equity that might be used at various times as a firm develops in size and reputation. What follows will be a discussion of these "tools" of finance, starting with various types of stock.

HISTORICAL PERSPECTIVE AND COMMON STOCK

Our focus is not on plain vanilla common stock but rather on types of securities of special use to a developing firm. Nonetheless, we should look first at the basis upon which innovations rose.

Goodness only knows when and where the first use of common stock was, but it probably occurred in England. Even in the sixteenth century, shares in enterprises, usually shipping ventures, were issued to investors. But in those days, perhaps because of the paucity or absolute absence of financial and accounting information, common stock was more akin to partnership shares than to the anonymous form of security it is today. "Outside investors"—people who were not insiders and thus not privy to what was really going on in the firm—sought securities such as bonds and preferred stock.

Today **common stock** is the standard to which all other equity securities are compared. In the simplest form, each share of stock has one vote and each share has equal rights to dividends. In some states and for some companies, there is something called "cumulative voting." In this case a shareholder gets one vote for each director to be elected. Under this arrangement, it is possible for a minority shareholder to have representation on the board, even if he or she does not have voting plurality of 50 percent plus one share of the shares outstanding. Obviously, this arrangement is designed to give minority interests representation on the board of directors. If it were not for cumulative voting, the majority shareholder could vote 50+ percent for *every* director and, therefore, elect *all* of the board's directors.

TRADING STRATEGY

EVALUATING A COMPANY

Some years ago, Robert Bullington published[a] a short paper about how Standard and Poor's rated corporate bond issues. At the time it was news, as nothing had been written publicly prior to this to explain how this important rating agency rated bonds. While it may be informative to the reader to know what criteria the rating agencies use to rate bonds (and other securities) far more valuable are Bullington's five criteria. If one were to put up on the wall of one's office some guiding principals, it would be difficult to do better than the first four of Bullington's points. In some ways, these four points represent what this book is all about; the subjective and objective guide points for a business.

THE FIVE CRITERIA FOR RATING BONDS

Management. What are management's objectives and how are they trying to achieve them? What are the financial and operating policies? Has management provided for the unforeseen? What is the overall evaluation of the company's management?

Level and stability of earnings. The level of earnings applies mostly to the other companies in the same industry. How does this firm's earnings stack up against their competitors? The "stability" refers to the volatility of the firm's earnings. When referring to debt, the

[a] Robert A. Bullington, "How corporate debt issues are rated," *Financial Executive*, September 1974, 28–30.

reference here is to the "coverage ratios" but, in general, the idea here is that if a firm has a lot of volatility in its earnings, it is a strong negative. Good, consistent earnings (and cash flow, it might be added) are what rating agencies look for, but then so do banks!

Financial resources. A company's current liquidity and its ability to obtain external funds is examined. Here such things as the Current Ratio (alas, for better of worse!), Working Capital sufficiency, Inventory turns, Receivables turnover—these and all other factors, especially the *Balance Sheet characteristics*—that influence a lender to make a loan are what is meant by this criterion. Every firm can run short of cash from time to time, but the ability to borrow is what is looked for here.

Asset protection. Here they look at specific indices, e.g., total long-term debt/net plant, and net tangible assets/total long-term debt. These ratios—and you can say what you wish about *ratios, but if people think that these ratios are important they are important!*—are mostly mechanical but they try to get behind the ratios and see if there are real assets behind the numbers. But in general, this is the Debt/Equity test that was discussed in the chapter on capital structure, Chapter 7. If a firm has too much debt—whatever that means!—it is in *big* trouble.

The indenture provisions. This is a technical criterion that really applies only to bonded indebtedness. If a company issues bonds in an amount

(continues)

TRADING STRATEGY

EVALUATING A COMPANY *(continued)*

greater than $1 million, it must have an "indenture" (a contract between the company and its bondholders). If it writes this indenture in a biased manner, that is if it is slanted strictly toward the company, this will be a demerit for the company. What they are looking for here is an even-handed contract between the company and the bondholders.

IMPLICATIONS OF THE ARTICLE

This article is worth remembering for the *first four* criteria alone; the points that Bullington makes are essentially the guiding lights for financial management of a firm. And if the reader will notice, every one of these four points reflects good—or bad—financial management of the firm. *And none of these four points can be fixed quickly.* Each of the points requires constant adherence to the best principals of financial management. Forget one, e.g., your Balance Sheet maintenance, and it may hurt the firm at the worst possible time. Financial management of the firm is not one-dimensional. If this seems like balancing several balls in the air at the same time, then so be it! This book is really directed to trying to achieve management of all four of these factors.

In most states, common stock also has what is called a **preemptive right**. This is a right to subscribe to any new issue of common stock by the company in proportion to the shares held. In this way it is possible for one to maintain his or her equal ownership of a company. This antidilutive measure also applies to all securities *convertible* into common stock. Convertible bonds, for example, would contain this antidilutive feature such that if the bond were convertible into 50 shares of common stock, for example, before the issuance of new shares, then it would be convertible into some additional proportion of shares if the stock were split up such that the same proportion of company ownership would be maintained. Obviously, if securities did not have this antidilutive feature, management could issues more shares to whomever and seriously erode an individual's ownership percentage in the company.

Par value is also an interesting feature of common stock. Presumably, many years ago stock was given a "par" value so that an unsophisticated investor would know what he or she was getting. In the United States, at least, stock ownership was not at all common before World War I. The first securities that many people outside the financial districts of the East Coast owned were victory bonds issued in World War I. (A farmer in Kansas paid money and received a piece of paper that said that the government would pay the bearer so much money at a certain time in the future.) But when it came to stock, states saw a chance to tax the wealthy and started to inflict a tax based on the par value the share carried, completely irrespective of the market price, if any, of the share of stock. Responding to this tactic, many firms then eliminated the par value and replaced it with a "stated" value for accounting purposes. When some states saw this, they responded by stating that if a stock had no par value, then the state would assume one, for example, $100. Well, this reaction prompted many firms to do what is, seemingly, the mode currently: They went to "low par" stock, for example, one cent per share.▲

MODIFYING COMMON STOCK

There are three ways to classify or modify common stock: (1) by voting rights, (2) by dividend preference, and (3) by liquidation preference. Some years ago in the course of working on a business deal involving real estate I realized that the ways that common stock can be classified can provide a technique for creative financing of a developing firm. An experienced individual with a remarkable track record of real estate development came upon a situation in which a trust wished to sell all of its substantial holdings of real estate, which included everything from 3,600 acres of land that could be subdivided into smaller lots (and sold for substantial prices for homes) to lots in the city. By buying all of this land as a unit and raising it to its highest and best uses (or selling off the single lots), this enterprising entrepreneur saw the possibility of making a lot of money for his backers and himself. To effect this purchase, he enlisted the services of an investment banking firm. When told of this trust's desire to sell as a lot all of these diverse parcels of land and the entrepreneur's track record for large real estate development (he had directed the development of one of the most illustrious new towns in California), an investment banker agreed to assist in the raising of the necessary funds.

Since this was a real estate deal—and thus subject to the Debt/Equity rules of real estate, as opposed to corporate finance—a determination was made to divide the pie into three pieces. The first would be the largest piece and would be the senior debt. This 90 percent piece of the purchase price was placed with a pension fund of a very large California firm which had expressed interest to the investment banker in doing a deal with California real estate. To get the "equity" piece of the amount needed, two other clients of the investment bank were solicited, one an investment arm of a major religious organization and the other was the real estate deal division of a huge American diversified company. The investment arm of the religious organization agreed to take approximately half of the equity part of the deal.

A BRIEF DIGRESSION: "PIGGY-BACK FINANCING"

The real estate division of the major diversified company that invested in the equity (Class B) stock of the above example expressed a problem, however. It said

▲ A company's by-laws provide for so many "authorized" shares, a figure approved by the state Corporation Commission. The company then issues shares up to this maximum. Usually, when the outstanding shares get even *close* to this maximum, with shareholder approval the company applies for an addition to this maximum.

it would like to take the other roughly half of the equity piece but that it did not have any investable funds available at the moment. It then asked the investment banker if it could find a bank that would lend it some money. At the time the country's banking system was experiencing a rather severe credit crunch. When a major bank was asked to lend money to the real estate division of the very large firm, it agreed to lend this firm the necessary money *if* the investment banker could find the requisite amount of money for the bank to *borrow*! Yes, if someone would loan money to the bank, the bank would be pleased to loan money to the division of the very large firm that needed the money *if* the lender of the money to the bank pledged the loan as collateral for the loan to the real estate division.

This sounds crazy at first, but it isn't. What happened is that the money market division of this huge firm, which also had an extremely large finance division, simply purchased a certificate of deposit from the bank in question and then pledged this CD as collateral for the loan. This gave the bank the necessary money, and because it was riskless to the bank, the rate that the bank charged the borrowing firm for this loan was only a few basis points▲ over the rate the CD carried. "Why," one might ask, "didn't the large firm just advance or loan the money to its own division?" A reasonable question but one for which there is a good answer. The division of the large firm that bought the CD *needed* a negotiable money market instrument for its portfolio; it did not need a "loan" for a real estate speculation. And a loan to its sister division was *not* a money market instrument! In short, the Money Market Division got what it wanted *and* the Real Estate Division got what it needed—and at a very low interest rate. Today, this practice has become quite commonplace and is called **piggy-back financing.** Currently, this technique will usually result in a loan at a rate about 35 basis points above the CD rate. A former student of mine told me recently of his acquisition of a company utilizing this very technique. He bought the target company, along with a note to the selling shareholders, with a bank loan that was guaranteed by a CD from the same bank, this CD being supplied by a relative. After he acquired the company, he boosted sales rapidly in the next 2 years and then sold an interest in the company in an amount sufficient to repay the bank loan. At this point, he owned a majority of the company for *zero dollars* of his money!

PREFERRED STOCK

The first innovation of common stock was **preferred stock**. And as one might suspect, necessity was the motive this time, too. In England in the mid-1850s, when the big push was on to lay railroad track, there was a law regulating the amount of debt a firm could have. So instead of issuing more debt, which paid

---

▲ A "basis point" is one one-hundredth of 1 percent interest, that is 0.01%.

a fixed return, the railroads switched to preferred stock.▲ In the United States, preferred stock was first issued apparently in the middle 1800s during times of stress and crisis. George Evans points out that railroads put off bankruptcy by paying interest on bonds with preferred stock. When the financial crisis was over the preferred stock was switched to common stock. Up until the 1870s, railroads were the sole issuers of preferred stock, but after that time other firms began using it.▲▲ The obvious drawback in issuing preferred stock is the fact that dividends are not tax-deductible; interest is. But before 1913, however, there was no corporate income tax, and for practical purposes, before the 1930s (when the corporate tax was very low) it did not matter much to a corporation whether it issued preferred stock or debt. Of course there are technical differences, but there are major similarities, too. They both carry a fixed payment: dividends for the preferred stock and interest for the debt. The debt has preference to the preferred stock in liquidation, but the preferred stock has preference to common stock in liquidation. With the advent of the high-tech start-ups in the 1980s, and especially in the 1990s, preferred stock became the vehicle of choice for venture capitalists. They classified it in permutations of the above three ways: voting, dividend preference, and liquidation preference. They also might have used the convertible feature.

With ordinary preferred stock, there is no voting privilege. But this situation can change. *Preferred stock is different from debt in that the board of directors must declare each and every dividend that is paid*. With debt, the board must approve the initial borrowing, but after that the Chief Financial Officer can pay the interest without consultation with the board.

DICHOTOMIZING PREFERRED STOCK

Preferred stock may be dichotomized in several ways, for example, **cumulative** and **noncumulative**. If the stock is "cumulative" and the board does not declare a dividend when it is supposed to be declared, the dividends accumulate in "arrears." If the stock is noncumulative and a dividend is omitted by the board, the dividend is *lost*. But to keep companies honest virtually all preferred stock issues have a clause that stipulates that if so many dividends are passed (if the stock is noncumulative) or if the arrearages reach a certain dollar amount (if the stock is

---

▲ For an excellent paper detailing the history of corporate financial markets in England and the United States see Jonathan Barron Baskin, "The Development of Corporate Financial Markets in Britain and the United States: Overcoming Asymmetric Information," *Business History Review*, Vol. 62 (Summer 1988), 199–237.

▲▲ George Heberton Evans, Jr. "Preferred stock in the United States," *American Economic Review*, 1929, Vol. 19 (March), 43–58; and George Heberton Evans, Jr. "Preferred stock in the United States: 1850–1878," *American Economic Review*, 1931, Vol. 30 (March), 43–58. Cited in Brian Grinder and Dan W. Cooper, "Applications of Financial History," *Financial Practice and Education*, Vol. 5, no. 1 (Spring/Summer 1995), 96–103.

cumulative), then the preferred stockholders get sufficient voting rights to elect a majority of the board. In this way the preferred stock-holders can take control of the company and manage it in a way such that they will get paid—if this is possible.

Another dichotomy is that preferred stock may be **callable** or noncallable. All preferred stock should be made callable at the company's option. If it does not do this, the company would be forced to tender for the stock in the market or otherwise. In this case, all the preferred stockholders would have to do is to refuse them, and the company would be forced to raise the tender price.

It is possible to make the preferred stock convertible into common stock such that the dichotomy would be *convertible* and *nonconvertible*. The absence of votes on preferred stock in a close (private) deal may be compensated for by having a provision that the preferred stock-holders have a certain number of seats on the board. This would seem like the same thing as having votes, but it is technically different.

MONEY MARKET PREFERRED

In recent years, firms have been using preferred stock as a surrogate for commercial paper or other short-term borrowing. Firms could do this because the firm had a "tax loss carry-forward" that meant that as long as the firm had this "tax loss carry-forward" (currently for 5 years maximum), it did not pay taxes and therefore the tax shield resulting from interest was not applicable. Because corporations have a substantial exclusion on *dividend income*—which they do not have on interest income—this means that for a corporation receiving dividend income the *effective* tax rate is only about 7 percent as opposed to 34 percent (Federal) tax on interest income. Because this is such an advantage to firms, they are willing to accept a *lower* yield on preferred stock than they would on the same company's commercial paper. This means that the company issuing the preferred stock gets *a lower cost of capital.*

To make this more like commercial paper, the rate on this kind of money market preferred stock will vary with some indexes, such as the London Inter-Bank Offering Rate (LIBOR) or some other index. Also, the preferred stock is "puttable" by the holder, meaning that the holder of the preferred stock can "put" the stock to the company that issued it—that is, make it repay the principal. While at first blush this innovation seems like it would not be applicable for a developing firm, this may not be the case since developing firms may have tax losses that could be carried forward.

While preferred stock was the first innovation in stock, it was not the last.

CREATING CLASSES OF STOCK

Returning to the story of the acquisition of the lot of real estate, the situation was thus: The pension fund needed a senior security as they were the equivalent of the debt position; the church and the large diversified company needed a security that would allow them to benefit from the resale of the different parcels of land; and finally the entrepreneur, and the investment banker needed a way to make a share of the profit after the other two received their money that they had invested. Since the whole idea of the exercise was to buy the land, upgrade it to its highest and best use, sell the land and then go out of business, *liquidation became the first means of classification.*

Accordingly, three **classes** of stock were created. Class A stock went to the pension fund which put up 90 percent of the purchase price. This class of stock had **liquidation preference** equal to an amount of the investment. The second class of stock, Class B, went to the equity investors, which also included the investment banker, who took money from its pension fund to invest in the deal, the church, and the diversified company. (Certainly this was a great way for the investment banker to inspire confidence in the deal by the other three parties who were investing in the deal.) This stock had liquidation preference equal to what these three parties contributed to the deal. Finally, Class C stock was issued to the entrepreneur who had the idea of doing this deal and the investment banker who put the deal together. This class of stock had no liquidation preference, but after the first two classes of stock received their money back, then this Class C stock would participate in any liquidation in the proportion of 20 percent for the Class A, 50 percent for the Class B, and 30 percent for the Class C stock. Since the entrepreneur was going to manage the enterprise, voting was not really a priority, so Class A had no votes, Class B had enough votes to elect two of the three directors, and Class C had enough votes to elect one director— the entrepreneur himself. Since the liquidation distributions were the equivalent of dividends, the third way to classify stock did not come into play. In summary, by simply classifying stock in a way that did the job needed, all parties were satisfied.

OTHER USES FOR CLASSIFIED STOCK

When doing a start-up, very often situations present themselves in which the use of classified stock is appropriate. For example, if an entrepreneur is getting someone to invest all, or almost all, of the money in a deal, this investor may feel that he or she does not want to be in the same room, so to speak, with the entrepreneur if the firm becomes bankrupt. The entrepreneur, on the other hand, wants to run the show as he or she sees fit. To the entrepreneur, then, voting rights may have higher priority than anything else. To solve this dilemma, classified stock might be used. The "hard money" investor may receive a stock that has *preference in liquidation* and only one vote per share. When asked what "hard money" was, a professor once remarked that it was "hard to get." Or, more simply, it means "actual cash." "Promotional stock" has also been called "sweat equity" as it was *earned* by the sweat of the brow.

The entrepreneur, on the other hand, could receive a class of stock that had multiple votes per share such that he or she could elect a majority of the board. On this point, however, it may well be worth noting that most *inexperienced* entrepreneurs feel that they have to have control over their own company. What they do not know, however, is that if the firm gets into trouble, the hard money investors are not going to sit back and watch their investment get diluted. For example, if more money is needed in the firm in order to avoid a serious liquidity problem, one can be sure that if the "hard money" investor puts up that money, he or she will *not* do so on the *same* terms as the original investment. Instead the investor may insist on revamping the board and/or issuing a disproportionate amount of the class of stock already owned for the investment made. Furthermore, most inexperienced entrepreneurs do not realize that small or new companies are managed by *consensus* of the board, not votes.

Whenever two or more classes of stock are issued it is well, however, to make the shares equivalent in some way, for example, as (plain) common stock equivalents. This means make every class of stock convertible into common stock; at least, state what their equivalence is. Later, for example, if the firm is being bought by a third party, it may be quite important to have equivalent values for all the shares. One of the strangest conundrums I have ever seen with regard to classified stock was a situation where an engineer/entrepreneur had stock issued to him that could *never* receive a cash dividend. Later, the problem arose as to the value of this stock. What was the stock worth, if the only attribute it had was one vote per share?

Another fairly common method of issuing stock in a start-up is to issue some senior security to the parties who invest cash (e.g., one share for each dollar invested) *plus* one share of common stock. For the entrepreneur who put the deal together and/or the management, these parties would receive just common stock. Then if additional money is needed subsequently, the number of shares of the senior security would be disproportional to the original arrangement. If this situation persists, the promotional stockholders would be reduced in importance in the ownership of the firm. For example, if the entrepreneur of a Leveraged Buyout deal had 20 percent of the company originally—not too unusual a percentage—he or she might wind up owning only 5 percent of the company after some additional financings have taken place. (With high-tech start-ups, this ownership percentage would be much higher to start.) Conversely, if things go as planned, the entrepreneur and the hard money investor get what they thought they were going to get in the first place. If there is this kind of classification it is still important to make the senior security convertible into shares of the common. At least the equivalency should be enumerated; if the firm is sold the proportional ownership will be known.

Whenever professional money comes into a deal, you expect to have at least two classes of stock: preferred and common. The last money "in," as John Morris remarks, is the first money "out." They do this with preferred shares.

WARNING ABOUT TERMINOLOGY

Before passing on to other forms of classifications, it may be well to strike a note of warning about classified stock. In the 1920s—when regulations were nonexistent or lax—unscrupulous individuals would go about the country selling stock to people who knew little or nothing about securities. One of the principal ways of cheating—if this is not too strong of a word—was to use classified stock. They sold Class A shares to the public and Class B shares were reserved for the management. Since it was logical to assume that Class A shares were better than Class B shares, most people that bought such shares felt that they were in a superior position to the Class B shareholders. What they may not have realized was that Class B shares may have had more votes *per share* than did Class A—for example, 50 votes for each share of Class B stock and one vote for each share of Class A stock. This voting classification, by itself, may not have been the misleading aspect of the classified stock but remember there are *two other ways to classify stock*. For example, the Class B shares may have been entitled to a certain amount of dividends *before* the Class A stockholders received anything. Well, the abuses of classified stock were such that the state Corporation Commissions, which regulated securities sales in their states, began to associate classified stock with fraud. Today, therefore, it may not be wise to use the terminology "Class A, Class B," etc. when issuing stock, even in a closely held deal. Instead, such designations as Senior Preferred, Preferred, and Common may provoke less anxiety on the part of regulators in the respective state Corporation Commissions.

INNOVATIVE DEBT SECURITIES

While innovations in stocks are impressive, they were matched by the innovations that have occurred in *debt* securities. Some of the more interesting for our kind of emerging firm follow. Note that in this discussion, the distinction that will be made between notes and bonds is convenient but perhaps not technically correct. Bonds will be assumed to be sold publicly; notes will be assumed to be privately placed. So if a debt security is to be sold to the public, it will be called a "bond." If the same type of security is to be sold privately, it may be called a note. For practical purposes, the innovative features that are added to a bond may be added to a "note."

"PAYMENT IN KIND" SECURITIES

Primarily started in the mid-1980s, when the "Go-Go" merger craze was in full swing, some securities, especially subordinated debentures, were issued where the interest and/or the principal was payable in cash or in the issuer's common stock. This is called "**PIK**," or **payment in kind**. While we, in the context of this book are not interested in exotic securities for takeovers of very large corporations, PIKs do offer the management of developing firms another tool.

For many firms, there will be situations when it is in the company's best interest to protect itself from the risk of failure to pay interest and/or principal on its indebtedness. This is true even if the debt is in issued to insiders in a closely held firm. By making the securities—usually debt, but it may be preferred stock—PIK securities, an effective hedge for a very uncertain future is created.

And of course by making the debt securities "subordinated" the firm creates debt that is, as mentioned in Chapter 3 *de facto equity*. In fact, it may be that the issuing firm and its managers/investors may intend from the beginning to basically pay off the debt with common stock, but get a tax deduction before maturity. The reverse of this, in a slightly different form, is where a firm issues preferred stock when it has a tax loss carry-forward, but with the announced intention of converting the preferred stock to debt instruments when the tax loss expires and the lack of "tax deductibility" becomes important.

SEVERAL OTHER DEBT INNOVATIONS

Making the interest rate on notes *adjustable* was another innovation of the 1980s. This rate could be adjusted according to some money market rate such as the bank prime rate or LIBOR. Or, it could be adjusted to some long-term rate such as a long-term Treasury bond. This doesn't appear to be particularly useful for developing firms as much as large, established firms, but when doing a deal and offering a subordinated note as partial compensation for the purchase price of firm in a Leveraged Buyout (LBO), the opportunity to index the interest rate on the note will surely be present. **Floating rate notes** are a variant of this indexing idea. In this case, the interest rate floats rather constantly—weekly or monthly, for example—as a function of some rate such as LIBOR.

There have been lots of other innovations in debt securities in the past 15 or 20 years—such as "receivables-backed" bonds or collateralized mortgage obligations (CMOs) but these are not particularly applicable to use by developing firms.▲ With respect to receivables-backed securities, however, one example does come to mind. A high-tech firm in Silicon Valley, with Sales of about $600 million, established a captive subsidiary to which it sold its Accounts Receivable. With the backing of a Clean Letter of Credit (discussed in Chapter 12) and the A/Rs as collateral, the subsidiary issued commercial paper which was used to finance the A/Rs at a much lower rate than if the company borrowed from a bank with the A/Rs as collateral.

▲ For a particularly interesting article on the subject of these innovations in debt and equity securities see John D. Finnerty's article "Securities Innovation: Where is the Value Added?" *Financial Management Collection* Winter 1988.

SUMMARY

This chapter discussed the kinds of securities that an entrepreneur is likely to use in the course of starting a new company or acquiring another company, or in the course of raising funds externally. The first part of the chapter was devoted to what are called "sweetened securities," meaning convertibles and bonds (or notes) with warrants. It is important for an entrepreneurial manager to know certain things about the types of securities before he or she enters into discussions with investment bankers or before doing a deal. Convertibles, which are popular during bull markets, are bonds that are convertible into stock. For the company, when it calls the bonds, the equity section is increased and the debt section reduced. Bonds with warrants, on the other hand, remain outstanding even if the warrant is "exercised"—meaning the holder pays the company for a share of stock with a warrant and cash. Bonds with warrants are not as popular as they once were, but when doing private deals, the use of shadow (or "make believe") warrants can be expected.

Subsequently the chapter dealt with the principal types of innovative securities that have been developed in recent years. It behooves someone trying to put together a deal, say, for the acquisition of another company, to at least be familiar with these "tools" of the deal business.

The use of classified common stock, it was noted, is particularly useful in doing private deals—start-ups or buyouts. Stocks may be classified three ways: 1) by liquidation preference 2) by voting rights and 3) by dividend preference.

If an entrepreneur does not even know what exists, it stands to reason that he or she will be oblivious to their use. These securities were created for various purposes, some of which the entrepreneurial manager may encounter.

QUESTIONS FOR DISCUSSION

1. When you as CFO or CEO of your emerging company go "downtown" to discuss issuing debt securities, you expect that the underwriter will insist on "sweetening" the offering. What "sweetener" would you prefer—a convertible feature or a bond with warrants? Discuss your reasoning.
2. If you want to borrow the money to make an acquisition of (another) company, and you feel that the economic climate is not right for bank financing, you will have to talk with finance companies. These finance companies want returns of about 25–35 percent per annum. When the finance company asks you for shadow warrants, how will you know if they are asking for too many such "shadow warrants"? Where would you get the money needed

9

CHAPTER REVIEW

QUESTIONS FOR DISCUSSION *(continued)*

to redeem these shadow warrants at their expiration date if your new company does not have all that is needed in available cash?

3. When you as an aspiring entrepreneur want to start a company or do a buyout of an existing company, you will need a certain amount of "equity" for the deal, that is, actual cash to invest in the deal. Suppose that is more than you have, how would you raise the remaining amount of money? Now in the course of raising the remainder of the money you may find it necessary to use certain securities to accomplish the certain specific needs of the deal. Discuss three or four of the securities that you might use in satisfying the needs of those participating in financing the deal.

4. Discuss how "piggy-back" financing might be used in raising the equity needed to do a deal—either a buyout or possibly a start-up.

JUST WONDERING!: A STUDENT ASSIGNMENT

Here are two assignments concerning CompuServe and Prodigy for the readers and students. However, first some background on both companies.

In 1980, the tax preparation giant H&R Block purchased the rock-solid CompuServe for over $500 million and kept its independence and position as a *business* service. On the other hand, IBM and Sears launched Prodigy in 1990 with a seed capital of $500 million and roughly another $500 million earmarked for future needs. Prodigy had been positioned as an online shopping place—mainly for records, clothes, and airline tickets. "We had the belief that goods will be sold electronically, so why not establish dominance in the marketplace?" Prodigy's Ross Glatzer stated.

1. Given different market niches and growth strategies, as well as deep pockets, for both CompuServe and Prodigy, why could neither grow significantly in the online business? Hint 1: In addition to niche and strategy for CompuServe *vis-á-vis* AOL, you may also want to look at the role that content plays in an online information service. Hint 2: In addition to niche and strategy for Prodigy, you may also want to specifically compare/contrast Prodigy of 1990 with Amazon.com of 1994.

2. What role did the envisioned "business model" (the way a venture makes money) play in the success or failure of each of: Prodigy, CompuServe, AOL, and Amazon.com?

9

CHAPTER REVIEW

10

Intermediate-Term Financing: Term Loans and Private Placements

The preceding two chapters have dealt with what might be termed "long-term finance," or raising funds externally from the public markets. This chapter deals with debt that is privately placed and intermediate in length: 3 years up to about 10 or 15 years. At the shorter length, this type of loan is primarily a **term loan**, meaning that it is paid back in installments over the tenure of the loan, monthly or quarterly. Term loans really originated in popularity, if not in fact, during World War II. But since that time, term loans from banks, finance companies, and other institutional lenders are used frequently by the kind of entrepreneurial growing firm that we are assuming in this book. With the "public" market for financing in a depressed state, as it is currently, much more attention is being directed to private placements, including intermediate-term financing. Institutional investors tend to be more farsighted than a sometimes whimsical market might be.

There are some significant differences between the bank term-loan market and the private placement market, both of which are grouped as "intermediate-term lending." Debt instruments in the private placement (intermediate-term) market are usually *securities* rather than loans. Some maturities tend to be much longer than bank loans. Interest rates, based on the LIBOR rate initially, tend to be fixed rather than floating, which is true for *short-term bank loans,* if not for term loans. While banks are the source of short-term loans and term loans, institutions, particularly life insurance companies and now junk bond funds (funds set up specifically to invest in below investment grade private placements and other similar securities)▲, are the source of most private placements. Even if banks make the intermediate loan initially, they may sell/"layoff" all or part of this loan to another institution.

THE FACTOR OF FIRM SIZE

Stephen Prowse describes three types of markets and differentiates them with respect to what he calls the **information intensity** of the firm. When firms are small, they represent a much more *information-problematic* situation than when they are quite large and, possibly, publicly owned. And in the middle, there are firms that are still information-problematic, but not as greatly as when they were smaller. Banks, by custom, are able and equipped to deal with the smaller, more *information-intensive* types of firms. In this market borrowers and lenders typically negotiate lending terms. Lenders evaluate and then monitor the borrower's credit risk. (Covenants—discussed at length under "Loan Covenants," later in this chapter—are employed to control that risk.) And, in general, really small borrowers lack access to the public markets.

When a firm is rather small, the term loan will probably be issued by the firm's bank or finance company, but as it grows the firm will probably turn to financial institutions, life insurance companies, and other financial vehicles such as junk bond funds for a private placement loan of the intermediate—or even longer—length. Before 1990, life insurance companies in the United States had about 20 percent of their loan portfolio in private placements in below investment grade (BIG) bonds.▲▲ Coincident with the **credit crunch** that started about early 1991—at the same time that the banks had to report highly leveraged transactions (HLTs)—there was a pronounced "flight to quality" by the insurance companies. This trend only started to subside in 2000; since then the insurance companies have gone back to a safe harbor somewhat as the "credit crunch" of 2001 has taken hold. In the present environment, many firms that are preempted from doing an LBO are doing private placements which are still available. What has happened since the life insurance companies' flight to quality is that the market has become quite diffused and now there are many sources for private placements other than the handful of life insurance companies that dominated the market prior to 1991.

▲ The so-called junk bond funds developed out of the void that ensued after the collapse of Drexel Burnham Lambert, the large investment banking house with Michael Milken as head of the West Coast operations.

▲▲ This section draws heavily on an excellent article by Stephen D. Prowse, "The Economics of Private Placements: Middle Market Finance, Life Insurance Companies, and a Credit Crunch," *Economic Review,* Federal Reserve Bank of Dallas, Third Quarter 1997, 12–24.

EXHIBIT 10.1 Credit Market Characteristics			
CHARACTERISTIC	**BANK LOAN**	**PRIVATE PLACEMENT**	**PUBLIC BOND**
CONTRACT TERMS			
AVERAGE LOAN SIZE	SMALL	MEDIUM	LARGE
AVERAGE MATURITY	SHORT	LONG	LONGEST
INTEREST RATE	FLOATING	FIXED	FIXED
COVENANTS	MANY, TIGHT	FEWER, LOOSER	FEWEST, LOOSEST
COVENANT RENEGOTIATION	FREQUENT	LESS FREQUENT	RARE
COLLATERAL	FREQUENT	LESS FREQUENT	RARE
LIQUIDITY OF INSTRUMENT	LOW	LOW	HIGH
BORROWERS			
AVERAGE BORROWER SIZE	SMALL	MEDIUM TO LARGE	LARGE
SEVERITY OF INFORMATION PROBLEMS POSED BY BORROWERS	HIGH	MODERATE	LOW
LENDERS			
LENDERS	INTERMEDIARIES	INTERMEDIARIES	VARIES
PRINCIPAL LENDER	BANKS	LIFE INSURERS	VARIES
LENDER MONITORING	INTENSE	SIGNIFICANT	MINIMAL

SOURCE: Stephen Prowse, "The Economics of Private Placements," *Economic Review* (Third Quarter 1997), p. 14.

CREDIT MARKET CHARACTERISTICS

Exhibit 10.1 presents the characteristics of the market for bank loans (meaning primarily short-term loans), private placements, and public bonds. Let us examine each of these characteristics.

It is reported that 80 percent of bank loans ranged between $10,000 and $1 million. Eighty percent of all private placements ranged from $10 million to $100 million, and 80 percent of all public bond offerings were between the range of $100 million and $500 million.[▲]

Mark Carey *et al.*[▲▲] report that maturities of private placements are generally longer than bank loans but not as long as the maturity of publicly issued bond issues. Bank loans, meaning the working capital loans, were for less than 1 year in 80 percent of the cases. Private placements are generally between 7 and 15 years maturity in half of the observations. Roughly 70 percent of the public bonds (issued in 1989) were longer than 10 years.

Banks have a preference for short-term loans over longer-term loans primarily because of the nature of the assets and liabilities of the banks. Banks follow

[▲] Prowse, *op. cit.*, p. 13.

[▲▲] Carey, Mark, Stephen Prouse, John Rea, and Gregory Udell, "The Economics of the Private Placement Market," *Financial Markets: Institutions & Instruments,* 1993, 2 (3).

the age-old practice of financing short-term assets with short-term liabilities (demand deposits). Banks could loan "long" and then "convert" their assets to short term by means of "swaps" but they have been reluctant to do so. It is speculated that, among other reasons, this is because of the costs of swaps, even though the cost is relatively low. If a bank did a loan with a fixed rate, it could convert that loan into a variable rate with a "swap" arrangement. It could swap their fixed rate loan to a party who wanted a variable rate in exchange for their variable rate loan. This "swap" process is so standard now that the price for such a maneuver is actually very small. Life insurance companies, on the other hand, prefer long term assets as they have long term liabilities. The new Junk Bond Funds also have primarily long term sources of money so they also prefer long term loans although they also make rather short term loans.

Since interest rates were already mentioned, the next characteristic listed in Exhibit 10.1 is the question of **covenants**. Since covenants are so important in the issuance of term loans and private placements a later part of this chapter will be devoted to this most important subject. Let us now focus on collateral.

With smaller firms—especially the ones that are information-problematic—**collateral** is frequently, or almost always, required. But as the size of the loan increases, and the information problems decrease, presumably, collateral becomes less frequently required. When collateral becomes less important in the loan, the loan is said to be a **cash flow loan**, meaning that the lender is relying almost solely on the firm's cash flow to repay the loan, whether it be a term loan by a bank or finance company or a private placement. For smaller firms, receiving a term loan usually is associated with financing secured by equipment. With *private placements* with institutional lenders there may not be any collateral, especially if the firm is *not* particularly information-problematic. With publicly issued bonds, virtually all are unsecured in the sense that they are not *specifically collateralized.* In general, these are called "debentures" in the United States.▲ Even though there is a rise in such collateralized bonds as CMOs (collateralized mortgage obligations), the so-called "unsecured" bonds are issued many times more than collateralized bonds.▲▲

The characteristic labeled "Liquidity of instrument" refers to the ability of the holder of the loan to sell or otherwise dispose of the loan. While bank loans might be syndicated to a group of banks, as mentioned, the smaller term loans are usually held by the bank until maturity. (An exception to this might be in the case of loans guaranteed by the Small Business Administration, which will be discussed in the next chapter.) Even private placement of loans with institutions, usually life insurance companies, remain as the "collection bank" with

---

▲ In other countries, e.g., South Africa, "debenture" means something different from the American meaning.

▲▲ "Unsecured" is really an inappropriate term for debentures of all types. These bonds have "general creditor" status and as such, in liquidation, they and the other "general creditors" are entitled to everything that is not otherwise secured specifically, after the payment of the "priority claims."

the institution negotiating the loan in the first place. Naturally, publicly placed bonds are freely traded and are expected to be so.

All firms have access to borrowing from banks, including the small or developing firm we are assuming in this book; the majority of loans made by banks are for smaller firms simply because smaller firms outnumber larger firms. To do a private placement with an institution, however, the firm should be medium to large. This is because the minimum is usually about $5 million. For access to the public market for straight bonds, the firm should be rather large (smaller, emerging companies can do this with sweeteners). For many small firms, doing a private placement is much more desirable than doing an S-18 public offering. (See Chapter 8.) This is due to the enormous increase in money available for private placements and the shorter time it takes to do a private placement. The other cited reason is the maximum dollar limit of $7.5 million. Why go through the strain of a public offering if only $7.5 million can be raised when it is much easier to do a private placement for $10 or $15 million? The other advantages of doing a private placement were covered in Chapter 8.

Since Prowse couches much of his article in terms of the information problems, the line in the exhibit referring to "the severity of information problems" speaks for itself. Banks perform all or virtually all the due diligence needed to make a loan of *any length*, so it is no surprise that they are staffed to do a proper due diligence review for term loans.

The low severity of information problems posed by publicly issued bonds might be a bit misleading, however. If the investment banker that is handling the bond placement does its job in an orderly and proper manner, then the *buyers* of the bond may feel that deep or intense investigation is not necessary on their part. Of course, this is subject to exception. If an institutional buyer of a firm's stock owns a significant amount of that stock, it probably will make it its business to learn a significant amount about that firm and its operation and management. And the same thing might apply if it owns a substantial portion of that firm's bonds. This involves a significant amount of investigation *before* it buys the bonds and a (somewhat) continuous monitoring after purchase of the bonds. But unless the amount of bonds is significant, the institution that owns the bond will only review the status of the company that issued the bond on a cursory basis. Additionally, if a bond is rated by one of the bond rating agencies, this rating agency will monitor the firm after issuance of the securities and issue warnings if the firm's position deteriorates.

THE EVOLUTION OF THE CREDIT MARKET

THE CHANGING POSITION OF LIFE INSURANCE COMPANIES

The flight to quality by life insurance companies alluded to on page 236 deserves some elaboration. Starting about 1991, the relative amount of money invested in private placements by insurance companies, in what are known as

EXHIBIT 10.2	Gross Issuance of Private Placements						
	1989	1990	1991	1992	1993	1994	1995
TOTAL ISSUANCE (IN BILLIONS)	$54.70	$49.90	$42.10	$29.50	$52.00	$31.00	$41.00
BELOW INVESTMENT GRADE (BIG) (IN BILLIONS)	$6.60	$8.10	$3.80	$3.20	$3.00	$2.00	$1.00
BIG AS PERCENTAGE OF TOTAL	12.1	16.2	8.9	10.8	5.8	6.4	2.4

Note: Excludes restructuring-related issues in excess of $250 million, issues to finance employee stock ownership plans, and related issues

SOURCE: Securities Data Corp. as cited by Prowse, *op. cit.,* p. 16.

below investment grade (BIG) securities, dropped dramatically. As Exhibit 10.2, taken from Prowse, shows, the gross issuance of private placements by nonfinancial corporations, primarily life insurance companies, dropped from $8.1 billion in 1990 to only $1 billion in 1995. Or expressed in percentage terms, it dropped from 12.1 percent to only 2.4 percent! This sharp drop-off in life insurance company investments resulted in what has since been called the "credit crunch of the early 1990s." Prowse defines a credit crunch as a situation where for a "given price of credit, lenders substantially reduce the volume provided to a group of borrowers whose risk is substantially unchanged."[a] Furthermore, the decline in lending did not result because of slack business conditions (1990 was the start of a business recession). The life insurance companies, feeling a variety of pressures from different sources, simply decided to lend less in the form of private placements. (Not to mention that five insurance companies were seized by regulators and two more wrote down their holdings of bonds and real estate investments.)

While the life insurance companies were pulling away from private placements, the banks were becoming extremely selective in their lending, too—a situation which was relaxed in the mid-1990s, has continued in the early 2000s. This noticeably affected attempts to do a deal, such as buying another company. The term loans that banks had been providing for this purpose declined precipitously due to the heightened concern by the banking authorities for the safety of bank loans. Having come from a reeling experience with Savings and Loans, the Federal Reserve and the other regulatory authorities were determined to keep banks from making questionable loans. As mentioned above, to this end they issued in late 1990 an order that the banks must identify "highly leveraged transactions" (HLTs) and *take a reserve against their capital* for these loans. This was something a bank never likes to do, since their capital is so limited anyway, and with this ruling the authorities brought this lending to an abrupt halt.

The result of this stoppage in making highly leveraged loans—which would really be BIG loans—was that many deals were simply not done. Serving as an

[a] Prowse, *op. cit.,* p. 16.

EXHIBIT 10.3	High-Yield Nonconvertible Debt Private Placement by Nonfinancial Issuers									
	1989	1990	1991	1992	1993	1994	1995	1996	1997	1998*
PROCEEDS (BILLIONS)	$25.8	9.4	3.0	1.8	1.6	1.8	1.6	1.8	1.7	.08
MARKET SHARE	52.9	19.4	6.2	3.8	3.3	3.7	3.4	3.8	3.4	.2
NUMBER OF ISSUES	267	152	79	34	38	62	43	48	39	2
*PARTIAL YEAR ONLY										

SOURCE: Securities Data Company, Inc. Used with permission.

alternative, finance companies were flooded with applications for financing, especially for acquisition deals, and this included term loans. So with life insurance company lending for BIG loans dropping, and the banks becoming very reluctant to make any below grade loans, the first few years in the 1990s were particularly difficult—especially for making acquisitions.

OTHER SOURCES OF PRIVATE PLACEMENT

As the United States came out of the recession of the early 1990s, there emerged a number of other sources of BIG private placements. Instead of insurance companies dominating the market, as they did up to their retreat and their flight to safety, now there are numerous sources for this type of financing. To fill the massive vacuum for what has become known as "junk bonds," precipitated by the failure of Drexel Burnham Lambert, a number of funds were set up to invest not only in low-rated publicly issued bonds but private placements of smaller (or larger) unrated or low rated firms.

Even the big investment banking companies got into the act. They either directed private placements to institutional sources, perhaps controlled by them, or, more importantly, helped these BIG firms tap the public market for equity or debt issues that would have been unavailable to this type of firm in the early 1990s. This means that for a certain segment of the demand for private placements, these firms were in the wild and wooly stock or bond markets of the second half of the 1990s. In this way smaller firms have a better crack at the old established sources of these private placement loans.

To illustrate the decline in the private placement market that characterized the 1980s, notice in Exhibit 10.3 the drop in private placements from 1989 to April 1998—an incomplete year. "High yield" here connotes lower quality; lower-yield bonds mean higher quality.

Offsetting this is the increase in public offerings during the bull market of the late 1990s. By the late 1990s, the tight credit situation of the early 1990s had been replaced with a market awash with loanable funds in a way that had not been seen for a long time, if ever. As mentioned earlier, the bear market of 2000–2002 reversed this and tapped into this hoard of loanable funds.

This abundance of loanable funds can also be shown in another way. Exhibits 10.4 and 10.5 plot how the spread between the top-ranked bonds and

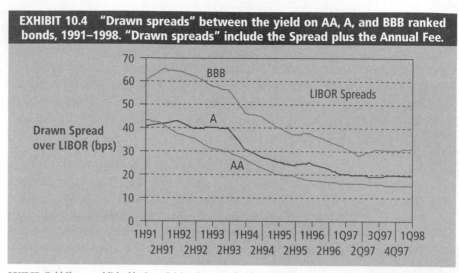

EXHIBIT 10.4   "Drawn spreads" between the yield on AA, A, and BBB ranked bonds, 1991–1998. "Drawn spreads" include the Spread plus the Annual Fee.

SOURCE: Gold Sheets, published by Loan Pricing Corp. Used with permission

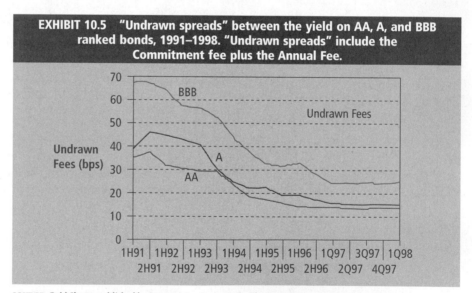

EXHIBIT 10.5   "Undrawn spreads" between the yield on AA, A, and BBB ranked bonds, 1991–1998. "Undrawn spreads" include the Commitment fee plus the Annual Fee.

SOURCE: Gold Sheets, published by Loan Pricing Corp. Used with permission.

the lowest-ranked (investment grade) bonds has narrowed over the 1990s. When loanable funds were desperately short in the early 1990s, the spread was about 25 basis points. By the late 1990s, the spread had been reduced to about 10–15 points. In these two exhibits you can see the effect of the loosening of credit between 1991 and 1998. The dramatic reduction in the spreads shows how money became more plentiful over this period of time.

LOAN COVENANTS▲

Inherent in any term loan or private placement are covenants—restrictions placed on the borrower by the lender. Essentially these covenants or restrictions are of two types: *affirmative* and *negative*. The former are not usually a problem to a borrower but the latter are.

AFFIRMATIVE COVENANTS

Affirmative covenants are what might be called "boilerplate" in the usual contract. They include promises such as the firm will remain in the same business as it is in, or that it will submit periodic financial statements—perhaps of a certain type, such as certified statements and periodic statements from a responsible officer of the company that the firm is in compliance with all the terms of the loan agreement. Other affirmative statements, such as proper insurance coverage, may also be required. It is not too unusual for a lender to require that the borrowing firm insure the chief executive or some similar officer's life, with the beneficiary being the lender. This requirement might come about if the lender perceives that the chief executive is *very* important to the firm's success—which is another way of saying that this person is important to the repayment of the debt to the lender. Other boilerplate restrictions might involve the statement that the firm's existence is assured, that the firm's assets are to be maintained in a safe and orderly way, and that the firm will pay its taxes, unless it has a legitimate dispute with the taxing authorities. Occasionally an affirmative statement will require that the top management—as defined—remain in place throughout the term of the loan. In one instance where this requirement was in place the board of directors fired the chief executive. This caused an immediate "call" on the loan of $5 million by an insurance company and this placed the firm in great jeopardy.

REPRESENTATIONS AND WARRANTIES

Other standard boilerplate statements include a statement that the firm is properly incorporated, or otherwise in good legal standing, and that the firm's board of directors has approved the borrowing in question. One should keep in mind that it is *always* necessary for the firm's board to approve borrowing from a bank or other institution. Once the broad statement by the board is passed, the actual specifics of the borrowing are be left to the responsible officer. Some other affirmative statements are that the firm is not in litigation, except as noted, and that it has "good and clear" title to its assets. Some statement about the firm being current with its taxes will probably also be included.

▲ This section regarding covenants draws largely from Jasper H. Arnold, "How to negotiate a term loan," *Harvard Business Review*, March-April, 1982, 131 ff.

NEGATIVE COVENANTS

While *affirmative* covenants and the *representations and warranties* are important, the major covenants that must concern management when negotiating a term loan or a private placement are the **negative covenants.** These covenants will be discussed individually, but they might be categorized as being either a type of covenant dealing with a *number* or a *specific act.*

For example, the firm must maintain a certain minimum working capital (a specific number type of covenant). In this case, the firm might be required to maintain a working capital of $5,500,000. It is felt that the "number" types of covenants are the ones that may be broken in the course of doing business. In this example, the firm is going to have a working capital of only $5,000,000. (This could be discovered in the course of doing an audit.) When this does happen, the accounting firm will advise the firm and the firm's chief financial officer will notify the lender and ask for a time-limited waiver of the covenant. With these types of covenants a breach might result in a technical default but this is one that the lender can waive if requested.

But a breach of the second type of covenant—for example, paying a dividend—might provoke a completely different and far more emphatic response from the lender. In the case mentioned on page 243, where the board fired the chief executive, the life insurance company did not even call the company to give the firm a chance to explain their position in the firing; it merely called the loan—it "**pulled the trigger.**" Starting a new store when the firm agreed not to do so would be another example of a violation of this type of covenant. Or paying a bonus. These would be construed as *deliberate* breaches of the agreement, something any lender would consider highly offensive. The manager who violates one of these "go, no-go" types of covenants deserves all the trouble his or her action will provoke from a lender.

Jasper Arnold▲ groups the *negative* covenants into five groupings.

Cash Flow Control

When the lender perceives the firm's Balance Sheet as sufficiently strong, it may not seek to inject covenants that control the firm's use of its cash flow. If it looks like the firm could easily *refinance* the loan in question, the lender will be much less concerned about placing restrictive covenants. Much was said about the importance of the firm's Balance Sheet in Chapter 3, but here is really where the importance comes into play. By managing the firm's Balance Sheet wisely—because it is so important to lenders—the firm can spare itself many an anxious moment watching to see if it will violate a negative covenant.

Cash flow control is really directed to the firm's NOCF (Net Operating Cash Flow) and more specifically to its NOCF' and its NOCF", a measure of its ability to service the debt. Such restrictions might include restrictions on the firm's capital expenditures, for example. This could be in the form of an absolute number or some sort of ratio. Or, the restriction might be a restriction on the firm pay-

---

▲ Arnold, *op. cit.*

ing dividends or bonuses, or perhaps restrictions on salaries to certain individuals. The more comfortable the lender is with the potential borrower, the fewer will be the restrictions placed on the firm's cash flow, as well as on everything else. The firm can start to perceive how the potential lender feels about the firm from early indications about these more restrictive covenants. In short, cash flow covenants will try to restrict how much the firm can plow back or pay out from its NOCF'. This is done, of course, to prevent dissipation of the firm's NOCF", which is the amount of money the firm has to service and repay the debt if it has periodic principal payments.

Control Over Strategy

Very often, a developing firm's management will approach a lender with great plans to expand the business in a dramatic fashion. While some firms can expand without the need for additional working capital, such as additional accounts receivable or inventory, most manufacturing firms cannot do so. One spectacular example of a firm that expanded like a rocket taking off is *Auto-by-Tel*, a major Web-based automobile dealer whose sales jumped from practically nothing to $1.8 billion in 1996 to be on course to hit $6 billion in fiscal 1998. *Amazon.com* had sales in 1997 of $148 million, which represented an increase of 825 percent from the prior year. But in both of these cases, little or no inventory was involved. *Amazon.com* may advertise that it has 2.5 million titles in its inventory but actually it has many fewer books in its inventory: It can merely relay the order to the publisher who keeps an inventory. *Auto by Tel* has a similar situation. This rapidly expanding company merely refers a potential buyer to a dealer near the potential buyer's zip code, who, in turn, calls the buyer with a deal on the car he or she wants. (This raises the interesting question, posed in Chapter 3, as to whether they actually had sales or just commissions, a lot less!) But with other "mortal" firms, an expansion of inventory and/or receivables will accompany an expansion in sales. And as we learned in Chapter 4, an *increase* in inventory or receivables means a *decrease* in cash—*dollar for dollar!* This is what is so scary to a potential lender. And this is why a potential lender will place restrictions on a firm's strategy if it looks like that strategy might impair the firm's cash flow (NOCF) with either excessive capital expenditures or working capital requirements.

In placing strategy restrictions, the lender may restrict the specific strategy or it might do so in a somewhat circuitous way. This could be by limiting the amount of the firm's capital expenditures or the amount it may spend on acquisitions or, possibly, it might place restrictions on the firm's Debt/Equity ratio or its working capital.

Balance Sheet Preservation

In Chapter 3 the importance of the Balance Sheet to bankers was mentioned. This is one good reason for the firm to concern itself with its Balance Sheet. In fact, the firm's Balance Sheet is probably the most important of the statements that the firm presents to a lender of a loan—*if* it is possible to say that one statement is more important. Also, the condition of a firm's Balance Sheet determines the ability of the firm to borrow additional funds if it runs short—and how many firms don't need some additional cash at some point in time? Arnold also stresses the fact that *it is considered to be bad financial management to finance long-term assets with short-term loans*. In order to put teeth into this proposition, the lender, as mentioned, will probably place a restriction on the firm's working capital, either in dollar terms or in the form of a minimum Current Ratio. If the lender has a secured position in a firm's current assets, it hardly makes any sense to concern itself with the firm's Current Ratio. This is so because the lender will be able to take *all* such current assets leaving *none* for the other Current Liability holders. Nevertheless, a lender may want, or at least try, to restrict the firm's incurring of other Current Liabilities.

Asset Preservation

If worse comes to worse, the lender will look to the firm's assets for the ultimate payoff for the loan. This means that the lender will be most concerned that the firm protect its assets and keep others from having a claim on these assets. To this end, the lender may restrict the disposition of assets *unless the proceeds from the sale of these assets are used to pay down the loan*. Also, the lender may require that the sale of the assets be for some reasonable price, such as fair market price. This restriction might be placed on the disposition of the assets to prevent the sale of the assets at an unreasonably low price to, perhaps, a related party for the purpose of getting the assets out from under the contractual control of the lender. An alternative restriction might be that the firm has to purchase replacement equipment (or some other asset) with the proceeds of the sale. This could be worded in such a way as to restrict the selling price, as well.

As a subset of asset preservation, one of the oldest restrictive covenants deals with what has since become known as the **negative pledge clause**. In short, in an effort to restrict the firm from borrowing from another lender—and upsetting the fine balance in debt and equity that the first lender has achieved—the lender may make it impossible for the firm to pledge its assets to another lender. They can do this in several ways. They can take a secured position in all of the firm's assets, even though they are really lending on only some of the assets. For example, they can take a secured position on, for instance, inventory and the receivables even though they are really only lending on receivables.▲ With term loans, the lender might take a secured position on more equipment than on the specific equipment on which it is really lending. Similarly, a private placement might include real property in excess of the real property collateralizing the private placement loan. But, as mentioned, private placements are quite often not collateralized.

What a lender would really like to do, however, is completely restrict the borrower from borrowing from any other lender. This would ensure that the sta-

---

▲ In the next chapter this "secured position" will be identified as the taking of a Financing Statement, UCC 1, on the asset if it is "personalty," meaning something other than real estate, or a trust deed or mortgage on real property (realty).

tus quo that the lender had achieved with the borrower would be maintained. Unfortunately for the lender, this sort of prohibition is illegal in the United States under the Robinson Patman Act of 1936 and, possibly, the Sherman Anti-Trust Act, since it would be a restraint of trade. The loan officers of large loans to major companies by major banks, for example, would not even think of putting such a clause in their contracts. But with smaller banks—and, possibly, some institutional lenders—there occasionally may be seen attempts at putting in a type of specific negative pledge clause.

Recognizing that lenders, in the bottom of their hearts at least, would like to have a negative pledge clause in their contract, wise finance managers might turn this desire to their advantage. Assuming that the borrower really intends to be a model customer and comply with the letter as well as the spirit of the loan agreement, why not proffer a negative pledge to the lender *before* being asked? Even if the borrowing firm feels that for one reason or another the lender would not ask for such a covenant, something might be gained psychologically by offering such a covenant. At least this lets the lender know that you, the borrower, want to be a model borrower.

The Trigger▲

When the borrower defaults on an interest payment or principal payment or commits some other serious breach of the loan agreement, the lender may call the loan. This is called in the vernacular of finance "pulling the trigger." Lenders seldom pull the trigger, because this is a particularly nasty procedure. But the first time the lender calls the loan usually does not mean that the lender *really* wants to (actually) "call" the loan, that is, demand repayment of the loan. Rather it usually means that the lender wants to get the borrower's attention and—quite importantly—revise the terms of the loan in order to recognize what is now, obviously, a higher credit risk. Usually this "revision" means that the interest rate will be raised, but it could mean that there might be a demand for more collateral or a revision of some other covenant.

The second time the lender pulls the trigger, however, is different. Usually this means that the lender wants to be repaid the outstanding balance—period. When this happens, whether it is a term loan (or **revolver loan**) with a bank or finance company, or a private placement with a junk bond fund, life insurance company, or other institutional lender, the firm will find itself in a most difficult position. I can attest to the dilemma clients have confronted in this regard. A substitute lender has to be found, and this is not easy. Trying to explain why the original lender wants to be repaid can be more than daunting.

All this raises an interesting point in which the borrower and the loan are really too "big" for the lender to call. This curious situation existed in Japan in the

---

▲ By considering this topic as a separate group of "negative pledges" I am merely following Arnold's classification. It would seem that the "trigger" is what is effected when there is a breach of any of the negative covenants.

early 1990s when property values fell dramatically. If the bank had foreclosed it would be stuck with property that was worth a mere fraction of what it was owed. This would mean that the bank would have to "mark to market" the loan. The lender in many cases refused to "bite the bullet" and "carried" the loan.

When reviewing the covenant that contains the trigger, it is important for the borrower to realize how sensitive the trigger really is. If the company presents a strong Balance Sheet to begin with, a lender will usually set the trigger much looser than if the lender is seriously concerned about the borrower's safety. A hair trigger, using the analogy of the Old West, really presents a dilemma for both the lender and the borrower. Lenders do not really want to pull the trigger—at least the second time—as this frequently means bankruptcy, a messy business, at best. But they may not have any choice. It may appear necessary to do so in order to protect the collateral. Some of the conditions that might cause the lender to put a tight trigger into the loan would be considerable uncertainty regarding the firm's cash flow stream—what was called a "spread-out" distribution of sales in the chapter on leverage—or noticeably weak collateral, probably implying a weak Balance Sheet.

NEGOTIATING A STRATEGY

Once a borrower realizes the nature of the covenants that a lender is likely to impose, it behooves the borrower to devise a strategy to contend with any and all possible covenants. In short, if the borrower wants to be prepared for a meeting with the lender (a good idea for several reasons, including impressing the lender with the competence of the borrower) it is *imperative* that the borrower put himself or herself in the head of the lender and carefully evaluate his or her own company's strengths and weaknesses.

PUTTING YOURSELF IN THE HEAD OF THE LENDER

Putting yourself in the head of the lender means that you must look at this potential loan through the eyes of the lender. How will the lender perceive the company? If you were the lender would you be excited about making this loan or extremely reluctant? How do the things that concern a lender (or, banker, in general) appear? Where are the weak points of the company? Is there a serious concern about the firm's cash flow? Having said this, the next thing that the borrower must do is to evaluate the company's strengths and weaknesses. This may take some discipline, but it must be done.

DEVISING A STRATEGY TO CONFRONT THE LENDER

A borrower who *knows* the kind of covenants that the lender is most likely to propose will be able to devise a strategy to defuse the most onerous of these covenants. You know that the lender will propose covenants that will restrict the

WIN THE WAR OR GO FOR BROKE!
AOL'S SURVIVAL AND GROWTH STRATEGY

Focus on Technology

Until recently, AOL—now the giant AOL/Time Warner—commanded little respect among the technology elite. Many had given up on this company and its subscription-based business model. Someone even wrote that AOL had come back from the dead more often than Elvis! AOL buying CompuServe? Joking! AOL buying Netscape? Unthinkable! And AOL buying Time Warner? Who could believe it a few years back? (Now, I'm sure most stockholders wish this idea had never come up!)

But things did change, and AOL really came back from the dead! Here are the key elements of AOL's strategy for survival and hyper growth. These are the strategy pieces that set AOL apart from its well-funded (Prodigy) and well-established (CompuServe) competition and paved the way for its stardom.

I. Growth Objective and Business Model—The Carved Niche:

"Land grab" in the cyberspace—for the main purpose of creating "communica-tions and communities" (mainly e-mail and chat) for the masses; of course for a subscription fee.

II. Implementation Strategy—Growth Vehicle:

Disk Marketing—mass mailing of floppy disks containing AOL software and taking advantage of Windows' popularity.

III. Growth Mantra:

Keep it simple!

The above strategy delivered the following results for AOL:

YEAR:	SUBSCRIPTION BASE:
1993	300 K
1994	1000 K
1996	6,000 K
1998	11,000 K
2000	18,000 K

Such a subscription base was the main reason that Time Warner entered into its deal with AOL.

use of the firm's *cash flow*, and that it will try to regulate the firm's *strategy*, however this term applies to the firm in question. Protecting the Balance Sheet and preserving the firm's assets will also be in the mind of the potential lender. So how is the firm going to respond to this frontal attack that the lender will, undoubtedly, mount? To respond to this, the borrower must seriously analyze his or her strengths and weaknesses. Is the firm's *strength* its Balance Sheet or its cash flow? If both are strong, fine, but if not, which is *stronger*?

If it perceived that the firm's strength is its cash flow stream, then the borrower knows that he or she can yield on covenants that pertain to the cash flow stream. If the strength of the firm appears to be its Balance Sheet, meaning that it has good ratios—both Current and Debt/Equity—and lots of *unencumbered* assets, it knows that it can give in on the covenants that pertain to the Balance Sheet.

Once the borrower appraises his or her strengths and weaknesses, he or she is in a good position to know what covenants will be most inconvenient to the borrower and which covenants the lender will fight hardest to achieve. When negotiating with a lender it is important to realize that it may not be possible—or even desirable—to try to win all the skirmishes with lender. In this negotiation, as in any negotiation, one side should not expect to win *every* point of contention. But the important thing is to win the *critical* points that will hurt you, the borrower, most. By yielding on some points and fighting hard on others, the borrower will let the lender walk away from the negotiation feeling that he or she made all the important points that he or she wanted to make. Another important point is to try to eliminate duplicate restrictions.

And, most certainly, the borrower should constantly stress to the lender the need for *flexibility.* If the lender ties up the borrower in such a way that the borrower operates inefficiently, this is really no advantage to either the lender or borrower.

Going into a negotiation with a lender and being ignorant of the types of covenants that the lender will propose is a good way for the borrower to *lose on all points*! The *lender* knows the process of making the subject loans, and if the *borrower* is totally ignorant of the process and the covenants that will be used, guess who is going to come out ahead at the end of the negotiation?

SUMMARY

The first part of this chapter discussed the various types of debt. It was noted that the more "information-problematic" a firm is, the more likely the loan will have to be by a bank or perhaps an institutional investor. Only when the company is perceived to be quite transparent can it go to the bond market.

The second part of the chapter deals with the types of covenants that an emerging firm is likely to encounter and then a strategy for negotiating a term loan. It was noted that the negative covenants—cash flow control, strategy, Balance Sheet preservation, asset protection, and the trigger—are the ones of main concern. In the latter section, it was noted that it behooves the entrepreneurial manager to be aware of his or her company's strengths and weaknesses and use this knowledge in the strategy session with the lender. Fight hard where you are weak and give in where you are strong. It is unrealistic to think that the borrower is going to win all the points of discussion. A smart borrower will let the lender "score some points," too.

QUESTIONS FOR DISCUSSION

1. As CFO for your company, you are anticipating a meeting with your potential lenders for a private placement of $20 million. How would you prepare yourself for this meeting? What factors would you review before meeting the lender?

2. Your commercial bank is a fairly small regional bank. You are negotiating an increase in your outstanding loan with them. In preliminary meetings you were told that the bank wanted you to execute a "negative pledge clause." Knowing that this is illegal and unenforceable, how would you as CFO treat this request from your bank?

10

CHAPTER REVIEW

11

Short-Term Financing—Including Equipment Financing

Far and away the most important of source of debt financing for the developing firm is the pledging of Accounts Receivables and inventory. This chapter discusses this subject in the context of borrowing from banks as well as from finance companies and includes term loans on equipment. Before turning to the various aspects of receivables and inventory financing, we will first discuss the legal forms used by both banks and finance companies in the United States to secure personal property as collateral. Personal property, or *personalty* as it is called technically, includes cash, money market securities, Accounts Receivable, inventory, and equipment. In short, anything that is not real property or something attached to real property (which is called *realty*).

THE UNIFORM COMMERCIAL CODE

In the mid-1960s, most of the states passed something called the **Uniform Commercial Code** in response to a crying need of banks and finance companies. Up to this time, lenders would make loans to businesses based on Accounts Receivables or inventory, but when it came time to repossess the collateral, lenders would all too often find themselves considered "general creditors" by the court instead of a secured lender. (See Chapter 3 for discussion of credit priorities.) Even the slightest discrepancy in the itemization of the collateral would be enough for courts to throw out the secured claim of the bank or finance company, placing this lender with the general creditors.

With the passage of the Uniform Commercial Code, however, lenders could be assured that their claim for specific collateral would stand up in court. This was a great day for the lenders, but it was even a better day for the borrowers. As long as they experienced trepidation that they would have a valid security claim, most lenders felt that they were, in fact, just general creditors. They felt that in case the firm defaulted on its loan they would be hard pressed to get much, if anything, of the principal that was owed. This meant that the banks and finance companies were reluctant to loan except to the most creditworthy of firms—much to the dismay of many developing firms! The really important thing to the developing firm is not whether the bank or finance company would be considered a "secured creditor" or a "general creditor" (really, the borrowing firm could care less), but whether they would get the loan. With lenders reluctant to lend to developing firms in situations where they felt that they could not adequately collateralize a loan, the real loser was the developing firm that needed a loan. With the passage of the Uniform Commercial Code, this situation has come to an end.▲

THE UCC FORMS

There are three forms that one should be familiar with in respect to the Uniform Commercial Code. The first is called UCC 1, the **Financing Statement**, which basically states who is borrowing from whom, using what as collateral. This form is filed with the Secretary of State of the respective states where the borrowing or lending firm is located—except for aircraft where the filing place is Oklahoma City. Basically this form tells the whole world that this lender (bank or finance company) has a secured claim on this borrower's specific assets, such as its accounts receivable, inventory, and equipment. Now these claims can be prioritized such as a first claim, a second claim, etc.

The second form, **UCC 2**, is called the **Security Agreement**. These are specially preprinted forms for the type of collateral that the firm is using, such as inventory, vehicles, or Accounts Receivable. Under some borrowing arrangements, the borrower must indicate exactly the collateral that is being used *each* time the borrower wants to borrow additional funds. This form is sent or delivered to the *lender*; it is not sent to the Secretary of State.

The third form is called the **UCC 3**, the **Inquiry Form**, which is used when someone wishes to inquire if someone has already laid claim to the firm's specific assets. Whenever one is in the process of trying to buy a company, it is mandatory to file a UCC3 form to see just who has a claim on the firm's assets. Unfortunately, what is so often found is that there are UCC 1s

▲ China, the "mother of all developing firms" at the present time, could surely use a Uniform Commercial Code. If they had one—with teeth in it—commercial finance companies would gladly go to China and supply what China needs most: capital.

still on file for assets—for example, equipment—where the loan has been re-paid long ago but somebody just forgot to remove the UCC 1. This UCC 3 form is sent to the Secretary of State, with the necessary fee, and the Secretary of State will respond by sending a list of all the UCC 1s that are outstanding. You can also use the services of a law firm in the capital which will, for a fee, hand deliver the UCC 3 to the Secretary of State, and, in general expedite the processing of the form. This is the usual way to file this form.

BANK LOANS

Now that these UCC forms have been introduced and we have discussed choosing a bank, we will now take up the various types of short-term loans that banks and finance companies make to business firms. First we will discuss the loans from banks and, later, loans from finance companies.

THE PSYCHOLOGY OF BEING A BANK'S CUSTOMER

It is ironic that a typical firm's management gives so little thought to the bank with which their company does business and the relationship they have with that bank, considering the importance the bank represents in the financial affairs of the firm. When asked why a particular bank was chosen, a manager might say something like "Because they are across the street!" Whether the company is doing business with the "wrong" bank may never occur to some managers.

There are three ways to approach the question of bank relations:

- The choice of the right bank, meaning an appropriate bank

- The selection of the bankers

- The building of rapport with your bankers

While the differences between banks is blurring, there are, generally speaking, three different types of banks, classified by the types of customer they are designed to serve.

Retail Banks

First, there are the **retail** types of banks, set up to serve individual or retail customers like you and me. These banks are prepared to receive your checking and savings accounts, to make loans for such things as car purchases or home improvements, anything that an individual requires. Some retail banks cater to a wide cross section of retail customers, and some are focused on high-net-worth individuals and offer all sorts of sophisticated investment advice.

These banks are *definitely* not the type of bank that a growing business needs. While they know a lot about cashing checks and all the other minutiae associated with operating a retail bank, they probably know little if anything about the complicated and sophisticated world of corporate finance. Even the financial statements of the aspiring firm might seem foreign to such a bank. If they loan to a business, the chances are that they are loaning only on the *owner's personal financial statement*. When this is the case, the borrowing capacity of the growing firm will hit a ceiling when the owner's personal credit limit is reached. Furthermore, when a problem arises, the usual response is "No." Ignorance usually provokes a negative response. If the bank officer does not really understand what the firm is trying to do or is encountering, the bank officer will most likely take a defensive position so as to protect the bank—and his or her reputation! You can very often recognize these banks by their name. The People's Bank or Citizen's Bank of Pasadena. Also, their advertising alerts you to their orientation. If the ads feature pictures of a romantic vacation spot or a new sailboat, you can be sure that this is a retail-oriented bank and your firm's business had better stay away.

Wholesale-Oriented Banks

Today there are few strictly **wholesale-oriented** banks, meaning banks that are established expressly for the purpose of serving business needs, but they do exist, especially in the larger metropolitan areas. Today, these banks will also take personal accounts, but their focus is on the business account. Many of these wholesale-oriented banks have a particular niche that they fulfill in their community. In the Los Angeles area, for example, there is a bank that is known as the "garment maker's bank" (Manufacturer's Bank), a bank that is known for wholesale car financing (United California Bank), and so on. Dealing with this kind of bank means that you are dealing with knowledgeable loan officers who can understand your problems when they arise and who understand the condition of the industry at any given time. If your company is having problems that are industry-specific rather than firm-specific, this kind of bank will know that and, probably, be more tolerant than if they had no idea of what is happening in the industry overall. Also, these kinds of banks will understand sophisticated types of financing instruments and be able to provide such useful services as Letters of Credit. Without this sophistication on the part of the lending officer, the business executive is forced to explain the most mundane things, something that can be trying at best. And, as mentioned above, ignorance usually leads to a negative response from a lending officer.

A business firm may have to *seek out* a wholesale-oriented bank that specializes in its type of business, because they are not as numerous as the typical retail-oriented bank. But driving some distance will surely be worthwhile if the bank can provide the type of service the firm really needs.

Combination Banks

Combination banks offer a whole range of services to both retail and wholesale customers. With the consolidation of the major banks in the United States, these combination banks are getting bigger and fewer. Citibank and Chase Manhattan are the largest such combination banks in the United States, but the newly reorganized Bank of America is close behind. Because of their size and the number of branches, these combination banks are the ones most familiar to the public. Down the street from most business establishments is an office of a Wells Fargo or Citibank. But not all these bank offices or branches are the same. Within these combination banks there are *retail* and *wholesale* and *international* divisions that are set up to serve specific needs of customers, whether they be individuals or business firms.

The mistake that many business entrepreneurs make, however, is that they do not recognize that one branch may be profoundly different from another. Bank of America, for example, does not hang a sign outside of its offices that says "Retail-oriented—Business Stay Away!" If the management of a business firm walks into a *retail* bank and asks to open an account, the bank may very well accept the account. If a loan is made to a developing firm, it will probably be based on the owner's personal financial statement—without ever telling the business owner that this is the case. This can create all sorts of problems for a firm, with the management taking its wrath out on the (fill in the name) bank. The problem is not that the bank is at fault, the problem is that the business is just in the *wrong* office of that bank. These combination banks, for the most part, have regional wholesale banking centers designed to service business needs. Furthermore, they probably have specialized banking offices for specialized business needs, such as the entertainment industry, the car dealership industry, etc. The trick in doing business with these *combination* banks is to find the appropriate office for your business.

Choosing the Right Bankers

Bank officers have a lot of mobility and if you have only one bank officer with whom you do business, and that person leaves the bank, all of the rapport that you have built up may be lost. Instead, it is better to have close relations with at least *two* bank officers. In this way, if one leaves, you still have one officer who is familiar with your business and situation. Selecting the right loan officer will depend on the situation, but logic says that you would be better off selecting someone who might have something in common with the CEO or the chief financial officer of the customer firm. Some banks routinely assign two bank officers to a new customer. If this is not the case, it might be well to use the branch manager as the second loan officer.

Banks generally fall into two categories: there are those banks that have a *loan committee* to review credit applications and there are banks which give an *individual loan officer* this authority. This latter group is definitely in the minority. If—and this might be a big "if"—the company has a choice in the selection of a loan officer, it is well to keep in mind that it is your loan officer who will make your presentation when you apply for a loan. If the loan officer is really junior to the others on the committee, the company faces the dual challenge of having to present a viable plan for the loan *and* overcoming the suspicion that the senior members of the loan committee have regarding the junior loan officer personally. Of course it would help, therefore, if the firm can somehow secure the services of a senior member of the bank, so that when he or she makes a presentation on behalf of your company to the loan committee there already would exist a certain respect that might convince the others to go along with the request without unduly scrutinizing it.

Building Rapport with Your Banker

Once the right bank has been chosen and an appropriate banker (or, better, pair of bankers) selected then the task begins of building rapport with this person or persons. Unfortunately, there exists in many owner/managers a feeling of hostility toward banks and bankers in general. Most of us resent having to reveal financial data that is considered quite private. But to paraphrase a Deputy Secretary of Defense when referring to China, "If you treat them like an enemy, they are going to be an enemy." If you treat your bankers as enemies, they are not going to have the enthusiasm for your company that will be needed when the company makes a presentation to the bank. What would be ideal is for the bank officer to have great admiration and respect for your firm and your management. The most contagious thing in the world is *enthusiasm*. If this loan officer is enthusiastic about you and your company, this will go a long way toward convincing others of the worthwhileness of the company.

How can one build this kind of rapport with a loan officer? The best way to start is to realize what the banker's "hot buttons" are. These are different from the ones mentioned in the cash flow chapter, but the idea is similar. What are the things that annoy the banker and what are the things that make him or her pleased? One of the things that most annoys a bank officer is going to the company's file and finding that the latest financial statements are not there. "There has been adequate time for the company to get the statements and forward them to the bank. Then why aren't they here? There must be something wrong!" To a banker, the company is really a set of financial statements and when they are not forwarded to the bank in a timely manner, all sorts of negative thoughts rise up. Immediately there is suspicion that there is something wrong with the company or that the company's management is trying to hide something. In many cases this is not the case at all. The company's outside accountant just got busy, or it was tax time, or he or she was on vacation and the statements were delayed. For the management of a developing firm getting the statements from the accountants on time so that they can be passed along to the banker is not very high on the priority list. This is a pity because statements *really are important* to any banker. Taking care that statements are forwarded to the banker in a timely manner will surely win commendation and avoid negative thoughts.

Realizing that the worst time to ask for a loan is when you need it, this brings up the matter of periodic briefings of your banker. Once a quarter or at least once every 6 months, it would be a good idea to have a formal presentation to your banker in which you review the past period and present a forecast of the upcoming ones. This gives the firm the chance to ask for a loan *before* it is needed! And what better way is there to impress the banker with the firm's management acumen than by successfully forecasting a cash flow problem *before* it happens. What so often happens is that the firm calls the bank officer with an "emergency." Surely this is one of the best ways to reduce your company's image in the mind of a banker.

If something really bad befalls the company, such as the cancellation of a major contract, trying to hide this fact from your banker will certainly be met with failure. Instead, making a full presentation to your banker—and then following this up with periodic reports—will surely win kudos for your management. If nothing else, your company will most likely be the only one that does this sort of thoughtful thing, which in itself is enough to gain the respect of your banker.

Another way to show your respect for your banker is to offer to pay for lunch or dinner instead of always having the bank pay the check. Subtle, perhaps, but this offer will be noticed.

Finally, a bit of advice when dealing with the company's banker(s). *Never go "off the record" with your banker*. There is no such thing as "off the record" if you have a decent, honest, hard-working banker. This person always has you and your firm under a microscope and anything that is so adverse as to invoke an off-the-record remark will only hurt the firm. One company manager, in chatting with his banker, told him how "clever"(read "dishonest") he was with his tax return. The banker was undoubtedly thinking that if the business owner would do this with his tax return he may, very likely, do it with his statements to the bank! Again, you never want the banker to have occasion to harbor a negative thought about your company or you.

SIGNATURE LOANS

The litmus test for a firm in appraising its relations with its bank is to receive a **signature loan** from its bank. The only way a bank would agree to make a signature loan, which is *uncollateralized*, would be if the bank held the borrowing firm in the highest esteem.

As with *all* loans, the first step in securing a signature loan is for the firm's board of directors to approve a resolution authorizing the firm to borrow money from the bank. Then, an authorized officer (e.g., the chief financial officer, the controller or, perhaps, the president) contacts the bank and requests a loan of so much money for a period of time—in the case of short-term loans, a relatively short period such as 30 to 120 days. Presumably the bank has already verbally or otherwise told the firm's management that they (the bank) would be receptive to a request for a signature loan.

Before one thinks that this is the best of all types of loans, it should be remembered that signature loans *must* be repaid at least once yearly. *They are not "evergreen" loans.* **Evergreen loans** are loans that can be rolled over any number of times and may go on for years like Accounts Receivable pledging, which will be discussed next.

ACCOUNTS RECEIVABLE PLEDGING

By far, the most important source of short-term financing available for most types of developing firms is what is called "Accounts Receivable pledging." By **pledging** we mean that the business company merely *pledges* its receivables as collateral for a loan; the firm itself retains title to them. In this form of financing, the firm executes a UCC 1 Financing Statement in favor of the lender. Then, depending on the arrangement with the bank, it proceeds to borrow from the bank. While there are about as many arrangements for carrying out this financing arrangement as there are banks involved, there are some characteristics that can be generalized.

ELIGIBLE RECEIVABLES

First, all banks lend a certain percentage on the so-called **eligible receivables**. Eligibility is discussed below. This percentage can run from an abysmal 30 percent to about 95 percent—and higher on special occasions. The typical lending percentage is in the range of 75 to 90 percent. If the firm has the right rapport with its lending officer (or officers) it may ask the bank to go higher for a short period of time, even over 100 percent for a few days.

The big determinant here is the overall appearance of the firm's Balance Sheet and the firm's record in "Returns and Allowances." Banks are naturally concerned about taking a receivable against which a customer supposedly owes the firm only to find out that the customer *returned* the merchandise for credit! If the bank had foreclosed on the firm's Accounts Receivable, it would have found itself holding some worthless paper. So if a bank—or other lender—sees that the firm has an unusually high level of returns and allowances, it will lower the borrowing percentage that it will allow the firm. That is, *if* the bank will lend on the firm's receivables at all.

I was involved in a buyout of a company owned by an individual who made it a practice to *not* issue credit memos to its customers who returned merchandise for quality reasons. What he hoped to do was to create a situation in which the customer would accidentally pay for the replacement shipment *and* the original shipment as well. What this obviously underhanded procedure did for us, the buyers of the company, was to create a situation that made it look as though there were many more returns than, in fact, there were. Naturally, we had some convincing to do with the bank when we applied for receivables financing.

"Eligible" means one of two things, usually. It means "not over 90 days *overdue*" or it means "not over 90 days *old*." The latter is, of course, more restrictive than the former. But on this point I am aware of a number of occasions in which the management did not communicate with the clerk or accountant actually handling the paperwork for the financing what the practice of the bank was. If the bank says, "Not over 90 days overdue," it may mean 120 days from the date of invoice, not 90. So it is well to actually make it quite clear to the personnel involved exactly what is meant by "eligible."

This discussion reinforces the importance of having the right bank as well as being in the appropriate office of the right bank. When you apply to your bank for an Accounts Receivable line and the bank officer says that they have an office downtown that handles receivables financing, you know that you are in the "wrong" bank. Every developing firm runs short of cash sometime and needs to call their bank lending officer and ask if they can go over the limit for a few days. If they have the "right" bank and the appropriate rapport with their lending officer, they are more likely to have the bank acquiesce to their request. If the Accounts Receivable financing is being handled by a downtown department of the bank, there is absolutely no reason for the person handling the firm's account at your local bank to say "yes" to such a request. That person is in that position to protect the bank, and if he or she is doing his or her job, they will most likely hold the line.

The Case of Service Companies

Many banks consider receivables to be "ineligible" if they are generated by a firm that is considered to be a service company. Engineering consulting companies, construction companies, radio and television stations, and, perhaps, custom computer software firms come immediately to mind as being suspect when it comes to whether or not a bank would finance their receivables. One must keep in mind that this A/R financing is the essence of what is called **asset-based lending** and if a bank thinks that there is nothing to recapture, then it may rule that the firm's receivables are ineligible because the firm is a service company.

Personally, I find this type of reasoning to be irrational. If there is a valid Accounts Receivable then there is some contract between the firm and its customer. The customer legally owes the firm, its supplier, the money indicated. If the bank had to repossess the receivable, it would have the same rights as the selling firm had in the first place. As far as repossessing the material and taking it back to be resold, suppose the material were steel and this steel were made into some product. Would the bank repossess the steel, melt it down, and the reconfigure it into coils of steel like the ones originally sold? Well this seems just as absurd as saying the service company really didn't sell anything of substance. Of course, there are banks that will finance Accounts Receivable from a service company so, again, it behooves the firm to make the right choice of a bank. One should keep this thought in mind when evaluating a prospect for a leveraged buyout, however. If in doubt, ask the bank if a particular target's Accounts Receivable would be considered eligible.

Government Accounts Receivable

Banks also do not usually loan on Accounts Receivable when the government is the customer, whether it be state, local, or federal. The reason most banks give for this policy is that it is too difficult to force a governmental unit to pay. If the firm's main customers are governmental, most banks would most likely not lend on *any* receivables generated by the firm because it would be akin to a *concentration problem*, discussed below. If the firm has an occasional receivable from the government, and the order is of sufficient size, there is a way to get the bank to lend against the receivable. The firm can have the contracting officer for the government execute what is called an "assignment of proceeds" form. This gives the government the authorization to pay the lender—bank or finance company—directly. In these cases the lender is made much more comfortable. But it should be remembered that this procedure is available only for large orders—receivables—and not for *all* orders. The amount of time and paperwork involved by the contracting officer and the bank argues for limiting this procedure to only significant orders, however that may be construed. If nothing else, the government contracting officer has to do extra work for which he or she is not compensated.

The Concentration Factor

Another aspect of whether a firm's receivables are eligible involves the issue of what is called a **concentration factor**. If a firm has a large percentage of its orders concentrated in one of a very few customers, the bank may likely gauge *all* the firm's receivables *ineligible*. At first, this may seem to be an unreasonable restriction by the lender. But on reflection, this is quite understandable.

In one case, 85 percent of a firm's Accounts Receivable were concentrated in one customer. Even though that particular customer was extremely financially well off (it was Ford Motor Company), no bank would take this firm's Accounts Receivable because of this blatant concentration factor. Finally, a finance company was found that knew and had a good business relation with the prospective owner of the target company that would supply the receivables (it was a target in an LBO attempt). But as it worked out, the banks were right! About a year after the deal was done, a crisis hit the business and Ford virtually stopped ordering the few parts that this firm made for them. This situation, which lasted for some months, almost forced the company out of business.

In other cases, it may not take a crisis to provoke a halt in orders from the concentrated customer to the firm. In dealing with aerospace companies, for example, disputes will arise in which a quality-control inspector might stop all further billings to the aerospace contractor until the dispute is cleared up. So it is situations like this that banks try to avoid by invoking the concentration argument in denying Accounts Receivable financing to some firms.

The Diffusion Factor

The opposite situation is what might be called a **diffusion factor**. It first came to my attention during the course of trying to buy a manufacturer of hearing aids. The company had a very low "bad debt expense," which made it appear that they would have good receivables that could be used as collateral. But it soon became apparent that even though the company had solid paying customers, they were spread out over about seventeen states, with the invoices being, typically, of two denominations: either about $650 for a new unit or a repair order for about $200. This meant that it would be impractical to try to collect the many accounts receivable from around the country. This being the case, the Accounts Receivable were worthless as collateral for a working capital loan.

Incidentally, just having lots of receivables is not a reason to say that the firm has a diffusion factor. For example, a company that is in the reprographics business may generate lots of rather small Accounts Receivable, but these may be acceptable collateral because the customers of the firm were all within about a 5-mile radius of the company and there were many receivables with any one customer. This meant that it would not be a particularly difficult job to collect the receivables in the event that situation became necessary.

ACCOUNTS RECEIVABLE PLANS

Most banks will establish a line of credit for their borrowing customer that will usually be stipulated as a dollar amount maximum. Then they will set up a time when they will review the arrangement. Of course, if the firm is growing so rapidly as to require more frequent review, this could be done as well. The cost from banks for Accounts Receivable financing will usually be based on the dollar amount of financing outstanding and will usually be calculated on a daily basis. The yearly cost will usually be about 2 to 4 points above prime, for smaller accommodations. If the firm has unusually strong financial statements, the cost can be lower, perhaps prime or even a bit below prime. With less creditworthy customers, smaller banks might charge 4 to 8 points above prime. But when the pricing gets to be over 4 points above prime banks will, most likely, start bowing out and suggest that the firm use a finance company.

As mentioned earlier, the actual plan that any one bank has in its Accounts Receivable financing program differs markedly. On the one hand, there is the situation where the bank really likes the customer and takes out a UCC 1 just to appear to be doing everything according to the book, in a manner of speaking. Under this cozy arrangement, the bank might say something about the fact that the company has an upper limit on the amount of credit the bank wants to have outstanding at any one time, such as $5 million. As long as the company does not go over that amount, and the amount of the Accounts Receivable does not go under some amount, $6 million, for instance, then the bank will consider the account to be in good shape. In this case, the bank may say something like "We'll come in about once or twice a year and audit the Accounts Receivable." This means that the bank does not even intend to use the UCC 2 Security Agreement to keep track of individual Accounts Receivable. To be in this enviable position, the borrowing firm would most likely have an unusually strong Balance Sheet and a healthy Income Statement, too. The firm may be growing rapidly and the bank is lending on the Accounts Receivable to provide working capital.

Contrast this situation to the case where the bank requires a UCC 2 to be completed for *each and every time* the borrowing firm wants to borrow more money. The bank would check every invoice to determine its eligibility and then, when all the checking is complete, loan a stipulated amount against the Accounts Receivable. This represents about the toughest situation that the borrowing firm might find itself in when utilizing this form of financing with a bank. This means that the firm probably has weak financial statements and/or the bank is suspicious of the firm's management. The bank's suspicions may lead it to make a surprise visit to the borrower and announce that they are going to start an *audit* of the firm's Accounts Receivable the next day. What the bank may suspect is that the firm is listing orders that have not even been shipped yet as *bona fide* receivable. In an effort to get enough receivables to borrow a certain amount of money needed—for example, to meet a payroll on Friday—the firm's management might "anticipate" a shipment by a few days or more! The announcement of a surprise audit would surely put the firm in a precarious position if this audit revealed this underhanded operation. How finance companies handle this possibility will be discussed below.

INVENTORY FINANCING

When Adam Smith wrote the *Wealth of Nations*, published in 1776, he addressed the matter of what he thought should be a proper loan by a bank to a business firm. He reasoned that the only proper loan should be based on inventory. He apparently thought that if banks loaned to businesses on the basis of their inventory, then, as this inventory turned over in the normal course of trade, the business firm would have the money it needed to repay the loan. Making loans on inventory, which has since been called "the real bills doctrine" was a cardinal rule for bankers for all the years after 1776 until about the 1960s, when the Uniform Commercial Code came into being.

Today, this situation is quite reversed. Banks really do not like to loan on inventory. If they do, it is most likely because they wish to *rationalize* a loan to a customer and/or they wish to prevent the customer from borrowing from some other lender. What seemed perfectly logical to Adam Smith suddenly came to be viewed as something less than ideal. With a receivable the customer already owes the firm the money; the firm only has to collect the money. With inventory, there is no compulsion on the part of the customer to *buy* the inventory from the company. In short, it is much better to have a claim on a debt that some firm owes the borrower than to have a claim on something that has to be sold!

Nevertheless, banks do make loans to businesses on the basis of their inventory following some general guidelines. Of the three types of inventory—raw material, work-in-process, and finished goods—the first and last are usually the only inventory eligible for borrowing against. When a bank *really* wants to make a loan to a customer or customer-to-be, however, it may offer to lend against work-in-process. In the 1970s, when banks were trying to get a larger share of the middle-market business and were just starting to make leveraged buyout loans, loaning against W-I-P was routine. Today it is rare.

CRITERIA FOR BORROWING

Banks prefer to lend no more than about 50 percent against most inventory because that inventory has a way of really shrinking when subject to forced sale. Furthermore, liquidators will take a large piece of the selling price, which will be discounted to begin with. This leaves only a small portion of the original inventory value. What, then, determines what inventory makes good collateral? In a word, it is the inventory's *resale* value. How easy would it be, for example, to send a truck to the borrower's premises, load the inventory, and then resell it? Coils of galvanized steel, for example, would qualify beautifully under this criterion. Certain raw materials might also qualify, if the manufacturer or distributor has indicated a willingness to take back returned material. Also, certain raw material in the borrower's inventory might come from a supplier who has an announced policy of taking back the part for a "restocking charge" of something like 15 percent. If the inventory consists of bolts of fabric, most lenders will not lend on this at all. This is because the fabric is considered to be "fashion" material and subject to style obsolescence. The reasoning here is that by the time the legal proceedings cleared and the bank had the legal right to sell the repossessed inventory, fashion might have changed rendering the material virtually worthless.

Finished goods that involve a guarantee or warranty from the manufacturer might also be quite ineligible as collateral. This is so because the only way the bank could get the goods to sell would be if the firm were out of business. In this case, what would be the status of the guarantee or warranty? It might be argued that *any* finished good would involve *some* degree of guarantee, but then this is all relative. If what you see is what you get, the inventory might be considered acceptable for collateral. But, still, this means that the most any bank will lend is a maximum of about 50 percent of the inventory's value.

This raises the interesting point about the way the inventory is valued: First In, First Out or Last In, First Out. If LIFO, the inventory might be shown on the company's books at a small fraction of what the value would be if shown as FIFO. If there is great disparity, the bank might make some concession to the way the inventory is shown on the company's books. This is why it is a good idea to show a LIFO reserve—meaning what the value of the inventory would be if it were valued at FIFO—on the company's financial statement.

OTHER WAYS OF FINANCING INVENTORY

In addition to pledging inventory as collateral, another way of using inventory to secure financing is through the use of **warehousing**. Warehousing was widely used until the passage of the Uniform Commercial Code drastically reduced its use in the United States. But the situation still exists, and if the 50 percent limit is too restraining, a firm might consider the use of a public warehouse or a field warehouse.

Public warehouses exist in all large cities, especially port cities. Under this arrangement, the borrower takes the inventory to the public warehouse and receives a receipt which it then takes to the lending institution. On the strength of this receipt, the bank or finance company loans a certain percentage, sometimes a lot more than 50 percent. When the borrower wants to use the inventory, it pays the lender the amount borrowed and receives the receipt which is needed to obtain the inventory. Sometimes import/export firms use an arrangement like this to finance their inventory. In this case, the warehouse may be in a special "duty-free" zone or warehouse. Often this is done in the course of transshipping the material.

Another type of warehouse that might be used is called the *field warehouse*. Under this arrangement, a public (bonded) warehouse is retained to supervise the field warehouse. Often, an employee of the borrowing firm is selected to be bonded and to act as the agent of the warehousing company in the warehousing arrangement. For example, if the inventory were gold, a field warehouse might be set up on the borrower's premises. An employee in the warehouse area is selected and bonded. The gold (or other very valuable material) might be stored in a safe. When the firm wishes to withdraw some of the gold, it would pay the bank or other lender and authorize the warehouse person to release the specified amount of gold. In other cases, a field warehouse might be set up merely by putting a rather temporary fence around the inventory that might be stored, for example, in a field on the borrower's property. This might be used, for example, for a large quantity of steel. But with the security that lenders feel today under the UCC, even this kind of field warehouse might be unnecessary.

EQUIPMENT FINANCING

Virtually every developing firm that is involved in manufacturing utilizes equipment financing at one time or another. This may be from the manufacturer of the equipment itself or an affiliate. If it is new equipment, the amount loaned is in the order of two-thirds to three-quarters of the purchase price. The term is typically about 3 years. But what about financing *used* equipment?

Banks and finance companies lend on equipment based on the "quick sale" or "liquidation value" on an appraisal of the equipment. But when getting an appraisal it makes a difference as to the type of appraiser one selects.

TYPES OF APPRAISERS

There are basically three types of appraisers that might be selected. First, there are the **appraisal companies** such as American Appraisal Co. or Marshall and Stevens. There are all types of appraisals for all types of property. For our purposes, however, an appraisal company will give the usual *market price appraisal*— which all appraisers do—and this value tends to be the same for all appraisers. But you can specify which type of "quick sale" you want. You can have your choice of a "knockdown" (also called "at auction") quick sale value *or* you can specify an "orderly resale" value, which means what the machine would bring if sold in an orderly manner over 6 months or so. I feel that the orderly resale value is the higher of the *quick sale* values, but I have seen instances when this did not hold true.

Secondly, there are the so-called **liquidators**. These are what might also be called "auctioneers." These companies—for example, Tauber Aarons or Worshow—actually do the auctioning of equipment, so what they are saying in their quick sale value is that this is what the company thinks this particular piece of equipment would bring if it were placed up for auction the next week. So with an appraisal company, you are restricted to only the one type of quick sale value, the importance of which will be discussed below.

The third type of appraiser is the **used equipment dealer**. If properly selected, i.e., the dealer *actually* deals in the type of equipment involved, this type of appraiser should be rather reliable. Unfortunately, my experience has been the opposite. In fact, this type of appraiser may not be acceptable to the lender. Some equipment dealers may actually guarantee an appraisal for some period of time. They charge some percentage of the appraisal price for this guarantee, perhaps, 10 percent.

FACTORS THAT INFLUENCE AN APPRAISAL

When seeking financing on equipment, whether this be for the company which owns the equipment or for a prospective LBO buyer, the value of the quick sale is quite important. But what determines the market value and the quick sale value? Obviously, the *age and condition* of the equipment is quite important. Equipment that is properly maintained is going to bring a higher appraisal value than equipment from a dirty shop or one in which the equipment's maintenance has been deferred. When buying a company, one of the dangers is that the equipment would not be maintained properly. Here, the problem is not so much that repairs would have to be made, but *how much* repair work would have to be made? Sometimes, many thousands of dollars can be expended and still the machine would not work properly. So when buying a manufacturing business which has a lot of equipment, it behooves the buyer to notice the cleanliness of the shop for an indication that maintenance has been properly performed when needed. True, this is not a certain indication of well-maintained equipment, but it is at least some indication. The odds are that a dirty shop will have a lot of poorly maintained equipment. Remember the old saying that "cleanliness is next to Godliness!"

Another factor that determines market value and, thus, quick sale value is the *state of the economy*, especially as it relates to the demand for the product that the machines produce. For example, if the machines produce aircraft parts and the aircraft industry is in a severe downturn, then the market value will be unusually low for that piece of machinery. One example of this may make the point. In 1968, a new Cincinnati Milicron CNC Hydrotel (a computer-controlled mill) would sell for about $35,000. In 1971, this machine sold at auction for $4,000 (and the aerospace recession was so severe that observers wondered who was crazy enough to pay that *much* for the machine). If properly maintained, today, 30 years later, that same machine would probably bring $20,000 to $25,000 because the market for airplanes is quite good. What can we infer from this story? When buying a business and needing to borrow on the equipment, the best time to do so is when the business conditions are good for that type of equipment. The market price will not only be higher than in depressed times, but, more importantly, the *quick sale* price will be higher absolutely as well as relative to the market price.

BORROWING PERCENTAGE ON EQUIPMENT

Banks and finance companies typically loan between 85 and 100 percent of quick sale value. This means that market value is really redundant. The only thing that is important is the quick sale value, however defined. So in order to get a higher borrowing base, one might select the *"orderly resale"* quick sale value offered by the appraisal companies instead of the auction value. This is, of course, assuming that the lender approves of your choice of an appraiser. Some banks and finance companies have their own in-house appraiser to check the accuracy of the outside appraiser. The opinion of this appraiser might alter either the lending percentage or the appraisal value.

COST OF EQUIPMENT APPRAISALS

It is difficult to pinpoint the cost of an appraisal. Many factors are involved and the price might vary by geographic region. Members of the National Appraisers Association are prohibited from charging for an appraisal based on the *value* of the equipment, however. They are supposed to charge on a "time required" basis. This means that the cost could vary based on the number of pieces of equipment and the difficulty of getting prices on the particular equipment. An appraisal cost for used equipment valued at $3 to $10 million (fair market price) might run about $5,000 to $10,000. But keep in mind that this may be quite misleading given the exact nature and quantity of equipment involved and the hourly rate that the appraiser uses. Don't forget to get an opinion from a prospective lender (if doing an LBO) that a certain appraisal company is acceptable before paying for an appraisal that may *not* be acceptable.

BORROWING FROM FINANCE COMPANIES

The preceding discussion was centered upon bank lending. In this section we will specifically discuss borrowing from finance companies. Finance companies in the United States vary from very modest companies (in size) to very large companies, e.g., General Electric Capital. Accordingly, the size of the deal involved will usually dictate the finance company approached. When appropriate, we will note the differences between borrowing from finance companies and banks. Before we contrast finance companies with banks and what they each prefer, the different types of loans made by finance companies will be discussed.

ACCOUNTS RECEIVABLE PLEDGING

Like banks, finance companies will make loans based on Accounts Receivable. Their methodology will be generally similar to the banks' but generally they tend to scrutinize the accounts more than banks might do. By this I mean that an individual will be assigned to monitor the Accounts Receivable and this will be this person's primary job. If anything goes wrong with the account or with the borrowing firm, this person is held responsible. In the course of exercising this scrutiny this individual may start to anticipate slow-paying customers—even those whom he or she has no reason to believe will become slow pays! This may start to grate on the firm's customers, impairing the goodwill between the vendor and the customer.

In general, finance companies tend to be more suspicious than banks in this type of financing. For example, many finance companies have a policy of requiring that all UCC 2s that are submitted be accompanied by what are called "shippers." **Shippers** are the paperwork that attest to the fact that the goods covered by the invoice have actually been shipped. This means the actual documents that the shipping carrier executes when accepting a shipment for delivery. Of course, this does not mean that *all* finance companies do this with *all* of their client borrowing firms, but it is much more prevalent than with banks. The practice of "anticipating" the shipment of goods, in order to be able to list the invoice as a new invoice in order to be eligible for borrowing is prevented by the finance company's insistence that there be actual evidence of shipment *before* any money is loaned against the invoice.

Finance companies also might be more lenient with a potential or actual concentration factor than banks might be. If they feel that they know the financial condition and the circumstances of the borrower, the finance company might feel that it can take a chance with the concentration factor that a bank might not take. (Of course the borrowing firm must itself be in good financial condition for the finance company to lend in a situation in which there is a "concentration factor" problem.) The finance company will charge more for this increase in risk.

The borrowing percentages on receivables that finance companies utilize are approximately the same as for banks—30 to 95 percent with the most common range being 70–85 percent. As with banks, the borrower's returns and allowances will greatly influence this percentage.

While *banks* generally might consider receivables to be eligible if they are not over *90 days overdue*, most *finance companies* will be more strict than this and require all eligible receivables to be not over *90 days old*. Under the Robinson-Patman Act, it is illegal for a selling firm to discriminate between customers with respect to credit periods but in fact many selling firms do this—quietly! The difficulty comes in explaining to the lender that this customer really has "permission" to pay late, and he or she really does pay. It also behooves the borrowing firm to school the personnel in their Accounts Receivable Department to watch the dating of the receivables to make sure that it agrees with the lender's requirement and that they do not eliminate some receivables by mistake.

ACCOUNTS RECEIVABLE FACTORING

Another way some firms raise money with their Accounts Receivables as collateral is through the process known as **factoring**. This practice began in colonial America and was used in lieu of Letters of Credit. The cloth mills in New England found that they had customers spread out all along the Eastern Seaboard and as far away as New Orleans. Shipping the material was problem enough, but the other serious problem was how to get paid for a shipment. Out of this dilemma arose what we call today the "factoring industry." A factor would say to a manufacturer "I'll buy that receivable. And I have people in the distant city who can collect the amount owed."

Factoring differs significantly from *pledging* in that the factor actually *takes title* to the account receivable. The factor *buys* the account receivable at a discount to the face amount. In pledging, the lender only has a lien on the account receivable, and the selling company still owns title to the receivable. Naturally, if the factor is going to *buy* the receivable, it will do so only if it approves of the customer's credit rating. This means that the factor will have to screen every possible order that the selling manufacturer wishes to make. The advantage of this is that the seller does not have to maintain a credit department in order to screen a potential customer for acceptance. All the seller has to do is to ask the factor if a certain customer is acceptable. Of course, the manufacturer can still sell to the customer if he or she wishes, but if the factor declines to buy the receivable, the manufacturer will not receive any financing on the receivable.

Predominant Use in the Garment Industry
Factoring grew up in the garment trade, but it has not become popular in other industries. Consequently, if a manufacturer tries to use factoring in an industry

that is not accustomed to factoring, it risks potential backlash from customers. This is because factors make their rate of return if and only if the customer pays *on time*. If a customer is late, the factor will most likely start to dun the customer to pay. This can lead to what might be called a "negative demand" effect. The firm will simply start to lose customers—customers who do not wish to be dunned into paying, even on time.

A manufacturer is unwise to elect to sell to a customer who is an unknown if the factor declines to accept the customer. If a factor declines to accept a customer, it means that the factor has knowledge that the customer is not a good credit risk. In the garment industry, even though there are buyers spread across the United States, the factors know practically every one of these customers (buyers) and is in a much better position to evaluate the credit worthiness of potential customers. This can save a manufacturer much time, angst, and money.

Other Features of Factoring

A manufacturer can elect to sell the receivables to a factor either *with recourse* or *without recourse*. This refers to who is going to be responsible if the customer does not pay. **With recourse** means that the manufacturer/seller will stand the bad debt. "Without recourse" means that the factor will absorb the bad debt. But before getting excited about what a wonderful benefit it would be if one did not have to worry about bad debts, you should remember that the factor charges more for this privilege—substantially more, usually.

The factoring plan may also be *with notification* and *without notification*. **With notification** means that the factoring plan is quite open to all. The Accounts Receivable invoice will clearly state that the payment should be made to such and such company (the name of the factor, such as United Factors). In other cases, the identity of the factor is concealed.

When the invoice is collected by the factor, the factor will then pay the remaining balance to the seller, less the fee. Remember, when the factor approved the order it advanced the manufacturer a percentage of the selling price. But this advance percentage is a variable depending on a number of things; one important one is the firm's Balance Sheet. The other is "Returns and Allowances"—tendencies and behavior patterns of the various stores that purchase clothing. This is one reason why factoring is so predominant in the clothing industry. In this industry the factor brings more to the manufacturer than just money. Its knowledge of all the potential customers may be invaluable in the credit-granting decision process.

It is easy to say that factoring is expensive. Factors charge about five percent for a normal 30-day receivable, and if this is extrapolated for a year it looks like 60 percent! But the good news, remember, is that the company that is factoring does not have to maintain a credit department and this, in itself, is a saving. Also, being relieved of this responsibility may save the firm a large potential bad debt loss on some transaction—a transaction that would be avoided if a factor were consulted. Also, many of the garment manufacturers that use factoring feel that there is sufficient price elasticity of demand for the product that really they can pass on the factor's charge to the buyer.

While factoring is done largely with the garment manufacturers, a number of other firms—both commercial and professional—do use factoring. It is this author's opinion that this is *not* the best approach to financing receivables for companies other than those in the garment trade. This is said because of the possibility of the negative demand effect as well as the cost. Using factoring should be as a last resort, not the first, most desirable way.

INVENTORY PLEDGING

Because finance companies have been dealing in asset-based lending longer than banks, generally speaking, finance companies are more knowledgeable than banks with regard to inventory financing. Banks really try to lend in such a way that they do not have to contend with repossessing collateral such as inventory. Finance companies, on the other hand, have had to contend with this possibility for many years before the banks found the middle-market business attractive. In a way, finance companies got their start by making loans on such things as refrigerators and cars (consumer finance companies) or inventory and equipment (commercial finance companies) on which banks had turned their backs. When making loans on inventory, however, finance companies tend to be much more cognizant than banks are of such things as inventory turnover. Finance companies can be seen conducting tests of a firm's inventory turnover where banks would not even think of doing such tests. Again, this is in part due to the fact that finance companies did this kind of lending long before banks moved in a big way into the middle-market lending arena. Finance companies are able to recognize inventory that can be sold after repossession quickly, whereas banks may not be as discerning.

Interestingly, the borrowing percentages that finance companies use on inventory tend to top out at the same 50 percent that banks use as their maximum. The difference is, however, that the finance company might make a loan against some inventory that a bank would not consider.

Also, finance companies—like banks—may take a UCC 1 on a firm's inventory when, in fact, they are only lending on that firm's Accounts Receivable. As with banks, this is done to prevent other lenders from using the inventory as collateral for a loan.

The irony of all this is that the finance companies, in the early years, got the money they loaned on such collateral from the *banks*—the very institutions that would not lend on that collateral! And to show that history really does repeat itself, when Real Estate Investment Trusts (REITs) got into trouble in the mid-1970s, it came out that the banks were financing the REITs to make the loans that the banks would not make.

DIFFERENCES IN THE PRIORITIES OF FINANCE COMPANIES AND BANKS

It may be useful to compare banks with finance companies to see how they differ in their priorities and methods. To *banks* the most important thing is the firm's Balance Sheet. This is followed by the firm's Income Statement, the Cash Flow Statement and then, the collateral. (The Cash Flow Statement is gaining rapidly in importance and stature. It may be second.) Finally, the guarantees that the principals of the firm give the bank come into play. *Finance companies*, on the other hand, place greatest reliance on the collateral and the firm's Cash Flow Statement, and *then* they look at the firm's Balance Sheet and Income Statement. Personal guarantees tend to be much more important to finance companies than to banks, although the banks will really insist on the guarantees.

In both cases, the **insistence on guarantees** is a way the lender—bank or finance company—has of making sure that the borrower keeps his or her attention focused on the business and works always toward paying off the debt. The lender does not want the borrower walking if things get tough.

For banks a loan is *only one part* of the relationship the bank has with a firm. It also has a deposit relationship (the corporate checking account and the payroll account) as well a being a provider of other services such as Trust Department services and Letters of Credit. Also, the bank may benefit from providing personal financial services to the owners and principal officers of the business or checking accounts for the employees. Finance companies do not have this general sort of relationship with a company, however. The *only* relationship they have is the loan, which is the only way the finance company can make money from the relationship. This is why finance companies tend to be more aggressive with the company borrowing the money and with the customers of the firm.

The finance company will, most likely, remind the potential borrower that "If you get into trouble, we'll work with you." And, indeed, they very well might be inclined to help solve a difficult situation with their borrower. But there is a "catch" in their offer. Finance companies typically use what is called the **Rule of 78** when calculating interest paid on a loan. Essentially, what the finance company will do is to calculate the proportion of interest and principal in every month's payment—and the monthly payment will be fixed and constant—by using this "Rule of 78." (The 78 comes from the fact that the sum of the digits from 1 to 12.) So if the loan were for just 1 year, in the first month the finance company would take the total interest to be paid during the year and apply 12/78ths of this amount in the first month, 11/78ths in the second month and so forth until 1/78ths in the twelfth month. If the loan were for longer than a year, the proportions would then apply.

If a borrower went to a finance company and complained that he or she could not service the monthly payments with the available cash flow, the lender might offer to tear up the loan and write a new one with *lower payments*. But if the cancellation of the old loan and the start of the new loan came early in the tenure of the loan, the finance company would keep all the interest paid—which was disproportionately high in percentage terms *for the period of*

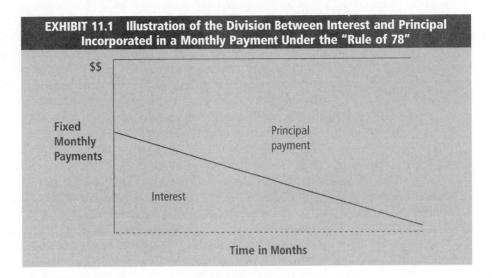

EXHIBIT 11.1   Illustration of the Division Between Interest and Principal Incorporated in a Monthly Payment Under the "Rule of 78"

the original loan. But to the "cash-sick" entrepreneur, getting relief from a monthly payment that was too stiff for the company's cash flow (NOCF"), he or she could care less if the finance company makes a very high rate of return. This is illustrated in Exhibit 11.1.

GOVERNMENT SOURCES OF SHORT-TERM FINANCING

There are a number of government agencies providing financing and other help to developing firms, too many to mention in this book. But there are two that provide financing nationally and are worth mentioning.

SMALL BUSINESS ADMINISTRATION FINANCING

Founded in 1960, the SBA provides guarantees for loans for working capital and term loans for such things as equipment purchases and other fixed assets. Loans can be for up to 8 years or more if buildings are involved. There are a number of criteria that must be met and these include the fact that the business must be a for-profit company. Nonprofit organizations, no matter how beneficial they might be, are not eligible. No business involved in newspapers, radio, television, or movies are eligible as this would be construed as government interference in First Amendment activity—"free speech." The loans must not be for "speculation," whatever that means. For example, buying land for possible resale would not qualify. Building a hotel or motel, on the other hand, would qualify. Also, the firm must have been turned down for a "normal" loan from a lending institution. This requirement is quite easy to get around. On more than one occasion, the author has called one of his friends who was a banker and asked for a "turn down" letter, which arrived soon thereafter.

Also, a bank may not request an SBA guarantee in order to bail itself out of a troubled loan. But it should be remembered that in trying to buy a company it might be possible to get an SBA guarantee *on a piece of the overall price*. For example, if the lender will only go part of the way toward providing the necessary financing, it may be that an SBA guarantee can be secured for the remaining part—the inventory, for example. The maximum loan guarantee provided by the SBA varies depending on loan or regional demand for such loans and the general financial condition of this U.S. agency.

When first founded, the SBA was used as an instrument for addressing human rights issues. It was popularly believed that if one were not a minority—however that was defined at the time—one would not qualify. For example, women, at one time, were considered to be a minority, but today a woman has to show special need to be considered a minority.

In addition to the loan guarantee program, the original act authorized the creation of Small Business Investment Companies (SBICs). In this case, the SBA advanced money to a private investment company (venture capitalist) in proportion to what the private company provides. Most venture capital firms have an SBIC arrangement for smaller or special cases.

THE RURAL BUSINESS-COOPERATIVE SERVICE

The Rural Business-Cooperative Service, a division of the U.S. Department of Agriculture, and formerly called the Farmers Home Administration, is little known in urban areas of the United States because it operates solely in towns with less than 50,000 population and the areas around them. Somewhat resembling the SBA, the Rural Business-Cooperative Service operates a number of programs designed to "enhance the quality of life for all rural Americans by providing leadership in building businesses and cooperatives that can prosper in the global marketplace."▲ These programs, like the SBA, include guarantees of up to 80 percent of loans made by a commercial lender. The *big* difference is that the maximum amount of the loan guarantee is currently $25 million. There is also a direct loan program for private parties (and public entities) when financing is not obtainable from other sources. This, also, has a maximum of $25 million.

For an entrepreneur wishing to acquire a manufacturing or other business in a rural area, this might be an excellent—and overlooked—source of financing. This is particularly true if you can show that jobs can be retained or created by such a loan.

THE EXPORT-IMPORT BANK

For businesses that are interested in exporting, the Export-Import Bank may provide financing when other sources might not; at least, they, like the SBA, provide guarantees for bank financing. This financing might also be available for financing early financing so that materials might be purchased to make whatever it is that is being exported.

▲ From a promotional flyer published by the Rural Business-Cooperative Service.

SUMMARY

Borrowing from banks using Accounts Receivable as collateral is the most common form of short-term financing available to emerging and middle-market companies. Before getting into details of the types of loans made by banks, there is a discussion of the types of banks, selecting a bank, and building rapport with a banker—something that is particularly important. In this chapter the criteria that banks use in making such loans are examined. It is true that a company's management will learn soon enough if it qualifies for A/R financing, but it may be helpful to know what the criteria are, in general, when looking to acquire another company, especially through the medium of a leveraged buyout (LBO). This is quite important when doing an LBO on, for example, a manufacturing company. Borrowing from finance companies is discussed in the second part of the chapter. It is important for management to know the differences in borrowing from banks and finance companies such that

when a choice has to be made it will be a more informed choice. A small but possibly important difference is in what is called the "Rule of 78" used by finance companies. This will help explain why finance companies can say to prospective customers "If you get into trouble, we can help you." Indeed tearing up the old contract and writing a new one for a lower monthly (periodic) payment may do just that, but the finance companies keep the interest already paid. The **rate paid for period** may be much more than the agreed upon rate. But many entrepreneurs, thinking mainly of *cash flow*, could care less. This situation comes about because finance companies customarily have more of the early payments devoted to interest than principal.

The way lenders make these loans, including a discussion of the several types of appraisals that may be obtained as well as the three types of "appraisal companies," is also covered.

11

CHAPTER REVIEW

QUESTIONS FOR DISCUSSION

1. You are in a fairly new relationship with a bank. Since you feel that you must do some borrowing with your receivables as collateral, you mentioned this to your banker. He suggested that they do this kind of lending "out of their special office downtown." How would you react to this?

2. You need some equipment financing and a finance company has approached you for the business. They said that they will quote you a competitive interest charge and "if you need help along the way they will work with you." What did they mean by this? If their rate is approximately the same as your bank's rate, which source of financing would you choose, and why?

3. How do you know if your company would be better off doing business with a commercial finance company or a bank? What factors would these two organizations use when they evaluate your company as a potential customer?

4. You are looking at a company as a potential LBO candidate. How would you evaluate this target's Accounts Receivable as collateral? Also, would their inventory be eligible for borrowing purposes?

Part 4

L/Cs and Working Capital Management

Chapter 12: Letters of Credit

Chapter 13: Cash Management and Money Market Securities

Chapter 14: Management of Accounts Receivable

12

Letters of Credit

Why a separate chapter on Letters of Credit? Years ago, in the United States, it was the rare business that dealt in international trade—where L/Cs are widely used. But today, the world has shrunk for all businesses, and if managers do not think internationally they are decades behind the times. Today, especially with the dramatic opening up of China, international business is a way of life for many firms, especially in distribution and manufacturing.

For many business people, Letters of Credit represent one of the most forbidding or intimidating aspects of business. Just about everything written to explain them has been prepared by technical experts and lawyers, to keep bankers from making a mistake. The detail can be stifling. But businesspeople do not have to know all the nuances of Letters of Credit to use them. So, this chapter aims to remove some of the mystery of Letters of Credit and make them, generally speaking, more understandable to an entrepreneurial manager. The kind of detail necessary for a *banker* has been deliberately omitted in the interest of clarity and relevance to the type of company this book assumes.

In this section, we deal with what is commonly called working capital management. Before discussing the management of cash and accounts receivable, we discuss Letters of Credit—not to make the reader an expert in L/Cs, but rather to show the useful applications of L/Cs. American managers in particular are relatively ignorant of L/Cs, but their use has mushroomed in recent years. Not just in international trade, but also in doing deals in general, L/Cs can play a part.

WHAT IS A LETTER OF CREDIT?

Simply stated, a **Letter of Credit (L/C)** is a letter from one bank to another requesting the second bank to do something, typically to pay money to someone upon fulfillment of certain conditions, such as shipment of merchandise. Use of this document started in the late Middle Ages, when merchant marine ships, especially the British and the Dutch, were exploring the world. The merchantmen had to have some way of paying for their purchases. Since banks kept deposits from other banks, they could merely offset a balance with a payment. In the Colonial days of the United States, however, this practice of using Letters of Credit was limited; instead, as mentioned in the preceding chapter, finance companies sprang up to take over the function of paying the supplier of goods. They did this by purchasing the accounts receivable. American businesspeople thus do not have a long history of acquaintance with Letters of Credit and are today reticent to use them. If one lived in ports like London, Rotterdam, Shanghai, Singapore, or Hong Kong, one would cut his or her business teeth on Letters of Credit.

When discussing Letters of Credit one has to realize that *getting* Letters of Credit in the United States is a major advantage; *giving* a supplier a Letter of Credit here can be painful, however. This is because many (most?) American banks consider the writing of a Letter of Credit for a customer the equivalent of granting a loan. Alternatively, a bank might take out of the company's checking account the amount of the Letter of Credit—even though the bank will not have to surrender that money to another bank for, possibly, 2 or 3 or more months. So to *buy* with a Letter of Credit is not the same as *selling* with a letter of credit.

There is one salient feature of Letters of Credit that should be understood before any other. Banks *do not have to* issue a Letter of Credit for a customer; they do so as a courtesy for that customer even though they charge the customer for this service. A customer cannot demand that the bank write a Letter of Credit on his or her behalf.

TYPES OF LETTERS OF CREDIT

There are several types of Letters of Credit, including commercial, revolving, confirmed, and performance, and all these fall into two main categories: international and domestic. International Letters of Credit naturally are used in international trade, and the protocol for using them is regulated by an international conference. Domestic Letters of Credit, used for domestic transactions, were probably one of the most little-used financing instruments until about 10 years ago. Since the increase in international trade, and with it an increase in the use by businesspeople of Letters of Credit, and since CPAs have been taught the use of domestic Letters of Credit, the issuance of domestic L/Cs has mushroomed in the United States. This chapter later deals with the special issues in domestic Letters of Credit. As we look first at the basic characteristics of Letters of Credit, examples of their international use come into play. Besides the international/domestic classification there are many others that might be made in the course of understanding the use of Letters of Credit.

THE USE OF A L/C: AN EXAMPLE FROM INTERNATIONAL TRADING

Suppose you are an American manufacturer and you want to buy from a company in Hong Kong. How would you pay for the goods? You could send a check to the seller in Hong Kong or you could wire transfer the money. But how would you know if the seller is shipping the right goods? You can't. Or, the seller could ship you the goods and send you a bill for the amount due, but then the seller would really have to trust you for this to happen.▲ Instead, the usual way for this transaction to happen is for you, the buyer, to offer to open a L/C in favor of the seller. Early on in the negotiation between the buyer and seller, the question arises of when the seller will get paid.

This is where the practice of many (most) American banks comes into play. If the buyer's bank is going to take the amount of money that is called for in the L/C from the buyer's account just as soon as it **opens the L/C**, the buyer really does not care if the seller gets paid **on sight**—upon presentation of the appropriate paperwork—or if the payment is delayed for some period of time. But in other situations, and especially in other countries, the payment date might be of extreme importance. For example, if the buyer's bank will not take the amount of the L/C from the company opening the Letter of Credit until it (the bank) has to make payment to the "advising" (paying) bank, then deferring payment for 60 or 90 days might give the buyer enough time to receive the goods and possibly resell them to secure the money necessary to pay for the L/C. Unfortunately, many American banks take the buyer's money as soon as the bank opens the L/C, so this credit extension is lost to such buyers.

If the payment is specified at some future date, the seller can get most of the face amount of the L/C by simply drawing a draft on the L/C when he or she takes the paperwork to the advising bank and asking the advising bank to **discount the draft**. The bank can do so at the prevailing rates for **Banker's Acceptances** in the location of the advising bank. In our example, this was Hong Kong. If this rate were, for example, 6 percent per annum and the deferred payment is for 60 days, then the discount will amount to only *1 percent* of the face amount of the L/C (one-sixth of 6 percent). Any businessperson would jump at such a chance to get money now instead of 60 days from now if it only cost 1 percent! And yet by accepting deferred payment terms, the seller may really be helping the buyer in a credit sense. If the seller were making a domestic sale in America, it might willingly offer a 3 percent discount if payment is made in the first 10 days of receipt of the bill. But that is the equivalent of 54 percent per annum—if paid in 30 days! Compare this to the 6 percent annual rate of discount-

---

▲ There are two other ways the seller could ship the goods to you, either by Documents on Payment or Documents on Approval, both of which will be discussed at the end of this chapter.

ing the L/C in this example. Now you can see one of the really beautiful things about doing business with L/Cs, assuming you are *getting* the L/C.

There is another interesting angle concerning the discounting of a draft against the L/C. The discounting does not have to be done in the seller's place (country) of business. For example, if an American company is buying from a company in Hong Kong, and the Hong Kong company has an office in Tokyo, for instance, where interest rates are quite low currently, it can arrange to discount a draft against the L/C in Tokyo instead of Hong Kong, where interest rates might be considerably higher. This sort of thing is typically done on really large L/Cs, however.

REVOCABLE VERSUS IRREVOCABLE

Whoever initiates a Letter of Credit may make it revocable or irrevocable. If the L/C is **revocable**, the party that initiates the L/C can revoke the L/C at any time before it is consummated by the (selling) party who has received the L/C. Naturally, if one is *selling* on the basis of a L/C that is revocable, there is a great deal more risk involved than if the L/C is irrevocable. If the seller is making something to rigid specifications and accepts a revocable L/C, and the buyer revokes the L/C before shipment, then the seller has no one to blame but himself or herself. It does not matter *why* the issuing party revokes the L/C; the only thing that matters is that the L/C *was revoked*. Because of this, revocable L/Cs are seldom used.

Irrevocable L/Cs, on the other hand, are not revocable by the issuing party. It does not matter what circumstance arises that might provoke the buyer (initiator) to want to revoke the L/C. The irrevocable L/C, once issued, cannot be revoked. The only way that the initiating party can escape paying on this L/C is if some provision of the L/C is not honored and the L/C expires. *Most L/Cs are irrevocable.*

It must be understood well that banks pay on a L/C on the basis of the paperwork called for in the L/C. There is *no discretion* allowed on the part of the paying bank. If the paperwork that is called for in the L/C is presented to the paying bank, the paying bank will make the payment. It does not matter if the buyer, the one who initiated the L/C, is unhappy with the merchandise involved or no longer needs it. If the seller presents the proper paperwork to the paying bank, he or she will get paid. Someone in Africa once ordered a train car load of cement and forgot to specify that the car in which the cement was to be shipped had to be covered. Unfortunately for the buyer, the cement was shipped in an open car and it rained en route! The bank, paying on the basis of the paperwork, paid the seller, much to the chagrin of the buyer.

If there is any question of quality, this situation must be provided for in the paperwork instructions to the bank. For example, there may be a requirement that the paperwork include an *inspection certificate* signed by a known person. If this person does not sign off on the quality report, the bank will not pay the seller. If in importing from abroad the buyer does not have someone in the particular country or locality, there are professional inspection services available which can be retained for this purpose. These inspectors can be a nuisance at times. When a shipment is ready to be shipped, it is necessary for the inspectors to work within the time schedule dictated by the shipment date. Sometimes these inspectors fail to arrive in time for the inspection prior to the shipment date. This might mean that the shipment is delayed to the consternation of all. The L/C might even have to be amended.

Whether or not it is convenient for the buyer to inspect the goods, it is incumbent upon the buyer, using a L/C, to provide for this inspection, because the paying bank will not! When the paying bank pays the seller, the deal is done. True, if there is a continuing arrangement with the seller, the buyer may have recourse, but when dealing abroad one does not have the sort of recourse available in the United States.

DOCUMENTARY VERSUS CLEAN

A **documentary** L/C means that there is merchandise involved. If no merchandise is involved, the L/C is called a **clean** L/C—meaning that it is clean of merchandise. (More on clean L/Cs later in this chapter.)

"ACTUAL" VERSUS STANDBY

"Actual"—my term, not an official designation—means that the bank is expected to pay on the L/C. **Standby** L/Cs mean that the bank is *not* expected to pay on the L/C; it will pay *if* and only *if* the maker of the L/C does not pay. Standby L/Cs are a form of bank guaranty. They are used more in domestic trade and will be discussed more fully later in this chapter.

CONFIRMED VERSUS UNCONFIRMED

Confirmed means that the paying bank can pay the seller when the proper documentation is present. This paperwork might include the Bill of Lading, an insurance certificate, country of origin certificate, invoices in the proper number of copies, and a way bill, among others. It does not have to send the paperwork back to the issuing bank for approval to pay. Practically all L/Cs issued between parties in developed countries are confirmed. But when dealing with China, Iran, and a number of other countries, it is *usual* for the L/C received by the selling firm to be **unconfirmed**. This means, for example, that if an American vendor is selling to a company in China and receives a L/C for payment, it very well might not be confirmed. So when the American seller takes the material to the shipper, such as an agent at the airport or shipping dock, and receives the shipping documents necessary to get paid, he or she might be in for a big surprise. Instead of being paid at once by the paying bank, even if through a discounted draft on the L/C, he or she might be told that the paperwork has to sent to China for payment. Or, even more aggravating, that the paperwork has to be sent to New York (or Los Angeles, or wherever) and then they have to send the paperwork to China for approval.▲ This approval process can take a minimum of 2 weeks and possibly more than a month. And during this time, the exporting company in the United States, which may have paid for the goods or manufactured them, can receive no money until the L/C is confirmed. Since time is money, this can be reasonably expensive for the American exporter, unless, of course, the seller has figured this delay into the pricing of goods. It behooves an exporter to China who is selling to a government-owned company to ask for a confirmed L/C, but unless the *buyer really needs* the goods, the attempt is apt to fail.

Another difficult thing about unconfirmed L/Cs is that they do not *say* that they are unconfirmed. It is sometimes quite difficult for someone to read the L/C and know immediately that the L/C is not confirmed or whether it is confirmed. If the L/C comes from China, however, it should be suspected that the L/C is *not* confirmed. If the L/C says "payable at any bank," it is a good indication that the L/C is confirmed.

GENERAL FEATURES OF THE APPLICATION FOR A LETTER OF CREDIT

Before a Letter of Credit is written, the company that is applying for the L/C completes an application form in which all the details are presented: who's buying from whom, what it is that they are buying, etc. On this form the buying company specifies *everything* that it requires in the L/C. Exhibit 12.1 is a sample of this application form. With this information, the issuing bank drafts the Letter of Credit.

The top of the application (labeled 4 in this exhibit) states the name of the bank that is to *issue* the L/C. What is labeled section 2 refers to the party for whom the L/C is being *written* (the buyer), the ABC Toys Import Co. of San Francisco. Section 3 is the name of the *beneficiary* of the L/C, the seller—XYZ Toys Export Ltd. of Kowloon, Hong Kong, in this case. In section 5 is entered the name of the bank that is designated to *pay* the beneficiary. Sometimes, the beneficiary will specify the name of the advising bank (the paying bank). In this example, the Bank of America branch in Hong Kong was specified. In other times the paying bank might be specified as "any bank."

Section 6 stipulates the *amount of the transaction*. The company that is buying the merchandise or the seller can specify any major currency. Fortunately, for American traders, the U.S. dollar is widely used in international trade, even between countries neither of which is American. For example, if an export company in China is dealing with an English importer, the amount might be

---

▲ Under the state ownership that has been the case in China, this practice of using unconfirmed L/Cs is an understandable one. Companies can purchase goods abroad but may not have the requisite foreign exchange. By making the L/Cs unconfirmed, the Chinese bank can make sure that the money is available before it authorizes payment on the L/C—that is, by *confirming* it. Like many things in China, this practice is changing also.

EXHIBIT 12.1   Sample Application for a Letter of Credit

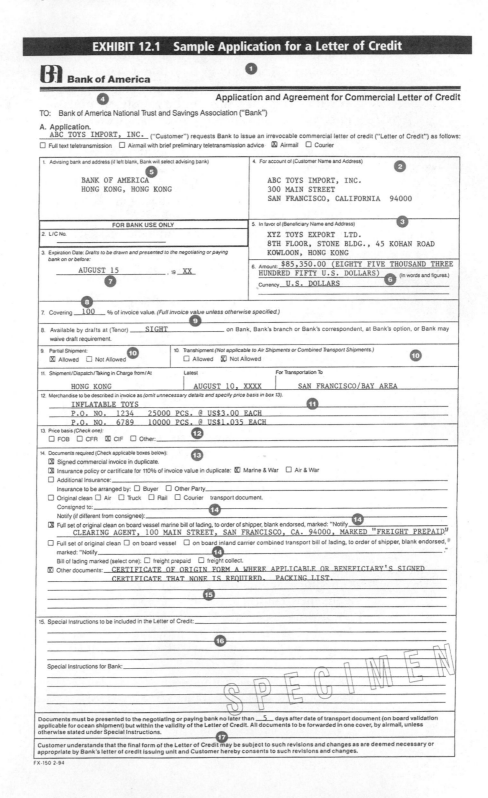

Bank of America   ①

Application and Agreement for Commercial Letter of Credit

④

TO: Bank of America National Trust and Savings Association ("Bank")

A. Application.

__ABC TOYS IMPORT, INC.__ ("Customer") requests Bank to issue an irrevocable commercial letter of credit ("Letter of Credit") as follows:

☐ Full text teletransmission   ☐ Airmail with brief preliminary teletransmission advice   ☒ Airmail   ☐ Courier

1. Advising bank and address (if left blank, Bank will select advising bank) ⑤	4. For account of (Customer Name and Address) ②
BANK OF AMERICA HONG KONG, HONG KONG	ABC TOYS IMPORT, INC. 300 MAIN STREET SAN FRANCISCO, CALIFORNIA 94000

FOR BANK USE ONLY

2. L/C No.

5. In favor of (Beneficiary Name and Address) ③
XYZ TOYS EXPORT LTD. 8TH FLOOR, STONE BLDG., 45 KOHAN ROAD KOWLOON, HONG KONG

3. Expiration Date: *Drafts to be drawn and presented to the negotiating or paying bank on or before:*

   AUGUST 15 , 19 XX
                    ⑦

6. Amount: **$85,350.00 (EIGHTY FIVE THOUSAND THREE HUNDRED FIFTY U.S. DOLLARS)** *(In words and figures.)* ⑥

Currency: __U.S. DOLLARS__

7. Covering __100__ % of invoice value. *(Full invoice value unless otherwise specified.)* ⑧

8. Available by drafts at (Tenor) __SIGHT__ on Bank, Bank's branch or Bank's correspondent, at Bank's option, or Bank may waive draft requirement. ⑨

9. Partial Shipment: ⑩ ☒ Allowed ☐ Not Allowed	10. Transhipment *(Not applicable to Air Shipments or Combined Transport Shipments.)* ⑩ ☐ Allowed ☒ Not Allowed

11. Shipment/Dispatch/Taking in Charge from/At	Latest	For Transportation To
HONG KONG	AUGUST 10, XXXX	SAN FRANCISCO/BAY AREA

12. Merchandise to be described in invoice as *(omit unnecessary details and specify price basis in box 13).* ⑪

   INFLATABLE TOYS
   P.O. NO. 1234 25000 PCS. @ US$3.00 EACH
   P.O. NO. 6789 10000 PCS. @ US$1.035 EACH

13. Price basis *(Check one)*: ⑫
☐ FOB ☐ CFR ☒ CIF ☐ Other: _____

14. Documents required (Check applicable boxes below): ⑬
☒ Signed commercial invoice in duplicate.
☒ Insurance policy or certificate for 110% of invoice value in duplicate: ☒ Marine & War ☐ Air & War
☐ Additional Insurance: _____
    Insurance to be arranged by: ☐ Buyer ☐ Other Party _____
☐ Original clean ☐ Air ☐ Truck ☐ Rail ☐ Courier transport document.
    Consigned to: _____ ⑭
    Notify (if different from consignee): _____
☒ Full set of original clean on board vessel marine bill of lading, to order of shipper, blank endorsed, marked: "Notify _____ ⑭
    CLEARING AGENT, 100 MAIN STREET, SAN FRANCISCO, CA. 94000, MARKED "FREIGHT PREPAID"
☐ Full set of original clean ☐ on board vessel ☐ on board inland carrier combined transport bill of lading, to order of shipper, blank endorsed,
    marked: "Notify _____ ⑭   ."
    Bill of lading marked (select one): ☐ freight prepaid ☐ freight collect.
☒ Other documents: __CERTIFICATE OF ORIGIN FORM A WHERE APPLICABLE OR BENEFICIARY'S SIGNED__
    __CERTIFICATE THAT NONE IS REQUIRED. PACKING LIST.__
    _____
    _____ ⑮

15. Special Instructions to be included in the Letter of Credit: _____
    _____
    _____ ⑯

Special Instructions for Bank: _____
    _____
    _____
    _____

Documents must be presented to the negotiating or paying bank no later than __5__ days after date of transport document (on board validation applicable for ocean shipment) but within the validity of the Letter of Credit. All documents to be forwarded in one cover, by airmail, unless otherwise stated under Special Instructions.

Customer understands that the final form of the Letter of Credit may be subject to such revisions and changes as are deemed necessary or appropriate by Bank's letter of credit issuing unit and Customer hereby consents to such revisions and changes.

FX-150 2-94

specified in U.S. dollars. Presumably, with the introduction of the Euro, there will be another standard currency in the future. But even Japan's yen has not replaced the dollar, or even come close to it.

Section 7 is the *date* on which the L/C expires. *This is an extremely important date.* If the beneficiary presents the paperwork—even if it is "proper"—*after* this date, the paying bank has no obligation to pay on this L/C. The buyer must request an amendment to the L/C to authorize payment. When there is a rather short period between the order date and the shipping date, and there is any sort of mistake in the L/C, then there will need to be an amendment to extend the L/C. In the sample application for a Letter of Credit (Exhibit 12.1), the buyer will have to pay the issuing bank for the revision, which is not only annoying but reasonably expensive. The kinds of errors that happen, in my experience, frequently stem from the fact that several languages are involved—for example, a South American buyer and an export company in China, with English used in the L/C. If the export company's name and address are not specified correctly—not just close—then the L/C must be amended.

Another reason for missing the expiration date is inefficiency on the part of the clerks handling the L/C for the seller. They might simply be late getting their paperwork to the paying bank. When this happens, the buyer is notified and puts through an amendment to the L/C to correct the situation. Obviously, this can be annoying to the buyer and, if repeated, can lead to considerable friction between buyer and seller. If the goods are already shipped and the seller lets the L/C expire, the buyer may collect the goods at his or her end without paying. Obviously, this situation would not go on long. If the buyer ever expects to order again from the seller, an amendment must be offered.

The section numbered 8 in the exhibit states what *percentage of the purchase price* is covered by the L/C. Sometimes there is a down payment and the L/C will cover only the remaining balance. Or, the buyer may specify that the L/C is for some portion of the purchase price, with the balance due upon receipt. This practice can lead to, for example, a buyer giving a seller an L/C for, say, 75 percent of the purchase price. When the buyer receives the material, he or she objects that the quality is not according to the order and requests (demands) a discount. (This can present a confusing situation, if the buyer receives merchandise that really is substandard, but the seller may think the buyer is just trying to cheat him or her.)

Section 9 stipulates *how* payment is to be made. Is it to be "at sight," meaning upon presentation of the appropriate documents, or at some future time? This is strictly the result of an agreement between the buyer and the seller. There is no rule about this. Even though the L/C specifies that the amount is payable at some future date—for instance 60 or 90 days—the seller can get virtually all the amount due by discounting a draft drawn against the L/C. (This will be explained in more detail below.)

Section 10 merely states *whether or not a partial shipment is allowed.* This is an agreement between the buyer and the seller. Section 10 also specifies whether or not a **transshipment** is allowed. Generally, this refers to whether or not the goods can be sent to one place and then reshipped to the final destination. It does not mean, for example, that a container cannot be shipped from some port in China to some port in the United States via Hong Kong, which is the most common way to ship out of China. It might also mean that the goods can be unloaded and/or repacked for further shipment. (This mostly concerns the shipping company.)

While not marked with a number on the exhibit, the "latest shipping date" must also be specified. This, like the date of expiry, is a most important date and care should be exercised in setting this date. If a delay occurs, an amendment to the L/C will have to be made. Section 11 contains a brief *description of the merchandise* that is being ordered. The purchase order or purchase contract contains the full description of the merchandise.

Section 12 states the *terms* under which the merchandise is being shipped. FOB, for example, means "free on board." This means that it is the *buyer's* responsibility to arrange shipping of the merchandise (typically in a container). For shipment between the United States and European ports this may not be much of a problem, but if the shipment is from China, Southeast Asia, or Japan, and the buyer is American or European, this requirement may be, indeed, daunting. Under these circumstances, the typical way to ship from these areas is **CIF**, which means "cost, insurance, and freight." Under CIF, the selling company undertakes to arrange shipping, for which it pays, and for the appropriate insurance to make sure that the merchandise gets to the buyer unharmed. A sleazy trick of some exporters is to stipulate in the shipping documents that, for example, 11,000 kilos are being shipped, but only 10,000 kilos arrive at the buyer's address. The seller explains "Those thieves in Hong Kong [where much of the trade between China and the rest of the world is reshipped] must have stolen 1,000 kilos because when we sealed the container it contained 11,000 kilos." Sure! When this happens it is time to get a new supplier.

CF means "cost and freight," no insurance. Some countries—Ecuador, for example—require that the insurance on imports be carried by an Ecuadorian insurance company. In this case the shipper (seller) will not procure the insurance.

Section 13 cites the *documents* that are required. Remember earlier the point was made that banks pay only on paperwork? This section of the application is where the buyer specifies what paperwork he or she wants. The area of the application numbered 14 provides space for the buyer to specify the name and address of the party to whom the shipping company should send notice of arrival. This party may be the buyer itself, the buyer's agent, or a customs house broker. The "Other documents" mentioned in Section 14 contain such requirements as the "Place of origin" and health certificates. But it is in this section that the buyer can place the requirement for inspection. *The fact that it is the buyer's responsibility to see to it that the quality of the goods is acceptable cannot be stressed enough; it is not the bank's responsibility.* How the buyer will exercise this responsibility varies with the circumstances. If the buyer is just getting to know the seller, he or she may insist upon inspection by the buyer's own representative or by a hired professional inspector. After confidence is built because of satisfactory shipments, the buyer may waive this requirement. Hiring a professional inspector—from one of the several inspection companies operating worldwide—may be a bit of a problem, however. If, for example, the inspection is to be carried out after the goods are made, but before shipment, it behooves the inspector to get to the seller's plant in time to do the inspection and not miss the shipping date. Depending on the destination, there may not be many carriers for the goods, so if the inspectors are late, the shipment may "miss the boat" literally.

Section 16 contains space for *special instructions* to the bank (Bank of America in this case). Below it, in Section 17, one specifies the *time allowed for the presentation* of the documents to the "advising" (paying) bank. If this section is left blank, then the documents must be presented no later than 21 days after shipment.

GENERAL FEATURES OF A LETTER OF CREDIT

Once the application is completed, the actual L/C is easy to prepare. Most of the features are the same as on the application but they will be repeated here. Exhibit 12.2 shows a sample L/C. In the first section, the name of the *issuing bank* as well as the Letter of Credit number is given. Also, a statement is made about the nature of the L/C. In the sample it states "IRREVOCABLE DOCUMENTARY LETTER OF CREDIT NO. 000000." We have already discussed the meaning of "Irrevocable," and "Documentary" means that merchandise is involved.

Section 2 states the name of the *buyer*. Section 3 states the name of the *advising bank* that has been selected to notify and forward the L/C to the beneficiary. They can do this by such methods as courier, airmail, or fax. Section 4 states the *beneficiary*, the seller.

Section 5 states the way the beneficiary is to be *paid*. The statement "Credit available with ANY BANK" means that the beneficiary can get paid on the L/C at any bank of its choosing. (This is also a clue that the L/C is "confirmed.") When receiving a L/C from some countries such as Russia and third-world countries, it behooves the seller to make sure that the bank on which the L/C is drawn is sound. Some are not. There are four kinds of payments that might be specified. "At sight" means that as soon as the beneficiary presents the paperwork to the bank it can get paid, assuming that the L/C is "confirmed." **Deferred payment** means that the payment date will be sometime in the future—for example, 60 or 90 days. As mentioned, this is something that the buyer and seller agree upon; the bank has nothing do with this decision. If the payment is deferred the seller can still get paid when he or she ships, and this process will be explained below. **Acceptance** means "acceptance by the drawee bank"—the buyer's bank. If "negotiation" is specified, the seller can get paid by any bank willing to negotiate the L/C. (These last two definitions are overly general to keep our discussion from getting too technical.)

Section 6 refers to the possibility of a *partial shipment*, which was already discussed. Section 7 was also previously discussed but bears repeating. First, there is a description of the merchandise. Secondly, the *documents required*, the

EXHIBIT 12.2 Sample Copy of a Letter of Credit

Bank of America

TRADE OPERATIONS CENTER #5655
333 SOUTH BEAUDRY AVE., 19TH FLOOR   Place:
LOS ANGELES, CA 90017

Cable Address: BankAmerica

☐ This refers to our preliminary teletransmission advice of this credit.

IRREVOCABLE DOCUMENTARY
LETTER OF CREDIT NO.   000000

DATE OF ISSUE: JANUARY 6, XXXX

APPLICANT
ABC TOYS IMPORT, INC.
300 MAIN STREET
SAN FRANCISCO, CALIFORNIA 94000

ADVISING BANK   REFERENCE NO.:
BANK OF AMERICA
G. P. O. BOX 472
HONG KONG, HONG KONG

BENEFICIARY
XYZ TOYS EXPORT LTD.
8TH FLOOR, STONE BLDG.
45 KOHAN ROAD
KOWLOON, HONG KONG

DATE AND PLACE OF EXPIRY
AUGUST 15, XXXX
HONG KONG

AMOUNT
US$85,350.00 (U.S. DOLLARS EIGHTY FIVE
THOUSAND THREE HUNDRED FIFTY AND
00/100)

Covering: 100   % invoice value

Credit available with ANY BANK
by   ☐ sight payment   ☐ deferred payment   ☐ acceptance   ☒ negotiation
against presentation of the documents detailed below and your draft(s) at SIGHT
drawn on BANK OF AMERICA, LOS ANGELES

Partial shipments: ☒ allowed   ☐ not allowed   Transhipments: ☐ allowed   ☒ not allowed

Shipments/dispatch/taking in charge from/at HONG KONG PORT   SHIPMENT LATEST: 08/10/XX
for transportation to   SAN FRANCISCO/BAY AREA, CALIFORNIA, USA

MERCHANDISE DESCRIPTION:

INFLATABLE TOYS
P.O. NO. 1234 25000 PCS @ US$3.00 EACH.
P.O. NO. 6789 10000 PCS @ US$1.035 EACH
CIF SAN FRANCISCO/BAY AREA, CALIFORNIA, USA.

DOCUMENTS REQUIRED:
1. SIGNED COMMERICAL INVOICE IN TRIPLICATE.
2. MARINE AND WAR INSURANCE POLICY OR CERTIFICATE FOR 110 PERCENT OF INVOICE VALUE IN DUPLICATE.
3. CERTIFICATE OF ORIGIN FORM 'A' WHERE APPLICABLE, OR BENEFICIARY'S SIGNED CERTIFICATE THAT NONE IS REQUIRED.
4. PACKING LIST.
5. FULL SET ORIGINAL CLEAN ON BOARD VESSEL MARINE BILLS OF LADING, TO ORDER OF SHIPPER, BLANK ENDORSED, MARKED FREIGHT PREPAID AND NOTIFY CLEARING AGENT, 100 MAIN STREET, SAN FRANCISCO, CALIFORNIA 94000.

SPECIAL INSTRUCTIONS:

1. WE WILL DEDUCT US$XX FROM PROCEEDS ON EACH SET OF DOCUMENTS CONTAINING DISCREPANCIES.
2. ALL BANKING CHARGES OTHER THAN OURS ARE FOR BENEFICIARY'S ACCOUNT.
3. ALL DOCUMENTS MUST BEAR OUR LETTER OF CREDIT NUMBER.

Documents to be presented within   5 days after the date of issuance of the shipping document(s)
but within the validity of the credit.

We hereby issue this Documentary Credit in your favour. It is subject to the Uniform Customs and Practice for Documentary Credits, 1993 revision, ICC Publication No. 500, and engages us in accordance with the terms thereof. The number and the date of the credit and the name of our bank must be quoted on all drafts required. If the credit is available by negotiation, each presentation must be noted on the reverse of this advice by the bank where the credit is available.

All documents to be forwarded in one cover, by airmail, unless otherwise stated above. Negotiating bank charges, if any, are for account of beneficiary. The advising bank is requested to notify the credit to the beneficiary without adding their confirmation.

This document consists
of 1 signed page(s)   Mary Smith AUTHORIZED COUNTERSIGNATURE   John Doe AUTHORIZED SIGNATURE

Please examine this instrument carefully. If you are unable to comply with the terms or conditions, please communicate with your buyer to arrange for an amendment. This procedure will facilitate prompt handling when documents are presented.

FX-1310 3-94

importance of which is paramount. It is here that the buyer states the things that he or she requires, including an inspection report if needed. Thirdly, there is space for *special instructions*. It is here that the buyer states anything that is left out above, such as who will pay for any amendments.

Section 8 is the standard boilerplate regarding the L/C. Section 9 contains a statement that the bank will make about charging a fee if there needs to be an amendment to the L/C. Section 9 is interesting, and often overlooked. It tells the *seller* that he or she had better look over the L/C to see if he or she can comply with the terms of the L/C. If they cannot, then they will have to request an amendment to the L/C, which will cost both in time and money.

COSTS OF LETTERS OF CREDIT

It is difficult to state what the cost of a L/C is because there are, generally speaking, two charges for a L/C. There is the charge for writing the L/C itself and then there is a percentage charge for the monetary amount involved. The first charge can vary from as low as about $25 to $100 or more. The second charge can vary from about 3/8ths of 1 percent to about 1.5 percent. As mentioned, if amendments have to be made to the L/C once it is written, then the bank will levy additional charges, such as $25 to $50 or more.

DOMESTIC LETTERS OF CREDIT

Domestic Letters of Credit were approved by the Federal Reserve Act of 1913, but were little used until recently. Domestic L/Cs can be used in quite the same way as international L/Cs: to guarantee payment for merchandise that is being purchased, or for other guarantees, to be discussed below.

There are some rather minor technical differences between an international and a domestic L/C, but these should not bother a selling business. For example, the Federal regulations provide that the bank that issues the L/C must be in receipt of **title to the goods**, but this is really no major barrier to the use of domestic L/Cs. When discounting a draft against a domestic L/C, the discount rate is a bit higher than if the L/C were an international L/C, but, again, this is really not very significant to a manufacturer selling goods.

EXAMPLES OF THE USE OF DOMESTIC LETTERS OF CREDIT

Typically, we in the United States give **open book credit** to customers in this country, but there are situations where this may not be desirable or even possible. For example, an electronics manufacturer in California gets a chance to book a huge order from an East Coast "Baby Bell" company. If it took the order, it would represent an obvious **concentration factor** to the California manufacturer. This means that the manufacturer's bank would not only not loan on the receivables generated from this sale—actually a series of sales over an extended period of time—but may, in fact not loan on *any* of the company's receivables because of the danger this amount of concentration presents. The solution to this dilemma would be to have the Baby Bell (customer) open a **revolving** L/C arrangement for the California manufacturer. A revolving L/C arrangement is when the buyer sets a limit on how much money represented by L/Cs can be outstanding at any time. For example $1 million: when the dollar value of the outstanding L/Cs reaches this point, additional L/Cs will not be issued (or accepted). In this way, as soon as the goods are shipped to the customer, the manufacturer can go to its bank, draw a draft against the L/C, and get its money without waiting. In this way, there is no need for accounts receivable financing.

A domestic L/C might involve the use of **deferred payments** on the L/C. Suppose a manufacturer were invited to bid on supplying spare parts to a major midwestern manufacturer of engines. Again, if the selling firm were to take the order, it might represent a significant concentration factor, making the financing of the receivables difficult if not impossible. Again, a solution might be to use a domestic L/C. Now if—and this is a big *if*—the bank for the midwestern manufacturer will open a revolving L/C arrangement and not take the money out of the midwestern's company account as soon as the L/C is opened, then the selling company can say to the engine company "If you do business with us, we can virtually finance your spare parts inventory." If the engine company turns over its inventory four times a year, for example, and if the selling company agrees to take a L/C payable in 90 days (equal to four times a year), then it would virtually finance the spare parts inventory for the buyer! If the buyer says, "Yes, but what about the charges the bank will make for the L/C?" the seller can say that he or she will make up for this by a "quantity" discount. This is how a domestic L/C could be used for marketing purposes while making possible an otherwise impossible financial situation for the selling firm.

STANDBY LETTERS OF CREDIT

While the preceding discussions have dealt with documentary, or what I have called "actual," L/Cs, there exists another type that is gaining in usage: the **standby** Letter of Credit. Usually you do not have standby L/Cs in international commerce if there is merchandise involved, but domestically there is a good chance you may use them.

Here is how they might be used. A computer software company in Virginia wants to order a computer from a major manufacturer in some western state. Someone in the computer manufacturer's credit department does a credit analysis on the software company and decides that there is already too much credit extended to the software company for the size and condition of its Balance Sheet. "But software companies don't have big Balance Sheets," the software firm explains. The incantations fall on deaf ears. "Sorry," says the computer manufacturer, "rules are rules." The software company calls its bank and explains why it needs to buy the computer: it can install some software on it and sell it to a prime customer as a stand-alone computer system. Understanding the situation, the bank can offer to write a standby L/C for its customer. By so doing, the bank is saying, in effect, "If this little software company does not pay you, we will." When the computer manufacturer sees this standby L/C, it calls the software company and asks, "When do you want the computer shipped?"

What this standby L/C does is to change the apparent risk. Instead of looking at the little software company's Balance Sheet, the seller is now looking at a substantial *bank's* Balance Sheet. But there is one caveat in the use of standby L/Cs. *The bank does not expect to pay on the standby L/C; if it does it will most likely be very upset with its customer for whom it wrote the standby L/C.* Whether or not the issuing bank will consider the issuance of the standby L/C—the equivalent of a credit-granting decision—depends on the circumstances of the customer and the bank's policy.

ADVANTAGES OF L/Cs

THREE WAYS TO DO BUSINESS WITHOUT A SUBSTANTIAL BALANCE SHEET

One of the beauties of using Letters of Credit is the ability to use them to do business when you do not have a substantial Balance Sheet. By this I mean the ability to buy and sell without substantial Net Worth. Three ways to do this come to mind.

"Back to Back" Letters of Credit

Suppose you are able to sell computers to someone in Australia. You receive a purchase order and with it a L/C. Now all you have to do is to place an order with the manufacturer for the requisite computers. When you go to place the order for the computers with the manufacturer and have them drop ship the computers to your customer in Australia, you are asked to submit your financial statements for consideration by the computer manufacturer's credit department. Unfortunately, you do not have much of a Balance Sheet. But you do have a friendly banker who knows you and respects what you are doing. So you go to your banker and ask him or her to write for you a **back-to-back Letter of Credit** to the computer manufacturer so they will accept your order. If the banker feels that the L/C is in perfect order, he or she can write a new L/C, and then you can send this new L/C to the computer manufacturer. The banker will make absolutely sure that every important part of the first L/C is replicated in the second L/C, especially the dates.

Because the L/C changes the *apparent risk* to the manufacturer, he or she will ship at once because you have substituted your bank's Balance Sheet for your anemic Balance Sheet. While this sounds like a perfect way to do some business it is *most difficult to do this today*. At one time this was a rather usual way to do business without a strong Balance Sheet or Net Worth. Today, however, banks feel that by issuing a Letter of Credit on your behalf—even if backed up by another L/C—they are, in effect, granting you a line of credit. Of course they will issue the second Letter of Credit on your behalf if you will deposit the amount of the Letter of Credit with the bank! Although this is the normal posture for American banks today, you might get lucky and find a bank that would write a back-to-back L/C on your behalf. But if you cannot, there is, fortunately, a way out of this conundrum.

A Transferable Letter of Credit

If your bank will not write a back-to-back Letter of Credit for you, you could request that the L/C you receive from your customer be made **transferable**—and this is easy to do. As mentioned in the explanation of the L/C terms (pages 283–287), if the L/C you receive is marked transferable you can go to your bank and they will happily transfer your L/C to your supplier and make two changes in it for you. They can change the monetary amount and shorten the time of the L/C. In this way you can get your markup on the sale and your customer will never know how much you had to pay for whatever it is that you are selling to the customer. If something has to be done with the expiration date or the shipping date in order for you to receive the goods and reship them to your customer, that, too, can be accomplished. Because banks do not feel that this arrangement is akin to granting you a line of credit, banks today willingly write transferable L/Cs. But what do you do if the L/C is not marked transferable and you do not want to go back to your customer and ask that the L/C be amended and made transferable? Fortunately, again, there may be a way around this dilemma as well.

An Assignment of Proceeds

If you are dealing with a supplier that is in a highly developed country—for example, the United Kingdom or Germany—and you receive a L/C that is not transferable, you can go to your supplier and ask if he or she will accept an **assignment of proceeds** for the amount of your order to them. This means that your bank will issue to them a promise that when your L/C is "cashed"—when you have delivered on all the requirements (paperwork) that you have to get paid on the L/C—the bank will withhold an amount necessary to pay your supplier for the amount owed to him or her. In this way, you can effectively pay your supplier even though you do not have a substantial Balance Sheet to impress your supplier's credit department.

Unfortunately, this technique of assigning the proceeds of a L/C may only work if you are dealing with a supplier in a highly developed country. Trying to do this with a supplier in China is likely to result in your supplier expressing an unwillingness to accept this strange instrument. Of course, times change, and eventually even suppliers in the less developed countries will develop and they, too, will start to accept an "assignment of proceeds."

USING LETTERS OF CREDIT WITH A REVOLVING LINE OF CREDIT

It is possible, and in fact reasonably common, to use Letters of Credit in connection with an established **line of credit**. For example, if a car dealer is buying cars from a foreign manufacturer, he or she might set up some monetary limit on the amount of L/Cs outstanding—for example, $5 million. This means that the seller (the car manufacturer) can ship cars to the buyer until the total amount of L/Cs outstanding reaches the limit, $5 million. Once this limit is reached, the buyer has to pay down on the line before more L/Cs can be honored. This can be quite a useful arrangement, but it must be used with caution. Unless provision is made to prevent unwanted shipments, the seller might ship goods and draw down against a L/C at a time inconvenient to the buyer. By giving the seller discretion as to when to ship, this could mean that the buyer winds up with a lot of material or goods when they are not wanted. When a seller suggests a revolving L/C arrangement, *be careful!*

CLEAN LETTERS OF CREDIT

Up to this point we have been discussing Letters of Credit in which merchandise is involved. But there are billions of dollars of L/Cs outstanding that do not involve merchandise. These are called **clean** Letters of Credit, meaning "clean" of merchandise. These clean L/Cs can be of either the type on which the bank *expects* to pay or they can be standby clean Letters of Credit. In the first case, a clean L/C might be used to pay someone in a foreign country for services rendered, for example, your own employee stationed in a foreign country. It is prearranged that all that person has to do is to present himself or herself to some appointed bank on certain dates, show proper identification and receive his or her salary.

But the more interesting use of clean L/Cs is as standby L/Cs. There are many examples of these, including as "guarantees" for municipal bonds. If a small municipally owned water company in Idaho, for example, wishes to issue bonds, what chance would such an unknown entity have of getting a good bond rating? But if, for example, Citicorp issued a clean L/C guaranteeing payment by this little water company, it could, in all likelihood, issue bonds with a higher rating. So, even if the municipality paid the bank for its guarantee it would save money in the issuance of the bonds.

American banks have issued so many guarantees of this type that the outstanding amount is equal to or greater than their combined capital.▲ Technically, these bank L/Cs are not "guarantees," as it is against bank laws in the United States for banks to make financial or performance guarantees, to ensure the completion of a building, for example. Under a standby or commercial L/C, the bank makes payment only on the presentation of documents. Banks also issue clean L/Cs to guarantee commercial paper issued by corporations. This will be discussed in the next chapter.

Another more common use of clean L/Cs today is to guarantee contracts of indebtedness from one party to another. Since this practice has been added to the CPA review courses, this relatively unknown practice of 10 or more years ago

▲ While a bit dated, see Barbara Bennett's article "Off Balance Sheet Risk in Banking: The Case of Standby Letters of Credit," *Federal Reserve Bulletin of San Francisco*, Winter 1986, 19.

"YOU KNOW, WE OUGHT TO START A COMPANY": AGAINST ALL ODDS!

Focus on Technology

Starting a company is one of the most daring journeys that one can embark upon in a lifetime. However, it seems that such a journey will be twice the hassle if the entrepreneur happens to be a woman. I am saying this certainly not to discourage female entrepreneurs—quite the contrary. I want to bring in a sense of appreciation for the extra work female entrepreneurs have to put in to overcome the apparent stereotype. "I think sexism was in the mix. But my reaction . . . was not concern about sexism, but disappointment on behalf of my company, my co-founders and our customers," Marimba's Kim Polese said once in an interview. "'There's substance here, in me and in my company . . .'"

Marimba's primary product is Castanet, which allows corporations to efficiently deliver software and information across the Web. Marimba is basically an Internet infrastructure company, in the same league as Inktomi Corp., VeriSign Inc., and Vignette Corp. The company employs over 200 people.

Marimba's story is a good case in point. Kim Polese, along with three of her coworkers started Marimba back in 1996 on a shoestring budget. The idea came from group discussions during the previous year on starting a business. After doing some major brainstorming on everything from the type of product/service to be offered, to design, production, distribution, sales, and financing, the group members made some key decisions—including quitting their well-respected jobs—and Marimba was born. Initial funding came from founders and later on from VCs. The company went public very successfully 3 years later in 1999.

Given the technology shakedown of Spring 2000, Marimba has managed not only to stay alive but also to solidify its position in the marketplace and broaden its offerings and customer base.

As a final point, if you are an entrepreneur, nothing seems to matter to you. If you are focused enough and know what you are doing, somehow things will work out for you. "Everyone in our company was working really hard to build a great company, and everyone knew we have a fabulous product that works very well. But it didn't really bother me at the end of the day because I knew we were going to execute, I knew we were going to be successful, and I knew we were going to kick butt!"

is now quite common. For example, if one company is buying another company and there is a note involved from the buyer to the seller, today one would almost expect the seller, on the advice of his or her CPA, to request that the note be guaranteed by a clean L/C.

One of the greatest uses of clean L/Cs developed in the 1970s with project financing in the Middle East and Africa, where there were many large building projects. As is customary, the contracting party requested that the construction company post either a bond or 10 percent of the contract price in cash to assure completion. But the large banks situated in London—Citicorp and Bank of America, for example—which had banking relations with these large contractors said to the contractors "Why pay a bonding company to 'guarantee' your performance when we can do it for less." They could do it for less because they knew the company thoroughly and because they had what might be called a "total" relationship with the contractor: loans, demand deposits, foreign exchange, etc. The bonding company would have only one way to be compensated for the risk it took, and that was by charging a fee for its service. At one time the major banks had billions of dollars worth of clean L/Cs outstanding serving as guarantees for construction projects in the Middle East and associated areas. Only now is this practice of using clean L/Cs to guarantee building projects starting to take hold in the United States.

Another use of a clean L/C is illustrated in the following. A large second-tier aerospace manufacturing firm was approached by a large aerospace manufacturer and asked to install several pieces of very expensive computer numerical controlled (CNC) five-axis metal-cutting machines. Once before this firm had been asked to put in expensive equipment with the *verbal* promise from his customer ("Don't worry, we'll give you all the contracts you need to keep these machines busy."). But when a big aerospace recession came and the orders stopped abruptly, the large aerospace firm merely said "Sorry." Well, "sorry" did not make the payments on these machines and the manager remembered this. When the new request came in, he wisely said, "Certainly I will put in the multimillion dollar machines if you will put up a clean L/C to guarantee the payments I will need to make on them!" The large aerospace company did do this and the machines were installed. Several years later, the orders did slow and the second-tier manufacturer was pleased he had his "insurance" in place.

ADDITIONAL BANK SERVICES

In addition to the Letters of Credit that a bank can write for a customer, there are other services that a bank can provide for customers doing business internationally.

DOCUMENTS ON PAYMENT

Suppose that you have a customer in Italy who wants to buy from you but really chafes at issuing a L/C, probably because in Italy it is quite common for the banks to withdraw from the customer's checking account the amount of the L/C, much as in the United States. You, the seller, have reason to believe that the customer could pay for the goods at the time of arrival in Italy. Under these circumstances, you can ship the goods (e.g., in a container) to your customer in Venice, Italy. But in the process of doing this you can ask your bank to have their office in Venice act as your agent.

When the container of goods arrives in Venice, the customer is notified and goes to the local office of your bank or your bank's appointed bank. The customer pays for the merchandise and is given the paperwork necessary to collect the container at the dock. If, for some reason, the customer does not pay for the container, it is shipped back to the sender (you) at his or her expense.

The **Documents on Payment** service does have several advantages. First, it is good for the customer because it means that the customer does not tie up money while the goods are being made and *shipped*—and remember, shipping can sometimes take up to a month, or even a little more if coming from Asia. This may be a major advantage to the customer, thus building good customer relations. Second, for the seller, this is an improvement over just granting the foreign customer "open book credit." Because the customer is in a foreign country, it may be difficult to collect if the customer does not voluntarily pay when the invoice is due. Also, the seller can specify the paperwork necessary to get paid, such as an *inspection report* when quality is an issue—and isn't it always? Using this service, the seller knows that he or she will be paid if the customer receives the goods. The question of collecting on the invoice is obviated. With this method, the terms can be "DP on sight" or "DP on arrival"—meaning the buyer's bank will not forward the money to the seller—even if it has the paperwork—until the goods are actually received by the buyer.

DOCUMENTS ON APPROVAL

A slight variation on the preceding arrangement is for the goods to be shipped **Documents on Approval**. This means that the buyer has the right to inspect the goods when they are received at the foreign port *before* he or she has to pay the bank (in that foreign port) to obtain the paperwork necessary to take possession of the goods. This is more like open book credit, but you have the comfort of knowing that your bank will collect the money owed you before your customer can have possession of the goods.

SUMMARY

With the world shrinking, businesspersons today must think internationally. And this means that business must get involved with Letters of Credit. In this chapter, we have tried to remove some of the mystique associated with Letters of Credit. Perhaps it would be sufficient for someone just to learn to use international Letters of Credit, but it would be a pity. Knowing all the intricacies of an international L/C is not necessary for managers, but knowing the general details certainly helps. In this chapter, we looked at all the sections of a L/C and explained their use, mentioning caveats on some. There are many uses for domestic Letters of Credit, and an alert businessperson should be aware of their existence and use. The adroit use of domestic L/Cs was mentioned next. Using these instruments can solve some difficult problems, such as a "concentration" factor with your customers which might make *all* your receivables ineligible for bank or finance company lending. And then there are the "clean Letters of Credit" which can be used in many situations. Doing deals will probably never be the same since many businesspersons discovered Letters of Credit. Knowing of the possibility of replacing your credit—or someone else's—with what amounts to a bank "guarantee" is certainly a mark of an adroit manager. For example, using a clean L/C to back commercial paper (mentioned in Chapter-13) has been quite beneficial to some forward-looking companies. In fact there is a whole world of opportunities that will provide convenient uses for clean Letters of Credit.

Discussion of the types of L/Cs provided information on the various uses of L/Cs. But one point in particular bears special attention: the difference between confirmed and unconfirmed L/Cs. With so much business being done with China, especially, it behooves a businessperson to be aware of the difference. An unconfirmed L/C means that the paperwork has to be sent to the originating country, and only after approval and the return of the approval to the seller's bank will the seller get paid.

The beauty of L/Cs is in the *receiving* of a L/C with a purchase order—not in the *giving* of a L/C. Receiving a L/C may greatly reduce or eliminate a selling firm's accounts receivables, and this means that a given firm can do more business with *less working capital!* In fact, it might be possible to do business with virtually no Balance Sheet, at least, not a very substantial one.

12

CHAPTER REVIEW

QUESTIONS FOR DISCUSSION

1. You are talking with a company overseas about doing business with them. How would you expect to get paid if you did sell to this potential customer?

2. You are talking with a large company across the country about selling them parts for their cellular telephones. If you get the order, it would be the biggest order so far for your company and it would mean that you would have to have financing. What would you suggest as the company's CFO with regard to this order?

3. You have a customer in Venice, Italy. The customer does not want to give you a Letter of Credit for your order. You think they could pay you when the shipment gets to Venice. How would you handle this transaction?

4. As CFO of your company, you are negotiating to sell a portion of your business to another company. They want to pay you 25 percent down and the balance over 5 years. How could you increase the chance that this potential buyer will meet its responsibilities over this period of 5 years?

5. You are a software company and you have an order for a "turnkey" installation for a prime customer. When you tried to order the computer from the manufacturer, you were told that your Balance Sheet did not support any more credit. How could you handle this dilemma?

6. You have just graduated from college. You like to travel and you know something about computers. You talk with a computer manufacturer about selling their line of computers overseas. Unfortunately, you do not have a substantial Balance Sheet for your credit reference when the computer manufacturer checks on your credit worthiness. How could you sell their computers and have the computer manufacturer ship the computers you might sell without this required credit standing?

13

Cash Management and Money Market Securities

While cash is different from money market securities, it has become common to speak of them in a joint sense. Even listing them on the Balance Sheet should involve grouping them together—one is a good substitute for the other. In this chapter we deal with cash first and then we turn the discussion to what money market securities are.

CASH MANAGEMENT

If a firm is carrying too little cash, its bank will let it know soon enough. But what if a firm is carrying *too much* cash? Does it matter? Yes, it does. Cash is about the most unproductive asset a company can have. Except for psychological reasons, such as impressing a reader of the firm's financial statements, excess cash should be employed in the firm in productive ways, instead of lying idle or merely making money market rates. A firm should *employ* cash so as to make a higher rate of return. In short, leaving cash in the cash account means incurring (suffering) an **opportunity cost**—the amount of money you lose by not taking an alternative approach with this amount of money.

Years ago, the problem of optimizing the amount of cash was a much more complicated process than it is today. Currently, banks relieve much of this worry through what are known variously as *sweep accounts* or zero balance accounts or some other such name. Under this arrangement, a bank—through its computers—looks at a firm's cash account every night. If the company has cash in the account, it *sweeps* this money into the firm's money market account, where it can earn interest. If the account does not have any cash—that is, if it is overdrawn—the bank's computer sweeps some cash out of the company's money market account and back into the firm's cash account. It's that simple. But not all companies have a bank with this kind of service. How then does a firm know if it has too much money in the "near cash" money market account? Cash that could be employed more profitably elsewhere in the company? In short, how can a company's management determine if it is carrying too much cash? Before we work out a method of providing this information, a basic issue needs to be addressed—the attitude firms have regarding being overdrawn.

DETERMINING MANAGEMENT'S WILLINGNESS TO BE OVERDRAWN

What determines management's willingness to be overdrawn? It appears that there are two main bases.

First, there is the relationship the firm's management has with its bank. Unlike 20 or more years ago, American banks are moving closer and closer to the English system of overdraft privileges. In this system, if a firm is overdrawn in its checking account, it pays the bank interest on the amount overdrawn. If it has cash in the account, the bank pays it interest. But the United States is not yet on this system. Technically, American banks are still mostly on the old system in which banks were prohibited from paying interest on a firm's cash balance in its checking account. This was a system that undoubtedly pleased banks to no end.

But times change. Starting in the 1950s, banks realized that they had to start paying interest on these funds or lose them. By sweeping these funds into money market accounts they are, technically, not paying interest in the checking account, but the effect to the firm is about the same. So if the bank really likes the customer, it may "wink" at being overdrawn sometimes. On the other hand, relations with your bank may not be very good ("Don't you dare overdraw your account one penny or I will bounce every check that comes through!"). In this latter case, using a statistical model for determining optimal cash balance simply does not work.

The other determinant of the chance of being overdrawn is simply management's aversion to being overdrawn. Some managers are simply paranoid about being overdrawn. Such a feeling might be subjectively valid, but it is unrealistic. Statistically speaking, this implies that the decision maker wants to be something like 5 or 6 standard deviations away from the mean. This may be psychologically comforting, but it will be an extremely expensive policy from the point of view of the opportunity cost of money. As mentioned, having a surplus of cash means that the firm's management is forgoing profitable alternatives for

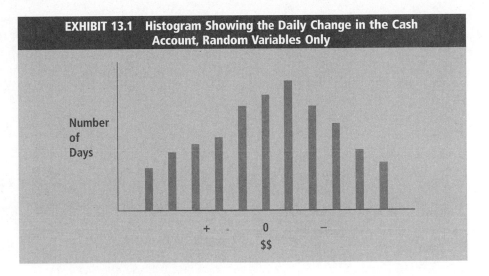

EXHIBIT 13.1   Histogram Showing the Daily Change in the Cash Account, Random Variables Only

the money. Sometimes, when accountants or bookkeepers are left to their own discretion, they may be observed following the policy of "not taking any chance" of being overdrawn, perhaps because they do not want to be criticized.

DETERMINING THE OPTIMAL AMOUNT OF CASH

If the company is not getting calls from its bank saying that it is overdrawn it may suspect that it has too much cash. It can check this by doing a simple statistical check of its cash account. To get the necessary input for this model, the firm should divide the checks that flow through its checking account into two groups: a **random group** and a **controllable group**.

Random Variables

In the random group there will be the checks for its Accounts Payable, Accounts Receivable, and the cash from its cash sales, if any. Using only these random items, next construct a histogram (Exhibit. 13.1) showing the "daily *change* in the cash account." The key word in this model is *change*. It does not matter what the level of the cash balance is; only the change in the cash balance is significant. As will be discussed more thoroughly below, the question we are trying to answer with this histogram is "What chance are you willing to take of being overdrawn?" To say that you are not willing to take *any* chance of being overdrawn is to talk nonsense in statistical terms. There is always some chance of being overdrawn, even if the chance is remote, for instance, 5 or more standard deviations from the mean. So the problem becomes *choosing a chance* that the firm's management is willing to take of being overdrawn and then locating that chance on the histogram of its changes in the cash balance, random variables only.

You will note also that this is a *statistical model*, implying that the underlying process going on in the firm's cash account is stochastic, or random. But to

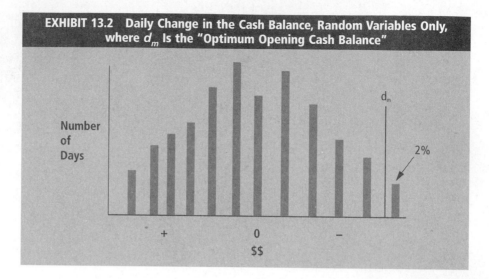

EXHIBIT 13.2   Daily Change in the Cash Balance, Random Variables Only, where d_m Is the "Optimum Opening Cash Balance"

say that in all cases this process of *changes* is stochastic would be naïve. When you see the company's checkbook on the desk of the chief executive, you can be reasonably sure that that manager is not using some statistical model for determining whether to write a check or knowing when a check has been received in its account at the bank. Or consider the vendor who has just delivered material to a company's Incoming Receiving and Inspection Department, and asks if the invoice could be approved so he or she could get paid in order to meet the company's payroll. Of course these managers are not relying on some stochastic process! But as the firm gets bigger, the amount of checks received each day does start to take on stochastic properties. For example, it you reviewed the checks *received* every day by the Accounts Receivable Department and showed the dollar amounts in a histogram, you surely would see an example of the stochastic process; you would not receive the *same* amount every day.

Suppose management decides that it is willing to take a 2 percent chance (meaning 1 day in 50) of being overdrawn in its main checking account. How can it translate this 2 percent chance into a daily opening cash balance? By looking at the histogram in Exhibit 13.1 and finding the area in the *negative tail* that corresponds to 2 percent of the observations, you have found the dollar amount for the **Daily Opening Cash Balance**, called d_m. What this means, in simple words, is that if the firm were to have this amount of cash in its checking account to start the business day it would be taking a 2 percent chance of being overdrawn on that particular day. This number should be seasonably adjusted if taken quite literally, which is improbable. Exhibit 13.2 shows such a distribution.

Including the Controllable Variables

What would happen if the firm's management made a histogram of the daily change in the cash balance *without* taking out the **controllable** items such as

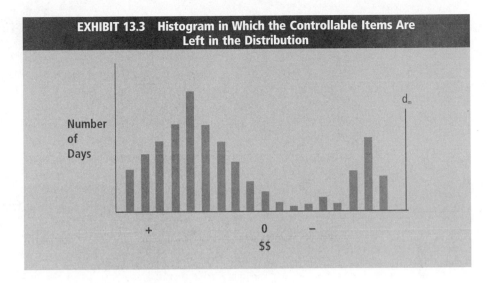

EXHIBIT 13.3 Histogram in Which the Controllable Items Are Left in the Distribution

payroll checks, tax checks, and the like? Because these controllable items are all *decreases* to the cash account, leaving in these controllable items will result in a blip in the negative tail of the histogram farther away from where the d_m value would be if the controllable items were removed. Exhibit 13.3 shows this type of situation.

The blip at the negative end of the histogram would result, for example, from hitting the main checking account every 2 weeks with a check (or account transfer) to fund the payroll account or to pay the payroll taxes. This is the simplest kind of histogram that might be made of the corporate checking account. But what if the firm's opening cash balance, d_m, is, on average, still *above* the outer limits of the negative side of this histogram? *In this case, the model clearly shows that management is carrying too much cash in its checking account.* And this is certainly something that management should know!

A Picture of Dissynchronization

What this histogram shows is really a picture of the firm's **dissynchronization** in its corporate checking account. It is apparent that if the firm had *less* dissynchronization in its checking account, implying that the distribution was more peaked and less spread out to the negative side, then its d_m would be closer to zero—or, simply, a lower number. Since this is a desirable situation, how can the firm's management *reduce* the dissynchronization in its checking account? Exhibit 13.4 is a picture of the dollar amounts put into the cash account and taken out each day over a period of several months.

When the *inflows* exceed the *outflows,* the cash balance will be increasing—that is putting more data points on the side of the *positive* changes. We need not really be worried about this side of the histogram. Instead, we are more concerned with the *negative* side of the histogram because this is where d_m will be found. How then can we get d_m to be closer to the zero line? By *reducing* the

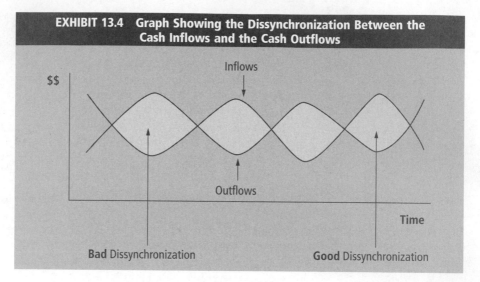

dollar amount between the cash outflows and the cash inflows, we would be bringing the d_m closer to the zero line. How can we do this? By focusing attention on when the firm pays its bills *vis-à-vis* when it receives its accounts receivable checks, it can effectively reduce this dissynchronization in its cash account. If the firm's accounting department delays in sending out its invoices, then it stands to reason that the payment of these invoices will be delayed. For some production managers, getting out the shipments is far more important than getting out the invoices for these shipments. This may make a lot of sense to the production manager who is trying to fill the customers' orders, but it will surely put a strain on the firm's cash flow *and* its checking account balance. If the invoices were sent promptly when an order was shipped, and if the firm followed a policy of paying the invoices received in an orderly and systematic manner, it would draw together the inflows and the outflows. This means, of course, that the firm could keep a lower cash balance, thus having more cash to invest in other more profitable ways.

OTHER WAYS OF REDUCING UNDESIRABLE DISSYNCHRONIZATION

Utilizing a Lock Box

Another way to improve cash management is through the utilization of a lock box. Simply stated, a **lock box** is a post office box in another city that is utilized for the purpose of accepting checks mailed to the company. When properly utilized, the use of a lock box will reduce the time it takes a check mailed from a customer's accounting department to be received and cashed, thus making the funds available sooner, and by so doing reducing the undesirable negative dissynchronization in the main cash account. The idea behind this arrangement is that the receiving company will appoint someone in a distant city to go to the lock box daily, perhaps more than one time a day, retrieve the checks, present them to a local bank, and then wire transfer the funds to the company's main checking account. This type of system assumes that the firm's customers are located a considerable distance from the company or, at least, concentrated at a considerable distance from the company's main bank. The assumption continues that it takes a number of days for the checks to reach the company through regular mail. And while this was true in times past, the U.S. Postal Service has greatly improved mail service from East Coast to West Coast and points in between. Now, letters mailed across the country might take only overnight or about the same time as checks mailed to the company from local customers. This is because all First Class mail goes air mail.

Another change that has made the use of lock boxes less advantageous is the fact that the Federal Reserve System now clears checks with a maximum of 2 days' delay, instead of the 4 days that it formerly took. And on this point, it is worth noting that if a bank is pleased with a customer, it might give that customer use of the funds as soon as they are deposited, instead of when the check actually clears the system in the guaranteed 2 days by the Federal Reserve. Also, it should be mentioned, the operation of a lock box is not without its own expense. It costs money to have someone monitor the lock box in a distant city and to deposit the checks and then to wire transfer the funds (another cost) to the main account of the company.

Playing the Federal Reserve Float

Realizing that the Federal Reserve System promises to clear a check in 2 days or less, some enterprising cash managers have used this information to reduce their undesirable dissynchronization by *slowing down* the length of time it takes a check the company has written to get back to the company's checking account after it is sent to pay a supplier. They do this by setting up checking accounts in distant banks, for example, in small towns located in the four corners of the country. Walla Walla, Washington; Las Cruces, New Mexico; Ocala, Florida; and Portland, Maine might be examples of such places. When the company goes to pay a bill, a computer program, on the basis of zip codes, selects the bank account that is located at the greatest distance from the addressee supplier. In this way, the supplier gets his or her money within the promised 2 days, but it may take longer than that for the check to actually get back to the bank on which it is drawn, possibly 3 or 4 days or, in cases of bad weather, even longer. This delays the check in actually hitting the company's checking account—the thing that really counts to the company writing the check.

Whether this is ethical or not is moot; the practice goes on for a number of large companies. The Federal Reserve knows that this practice is going on, but unless the dollar amount of this adverse Federal Reserve float increases— it's only about $700-800 million on average—they put up with it. Now while this seems like a clever tactic for managing cash, it obviously is not something that a small, developing firm might put into place. But some approximation of this practice might be attempted. Instead of four accounts spread around the country, perhaps one account in a distant city that is not too big might be used. In this way, there might be a delay in the time it takes for the company's checks to come back and be cleared. Any delay and the company's *adverse* dissynchronization will be lessened. If this happens, the company's d_m would be pulled closer to zero; the desired daily opening cash balance would be reduced.

PAYMENT WITH DRAFTS

A **draft** is something like a check except that it requires the person who controls the account at the bank on which the draft is written to approve it before the bank can pay on the draft. A person can write a draft on another person's account and present it to a bank for payment. Before the bank will pay on this draft, however, the bank must check with the person who controls the account and ask if payment is authorized. The most common usage of drafts is by insurance companies. When their agent pays an insurance claim, the odds are that this payment is being made with a draft. The insurance company can give the bank specific instructions regarding how they are to handle this kind of document, so there is usually no inconvenience to the person receiving the payment.

But when a company starts to use drafts for other than specific and unusual situations, there is a question of the ethics and morality involved. For example, if a company used drafts to pay its employees, there would be considerable inconvenience caused the employees and their banks. Even paying suppliers with a draft would be considered quite discourteous, to say the least.

BACKING UP THE CASH ACCOUNT

The preceding model for the determination of the optimal opening cash amount, d_m, assumes that the company will have a pool of money market securities to back up the cash account. This account will be called m_o. The amount of funds that are kept for the "controllable" items—payroll, capital expenditures, dividends, etc.—will be called m_c. The total amount of money market securities that the company has will be referred to as M. Thus:

$$M = m_o + m_c$$

If M does not equal $(m_o + m_c)$, but instead is greater than the sum of $(m_o + m_c)$, or

$$M > m_o + m_c$$

then

$$M_f = M - (m_o + m_c)$$

where M_f means **free money market securities**. These money market securities are not needed for either the operating cash account or for controllable items. Because m_c is for specific items, such as payroll, and their quantities are known, the amounts for this item—and there may be a number of accounts that collectively are referred to as m_c—is known. But the amount of money to put into m_o is another matter. This account has to have enough money in it so that money can be transferred to the company's main checking account when the daily opening cash balance is less than desired.

Presumably there are numerous models for how much money should be in the m_o account, but the following model is offered as a best effort:

$$m_o = d_m + [d_m / (1 - P)]$$

P represents the probability of *any negative change* in the histogram for the determination of the daily change in the cash account, random variables only. What this model does is to provide a pool of funds that would amount to a little bit more than the amount in d_m to a pool of three, four, or even more times larger than d_m. If the company's cash account is skewed toward the negative side, creating a relatively large d_m, then m_o will be larger on two counts: Because the distribution is *skewed* to the negative side, and because the divisor, $(1 - P)$, will be larger. By analogy, this m_o account is to the company's main cash account as a shock absorber is to an automobile. If the car is traversing a smooth road—similar to a company whose histogram of changes in its cash account is skewed to the positive side—then the m_o account will be small. If the vehicle is going over rough terrain, similar to a company whose cash account is getting battered by negative cash changes, then the m_o will larger, like a big shock absorber.

Remember that where m_o is ostensibly the amount of money market securities in this pool, if the firm does not have the money to fund this pool, it needs this amount of money as a *line of credit* from its bank to back up its checking account.

SECURITIES APPROPRIATE FOR THE M_O AND M_C ACCOUNT[▲]

Because the duration of the time securities need to be in the m_c is known (for example, you know when the payroll is due or taxes have to be paid), the kind of securities that are appropriate for this account may be different from the m_o. There are only two types of securities that are appropriate, T-bills[▲▲] and money market funds, both of which provide **same day delivery of funds**. Because we do not need this type of liquidity, we have a number of money market securities from which to choose, if the company elects to invest directly in these securities rather than in a money market fund. A brief explanation of these securities follows.

[▲] For a most complete explanation of all sorts of money market securities see Marcia Stigum, *The Money Market*, Richard D. Irwin, 3rd Ed., 1990.

[▲▲] Remember that Treasury bills are exempt from state taxation, a factor to consider for corporations that pay state income tax.

COMMERCIAL PAPER

Far and away the largest amount outstanding of any one of these securities is **commercial paper**—corporate IOUs with a maximum maturity of 270 days. (Short-term obligations are issued to investors who have discretionary cash at a given time.) In fact, the amount of commercial paper currently outstanding is now in excess of the amount of T-bills. Today we distinguish between *industrial* commercial paper and *financial* commercial paper. Issuers of financial commercial paper generally sell their paper directly to investors while the issuers of industrial paper generally sell their paper to dealers for resale. Commercial paper is, essentially, corporate IOUs, but in recent years banks, municipalities, foreign entities—even sovereigns—have been issuing commercial paper. For banks, this is at the expense of issuing Certificates of Deposit (CDs) or Bank Deposit notes. Regulated by convention, commercial paper is deceptively simple. Looking like an oversized check, the security states the name of the beneficiary, the term of the loan (when the commercial paper expires), the face amount of the paper, and the name of the company borrowing the money and the signature of a representative of this company. Commercial paper is sold at a discount, which means that the company buying the commercial paper pays an amount and receives a larger amount at maturity—this latter amount representing the interest on the paper for the period. The maximum length of commercial paper is 270 days. In fact it is reported that practically all commercial paper carries a maturity of 30 days or less. Financial commercial paper traditionally carries an interest rate that is less than industrial commercial paper.

The Development of Commercial Paper

Commercial paper originally was used by industrial firms such as General Mills, which had a decided seasonal demand for funds. During harvest time these cereal manufacturers had a great need for cash to pay for the grain they purchased. As they converted this grain to cereal they received cash in return. They then could pay back the commercial paper which they issued to borrow the money required. When finance companies came into being around the time of World War I, they found that they could go into the commercial paper market and borrow for less than the banks would charge to loan them money. This is because money market rates of all of these securities are less than bank's **prime loan rates**. In years past, the bank prime loan rate meant something different than it does today, however. Originally, the bank's prime rate meant the lowest rate the bank charged its most credit-worthy customer. When the banks got into trouble in the 1970s, they found that they could earn enough money to get themselves out of their predicament by raising the prime rate that they charged their middle-market business customers and the individuals who borrowed from them at a point or more over prime. After all, what alternatives did these borrowers have? Also, after the credit crunch of the early 1970s—the first real credit crunch anyone had seen in many years—a number of business firms, mostly large ones, turned to their investment bankers and

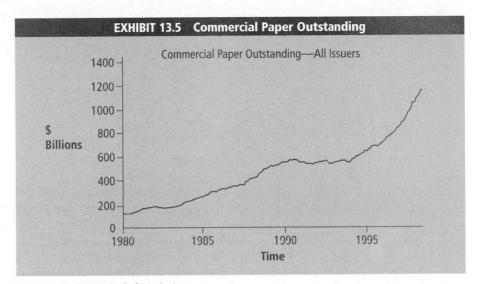

EXHIBIT 13.5   Commercial Paper Outstanding

Commercial Paper Outstanding—All Issuers

$ Billions

SOURCE: Federal Reserve Bank of Saint Louis.

asked whether they could get into the commercial paper market and borrow funds, not at the inflated prime rate but at rates less than prime. In fact, the banks came up with such euphemisms as "super prime" to denote a rate that was lower than their inflated "prime." If they wanted to loan to a business entity that could and would go elsewhere to borrow money, including the money market, they would quote such a rate. This practice still exists.

To make their paper more appealing—that is, to get a higher rating on their commercial paper—they turned, of all places, back to their banks. They would ask their banks to write clean Letters of Credit to back up their commercial paper. (Remember, banks in the United States cannot "guarantee" such things as commercial paper, but their L/C amounts to a guarantee for all practical purposes.) The banks were perfectly willing to do so as they were now making money where they would not otherwise be making interest on a loan to the business. Better to make a little than to make nothing, which would be the case if the business went to the money market and borrowed there instead of from the bank. Furthermore, almost all issuers of commercial paper have back-up lines of credit with a bank, for which they pay the bank a fee.

Before the early 1970s, the issuers of commercial paper were a close-knit fraternity of about 400 issuers. After the dike burst, so to speak, in 1970 there were several thousand issuers of commercial paper. With the demise of Penn Central Railroad, and the subsequent loss associated with their commercial paper, it became necessary to grade commercial paper. Today commercial paper is graded by Moody's, Standard and Poor's, Duff and Phelps, and Fitch. Today almost all commercial paper sold carries the highest prime ratings, such as Moody's P1 or P2, or Standard and Poor's A1+ or A1. Anyone buying commercial paper would be rather foolish to buy anything other than Prime One or, possibly, Prime Two. It is bad enough to have interest rates turn against you, but it is inexcusable to lose money because the issuer defaulted. The rates on commercial paper are not high enough to warrant speculation, just trying to get a little more yield.

Today, even firms that are not in the Fortune 1000 can use commercial paper, thanks to clean L/Cs by banks. This is because it is the reputation of the bank—not necessarily the reputation of the issuer—that governs whether somebody buys the commercial paper.

An Example for a Developing Firm

Recently a fast-growing computer products firm had a lot of accounts receivable that needed financing. They could have used bank pledging (see Chapter 11) for a rate about prime or a little less, but remember that prime today is really a phony, inflated prime. What they did instead was to sell the accounts receivable to a **captive finance company**—meaning one they established themselves—and then this finance company sold (issued) commercial paper, at rates considerably less than this inflated prime (even less than super prime). They did this by securing bank guarantees through a Letter of Credit. Even with paying the bank for their L/C, the cost of financing the accounts receivable—which amounted to several hundred millions of dollars—was less than going through a bank. And the interesting thing about this kind of issuance of commercial paper is that the issuing firm need not be large, in the traditional sense, or even publicly owned.

As said, commercial paper may be bought directly (typically from a *finance* company) or from a dealer (*industrial* paper). It is quite easy to go directly to an issuer. You do this by calling the issuer, such as Household Capital, and saying that you want a certain amount of commercial paper to mature on a certain date. You then instruct your bank to wire transfer the amount of your purchase (not the face amount of the paper) to the issuer. When the commercial paper matures, the face amount of the paper is wired to your checking account with automatic precision. The good thing about commercial paper is that it can be written for any amount the buyer wants (e.g., above about $5,000, although about $25,000 might be the usual minimum) and it can mature whenever the buyer wants, up to the maximum of 270 days. The reason for the 270-day maximum is that for securities with a maturity of more than 270 days, the security must be registered with the Securities and Exchange Commission, an expensive and timely process. The bad thing about commercial paper, however, is that there is not a well-defined secondary market for commercial paper. True, there are dealers, but selling commercial paper before maturity may be quite expensive in the sense that the rise in price, representing the buyer's "interest," might be seriously impaired by selling before maturity. If the buyer is a regular customer of an issuer of commercial paper, and the buyer needs to cash the paper a few days before maturity, sometimes the issuer will redeem the commercial paper for the buyer, possibly at face amount. Generally speaking, however, it is *not* a good idea to attempt to sell commercial paper before maturity.

CDS AND BANK DEPOSIT NOTES

Originally approved for issuance with the passage of the Federal Reserve Act of 1913, **Negotiable Time Certificates of Deposit (CDs)** were virtually never used until the early 1960s. The reason for this was that a maximum interest rate of one-half of 1 percent (0.5%) per annum was mandated for these CDs. During World War II, interest rates were extremely low. The T-bill rate was pegged at three-eighths of 1 percent ($^3/_8$ of 1%) until the late 1940s. As interest rates started to rise in the 1950s, banks saw their customers' bank accounts decline markedly as corporate treasurers sought out opportunities to earn something more than a trivial amount on the spare cash. Realizing that it would be better to pay for the cash that they formerly were getting free, banks appealed to the Federal Reserve to raise the rates on the CDs, which they did. When the ceiling was raised to 5 percent, the popularity of CDs soared, almost reaching a volume outstanding equivalent to commercial paper. The volume of outstanding CDs continued to keep pace with commercial paper until the late 1980s when their popularity dropped dramatically. Marcia Stigum,[▲] a leading authority on the money market, attributes this great fall to a number of factors, including a weakness in bank credits, the rise in the interest rate swaps market, deregulation of rates banks pay on deposits, and the creation of the *demand deposit note*. In fact, the volume for domestic CDs is currently so low, the Federal Reserve does not even track it anymore. With the decline of CDs, especially, the volume of commercial paper has soared.

Coming out of the ashes of CDs has been an instrument called the **deposit note**. Looking like corporate notes or bonds, these instruments are really bank deposits. The original maturities run from 18 months to 5 years. For banks the reserve requirement drops to zero for maturities of 18 months or longer. Deposit notes pay a fixed interest but this not what banks want. They want a floating rate so when they issue a deposit note they effect an **interest rate swap** to convert their fixed rate to a floating rate.[▲▲] The usefulness of deposit notes is quite questionable for developing firms, however, because the dollar amounts usually involved are not large enough to make investment in these instruments justified considering the ease of investing in other money market securities or just money market funds.

BANKER'S ACCEPTANCES

When a bank receives a draft drawn against a Letter of Credit, it may present the draft for payment. But if the bank accepts a draft that is not due for payment until a future date—30, 60, or 90 days hence—it will do so by discounting the draft at a money market rate called the **Banker's Acceptance** rate. If the

▲ Marcia Stigum, *op. cit.*, 54.

▲▲ A variation of the *deposit note* is the *bank note*. And while interesting to money market managers of sizeable amounts, this instrument is also not very useful for the developing firm seeking to fill its m_c portfolio.

bank chooses, it may continue to hold this discounted draft until it matures and then receive the interest represented by the Banker's Acceptance rate. If the bank feels that it can make better use of this money than having it invested at this low money market rate, it can stamp the draft "Accepted" and then sell this discounted draft in the money market. It now becomes a Banker's Acceptance or **BA**. The acceptability of these Banker's Acceptances usually turns on the reputation of the bank which accepted the draft, meaning the bank that is, itself, promising to pay at the expiration of the draft, rather than just the maker of the L/C who is responsible for paying the amount of the draft at its expiration. This situation contrasts with commercial paper, in which the corporation that issued the commercial paper is the only one responsible for paying the face amount when due—unless, of course, the paper is guaranteed by a bank's L/C. For this reason BAs sell for a slightly lower yield than commercial paper.

The problem with Banker's Acceptances for use in the firm's m_c accounts is that they come already prepackaged with a certain dollar amount and a date for maturity, which may not coincide with the need for liquidity for the developing firm. But if the developing firm is buying money market securities from its bank, the bank may be pushing its own Banker's Acceptances for purchase by the firm. And when this happens, the developing firm will be hard pressed to say "No" to its bank when it is trying to build rapport with this bank. So, the developing firm winds up having securities that do not mature *exactly* at the desired date and perhaps for amounts that are close to, but not exactly, the desired amounts. No really good established secondary market exists for Banker's Acceptances in small dollar amounts. And BA amounts can be quite small. So, again, BAs are not ideal for investment in m_c accounts, although they might be good for banks and other large institutional money market investors.

REPURCHASE AGREEMENTS

There is one money market security which is *not* in fact a security, as are the aforementioned securities. Instead, it is a *contract* to repurchase securities at a certain date, or from day to day. **Repurchase Agreements**, or **repos**, got their start in the 1920s when the banks which were financing the inventory of bonds for the nation's government bond dealers (primarily in New York) found that they could make more interest on their money by loaning it to the stock brokerage firms for covering **margin accounts** than by lending it to the government bond dealers. Margin accounts are ones in which the owner of the account honors a portion of the cost of the securities. Seeking alternate financing, the dealers discovered that they could find investors who would be willing to take an amount of U.S. government bonds on the condition that when the government bond dealer (there were approximately eleven at the time) needed the bonds to give delivery to some party who bought the bonds, they would repurchase the bonds for a higher price than the bond dealer received from the investor. The daily rate that the government dealer paid varied substantially depending on whether banks had a particular need for cash, such as at statement dates.▲ Over the years, this general idea of buying bonds for a relatively short period—such as overnight or over the weekend—grew, and the practice expanded outside of New York City. Eventually, the practice changed and instead of using government bonds, banks would set aside *any* high-grade security as the collateral for the transaction. Now, even small banks are effecting Repurchase Agreements with their customers for amounts as small as $25,000. When the bank needs more cash, it sells more *repos;* when it needs less cash for reserve requirements it can sell fewer repos. Liquidity, meaning a good secondary market for the sale of the securities before maturity, or price risk, is not a factor here. Also, credit risk is not a factor with regard to *repos.* True, this arrangement can be for more than just a day or over the weekend, but it is rarely for an extended period of time. Therefore, if cash is needed, all you have to do is unwind the arrangement and, typically, you can have your money the next day. The reverse of a repo is called, simply enough, a **reverse**. In this case, a dealer can "purchase" securities from some entity and offer to sell back the securities at a future date—e.g., 30 days. A *reverse* and a *repo* are really the same thing.

SHORT-TERM MUNICIPAL NOTES

Although most people are familiar with tax-exempt bonds, issued by municipalities, states, or other tax-exempt entities, many do not know that there are numerous issues of short-term notes that are also tax exempt. Municipal notes come in maturities of 1 month to 1 year. They are usually general obligations of the entity issuing them, as opposed to "revenue notes." **General obligation** means that they carry the full faith, credit, and taxing powers of the entity issuing them. These notes can be packaged in relatively small sizes, such as $5,000, but procuring them and selling them in an after or secondary market may be more of a problem than they are worth for a developing firm. True, they offer federal tax-exempt (or partial tax-exempt) interest and exemption from state tax in the state in which they are issued, but because the yield is lower than for taxable securities, much of the benefit has been removed. Over time, with changing tax rates, this "tax exemption" has lost some of its former importance, so that sometimes the "tax exempts" sell for a bit *higher yield* than Treasuries, rather than lower. For large companies with large cash portfolios, these securities may be quite appropriate, but for developing firms with smaller portfolios, this is probably not the case. The tax-exempt notes that are available may be found on the Standard and Poor's tax-exempt sheets that are published for the brokerage trade every evening and sent nationwide. Most of the offerings on these sheets are tax-exempt bonds, but the first two or so pages contain the information on the note offerings and which dealers have them for sale. Or, more simply, go directly to the dealers.

▲ Banks have a weekly "cycle" with their deposits at the Federal Reserve, so rates on Wednesday can be quite diverse.

MONEY MARKET PREFERREDS

As mentioned in Chapter 9 on security innovations, so-called money market preferred stocks were developed in the 1980s and have had a following since then, especially among major money managers. These preferred stocks have one thing in common: They all take advantage of the tax exclusion of dividend income to corporations. Instead of a marginal tax rate on taxable (interest) income of 34 percent, the dividend exclusion gives this income to the receiving corporation at a marginal tax rate of about 7.5 percent, a significant difference. The preferred stock is structured essentially to give the holder of the preferred stock a **put option**. In this way, the holder can *put* the preferred stock back to the issuer when it wants to convert to cash. Or, it may just sell the stock on the open market.

Whereas dividend income *to* a corporation may be mostly tax excludable, it is not tax deductible to the corporation paying it. The only corporations who would issue this type of preferred stock are those corporations which have a "tax loss carry-forward." Because they do not have to pay taxes as long as the tax loss carry-forward lasts,▲ these companies get the benefits of lower interest rates on their short-term borrowing. Because the yield is largely tax excludable, it can offer a lower yield and still be competitive with fully taxable instruments such as commercial paper. Knowing that these money market preferred stocks are taking advantage of a quirk in the tax laws, Congress and the Treasury are keeping a close eye on these securities, but unless they become much more popular, they will most likely leave them alone.

WHERE TO PROCURE MONEY MARKET SECURITIES

There are essentially two approaches to procuring money market securities. On the one hand, you can go to the actual issuer of the security or a dealer in the security, or you can utilize the services of your bank's money market division. Large, major city banks have huge departments that are constantly buying money market securities for their own behalf or for their trust accounts, which run into the billions of dollars. Although these banks used to buy and sell securities for their customers free of charge, they now charge a small fee for this service. But this service is really worth this fee because it may give the developing firm an added degree of liquidity for the money market securities it holds. This might be particularly true for something like commercial paper. If the firm needed to cash the paper prematurely, its bank might be quite willing to purchase these securities from the firm in view of the fact that they are almost constantly buying that same type of security. So this is what I call the easy way to purchase these securities. If your bank does not have such a money market department, then you will be forced to go direct or you might use the services of a major investment banking firm.

As already mentioned, the advent of money market funds has drastically changed the environment for trading in money market securities. Now it is

▲ Corporations can carry forward a tax loss for 5 years or go back 3 years to recover taxes paid.

possible to obtain yields that are about as good as you can get from direct investment in the individual securities such as commercial paper, but with much less hassle. Furthermore, you are able to obtain same day delivery of funds from most money market funds, which makes timing so much easier for the finance manager for the developing firm. Of course, these funds may not be used for such things as Repurchase Agreements (repos), so for this you will have to go directly to your bank. Also, the money market funds do not have the Money Market Preferreds or the tax-exempt notes (although there are tax-exempt funds), so, again, these are the securities that must be gotten from a securities broker or directly from the company issuing the security. *For practical purposes, the only real source of money market securities for our type of developing firms is the money market funds.*

Focus on Technology

ON GROWTH AND GROWTH STRATEGY—ESPECIALLY IN A "NET-CENTRIC" ENVIRONMENT

Two points as background:

1. The Internet has already changed the way we learn, the way we work, and in a nutshell, the way we live. Although temporarily slowed down by too many bad deals, all as a result of what has been referred to as "irrational exuberance," the Internet is here to stay! The reason: Efficiency! Efficiency in terms of cost savings and convenience. If you ever doubt this statement, just take a look at the annual reports of companies like Cisco Systems, Sun Microsystems, Oracle, and many similar ones. I guess I could also refer to the AOL/Time Warner deal, as well as Microsoft's ".Net Strategy," as other points of reference.

2. The Internet—especially given its infancy stage at the present time—has turned out to be the greatest "equalizer" of our time. This is especially true for entrepreneurs with minimal resources. And this takes me right to the main point I want to make in this box.

Here is the new reality: Growth in the Internet Age has a very expanded and all-encompassing meaning. The following quote from Sun Microsystems's Annual Report for year 2000 says it all. As you read the quote taken from their report, also remember that Scott McNealy, Sun's Cofounder and still Chairman and CEO—just like AOL's Steve Case—had been written off so many times by his colleagues in the industry. (Incidentally, both of these people had business, not technology or engineering, as their backgrounds.)

"Growth is just a *single metric of our success.* At Sun, we have a long history of making the right decisions at just the right time, positioning ourselves to set the agenda for our industry, grow market share quickly, *and become the thought leader that others look to in a fast-changing world.*" [Emphasis added]

From Sun Microsystems's Annual Report, 2000

SUMMARY

The principal question explored in this chapter was whether or not a company is carrying too much cash. If it is carrying too little cash, their bank will let them know soon enough. But what about the opposite situation? The secret in determining if the company is carrying too much cash—and how much—lies is an examination of the *daily change in the cash account, random variables only.* This will indicate the optimum daily opening cash balance, d_m. If the company is carrying more than this, it is carrying too much. But what makes d_m be the number it is? It would be best if d_m were zero. The answer to this is what is called *dissychronization* in the cash account. By paying more attention to the prompt sending of accounts receivable bills, a company can cut down on this undesirable dissychronization. The new use of "zero balance" accounts and similar accounts attempts to assist a company in its cash management. In this case, the only question that remains is "How much should the company keep in its money market account to service its cash account?"

The second half of the chapter was devoted to a most elementary description of the money market securities available. The main one of interest is commercial paper. Currently there is a huge amount of commercial paper existing— more than $1.3 trillion—but the thing of interest to emerging middle-market companies is the possibility of their issuing commercial paper. With bank backing, even rather small firms or privately owned firms might use commercial paper. Other variations in the use of commercial paper were also suggested. The discussion of the various money market securities concluded by noting that for many emerging or middle-market companies, money market funds provide a very good way of investing unneeded cash.

QUESTIONS FOR DISCUSSION

1. You are the CFO for a company that manufacturers large thermal oxidizers. You customarily receive about 10–25 percent down with the order and the balance in two to five more installment payments. You currently carry a large cash balance. You are wondering if you are carrying too much cash. How can you check on this?

2. How can you tell how much your company should have in your money market securities? You currently have a "zero balance" account with your bank.

3. Compare the rates your company would receive from the money market securities mentioned in this chapter.

13

CHAPTER REVIEW

14

Management of Accounts Receivable

One of the most frustrating areas of financial management is the management of Accounts Receivable. This is because the process is fraught with such uncertainty and subjectivity. In this chapter we examine the various parts of this puzzle and conclude with a model for granting credit. We begin with an analysis of how the parameters interface with what are called the "variables." The parameters are:

- The cash discount

- The cash discount period

- The credit period

- The collection effort

The variables that we examine with respect to these parameters are:

- Sales

- Net income

- Rate of return on sales and ROA

- The volume of receivables

- Net operating cash flow (NOCF)

- Bad debt expense

ANALYSIS OF THE CASH DISCOUNT

We begin with the analysis of the cash discount. By definition the **cash discount** is the amount of the invoice that the customer might deduct if the invoice is paid before the expiration of the cash discount period. But why is a cash discount offered? As always, it appears that there are two reasons: the "good" reason and the "real" reason. The good reason is to try to induce the customer to pay sooner rather than at the end of the credit period. A typical cash discount period is 10 days, while a typical credit period is 30 days. So if the vendor can induce the buyer to pay in 10 days, the vendor receives the payment about 20 days sooner than otherwise.▲ Presumably the vendor can use this money to make more than the interest rate implicit in a cash discount. For example, if a customer takes a 2 percent discount and pays in 10 days instead of 30, the customer is earning the equivalent of about 36 percent interest. This is figured as 2 percent is to 20 days as 3 percent is to 30 days, and 30 days times 12 months equals 36 percent. If the customer takes a 3 percent discount and pays in 10 days instead of 30 days the equivalent rate is approximately 54 percent. A 1 percent discount is the equivalent of approximately 18 percent and a .5 percent discount is the equivalent of approximately 9 percent.

It used to be that customers were quite oblivious to the *amount* of the cash discount, but in recent years managers of Accounts Payable have gotten much more sensitive to these implicit interest rates and have started to compare the discount offered (and its implicit interest rate) to its "opportunity cost of funds" in making rational choices between taking the discount or paying at the end of the cash discount period. If, for example, the vendor is offering only a 1 percent cash discount, the customer might feel that this is cheap money and decline to take the discount and pay in 30 days.

The possible "real" reason for offering the cash discount—as an early warning signal of a customer in financial trouble—will be discussed below.

Now, let's discuss the cash discount in the context of what we are calling the "variables." How does the cash discount affect the firm's sales? What are the determinants of the **elasticity of demand** with respect to the cash discount? This elasticity is shown in Exhibit 14.1.

DETERMINANTS OF ELASTICITY

When dealing with large-dollar amount purchase orders—for example, paper to a newspaper, or steel to a fabricator of steel products—it is expected that every

---

▲ Exceptions such as where the customer takes the discount and pays later anyway or seasonal billing will be discussed below.

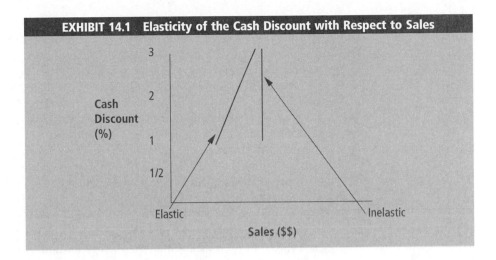

EXHIBIT 14.1   Elasticity of the Cash Discount with Respect to Sales

detail of the price, *including any cash discount,* will be scrutinized in minute detail. Varying the cash discount may make a substantial difference in the total price of the order. To think that one could slip a changed cash discount past a buyer in these circumstances is probably wishful thinking. In this case you have *elastic* demand—or, possibly, *highly elastic* demand. But reverse the situation and you could have quite a different result.

On small-dollar orders or orders for something that is considered insignificant, such as stationery supplies to a manufacturing company, experience indicates that the cash discount has *no* effect on the order. Buyers are usually in such a hurry to place these orders, so they can get on to the significant orders, that they will hardly notice the cash discount that is quoted by the vendor. In fact the vendor will, in all likelihood, not even mention the cash discount in such cases; this will appear on the printed sales order form. When this is the case, you have *inelastic* demand. But how does one know whether the company's sales are elastic or inelastic? Generally, it is not difficult to determine. Most salespersons should know why the customer is buying from them. Take the case of custom printing that has to be produced on sheet-fed printing machines, for example—calendars or stationery. What are the reasons a buyer selects one printing house over another? Overall quality? Service? Delivery? Personal attention of the salesperson? Possibly price. But certainly *not a cash discount.* So why should a sheet-fed printer offer a cash discount? To get prompt payment on an item like this they could shorten the credit period to 10 days. But industry practice is rather strong. In Los Angeles they offer a cash discount and in Chicago they do not. But "industry practice" does not mean that some selling firm could not do things differently!

Another example involves the manager of a paint company. He analyzed his customers and decided that they fell into three categories. First, there were the *retail* customers. He felt that he had tweaked these customers as much as he dared. Then there were the *special* customers: the Airport Authority, the Highway Patrol, the City and County governments, etc. He felt that these customers were sufficiently different that he did not want to tamper with the terms of sale for them. But about 35 percent of his sales were to *manufacturing firms*. Why, he reasoned, did they buy from his company? Lots of reasons could be offered but none of them was the *cash discount*. Can you imagine the reaction of a paint shop if a buyer said that he or she was changing the preferred paint supplier, from one which had been supplying the company paint for many years because of the *cash discount*? Astonishment would be an understatement! So what this manger did was to reprint the invoices and delete the cash discount and make the credit terms "Net 10." Subsequently, what did this do to the sales for this group of customers? Nothing. The sales to this group of customers were truly *inelastic* with respect to the cash discount. The inelastic sales were only part of the effect, however; the effect this might have on the A/R Balance Sheet and cash flow will be discussed below.

Another aspect of this matter of the cash discount is the question of whether or not a cash discount really does prompt the buyer to pay promptly. The question of the different cash discounts was already treated but another example might be informative. An aerospace subcontractor was selling to only several very large prime contractors. When a severe recession set in, other subcontractors were scrambling to cope with great downward price pressure. This machine shop's competitors were cutting the prices they quoted so that there was little gross profit left in their bids. And to make matters worse, they raised the cash discount to 5 percent, in some cases, in order to get the desperately needed payment sooner. One enterprising subcontractor visited a customer and asked a clerk in the Accounts Payable department what rule they followed in paying the invoices. "Well," this clerk said, "if there is a cash discount we take it and pay on the tenth day." So this subcontractor machine shop merely reprinted his invoices stating "½%/10, Net 30" and the payment came through punctually.

Elasticity of the Cash Discount Versus Pre-Tax Income

If the company's sales are inelastic with respect to the cash discount, there exists an interesting situation with respect to the firm's pre-tax profit. If the cash discount is *reduced*, what would happen to the firm's pre-tax profit?

If sales are inelastic with respect to the cash discount, one of the most remarkable results would be as shown in Exhibit 14.2. *Pre-tax income could rise substantially*, especially if the company's rate of return on sales is quite weak. For example, if the company were only making 7 percent pre-tax profit and, for instance, 5 percent after tax, and if the company *reduced* its cash discount from 3 percent to 1 percent, this means that 2 percent of sales would drop down to the pre-tax profit line, increasing pre-tax profit by a whopping 28.6 percent! And after-tax income would jump by 24 percent. All for reprinting the invoices or changing the cash discount on computer-printed forms. While this seems like a startling result, it is not without other implications. If the company's sales were inelastic to the cash discount and the company was making "only" 7 percent pre-tax, one wonders if the company's price elasticity of demand would be such that the company could raise prices of its products and get an increase in its pre-tax profit that way. But, if nothing else, this maneuver of the company may go unnoticed while a price increase might attract quite a bit of attention.

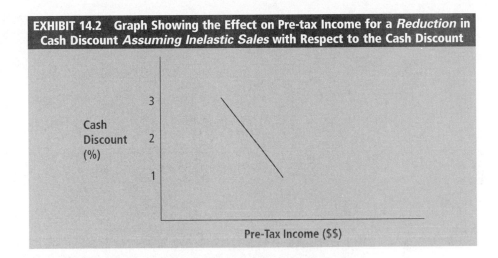

EXHIBIT 14.2   Graph Showing the Effect on Pre-tax Income for a *Reduction* in Cash Discount *Assuming Inelastic Sales* with Respect to the Cash Discount

Elasticity of the Cash Discount Versus the Volume of Receivables

One of the reasons for offering a cash discount period is to get the customer to pay early. But by lowering the cash discount what effect would this have on the firm's volume of accounts receivable? If the firm's sales are inelastic with respect to the cash discount, this means that sales will not go down if the cash discount is lowered, but it also means that the company has reduced the incentive to pay promptly, or, at least, within the cash discount period. See Exhibit 14.3. This means, therefore, that some firms will not take the cash discount and pay promptly. When this happens, the volume of accounts receivable *will increase*. If the company's sales with respect to the cash discount are *elastic*, then two things will be happening. The fact that there will be fewer sales if the cash discount is reduced means that there will be a lower level of receivables. Offsetting this is the fact, however, that the company can expect to have their remaining customers pay slower on balance (because some would not take the cash discount), thus resulting in an *increase* in the accounts receivable balance. So the overall effect would, most likely, be some increase in the firm's accounts receivable balance.

Elasticity of NOCF Versus the Cash Discount

If the firm reduces its cash discount it will have an increase in its volume of receivables even if its sales stay the same or decline a little. This increase in receivables will mean the Net Operating Cash Flow (NOCF) will decline until the new level of receivables is achieved and then level off, but at a somewhat higher level—because 2 percent more of the sales dollar is reaching NOCF assuming steady sales. See Exhibit 14.4.

A Reduction in the Cash Discount Versus Bad Debt Expense

Anytime you give your customers more time to pay, you are going to put upward pressure on the company's bad debt expense. Whether you actually have an *addition* depends on the circumstances of the firm itself. For example, some firms might have virtually no bad debt expense whether they give their customers a short time (e.g., 10 days) or a long time (e.g., 60 days) to pay.

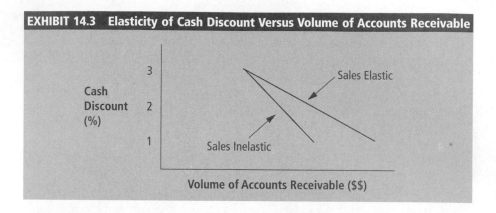

EXHIBIT 14.3   Elasticity of Cash Discount Versus Volume of Accounts Receivable

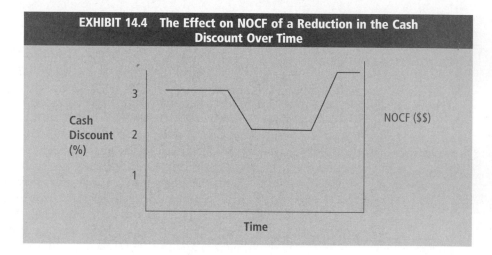

EXHIBIT 14.4   The Effect on NOCF of a Reduction in the Cash Discount Over Time

One of the possible undesirable effects of a reduction of the cash discount—or, even, the elimination of the cash discount—is the signaling effect referred to earlier. *Perhaps this is the real reason for offering the cash discount!* One of the most useful by-products of offering a cash discount is the warning it might give management when a customer who had been taking the cash discount suddenly stops doing so. In this case, the firm has to decide whether the customer stopped taking the discount because it felt that the implicit rate of interest is below their opportunity cost or, most importantly, because it is having liquidity problems, something any vendor would like to know about its customers. That is why the discussion above is focused on *reducing* the cash discount rather than eliminating it. At 1 percent, a cash discount may be enough to get virtually all those customers who would take the cash discount—as opposed to that group of customers who most likely would not take the cash discount at 1, 2, or 3 percent, to reveal their situation if they did not take the discount. This "early warning system" would thus be quite effective and, certainly, worth its price.

THE CASH DISCOUNT PERIOD

The **cash discount period** is the amount of time allowed the customer to pay and still take the cash discount. By tradition this period is 10 days. This is, practically speaking, about the minimum time that a sizeable firm needs to receive the merchandise, process the paperwork through the Incoming Receiving and Inspection Department, and forward the paperwork to Accounting for payment. So, tinkering with this parameter does not seem worthwhile. With the exception of "dating"—postponing the payment date until some future date for seasonal merchandise—10 days seems a reasonable time for the cash discount period. But when does the "cash discount period" begin? Ask a dozen businesspeople and the chances are you will get a diversity of answers. Does it begin with the date of the invoice? Or the date the material was received? Or the date the material was shipped? Who is to say? Frankly, there are no universally accepted rules, but paying before the merchandise arrives is not one of the most likely actions.

THE ROLE OF THE COMPUTER

In this age of computers, practically all developing firms (above the very smallest) produce their invoices on the computer. If this is the case, why not really utilize the computer's ability a little bit more than just printing out the customer's name and all the shipment information? For example, instead of using the old-fashioned term "$^2/_{10}$ Net 30," why not have the computer actually calculate the dollar amount of the discount? And furthermore, why not specify a date such that if the payment is postmarked by this certain date, the discount can be taken? To calculate when this date would be would not be such a difficult matter: A program could be set up to read the zip code of the customer's shipping address and then to generate a reasonable period for the merchandise to get to the customer's address. Next a standard period, maybe 10 days, could be added for the time it takes for the paperwork to be processed and the check mailed. For example, if something was shipped from Phoenix to Denver on the first of the month and it was known that it takes about 2 days by truck to get there, then the invoice could be printed to say that *"If you Postmark the payment of this invoice by the 12th of [name of month] you may take a discount of $317.07, or you may make a net payment of $10,251.93 by the 30th of [name of month]."* This way you are eliminating all the guesswork that goes on with respect to the cash discount period—when it begins and ends.

TAKING A DISCOUNT AND PAYING LATER

In a number of industries one may find companies that take the discount and pay when they please, in 30 or more days. For some companies in some highly competitive industries, taking a discount is a matter of competitive survival. But for others, this abhorrent practice is a matter of policy. This is to be deplored as "economic bullyism." A company would not do this if it knew that the vendor would retaliate in a severe way. It does it because it feels that it can take advantage of an economically weaker vendor. If, in fact, the vendor really needs the business of a bully customer, it can bite its collective lip and put up with this indiscretion. But firms that act like bullies usually get their comeuppance in time. In some industries—canned food, for example—it is commonplace to "pay late and take the discount." In these cases, economic reality says that a firm should " . . . do like the Romans do."

Taking a discount and paying late is one thing, but what should a firm do if the vendor prints a notation on the invoice that *"If this bill is not paid in 30 days, a finance charge equal to 1½% per month will be charged."* The answer to this depends on whom the vendor is. If the customer is a local stationery store, it might be quite all right to pay the small increased amount; it is inconsequential. But if the vendor is a principal supplier of some raw material to the company, then the company would take this under consideration. If the company has been paying promptly over a considerable period of time, but because of a recession decides to pay late, then it should not be paying a finance charge. "My late payment is because my customers are paying me late and that is the reason why we are paying late."

A manufacturer of equipment that is used on road construction had a policy of offering the customer the option of paying in 10 days with the discount, paying in 30 days net, *or* paying later and incurring a finance charge equivalent to 18 percent per annum interest. The customers in this industry, who are chronically undercapitalized, loved this option and a number took advantage of it. In fact, the manufacturer was running a little finance company with about $250,000 in these accounts. He was not only making a good interest return, he was winning the goodwill of his customers. I doubt if the manufacturer ever checked on whether he was violating the **usury laws** of his state, however!

THE CREDIT PERIOD

The **credit period** is the "sledgehammer" of accounts receivable policy. It is certainly *not* something that is "tweaked" a little bit. When the credit period is changed, the customer, depending on the industry, will probably notice the change. Unless, of course, the vendor is selling something rather inconsequential. For example, if a small stationery store were to change its credit period from 30 days to 60 days, would an industrial firm really take notice of this and would the large industrial firm do more business with this small stationery store? Hardly. It may be that it gave *all* of its stationery business to this store because it likes its service or delivery or because it is convenient.

Abstracting from this example, what would happen if a firm *increased* its credit period? If the customer were a retail firm, this increase would almost surely be noticed. The name of the game in retail is *turnover* and differing credit periods. If a retailer or wholesaler can get extended terms from a supplier, it may be able to sell the goods, get paid, and only then would it have to pay its supplier. Exhibit 14.5 illustrates this elasticity of the credit period with respect to *sales*.

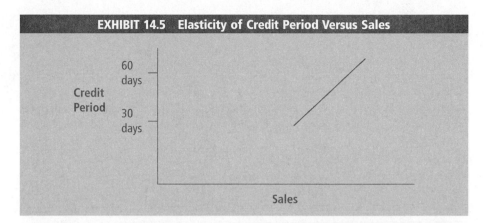

EXHIBIT 14.5   Elasticity of Credit Period Versus Sales

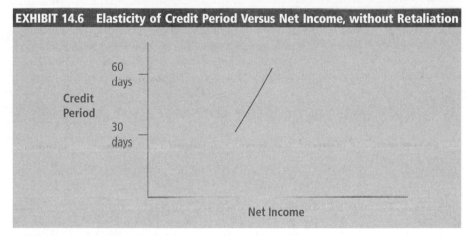

EXHIBIT 14.6   Elasticity of Credit Period Versus Net Income, without Retaliation

If the firm's customers increased their sales with an increase in the company's credit period, as assumed in Exhibit 14.5, then what would be the effect on the firm's Net Income and Rate of Return on Sales and ROA? First, let's look at the effect on Net Income. Exhibit 14.6 shows this.

This increase in Net Income as a result of an increase in the credit period assumes, perhaps naïvely, that the company's competitors would let it get away with this tactic. Some might call this trying to steal the business. If the firm has active competitors and they retaliated with increases in their own credit periods, this increase in sales and net income would be short lived. But other effects would continue. Nothing would happen to Rate of Return on Sales, but look what might happen to Rate of Return on Assets (ROA).

As Exhibit 14.7 shows, there is likely to be a *decrease* in the firm's ROA if competitors retaliate and sales drop back to where they were before the increase in the credit period. This is so because the firm will have *more* accounts receivable for a given level of sales (an increase in the day's sales outstanding) because the firm is giving its customers more time to pay. And when accounts receivable increase, we know what will happen to NOCF (and the company's

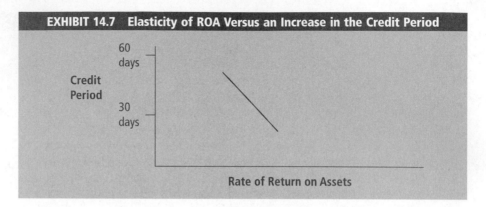

EXHIBIT 14.7   Elasticity of ROA Versus an Increase in the Credit Period

cash balance). Just as with the change in the firm's cash discount and the subsequent increase in the firm's Accounts Receivable balance, NOCF will go down until the new level of accounts receivable is achieved. The cash balance will go down *dollar for dollar* and stay down until something happens to change the level of receivables with respect to sales.

EFFECT ON THE VOLUME OF RECEIVABLES

It is important to note that Accounts Receivable would go up with a lengthening of the credit period, but the actual change may be more than at first thought. Exhibit 14.8 shows this. Instead of Accounts Receivable increasing from A to B, the actual increase might be from A to C, because of what might be called the **demand effect**. This demand effect may come about because the company's sales increase as a result of the lengthened credit period, assuming, of course, that competition does not react and nullify the sales gains.

CREDIT PERIOD VERSUS BAD DEBT EXPENSE

As was mentioned in the discussion of the cash discount, whenever you give the customer more time to pay rather than less time, there will be upward pressure on the firm's bad debt expense. So, for example, doubling the firm's credit period may increase the firm's bad debt expense. How much of an increase will depend on the firm's experience with its customers. For example, if, as mentioned earlier, the company has practically no bad debt, increasing the credit period may have minimal effect, if any. On the other hand, if the company is engaged in an industry that is plagued with questionable accounts, increasing the credit period may be disastrous. The reason, of course, is that it will take longer to discover that a customer is not going to pay, at which point it may be too late to get any payment. Giving a longer credit period may also encourage a customer to overextend his or her credit with subsequent bad experience. This may happen if the customer is given as much credit as it wants if it pays each invoice by the end of the credit period. (Contrast this to giving the customer a dollar amount of credit as its limit.)

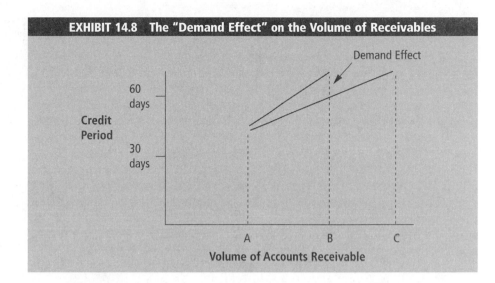

EXHIBIT 14.8   The "Demand Effect" on the Volume of Receivables

THE COLLECTION EFFORT

Because we are dealing with growing, emerging firms, this section is called the **collection effort** as opposed to "collection expense." With large corporations, it would not be too unrealistic to correlate "expense" with "effort." But because the companies that we are discussing are not really this large, the word "effort" is used to describe the activity of *both* screening a potential customer *and* following up to see that the customer pays his or her invoice. For many developing firms, the entire collection effort might be entrusted in one person, whether full time or part time. So what is meant by "collection effort" embodies not only the *system* employed by this one person but also the degree or strenuousness of effort devoted to collecting a past due account.

THE VARIABLES

Collection Effort Versus Sales

It is not unreasonable to expect some *increase* in sales with a bit more collection effort regarding the screening process. Some firms have the simplest—and perhaps most naïve—screening criteria possible. If these firms establish even a *somewhat* more sophisticated screening procedure, this may allow some potential customers to get credit where the more simple screening might reject them. But as the screening gets more rigorous and refined, it is probable that some potential customers will be declined credit and other firms will be denied increases in their credit facility. This is shown in Exhibit 14.9. This screening process could also take into account the Gross Profit of the sale (as will be discussed at the end of this chapter).

Assuming company-to-company sales, beating on a customer to pay is not exactly the way to please customers and gain new ones. So if the collection

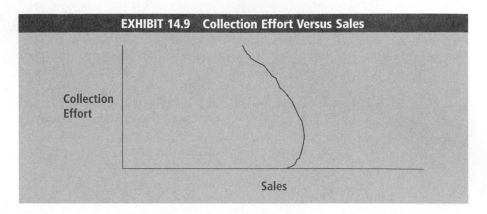

EXHIBIT 14.9   Collection Effort Versus Sales

effort becomes too aggressive, undoubtedly some customers will leave to find more peaceful environs. Thus the decline in sales as the collection effort gets more serious and forceful.

But dealing with "slow pay" and seriously deadbeat customers is a frustrating experience at best. To have a customer declare bankruptcy after assuring you that their company is in good financial shape is a perfectly maddening experience—one that is likely to provoke sentiments like "Never again will I be that agreeable." At this point, the collection manager or general manager may be on the verge of making an irrational decision with regard to a customer or potential customer. But tightening credit to one customer in knee-jerk response to a bad debt experience from a different customer is an irresponsible reaction. Human, perhaps, but this is possibly not in the best interests of the business. The reasoning for this will be developed in the subsequent section in which the credit-granting decision rule is developed.

Collection Effort Versus Net Income
Even though bad debt expense is reduced by precautionary action, overall sales may go down. By denying credit to firms that should have credit, not only will sales be affected but net income as well. What is better? More net income or fewer bad debts?

Collection Effort Versus ROA and Rate of Return on Sales
When we start to consider rate of return on assets, we must deal with the volume of accounts receivable that the firm has in the present state of its collection effort. Obviously, if the firm can reduce the volume of accounts receivable, with sales holding steady, ROA will increase. But for many managers of developing firms, the volume of receivables is simply not their first concern. Getting the product out the door usually ranks ahead of something like accounts receivable management. "After all," one might say, "it isn't like we aren't going to get paid. They will pay us soon enough." Allowing accounts receivable to build up unreasonably is a sure way to hurt the company's cash flow (remember: dollar for dollar!) and hinder the cash needed for expansion. So for some firms, little effort, if

any, is put into collecting the accounts receivable. But even rudimentary management may be able to lower the level of accounts receivable significantly. Such efforts may include calling up a customer who is late in paying and politely asking if the customer is aware that the bill is overdue and when the customer is going to pay the invoice. This could be followed by a telephone call to ascertain whether the payment was actually made. Sometimes this first call reveals that the customer either never got the invoice or misplaced it. In these cases payment is soon to follow. It is beyond the scope of this chapter to explore all the ways that a firm might go about enticing a customer to pay an overdue bill, for such a discussion may take up a whole chapter itself—or even a whole book!

Collection Effort Versus Bad Debt Expense

If someone were appointed credit manager and a year later his or her manager noticed that bad debt expense had *increased*, how would this credit manager feel? Would he or she feel that he or she had done a good job? Well, this depends on what one means by a "good job." Is it the job of the credit manager to *minimize* bad debt expense? Perhaps to some, but I believe this is quite irrational. Rather, it is the job of the credit manager to *optimize the bad debt expense*. By this is meant that the credit manager should take actions that would increase net income even though bad debt expense increases somewhat—or even a lot! For example, by denying credit to a potential customer because this customer exhibits some of the characteristics of an account that went bad may be an example of this "minimizing" attitude rather than an "optimizing" attitude. Here again, when an account goes bad it is likely to leave the credit manager embarrassed if not emotionally wounded. (And this is particularly telling in a developing firm where the bad debt in question might be really significant.) But all of this leads up to the question "How should a rational firm make a credit-granting decision?"

THE CREDIT-GRANTING DECISION RULE

In the simplest context, and utilizing marginal economics, the "expected gain" on a sale should exceed the "expected loss." In this case the **expected gain** is the profit that would be gained on *this sale* versus what we would lose on this sale if the customer did not pay the invoice. Thus, grant credit if:

$$\text{Expected gain} > \text{Expected loss}$$

Where the expected gain is equal to the probability of collection times the firm's Gross Profit on this one sale. Thus:

$$\text{Expected gain} = P(G)$$

P equals the probability of collection and G equals the firm's Gross Profit on this one sale. The *expected loss* is the probability of not collecting the invoice, or $(1 - P)$, multiplied by the firm's Cost of Goods Sold *on this one sale*. Thus:

$$\text{Expected loss} = (1 - P)\, C$$

$(1 - P)$ equals the probability of not collecting and G equals the Gross Profit *on this one order*. Therefore:

$$P(G) \geq (1 - P)C$$

If a customer does not pay on time, if it is what we call a "slow pay" but does pay eventually, the firm realizes something less than the whole gross profit. In this case we have to subtract a "slow-pay" factor, which we will define as $i(t)S$, a function of the time that the bill is expected to be delinquent, times the Sales amount. Earlier I had thought that this amount should be the "Cost of Goods Sold" amount, because this is all that the firm has invested in the account receivable. But this is forgetting that the account receivable affects the cash flow (and cash balance) dollar for dollar, not just a *fraction* of the amount of the invoice. Incorporating this "slow-pay" factor into the preceding equation yields:

$$P(G - i(t)S) \geq (1 - P)(C + i(t)S)$$

Note that the slow-pay factor *reduces* the Gross Profit that will be received, because of the *implicit* interest charge, if nothing else, that the company should make for the slow pay or even because of the *explicit* interest the company might pay for having to finance the account receivable. Furthermore, the slow-pay factor *increases* the loss for the same reason in the event that the customer does not pay. If the company pays interest in the course of financing the account receivable, then this exacerbates the loss. Also, it is necessary to couple the slow-pay factor with either the Gross Profit (G) or the Cost of Goods Sold (C); we would not want to be able to put two times the slow-pay factor on one side or the other.

AN EXAMPLE

Suppose the firm has a Sales price *on this order* of $1,000, a Cost of Goods Sold of $700, and a Gross Profit of $300. Let's assume that the company is reasonably sure that the customer will pay in 90 days, or 60 days past due. Plugging these numbers into the preceding equation, and assuming that the company's *opportunity cost of funds* is 24 percent per annum and the probability of collection is .9, we have:

$$.9(300 - (.04(1,000))) \geq (1 - .9)(700 + (.04(1,000)))$$

$$\$324 \geq \$74$$

Since the *expected gain* of $324 is greater than the *expected loss* of $74, the decision should be to grant credit.

AN ABBREVIATED DECISION RULE

In the preceding example, it can be seen that the probability of collection, P, is quite important to the model. But determining the probability of collection for a customer is not a particularly easy task. It would be a lot easier if we had a probability cut-off rate such that if we can say that if the customer's probability of collection is *greater* than some percentage—70 percent, for instance—then we should grant credit. Fortunately, there is a way to calculate such a probability cut-off rate. It can be shown that

$$\overline{P} = C/S \text{ or } (S - G)/S$$

$\overline{P}$ is the cut-off rate of probability that makes the expected gain of the equation equal the expected loss. Also, $\overline{P}$ *is the minimum probability of collection that is needed in order to grant credit.* If we add in the slow-pay factor, the preceding equation becomes:

$$\overline{P} = (C + i(t)S)/S \text{ or } (S - (G - i(t)S))/S$$

An example of this using the numbers in the example on page 330 might be:

$$\overline{P} = (1000 - (300 - 40))/1,000$$

$$\overline{P} = 74$$

$\overline{P}$, the minimum probability of collection, equals 74 percent.

If the customer's probability of collection is at least 74 percent, the company would be better off selling the customer this order. Thus, if $P \geq \overline{P}$ Sell!

IMPLICATIONS OF THE MODEL

The usual probabilities of collection run in the order of something greater than 90 percent. Most likely the distribution is *bimodal*—that is, most of the company's customers will bunch up at the high end of the distribution while a few (the deadbeats) will be bunched at the low end.

But notice that the firm's gross profit, as a percentage of sales, also takes on increasing importance. If this particular sale has a narrow gross profit, even without a slow-pay factor, the $\overline{P}$ for this sale will rise, perhaps significantly. In this case it behooves the firm to make sure that the customer pays. Aside from asking for payment up front, the selling company can raise the probability to 100 percent (certainty) by asking for and receiving a Letter of Credit essentially guaranteeing the customer will pay. If the customer is thought to be a "slow pay," then by introducing the slow-pay factor this will raise $\overline{P}$, thus raising the hurdle probability of collection.

If the selling company has an extraordinarily high gross profit, for instance, 60 percent or more, then it should *not* take strenuous action which would curtail the granting of credit. Or at least, it should not be stingy with credit. For example, if the firm is selling a software package that cost the firm, for example, $400 with a selling commission of $500, and a sales price of $4,500, it would be better off if it filled every sales request as long as it appeared that it was a legitimate sales order from a *bona fide* company, as evidenced by perhaps a printed letterhead or purchase order. With such a high gross profit (80 percent in this example), the company would not want to take any significant chance of *not* filling the order.

SUMMARY

This chapter treats accounts receivable management by examining the elasticity of demand for what were called the *parameters* (especially, cash discount) and *variables.* It behooves a manager to know what the elasticity is of such things as cash discount to sales and of the credit period to sales. If sales are relatively *inelastic* to a variable, it may permit moving the parameter (for example, reducing the cash discount and thereby increasing pre-tax income). This may seem like a trifling thing at first look, but if a company is operating on a very low pre-tax profit, it may actually increase this measure of profit substantially. But improvement on the Income Statement may mean changing more A/Rs, and this will affect cash and weigh down the Balance Sheet.

The last part of the chapter deals with the credit-granting decision rule. Realizing that the critical factor to consider in granting credit is the selling gross profit and the customer's probability of collection, a business firm can afford to be quite lenient in granting credit if it has a substantial gross profit on that sale. On the other hand, if the selling firm has a rather low gross profit, it must be much more selective in granting credit, especially if there is a "slow-pay" factor involved. But, if need be, the selling firm can raise the probability of collection to certainty by asking for and receiving a Letter of Credit from the customer.

When using this analysis, it is important to remember that this is *marginal analysis*: the next sale. Furthermore, it is equally important to remember that a selling firm can "kill" a customer by granting too much credit to the customer. If the customer, who may have started out as a perfectly "normal" paying customer, buys too much and finds itself unable to pay, then P, its probability of collection, may have shrunk to the point where it is no longer greater than $\bar{P}$, the minimum probability of paying. One important thing to remember is that growing a firm isn't only about managing your own company. Often you have to manage your customers as well!

QUESTIONS FOR DISCUSSION

1. Your company is selling to a customer on terms that discount your regular prices. But this time the customer says that if you want the order you had better drop the price—to a point where you can only make about 12 percent over your "cost of goods" sold. You know that your General and Administrative Expenses run about 15 percent of your sales dollar. Should you take this order?

2. You have a potential customer who says that he will pay you but he will be late—about 2 months—in doing so. How can you factor this information into your decision to sell to this potential customer? Do you want to take this business? What factors should run through your mind in deciding to do business with this potential customer?

3. How can you get the probability of a particular customer paying you up to certainty?

4. When should you offer a cash discount? When should you eliminate one you already have?

5. What risks are you running when you offer longer credit terms to your customers? What factors must you consider?

6. Is it all right to offer longer credit terms to a few of your customers and not hide this fact? How would you "hide" this fact?

7. If you were the credit manager for your company, would you think you were doing a good job if the company's bad debt expense went up? In the absolute and as a percentage of sales? Explain your reasoning.

14

Part 5

External Expansion: Mergers and Acquisitions, Including Doing a LBO

Chapter 15: External Expansion: Searching for an Acquisition

Chapter 16: External Expansion: Technical Aspects of Acquiring a Firm

Chapter 17: The Able Company Case: Doing a Leveraged Buyout

15

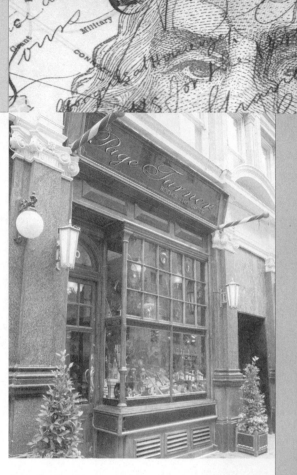

External Expansion: Searching for an Acquisition

In Chapter 5, we discussed "growing a firm," referring to the attempt to increase the firm's earnings. We noted that there were two basic ways to grow earnings: *internally* and *externally*. In this chapter we begin our discussion of expansion by acquiring another firm through the process of what is generally called mergers and acquisitions.

Our discussion, however, is not limited to the process of acquiring *another* company if you already have one (or more companies). It also focuses on an *initial* acquisition. Trying to acquire another company from the position of being president of a company is much easier than trying to acquire a firm without this position, but for many entrepreneurs or wannabe entrepreneurs this is their situation and it will be addressed. Furthermore, this discussion will not be limited by assuming that an acquiring firm will buy another firm *without* leveraging the transaction. Instead, we will assume that such a purchase will be what is now called a **Leveraged Buyout**, or **LBO**. In Chapter 16, we discuss the technical details of acquiring another firm, but before worrying about this, we need to find a target company.

We begin, however, with discussing how "conglomerates" were formed through the process of getting a "**pop in earnings**." The "trick that was used in building some very large companies is still applicable today, even though the word *conglomerate* now is anathema to most businesspeople.

In the second part of this chapter we will look at the criteria that one would use in doing a LBO, and in the third part of this chapter we deal with how to find a LBO target company. Finally, we will discuss what ought to go into the introduction letter to the potential seller.

HOW CONGLOMERATES WERE CREATED—A SLIGHT DIGRESSION

Before we get into a discussion of the criteria for a leveraged buyout—or, as a variation is sometimes called, a *leveraged buildup*—it may be informative to note how conglomerates evolved. This has lessons useful to our study of how to grow a company externally.

Suppose the owner of Company A meets the owner of Company B and asks if the owner of Company B would be interested in being acquired. If the owner of Company B replies in the affirmative, saying that he or she would like to retire, perhaps, then it is up to the CEO of Company A to make an offer. Suppose Company A says "I will pay ten times your after-tax earnings in stock for your company." At this point, the owner of Company B will probably say something like "I will talk to my adviser about your offer." At this point, the "adviser" that the business owner seeks out will be quite instrumental in whether or not a deal is consummated, especially if the deal is to be a LBO. If the business owner asks his or her outside CPA for advice, he or she might get quite a different response than if he or she asked the company's outside lawyer. In the former case, the outside accountant will most likely conclude—correctly—that if he or she helps with the acquisition of this client company, it will no longer be a "client." In short, Company A will be "taking bread off the table of the accountant." If the company's outside lawyer is asked for advice on whether the owner of Company B should be acquired, the financial situation might be quite different. The outside lawyer will probably see the possibility of the largest fee the company has ever paid out. We will return to this decision-making process, but first let's get back to the deal from Company A's point of view.

THE MAGIC OF THE "POP IN EARNINGS"

Suppose Company A, a public company, has $1 million in earnings and has outstanding 1 million shares. This means that Company A has $1 in earnings per share; if it sells for $20 a share it will have a Price/Earnings ratio of 20/1. Now Company B has earnings of $500,000 and, for simplicity, let's say it has 500,000 shares outstanding. Since Company A is acquiring *all* of B's shares, it does not matter how many shares Company B has outstanding; it could be as few as one share or as many as millions. This situation is shown in Exhibit 15.1.

After the acquisition, the combined company, Company A_B, will have earnings of $1.5 million and shares outstanding of 1,250,000. This is because Company A paid ten times Company B's earnings of $500,000 *in stock*, or a total of 250,000 shares ($5,000,000 / $20.) Now let's see what happened to Company

EXHIBIT 15.1	Table Showing the "Pop in Earnings" by Company A Acquiring Company B		
	COMPANY A	**COMPANY B**	**COMPANY A$_B$**
EARNINGS	$1,000,000	$500,000	$1,500,000
SHARES	1,000,000	500,000	1,250,000
EPS	$1	$1	$1.20
STOCK PRICE	$20	—	$24
P/E	20/1	10/1	20/1

A$_B$'s earnings per share. Almost like magic, the earnings have risen to $1.20! How? Did this acquisition cause the firms to have a burst in productivity? Was there some sort of wonderful synergy going on as a result of the acquisition? What did cause Company A's earnings (those of what we are calling Company A$_B$) to jump by 20 percent? How did it get this **"Pop In Earnings"**? Simple. Company A paid *ten* times Company B's earnings whereas it was selling for *twenty* times earnings. This simple fact, of paying a *lower* P/E for the firm acquired, is the reason Company A$_B$'s earnings increased 20 percent.

And, of course, if Company A had purchased Company B for cash instead of stock, the increase would have been even greater—50 percent instead of 20 percent. But in those halcyon days of the 1950s and 1960s, when this game was being played to the extreme, few thoughtful business owners of midsized firms would have taken cash in payment in lieu of stock unless they thought the offered stock was quite overvalued. The process was repeated somewhat in the same way in the 1990s when the high-tech and dot.com firms went on an acquisition binge using their highly overvalued stock as currency.

Why would some business owners take *cash*? If the owner of Company B had taken cash for payment, after the transaction, he or she would have had only $5 million before tax. But by being "smart" and demanding stock, the owner of Company B would now be worth $6 million *in stock*. And if Company A continued to play this acquisition game, it might have had a steady increase in earnings—and stock price—for a considerable time.

THE KEY TO THE GAME

The catch in this game is the assumption that the P/E ratio of Company A (or A$_B$) will *remain the same or increase* with each successive acquisition. What stopped the conglomerates about 1970 (even though they later sprang up again) was the fact that they were not able to keep increasing earnings and their P/E ratio slipped. And this was the kiss of death for the so-called conglomerates. If the stock market perceives the acquisition as undesirable, it may indicate its displeasure by dropping the P/E for the acquiring firm, in which case the exercise will be one of futility.

With regard to the mergers and acquisitions of rather large firms, studies show that the market price of the acquiring firm drops some when an acquisition is announced and the market price of the target firm goes up with the announcement. This is not true with all merger announcements. Sometimes the stock price of both firms goes up, but this is generally not the case. This does not contravene the above example, however, for it takes some time for the earnings to be reported, by which time the stock price of the acquiring firm may change for a variety of reasons.

The typical way for the acquiring firm to "pay" for the target firm was with what is called "lettered stock." (The word "pay" is in quotes because the transaction usually was technically a merger and not a purchase transaction.) **Lettered stock** has been authorized by the acquiring company, and is legally issued, but it has not been registered with the SEC. The company would put a letter (now a rubber stamp) with the stock certificate(s) saying that the stock could not be sold, except pursuant to Rule 144, until the stock was registered. Rule 144 is an SEC regulation that provides for the legal sale of unregistered stock in small amounts over time. This is a sort of "dribble rule" in which the owner of a relatively small amount of stock in a very large company can "dribble out" the sale of stock every month. The letter usually provided that the stock of the acquiring firm would be registered by that company usually within 2 years. If the company had a registration within the 2-year period, it would include the unregistered shares of the acquired company's former owner(s) with this registration; otherwise it would make a special registration before the agreed-upon period. The acquiring firm would want a period of time before the stockholders of the acquired firm could sell their stock because they felt that a quick sale would upset the market.

Before 1970 or 1971, when the bull market of the 1960s came to an end, the typical way for an acquiring firm to acquire another small firm was through the form of transaction known as a **pooling of interest**. This is the form of transaction, which will be discussed in the next chapter, that is commonly called a **merger** and is a tax-free exchange of stock for stock, or something convertible into stock. The stockholders of the acquired firm did not have to pay tax on the sale of their company until they actually sold the shares of the acquiring company which they accepted in exchange for their shares. This led to great abuses of this tax-free exchange and today tax-free "mergers" of disparate firms is difficult, if not impossible, to do. Currently, the thinking of leaders in the accounting profession is to do away with all "mergers" and treat all transactions as **purchase transactions**, a distinction that will be made clear in the next chapter.

CRITERIA FOR A LBO

Before embarking on a search for a leveraged buyout, it is well to consider what it is that makes for a good LBO target. What are the criteria for a LBO? In the course of discussing these criteria, we will make use of principles and information learned in prior chapters, especially Chapters 4 and 10.

"HOCKABLE ASSETS"

Because the whole idea in doing a LBO is to *borrow on the strength of the target's assets*, the most important aspect of a good target is that it have assets against which the buyer can borrow. This attribute of being good for borrowing is what I call **hockable assets** (when borrowing on one's assets from a pawnshop we speak of this as "hocking" the asset).

What, then, are really good hockable assets? First of all, there are *Accounts Receivable*. How good are the target's receivables? If they are really good, lenders will loan something on the order of 70–80 percent of their face amount. Typically, when the transaction is a LBO, banks and finance companies will loan somewhat less than if the original owner were borrowing without the use of a LBO mechanism. By doing a LBO the apparent risk to the bank has increased, thus prompting the bank to lower the borrowing percentage.

The second most important asset is usually the target's *equipment*. As mentioned in Chapter 11 lenders will usually loan 85–100 percent of the "quick sale" value of a firm's equipment. Remember, there are two types of quick sale values: *orderly resale* over a period of, say, 6 months, and the so-called *liquidation value*. The former usually will result in a higher quick sale value, so this is the one to request when retaining an appraisal company. However, the appraisal company must be one that the prospective lender will approve. If the prospective lender insists on the appraisal being done by an appraiser who is actually an auctioneer, then the quick sale value will most likely be a liquidation quick sale value. (Remember, the asset's "market value" really is redundant in the process of borrowing on the asset's value.)

Without having an actual appraisal, which costs usually from $5,000 to $10,000 for a middle-market firm, it is quite tricky trying to estimate what the quick sale value of equipment might be. We know that really "clean" machine shops will have a positive effect on an appraisal, so being sensitive to this when looking around a shop with lots of equipment will help a little. But for most situations, the prospective buyer will have to risk the price of an appraisal if he or she wants to know how much might be borrowed on the target's equipment. While I hesitate to mention this, as it is not at all verifiable, sometimes the "quick sale" value for a company's equipment is close to the *depreciated* value of the equipment.

Real estate is another fairly good asset on which to borrow, if you have a sense of the real estate market in the area where it is located. This information is usually readily available from local real estate sources, for free. Here, *market value* is the basis of the appraisal. But one intangible is whether the building has been properly maintained, which might be ascertained by inspection. Another intangible is whether there is pollution on the subject property. This latter factor will be specifically mentioned as one of the criteria below.

The asset that has the worst "hockability" is, of course, the target's *inventory*. Usually, the most that a bank will lend on inventory is 50 percent of raw material and 50 percent of finished goods inventory. They will not lend on work-in-progress. Finance companies will usually be more understanding when it comes to inventory, but that does not mean that they will lend more on that than a bank will. If a lender is generally pleased with the LBO deal, meaning that it likes the price and terms, it will be much more inclined to lend on inventory than if it feels that the deal is a "tight" one, meaning that the price is high or the payment of the debt is stretching the firm's ability to service the debt. But, in general, if the target has a lot of inventory, this will make doing the deal quite difficult, if not impossible, in the usual sense. This means that distributive types of companies, where inventory is quite important, are difficult targets from the point of view of doing a LBO. And, of course, service companies with virtually no inventory are *really* difficult.

It should go without saying that if the target has a significant amount of "intangible" assets, such as goodwill, this will complicate the borrowing strategy immensely. True, the intangible asset might be worth a considerable sum, but borrowing against this will be quite difficult. Unless there is rather clear value, the typical middle-market LBO lender is not going to consider this intangible to have much, if any, value. With much bigger deals intangible value might take on a completely different complexion, however. "Proven oil reserves" might be considered in this same light when valuing an oil company's assets.

So, to summarize, assets are the most important aspect of a LBO. Without good "hockable" assets, the typical technique of a LBO transaction would not be possible. And yet people try continuously to do LBOs on service companies and distributive companies, without adequate assets. In the vernacular of finance they are trying to "break their pick."

There is an exception to the rule here, however. With smaller deals, assets are of particular importance, but as the deal gets larger—to say, $20 million in purchase price—assets become less and less important and cash flow becomes much more important. In fact, with larger deals, cash flow might be dominant and hockability is not even mentioned. These deals are called, naturally enough, **cash flow deals**.

LOW OR NO LONG-TERM DEBT

It is quite necessary that the target company have little or no long-term debt. This is so because if some debt is outstanding against an asset, this debt will, most likely, have to be repaid before more debt can be placed against the same asset as collateral. This means that there will be that much less to give the seller at closing, something that is very important to making the deal happen.

STATUS AS AN OLD FIRM

Usually the target firm will be a rather old firm, meaning at least 20 years old. This is because the prime reason for selling for the owners of many middle-market firms is to retire. An owner might be in his or her sixties after 20-odd years in business, a time when many people are thinking of retiring. The firm might even be 30 or 40 years old and still be owned by the same owner. I negotiated a deal in 1983 for a rather large sheet-fed printing company that was founded in 1921 and owned by the same man for the entire time. He had two children but neither was able to succeed him in the ownership of the business. The owner was 82 at the time of the sale and his eyesight had suddenly failed.

Also, older firms tend to have no debt outstanding. If they do, this may be cause for concern beyond the reason mentioned above, in our second criterion. The existence of long-term—and sometimes short-term debt—may indicate that the business is just not very profitable, despite what the statements say. Alternatively, outstanding debt might indicate that the owner was taking too much out of the business in the way of salary or bonus or both. If this can be verified, it might be something that could be accepted by the prospective new owner. This would show up in valuing this closely held firm, a subject discussed in the next chapter.▲

Another interesting thing about relatively old firms is that they very often have **hidden assets**. This means they were written off the books, because they were fully depreciated, or they never appeared on the books. Land, which is carried on the company's books at cost may have appreciated dramatically, a fact that may escape the owner(s). This is particularly true if the target happens to be a subsidiary of a large corporation that may be geographically removed.

GOOD DEPENDABLE CASH FLOW

The necessity of having an observable cash flow should be obvious to anyone reading this book. Here the key features are not only the *adequacy* but the *dependability* of the cash flow stream. (Chapter 1 deals with this matter extensively. Taking on debt is the essence of a LBO.) This gives great comfort to the lenders in a LBO transaction. And, indeed, it should give great assurance to the individual attempting the LBO. But invariably some individuals forget the obvious, and they attempt to do a LBO on a company with inadequate or "spotty" cash flow. Inadequate cash flow should be picked up in calculating the price, because it will result in a very low "ceiling price" (see Chapter 16).

There are always the individuals who see a "bargain" and cannot resist trying to take advantage of the "great" price for a certain company. The mistake they make is not realizing that it does not matter if the prospective target is low priced if the *deal is not doable!* It would be better to find a target that is priced "higher," whatever that means, than to try to buy a company that does not have adequate cash flow. A "bargain" is no bargain if a lender will not loan enough to make the deal doable. If an individual is paying all cash—cash that is not borrowed—for a target, there is some reason to jump at a bargain. But one has to remember that to acquire a target company in a LBO deal, a lender has to be ready and willing to make the necessary loans to provide the money to make the deal happen. *Turnarounds do not make good LBO targets.* Of course, turnarounds (companies that are currently losing money) are priced "cheaply," but

---

▲ This will be discussed in the section of Chapter 16 that deals with the "ceiling" price for a business which is determined by taking the "adjusted EBITDA." This could be one important factor in the *adjustment* process.

that does not make buying them particularly smart. And, besides, suppose the "turnaround" does not turn? Doing a middle-market LBO will invariably require an individual to guarantee the loans that are secured to make the deal happen. If the cash flow is adequate to service the loans, and bankruptcy or some other terribly serious result ensues, the individual who made these guarantees will lose materially, perhaps everything he or she has. So why would a thoughtful individual want to risk everything? Because the target company is a bargain that can't be resisted? Sometimes something quite unforeseen and disastrous happens to the company acquired via a LBO, which is lamentable, but to try to buy a company via a LBO when it is *known* that the company's cash flow is inadequate or even suspect is inexcusable.

SIZE

What is the *size of the target*, meaning, usually, the volume of sales? There are several aspects of the question of size.

Is this target a good size considering the track record of the individual who is trying to do the deal? The lender and the selling owner have to feel "comfortable" with the individual who is trying to do a LBO, which is one reason it is so much easier to buy another company once an individual already has bought and successfully managed a company. For the first-time buyer, the question of size is invariably raised. If the individual who is attempting to do the LBO is to be the general manager, the question will be raised as to whether that individual has sufficient experience to manage such a company. Has he or she ever managed a similar or larger company before? As was discussed in Part One on doing a start-up, having a track record answers the question Has the individual ever managed an Income Statement and made any money with it? If the answer is "No," then the individual seeking to do the LBO should, perhaps, try to ally himself or herself with an individual who has such a track record. Perhaps this individual is already managing the target company, in which case the individual who engineers the deal might become the chairman of the target company.

Another aspect of the "size" question is the matter of managerial competence in the principal functions of the company. For example, if the target company badly needs marketing expertise, will the prospective owner be able to compensate for this weakness? Or how about the manufacturing side of the business? Will this managerial position be adequately covered after the acquisition? For middle-market companies, the finance and accounting functions are reasonably easy to fill by hiring a competent person, but usually these positions are filled sufficiently at the time of acquisition. This is not to imply that the new owner has to be expert in all aspects of the target company. If this were the case, few, if any, companies would be acquired by a LBO or otherwise. Rather, the prospective owner must feel that either he or she or someone else will be able to manage all aspects of the business once the new owner has taken over.

The opposite situation might also arise. Is the target company *big enough* for the individual seeking to do the LBO? If not, the target might be so small that the entrepreneur/owner has to do virtually everything of managerial importance. True, if the entrepreneur sticks with the new company, he or she might grow it into something rather big, something certainly worthwhile. But what is disturbing about this scenario is the fact that the cash flow is so small that after servicing the debt there is little left for the owner to receive as salary. And if the new owner is going to pledge everything he or she has by way of guarantees, the reward should be commensurate with the risk. If the target is "too small," it seems like this is not the case. Conceivably the target could be so small that the "owner" could not make more than he or she could make working for someone else. It is true, that in this circumstance the entrepreneur can boast of being his or her own boss, but it would seem that in this case there is an *opportunity cost* present in no small way.

TYPE OF COMPANY

The prospective owner should consider if this target company is really the kind of company that he or she would be *proud* to own. And what kind of work style would ownership present? Would the ownership of this target company involve doing things that would be distasteful to the new owner? These and other related concerns must be considered before pursuing the target company. Even though the target might appear to be a wonderful business opportunity, the savvy entrepreneur should back off from a situation that would not be pleasant and rewarding if pursued.

Unfortunately, to a very ambitious entrepreneur this might seem like the "one and only" opportunity he or she will ever see. This "golden opportunity" might dominate situations where the acquisition of a target company is simply not "doable," and the wannabe owner continues to pursue the target to the point where the people associated with the deal—e.g., potential lenders—get tired of hearing about it. If a deal is beginning to look like it is going to be impossible to do, either because the price is too high or because the assets are not going to support the necessary borrowing, then the wannabe owner should back off and forget the target company. Persistence may only waste time and incur animosities from others.

COMPELLING REASON TO SELL

It is tempting to think that any one of these criteria is "most important," and there is one criterion which might emerge with that distinction. It is *quite necessary for the owner/seller to have a compelling reason to sell* or else the chances of getting the concessions in terms that are needed to do a LBO might not be met. If you ask any business owner if his or her company is for sale, the answer might very well be "Of course, for the right price." (This is why an owner in his or her 40s, for example, would be a suspect target. They have no incentive to yield on terms.) But when attempting to do a LBO, the price not only has to be "reasonable" but the *terms* must be present to favor the wannabe owner. For example, it is mandatory for the seller—or a surrogate for the seller—to accept a *subordinated note* for a portion of the purchase price. If the seller does not have a compelling reason to sell, there will be no incentive to accept anything less than a deal completely slanted in favor of the seller. Furthermore, the inclusion of contracts such as a consulting contract, as part of the purchase price—these are called "soft-dollar" contracts—would not be acceptable to the seller, thus denying the buyer a chance to "write off" part of the purchase price.

What incentive would the seller have for accepting anything but terms that were perfect for him or her? Reference was made earlier to the sale of a large sheet-fed printing company by someone who had been the owner of the business for 61 years. Undoubtedly, the owner had many chances to sell the business over this period of time, and especially for the last 10 years of ownership, but it took a medical emergency to force the owner, on the strong advice of his lawyers, to put the company up for sale. The sudden failure of his eyesight provided the stimulus to sell where there had not been one before. In the negotiations, the lawyers were extremely astute and aware of all the "angles" present in the proposal, such as collateralizing the subordinated note, but even the lawyers sensed the compelling reason to sell that was present with the owner and eventually yielded to the final offer.

This specific compelling reason to sell was rather easy to ascertain, but sometimes it is not as easy to perceive. The prospective buyer must ask discerning questions to try to find out the "real" reason the owner has for wishing to sell. Such answers as "Oh, I just want to travel" leave a lot to the imagination. Is the owner trying to unload the business on an unsuspecting wannabe entrepreneur/owner? Does the owner really want you to "put your neck in his or her noose"? If you as a potential buyer have a strategic reason for trying to acquire the firm and will pay what it takes to succeed, you do not have to worry about the presence of a compelling reason to sell. But as a prospective LBO buyer, you do not have this luxury. You must have a valid and compelling reason to sell by the owner or you will, most likely, not get the terms that you need to do a deal.

NO INSURMOUNTABLE POLLUTION PROBLEMS

In the past 20 or so years, the problems connected with environmental pollution problems have grown almost exponentially. And the leading kind of company facing these "problems" is the manufacturing firm. Unfortunately, these are the kind of companies that make good LBO targets. So in the pursuit of "good" targets, it is quite common to find a company with a pollution problem. This, in and of itself, is not a reason to discard the target, but the trick is to try to ascertain if the problem is *insurmountable* or not. If it appears that the problem is too big for a "quick fix," then the correction of the problem could become part of the whole plan for the acquisition of the company. Remember, lenders typically cannot or will not lend on troubled properties.

Once I was involved with a situation in which the manufacturing company was situated on land that was part of a large toxic spill that occurred many years earlier and had become part of a major "superfund" remedial action. What made this problem a bit different was that the authorities were looking for a "deep pocket" which could be tapped to help pay for the remediation, even though the new company had not had anything to do with the initial contamination. In fact, the target company had nothing to do with the big toxic spill, it just happened to be located on land that was covered by the superfund jurisdiction. As a LBO group, we did not qualify for this deep-pocket status while a large, well-financed corporation would have qualified. In this case, competition for this target was substantially reduced.

This suggests a somewhat similar problem that presented an "opportunity" for a buyer. An American company had such a high product legal liability "problem" that no substantial corporation could be found as a buyer. An individual, who did not represent a publicly owned firm but was acting for himself, was able to buy this company. The buyer "solved" the insurance problem by forming an insurance company in the Bahamas. So, while this was a problem for large, publicly owned firms—the most logical prospective buyer for this company—it was an "opportunity" for this entrepreneur.

A somewhat common problem involving pollution is of the type where the ownership of the contaminants cannot be sold or gotten rid of, for example, asbestos. A company can have the asbestos removed from its premises and "stored" in an approved site, but the company that owned the asbestos can never effectively rid itself of the responsibility for this toxic waste. Whether this presents an "insurmountable" obstacle depends on the scope of the problem. It may be that ownership of this toxic whatever would present no serious problem. This condition would cause any thoughtful buyer to hesitate, if not drop the deal, however.

One of the most common problems with contamination is the case of oil or some other substance spilled on the grounds of a manufacturing plant. This might be major in scope or relatively minor. In the latter case it may be that someone spilled some motor oil on the property sometime in the past; where this spill is caught in an examination of the property, some remediation will be required in the purchase of the land (and building). In these cases, remediation would be a relatively easy matter; it would be probably more of a nuisance than an expense. Where the contamination is found under the floor of the building, however, this can represent a major problem, one that might be quite insurmountable. This could be a deal killer.

LONG-TERM FUTURE

Today we live in a world that is truly getting to be "one world." Now, manufacturing can be performed, in many cases, in lower-cost environments such as China or Mexico. The expression "You don't have to make what you sell" seems to be taking on increasing importance. So why, then, would some wannabe entrepreneur want to buy a manufacturing firm when this sort of manufacturing is moving offshore? Because it is doable, for one reason! But even with the movement of manufacturers to offshore locations, there are still going to be situations or niche markets that can be serviced with local manufacturing companies. If nothing else, once you have control of the target company, you may be able to move some or all of the production offshore, assuming the lender is in agreement. Outsourcing production to, say, China, may be advantageous, but what do you do with the equipment on which you borrowed a substantial part of the down payment? This is the conundrum that the wannabe owner must explore.

A QUIET DEAL

When trying to buy a company via the LBO route, the ideal situation is for you, the potential buyer, to be the *only* buyer. Competition with other potential buyers makes for not only a *rising price*, but more importantly *decreasing terms*. And in this category of "decreasing terms" is the expectation that the *cash down payment* will *go up*. To do a LBO, it is important to get the necessary terms from the seller. When there is competition with other buyers for the company, one or more of the potential buyers may offer not only a higher price, but more "front-end" money. This, effectively, would knock out a wannabe LBO buyer.

Although it appears that it would be to the advantage of the seller to have more than one party bidding for the company, this is precisely what *most sellers do not want*. Experience teaches that many, if not most, of the sellers want their whole negotiation to be held in the strictest confidence. If there are multiple bidders on the company it will be much harder to maintain confidentiality. Furthermore, they do not want their customers to know that the company is for sale, they do not want their competitors to know, and   Horrors of Horrors!— they do not want their employees to know. There could be many reasons for each of these positions, but as far as the would-be buyer is concerned, it is sufficient that the seller has these feelings. If the seller really wants the deal to be kept a secret, this only plays into the hands of the potential LBO buyer.

This is why it is important for the potential buyer to make sure that confidentiality is maintained at all costs. You must reassure the seller that by dealing with you as a potential buyer, his or her secret is safe. But it is also necessary to make sure that someone else does not get in on the action and propose another purchase proposal. By being extremely secretive, the seller may advance his or her purpose, but he or she is also working against getting the best possible price for the business. Remember, most middle-market company owners have never sold a business before and know little about the process. Furthermore, they do not know much about the pricing of these middle-market companies. True, these sellers will have some advice from their CPA or corporate attorney, or both, but this is not to say that these "advisers" are fully apprised as to the current state of the (price) market for companies such as the one under consideration. It may be that this is the first acquisition deal that either the accountant or lawyer has ever personally done. In any case, it is the "feeling" of the seller that is likely to carry the day in the final negotiation.

On this latter point, this is why it is quite important for the potential buyer to do what he or she can to win the "favor" of the seller. If the seller really likes the prospective buyer, the road to acquisition will be remarkably easier. For many retiring sellers, it is comforting to think that a "bright" young(er) person is going to continue to keep the (family?) business running. If this feeling exists, it behooves the buyer to do everything he or she can do to encourage it, and keeping this deal quiet would be quite consistent with this predisposition.

WHAT OTHER CRITERIA ARE THERE?

It seems like the ten above-mentioned criteria would serve, but no one would be foolish enough to say that these are the *only* criteria that one might have for selecting a target company for a LBO. So it goes without saying that the astute potential buyer will use these as a starting point in his or her quest for the ideal target.

It is important to keep in mind each of these criteria, because if one or more of them is forgotten, the whole quest might be for naught. Obviously, hockable assets are a necessary ingredient; nevertheless many a person brings a potential LBO deal to an adviser for consideration only to realize that the assets do not have sufficient borrowing power. Or everything looks "great," except the cash flow is weak. Or the selling owner is 38 years old, and has no incentive whatsoever to do the deal. And so forth and so forth!

FINDING A LBO TARGET

Once the criteria for finding a LBO target are carefully understood, finding a target may be easier than at first thought.

PERSONAL KNOWLEDGE

If someone is working in an industry composed of companies that, in general, meet the criteria of a LBO, such as good hockable assets, then spotting a potential target might be just a matter of observation. Or you might know of a company with an owner who might be reaching retirement age. This company does not have to have to be in the industry that a potential buyer is already working in; it could be in another industry. The fact that the target is in an industry that is unfamiliar to the potential buyer is a bit of a challenge, but it should not preclude the wannabe business owner from, at least, investigating the potential target to see if that business is of interest. Many a new business owner *learns* a new business during and after the acquisition. Doing sufficient "due diligence" can bring the wannabe entrepreneur up to speed, so to speak.

When "personal knowledge" includes a situation where some business owner becomes seriously ill, the criteria of a "compelling reason to sell" will be amply met. If the owner gets quite ill, or terminally so, he or she may realize that his or her spouse could be left with the responsibility of running or disposing of the business but without any experience. And while it may be that the new widowed spouse might, in fact, manage the business better than the deceased owner, this would be the exception. So, the logical presumption is that the business is "for sale" and one of the most important criteria is about to be met. Buying out a relative of the family also comes under this category. Once a potential business owner *knows how* to acquire a business using leverage and some other "tricks" of the trade, buying out a relative might suddenly become a definite possibility. Knowing that one does not have to have the whole purchase price in his or her checking account is, indeed, a revelation to many a potential business owner.

ADS IN THE *WALL STREET JOURNAL* AND OTHER CITY PAPERS

When a business comes up for sale, some owners do as they might do if they wished to sell a car: They put an ad in the paper. If the newspaper happens to be the *Wall Street Journal*, either in the national edition or one of the regional editions, the chance of getting a "quiet" deal may be slim. But nevertheless, it has happened. It may be that you are the only potential buyer to answer the ad, or at least to answer it in such a way that the potential seller selects your letter for reply.

Answering ads in large city newspapers is fraught with the same problem of competition. But there are many situations in which a business owner has to sell the business and, not knowing any better way, places an ad in the local city paper. Such cases might include the split-up of a partnership, or a divorce, or simply someone wishing to retire. Finding an appropriate target candidate may be a bit of a chore, however, as it might be that you will have to answer a number of ads before an appropriate one is found. It might be that you have to look at many separate listings in order to find, for example, an appropriate manufacturing firm for sale. The reason for this is that the newspaper might not always list the manufacturing company under the general category starting with "Manufacturers" and instead list it under some other title such as "Machine shop" or "Injection molding company."

BUSINESS BROKERS

Under this generic heading, there are two types of brokers: "business opportunity brokers" and "merger and acquisition brokers."

Business Opportunity Brokers

These consist really of specialists in selling mom-and-pop businesses, including retail stores. These brokers, who often are also real estate brokers, have a number of listings, and their names and the companies they are trying to sell are often found in the city newspapers under "Businesses for sale." For someone who has never "looked" at a company for sale, starting with these "brokers" might be good way to gain some experience. But the odds of finding a good middle-market LBO target in the listing of one of these brokers are slim, at best. A number of the companies these brokers have for sale are not *really* for sale—in that their price is unrealistic or the seller is not "motivated." Instead, the manufacturing companies they have "for sale" got there because the *broker* solicited the owner of the business with a letter saying "Wouldn't you like to sell your company?" For many of the owners, saying "Yes" is a way of answering the question "I wonder how much my company is worth?" This is about as close to idle curiosity as you can get. And then there are the owners who like to be "romanced" by potential buyers, although they have no real intention of selling.

Another "problem" of dealing with "business opportunity brokers" is that they might try to be "helpful" to the seller in the negotiations. Consequently, their "suggestions" might be quite contrary to the terms being offered by a potential LBO buyer. In short, they are useful in helping really small business owners sell their businesses for cash or a healthy down payment and a note.

The tools used by the LBO buyer are very often foreign to these mostly real estate brokers turned business brokers. They might reveal their ignorance or naïveté by asking to see your personal Balance Sheet. When this happens, it might be best to say "When I give you the certified check, you could care less where the money came from." To accede to the request would be naïve on your part. You have nothing to lose by *refusing* to show your personal Balance Sheet. If you show it, you will not get to see the kind of companies you want. This is so because it appears that you do not have the financial resources to buy the company. As the deals get bigger, these questions tend to be not asked.

It is important for the would-be buyer to realize that he or she must "look the part." Do you have the creditability to impress the two people who matter most—the seller and the banker whom you approach to finance the deal? If you have the necessary experience, whatever that means, to manage and/or own the target company, this fact, more than anything else, is the one that will matter. It may be that you have the ability to own the company, but that you need an experienced manager to run it. "Ability" to own the company means that you have the money to buy the business or, at least, know how to get the money—and all of the other instruments needed to do a LBO deal—to buy the business.

Merger and Acquisition Brokers

These professional brokers will not deal with the small retail or service type of companies the above-mentioned business opportunity brokers will handle. Instead, these brokers will accept a company, say, a middle-market company, for sale on a discrete basis. Usually these brokers will know the buying "appetite" of other companies and, accordingly, usually know just where to go to find a buyer. But there are all sorts of degrees of M & A brokers, some of whom might be willing to let a potential LBO buyer look at a prospect that he or she has for sale. On the other hand, some of these brokers might not wish to expose one of their companies for sale to a potential buyer if it is known that the buyer will have to do a LBO to do the deal. An experienced broker knows that it is difficult to do a LBO, as opposed to selling the company to another company or individual who will have no trouble financing the deal. In short, it is easier to sell to a known "customer" of the broker, perhaps someone who has bought a company from him or her before, than it is to get involved with a LBO buyer, who may be a first-time buyer. Again, it is so much easier to buy another company once you already own a company.

If—and this is a big "if"—a professional M & A broker can accept you as a *bona fide* buyer, this may be an excellent source for finding a target company. Some of the M & A brokers specialize in a particular industry—the food industry, for example. If you know that you want to stay in a particular industry, it may be advantageous to patronize one of these specialized brokers.

The fees for the broker may be "charged" to the seller, but the buyer can be sure that he or she is actually paying the fee. In fact, it may be good psychology to offer to pay the broker's fee in an up-front conversation. At least this will relieve the broker of wondering whether he or she will get paid for his or her work.

CORPORATE FINANCE/M & A DEPARTMENTS OF BANKS AND MAJOR ACCOUNTING FIRMS

Some banks and large accounting firms maintain departments that offer brokerage services to their customers and others, too. Not as popular as they once were, these departments will function rather like any other professional M & A brokers. On first thought, these departments should have a tremendous edge over other brokers because they know the client who wishes to sell his or her company or, conversely, who wishes to buy another company. Unfortunately, the bank officers or accountants who handle the company's account do not always convey this information to their own brokerage department. Without this information, the brokerage unit is hurting. If the unit is a bank, however, there is something of an advantage in that this bank may be the most likely source of financing for the deal, if for no other reason than desire to keep the account. The problem with these types of brokers is the same as with professional M & A brokers: They may shun individual buyers who are known to be "LBO buyers." If they have a particularly attractive sale candidate, they may have a favorite buyer already in mind. Also, there is somewhat more likelihood that the deal may not be a "quiet" deal, something the LBO buyer wants.

TRUST COMPANIES

If a business owner dies and leaves his stock in trust to someone, he or she may appoint a *trust company* to administer the will. If this is the case, the company will be almost surely for sale. This is because the trust company knows that it can do two things with the company for which it now holds the stock: It can manage it and, with some probability get sued for mismanagement, or it can sell the stock and invest the funds in one of its pooled investment accounts for which it knows that there is little chance of being sued for mismanagement. It is not hard to guess which choice the trust company will make.

I used to think that this would be an excellent source of finding a LBO target, but I no longer do. There are two reasons for this. First, if the seller is the trust company, they, in all probability, will *not* take a note, subordinated or otherwise—something that is absolutely necessary for doing a LBO. This is because, as one trust officer once told me, "If we take a note, we really haven't sold the business." The fact that the criterion of "a compelling reason to sell" is met most assuredly is little consolation if it is not possible to do the deal. In the situation of a trust company selling the company, it becomes necessary to find a third party to take the subordinated note that is requisite to doing a LBO. This may be possible, but for a higher price than if the seller took the note as part of the whole purchase price. For example, you may need to offer a wealthy individual or a finance company a deal where they put up, say, $2 million for a subordinated note for $4 million. Without the subordinated note, there is no deal, so the party approached to take the note is in a commanding position in any negotiation. In recent years, as mentioned in Chapter 10, we have seen an appetite for these subordinated notes from institutional lenders. Currently the minimum is about $5 million and the usual interest rate is in the order of 20–25 percent, but the fact that these financing possibilities exist is good news for LBO buyers.

If the potential buyer knows who the beneficiaries of the stock in trust are, he or she might make a deal with these persons. In this case, the trust company might approve the deal with the concurrence of the beneficiaries. In one such case there was quite a line of prospective buyers wanting to make an offer on the business. Two aspiring business owners, with help from one of their fathers, went directly to the beneficiaries and made a deal that they accepted, thus preempting the other would-be owners. The helpful father took the place of the selling owner in providing the *de facto* equity for the buying partners.

The second reason this potential source of targets is not very attractive is because it takes a lot of time to "cultivate" any one trust company. Taking time to cultivate this "source" might be expensive in terms of your time and could be full of frustration. But it is one source—and may be the one you need in a particular situation.

While on the topic of trust companies, another potential source of leads for a LBO target would be lawyers and other estate planning advisers. If one of these individuals knows that you are trying to buy a certain kind of company, and he or she has a client who owns such a company and is thinking of retiring, this could be an excellent lead. Bank officers will surely know if one of their customers is thinking of putting the company up for sale.

MANUFACTURERS' DIRECTORY

For many if not all of the industrial states, there is published in hard-copy form or electronically a directory of the manufacturing companies in their region. Now, there are other services on the Internet that offer similar information. Typically, these directories have these firms listed three ways: By SIC Code, by city or county, and alphabetically.

The SIC Code makes looking for companies in a particular field quite convenient. And while it is true that these directories cannot be guaranteed to contain *every* company in that field, by talking to the owners of some of the firms listed, you may find owners who are now selling. By concentrating on companies in a particular industry that is appropriate for a LBO deal, such as an industry where the firms have lots of "hockable" assets, it may be possible to save time in the search for a good target.

The listing by region needs no particular amplification. The *alphabetical* listing is the one that contains the information needed in searching for a target. In reviewing this section you need a good deal of *deductive reasoning*. Of course, there will not be any "For sale" signs displayed in these listings, but with just a little bit of practice and imagination one will surely find a company for sale. Knowing that a business owner might want to retire can be a sure way of spotting a LBO target. Let us see how this might be deduced from the directory.

What to Look For

First, observe the name of the business and its age. When was it founded? What is the size of the business? Most listings will give some range of size in terms of sales. Is it approximately the size that you are looking for? Is the business name a person's name like "Taylor Co."? If it was founded at least 20 years ago, there is a chance that the owner now wants to retire. (Of course, this is not a certainty, but if it works for some proportion of business owners, it is worth the supposition.) *And remember, the very best time to get to the owner of a business for sale is when he or she first decides to sell!* When the "For sale" sign is posted it may be too late. If you could have a meaningful letter on that person's desk the day he or she says "I think I'll sell the business" you would be doing that person a great favor by relieving him or her of the burden of trying to find a buyer!

Secondly, you look for the names of the officers of the company. If the president is Tom Taylor and Tom Taylor, Jr. is vice president, I think it is a safe bet that you can go on to the next company listed. This one is probably not for sale. Or if the vice president is Tania Taylor, this may be the owner's daughter, who is going to succeed her father in the business. Here, too, you had better skip on to the next possibility. If, after the president, there is a listing for "Chris Taylor, Secretary," this probably denotes the owner's wife, who is Secretary of the corporation. This is not the situation that a son or daughter presents.

You next look at the kind of business described in the write-up. Is this the kind of business you would like to be in? The good thing about reading through these directories is that you will come upon all sorts of businesses—businesses that you had never thought about! And then, what kind of assets would a business like this have? Is there likely to be a number of pieces of hockable assets? Like machine tools or injection-molding machines? Or are you looking at a company that has few, if any, machines that could be used as collateral?

For example, a plating company had wonderful cash flow, never having a loss on the Income Statement in over 30 years. Furthermore, it had all of the requisite permits from the environmental authorities, so there were no "insurmountable environmental problems." But what kind of hard assets did it have? The "assets" the company used to plate metal parts were nothing more than a series of galvanized dip tanks, with little commercial value. Hardly the kind of asset that would be "hockable." So although this company had a lot of good characteristics, it did not have the one that may be most necessary: hockable fixed equipment. (If the target were bigger, it might qualify for what is called a "cash flow LBO," one in which the cash flow becomes more important than the assets, but it did not so qualify.)

Focus on Technology

INVESTING IN HIGH-GROWTH, HIGH-POTENTIAL BUSINESSES: THE "SEARCH FUND" MODEL

It is said that entrepreneurs are made of passion! And that is true for many real entrepreneurs who have come up with new ways of doing things. In fact, many venture capitalists base their funding decisions on the presence, or the lack, of genuine excitement displayed by the entrepreneurs who seek funding. However, there are less "heartfelt" ways for one to engage in a real business and make a living. One such approach is the "search fund model." This model has been used by some entrepreneurial-minded business school graduates in their journeys toward job independence.

Under the search fund model, the entrepreneur (principal), usually working as part of a team, raises a "blind" pool of capital from usually a group of angels in a given area. To obtain funding, like any other business, the principal has to prepare a funding proposal and a business plan along with all the credentials and qualifications. Once raised, such seed capital will fund the principal's search ex-penses and efforts until he/she finds some attractive business opportunities—usually involving some LBO or even turnaround candidates.

The efforts may take up to 2 years depending on the investment agreement. The process is not dissimilar to raising venture capital. The main difference is that in the blind pool arrangement, the principal already has a specific operational and technical experience that could be fully utilized in running and growing the acquired business.

Once promising opportunities are identified and approved for investment, the principal brings all parties—usually including a financial institution—together to close the deal. Needless to say, the original investors/angels keep the right of first refusal on all deals brought in by the principal and his/her team. At the end, the principal creates value by growing and later selling the acquired business(s). The final buyer may be the principal him/herself through a management buyout.

How someone is supposed to know the kind of equipment that a company has by looking at a listing in a directory is a good question, but a bit of experience or practice will quickly fill this lack of knowledge. For example, if the company is engaged in sheet-metal work, it most likely will not have lots of hockable equipment. All it really needs are some shears and breaks, equipment that is not very expensive, and which does not have much borrowing capacity. If in doubt, send the approach letter, discussed below, and later, when you call the owner, you may ask what kind of equipment the company has.

Admittedly, this approach is an exercise in logical deduction, but it works! And as was stated earlier, if you can get to an owner as he or she is in the process of deciding that the time has come to retire (or sell for whatever reason), you have an excellent chance of being the only potential buyer to whom the seller will talk. Truly, *a Quiet Deal!*

THE APPROACH LETTER

Once a potential target has been identified, it is necessary to contact the owner. The best way to do this is with a letter, followed by a telephone call.

THE LETTER ITSELF

The letter should be carefully crafted to hit the potential seller's "hot buttons," for you may never get a second chance to communicate with the seller. It appears that there are three main points to emphasize in the letter.

First, say something like "we would offer all cash or a substantial amount of *cash*, depending on the deal." Referring to cash is telling the potential seller that you are not trying to offer him or her stock (which to some business owners is "funny money" and something that may have cost this seller's friends dearly). It is quite unlikely that you would offer "all cash"—but you never know. The company may represent such an unusual opportunity that partners could be found that would provide the cash needed for an "all-cash" deal. Rather, it is what is referred to in the second part of this sentence that you probably will have to offer: a substantial amount of cash. What does "substantial" mean? Well, that depends on the situation and the company. Fifty, 60, or more percent is surely "substantial" in most people's minds. So, you are not saying something that is deliberately misleading. But certainly eye-catching!

The second point to emphasize is one of the most likely "hot buttons" which any entrepreneurial owner has: *an abhorrence of taxes*. Take advantage of this predisposition of a potential seller. Include a sentence such as "And we will try to structure the deal to be tax advantageous to you" to address this hot button. Again, if you structure the deal to be what is called a "purchase/sale of stock," something discussed in the next chapter, you would be doing what you say in the letter and, again, not be misrepresenting yourself. But certainly, you would be hitting one of the things that is near and dear to the heart of most every entrepreneur: *taxes*.

The third thing to emphasize in the letter is the matter of *confidentiality*. As already mentioned, most business owners are almost paranoid about keeping the fact that they are for sale confidential, so if you emphasize this fact to them in your initial letter, you will find fertile ground in which to plow. Saying something like "Naturally we will keep our conversations strictly confidential" may do the trick in this regard. If you later talk to the owner, you must continue to be discreet. Sometimes owners will not want to turn over their financial statements to a potential buyer unless the buyer gives the seller a "confidentiality agreement." This is relatively easy to do and does not need to be prepared by a lawyer. Merely a letter will suffice.

THE TELEPHONE CALL FOLLOW-UP

About a week after the letter should have been delivered, you should call the company president and inquire if he or she has received your letter. If the answer is affirmative, and the owner indicates a possible willingness to sell, you should at this point ask if the company is profitable. If it is *really unprofitable*, the company is most likely for sale! But if the owner can explain why he or she is not showing a profit, you might proceed. If a firm is not profitable, why waste time trying to do an "undoable" deal? Also in this conversation you can ask about such things as the extent of equipment, if you don't already know this. If this conversation goes well, you arrange to meet with the seller at a place of his or her choosing.

THE DUE DILIGENCE PROCESS

Assume that you have found a company that apparently meets all your criteria and is for sale. After you have gotten to meet the owner and reviewed, preliminarily, the company's financial statements, you now have the difficult process of doing what is called the **due diligence**. Describing the due diligence process is almost as difficult as doing one. But the whole process may be summarized this way: Why are you interested in this company? What are the factors that led you to think that this company would be a good target? To do a due diligence, you now have to fashion questions and an investigative process that that will get answers to these questions. It is simply not feasible to say "I want to know everything about this company." You probably don't have the time this extensive an investigation will take. Remember: Time will kill any deal!

Usually, you begin with sales. What is the foundation on which you build your sales forecast? Can you substantiate the numbers? Are your assumptions reasonable? (Much easier said than done!)

VERIFYING FINANCIAL STATEMENTS

To verify the financial statements, it is usually necessary to retain an accounting firm to do what is called an **accountant's review**. This means that the accounting firm you retain will have to go into the company and review the company's books of account, and in so doing, pass judgment on the target company's financial statements. This process can be a really troublesome one because the accounting of many middle-market firms leaves a lot to be desired.

The trick in this process is to be able to say whether or not there are substantial changes that need to be done in order to make the statements realistic—and how substantial these are. A friend of mine once was in the process of doing due diligence on a company that he wanted to buy. It was in the mail-order business, with most of the company's sales occurring over Christmas. In the course of negotiating, the potential buyer suspected that the owners were trying to conceal the fact that they were playing games with inventory in order to improve the company's Income Statement. Thinking that this was the problem, the buyer made a "Take it or leave it" offer to the sellers with a substantial reduction built in for "inventory obsolescence." The owners agreed, and the deal was completed—*without an accounting review.* The buyer said he wasn't concerned as he knew that the sellers were lying about their inventory. *After* the deal was completed, the buyer sent a major accounting firm in to do the accounting review. Some time later, the auditors called the buyer to report that they had found some discrepancy. "Not to worry," the new buyer said, "I know they were playing games with the inventory." The auditors replied, "Did you know the extent of the games they were playing?" When the owner heard the extent of the overstatement, he had to report this to the bank from whom he was borrowing the money to buy the company. When the bank heard the extent of the overstatement, they immediately called the loan. The brand-new buyer had no recourse but to file bankruptcy! A bitter lesson!

Another example of problems encountered in an accounting review occurred when a large company that was selling a division was asked for certification of the financial statements provided. The selling company agreed, and for a small sum the major accounting firm produced "certified" statements. Unfortunately, when an accounting auditor went in to verify these "certified" statements, the worms started to climb out of the books! How could these accounting records be so bad? How could the major accounting firm certify these statements? The answer was really simple: The company on which the statements were made was so small relative to the parent's statement that they were inconsequential to the parent company's statement! So don't think that just because the seller presents you with "certified" statements that you do not have to do an accounting audit.

The cost for an accounting audit for a typical middle-market firm might easily be in the order of $5,000 to $10,000. But instead of paying the accounting firm selected, you could make a deal with the accounting firm that if the deal goes through, the accounting firm will be hired to be the company's accountant. In this case the charge for the review will be blended into the first year's retainer fee. But if the deal does not go through, there will be no charge for the audit. Most middle-sized or small accounting firms will be hungry enough for new business to snap at this offer. Major accounting firms will not do this.

ASSET VERIFICATION AND APPRAISAL

If assets are a significant part of the selling firm's assets, it is usually necessary to hire an appraisal firm to verify the value of the assets. (Remember, as the LBO gets larger in price, the necessity of an appraisal diminishes; the deal then becomes a "cash flow" deal.) This process of hiring an appraisal firm was discussed in Chapter 11, so it will not be repeated here. But, in addition to the appraisal, it is quite useful to try to ascertain the condition of the equipment and/or building. If equipment has been neglected, large expenditures may be needed to place the machines in proper running order. True, the appraisal may catch this problem by giving the machines a lower value, but this does not always mean the buyer is aware of the "maintenance make-up" expense waiting once the company is purchased. A little observation and common sense can go a long way in this regard. What are the seller's repair policies? Does he or she have in-house repair capability? If so, how good is (are) the mechanic(s)? Is the plant dirty? If it is spotless, this is a good sign that the machines are well kept. If the shop is dirty, this is a good sign that the maintenance has been neglected—particularly if you know that the seller has been planning on selling the company for some time.

If real estate is involved it may be wise to retain a company to see if there is any pollution involved that is not obvious.

CUSTOMER SATISFACTION

When buying a business it is quite useful to be able to ask the customers what they think of the target. But getting to do this is often quite difficult or impossible. The reason for this is the typical seller's desire for strict secrecy in the sale. So how do you call up a customer and ask him or her what he or she thinks of the target company without revealing that you are trying to buy the company? Usually, about the only way you can do this is by some circuitous route. Perhaps you can get some friend in the industry to give you the impressions you need. Or, if you already know the industry, this problem is solved.

With regard to customer satisfaction, another problem that must be reckoned with is the problem of customers leaving after you buy the business. I doubt there is a sure way to prevent this, but *customer concentration* may be a clue. This problem is not only one of "losing a customer" but it is also a problem when trying to finance the target's receivables, as was discussed in Chapter 11. This is because there is a *concentration factor* that may preclude borrowing on any of the receivables. One buyer did a deal for a company only to find that several of the company's customers "took a hike" after he bought the company. This almost caused the buyer to fail. It is difficult to say how to prevent this, but one should always be on the alert for this contingency. As will be discussed in the notes to the Able Case, in Chapter 17, getting a seller's "noncompetition" agreement is certainly useful in this regard. If the seller is a large company spinning off this smaller subsidiary, the problem may be complicated. In any case, awareness of the problem may suggest a logical solution if one is possible.

DUE DILIGENCE "COOK BOOKS"

Lots of articles have been written purportedly to tell wannabe buyers everything they ever wanted to know about doing "due diligence." Some of these sources are voluminous and cover every imaginable question that might be asked. But a buyer should realize that no company is "perfect." And if you try to analyze the target to the bitter end you may, in fact, lose the target out of frustration on the part of the seller. It appears that the critical point to be considered is not to check on everything, but only the *critical* ones. Knowing everything about the target may seem like a good idea at the time, but if this prolongs the due diligence investigation unduly, antagonisms may arise—and for what purpose? To do the deal, or to be absolutely certain that you have not overlooked anything? To me this overexuberance in doing the due diligence merely reflects a lack of confidence on the part of the buyer.

This lack of confidence is not unlike the buyer who says "I am not going to buy any company until I have looked for at least 2 years." If you know what you are looking for, you may find it on your first attempt. "Just looking" for 2 years in and of itself is no guarantee that you will find the perfect target. This is where the criteria checklist comes in handy. It's not perfect, but it should take care of the most important points.

TO SUMMARIZE THE DUE DILIGENCE PROCESS

Aside from the obvious—doing an accounting audit and an appraisal of the target's equipment and/or building—how you do a due diligence investigation has to depend on the individual target. To not do a sufficient due diligence investigation is inexcusable; to overdo a due diligence may result in great satisfaction that you now know "everything" about the target, but this might be indeed a Pyrrhic victory. If the company is really a good target and you lose it because the seller lost patience with your investigation, then what satisfaction do you have?

SUMMARY

For many wannabe entrepreneurs without an exciting idea for starting a company, buying an existing company may be the best and fastest road to success. This chapter is the first of three that deal with this process. And for many companies, the road to expansion lies through doing acquisitions. This may be the best way to "fill the earnings gap."

After briefly mentioning how the so-called "conglomerates" were built—by getting a "pop in earnings" by paying a lower P/E price than the buying firm's P/E, ten criteria for a LBO were discussed. What is necessary to do an LBO, meaning that you are buying a company with mostly "other people's money"? Such critical factors as "hockable" assets were mentioned, and, of course, cash flow. While not pretending to be all inclusive, these ten factors cover most of the requirements necessary to do a LBO.

Once these criteria are understood, finding a likely target is next. Sometimes the wannabe entrepreneur may already know of an appropriate company that could be purchased through the medium of a LBO. Perhaps a relative has a business that would qualify. You never thought about buying the company because you thought that you did not have enough money. But knowing the secret of doing a LBO—especially the use of subordinated debt—may make the purchase possible. Other sources of finding a target were mentioned, but possibly the best way to find a target is through the use of deductive reasoning coupled with the use of a business directory. The best time to approach a would-be seller is at that moment when he or she finally says "I guess it is time to sell." If you have a letter on that person's desk asking in a proper way if he or she would be willing to talk about selling the company, it may be that you will have a good target and one that is a "quiet deal." Of course one does not know for certain that someone may want to sell their company, but with the right factors (e.g., time the company has been in existence) a certain amount of "good" possibilities will turn up. Then comes the introduction letter. Once a meeting with the owner is established and some basic ground rules established, it may be time to perform some due diligence. It was mentioned that this process requires a generous amount of "good faith" because it may not be possible—or *desirable*—to do the due diligence to an ultimate degree.

QUESTIONS FOR DISCUSSION

1. If you were the CEO of an emerging publicly held company, how could you get a "pop in earnings"? What risk do you take in doing this?

2. Go to a directory of manufacturing companies in your state—if possible—and select several possible companies for acquisition via a LBO. Next, evaluate these possible targets with respect to the criteria mentioned in this chapter. If such a directory is not available, look at the "For sale" listings in the *Wall Street Journal* or another newspaper and try to select several target companies for your review.

3. Other than using directories of manufacturers, what sources do you have for finding a company for sale? Discuss each source with respect to potential problems you might have in using these sources.

15

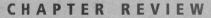

CHAPTER REVIEW

16

External Expansion: Technical Aspects of Acquiring a Firm

VALUING A CLOSELY HELD COMPANY

In Chapter 15 we discussed the criteria for a target for a leveraged buyout (LBO) and how to find a suitable target. But once a possible target has been found, the first thing that might be done is to value the prospective target to ascertain whether a deal is realistically possible. The approach taken here is to try to establish a "floor" and a "ceiling" price and then to negotiate between the two.

The calculation of a *ceiling* price seems intuitively reasonable from the point of view of an *acquiring* party, but why would the buyer want to calculate the *floor* price? Isn't this virtually bottomless? The two reasons to calculate a **floor price** are, first, to have a feel for the minimum price that the seller would accept. If you start to try to negotiate *below* this price, the conversation is likely to be rather short indeed. You may insult the potential seller and be asked to leave summarily. Insulting a seller is no way to start a negotiation! The second reason for calculating a floor price is to be able to "brag" to a potential lender how close your price is to the floor price. And, of course, this is a reason to calculate the **ceiling price**, as well, if the "agreed-upon price" is well short of this ceiling price. This ceiling price is really the maximum that you want to pay for this business. "See what a good deal we are getting?" If a potential lender feels that you—the buyer—are, in fact, getting a very good price, this will surely facilitate the procurement of the necessary financing. If the potential lender feels that you are paying "too much" for the target company, securing the requisite financing will be difficult at best and maybe impossible.

CALCULATING THE FLOOR PRICE

There are a number of factors that may be considered when calculating the floor price, some of which are reasonable and some which are quite unreasonable—but voiced, nevertheless!

ACCOUNTING BOOK VALUE

Accounting book value is probably the value most often cited as a *floor* price. Individual owners of a business may feel that there is some importance to this value ("Otherwise, why would accountants calculate it?"). But what is the firm's book value? And how did it get to what it is? Simply stated, the firm's *book value* is an accounting definition which results from the exercise of *accounting rules*. Does book value represent *economic value*? Possibly, but most likely not. Assets are listed at historical purchase price or some other value lower than that. When an asset is fully depreciated, it is written off of the company's books, even though it may have substantial value. And some assets may have appreciated in value enormously. For example, real estate (which is not depreciated) that might have been purchased in 1950 for $50,000 might be worth millions today. And it would be easy to cite other examples. No, book value is not a very good measure of what a firm is "worth," but saying that does not mean a thing if somebody *thinks* it means a lot!

There is a situation where book value takes on greater importance: the purchase of a subsidiary of a larger corporation. If a corporation sells a subsidiary at *less* than book value, the parent must take a hit to its Income Statement for the difference. This is definitely something a publicly owned company would not want to do, even if they agree that the subsidiary is "worth" less. How to get around this conundrum is difficult at best.

MARKET VALUE

When introducing **market value** into the question of a floor value, one factor is difficult to dispute. *If* the market value of some asset—say, the company's land and/or building—is known, this fact becomes rather indisputable. But very often in the purchase of middle-market firms, the market value of some or all of the assets is not known. An individual owner may or may not know the market value of all of the company's assets. An example of this was when two friends of mine were trying to acquire a manufacturing firm that was situated on a parcel of land of ten acres in a growing suburb of Los Angeles. The purchase price was fair for the business itself, without any consideration of the land! The two partners purchased the business and then proceeded to sell the manufacturing unit for what they had paid for the whole "package" and they were left with the land. They now owned *ten acres* of desirable land for a *zero* cost! Undoubtedly, if the East Coast parent company had known the market value of this ten acres of land, the price would have been substantially higher. But it didn't!

REPLACEMENT VALUE

One of the values that the seller will most likely mention is **replacement value**. And of all the possible values that might be mentioned, replacement value is probably the most irrelevant. But being a *higher* value than, say, book or market value, the seller might want to interject this value in an attempt to boost the value of the firm. "Why, you couldn't replace this machine for $100,000!" OK, but so what? Who would want to replace this machine with an identical one anyway? "Today, we might do this whole operation some other way, for example. . . ." So even though the replacement value is higher than some other value under discussion, it still is rather meaningless. But hope springs eternal. Prospective sellers will keep trying.

LIQUIDATION VALUE

While replacement value is of little value, **liquidation value** may be of enormous value to the party who knows what it is. This is why you the buyer do not want the seller to know what the appraisal value of the equipment is. Naturally, as a buyer I want to know what the "market value" and "quick sale value" of the equipment is, but I would very much prefer to have the owner unaware of this value. If the owner knows this value, especially the "quick sale" value, then this, combined with the low value of the other assets, will most likely be the *floor* in fact!

But "liquidation value" means more than just the *market* or *quick sale* value of equipment. It may involve all of the other assets, including the receivables and the inventory. Any questionable Accounts Receivable should be subtracted as should obsolete or otherwise questionable inventory. Potential buyers might be better able to face up to reality than some owners regarding these assets, especially the obsolete inventory. Remember, hope still springs eternal! Some owners may think that even though some inventory may not have turned over in years, it is still quite valuable. Trying to get good estimates of such items as obsolete inventory may be easier said than done. Liquidation value should apply to the *liabilities* side as well. Are there items that should be written off? Or added? Are there impending judgments that should be entered onto the statements? These might be items that would be added to certified statements but which were omitted from the *compiled* statement with which you are working.

ADJUSTED BOOK VALUE—THE SUGGESTED METHOD

When making an "adjusted" book value estimate of the target's assets and liabilities, you are trying to put economically reasonable values on the firm's assets and liabilities. You can begin with the company's cash. Is this a reasonable number? Or was this a quirk, an aberration due to some point in time? Perhaps it should be less. How does the balance compare with prior years?

Next, the firm's Accounts Receivable. Normally you subtract the value of the Accounts Receivable that are more than, say, 90 days overdue.

INVENTORY AND EQUIPMENT

Then the inventory is valued. How much of the inventory is *obsolete*? If you, the buyer, can get the seller to estimate how much of the inventory is obsolete, then this amount would be subtracted from the inventory total. A friend of mine, when doing a "walk-through" of the seller's plant, would ask the owner/seller how much of the inventory was obsolete? If the seller said "None," the would-be buyer would start to take a very skeptical approach to the whole deal, for virtually *every* manufacturing company has some obsolete inventory. If the potential seller gave an estimate, the buyer would respond "And you will take a note for this?" If the seller said "Yes"—and how could he or she say anything other than yes—then the potential buyer felt that he had established a *principle* with this statement. The seller said he or she would take a note! Now all that needed to be decided was the *amount* of the note!

Sometimes it might be necessary to calculate or estimate the *turnover ratio* of the inventory. If a good bit of the inventory is turning over quite slowly, compared to what might be considered "normal," then some percentage might be applied to the value of the entire inventory, thereby reducing its value. A more normal problem that might arise with putting an *adjusted* value on inventory is whether the inventory is valued on the company's books under the FIFO or LIFO method. If it is LIFO, the inventory might have old, and thus quite unrealistic, values. More up-to-date values might be placed on the inventory. When working with a seller who is presenting you with *compiled statements* (remember from Chapter 3 that most middle-market firms have only compiled statements), it is wise to check to make sure that the seller did not put an artificial value on the inventory. Such a value might result from carrying the inventory at the *higher of cost or market*. This would do wonders for the profit and book value of the firm, but it would be strictly contrived. Even though a compiled statement says nothing about the statement complying with GAAP, such a presentation is so blatant as to represent deception. (See Chapter 3.) Appearing to use FIFO and then stating the inventory at NIFO (Next-In-First-Out) is equally deceptive. Cheating would be more to the point! But some sellers are so greedy that they might resort to any manner of deception.

It is useful to point out here that most sellers are not sophisticated in the technique of selling their company. These sellers may have been extremely adroit in running their business, but the odds are that they have never sold a business before and do not really know the technique—not to mention the "tricks"—of selling a business. And many of these very independent entrepreneurs/owners are too proud to even ask for advice for selling their business. This puts the knowledgeable buyer at a tremendous advantage in the whole process of buying a middle-market business.

Perhaps the most important adjustment that is made to the company's assets concerns its equipment, especially if the company is a manufacturing firm. "Book value" might be quite misleading, as many assets might be written off the company's books, even though they are still in operating order. When an appraisal is made, the potential buyer has a choice of listing the equipment at *market* value or *quick sale* value. If the buyer feels that he or she is in a strong position relative to the seller, it would seem natural that the buyer would list the equipment at *quick sale* value, for this really is the lower of the two. But otherwise the buyer might feel that listing the firm's equipment at *market value* might be advisable. This will produce a higher value for this "floor" value, but this might be quite useful when discussing the company's floor value with a prospective lender. By having a higher floor, the potential buyer might be able to show how close he or she was coming to the floor for this target. Again, something akin to bragging rights!

Also, if property has been written off the company's books, in this adjustment process it is important to put it back in. A knowledgeable LBO lender will do this as a matter of course, but you do it too.

Incidentally, in my experience, a rough estimate of the quick sale value of the target's equipment might be the company's depreciated book value of the equipment. One should not take this suggestion too literally, but it is a crude estimate of quick sale value in a number of cases. At least it suggests the order of magnitude.

LIABILITIES

Two of the most common liabilities that should be adjusted are "Loans from Stockholder" and "Reserve for Deferred Federal Income Tax." The latter, which may be either an asset or a liability, is, technically, not an asset or a liability; it is simply a **reserve**. This reserve simply goes away when the target company is purchased via a purchase of assets. There is not really an asset or liability in the usual sense. So, by removing this item, you are actually *decreasing* the adjusted book value if the reserve is shown as an asset, or *increasing* the adjusted book value if it is shown as a liability.

The often-seen "Loan from Stockholder" is another matter. I feel strongly that this item amounts to *de facto* equity and, as such, should be treated as you do the Common Stock account on the Balance Sheet. The fact that the owner(s) elected to put the additional money into the company as a "loan" instead of a stock purchase is really a matter of form and not substance. If you are buying the company—assets or stock—you are not buying the company *and* buying the stock as well. This would be a case of double counting! Unfortunately, some owners do not see it this way. They feel that they "loaned" the money to the company and they are entitled to be repaid the amount the same as any other lender. Sometimes this can be a very nettlesome problem.

DETERMINING THE CEILING

There are two basic approaches to determining the **ceiling price** that *you want to pay for the business*. First—but of least importance—is a practice familiar to students of a basic corporate finance course: discounting the cash flows back to the present time to arrive at a purchase price. Alfred Rappaport's Alcar model is an example of such a process and is summarized in the Appendix to this chapter. While quite common in valuing rather large deals, it is practically *never* used in middle-market transactions.

The most common way of valuing middle-market firms is by taking the **adjusted EBITDA** (EBITDA stands for Earnings Before Interest and Taxes [EBIT] plus depreciation plus amortization of intangibles such as goodwill) and multiplying it by some multiple. This multiple usually is between two and nine. For most leveraged buyout situations, the multiple most often used is now between $3\frac{1}{2}$ and 5. Interestingly enough, this rule of thumb is independent of the industry that the target is in, with the exception of high-tech deals and computer-related deals. And of course Internet deals! But for "plain-vanilla" deals—metal cutting or plastics forming deals, for example—this span of multiples probably accounts for about 75 to 80 percent of them (this is strictly a guess, however). There is no way of knowing exactly what this multiple might be for two reasons. First, no outsider would know how and how much the EBIT figures are being "adjusted," and, second, so many of these private deals are not reported to services such as the ones which report on the public (and large) deals. Personal experience also suggests that that if a target is priced at much more than about five times adjusted EBITDA, the deal does not provide enough NOCF" (cash flow) to service the loans.

It sometimes happens that the price estimated by using adjusted EBITDA is actually *less* than the "floor" price. This is occasioned usually by a firm having very anemic earnings—even if it is still "making a profit." In this anomaly, it may be that the deal is "doable," but one would suspect that something was "wrong" with the deal. It does happen, and one should be happy when a doable deal does come up this way.

To adjust EBITDA you start with the reported pre-tax profit. To this you add the amount of depreciation that is over and above what we called "Necessary discretionary" expenditures, capital expenditures that must be made (see Chapter 7). On many leveraged buyouts of middle-market firms, this figure might be low or even zero. This is so because many targets for a LBO are rather old firms that have all the equipment they need and are situated in a building that does not need repairs or replacement. To this is added any amortization charge that the target company is taking, which is rare for middle-market firms. Such an amortization might be the amortization of goodwill from making an acquisition of another company. In the past, accountants called this "Excess of Purchase Price Over Asset Value," but CPAs are trying to wean themselves from this euphemism, and now they call it simply "goodwill."

For middle-market, privately owned firms, however, the *real* adjustment to EBIT comes from the deletion of all of the "personal" expenses that the old ownership incurred and which will "go away" with the new ownership. Typically, outgoing owners will volunteer what these "goodies" are because they will realize all too soon that by doing so they can elevate pre-tax profit—the item on which the value of the company is based. In fact, it is surprising how many older business owners who want to sell their business and retire will volunteer these admissions on the telephone when approached by a prospective seller. Admissions that might seriously get them into trouble if the "prospective buyer" turned out to be an Internal Revenue agent! Many are the kinds of things that private business owners "load" onto their companies. Excess autos and airplanes, excess expense accounts, improvements to their personal homes (blatant), and, most commonly, relatives on the payroll who do not really work or, at least, do not earn their salary are easy examples of these "extra" expenses that would not be there under new ownership. Do not assume that these "goodies" would not amount to much! In many cases, the pre-tax profit might be doubled or even increased more by the removal of the questionable items. Sometimes, one finds that the reported loss actually becomes a profit.

When discussing the "adjustment" process of EBIT, we should give special attention to a statement by some sellers of businesses which do a substantial amount of cash sales. In these cases, the seller might "suggest," if not outright say, that they were taking a certain amount of cash from the proceeds and not reporting it. If this is factored into the "adjustment" of EBIT, the buyer might be in for a huge surprise. "What, you didn't get that much?" might be the reply to your query if, after the fact, you found that you were not able to realize the suggested cash amount. But at that point, what can you, the buyer, do about it? There will be no written record of this "extra" amount, so how can you go back to the seller and complain? There will be no written record because the seller, unless he or she is stupid, will not put something that is blatantly illegal—not reporting cash sales on the Income Tax Report—in writing. No, if some seller suggests that there is "tax-free" money to be had, the buyer will be well advised to ignore all such incantations. The difference between these "suggested dollar amounts" and the goodies alluded to above is that the goodies can be verified with actual accounting records. No record, no addition!

NEGOTIATING BETWEEN THE FLOOR AND THE CEILING

Once the buyer settles on the floor and ceiling price, he or she then has to negotiate a price with the seller. It is wise to be aware of the floor value in particular, because it would be unwise to approach the seller with an offer so low that he or she is insulted. It would be much better to ask the seller what he or she wants in the way of a selling price than to make the first offer. Whatever the seller says suddenly becomes the "ceiling" and you can bargain from there. If the price the seller suggests is *equal to or less than* the ceiling the buyer has calculated, then the potential buyer has reason to continue the negotiation.

But if the seller's asking price is well above the ceiling price, the buyer would do well to retire from the negotiation. It may be that the seller will come down in price, but he or she might want, in return, such a high percentage of cash in the down payment as to make the purchase impossible for a buyer doing a leveraged buyout. Ideally, the "right" target will have a price suggested by the seller that is within the floor and ceiling. Then the buyer can make a point of saying "Hey, I'm offering you just about what you asked, so can't you give me some benefits?"

Remember, the name of the game in doing a LBO is terms, not necessarily the lowest price. If you are offering an "all-cash deal," it is reasonable to bargain as hard as you like and still get the deal. But when doing a LBO it is imperative that the seller grant some concessions, like taking a subordinated note and some "soft dollars"—contracts for such things as consulting that can be written off for tax purposes and the face amount of which is counted as part of the purchase price. (More on these two things below.)

Bargaining the seller down from what might be a reasonable price might be quite counter-productive. It does not make sense to take pride in getting the seller "down" in price if the deal is not "doable"! If a seller feels that he or she is getting approximately the "asked" price, he or she will be much more agreeable when asked to grant terms—terms that might make the deal possible for a LBO buyer. It cannot be stressed enough that in doing a successful LBO, there must be a feeling of "win-win" for the parties. You really can't have an "I win, you lose" situation; at least, I have never seen or heard of one. If the seller's advisers feel that you the buyer are getting "too much" in the deal, the odds are that they will discourage the seller and there will be no deal! Successful negotiation in a LBO is very definitely a win-win situation.

FORMS OF TRANSACTIONS

Once the floor and ceiling prices have been determined, it may be time to contemplate the **form of transaction** that might be used to acquire the target firm. By "form of transaction" is meant the type of purchase for the deal. There are two types of transactions that might be used:

- A purchase/sale of assets, in which you purchase any or all of the assets and any or some of the liabilities,

- And purchase/sale of stock, in which you purchase the stock of the selling shareholder, which means you have purchased all the assets and all the liabilities including the contingent liabilities.

Each of these two forms has its own peculiarities and advantages and disadvantages. *In order to work effectively in the field of acquisitions it is imperative that one know the advantages and disadvantages of each method.* First we will discuss purchase of assets, after which we will discuss the purchase of stock.

PURCHASE/SALE OF ASSETS

In a **purchase/sale of assets**, the buyer buys *any or all of the assets and any or none of the liabilities*. The seller of these assets is the corporation that owns these assets; no individual is involved. The board of directors must pass a resolution to sell the assets. It may come as a surprise to some to learn that under most charters of corporations in the United States, the board of directors may sell the corporation's assets without asking permission or approval of the corporation's stockholders. With primarily privately owned middle-market firms, this issue practically never comes up because the ownership/management/board of directors of the corporation are all one and the same, or practically so.

In a sale of assets, the corporation sells the assets, and, following the sale, it must determine the **depreciation recapture** tax, if any, that must be paid on the depreciable assets subject to such recapture. Only after this tax is paid can the corporation pay a **liquidating dividend** of the assets (net of any liabilities) to its stockholders and go out of business. At that point the stockholders will have to pay capital gains tax (or ordinary income tax under rare circumstances) on all the amounts above their "basis" in the corporation. **Basis** is a tax term meaning what an individual paid for the assets—or stock. Before continuing this discussion of the purchase/sale of assets, it may be well to review the mechanics of *depreciation recapture*.

Depreciation Recapture

There are two sections of the tax code that collectively deal with what is called depreciation recapture. This tax came about when companies were selling their equipment and, possibly, leasing it back. The buyer would then depreciate the same piece of equipment and reduce its tax accordingly. Section 1245 deals with depreciation recapture on depreciable "personalty," meaning usually equipment and rolling stock—something other than real estate. Under Section 1245, if a depreciable asset is sold for more than the depreciated book value, the gain above this amount is subject to ordinary corporate income tax. Consider the following example.

Original price of a piece of machinery:	$100,000
Amount of depreciation taken at time of sale:	$ 70,000
Depreciated or "book value" of the machine:	$ 30,000
Sale price of the machine:	$ 80,000
Amount subject to depreciation recapture:	$ 50,000
Tax due on this "ordinary" income at 34 percent tax rate:	$ 17,000

Depreciation recapture of real property falls under Section 1250, concerning land and buildings attached thereto. This applies only to the amount of depreciation over and above *straight line depreciation*. This may mean that *no* depreciation recapture tax is due on the real property.

When selling assets, it will not take long for the seller to realize that it makes a considerable amount of difference how the purchase price for *all* of the assets is distributed to the different categories of assets and the specific assets themselves. If more of the "purchase price" can be allocated to assets that would not be subject to depreciation recapture, and less to those assets that are subject to recapture, then the selling corporation and its stockholders will be much better off financially. To do this, an astute accountant, who is in charge of doing the accounting for the liquidation of the business, can allocate more of the purchase price to such things a inventory and real property not subject to recapture. If value is ascribed to such "intangibles" as lists of customers, "goodwill" may result which may make the buyer unhappy if he or she cannot depreciate these assets for tax purposes. This is another reason for having the support of competent and imaginative accountants (and tax advisers) for both parties to the deal.

When specific value is ascribed to such things as equipment, the problem of depreciation recapture tax is exacerbated by the fact that the sale of the equipment is subject to sales tax in states that have applicable sales tax. This is usually a problem in very small deals where the principal assets are equipment and, possibly, inventory. Some buyers attempt to keep the deal as small as possible, so instead of buying all the assets and liabilities, they want to buy only the inventory, equipment, and name of the company. The seller is left to collect all the receivables and pay off all of the liabilities. I feel that this is usually not a good practice for doing a LBO, because the buyer is giving up the assets that can be "hocked" for the most money and buying the ones on which one cannot borrow as much, such as inventory. Also, it is convenient to take over the payables and, in so doing, to keep the suppliers that the "old" company had. These suppliers can then be paid off in the normal course of trade. Doing this kind of "short-cut" deal will usually result in a lower percentage of "cash down payment" than will buying all the assets and all the liabilities.

When many sellers are reminded of the dreaded "depreciation recapture" tax, a great deal of emotion takes over their reasoning. Anything that pertains to that utterly distasteful word *taxes* is anathema to most entrepreneurial business owners. By talking about the prospect of paying taxes on "all that depreciation" one would surely be touching one of the seller's hot buttons. Instead of very carefully calculating how much tax would have to be paid, many a business owner would quickly opt for "What other choice do I have?" When this happens, there might be an advantage for the buyer, an advantage that will be discussed subsequently.

ADVANTAGES AND DISADVANTAGES OF AN ASSET PURCHASE

As we have already seen, the sale of assets is decidedly something that the seller wants to avoid. If he or she can sell stock, this "terrible situation" of paying depreciation tax—and maybe a substantial amount of sales tax—can be avoided. So, from a seller's point of view, there is little if anything to recommend the form of transaction known as purchase/sale of assets.

From the buyer's point of view, however, there is much to recommend the "purchase of assets" form of transaction.

Taxes

First, there is the tax advantage. The buyer can write up the assets to the lower of cost or market. This means that depreciable assets such as machinery can be written *up* to market value (or less, if that is what was paid for the asset) and then depreciated *down* from there. This could have a significant positive influence on the rate of return that one would expect to receive from an investment.

Contingent Liability

As if the ability to write up the depreciable assets were not enough, there are two other advantages to the buyer in an "asset purchase." One is the ability to escape any **contingent liability**. Contingent liability can come from a number of situations—product liability, for example. Suppose the company you are purchasing is an old manufacturer of machinery. Back in 1960, the company made a machine with a guardrail attached. Over the years, someone took the guardrail off the machine, with the result that recently, someone was hurt by operating this machine. The injured party sues the company that made the machine. If this were a "sale of stock" transaction, the company might still be held liable, and you as the new owner would have to contend with this problem. Fortunately, the corporation might have product liability insurance that would cover this lawsuit.

There are other situations—a medical claim, for example—in which insurance might cover the contingent liability in a sale of stock transaction. After a sale of stock transaction, someone might appear at the company and claim that he or she was injured on the job in the past. Because it was a job-related injury, the corporation is responsible. The company's health insurance might cover part of the claim, but what if the claim is for more than the insurance will pay? I saw such a situation in which someone claimed a back injury and the ultimate claim was for about $290,000 over and above what the company's insurance would pay. A very unpleasant surprise. For the most part, however, these liabilities can be protected against by insurance.

The most important contingent liability that might crop up in the purchase/sale of stock transaction is the matter of taxes. The Internal Revenue Service may audit the company's books and go back 3 years (7 if there is fraud). And this is where the problem comes in. Virtually every privately owned firm has items of expense that *might be disallowed* by the IRS. The fact that these items occurred *before* the purchase of the company by the new owners is completely immaterial. It is the *corporation* that is being audited, completely independent of its stockholder(s). If the corporate "goodies" are excessive, and the IRS disallows these items as legitimate expense items, the tax bill, including interest and, possibly, penalties can be significant. By "purchasing assets" the buyer effectively escapes this contingent liability. In rare cases, particularly if there is fraud, the IRS might be able to "follow the assets" and go after the buyer of the assets to recover the assets for liquidation and recover money owed the IRS, but this is quite unusual. If the buyer purchases stock, however, there is a way that he or she might be able to protect himself or herself from being harmed by such contingent claims, including taxes owed.

The Right of Offset Clause

If the buyer gives the seller a note for a portion of the purchase price—and this will always be the case in a leveraged buyout—then the buyer can insert into the note a clause that is called the **right of offset**. In this clause it is stipulated that if the new buyer has to pay some claim, such as taxes, for "something" that happened before the new buyer purchased the stock of the company, then the buyer has a right to *subtract* that amount from the amount of the note that is tendered to the seller. More on this below.

Fraudulent Conveyance

The third major advantage of a "purchase of assets" transaction is the fact that under this form of transaction, the buyer's lender can escape the provisions of what is known in some states as **fraudulent conveyance**. In California, for example, there is a state statute that applies to a company that is sold via a purchase of stock, then goes bankrupt during the first year after the sale because of the excessive debt incurred to purchase the company. There are Balance Sheet tests for whether the debt is excessive; the secured lender(s) that provided the loans might be reclassified as having lower priority than the former debtors who might get hurt because of this bankruptcy. In short, the court would place the *new secured lender after* the company's old creditors, even though they were unsecured general creditors. This whole problem of fraudulent conveyance can be avoided through a purchase of assets form of transaction. This is why most finance companies that finance leveraged buyouts will not touch a deal if the form of transaction is a "purchase/sale of stock."

Interestingly enough, if a bank is brought in to provide the financing for a LBO, the buyer will have to pay the bank to retain a lawyer to advise the bank on the legality of the loan. Invariably, the lawyer who is retained (at the *expense* of the potential buyer; the fee for this might be in the order of $20,000 to $50,000 for a middle-market size deal), will advise the bank that the amount of leverage employed by the buyer's corporation would mean that the provisions of the fraudulent conveyance rule would apply.[▲] The bank's loan officers will then make a "business decision" that they do not believe that the company will

---

[▲] A similar law, called "Illegal Redemption" might be applied where the owner of a business borrows an "excessive" amount of money and gives the lender a secured position that places the company's existing creditors in a disadvantageous position. The owner then takes this newly acquired money and redeems some of his or her stock. In this case, the court can step in and waive the secured position of the secured lender.

go bankrupt in the first year of operation by the new owner, and therefore they will disregard the warning of their lawyer. (And if they were to assume bankruptcy in the first year, they would not make the loan!) This exercise seems a bit unwarranted from the buyer's point of view, but, unfortunately, this is just one more of those necessary expenses of doing business.

PURCHASE/SALE OF STOCK

In a **purchase/sale of stock** the buyer buys from the selling stockholder(s) all, or sometimes part, of the stock of the corporation. Actually, the exact process of the transaction is for the buyer to establish a new corporation, usually with the name of something like XYZ Acquisition Corporation. This new corporation will then be the one to buy the stock of the selling shareholder(s). When this happens, there is arranged a tax-free merger of the old (XYZ) corporation into the new (XYZ Acquisition) corporation. The old corporation then relinquishes its name and the new corporation assumes the name of the old corporation and drops its "acquisition" name.

When the buyer buys the stock of the target company it buys *all the assets and all the liabilities, including any contingent liabilities*. The old corporation is not affected at all. The transaction is entirely outside of the old corporation; it is strictly with the selling shareholder(s).

The major—and only?—apparent advantage of a purchase/sale of stock is to the selling shareholders, who will receive capital gains treatment on their capital gains all over their "basis" in that stock. If the company was founded 30 years ago with a relatively small (by today's standard) amount of capital, say $50,000, and the sale price is $5 million (excluding "side" contracts that will be called "soft-dollar contracts"), then that stockholder has capital gains treatment on $4,950,000! And at today's low capital gains tax rate of 20 percent *versus* the maximum ordinary income tax rate of 39.7 percent, this advantage is, indeed, worth noting!

Furthermore, the seller does not have to worry about *any* contingent liability after the sale. Any such problems are now the worry of the buyer, or more correctly, the buyer's corporation. For many sellers this is more important than even the tax advantage. This is, of course, precluding any fraud on the part of the selling shareholder.

With these important advantages all going to the seller, what are the advantages to the buyer of this form of transaction? On the surface, there are none. With a purchase/sale of assets the buyer can write up the assets and then depreciate them from this higher basis, thus getting a tax advantage that might be highly significant. Under a purchase/sale of stock, it cannot do that, unless it wants to pay a depreciation recapture tax and then start depreciating the asset from its new value—something practically no one would do. Under a purchase/sale of assets, the buyer can escape virtually all contingent liability; under a purchase/sale of stock, the *buyer gets any and all of the contingent liability*.

So why would a buyer agree to a purchase/sale of stock? It is precisely because *all* of the advantages fall on the seller that a *buyer* might agree to a purchase/sale of stock. If the buyer is giving these really valuable advantages to the seller, the buyer should feel that he or she may ask the seller for some advantages or concessions in return. The buyer could ask that the seller take, as part of the purchase price, "soft-dollar contracts" that can be written off as expense by the buyer. Or that the seller take a (subordinated) note for part of the purchase price—with a "Right of Offset Clause" included, naturally.

In short, because the buyer is giving several significant advantages to the seller, he or she should feel that he or she can ask for concessions from the seller that make the WHOLE DEAL doable.

The buyer must remember that the name of the game in doing a leveraged buyout is *terms*. What difference does it make to the buyer if he or she cannot get larger depreciation charges, if the deal is attractive at the current depreciation (and tax) level? And what difference does it make to the buyer if the seller gets highly advantageous tax treatment on the sale of his or her stock? None, if the buyer gets what he or she wants: the terms that make the deal possible! Remember, for a deal to be successful it must be a "win-win" situation. Seldom, if ever, is a deal done where the situation is "I win, you lose."

Probably the single most important concession that the seller can make to the buyer is the *acceptance of a subordinated note*. By accepting this subordinated note, that is subordinated to any bank borrowing that the buyer makes, the seller is essentially putting up the bulk of the equity required by a bank when it calculates the all-important Debt/Equity ratio for the LBO deal. Remember that subordinated debt—and in this case it will be "specifically subordinated" debt to the lender—represents *de facto equity*. It is debt, but it serves as equity!

Incidentally, it is not a good idea to make a point of saying to the seller that the note is subordinated. Instead, make a statement in the offer letter that ". . . naturally this note would be subordinated to any bank borrowing that might be made in the course of buying the business." If questioned about this, one might say "Oh, that is standard. Remember, if you and I were to collude, we could take the bank to the proverbial cleaners." And if pushed, I would merely shrug my shoulders and say "I'm sorry but this is a deal breaker. I can't do anything about this." Without making any more of this, the seller will usually acquiesce and the matter is dropped. Seldom, if ever, does a seller realize that he or she is actually *putting up the buyer's equity*. But even if the seller realizes that he or she is, in effect, putting up the bulk of the buyer's equity, this is not as significant as a tax or other advantage. So does a purchase of stock transaction give *all* the benefits to the seller? I think not.

Soft Dollars

As mentioned, it is possible to put part of the purchase price, whether the form of transaction is purchase/sale of assets *or* purchase/sale of stock, into contracts between the acquiring corporation and the seller(s). Because these contracts can be written off to ordinary expense to the acquiring corporation, they are called "soft-dollar" contracts or, simply, *soft dollars*. Other parts of the purchase price cannot be written off as expense; they must be paid for with after-tax dollars. The "cash-down" part of the purchase price and the (subordinated) note cannot be "expensed" to the acquiring corporation. So making part of the purchase price "expensable" adds quite a bit to the attractiveness of the deal from the buyer's point of view, especially if the buyer agrees to a purchase/sale of stock. Under a purchase/sale of stock, the buyer gives up the option of raising the depreciable basis of an asset in order to take an increased depreciation charge against the asset—and thus reduce its taxes. But by putting part of the purchase price into these soft-dollar contracts, the buyer recoups all or part of the tax break that had been given up in agreeing to a purchase/sale of stock form of transaction.

Perhaps the most typical soft-dollar contract is the one restricting competition from the selling shareholder or the shareholder(s) of a corporation that is selling its assets. This contract, called a *noncompete agreement*, provides that the selling shareholder cannot go into the same business within a certain geographic distance and for a specified period of time. The trick in writing such an agreement is to make it "protective" of the buying corporation, but not so restrictive as to be thrown out in a subsequent legal challenge. In general, the law provides that no person shall be denied an opportunity to "make a living." This means, loosely that the terms of the noncompete agreement have to be such that the seller cannot be denied *unreasonably* an opportunity to engage in the business he or she knows. For example, if the acquired firm does business in a four-county area, it may be reasonable to prohibit the seller from engaging in that business in those four counties, but not outside of those four counties. If the acquired firm does business nationally, the problem of writing a noncompete agreement becomes trickier and requires the service of an experienced lawyer to write a contract that will stand up against challenge. But no matter how difficult the problem may be, the buyer should write such a contract to keep the seller from going out and starting a business with his or her "old" customers in direct competition with the buyer's new corporation.

Furthermore, even if the buyer is paying *all cash*, it behooves the buyer to specify that *part* of the purchase price be attributed to a noncompete agreement. Because this contract is "expensable" to the corporation, one might think that he or she could put a large part of the purchase price into this contract. Such thinking is, however, naïve. The amount of this expense item must be "reasonable" in the eyes of the IRS. This is another reason for using the services of an experienced lawyer and accountant in doing an acquisition. Knowing how much the IRS will approve comes with experience in doing deals, and this is what the buyer is paying for.

Perhaps the second most common "soft-dollar" contract is one for "consulting services." This is another contract that should be in the purchase price even if the buyer is paying all cash. This contract provides that the seller (typically) will provide consulting services to the new owners over a period of time. A typical contract might provide that the seller be "on call" for a certain number of hours per month. This usually means that the seller be available for a telephone conversation; it typically does *not* mean that the seller has to physically come to the business for the stipulated period of time.

Aside from the obvious advantage of being able to write off against taxes a portion of the purchase price, this soft-dollar contract is quite useful to the new owner(s) when questions arise concerning something that happened in the past that only the former owner knows. But the new owner must exercise prudence when putting a portion of the purchase price into this soft-dollar account. The dollar amount that might be placed on this expense item should also bear some resemblance to the salary earned by the former owner. The higher the former owner's salary, the higher the per-hour fee for his or her "consulting services," and thus the higher the amount of this soft-dollar amount that might be considered "reasonable."

Another "soft-dollar" item that might be used is the royalty on patents. As long as the owner of the business personally owns the patents, if the company which he or she owns pays him or her a "royalty," this payment is "ordinary expense" to the company paying the royalty and "ordinary income" to the individual receiving the payment. But assuming that the patent(s) is a capital asset as soon as the owner sells the business, this royalty payment becomes a capital gain to the person receiving it. This is quite an interesting soft-dollar item that might be included in the purchase price; it is the best of both worlds for the new company paying it and the individual receiving it.

SUMMARY

In the initial meeting or sometime soon thereafter, it is customary for the seller to provide the prospective buyer with the company's financial statements. At this point the buyer-to-be may ask the seller what price he or she was "thinking about." With the statements in hand, one can make a quick guess of the reasonableness of this "asking price." But it behooves the would-be buyer to let the seller name the first price. (That then becomes the ceiling.) Determining the "price" for a privately held company is usually done by establishing a *floor* and a *ceiling* price. Why a "floor," one might ask. Isn't zero the floor? The reason for establishing a floor price is to get an idea of the point at which the seller will feel that an offering price is insulting. The ceiling price is what you, the buyer think is *your* ceiling price. This may not be the most someone else might pay, but that is immaterial. The main thing about establishing the ceiling is to get an *adjusted EBITDA*. The secret is in making the adjustment to the raw EBITDA. What would EBITDA look like with you owning the business?

The critical thing to keep in mind is that if the deal is to succeed, it must be a *win-win* situation. Thinking that you the buyer are going to "beat" the seller is usually a good way to squelch a deal.

After getting the price range, the most important consideration is the form of transaction that you the wannabe buyer will offer. Understanding the advantages of the "purchase/sale of stock" form of transaction and the "purchase/sale of assets" form is absolutely critical whenever negotiating the purchase/sale of a company.

As part of the payment of the purchase price, the buyer will offer the seller a subordinated note—specifically subordinated to the buyer's bank. It is the acceptance of this subordinated note that really makes a LBO possible. By adding this note to the buyer's equity when computing the D/E, the deal becomes possible, where otherwise it would be impossible because of the (terrible) D/E ratio resulting if the subordinated debt weren't counted as equity.

The chapter concluded with a discussion of what are called "soft dollars." Certain contracts between the new, acquiring company and the seller can be used as part of compensation for the purchase price. This makes that part of the purchase price tax deductible, something that may be quite important.

QUESTIONS FOR DISCUSSION

1. You are discussing the purchase/sale of a company with the seller. You are told that the seller wants to do a "purchase/sale of stock" type of transaction. What do you think of this request? How would you respond to this request? Does your source of financing influence your decision to accept or reject this request? Explain your reasoning in selecting the type of transaction.

2. You have just started discussions with a potential seller for his company. You intend to do a LBO on this transaction. He advises you that he wants to talk to: (a) his accountant, or (b) his attorney. What difference does it make to you as to whether he talks to his accountant or his lawyer? Explain your reasoning.

3. Write a letter of introduction for yourself to a company that is a potential target for a LBO. What points do you wish to make in this letter?

4. How would you value a closely held company that you are considering to purchase via an asset-based LBO? Would you bother to compute a floor value *and* a ceiling value? Why?

16

CHAPTER REVIEW

Appendix: Summary of Rappaport's Alcar Model

One of the most-used models for valuing large firms is one Alfred Rappaport first introduced in an article in 1979, and later in a book, called the Alcar model.▲ He says that the process of analyzing acquisitions lies in three broad stages: planning, search and screen, and financial evaluation. As a prelude he urges firms to do a self-evaluation of their own company, asking such questions as "How much is my company worth?" and "How would it change with some hypothetical acquisitions?" With this self-evaluation done, the reader is then taken through the six steps involved in the model.

THE SIX STEPS

STEP 1

Assuming an acquisition for cash, the first step is to project the target's cash flow. For this purpose he uses the following formula:

$$CF_t = S_{t-1} (1 + g_t) (p_t) (1 - T_t) - (S_t - S_{t-1}) (f_t + w_t)$$

Where

CF = Cash flow

S = Sales

g = Annual growth rate in Sales

p = EBIT as a percentage of Sales

T = Income tax rate

f = Capital investment required (i.e., total capital investment net of replacement of existing capacity estimated by depreciation) per dollar of Sales increase

w = Cash required for net working capital per dollar of Sales increase

The reader will notice that is not unlike our Item 7, Net Change in Cash (see Chapter 4), except that in this model no account is taken of any Priority Outflows. Working capital and capital expenditures (Discretionary Outflows) are included as they are in our model.

▲ Alfred Rappaport, "Strategic analysis for more profitable decisions," *Harvard Business Review*, July–August 1979, 99–110. Alfred Rappaport, *Creating Shareholder Value*, New York: The Free Press, 1986. Two other DCF models that might interest someone doing "big company" valuations are: G. Bennett Stewart, *The Quest for Value*, New York: Harper Business, 1991; and Tom Copeland and Jack Murrin, *Valuation: Measuring and Managing the Value of Companies*, New York: John Wiley and Sons, 1994.

STEP 2

Estimate the minimum acceptable rate of return. Rappaport does this by utilizing the well-known CAPM model to estimate the cost of equity capital, such as was shown in the discussion of Weston's capital budgeting model in the Appendix to Chapter 5, and then he uses a weighted average cost of capital to include the "cost of debt."

STEP 3

Compute the maximum acceptable cash price. He does this by forming a matrix where the row stubs are the three possible scenarios (most likely, conservative, and optimistic). The heading of the middle column is the "cost of capital," and on each side of this are two lower rates and two higher rates. The cell values are the discounted cash flow values. This can be done for both share price and total market price.

STEP 4

Compute the rate of return for various offering prices and scenarios. Basically, this is just the inversion of the matrix for Step 3.

STEP 5

Analyze the feasibility of a cash purchase. It does this with an eye toward the company's liquidity position and its target Debt/Equity ratio. Does it have the cash and/or can it raise the necessary cash? If this raising of cash involves borrowing, what will this borrowing do to the company's Debt/Equity ratio? If the conclusion is that cash would not be forthcoming, drop the idea or recompute using just stock.

STEP 6

Evaluate the impact of this acquisition on your company's EPS and capital structure. (Remember, in an all-cash deal, the impact on the firm's EPS is likely to be positive, but if the medium of exchange is stock, then there might be dilution depending on whether the P/E paid is greater or less than your company's P/E.)

There is certainly nothing unique in Rappaport's model, but to his credit he was the first to unify this approach and present a systematic model. He later formed a company that sold commercial versions of this model, and was quite successful in so doing. For evaluating a target in the "big company" range, one is likely to see the Rappaport model or some variation being applied. But while this discounted cash flow (DCF) approach is quite usual in "big company" deals it is most unusual for valuing privately held middle-market firms, where a multiple of EBITDA is used almost exclusively.

17

The Able Case: Doing a Leveraged Buyout

This chapter presents the Able Case, a case study in doing a leveraged buyout (LBO). First the case itself is presented. Then an analysis of the case is presented to assist the reader in "solving" it—leading to a detailed walk-through to show the reader how to do a LBO, or, at least, *one* way of doing a LBO.

BACKGROUND OF THE ABLE COMPANY

The company was founded in 1969 to manufacture a diverse line—about 23 different items—of proprietary plastic molded parts for the medical field. The company occupies a 70,000-square-foot building in excellent repair with ample parking which it acquired in 1975. The company is owned by its founder, a 68-year-old man. The founder personally owns patents with between 5 and 12 years until expiration on the company's products.

The company's equipment is modern, well maintained, and capable of producing at least one-third more than current production. The equipment was recently appraised for a fair market value of $6,100,000 and a quick sale value of $4,000,000. The Accounts Receivable are well spread out among about 40 active customers and only $200,000 are over 90 days overdue. (Bad debt expense has been nominal.) About two-thirds of the inventory consists of raw material, which the company buys in bulk. The plant has an estimated market value of $6,000,000. The owner's salary and bonus was $850,000 in 2002.

Able Company Balance Sheet

BALANCE SHEET (in thousands)

ASSETS	2000	2001	2002
CASH	$ 500	$ 480	$ 1,860
ACCOUNTS RECEIVABLE	3,000	3,100	3,200
INVENTORY—LIFO	4,000	4,200	4,500
EQUIPMENT—COST	4,000	4,200	6,500
LESS DEPRECIATION	2,000	2,200	3,000
NET EQUIPMENT	2,000	2,000	3,500
PLANT—COST	750	750	750
LESS DEPRECIATION	680	690	700
NET PLANT	70	60	50
TOTAL ASSETS	$9,570	$9,840	$13,110
LIABILITIES AND CAPITAL			
ACCOUNTS PAYABLE	$1,000	$1,050	$ 1,200
ACCRUED TAX	700	50	20
DEFERRED FEDERAL INCOME TAX	1,000	1,100	1,200
NOTE DUE SHAREHOLDER	500	1,000	1,000
LONG-TERM DEBT			
EQUIPMENT FINANCING	300	250	200
EQUITY			
COMMON STOCK	50	50	50
RETAINED EARNINGS	6,020	7,340	9,440
TOTAL LIABILITIES & CAPITAL	$9,570	$9,840	$13,110

INCOME STATEMENT (in thousands)

	2000	2001	2002
SALES	$24,000	$22,000	$26,000
COST OF GOOD SOLD*	16,800	16,060	18,200
GROSS PROFIT	7,200	5,940	7,800
GENERAL & ADMINISTRATIVE EXPENSE	2,400	2,200	2,600
SELLING EXPENSES	1,200	1,100	1,300
PRE-TAX PROFIT	3,600	2,640	3,900
TAX	1,800	1,320	1,800
NET INCOME	$ 1,800	$ 1,320	$ 2,100

*INCLUDES DEPRECIATION OF $500,000 ('00), $550,000 ('01) AND $600,000 ('02)

Assumption: You want to buy this company through a leveraged buyout and you only have $500,000 to put into the deal.

Questions regarding the ABLE COMPANY

1. The owner says he wants $23 million plus whatever cash the company has. Is this a reasonable price? Discuss.

2. How much cash do you think you could borrow on the company's assets? State assumptions.

3. What type of transaction would you propose to the seller? Explain your reasoning.

4. The bank has told you that they will not go over 4/1 in Debt/Equity and that they want interest coverage of 1½ to 1. Can you design a deal to accomplish this? What would you propose? Or is it that you can't do the deal? Be sure to put into your answer your line of reasoning and **why** the **seller should accept** what you offer. Also be sure to discuss the tax and accounting aspects of the case. Include in your discussion how you are going to get around the seller's (or seller's attorney's) request to collateralize any note. In short, design an offer the seller can't refuse—but with which you can live.

REVIEW AND COMMENTS ON THE INFORMATION PROVIDED IN THE CASE

In this section we will take the information provided in the "Background" section and interpret it for us (the potential buyer).

The company was founded in 1969 to manufacture a diverse line—about 23 different items—of proprietary plastic molded parts for the medical field.

What does this sentence mean to us? The fact that this company was founded in 1969 means that it is now reasonably old and well established—a favorable attribute. It also suggests that the company is a logical "For sale" candidate (particularly since the company is still owned by its founder). The company is a manufacturing company, the best kind on which to do a leveraged buyout. The fact that it manufactures about 23 different items means that its production is probably reasonably well spread out and not too dependent on one or two products (another plus).

The key word in the sentence quoted above is *proprietary*. Companies that manufacture proprietary products are more valuable, other things being equal, than companies that manufacture "job shop" parts. Proprietary parts are products that the company owns and sells under its own label. "Job shop" products mean that the company makes products for other companies, products that are owned and sold by the other company usually under its own name or brand. Usually the products that are proprietary are sold at a price that is higher than the identical part made under a "job shop" situation. (This is because the company "jobbing" the part to our (target) company has to turn around and make a profit on it. When thinking of doing a LBO, you should not turn up your nose at job shop manufacturers, however, because they very often have the assets on which one can borrow enough money to effectively do a LBO. Also, the price might be lower than a manufacturer of proprietary products, something that helps in doing a LBO. And there are lots of these "job shops" in existence.

The part about "plastic molded" parts means that the company uses injecting molding machines, generically one of the best types of equipment on which to borrow. If properly maintained, these machines can produce high-quality work for many years. The fact that the company makes parts for the medical field is a plus (despite all the whining and groaning from the professionals in the medical field). There apparently will be a continuing market for the company's products, at least for the next 5 years or so. Looking downstream, one might think that if this company were to grow to two or three times its present size, either through internal expansion or external expansion, it might be a reasonable IPO in the future. And unless something very adverse happens to the medical field, one might expect a reasonably good P/E at IPO time. (But this is not really the reason for buying a company via the LBO route. Usually it is to pay off the debt over, say, 5 years and then resell the company for at least what you paid for it.)

The company occupies a 70,000-square-foot building in excellent repair with ample parking which it acquired in 1975.

The significant inference about this sentence has to do with both the "up-front" money that is needed and the implications it has for the required NOCF", the money required to service the debt that will have to be incurred to do the deal. If the company's building was crowded or if, for any other reason, the company had to change buildings, this would present a formidable problem for you, the wannabe buyer/owner. This problem would mean that you would need a considerable "bulge" in up-front money, money that may not be readily financed. True, the fact that the company has to move might be the reason the company is for sale, but this does not mitigate the consequences of this "problem" to the potential buyer.

The second implication is also of crucial importance. Any payments that cut into the "new" company's NOCF" will mean that much less that can go to service the debt of the acquisition itself. So having a building that is perfectly adequate in regard to both space and parking is, indeed, a big plus for this company.

The company is owned by its founder, a 68-year-old man.

This sentence is as significant as any other in the background material for it indicates that the owner most likely has a legitimate "compelling reason to sell," one of the most significant of the criteria one looks for in a candidate for a LBO. The significance of this compelling reason to sell will become clear as the analysis of the case proceeds in subsequent sections.

The founder personally owns patents with between 5 and 12 years until expiration on the company's products.

This is a very fortuitous circumstance, one that is very often not found in a LBO target. This circumstance and the advantage it provides the potential buyer will be discussed below in the analysis section under the topic of "soft dollars."

The company's equipment is modern, well maintained, and capable of producing at least one-third more than current production.

This sentence indicates that the "new" company will not have to purchase additional or replacement equipment anytime in the near future—and the LBO buyer's near-term future means, usually, the next 5 years. Again, the implication of this sentence is that the "new" company's NOCF" will be spared, but in a somewhat different way. Without the need to buy additional equipment, the "Necessary discretionary" part of NOCF" can be reduced. In fact, in this case it might be reduced to zero! This is not such an unusual circumstance for a LBO target because, like a lot of good LBO targets, the company is reasonably old. Also, since the company is not growing rapidly—a decided *plus* for a LBO—the company's equipment can take care of its current needs and some expansion, too. Conceptually, a LBO buyer should think first in terms of paying off the debt incurred in doing the LBO and only then think of expansion or, possibly, selling the company. If the debt is not serviced, the whole LBO deal collapses, to the chagrin—and personal loss—of the buyer!

Remember that growth in Sales is usually the *enemy* of cash flow, the vehicle on which the whole LBO process rides. The reason for this is that growth eats up cash to finance working capital, if for no other reason. This is the reason that individuals buying a company through the LBO route should not set their sights on aggressive growth in sales. This is contra to the inclination of an individual who is particularly *market oriented*—one who says "Boy, I think I can really grow this company!" Unless a generous amount of outside financing is provided, a LBO does not usually have enough *surplus* NOCF" to plow back into aggressive growth.

The equipment was recently appraised for a fair market value of $6.1 million and a quick sale value of $3 million.

This appraisal value of the equipment is necessary in order to estimate the borrowing capacity of the equipment.

The Accounts Receivable are well spread out among about 40 active customers and only $200,000 are over 90 days overdue. (Bad debt expense has been nominal.)

This, too, is a crucial bit of information for this case. Accounts Receivable are one of the two most important sources of borrowing (collateral) for a LBO. The fact that there are about 40 active customers means that there is not a "concentration" factor; it also means that there is not a "diffusion" factor with which to contend. The low bad-debt expense is also a real plus. In short, these Accounts Receivable should be looked upon by a bank as near "perfect" collateral, another very positive factor in this company's favor.

About two-thirds of the inventory consists of raw material, which the company buys in bulk.

This bit of information regarding inventory is a little difficult to interpret. If the company buys this inventory, presumably raw resin for the molding machines, in such a form as to be "hockable" this is good for our purpose. But will a lender loan money on this kind of inventory? If it can be moved out of the plant and resold readily, this makes good collateral for a loan. If it cannot be returned or resold, it makes poor collateral. As will be shown later in the discussion of this case, this inventory may be the "swing" vote that could go either way. The thing that may sway the lender is whether he or she really likes the deal. If so, he or she might loan money on the inventory in order to help make the deal "doable." Ordinarily the lender might not lend on this inventory but because the lender might like the deal so much as to want to do the deal, he or she might "rationalize" the decision by saying that the inventory has borrowing power.

The plant has an estimated market value of $6 million.

This information is needed in order to estimate how much can be borrowed on the real estate. The discussion of this will be contained in the next section.

The owner's salary and bonus was $850,000 in 2002.

This information is important in two ways. First, it tells us how much "extra" we can "adjust" the EBITDA. It seems rather evident that we would not have to pay a qualified manager $850,000 a year to manage this $20 million company. Perhaps $150,000 or $200,000 or even $250,000, but not $850,000.

The other reason this information is important is that it is an indication that this company really is profitable. Sometimes, companies seem to be "profitable," but the owner is not "making any money." This is decidedly not the case. One should always look for any clue that a company is or is not *really* profitable.

ADDRESSING THE QUESTIONS ASKED IN THE CASE

The first question that has to be addressed is the "fairness" of the asking price. The owner says that he wants "$23 million plus whatever cash the company has." To answer the question of whether this price is "fair" we have to do two things. First we have to ask ourselves "What is this owner really saying?" Is he saying that he wants $23 million plus about $1.8 million and he won't take a cent less? Hardly! If the man is acting rationally—and sometimes sellers ask completely unreasonable prices—he probably means that he wants "about $23 million." So let's read this into what he is saying. If our assumption turns out to be incorrect we can "tweak" the price later.

Secondly, we have to calculate the floor and the ceiling price and see whether the owner's asking price is within this range. If we are lucky, the owner's "asking price" as we now interpret it will be not only in the range, but close to the floor.

DETERMINING THE FLOOR PRICE

In order to determine the "floor" price we have to look at the Balance Sheet and make adjustments as we deem appropriate. The cash item is easy; it may not be the same when we settle, but we will count $1.8 million now. The Accounts Receivable of $3.2 million needs to be reduced by the amount of the Bad Debt of $200,000. The Inventory of $4.5 million presents somewhat of a problem because it is carried at LIFO. If the statements were more complete, they would tell us what the LIFO reserve was. One can only guess, however, without this information. An apparently conservative guess would be that the Inventory would have a FIFO value of $5 million.

The equipment is valued on the books at only $3.5 million but, presumably, we had an appraisal made that indicated that the equipment had a "fair market value" of $6.1 million and a "quick sale" value of $4 million. Which should we use in calculating our "floor" value? The first instinct is to use the quick sale value as this is the lower of the two values. If we thought that we were in a strong bargaining position with the seller, this would be the thing to do. But, as will be seen as we go along, this is an almost "ideal" target LBO company, and if we want to impress the bank with what a "good deal" we have it might be advantageous to use the higher of the two. Although this might seem like rationalization to an outsider, if this owner wanted to sell this company he would not be pushed to use "liquidation" as the value, as the owner of a less desirable business might. So, in this case, we would be using what the owner might use if he were to calculate his floor value.

The real estate has been appraised at $6 million, so we will use this number. Note that the real estate is valued at only $50,000 on the company's books, probably the value of the land when it was purchased many years ago. This is not an unusual observance for LBO targets if, as usual, they are reasonably old.

On the Liabilities side, we have $1.2 million of Accounts Payable—a number that we will leave alone. The Accrued Tax already will have been paid, so we can forget about this. The next item listed, "Deferred Federal Income Tax," does represent an interesting item. This item, shown in the "Liabilities" section is not really a "liability" in the usual sense. In fact, this item might be found as an "asset" also. The idea for this reserve came about when accelerated depreciation first was introduced in 1954. If a company takes more depreciation early on, then it will have to pay more income tax later when depreciation charges drop. Well, with inflation and the rise in technology, most firms found that their total depreciation charges never did drop. When the corporate tax rate dropped significantly in 1986, this presented quite a dilemma for the accountants. In any case, this is one item we can delete; certainly we will never have to worry about this item when and if we acquire the company. (It is for our purpose of calculating an "adjusted book value" and, in fact, if we do a purchase/sale of stock, it may remain officially on the company's books.)

The "Note due Shareholder" is also an item that requires attention. Some—many?—business owners lend their own companies money and take a note for the amount. They could buy stock, receiving stock in return, but they elect to "loan" the company money. I feel that this "loan" is really *de facto* equity and ought to be eliminated. We are not going to buy the company *and then* pay the owner for his "stock," so why should we buy the company and pay the stockholder for the money he "loaned"—instead of "invested" in—the company? But—and this is a big "but"—sometimes the owner feels that he or she is "entitled" to this money that was "loaned" to the company. If they "dig in their heels," this can be a deal breaker, as it effectively raises the price. Let's hope that this owner does not take this strong a position and demand return of his $1 million in addition to the price of the company.

The $200,000 owed for equipment financing stands as is.

To summarize, we have the following adjusted book value:

Assets:

Cash	$ 1,800,000
Accounts Receivable	3,000,000
Inventory	5,000,000 at FIFO ("guesstimated")
Equipment	6,100,000
Plant	6,000,000
Total Assets	$ 21,900,000

Less Liabilities:

Accounts Payable	1,200,000
Equipment Financing	200,000
Total Liabilities:	$ 1,400,000
Equals: Adjusted Book Value	$20,500,000

CALCULATING THE CEILING VALUE

As you will recall, there are two basic ways of calculating the ceiling value: (1) by discounting the "cash flows," and (2) by using a multiple of adjusted EBITDA. For middle-market companies like the Able Company, the widespread—or virtually universal—approach is to use the adjusted EBITDA. It is the latter that we will use here. So the problem becomes calculating the adjusted EBITDA and then deciding on a multiple.

We begin with the Able Company's Pre-Tax Profit. This is $3.9 million for 2002. To this we add the Depreciation charge for 2002. But in keeping with the spirit of "Necessary discretionary" expenditures in the NOCF" formula (see page 169), instead of automatically taking all of the $600,000 of depreciation, we should consider what "Necessary discretionary" should be in this case. From the facts given, it appears that we will not have to purchase any equipment in the near future, nor would we have to do anything to the building in the near term. So it appears that "Necessary discretionary" in this case could be zero. There are those, however, who would argue that you should put "some" money aside for "Necessary discretionary" in every case. In short, do not use all of the depreciation charge. Presumably, if something has to be purchased in the way of equipment or if some repair has to be made to the building, normal cash flow could be used or the equipment could be financed with a low down payment. This being the case, we can add all $600,000 of depreciation.

The next item that we can "adjust" is the owner's salary and bonus. The facts of the case tell us that the owner paid himself a salary and bonus of $850,000 for 2002. It would appear that we could easily hire someone very competent as president for less than $850,000. For a company of this size, it appears that we could hire a manger for $200,000 to $250,000. Even if we take the higher number, this results in a saving of $600,000. So we can add this to the total. To this we would normally add the "other" perquisites that the owner is most likely taking out of the business, but which we would not have to take after we owned the business. Undoubtedly, this owner, like almost every owner of middle-market companies, takes a number of "perks," some of which may not be legitimate for IRS purposes. In fact, it is surprising how many owners will admit to a prospective buyer the "perquisites" that he or she is taking, even though they would not be allowed by the IRS! But in this case, we do not know what these perks are, so we will exclude them. If the "adjusted EBITDA" were weak, we might have to go back and probe for some perks, but since we already have so much it does not seem necessary in this case. To summarize:

Adjusted EBITDA:

Net Profit Before Tax	$3,900,000
Plus: Depreciation	600,000
Plus: Adjustment to owner's salary	600,000
Total after adjustments:	$5,100,000

Making the adjustments to EBITDA that we did results in an "adjusted EBITDA" of $5.1 million.

Now we have to determine a multiple for this adjusted EBITDA. Experience shows that it is difficult to pay more than a multiple of, say, five or five-and-a-half times adjusted EBITDA in a LBO situation. This is because of the heavy debt-servicing obligations that we would have to take on in doing the deal. Usually, a multiple of four or four-and-a-half or five would suffice for setting the ceiling price. But this company looks to be well above "average." Let's see what the use of these multiples will do for calculating the "ceiling" price.

Ceiling Price Calculations:

$5,100,000 × 4.5 = $22,950,000
$5,100,000 × 5   = 25,500,000
$5,100,000 × 5.5 = 28,050,000

So it appears that the "ceiling" price that we should consider is between $23 million and $28 million. If the owner says that he wants "$23 million plus whatever cash the company has," this is lower than our calculated "ceiling" using five times adjusted EBITDA and certainly lower than 5.5 times. So, an offer to the owner of $23 million, without stating the terms, would look like a very feasible offer. If the owner accepted this "number"—and remember, with a LBO it is the *terms* that really matter—we would have, indeed, a very good buy! In fact if a banker were shown this range of prices for the low multiples used, he or she would undoubtedly want to do the deal. In fact, this good a company for this price would provoke great enthusiasm on the part of a banker in today's economy.

RAISING MONEY ON THE ASSETS OF THE COMPANY

The next question to be raised is "How much money could be raised by borrowing on the company's assets?" For this we return to the Balance Sheet. First, there is the cash. Forgetting for the moment the statement by the owner" . . . plus whatever cash the company has," we can use at least most of the company's cash for our down payment.▲ But of the $1.8 million that the company has on its Balance Sheet as of the end of fiscal 2000, how much do we dare take for the down payment? If we take too much, this will leave the company with, possibly, insufficient cash for operating purposes. If we did the deal, and then later the company got into a cash insufficiency situation, the fact that we "cleaned out the cash account" would undoubtedly become known to employees, with the result that morale would plunge. But, sight unseen—and not employing our statistical model in Chapter 13 on cash management—it would appear that if we left two or three hundred thousand dollars in the company's cash account, this would be enough for the company to get along, other things being equal. This means that we can plan on taking $1,550,000 of the company's cash at closing. (In the buy/sell agreement, we can specify the minimum amount of cash that has to be in the company at closing.)

Next, there is the Accounts Receivable. We know that there is only $200,000 in "overdue" Accounts Receivable, so if we subtract this amount it leaves us with $3 million of "good" receivables. As we discussed in our comments to the facts of the case, this company's Accounts Receivable appear to be excellent collateral. There is no "concentration factor," because the accounts are ". . . well spread out among about 40 active customers." Nor is there a "diffusion factor" present. If the owner went to his bank and asked to borrow on these receivables, he could undoubtedly get as much as 80 or 85 percent of the "eligible receivables." Perhaps 90 percent if he really pushed. But in a LBO situation, lenders tend to be a bit more conservative. So we can assume that we could borrow about 70 percent of the value of "eligible receivables." Maybe we could even borrow 75 percent. But 70 percent of $3 million is $2.1 million.

▲ The owner would not "pay" himself this cash as it would be subject to the highest ordinary income tax rate.

Then there is the Inventory. Typically banks do not like to loan on inventory—that is, if they can help it! But inventory is *bona fide* collateral and the problem is to find out just how much we can get for it. We know that the "raw material inventory," which is about two-thirds of the total, consists of raw material the company buys in bulk, presumably raw plastic material. Is there some "marketability" in this raw material? If there is, we might be able to borrow up to 50 percent of its cost. If we use the estimated FIFO Inventory value of $5 million and take two-thirds of this, we have $3,350,000. Fifty percent of this is $1,650,000. Our work-in-process has no borrowing power.▲ The finished goods inventory has borrowing power and we will assume that we can borrow 50 percent. Of the $5 million total, this might be $1 million, and if we take 50 percent of this we have $500,000. Together the amounts total $2,150,000 that we might borrow on the inventory. This is, of course, assuming that the LIFO reserve is no bigger than assumed.

Something to consider with regard to borrowing on the company's inventory is the fact that by so doing we can raise enough cash to make a respectable down payment to the seller. The bank will know this and, if as we suspect, they would very much like to do this deal, it appears likely that the bank would loan the "maximum" that would appear reasonable on the Inventory, if no for other reason than to rationalize a loan that will make the deal "doable." In short, where ordinarily the bank would shy away from Inventory, it might be willing to loan on this company's inventory to help "do the deal."

The company's equipment is our next asset for borrowing. We know from the facts that the equipment has a "fair market value" of $6.1 million, which really means nothing to us for the purpose of borrowing against the equipment. The relevant number is the "quick sale" value of the equipment, which in this case is $4 million. We should be able to borrow 85–100 percent of this "quick sale" value. Taking an aggressive estimate of 100 percent, because we think the bank will think this is a "good deal," means that we can borrow $4 million on the equipment.

The next item on which we can borrow is the real estate, the land and buildings that the company owns. Of course, we do not really have to borrow against this collateral; we could if we like, delete the real estate from the deal. Or, even, buy it and then sell it to some third party. But I think it would be an error to attempt to do this without first trying to include the real estate in the deal. If we can buy the real estate as part of the "package," so much the better. In my experience, owning the real estate might be the most profitable part of the whole deal. Real estate has a way of increasing in value over time! We know that the "estimated market value" of the real estate is $6 million. What borrowing rate to apply is a function of the local real estate market and the economy. During the recession of the early 1990s, the borrowing rate dropped, in some cases to about half of what it is today. But for the company's real estate, and the sound financial condition of the company—and the great price that it appears we can get

---

▲ When the banks were first getting into loaning on LBO deals, in the 1960s and early 1970s, they were so eager, they would loan even on WIP. But that time is gone!

from the seller—a borrowing rate of 70 percent appears feasible. This is particularly true if we elect a 15-year contract. Therefore, 70 percent of $6 million means that we might be able to borrow $4.2 million on the real estate.

It appears that the only liabilities we would have to pay off would be the $200,000 due on the equipment financing. The Accounts Payable of $1.2 million would not have to be paid at closing, particularly if we do a "purchase of stock" deal. This is so because we would notify the creditors of the change of ownership, and ask if they want to be paid off. But there is no reason for an Accounts Payable creditor—trade creditor—to demand to be paid off at closing, because this would mean that this creditor would lose a customer!

To summarize, it appears that we might be able to borrow the following amounts on the company's assets, net of the liability we would have to pay at closing:

Amount that could be raised on the company's assets:

Cash	$1,550,000
Accounts Receivable	2,000,000
Inventory	2,150,000
Equipment	4,000,000
Real Estate	4,200,000
Less:	
Pay-off of equipment financing	200,000
Equals	$13,700,000

To this amount we can add the equity money we plan on putting into the deal, $500,000. Together these two add to $14,200,000. Rounding off this number, it means that we could possibly have $14 million for a down payment on a $23 million price. Is this a reasonable down payment? At 60 percent it appears that this would be a perfectly reasonable down payment; one for which we would not have to apologize.

If, for any reason, it is felt that more cash should be paid at the front-end of the deal (or, even if we have to raise the price *and* the down payment), usually meaning as a down payment, for a deal that appears to be as good as this one, it would, most likely, be possible to bring in some "mezzanine" financing. Perhaps the bank would even be willing to make a term loan of some sort to raise the necessary down payment. If we need "mezzanine" type of financing, which could be provided by the bank, or more likely by a "mezzanine" lender such as a finance company or other institution, this is not really debt, in the sense of "secured debt," but it is not really equity either. Ergo the term mezzanine. Because it could be subordinated it is *de facto* equity, however. In fact, at this time there are number of institutional lenders who would make such a subordinated loan, but the "price" of such a loan is, now, about 20–25 percent per annum.

The minimum for such a loan, currently, is about $5 million. (Chapter 10 deals with this type of mezzanine loan.)

Again, this illustrates the importance of having an attractive firm as your target. Of course, life is not as perfect as one would like. It is important for the wannabe business owner to realize that if a deal seems to be "too difficult" to finance, there is probably a good reason for this and the best way to respond to this situation is to pass on the target and look for a better one. *Persistence in trying to do an "undoable" deal may irritate your prospective lenders and any others associated with the deal.* This is a most important lesson for wannabe entrepreneurs to learn. There is an expression about doing a deal that says "Don't break your pick on a bad deal."

SYNDICATING THE EQUITY

In the case of the Able Company we are told that you have "only $500,000" to put into the deal. What if you do not have this much? What is the minimum that you should expect to have?

To answer this, you have to look at your creditability from the viewpoint of the person putting together the deal. Would someone believe that you have the experience to be the owner of a company of this size? And that "someone" is really two people: the seller and the banker. Would they accept you as a *bona fide* buyer? If the answer is "Yes" then this suggests that you should have "some" money, given your success, to put into the equity of this deal. But whether this is $500,000 or a lesser or greater amount is conjectural. Also, remember, the "required" equity participation of the entrepreneur is a function of the economic times. When people first started doing LBOs in the late 1960s, it might have been possible to do a deal of this size—and beauty—for as little as $5,000 or $10,000 of pure equity! In the 30 years since then the "required" equity money, as a percentage of the deal, has varied from about 5 percent to as much as 20 or 30 percent—or even more! This is a function of both the economic times (the early seventies were good, after 1991 to 1993, and more recently, very bad), and the institution with which you are dealing. Also, the attractiveness of the deal to a financial institution is a major determinant.

But assuming that $500,000 seems like a reasonable number and you feel that you do not have this much cash to put into the deal, how can you get the balance needed in order to do the deal? This may not be very difficult, particularly for an attractive target that is as well priced as Able Company is. The way to raise the needed equity is to "syndicate" the amount. In **syndication** you solicit other investors to come into the deal with you. You may need one, two, three, or more people to join with you in order to put together the required equity. Two or three is probably better than one in order to permit you to maintain control. But as the "deal maker" you should be entitled to a bit more than your pro-rata share of the equity as determined by your dollar contribution into the equity pool. This is where it sometimes get a bit difficult, but, in general, investors in deals like this would expect that you, as the person putting the deal together would get some percentage as "promoter's" stock, say 20 percent.

Investors in such a syndicate may sometimes insist that two classes of stock be used, one portion which would include the "promoter's" stock and the other class for the "hard money"—the actual cash. So you might have Preferred Stock for the "hard money" and Common Stock for the other class, including promotional stock. In the distribution, each participant would get, say, one share of Preferred for each dollar he or she contributed and one share of Common Stock. Then the promoter, and possibly some members of management, might get additional shares of the Common Stock in an amount that is open to negotiation. These two classes of stock would have different preferences in liquidation, perhaps different voting rights, and the Preferred may have a different preference over the Common in any dividend distribution. But if you do something like this *it is important to give a conversion ratio for the Preferred in terms of the Common* if it ever becomes necessary to have only one class of stock. Such an occurrence might be if the company is sold. If someone offered so much money for the whole company, how would that be split between the Preferred stockholders and the Common stockholders? This is the question that has to be answered in deciding on this conversion ratio.

STRUCTURING THE DEAL

Now that we have an idea of how much cash we can raise by using the assets of the company and adding our equity, it is time to start to "structure" the deal. If we decide that we are going to offer $14 million cash as a down payment, how do we make up the balance of the purchase price?

This is also the time to try to decide on the form of transaction that might be used, meaning, of course, whether we are going to propose a "purchase/sale of assets" or a "purchase/sale of stock." As was mentioned in Chapter 16, it is to the advantage of the buyer to buy assets; and it is to the advantage of the seller to sell stock. Knowing this, the prospective buyer has to decide which of these two methods to propose to the seller. In making this decision, the wannabe owner must keep in mind, however, the "whole deal," meaning the price *and* the terms. By offering to buy the assets, you are not doing the seller any favor; in fact, you are really hurting the seller by making him pay more taxes, both corporate (for depreciation recapture) and, possibly, personal.

Whether you are going to go to a bank for financing or a finance company makes a difference in the type of deal proposed. If the deal is not good enough for a bank, and you expect to go to a finance company, you will have trouble getting a finance company to accept a purchase/sale of stock because of the possibility of fraudulent conveyance. But since this target company looks—at this point—to be quite good, assuming that you are going to go to a bank makes sense. A bank will most likely accept a purchase/sale of stock if the whole deal and company look good.

From the seller's point of view, a sale of stock would be unquestionably the better form of transaction. So if we offer this highly advantageous form of transaction, what does that do for us? We know that it will hurt us by making us pay higher taxes, because we will have lower depreciation allowances, but we can use this fact in our bargaining position. If this is such a good deal for the seller, what can we extract from the seller in return? Remember, the name of the game in doing a LBO is terms so what we can extract from the seller is *terms*. Our rationale for asking for these terms is that the seller is "getting such a good deal." So if we offer a "purchase/sale of stock" form of transaction this *gives* us the rationale for asking for terms, but we now have to figure out how we are going to make up for the difference between our down payment of $14 million and the offer price of $23 million—that is, the terms.

SOFT DOLLARS

The first form of "terms" that we should consider is what was introduced in Chapter 16: "soft-dollar payments"—*payments we make to the seller that are considered part of the purchase price but which, quite importantly, we can deduct for tax purposes.* Thus the term "soft" means they are "tax deductible." Unfortunately, these soft-dollar contracts that are tax deductible for the buyer are usually *ordinary income* items for the seller. And, when we discuss these "soft-dollar" contracts with the seller we remind him that by doing a "purchase/sale of stock" we are giving up additional depreciation charges (which would lower our tax bill) that we would have if we did a "purchase/sale of assets." These types of soft-dollar contracts were discussed in Chapter 16, so only a summary will be repeated here.

Probably the most common of these soft-dollar contracts is a *noncompete contract* This is a most important contract between the buyer and seller, so even if you were paying all cash for this company, as mentioned above, a wise lawyer would advise you to ascribe part of the purchase price to a contract "not to compete."

Next in importance is a contract for *consulting services.* In this contract, typically, the buyer agrees with the seller for the seller to provide "consulting services" to the buyer's new company for a period of time. This does not mean that the seller will actually be present in the company for so many hours a month—something that might be totally offensive to both the buyer and the seller! Instead it means that an officer of the company can call the former owner and ask him or her questions about some problem in the business. The amount of money attributed to this contract should, as with all the other "soft-dollar" contracts, be "reasonable." What this means will be different for each individual deal, but the amount of money paid to the owner before the sale will have a strong bearing on the amount paid. If the amount paid is substantially more than the prior owner was paid, the IRS might seriously question the reason for this.

Another possible soft-dollar contract is the payment of royalty fees for patents owned by the individual seller. If the company owns the patents, this scheme is lost; the patent must be owned by the individual. Also, the patent must also be considered to be a "capital asset." But, in general, if the selling owner owns patents that can be considered to have economic value, then a portion of the purchase price can be attributed to royalty fees for these patents. And, as was mentioned in the previous chapter, what makes these royalty fees even more attractive is the fact that for the company paying the fees, there is an ordinary tax-deductible expense. For the person receiving these fees, however, *the fees are capital gains!* Surely, this must be one of the only such cases of an "ordinary expense" on the one hand and a "capital gains" on the other.

OTHER EXPENSES

While they are not strictly soft-dollar expenses, it is not uncommon in doing a deal to attribute part of the purchase price to certain aspects of the business being acquired. An example might be the company's *customer list*. Or some special process that is proprietary to the company being acquired. Another example would be a brand name. Depending on the circumstances, these can be used to reduce the amount of goodwill resulting from the purchase. The required amortization of this goodwill and the fact that it is not tax deductible make any effort to reduce this amount worthwhile. Again, this is a good reason to have a savvy and experienced CPA to assist you in the acquisition.▲

Similarly, this is why so many acquirers of high-tech firms try to write off a significant portion—or all!—of the "excess of purchase price over asset value" at the time of acquisition. They call this a write-off of "Research and Development Expense" and use this as their rationale for expensing this sometimes considerable amount. They do this, of course, to eliminate the yearly charge that would have to be made in the future against their Income Statement. By taking a "bath" all at one time, they eliminate this onerous charge that would otherwise weigh down future earnings. At this writing, fearing abuses of this practice, the SEC is putting pressure on the Financial Accounting Standards Board to eliminate this practice. What is being circulated by the FASB is a proposal to have what amounts to "permanent goodwill," goodwill that does not have to be written off each year.

PUTTING VALUE ON THE SOFT-DOLLAR CONTRACTS

In the case at hand we now have to determine the amounts that we are going to put on the soft-dollar contracts we are going to offer the seller as part of the purchase price. In doing this we should remember that this will be a "first attempt" at these numbers because we have yet to decide on the amount of the subordinated note that we will offer the seller as part of the purchase price. Remember, the purchase price—in this case—will be made up of: (a) the cash down payment, (b) the soft-dollar contracts, and (c) the subordinated note. (In larger deals, the usual order is: cash down, senior debt, subordinated debt [or mezzanine debt] and equity, and there can be degrees within each category.)

▲ As mentioned above, in very small "purchase/sale of assets" transactions it is common to try to agree on higher values for such things as Inventory and lower values on equipment, the sale of which is subject to sales tax.

1. *The covenant "not to compete."* As with all of these contracts, we must keep in mind that they must be considered "reasonable," whatever that means. I think in this case that if we put a value of $1 million on the covenant it would not be "unreasonable." And we can pay this amount over 5 years at the rate of $200,000 a year. (Later on we will have to check to see if these payments and the various interest payments and principal payments will fit into the cash flow that is available.) But note also that no mention is made of the *present value* of these payments. By merely *adding* yearly payments we are violating the notion of the present value of money. The present value of this payment is not $1 million, but something less. I do not use "present value" unless the seller or his or her adviser brings it up, hoping, of course, to gain the psychological advantage of the larger number. Remember, also, that this is really *reducing* the price to the buyer—and sometimes the seller will not even think about what is being done.

2. *The "consulting contract."* In this case we have to pay attention to the salary that the seller was paid in the past year. "Consulting pay" should be more than regular salary on a "per time basis." So if we offered to pay $200,000 a year for 5 years, a total of $1 million, this would seem to be "reasonable."

3. *Royalty payments for the patents.* It is fortunate that this seller has registered the patents in his own name as this sets up the possibility of our paying the seller royalties—that will be capital gains to him, but ordinary expense to our new corporation that will pay the royalties. The value that we put on these royalties will have to have a bearing on the "economic value" of the patents. So for what products they apply and the length of time they have to run will be important. Let's assume that we can ascribe $2 million to these payments, spread out over 5 years. Since this is such a desirable device for paying the seller, one might wonder why we don't put more of the purchase price on this particular item. I think the only way to answer this is to say that if the royalty payment were attacked by the IRS, and we found that we could not defend the "economic value" that we placed on the patents, or in some other way the IRS knocked out this item, we would lose a lot. So to be safe—or "safer"—we had better not place too much of the purchase price on this one item.

To summarize, we have the following soft-dollar payments:

"Covenant not to compete"	$1,000,000
Consulting agreement	$1,000,000
Royalty payments	$2,000,000
Total	$4,000,000

THE SUBORDINATED NOTE

If we make a down payment of $14 million, and place $4 million on the soft-dollar contracts, this leaves $5 million as a balance. We can offer the seller a *subordinated note for $5 million* to make up the $23 million offering price. I suggest that this note be for 5 years, with interest only for 3 years, and 20 percent of the principal in the fourth and fifth year, interest and principal payable quarterly, with 60 percent of the principal payable at the end of the fifth year. The rationale for making this "interest only" for the first 3 years has to do with the fact that we are going to offer the seller a "purchase/sale of stock" form of transaction.

Remember, by purchasing the stock of the seller, we are purchasing all of the assets, all of the liabilities, and *all of the contingent liabilities,* if any. And, of course, potentially the biggest possible contingent liability is *taxes.* Since individual owners traditionally put a lot of possibly questionable expenses on the company's books—for tax purposes—the IRS may audit for the disallowed expenses. The sale of the company might trigger such an audit. Since the IRS has 3 years to audit, this is a perfect excuse for our asking for at least a 3-year interest-only period, *with a right of offset.* If we have to pay something that was rightfully the responsibility of the seller, we have a right to "offset" the note for that amount. So, since that amount is rather uncertain, we can say that we need the "interest-only" provision to protect ourselves from some contingency. It behooves you, the buyer, to make an educated guess as to how much this possible "contingency" payment might be, because this also has a bearing on the size of the subordinated note.

At least this provides us with a "good" reason for the size of the note, when, in fact, we know that the "real" reason is something else. The *real* reason includes the fact that we need a certain amount to fill the gap after the *soft-dollar* payments, and quite importantly, we need a subordinated note of a certain size in order to get our Debt/Equity ratio to come in under some target D/E, often 4 to 1. Remember, the reason we are making this note "subordinate" is to use it as *de facto equity.* Without knowing it, *the seller is actually putting up most of our "equity" in the deal!* At least as far as the Debt/Equity ratio is concerned. But isn't this enough!

Without a subordinated note the whole deal is not possible. With it the deal looks good to a banker.

SUMMARY OF THE FINANCING

Now we have all the "pieces" of our financing in place. This is, of course, before we go to the bank and request financing. It is usually necessary to get the seller's approval before you ask the bank. This can be a real problem. The bank doesn't want to talk to you until the seller has approved your deal; and the buyer is reluctant to talk to the seller until the bank has approved the deal. At least verbally! So what to do is a good question. The best way to handle this conundrum is to preliminarily consult with the banker with a *"pro forma* deal" and ask for a verbal approval. This implies that you can structure the deal as we have done here.

We have a respectable down payment of $14 million. Then we have soft-dollar contracts worth $4 million and a subordinated note for $5 million, for a total of $23 million. In this way we can say that we are giving the seller "virtually everything you asked for." This may not be literally true, but it is close enough to the truth to permit making the statement to the seller. If the seller objects to this price we can remind him that we are trying to match what he asked for. (Conveniently we are implicitly asking him to forget about the added portion of the asking price, namely "plus whatever cash the company has." I think it is reasonable to expect the seller to think that he will not get *all* of his asking price. But in this offer, we are giving him "virtually the asking price" and a lot of cash! This is important because we need to remind the seller of this fact when we get into other aspects of the bargaining process. What I mean by this statement is that if we are giving the seller "your asking price" we can ask him or her for some concessions on the terms. *And this is what we want!*

If the seller objects to the amount of the soft-dollar contracts, we might agree to rearrange the dollar amounts for the various items. For example, we might put some more money on the royalty payments, if counsel agrees that this is "reasonable." Or, in some other way, change the payments or dollar amounts. Remember, it is only the first two contracts that will be ordinary income to the seller, not the royalty payments.

As far as the subordinated note is concerned, the three possible objections that might be raised are: (1) it is "subordinated," (2) it is not "collateralized," and (3) the payment terms run out to 5 years.

With regard to the first objection, you can say, "Oh that's a bank requirement. They do this in order to keep people from swindling them. And, besides, this is just routine." Typically, this will calm the apprehension of the seller. Also, I make the point that the note is *subordinated* only in the offer letter and not when I am talking about the note to the seller. Often the seller does not really realize what "subordination" means; in fact, the seller's accountant and/or his or her lawyer may not really understand what it means! In the offer letter I make the statement "Naturally, this note would be subordinated to any bank borrowing I might make." If the seller and/or his or her advisers refuse to accept this, you merely say, "Sorry, but this a deal breaker. I can't do anything about this." If the seller is really motivated he or she will accept this.

The second objection may be met with the suggestion that the seller take a "second" position on the equipment and/or the building. Typically, I do not like to bring up the subject of "collateralizing the note" myself, preferring to wait until the subject is raised (very often it is not). By suggesting that the collateral be a "second" position on the equipment and/or real estate, you are admitting that you are doing a LBO. And this is something you never want to admit to the seller. There are several reasons for this. One is because some elderly business owners simply are disturbed that someone could buy their business—a business that took them many years to build—without much of his or her own money. "It's not fair" is a refrain I have heard more than once. So not raising the issue is the best way of avoiding feelings of angst on the part of the seller. Another reason is if the seller's accountant finds out that you are leveraging the purchase as much as possible, he or she might start to raise the possibility of a "fraudulent conveyance." In this way the accountant might be able to dissuade the seller from selling and the accountant gets to keep his or her client.

The third objection, the length of the note, may be met with a reply that you are doing a "purchase/sale of stock" and that you are buying all the assets, all the liabilities, and all of the *contingent liabilities.* You can say, with a lot of justification, that you need some time to let these contingencies run their course. True, taxes, as a contingency, normally last for only 3 years but there might be other "contingencies" that last longer, such as product liability. It is also true that product liability can be covered by insurance, so in this case it is not like another "contingent" liability, but you can argue "Suppose the claim is *larger* than the insurance payment?" I have not found too many objections to a 5-year note. Most sellers *expect* to take a note, and they probably expect it to be longer than 5 years.

THE OFFER LETTER

So now we have an offer that we can present to the seller. Exhibit 17.1 is an example of such a letter. Let's go over this letter and discuss what each part means. You will note that I do *not* have a lawyer draft this offer letter. If I did the seller would have to get a lawyer to review the offer letter and before you know what is happening, the lawyers would be acting "like lawyers" and incurring a bill that need not be. There is ample time for the lawyers to get involved once the seller agrees to the basic deal terms. With regard to the statement concerning the "legal work" and the accounting "due diligence," this encompasses a number of things. First, it will be necessary to file a UCC 3 Inquiry Form with the Secretary of State of your state to see if there are any UCC 1s on file against the company. Usually there are, if it is a manufacturing company with a lot of equipment. Many of these UCC 1s are for equipment that was bought and paid for long ago, but someone forgot to take off the Financing Statement. Usually your law firm will do this for you.

The accounting "due diligence" involves doing a "review" of the subject company's accounting records. And this can be more than you expect at first. Often the books of account leave a lot to be desired for the kind of middle-market companies that we are talking about in this book. But just *how bad* is really the question. Does your accountant feel that despite all the problems with the records—which may be endemic with the accounting computer program utilized, or may be just poor record keeping or management of the accounting system—that the system is good enough? Whatever is the case there is a judgment call to be made by you the buyer in conjunction with your CPA firm as to the "sufficiency" of the accounting records. In short, is what you see what you are going to get—accounting-wise?

EXHIBIT 17.1   Sample of an "Offer Letter"

MR. GREGORY WILLIAMS, PRESIDENT   YOUR NAME AND ADDRESS
THE ABLE COMPANY
ANY TOWN, USA

DEAR MR. WILLIAMS:

IT IS WITH PLEASURE THAT I MAKE THE FOLLOWING OFFER FOR YOUR COMPANY, **THE ABLE COMPANY.** THE FORM OF TRANSACTION THAT I PROPOSE IS A "PURCHASE/SALE OF STOCK." THE PRICE THAT I OFFER IS $23 MILLION PAYABLE AS FOLLOWS: $14 MILLION AT CLOSING, PLUS A NOTE FOR $5 MILLION, PLUS SEPARATE CONTRACTS FOR "CONSULTING SERVICES," A "NONCOMPETE AGREEMENT," AND A ROYALTY AGREEMENT FOR THE USE (AND SUBSEQUENT SALE) OF YOUR PATENTS COLLECTIVELY VALUED AT $4 MILLION. THE DOWN PAYMENT WILL BE IN THE FORM OF A CASHIER'S CHECK MADE TO YOUR ORDER. THE NOTE WILL BE FOR A PERIOD OF 5 YEARS, BEARING INTEREST AT 10 PERCENT PER ANNUM ON THE UNPAID BALANCE AND WITH PRINCIPAL PAYMENTS AS FOLLOWS: 20 PERCENT OF THE PRINCIPAL, PAYABLE QUARTERLY, DURING THE FOURTH YEAR, 20 PERCENT DURING THE FIFTH, ALSO QUARTERLY, AND 60 PERCENT OF THE PRINCIPAL AT THE END OF THE FIFTH YEAR. THIS NOTE WILL HAVE A "RIGHT OF OFFSET" ATTACHED TO IT, MEANING THAT IF MY NEW COMPANY WHICH WILL PURCHASE YOUR STOCK HAS TO PAY ANY CONTINGENT CLAIM FOR ANY ACTION THAT HAPPENED PRIOR TO MY PURCHASING YOUR STOCK, THIS AMOUNT CAN BE SUBTRACTED FROM THE AMOUNT OF THE NOTE. ANY EXCESS OVER AND ABOVE THE AMOUNT OF THE NOTE WILL ALSO BE YOUR RESPONSIBILITY. NATURALLY, AS A SELLING SHAREHOLDER, THIS NOTE FOR $5 MILLION WOULD BE SUBORDINATED BY YOU TO ANY BANK BORROWING THAT I MIGHT MAKE.

THIS OFFER IS SUBJECT TO THE SIGNING OF A DEFINITIVE "BUY-SELL AGREEMENT." IT IS ALSO SUBJECT TO THE COMPANY BEING IN SUBSTANTIALLY THE SAME FINANCIAL CONDITION AS IS SHOWN ON YOUR LATEST FINANCIAL STATEMENTS, THAT IS THAT THE ASSETS AND LIABILITIES WILL BE SUBSTANTIALLY UNCHANGED EXCEPT FOR THE NORMAL COURSE OF BUSINESS AND THAT THERE WILL BE NO LAWSUITS PENDING.

IF THIS OFFER IS ACCEPTABLE TO YOU, PLEASE SIGN ONE COPY OF THIS LETTER AND RETURN IT TO ME. UPON RECEIPT I WILL INSTIGATE THE LEGAL WORK, ACCOUNTING REVIEW, AND OTHER "DUE DILIGENCE" THAT WILL BE NEEDED TO COMPLETE THIS TRANSACTION. I HOPE THAT WE WILL BE ABLE TO CLOSE THIS DEAL IN THE NEAR FUTURE.

SINCERELY,

ROYCE MCNEILL

THE AGREEMENT IS ACCEPTABLE: SIGNED _____

                                   DATE _____

The other aspects of the "due diligence" process have already been alluded to, and will not be repeated here. But this is not to minimize the importance of a "proper" due diligence for the whole company. A whole chapter, if not a book in and of itself, could be written about doing due diligence. The best advice I can offer, however, is to do a "due diligence" of sufficient magnitude to keep you from making a major mistake, but try to not "overkill" the process. Some buyers try to do so much that they exhaust the time patience of the seller and effectively stop the deal. Whether you the buyer like it or not, there is a certain amount that you are going to have to learn about a company *only after* you acquire it. Just try to avoid the *big* surprises!

You will note that the offer letter is subject to the drafting of a "Definitive Buy-Sell Agreement." I use this phrasing instead of the more usual phrase "Subject to my obtaining certain financing." I feel that this latter phrasing is a decided tip-off to the seller that I am going to borrow money (as much as I can) to do the deal. And remember what was said about never revealing that you are doing a leveraged buyout? This clause, "Definitive Buy-Sell Agreement," accomplishes that same end result as the one about obtaining financing without drawing attention to this financing process. If you do not get the financing, you simply do not complete a "Buy-Sell Agreement."

The part about the note having a "Right of offset" clause attached is an important one. As the letter says, if you have to pay on any contingent liability, that amount can be subtracted from the note still due. This is quite useful *per se*, but it also provides a basis for making the note 5 years in length *and making it "interest only" for the first 3 years*. The "good" reason for this is that you need to have as big a cushion as possible *in case* you have to make a payment, but the "real" reason is that you want to make the note as painless as possible for your cash flow stream. By making the note "interest only" you relieve your new company of having to make the onerous principal payments in the early years after your acquisition. If the payment is not a strain on the cash flow, you can save money to pay it later.

The clause about the note being "subordinated" was also covered earlier. If the seller asks about this, I usually just say "Oh that's just boilerplate from the banks." And as I said, if the seller persists, I merely say "Sorry, but I can't do anything about this. This is just customary for a bank. If you object there is no deal." This will usually do the trick. If the seller still, objects, then you have to tell him that there is no deal. And as far as you are concerned, there *is* no deal. No subordinated note, no deal! It is as simple as that!

Of course, there is always the possibility that you can find a third party to take the subordinated note in lieu of the seller taking it, but usually this is a contingency that you wish you didn't have to resort to. With institutional lenders now more willing to do such deals, you may have an alternative. But the interest you will pay may be at least twice the price that the seller will accept! (Today it is typically approximately 20–25 percent for institutional lenders.) If your subordinated note is too small for institutional lenders—say, less than $5 million—you may have to offer an individual, say, a $6 million note to receive $3 million.

And finally there is the matter of the letterhead on which you present the offer letter. This letterhead, which presumably will be the same one that you used in your "letter of inquiry" deserves attention. Does your stationery represent you in the way that it should? Does it look "homemade"? Does it look like you have the money and wherewithal that one would expect from a legitimate buyer? Ideally, the letterhead would be from your corporation with the buyer signing the letter as president or chairman, or some such title. But for an individual buyer it behooves you to pay special attention to the letterhead that is used in the offer letter and the introductory letter, if you want the seller to take you seriously.

CHECKING THE BANK'S REQUIREMENTS

Now that you have an offer in mind, and *before* you actually present the offer letter to the seller, you must look at the deal from the point of view of the banker. After the deal is done, what will be your company's Debt/Equity ratio? The bank has told you that they will "not go over 4/1." Now you start to realize the importance of the subordinated note! Let's see what the new company's debt will be. This is summarized as follows:

Accounts Payable	$ 1,200,000
Revolver notes due bank (A/Rs & Inv.)	4,150,000
Equipment loan	4,000,000
Real Estate loan	4,200,000
Total Debt	$13,350,000

(The reason this does not add to $23 million is because of the soft-dollar contracts, which will be "off Balance Sheet financing" and the subordinated note to the seller, which here is not counted as "debt.")

The amount of equity we have is only $500,000, but to this we can "add" the amount of the subordinated note, $5 million. We can do this because the subordinated note will be "specifically subordinated" to the bank, thus making it *de facto equity to the bank*. Now we can calculate the Debt/Equity ratio as $13,350,000/$5,500,000 = 2.45/1. Yes, by counting the subordinated note as *de facto* equity we have a Debt/Equity ratio of 2.45/1 instead of 36.7/1 (= 18,350,000/500,000). So thanks to the seller accepting our subordinated note, we have a doable deal instead of an unworkable one. Now you can see the importance of the subordinated note and the fact that the *seller* is providing most of the equity needed for *your* deal. From a Debt/Equity point of view, a bank would be really excited about doing this deal and acquiring a customer company of this stature.

And what if the seller wants more than $23 million? In this case, you can raise the amount of the note and/or increase the amount of the soft-dollar contracts. But I really think a rational seller would accept the $23 million offer that we are going to make. If nothing else, he can pay his capital gains tax out of the

$14 million down payment▲ and invest the remaining money to realize more after tax than he was taking out of the company in salary. Furthermore, for the next 5 years your new company will be paying him for the soft-dollar contracts and the interest and principal on the subordinated note—more than he took in his salary. If the owner seems to be slow in accepting the offer, you can remind him of this important fact.

Next we have to check to see if the "times interest earned" criteria is met. We know, of course, that the real test of the deal is whether our company's cash flow can service the debt, but since most bankers use "times interest earned" it behooves us to check this.

The estimated interest payments we must make are as follows:

Interest on the Accounts Receivable & Inventory line	$456,500 @ 11%
Interest on the Equipment term loan	400,000 @ 10%
Interest on the Real Estate	378,000 @ 9%
Interest on the subordinated note	500,000
Total	**$1,734,500**

For the numerator of the ratio we use the unadjusted EBIT for Able Company of $3.9 million. Therefore the "times interest earned" is: 3,900,000/1,734,500 = 2.25 times. If the bank will accept the "adjusted" number, this ratio is 5,900,000/1,734,000 = 3.4 times! Compared to other LBO deals, this Interest Coverage ratio is spectacular. If the bank was not excited about this deal before, it would be now.

ABILITY TO SERVICE THESE COMMITMENTS

It is one thing for the bank to be excited about this deal, but we, the borrower, must be confident that our new company will be able to service the loans and soft-dollar commitments once the deal is done. Of course, the bank will be concerned about this, too.

The way that this cash flow "sufficiency" should be checked is to put all the numbers into the Cash FlowCast® forecasting program—the Excel spreadsheet available to the reader—and then see firsthand whether the cash flow will support these commitments. Since we know that in a "steady sales" scenario the EBIT is similar to NOCF", except for the taxes involved, we can make a quick check on whether we can service the loans and soft-dollar commitments by comparing this number to the total dollar amount needed for all the items. Let's list the dollar commitments that we need to take into account:

▲ If the current law persists, he may have to pay tax on the *entire purchase* price. But even this might not be enough to dissuade the seller.

Interest on the Accounts Receivable & Inventory line▲	$ 456,500
Equipment term-loan interest	400,000
Equipment term-loan principal	571,428
Real Estate loan interest	378,000
Real Estate loan principal	280,000
Noncompete contract	200,000
Consulting contract	200,000
Royalty payments	400,000
Interest on the subordinated note▲▲	500,000
Total	$3,385,928

With an "adjusted" EBITDA (our surrogate for NOCF") of $5.9 million, it is plain to see that the new company will not have any problem with this amount of debt and contractual fixed charges *if everything remains roughly the same.* If there is any reason to believe that sales will not hold steady, then this fact must be taken into account in a formal Cash Flow forecast. Remember the thinking advanced in Chapter 7?

CONCLUDING DETAILS

Once the seller accepts the offer "in principle" and the "due diligence" is complete, the next step may be the application to the bank for the requisite financing. Timing is rather critical here as the bank will want up-front payments from you for their legal fees and for the loan commitment. For this size deal this could amount to $40,000 to $60,000, which is *nonrefundable* to you. If it is possible to wait until the signing of the formal "Buy-Sell Agreement," you would hedge your bet that the deal will not go through, and in this case you would not lose your nonrefundable payments to the bank. Thus there would not be a slip-up if the seller did not sign the Buy-Sell Agreement. Sometimes, this is not possible due to the circumstances of the deal. If the seller does not sign the Buy-Sell Agreement, you have another bill to pay and that is your own lawyer's bill, which by this time will not be inconsequential. This bill cannot be hedged, but the payment to the bank can. So it is best to wait until after the signing to pay the bank, if possible. The downside to this is that you are now committed to pay the seller even if a bank does not make you the loans. What do you do then?

The Buy-Sell Agreement will be drafted by a lawyer. I feel it is preferable for you the buyer to have *your* lawyer do this, even though this will cost you more

---

▲ Since this line is an "evergreen" line of credit we do not need to include principal payments.

▲▲ This ignores the principal payment due starting the fourth year.

in legal fees than if the seller's lawyer drafts the agreement and your lawyer reviews it. I say this because there are subtleties in the drafting that your lawyer can place in the document that will favor you, whereas if the seller's lawyer does the drafting these subtleties will favor the seller. If the transaction is a "purchase/sale of stock" there will be more warranties and representations than if the transaction is a "purchase/sale of assets." This is another reason for you, the buyer, to have *your* lawyer draft the agreement.

In the course of drafting the Buy-Sell Agreement, your lawyer can file for the UCC 3s (as mentioned earlier) and also he or she will form a new corporation for the purpose of acquiring the stock of the target company. Typically, the new company will be given a name like "Able Acquisition Co." Once the closing takes place, the old company, Able Co., will be merged under a tax-free section of the IRS Code into the new corporation. The name of the old corporation, the Able Company, will be returned to the state registrar and the new corporation will then change its name to the name of the old corporation, the Able Company. The acquisition will then be complete.

AN ALTERNATE WAY OF FINANCING THE DEAL

In this illustration, we did an "asset-based" acquisition. With a company of this size and performance it may be possible to get a term loan for a substantial amount, enough to replace the money borrowed on the assets, at least. But this is dependent on the economic times. Furthermore, where this company may be bought with term loans, another may not be so fortunate. So to illustrate the rather complete process, this illustration utilized an asset-based approach. Remember, the smaller the deal, the more important the assets; the larger the deal, the less important the assets and the more important the cash flow. Where the cross-over line is depends on the times. Currently, about $25 million in sale price is about it. (So this deal could really be done as a "cash flow" deal.)

Part 6

Dressing Up Your Company for a Better Multiple

Chapter 18: Managing the Multiplier and Your Company's Image

Epilogue: Valuation and What We Learned from the dot.com Bust

18

Managing the Multiplier and Your Company's Image

Except for the last three chapters, this book has been focused on financial management of an emerging firm and on improving earnings (and, perhaps, cash flow). But when it comes time to sell the company, the value of the firm is a product of two things: the firm's earnings and the multiple of those earnings. In this chapter, we address the question of a firm's multiplier. Why do some privately held companies sell for, say, four times adjusted EBITDA, while another sells for, say, six times adjusted EBITDA? If one were to believe that the selling price of a firm, its P/E, is in the lap of the gods, and individuals can do little if anything to change that valuation, then this chapter would be irrelevant. But I strongly believe that there are positive actions that management can take to improve their market price. *This is particularly true for smaller middle-market companies.* In other words, it is possible to make the company more attractive to a potential buyer.

To make the company "more attractive" there are a number of factors that can be "managed." True, like so many other parts of this book, this chapter also makes "common sense" suggestions, but very often, management forgets even the most obvious. So let's take a look at the factors that go into making up the firm's multiple.

THE COMPANY'S INDUSTRY

In what industry is your company classified? Industry is probably the most important determinant in setting the firm's multiple; at least it tends to determine the "ballpark." Think back to the craze in the late 1990s, when any stock was swept up if it were looked upon as an "Internet stock"! And conversely, look what happened after the bubble burst to those stocks that still had "dot.com" as part of their names. Rather like the early 1970s when "conglomerate" was a dirty word. But sometimes, the apparent industry classification is not necessarily the best industry—or only industry—for the company.

For example, there was once a company that was lightly (publicly) traded. This company manufactured mundane metal parts, things that would not get any financial analyst excited. But this company on its own developed a state-of-the-art line of dental equipment, including chairs and lights. This new line of business was selling well, so well, in fact, that the sales of this "attractive" dental equipment soon eclipsed the sales of its nondescript metal items. But, the market still classified this company as a manufacturer of run-of-the-mill metals parts. Apparently, the market did not classify this company in a P/E range that would have accorded the company a better price. The company was not classified as to *industry* correctly. In this case, the parent company probably should have spun off the attractive part of the business, dental equipment, and made it separate from the other mundane company. In this way the *combined* market value of both companies would have been larger.

Another example: I was touring a company for sale with another individual who was most recently the head of Corporate Development for a very large diversified company that had done many acquisitions. The company that was being visited manufactured three or four electronic devices, including transformers. Hardly the kind of equipment that would make one think that the company had something going for it that warranted anything special in the way of a market price. Not until this very savvy individual had an inspiration. This company could be called a "manufacturer of testing equipment," an industry that definitely had a higher multiple than a mundane manufacturer of ordinary electronic equipment. True, this might also mean that the company's marketing might also have to be turned around, but this was merely a detail. So what's in name? A lot!

For most entrepreneur/business owners, their company's industry classification is beyond some simple "fix." If it is a mundane industry, and if there is not much that can be done about it, what can the owner do to improve his or her "wealth," meaning the value of the company he or she owns? In this instance, the best thing to do is to use the earnings and/or value of this nondescript firm to acquire another firm that is in a better P/E industry. It is possible for a reasonably intelligent entrepreneur to acquire another company that will have a higher market value when it comes time to sell or "go public." If you, as an entrepreneur, are going to spend many years of your life managing a business, only to have to sell it for the lowest of multiples, why not "change horses" and find a company that can sell for, say, five or six times EBITDA. Certainly this sounds easier than it is, but it is *possible*!

THE PATTERN OF EARNINGS

While the "industry" into which the firm is assigned sets the ballpark for the multiple of EBITDA, the historical and forecast *earnings* that the company presents will be the next fine-tuning device. During the Internet bubble, many Internet-type stocks traded on sales growth irrespective of whether or not they were making any earnings. But those times are gone, for the most part. And when it comes to discussing a firm's earnings, there are a number of patterns that might be discerned.

THE "WHERE ARE YOU GOING?" PATTERN

This kind of pattern, depicted in Exhibit 18.1, leaves the observer with the logical question "Just where are this company's earnings heading?"

In this pattern someone looking at the 5 years' historical earnings would likely wonder whether this company's earnings are going to be negative or positive. Remember that people looking at your historical pattern of earnings are not clairvoyant. If they look at the pattern you give them to examine, and they cannot easily deduce the direction of earnings, they surely are not going to assume the best possible scenario. Instead, they will probably conclude that your company is not doing as well as you would like. But how does your company get its pattern of earnings? This is what was meant in Chapter 3 about "managing your earnings." The management of the firm, within the constraints imposed upon

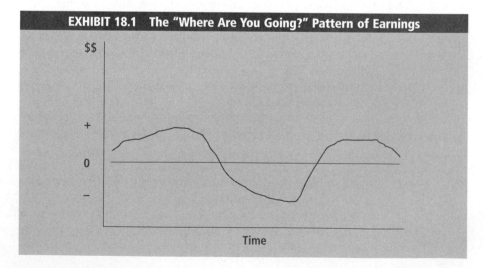

EXHIBIT 18.1   The "Where Are You Going?" Pattern of Earnings

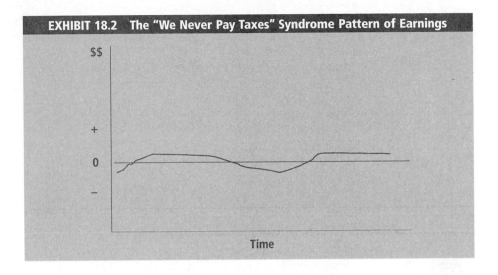

EXHIBIT 18.2   The "We Never Pay Taxes" Syndrome Pattern of Earnings

it, *sets* the pattern of earnings. And once you, the management, have set this pattern, it is not easy to change it once the "trail is laid."

THE "WE NEVER PAY TAXES" SYNDROME

Of course entrepreneurs do not like to pay taxes, but when it comes to selling your company, it had better be possible to explain away the lack of earnings. As Exhibit 18.2 shows, the company did not make very much, if anything, in the way of earnings.

Surely, this would convince anyone that this company does not pay any taxes to speak of. But can they show how they hide earnings? If this is a privately owned company and it is for sale, the owner(s) will probably have a chance to adjust EBITDA, but if this is a publicly owned company, it will be too late for explanations. Even if the company is privately owned, the "explanations" might be too embarrassing to reveal to a stranger (potential buyer). And by "too embarrassing" is also meant "too potentially dangerous," if the Internal Revenue Service should find out what was happening.

Another problem with this syndrome of not showing any earnings in order to avoid paying taxes is the situation that will confront the management of this company if they go to their bank and ask for a loan. How does one show the banker that the company can repay the loan if it does not have sufficient cash flow, which could be suggested by its earnings. Do you just wink when asked about the lack of earnings? Or, do you reveal the subterfuge that has been going on? In either case it would not look good for the management.

Another mistake a potential buyer wants to avoid is the situation where the seller explains that no profits were shown because of taxes but "don't worry, we take $5,000 a week out in cash that no one knows about." If you factor this "skimming" into your rate of return calculation, the company may look good.

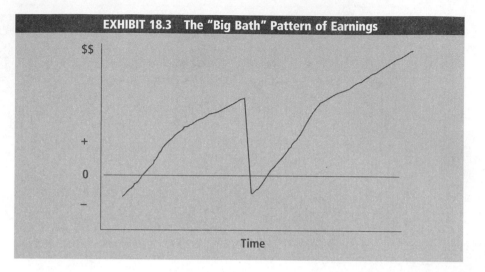

EXHIBIT 18.3   The "Big Bath" Pattern of Earnings

But what if you do not get this $5,000 a week? What can you do? Go back to the seller and complain? The seller might reply "What, didn't you get $5,000 a week? We always did!" And then what do you do?

THE "BIG BATH" PATTERN OF EARNINGS

As Exhibit 18.3 shows, the company had an unusual loss a year or two ago. Assuming the company's management can "explain away" this steep drop in earnings, perhaps as some extraordinary event, this "big bath" pattern should not hurt this company's valuation very much, if at all. And if this is a publicly held firm, this pattern of "nonoperating, extraordinary" loss is getting to be quite commonplace—especially in the bear market of 2000–2003. Broadcom, for example, wrote off $500 million of goodwill on its 2000 annual report, reducing its profit to virtually zero! Such a "nonoperating" loss might be a charge for "restructuring" or for writing off what would otherwise be goodwill in the acquisition of another company or a charge to correct for a pension fund discrepancy. These, and lots of other reasons, might account for this *one-time* steep drop in earnings. And, I repeat, this "big bath" pattern most likely will not hurt the company's value. As was mentioned in Chapter 3, a number of high-tech companies are taking a "bath" in this down market of 2001–2003 with an eye on bringing out really strong earnings in 2004 or beyond. Stronger earnings than they would have had had they not taken a financial bath.

THE "HOCKEY STICK" PATTERN

While on the subject of examining earnings' patterns, it is useful to comment on a pattern that might be exhibited by a company that you are attempting to

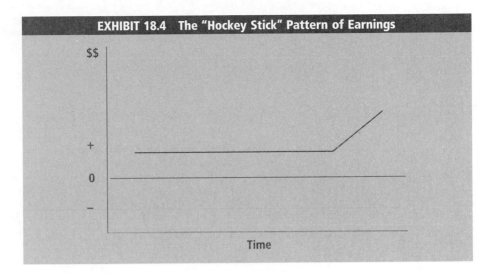

EXHIBIT 18.4   The "Hockey Stick" Pattern of Earnings

buy. This might be called the "hockey stick" pattern, for it looks like the shape in Exhibit 18.4.

Very often, when a company is put up for sale, particularly by a broker, it may be felt that it is desirable to project a good growth in earnings. So a year or two ahead of the sale, the company "finds" inventory that has been written off or otherwise disposed of over time. When this happens, the earnings suddenly come to life and the result is a "hockey stick" pattern. To check out whether this phenomenon is occurring, all you have to do is look at what has happened to the company's inventory from its Balance Sheet. If the inventory has gone up in tandem with the rise in earnings, the deception will be quickly revealed.

Another "trick" used by some brokers to sell a firm is to *project* the company's earnings with a "hockey stick." One large brokerage firm is known for making these kinds of projections on their client's earnings. They do this by making a lot of heroic assumptions about what the company's earnings will be when *you* are running the company. But why should any buyer want to pay for a company only in anticipation of what can be done when he or she owns the company? To me, this is a real pitch to what is called in the vernacular a "sucker." You have to be one to pay for these elevated earnings that are really nothing but a *projection* with you running the company. But hope springs eternal in the breast of many a broker!

THE IDEAL PATTERN

The "ideal" pattern would be one in which a normally intelligent person would extrapolate the earnings in a way that is complimentary to the company. Exhibit 18.5 shows one such pattern.

Perhaps one would argue that this pattern is too "ideal"; that someone would suspect that this pattern was "engineered." But if this pattern can be

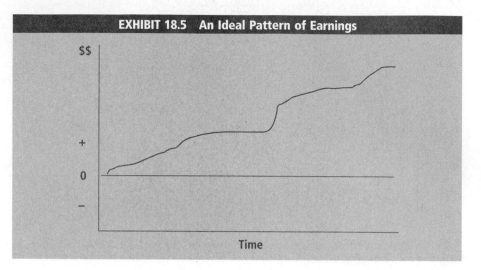

EXHIBIT 18.5   An Ideal Pattern of Earnings

reasonably explained, it would be easy for anyone to extrapolate these earnings into a very bright future for this company. If this were a private company, you expect this company to fetch a rather high multiple. But if history is a guide, the multiple may be higher, but not spectacularly so. But five times EBITDA is much higher than four times EBITDA! Of course, the higher the slope of the earnings line, the higher the multiple—assuming, of course, that the company's books were not "cooked." This is particularly true if the potential buyer is a strategic buyer instead of a LBO buyer.

ABSOLUTE EARNINGS PER SHARE

Although they are of no importance in a privately held company, in a publicly held firm, absolute earnings per share might somewhat influence the company's P/E ratio. This is because the desired price range for most types of stocks is, approximately, from $15 to $75. While less important today than it once was, in this range, an "even" lot of shares (100) would cost from $1,500 to $7,500, or what is considered (or used to be considered) to be within the range of *individual* buyers. (Of course, institutions, which usually prefer to buy blocks of stock over 1,000 shares, would not be affected by this generalization.) When the public company's stock price gets too low—whatever that means—it can effect a reverse split. You might get one share for every three you held. If the stock price gets too high—again whatever that means—then they might have a split up.▲

▲ If the transaction is a "stock split" there is no effect on the firm's Earned Surplus account; the number of shares is just increased. If the transaction is a "stock dividend" then a pro-rata amount will be deducted from the Earned Surplus account and used to increase the Capital Stock account. In the latter case this is called "capitalizing the earned surplus."

In the latter case this action usually connotes a sense of optimism by management and this usually results in a slightly higher P/E. In the former case, it may result in a lower P/E, but it makes the stock more respectable. It might escape the category of a very low-priced stock or even a penny stock. I once had a client who wanted to sell his company. He was approached by a publicly held company whose stock was selling at 75 cents per share. The owner dismissed the overture with the statement, "I don't think that's very good!" (Too bad he didn't take the offer. The publicly held company is now selling for about $25 per share.) Remember—in business, like in life, it's not really what you are, it's what people think you are.

Another more serious problem with having so many shares outstanding (such that your stock price is quite low, say, less than $1) is that of being delisted from NASDAQ. As will be mentioned more fully below, there are rules for a company to be listed on NASDAQ and one of them is that the price must be above $1 for a period of time. If the stock drops below this, and the company were delisted, the company would be placed on what is known as the "pink slip" or "bulletin board."[a] This will inhibit the trading of the stock somewhat—perhaps a lot. So it usually behooves the company to keep the number of shares high enough to avoid this problem. Of course, the reason for the low price in the stock might be operating losses or other "bad news" in the company. In this instance, merely changing the number of shares might have little effect on the value of the firm.

MANAGEMENT

How does your company's management *appear* to an outsider? Does it appear that your company has effective management? Does it appear that the company's management has everything under control? Does the company's management really appear to be professional? Whether the company is closely held or publicly held, an outsider's appraisal of management is crucial in the overall evaluation of the company. This includes not only the very top management but the second, and perhaps, third level of management as well. If this company got into trouble, would management be the company's strength or its weakness? And remember, it is the perception that makes the difference, not necessarily the facts.

STATE OF THE STOCK MARKET

For a publicly held firm, the state of the stock market is certainly something that must command management's attention. But if management feels that the company's stock is "high," what should this prompt management to

---

[a] During the serious bear market of 2001–2003—and maybe beyond—NASDAQ relaxed this rule for a number of stocks.

do? For a company that really wants to grow, this situation should present an opportunity to be somewhat creative. "Highly" priced stock—meaning a high P/E—is a tool for acquisition or, possibly, sale of more stock with judicious use made of the proceeds of the offering of new stock. By acquiring another firm with its stock that is "highly" valued, having a high P/E ratio, the company might validate the reason for the stock being valued highly. This is why Yahoo!'s acquisition of GeoCities made a lot of sense. Of course they paid a big premium for GeoCities, but they were playing with what's called in the vernacular "Chinese money," meaning currency that was grossly inflated in the 1930s. (This is *not* to imply that China's currency today is inflated!)

This strategy came back to haunt a lot of high-tech companies who deliberately *overpaid* for an acquisition because they were playing with Chinese money, so to speak. The new FASB made it necessary to evaluate the acquisition's value at the *new* time (when the statements were prepared) and write down the value of the acquired company against their current Income Statement.

Or, if an acquisition is not foreseen, then having a secondary offering and reinvesting the money in very profitable projects might also produce good results. To summarize this point, it behooves management to be aware of the state of the stock market and the company's own stock. If, for whatever reason, the market sends the company's P/E soaring, management had better do something proactive and not just sit back and "admire" the company's stock!

One individual took over a "turnaround" company and saw its stock rise dramatically. When it was suggested that the president do something proactive to "shore up" the company's earnings and, thus the stock—that is, do something with this apparently overvalued stock—he replied that he did not want to do anything "impulsive." He said that the company's stock was as "solid as Gibraltar." Shortly thereafter the company reported disappointing earnings and the stock dropped on a Friday from $35 to $19. On Monday the slide continued until the stock "bottomed out" at about $9. Solid indeed! This sounds like what happened to some of the Internet or computer stocks in the post 2000 period.

Whether or not a firm is listed on the New York Stock Exchange or NASDAQ is not as important today as it might once have been. With Microsoft on the NASDAQ and a lot of other very high value high-tech firms on the NASDAQ, this has brought a lot of respectability to what was once the "poor cousin."

When a firm thinks it might want to go onto the New York Stock Exchange or some other exchange, it will interview three possible specialists. The job of these "specialists" is to make an "orderly market" in the stock, selling when demand exceeds supply, and buying when sellers outnumber buyers, or, simply, matching buy and sell orders. The market crash of 1987 exposed the weakness of this specialist system when a few specialists simply ran out of money to support their stocks. The capitalization of specialists was definitely called into play. Today, numerous improvements in the specialist system go a long way toward correcting the failings of the past.

The NASDAQ is essentially a **quote-driven market,** meaning that the dealers are linked by computerized communications networks. On the NASDAQ there is an initial listing requirement that there will be three "market makers" in the stock. These "market makers" can match orders, or buy or sell for their own positions. Some of the more popular stocks have dozens of market makers working the stock. Obviously, with more market makers, the liquidity of the stock is improved. Also, more potential investment banking houses may recommend "buy" strategies. So, it behooves the company to do what it can to expand the number of market makers who are trading its stock. The NYSE is an **order-driven market,** meaning that with orders from a customer the specialist tries to fill the order.

The listing requirements for the NYSE differ depending on whether or not the applicant firm is domestic or foreign. Their requirements are found on their Web site, <http://www.nyse.com/listed/listed.html>. But, in general, they say that the company must be willing to keep the public informed on the progress of their affairs, and be a going concern. "Particular attention is given to such qualifications as:

1. The degree of national interest in the company;

2. Its relative position and stability in the industry; and

3. Whether it is engaged in an expanding industry, with prospects of at least maintaining its relative position."

There are numerous requirements for being listed on NASDAQ initially, and there are regulations for remaining on NASDAQ. These regulations may be found in detail at their Web site, <http://www.nasdaq.com/about/listing_information.stm>. In general, for *initial inclusion* these regulations require minimums on assets, shares of stock outstanding, and market value of all the stock.

A particularly important rule (usually) for continued inclusion is that the market price of the stock must be a minimum of $1 for a certain number of continuous trading days. Apparently, many of the firms that are "delisted" get into this position by not having the market price of their stock above $1 for the minimum period. There is some flexibility in this "minimum period" apparently, although the rule has been 10 trading days. For example, the minimum period of failure to meet the minimum bid price and market value of public float may be 30 days, with a 90-day warning period.

It is important for management to pay attention to these requirements, for as mentioned earlier, if they are not met, the company will be bumped off of the regular NASDAQ listing and be placed on the "pink slip" or the "bulletin board". That means that it will be harder for someone to get a quote on the stock and the price may suffer accordingly.

DIVIDENDS

It may be that if an emerging firm were to pay a cash dividend, it would, in effect, be saying that it had run out of investment opportunities within the firm. If it did this, the market might very well react negatively to such an announcement. Investors are investing in "emerging firms" for capital appreciation and not for dividend yield. This is one reason why the long-held notion of a reasonable P/E ratio for stocks is suspect today. Institutional investors do not need "current income" in the form of dividends to fulfill their investment goals. If they wish, they can sell some of the stock and, in so doing, make whatever "income" they might wish. So they are, in general, looking for appreciation in stocks. This excludes, of course, investment policies of funds that have as their goal strictly income. Another *bona fide* reason for paying a small cash dividend is that some funds are prohibited from investing in stocks that do not pay a dividend. So even though our developing firm is paying *only* a few cents per share, it is nominally complying with this requirement of some funds and, in so doing, expanding the market for its stock. Whether the proposal to make dividends deductible will spur emerging businesses to pay dividends is questioned for the reason cited above.

For an emerging firm—or a "growth" firm—to announce that they are "sharing" their good fortune with their stockholders would be misplaced good intentions. Instead, the market wants to hear other kinds of "good news." A prime example of another kind of good news would be an announcement of a stock split or stock dividend. This would be a way of saying to the market that the stockholders can expect continued increased earnings announcements or something akin to an earnings announcement such as an increase in market share or even sales. By declaring a stock dividend or split, thereby making the stock trade in the more popular range, as mentioned above, the company can expect to squeeze out of the market a slightly higher P/E ratio. This is in addition to the "good news" aspect.

THE DEBT/EQUITY RATIO

In Chapter 3, the firm's Debt/Equity ratio was discussed. There it was emphasized that no single ratio was nearly as important as this one. The Debt/Equity ratio is far and away a matter of great concern to management. But is it a critical determinant of a firm's market value? Yes, and no. Yes, because at the high extreme, the firm's Debt/Equity ratio could play a major role in determining the firm's market value. But other than that, it is quite questionable. When was the last time you bought a stock *because* of its Debt/Equity ratio? Or, did you even know what its D/E ratio was? Or, did you care? True, if the company was in big trouble, an astute investor would know this and factor this into his or her decision-making process. But whether a firm had a 40 percent D/E ratio or a 60 percent ratio, this fact in and of itself would hardly make any difference in the trading of a publicly traded company. If a publicly traded company has a "clean" Balance Sheet (as a firm's Balance Sheet with no long-term debt is called), and it is in a particularly volatile industry, such as recreational vehicles, then the "market" might reward it with a somewhat higher P/E ratio. Another reason for a "clean" Balance Sheet is that the firm is growing so fast that its cash flow could not support any debt-servicing payments. We saw this in Chapter 7 in our discussion of leverage.

With privately held firms, however, different D/E ratios are generally applied: Something like a 4 to 1 D/E ratio might be considered to be the limit of debt to equity. For many publicly held companies, this amount of debt to equity might be considered "extreme."

A common misconception among the owners of privately held firms is that debt "doesn't matter" when valuing the company. Nothing could be farther from the truth. The value of the firm, V, is equal to the value of the firm's debt (D) plus the value of the firm's equity (S). Thus:

$$V = D + S$$

For the management to "load up" on debt and then expect to sell the company for a price that disregards the debt is purely wishful thinking. In the vernacular of finance, you "already sold the company." When some owners have tried to retire and sell their company with a lot of debt on the company's books, this rude awakening has come as a shock. The company may not be worth anything close to enough for the owner to retire on what is left after paying taxes. So if a firm's owner is thinking of retiring and selling the business, it behooves him or her to reduce the firm's debt as the time for sale approaches. With the present difference between ordinary income and capital gains tax rates the way it is, paying dividends—with the usual "double tax" problem—would hardly be a substitute for selling at capital gains rates (unless the dividend is tax deductible). And even paying big bonuses is not as advantageous compared to selling at capital gains rates. So if the owner of a business is thinking of selling in the near future, it behooves him or her to reduce the firm's debt.

WHAT'S IN A NAME?

What's in a name? A lot and a little. Does a company's name matter? Sometimes Yes, and sometimes No. But this is no excuse for not giving a good deal of attention to the company's name. What does the company's name connote? If you are a food company, does your name connote that? Are you high-tech? Does your name indicate something hip to the high-tech crowd? Are you using an "old-fashioned" name for a new concept company? For a while any company with ".com" in their name prospered, then came the burst in the bubble. This same sort of thing occurred in the 1970s when any firm that even looked like a conglomerate was punished severely in their P/E.

Years ago, America went through phases where firms had to be called "International" something or "Industries." The word *industries* connoted diversification, which later became known as conglomerates. When conglomerates became a dirty word following the crash of the conglomerate stocks in the early 1970s, you could not insult a firm more than by referring to it as a *conglomerate*. Other phases followed. Animal names or names with an exclamation point sprung up all over the corporate landscape. "Quality Naturally! Foods" or, perhaps the most famous exclamation point name, Yahoo! "Master" was another phase. Companies were named "Flamemaster" or "Shufflemaster." This "master" tag was designed to indicate expertise in some field, and it seemed to work, at least for some. In the 1980s, "something-or-other-One" became quite popular. PlumbingOne or BankOne are examples. And then there was the phase of words with x's and y's and z's in their name. The infamous "ZZZZ Best" was an example. Or on the good side, Exxon.

And then there are the "big ego" and "little ego" names. The John T. Smith Co. would be an example of the *big ego* name. Calling the company the "Smith Co." would be an example of a *little ego* company. And, of course, naming a company today "Smith and Sons" labels the owner of this company as a male chauvinist or simply old-fashioned. It certainly would not be considered a modern or politically appropriate name. If the company is rather old and has "... and Sons" in the name, it might be acceptable, but not if the company were just named. Another problem with naming a company after the founder comes when the owner attempts to sell the company. Is this really a mom-and-pop business? If not, why is it named after the founder? How important is the founder to the success of the business? Fred Sands Realtors seemed like a reasonable name for a small real estate brokerage firm when it started years ago but as it grew larger, it presented real problems for it owner, Fred Sands. With adroit public relations work, the name survived without being too much of a hindrance, but it is probable that the owner wishes now that he had chosen a generic name, one that could be easily franchised, for example. Of course, they are franchising the company with its original name, so it proves that even an awkward name can survive and be all right.

Picking a name that tends to look like a well-known name is also quite commonplace. How many "Micro-somethings" do we have? Or the look-alike biotech names? And how about Internet suggestive names? If you have a ".net" or ".com" or "cyber" attached to your name, you are probably looking around for new name.

One aspect of naming a new company is the ease of remembering the name and pronouncing it. How will it look in print? Is it a name that people will think appropriate for the company? Does it fit what your company is doing? If you are high-tech, does the name sound high-tech? If you are biotech, does your name suggest biotech? This is what I mean by appropriateness. Also, the name should not necessarily be a "look-alike." And above all, it should not be really misleading. Possibly the most-noted example is the old Seaboard Airlines in the 1940s, which was a railroad, not an airline.

A major problem in naming a company is the ability to register in a desired state. And then there are the legal complications when it turns out that some little firm in some state is already so named. This can cause major firms enormous sums of money. They usually get around this problem by inventing a name.

GRAPHIC IMAGE

By graphic "image" is meant all those factors that influence whatever it is that can be seen that represents the company. This includes all signs and other exterior arrangements that project the corporate name. Most of the "exterior" image is, for many companies, the corporate name. But why is it that some emerging firms do not even have their name on the building? Obviously, there are exceptions, but to *not* have the company's name displayed in good taste is to miss an excellent opportunity to promote corporate goodwill and, quite importantly, personnel pride. To see a middle-market company without an exterior sign is to make one wonder just how cheap the owner must be. If he or she would just ask himself or herself the question "How would you like to work for a company that didn't even have its name on the building?" Or clothing certain workers in an attractive uniform might enhance the company's image.

If the company has delivery or other trucks, why not paint the company's name on the sides of these trucks? One sizeable clothing goods retailer had a number of delivery trucks, all completely devoid of any identifying marking because the owner of the company was so paranoid that the trucks would get stolen. The fact that the company had insurance against theft was beside the point. The owner just did not want the trucks stolen. The fact that he could have gotten substantial advertising by having the trucks painted apparently did not mean enough to suppress his paranoia. For some construction companies, painting their trucks is an open invitation to be taxed by some local city or municipal authority for "doing business" in their community. But recognizing this as an exception, the general point remains.

CORPORATE LOGO

For most people the corporate logo or symbol represents the company's name. How impressive is it? When asked about their logo, some business owners smile and, not modestly, admit that they designed it themselves. Unfortunately, many of these "homemade" logos look just that. There is a considerable amount of artistic know-how involved in making a good corporate symbol. For example, with color so popular today—for which we can thank Apple Computer—the logo's colors should be easily separated for printing. Also, the logo should be adaptable to media other than just paper. And the logo should not be misconstrued for that of another company. These and other reasons suggest that the expenditure of at least $5,000 or $10,000 for a professionally produced logo for a small or emerging middle-market firm might be a good investment for the long run. (For large or publicly owned firms, this amount might be ten or a hundred times this modest amount!)

One of the most important features of the company logo is appropriateness. How appropriate is the logo in conveying the "image" that the company wants projected? If the company is high-tech does the logo carry out this idea? Is it too demure? Or too traditional? Or too modern? If the company is trying to project a traditional image, can it still do this with a logo that will not appear "dated"?

CORPORATE STATIONERY

Nothing represents "image" as much as the company's stationery. This may be not only the first impression that one gets of the company, but the one and only image! Today, with the facility of computers and some wonderful software, almost anyone is "able" to design the company's stationery, but should just "anyone" do it? The one thing that the computer does not do is to impart a sense of class or real style to the stationery. This is the human ingredient. If someone has this sense of style and good taste, he or she can go ahead and design the company's stationery, but if not, this important job is best left for the professional graphic designer. Unfortunately, some people think they have a sense of style when they do not.

Stationery means not just the company's letterhead but all matter of printed goods, and all should be carefully designed and coordinated. Invoices and sale orders and personnel applications and everything else that is printed should be considered eligible for consideration. If something is *seen* by someone outside of the company, it is important! Who knows what piece of printed material will be the one to influence someone?

ANNUAL REPORT

For publicly held firms, the annual report should be looked upon as a chance to communicate with the company's stockholders and others in a meaningful way, and not just a nuisance. The amount of money spent on the annual report, however, should not be a question of "the more the merrier." The annual report does not have to be pretentious to be effective. In fact, a pretentious annual report speaks of a lack of judgment on the part of management. The report should be appropriate for the company in question. If you are a small developing firm, your report does not have to be the financial equivalent of a giant company. Good taste does not have to be expensive.

And instead of simply putting a cover on the company's 10-Q report, it would not take too much more to prepare an actual report to the shareholders complete with a review of the past year by the CEO. (This could be just a few pages inserted before the 10-K.) It is in this report to the stockholders that the management of the company can present their version of what happened in the past year, and not just leave this to the reader's conclusion by presenting the bare financial statements. If the past year was financially good, the company can extol this fact. If the past year was not as good as desired, the CEO can explain why the company did not perform as desired, that is it can put its own spin on the material. For large, publicly held firms, an attractive annual report is a given. But for many small publicly held but developing firms, the annual report is sometimes an afterthought. It should not be so.

What about a privately held company? Why should management take the time to write an annual report? There are lots of reasons for this. First, there is the impression this would make on the company's bankers. How many customers of a bank that are privately held take the time and effort to make an annual report? If a privately held company did this, it would surely distinguish its management as above-average. If the firm decides to go public or make a private placement, presenting an annual report, however brief, would also impress the investment banker with the professionalism of the management. A second reason would be if the company puts itself up for sale. Wouldn't it be a pleasant surprise to a potential buyer to be presented not just with the financials of the company, but a report of what happened during the years in question? But for management to say "But that's silly, we can remember what happened this year" fails to take account of the passage of time. Four or 5 years from now will the facts be as clear as they are now? Doubtful. So why not write a report on what happened during the past year when the facts and circumstances are fresh in management's mind?

FINANCIAL ANALYSTS MEETINGS

Every publicly held firm may have an opportunity to attend financial analysts meetings or meetings with large institutional investors throughout the country. As with annual reports, some of these meetings are a distraction and require a lot of preparation—two reasons management does not like them. But these meetings are a chance to tell your company's story and should not be missed if management is concerned about keeping the company's stock at as high a level as possible. How management deports itself at these meeting makes a big difference in most cases. A thoroughly professional "performance" before these discriminating analysts is the order of the day for management. A faulty and ill-prepared presentation will reflect badly on management, one of the most important factors determining the company's P/E ratio.

BEATING THE ANALYSTS' ESTIMATES

Every publicly held developing firm should be so lucky as to have financial analysts following the company and making estimates of what the company's earnings will be in the next reporting period. (This is one criterion for selecting an investment banking firm.) This would indicate that they are attracting the interest of these analysts and the market makers for whom they work. But in recent years, these analysts' estimates have become the "bogie" for which the company's chief financial officer shoots. Beat the analysts' estimates and your stock may go up, but there is a good chance that if all you do is meet the analysts' estimates, your stock will decline. This is particularly true if your company is in one of the high-tech or Internet fields. The investing public is usually investing on the assumption that your company will *beat* the analysts' estimates. So, it's a real game of cat and mouse. The *Wall Street Journal* quoted a finance official as saying: "If the Street's looking for 10 cents and you give them 9, you're a moron. If they're looking for 10 and you give them 11, you're a hero."▲

Analysts say they do not care if companies "lowball" their estimates, just so long as their report is better and the stock goes up! What they don't like is an estimate that is *not* met on the low side. The SEC has regulations regarding fallacious future estimates if they are too high. But, apparently, the regulations are a bit murky about low-ball estimates. So the game goes on with those public companies that are followed by analysts. Are the financial public relations firms that work for the company responsible? For the record, most will say they are not responsible for any really low estimates. But the jury is still out. Recently, the SEC has been casting a suspicious eye on some of these analysts who were still sending "buy" signals despite the declining market of 2000. Merrill Lynch has paid an enormous fine for their indiscretion. Fortunately, at least currently, this problem has not affected small emerging businesses.

FINANCIAL PUBLIC RELATIONS

Unless your company is one of that rare (and diminishing) breed of high-tech stocks that have to beat off the publicists with a stick, virtually every publicly held company needs to tell its "story" to the investing public. There are a number of financial public relations firms in every major city set up to cater to this need. Usually staffed by former writers and editors of major newspapers and business magazines, these professionals are able to get your company's story into print. They do this not only with well-written stories, but with the personal contacts they have with these newspapers and business magazines, some of which were their former employers. In fact, their reputation—and thus their price tag—is largely based on whom their former employers were. Usually the more prestigious the former employer, the more they can charge. This is because the company hiring this financial public relations firm assumes that the PR people involved will be able to get their story in their former employer's magazine or newspaper. This may or may not be true.

To say "All you have to do is a good job and people will notice you" is simply naïve. There are thousands of small developing companies in the stock market and why one does better, price-wise, than another is very often a matter of being noticed by the investing corps. You can have the finest product in your in-

▲ "Low-Balling: How Some Companies Send Stocks Aloft," *Wall Street Journal*, May 6, 1997, C1.

dustry and still not be selling for the kind of P/E ratio that you think is appropriate. The reason is that the investors have not been attracted to your company. To get noticed, firms need to tell their story through the media. And this kind of public relations does not need to be terribly expensive. Even small developing publicly held firms should be able to afford some sort of minimal coverage. For as little as $5,000 a month, a firm can have some coverage of its activities. If something really big breaks for the company, this coverage can be expanded as needed.

Companies should not forget general public relations if they are in an industry where something adverse could happen. For example, in the health care industry some patient might cause some catastrophe that would hit the press. Quick response would be needed and if the company does not have someone ready and able to respond, the consequences could be dire for the company. So money-saving miserliness would inflict a huge price of its own.

CORPORATE UNIQUENESS

What is it that is unique about your company? When someone asks the CEO of an emerging middle-market firm what is it different about his or her company, does that someone get an answer like "Well, we make a good product"? Of course, but so does everyone else! No, what is it that makes your company really different! What are some of the things that distinguish your company from all your competitors? Do you do something that no other competitor does? Is your quality demonstratively so different as to make your company "Number One" in some important classification? Have you qualified your product where no one else has? Do you have ISO 9000 certification? Do you have distribution that no other competitor has? Have you been written up in trade magazines? Do you have reprints ready for just such a question?

If you really want to reply to someone who asks "What's different about your company?", be ready with an answer that will leave them speechless. And why not? Aren't you the one who knows more about your company than anyone else? For some owners, this type of question takes them by surprise. But once you are forewarned, as you are now, you should have prepared an answer in advance.

SUMMARY

Selling a company is, for some, a once-in-a-life-time experience. It is no wonder that long-time owners are so amateurish about the process. But a little forethought can put a seller on top of any question asked. Amazing as it is, that when asked what is different about their privately held company, some owners say "Well, not very much, I guess." How do you expect to receive a better than average multiple of EBITDA if you, the owner, can't even think of what makes your company different? And it is not just the answer to this question that makes the difference between a three or four times multiple and five, six, or seven times your EBITDA! The *whole pattern* of earnings that you present to the possible buyer will make a big difference. Even the industry that you are apparently in will make a big difference. And if you happen to be in an industry that is characterized by a low multiple, use your company's cash flow and earnings (undistinguished as they may be) to buy another company in another field that will fetch a higher P/E when it comes time to sell, and, possibly retire. Others have done it, why can't you?

The pattern of earnings that a company presents is also crucial. In Chapter 3 we discussed managing the company's earnings. This does *not* mean hyping the earnings to unreasonable levels. But it does mean that top management must think about the trail of earnings they are laying. Once done, it is difficult or impossible to change. Top management should ask the question, "What would someone conclude when looking at the trail of earnings?"

What about the other things that potential buyers (and others) see? What is the graphic image of your company? Does it look like someone designed the corporate symbol in his or her spare time? Or does it make someone take notice of your company? How does your management look to outsiders? Do they appear to know what they are talking about? Are they really professional in their actions and deeds? If your firm is privately held and your personal name is in the company's name, it is critically important for you, the owner, to feature the expertise of the management staff so that your company does not look like a "mom-and-pop" business that is highly dependent on its founder. For example, an owner once contacted me to help him sell his business, an engineering consulting company. The name of the company was the man's full name. When I suggested that the company looked like a mom-and-pop business, the owner took offense. In order to make the management look "good" he showed me the company brochure. Sure enough, practically every page that featured a member of management also pictured the owner! He may have thought his company had "functional management" but the reader of this brochure would surely be left with the impression that the owner was "mighty important" to the company, if nothing else. What's wrong with a mom-and-pop firm? It is difficult to sell, at least for a premium price.

If your company is publicly held, what are you doing to enhance the company's P/E? Nothing? Many small, publicly held companies do precious little to make the market notice them. They are too stingy to hire a good financial public relations company to help tell their story to the investing public. And do they regularly make the financial analysts meetings?▲ Or do they even get asked? How is their presentation when they do get to make a presentation? Ama-

---

▲ Some developing publicly held firms try to avoid analysts meetings for fear that they will reveal information about the company that would assist competitors. This may be a good reason!

SUMMARY *(continued)*

teurish, or something less than really professional? Management can help convince any analyst that the company is in good hands; poor management may convince an analyst that even if the company is in a "good" industry, it will not go far because of diffident management. And remember, it is not what management really is, it is what people *think* your management is! *The difference between the apparent and the real.* And that's what this chapter was all about. Influencing the impression that one has of your company. If people *think* your company is really worth more, they will pay more for it; if they think you are "ordinary," they will pay only an *ordinary* price for your company, whether it be privately owned or publicly owned.

QUESTIONS FOR DISCUSSION

1. Suppose you buy a company in a mundane industry. How can you change this situation for yourself? How can you use this situation to get into a better P/E industry?
2. Discuss what the author means by "managing earnings" in your middle-market company. For what purpose would you be doing this? How do you do this?
3. If you were CEO of a privately owned firm, would you go to the trouble of making an annual report each year? Why?
4. If your company were an emerging publicly held firm, would you consider paying a dividend? If so, how much? Explain your reasoning.
5. What is meant by "managing your corporate image"? How can you do this? Suggest several ways.
6. If you are selling your company, and the potential buyer asks what is "different" about your company, how would you respond?
7. If you were thinking of starting a company, how would you go about naming this new company? What would be your line of reasoning? Does it make any difference?

18

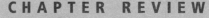

CHAPTER REVIEW

Epilogue

Valuation and What We Learned from the Dot.com Bust

If this epilogue were written in the early spring of 2000, I wonder what it would say. Would it be a complete recantation of all the principles that were espoused in this book? Would it say that doing a start-up was your divine right and that any old "dot .com" idea would fetch financing from "someone"? Would it say that making a profit was "dirty" and that we should disregard the adage that profit making was the point of free business enterprise? Would it say that "all we need is a share of this enormous market and we will be in 'fat city'"? With the advantage of hindsight, we look back on those halcyon days and say "How could we have been so wrong, so off base?"

Momentum—the word used then to explain the stock market of the 1990s—was also the explanation for our actions. This was the "New Way." Well, no "new way" lasts. As I said in Chapter 1, I truly believe that if you want a business, it is easier to buy an existing business—even if it is an Old Economy bricks-and-mortar manufacturing firm—than it is to do a start-up. Easier in the sense that it is emotionally, physically, and financially (most likely) easier. You should do a start-up only because it does not make sense to do anything else—that is, when it does not make sense to buy a similar business if there were one for sale. Software houses are a good example: If an individual were to buy such a business it would involve buying a considerable amount of "goodwill," something no intelligent individual investor would back. Or perhaps a shampoo company. When John Paul Mitchell Systems was started, the entrepreneurs had only $700. *Buying* a similar company was out of the question.

Am I saying that it is ridiculous to try to start a New Economy company? Of course I am not. The "new economy" is not going away even though the dot.com bubble has burst. No more so than saying the Internet is going away. It is here to stay, and as long as there are creative people, there will be new ideas on how to capitalize on it. No, rather what I am saying is that the idea that you have for the new start-up had better be a "pain killer" and not another "vitamin" that would be nice, but not necessary.

Of course, this is true if you look for outside financing. The angels have also been taught a lesson and they are not about to invest new, "good" money into a scheme that does not look—no, *look* is much too soft a word, demonstrate may be better—to be quite profitable. Yes, there is still some start-up money available, but you had better have an excellent idea *and* some experience—or track record—to back up your idea.

No longer are angels and venture capitalists gullible enough to invest money in a start-up being managed by a group of really young "computer-niks," by people who "know a gigabyte from a drill bit." Oh, yes, they know all about the ins and outs of the Internet and how to design a computer program to do what they want. But do they know anything about managing a new and emerging business? A reviewer of this book said that if more entrepreneurs had read this book (and taken to heart what it said) there would be fewer dead dot.coms littering the landscape.

HARVESTING

And then there was "harvesting," that magic word that drove all wannabe millionaires in the dot.com era. You would start a company and in a matter of a relatively few months, you would take the company public and reap—harvest—a fortune. How many of us know of someone who invested a $100,000 in April, saw a chance to sell the company for $10 million in October—but smartly refused—only to be taken "public" in November for 70 times their initial investment of $100,000? These stories were sufficiently plentiful to light a fire in the heart of any wannabe entrepreneur. Was the idea realistic, with a chance to really make a profit in the near future? Who cared?

When someone commented on this book and said there was not enough attention devoted to "harvesting," I wanted to write back and ask Have you looked at a calendar lately? Or, where have you been for the past few years? Oh, yes, there will be an IPO market again, but until that comes, there will not be any real "harvesting" of relatively new firms. And when the day comes when there is a chance to take your firm public for a respectively decent P/E, do you think that investors will forget the fleecing they took in the popping of the dot.com bubble? Hardly! Oh yes, there will be "excesses" again, as long as there are human beings with human memories, and not robots that don't forget. But one should not start out today thinking that that day is close at hand.

"VALUATION, THAT'S WHAT IT IS ALL ABOUT"

Remember when New Economy companies were valued at multiples of Price/Dreams? Remember valuations that were based on "imagining" how big the market was going to be ("and we are going to take a big piece of it")? To those people who were steeped in these notions of valuations, the pedestrian discussion of valuation in this book would have seemed like ancient history. Not at all "hip"! Well, hip or not, foolish valuations are a thing of the past—for now! Performing discounted cash flow on "imaginary profits" from "imaginary markets" will not stimulate an audience of investors now. Hard-nosed, realistic profit expectations are *de rigueur* now. Furthermore, as mentioned in Chapter 2, angels and venture capitalists are going to use profit as a rule of thumb, more than likely, when they talk to an entrepreneur about the value of a certain company. This may seem to dreamers to be "unrealistic" but it is the way it is!

To savvy investors of the 1990s, there were two important lessons they learned: (1) misestimation of the size of the market, and (2) misjudgment of the speed at which competitors can move into a market. In the first case, investors imagined huge markets that never realized anything like what was hoped for. To be sure, smart investors *want* a big market for the company and/or its product, or they will not invest. But in light of recent experience, they are more conservative in estimating the market size. In the second case, they learned the lesson not to believe in a wannabe entrepreneur when he or she says "there is no competition." Maybe today there isn't, but just get in there and show—prove out—a market, and there may be formidable competitors.

Index

Abandonment value, 155–156, 159
Able Case
  ability to service commitments,
    405–406
  addressing questions asked in,
    387–395
    determining ceiling value, 389–391
    determining floor price, 388–389
    raising money on company assets,
      391–394
    syndicating equity, 394–395
  background of company, 382–384
  bank's requirements, 404–405
  concluding details, 406–407
  financing alternative, 407
  financing summary, 399–401
  interpretation of background
    information, 384–387
  offer letter, 401–404
  structuring the deal, 395–399
    other expenses, 397
    soft dollars, 396–397
    subordinated note, 398–399
    valuing soft-dollar contracts,
      397–398
Absolute earnings per share, 416–417
Absolute priority in bankruptcy, 64
Accelerated Depreciation, 59–60, 165
Acceptance of Letter of Credit, 287
Accountants method, 125
Accountant's review, 356
Accounting, S-X, 190
Accounting book value of acquisition,
  363
Accounting firms, finding LBO target
  through, 351
Accounting Principals Board Ruling
  Number 15, 215
Accounting system, 70
Accounts Payable, forecasting, 104, 107
Accounts Receivable, 9
  elasticity of cash discount versus
    volume of, 321, 322
  eligible, 259–262
    concentration factor and, 261
    diffusion factor and, 261–262
    government, 260–261
    service companies and, 260
  factoring, 269–271
    with or without notification, 270
    with or without recourse, 270
  forecasting, 102, 104
  as hockable asset, 340
  managing, 317–332
    cash discount analysis, 318–322
    cash discount period, 323–324
    collection effort, 327–329
    credit-granting decision rule,
      329–332

credit period, 324–327
  pledging
    in Able Case, 391, 393
    to banks, 259–263
    to finance companies, 268–269
    sensitivity to, 90, 91, 98
Accounts Receivable Plans, 262–263
Accounts Receivable Turnover, 102
Accredited investors, 189
Accrued Taxes, forecasting, 103
Acid Test Ratio, 65
Acquisition
  start-up versus, 2–3
  See also Leveraged Buy Out
Actual Letters of Credit, standby versus,
  282
Ad hoc capital budgeting, 152, 153
Adjusted book value of acquisition,
  365–367
  in Able Case, 389
  inventory and equipment, 365–366
  liabilities, 366–367
Adjusted EBITDA, 367
  in Able Case, 390
Advertising, 10–11
Affirmative covenants, 243
After-tax earnings, 27
Alcar model, Rappaport's, 380–381
Alliance of Angels, 33
Amazon.com, 11, 75, 132, 245
American Appraisal Co., 266
AMEX, listing on, 185
Amortization of principal, 165, 168
Andreessen, Marc, 75
Angel round money, 37
Angels, 6, 33–34, 45
Annual report and corporate image,
  424–425
Annuity, 133
  table of Present Worth (Value) of, 140
AOL, 132, 249, 315
Apple Computer, 423
Appraisal companies, 266
Appraisals
  factors influencing, 266–267
  in Leveraged Buy Out, 357–358
Appraisal Surplus, 67
Appraisers, types of, 266
Approach letter, in Leveraged Buy Out,
  355–356
Arbitrage, 210
Arbitrageurs, 210
Arnold, Jasper H., 243, 244, 246, 247
Arnold, Jerry L., 189
ASK, Inc., 40
Asset-based lending, 260
Asset efficiency, 53
Assets
  hidden, 342

hockable, 340–341
  preservation of, in negative covenants,
    246–247
  priorities of, 64
  purchase/sale of, in LBO, 370–371
    advantages and disadvantages of,
      371–373
  raising money on, in Able Case,
    391–394
  Return on, 51, 52
  verification of, in LBO, 357–358
Assignment of proceeds, 261, 292
At auction quick sale value, 266
Audited Statement, 69–70, 71
Auto-by-Tel, 245
Autodesk, 18
Average Rate of Return, 125–126, 129

BA (Banker's Acceptances), 280, 311–312
Babies 'R' Us, 132
Back-to-Back Letters of Credit, 291–292
Bad debt expense
  collection effort versus, 329
  credit period versus, 326
  reduction in cash discount versus,
    321–322
Balance Sheet, 5, 61–67
  Cash account in, 62–63
  cash flow and, 76–77
  current portion of Long-term Debt in,
    63–65
  Debt/Equity Ratio, 66–67
  example of, 52
  General Creditor Ratio, 65–66
  money market securities in, 63
  period-to-period changes in, 79
  preservation of, in negative covenants,
    245–246
Band of Angels, 33
Bankers
  building rapport with, 257–258
  choosing, 256–257
Banker's Acceptances (BA), 280,
  311–312
Bank loans, 237–239, 254–258
  psychology of obtaining, 254–258
  signature, 258
Bank note, 311
Bank of America, 256
Bankruptcy, priorities of assets in, 64
Banks
  combination, 255–256
  finding LBO target through, 351
  priorities of, versus finance compa-
    nies, 272–273
  retail, 254–255
  wholesale-oriented, 255
Baringer, Bruce R., 117
Bartz, Carol, 18

Basic idea for start-up. *See* Idea for start-up
Basic Profitability, 6–7
Basis, 370
Baskin, Jonathon Barron, 227
Bath, financial. *See* Financial baths
Bell, Alexander Graham, 23
Below investment grade (BIG) bonds, 236, 240–241
Bennett, Barbara, 293
Best efforts offering, 196–197
Bezos, Jeff, 75
BIG (below investment grade) bonds, 236, 240–241
Biotech startups, sequencing of financing in, 32–34
Block, Frank, 165
Bond funds, junk, 236, 238
Bonds
    below investment grade, 236, 240–241
    collateral trust, 206
    convertible, 208–210
        Diluted Earnings Per Share for, 215
        interest rate on, 213, 214
        variations in, 216–221
    deep discount, 217–218
    guaranteed, 206
    income, 206–207
    joint, 206
    junk, 185, 241
    mortgage, 206
    notes versus, 231
    public, 237, 238
    ratings of, 212
        criteria for, 223–224
    receivables backed, 232
    spreads between grades of, 242
    unsecured. *See* Debentures
    with warrants, 210–214
        Diluted Earnings Per Share for, 215–216
        interest rate on, 213–214
        "in the money," 211–212
        number of warrants with, 212–213
        variations in, 216–221
    zero coupon, 217–218
Bonnett, David, 14
Book value of acquisition
    accounting, 363
    adjusted, 365–367
    in Able Case, 389
Bootstrapping, 32
Breakeven chart
    cash, 178, 180
    cash-flow with NOCF", 179
    with probability density function, 175, 176, 177
    with sales and total costs, 173
    with shift in probability density function, 179
    with shift in profit-loss line, 174
    traditional, 173
Brokers
    business opportunity, 349–350
    merger and acquisition, 350–351

Budgeting, capital. *See* Capital budgeting
Bullington, Robert, 223–224
Burn rate, 29, 44
Business opportunity brokers, 349–350
Business plan. *See* Private Placement Memorandum
Buy.com, 7, 44
Buy-Sell Agreement, 403, 406–407
Calculation of abandonment value, 155–156

Call, 208
Callable preferred stock, 228
Call date, first, 208
Call premium, 208
Capital
    Cost of, 126
    start-up. *See* Start-up financing
    sunk, 9–11
    venture. *See* Venture capital
    working, 9
Capital Asset Pricing Model (CAPM), 161–162
Capital budgeting, 119
    ad hoc, 152, 153
    criteria for, 122–124, 129
    decisions in, 154–156
    meaning of, 120–124
    methods of rationing money for, 124–129
    money available for, 120–122
Capital budgeting models
    computerized, 145–152
    conventional versus, 141–142
    format for comparison in, 142–143
    Hertz, 158–161
    internal rate of return in, 143–144
    practical importance of, 154
    using, without computer, 152–154
    Weston's CAPM, 161–162
Capital intensity, 9–11
Capital investment, 10
Capitalizing earned surplus, 416
Capital structure
    complex, 215
    optimal, 172
CAPM (Capital Asset Pricing Model), 161–162
Captive finance company, 310
Carey, Mark, 237
Case, Steve, 315
Cash Account, 62–63
    backing up, 306–307
    in Cash Flow Statement, 81
    determining optimal level of, 301–304
Cash balance
    Daily Opening, 302
    maximum negative, 30
Cash discount
    analysis of, 318–322
    computer use in, 323
    defined, 318
    elasticity with respect to, 318–322

reduction in, versus bad debt expense, 321–322
Cash discount period, 323–324
Cash flow approach to financial leverage, 168–172
Cash FlowCast©, 30, 31, 405
Cash flow deals, 341
Cash flow loan, 238
Cash flows
    concept of, 165
    controllable variables in, 302–303
    control of, in negative covenants, 244–245
    as criteria for Leveraged Buy Out, 342–343
    discounting, 120
    discretionary outflows, 80–81, 82
    dissynchronization in, 303–306
    financial, 81
    forecasting, 99–108
        ratio approach and regression compared, 107–108, 110
        ratio approach to, 102–104
        with regression analysis, 104–107
    Free, 82
    importance of, 76–77
    leverage and, 177–178
    measures of, 82–83
        evaluating, 82
        under growth scenario, 88–92
        under recession scenario, 92, 94, 96–99, 100–101
        under steady sales scenario, 83–88
    Net Operating. *See* NOCF; NOCF'; NOCF"
    operating inflows, 79
    operating outflows, 79–80
    priority outflows, 80
    random variables in, 301–302
    time shape of, 123–124, 129, 142, 146–148, 153, 154
Cash Flow Statement, 65
    capital budgeting and, 120
    components of, 77–81
    items not included in, 108
Cash management, 299–306
    determining optimal amount of cash, 301–304
    overdrawing and, 300–301
    payment with drafts, 306
    reducing dissynchronization, 304–306
CDs (Negotiable Time Certificates of Deposit), 311
Ceiling price, 362
    determining, 367–368
        in Able Case, 389–391
    negotiating between floor and, 368–369
Certificates of Deposit, Negotiable Time, 311
Certified Statement, 69–70, 71
CF (cost and freight), 286

Change
  minus positive (minus delta sign), 79
  period-to-period, 79
Character, of key person, 17–19
Charisma, of key person, 17
Chase Manhattan, 255
Chinese money, 47, 418
CIF (cost, insurance, freight), 286
Cisco Systems, 315
Citibank, 255
CitiCorp, 72
Clark, Jim, 16, 75
Classified stock
  creating, 228–229
  uses for, 229–230
  warning about, 230–231
Classify the loan, 167
Claw back provisions, 218–219
Clean Letters of Credit, 293–295
  documentary versus, 282
CMOs (collateralized mortgage
  obligations), 232, 238
Coefficient of Diffusion, 149, 153, 154
  CAPM and, 162
  Hertz model and, 160–161
  plotting Expected Rate of Return with,
    151
Coefficient of Variation, 159–160
Collateral, 238
Collateralized mortgage obligations
  (CMOs), 232, 238
Collateral mortgage obligations, 206
Collateral trust bond, 206
Collection effort, 327–329
  bad debt expense versus, 329
  Net Income versus, 328
  ROA and rate of return on sales ver-
    sus, 328–329
  sales versus, 327–328
Combination banks, 255–256
Commercial paper, 308–310
Commitment
  firm, versus best offering, 196–197
  letter of, 196
Common stock
  historical perspective and, 222,
    224–225
  modifying, 225–226
Common stock equivalents, 215
Company name, effect of, on multiplier,
  421–423
Competitiveness, of key person, 17
Compiled Statement, 68–69, 71, 365
Completed Contract Method of report-
  ing sales, 55
Compound interest, 129, 133, 135
CompuServe, 249
Concentration factor, 261, 289, 358
Conditioning, of key person, 15–16
Confidence, of key person, 16
Confidence scale, investor, 38–39
Confirmed Letters of Credit, noncon-
  firmed versus, 282–283
Conglomerates, evolution of, 337–339

Consulting services contract, 376–377,
  396, 398
Contingency amount, 30
Contingent liability, 372–373, 374, 399,
  401, 403
Convertible bonds
  Diluted Earnings Per Share for, 215
  interest rate on, 213, 214
Convertible debentures, 208–210
  arbitrage and, 210
  exercise price for stock in, 209–210
Convertible preferred stock, 228
Convertibles, 207
  synthetic, 210
  zero coupon, 217–218
Conway, Dolores, 149
Cooked books, 51
Cooper, Dan W., 227
Copeland, Tom, 380
Corporate logo and image, 423–424
Corporate stationery and image, 424
Corporate uniqueness, 427
Corporations commission, state,
  185–186
Cost
  fixed, 60
  going-in, 146, 152
  opportunity. See Opportunity cost
  variable, 60
Cost of Capital, 126
Cost of Goods Sold, 56–58
  forecasting, 102–103, 104–105
  sensitivity to, 88, 90, 92, 94
Cost-Volume-Profit Analysis, 172–174
Cottle, Sidney, 165
Coupon rate, 210
Courage, of key person, 17
Covariance, 149, 154, 162
Covenants, loan, 237, 238
  affirmative, 243
  negative, 244–248
    asset preservation in, 246–247
    balance sheet preservation in,
      245–246
    cash flow control in, 244–245
    strategy control in, 245
    trigger in, 244, 247–248
  representations and warranties in, 243
  strategy for contending with, 248–250
Credit, Letters of. See Letters of Credit
Credit crunch, 236, 240
Credit-granting decision rule, 329–332
  abbreviated, 330–331
  implications of, 331–332
Credit market
  characteristics of, 237–239
  evolution of, 239–242
  life insurance companies and,
    239–241
Creditors, claims of, in bankruptcy, 64
Credit period, 324–327
  bad debt expense versus, 326
  effect of, on volume of receivables,
    326, 327

Cumulative preferred stock, 227
Cumulative probability distribution,
  159
Current Assets, 64
Current portion of Long-term Debt,
  63–65
Current Ratio, 63
  liquidation and, 63–65
Customer concentration, 358
Customer satisfaction, in assessing LBO
  target, 358

Daily Opening Cash Balance, 302
Days Inventory On Hand (DIOH), 104
Days Sales Outstanding (DSO), 102
Debentures, 206, 238
  convertible, 208–210
Debt
  heterogeneity of, 168–170
  long-term
    current portion of, 63–65
    in Leveraged Buy Out, 341
  Subordinated, 66, 67, 214
Debt/Equity Ratio, 61–62, 66–67, 163,
  168
  in Able Case, 404
  effect of, on multiplier, 420–421
  and Modigliani and Miller approach
    to financial leverage, 166–168
Debt securities
  innovative, 231–232
  payment in kind," 231–232
  See also Bonds; Debentures; Notes
Debt service, in growth scenario, 88
Debt servicing capacity, simulation of,
  170–171
Decelerated Depreciation, 61
Deep discount bonds, 217–218
De facto equity, 66, 67, 232, 399
Deferred payment of Letter of Credit,
  287, 290
Deferred Tax Liability, Reserve for, 108,
  366
Deficiency letters, 185
Definitive Buy-Sell Agreement, 403
De Joria, John Paul, 9, 32–33
Delta sign, minus, 79
Demand, elasticity of, 318–322
Demand deposit notes, 311
Demand-driven product, 6
Demand effect, 326, 327
Department of Corporations, state,
  185–186
Deposit notes, 311
Depreciation, 59–61
  Accelerated, 59–60, 165
  Cash Flow Statement and, 79–80
  Decelerated, 61
  Net Income Plus, 166
  Reserve for, 108
  straight line, 59–60, 371
  Unit, 60–61
Depreciation recapture, 370–371
Detachable warrants, 210–211

Diffusion
  Coefficient of, 149, 153, 154,
    160–161, 162
  Index of, 149–151, 152
Diffusion factor, 261–262
Dillon-Gage Securities Inc., 197
Diluted Earnings Per Share, 215–216
Dilutions, 28
Discounting cash flows, 120
Discount the draft, 280
Discretionary outflows, 80–81
  Nec Discretionary, 82, 169
Dissynchronization, 303–304
  reducing, 304–306
Dividend
  effect of, on multiplier, 420
  liquidating, 370
Documentary Letters of Credit, clean
  versus, 282
Documents on Approval, 280, 296
Documents on Payment, 280, 295–296
Dodd, 165
Domestic Letters of Credit, 279,
  289–291
Dot-com bubble
  reflections on, 44–46
  valuation and, 430–432
Dot-com companies
  advertising by, 11
  multiplier and, 411
  public offerings by, 188
  revenue reporting by, 59
  See also New Economy start-up
Double Declining Balance, 61
Drafts, payment with, 306
Drexel-Burnham Lambert, 236, 241
Due diligence process, 356–359
  in Able Case, 401–403
  asset verification and appraisal in,
    357–358
  "cook books" for, 358–359
  customer satisfaction in, 358
  summary of, 359
  verifying financial statements,
    356–357
Duff and Phelps, 309
DuPont formula for profit, 53–54

Early Adopters, 131
Early Majority, 131
Earnings
  desired versus expected, 118–120
  growth of, 116. *See also* Growth
  mean, 148–149
  patterns of, 412–416
    "big bath," 414
    "hockey stick," 414–415
    ideal, 415–416
    "We never pay taxes," 413–414
    "Where are you going?" 412–413
  pop in, 336, 337–338
  Retained, 108
Earnings Before Interest and Taxes
  (EBIT), 76, 82, 83, 165–166

Earnings Before Interest and Taxes plus
  Depreciation and Amortization
  (EBITDA), 83, 166
  adjusted, 367
  in Able Case, 390
  multiple of. *See* Multiplier
Earnings Coverage, 164, 165
Earnings gap, 117, 119
  filling, 148–149, 153
Earnings Per Share, 119, 215–216
  absolute, 416–417
  diluted, 215–216
EBay, 18, 132
EBIT. *See* Earnings Before Interest and
  Taxes
EBITDA. *See* Earnings Before Interest
  and Taxes plus Depreciation and
  Amortization
Economic value, book value versus, 363
Economy
  New, 2, 431
  Old, 3
Efficiency
  asset, 53
  operating, 53
Efficiency Frontier, 151
  in Hertz model, 160
Elastic demand, 319
Elasticity of credit period, 325
Elasticity of demand, 318
  cash discount and, 318–320
    versus pretax income, 320–321
    versus volume of receivables, 321
  determinants of, 318–322
  of NOCF versus cash discount, 321
Elevator pitch, 14
Eligible receivables, 259–262
  concentration factor and, 261
  diffusion factor and, 261–262
  government accounts, 260–261
  service companies and, 260
Enron, 55
Entrepreneurial capital budgeting
  model. *See* Capital budgeting
  models
Equipment
  appraisal costs on, 267
  borrowing on, in Able Case, 392, 393
  borrowing percentage on, 267
  as hockable asset, 340
  in Leveraged Buy Out, 365–366
Equipment financing, 265–267
Equity
  de facto, 66, 67, 232, 399
  offer of, to investors, 26–28
  Return on, 51, 52
  syndicating, in Able Case, 394–395
  trading on. *See* Financial leverage
Equity holders, 64
ERR. *See* Expected Rate of Return
Ethics
  in accounting practices, 51
  in inventory valuation, 58–59
  in revenue reporting, 59

EToys, 8, 199
Evans, George Heberton, Jr., 227
Evergreen loans, 258
Ex ante rate of return, 128
Excess of Purchase Price Over Asset
  Value, 368
Exercise price, for stock in convertible
  bond, 209–210
Exit strategies, 12–13, 47
Expected gain, 329
Expected loss, 329
Expected Rate of Return (ERR),
  144, 152
  in CAPM, 161–162
  in Hertz model, 159
  plotting Coefficient of Diffusion with,
    151
  of Set of Proposals, 145
  weighting proposals', 145
Export-Import Bank, 274
Ex post rate of return, 128
External growth, 117
Face value, of bond, 211
Factoring Accounts Receivable, 269–271
  in garment industry, 269–270
  with or without notification, 270
  with or without recourse, 270
Farmer's Home Loan Administration,
  274
FASB (Financial Accounting Standards
  Board), 77, 215
Federal Reserve Float, playing, 305–306
Field warehouses, 265
FIFO (First-In, First-Out) Method of
  valuing inventory, 56, 264, 365
Finance companies
  borrowing from, 268–271
  captive, 310
  priorities of, versus banks, 272–273
Financial Accounting Standards Board
  (FASB), 77, 215
Financial analysts meetings, 425–426
Financial baths, 70–72
  value of firm and, 414
Financial commercial paper, 308
Financial flows, 81
Financial leverage, 163, 164–172
  cash flow approach to, 168–172
  Debt/Equity Ratio and Modigliani
    and Miller approach to,
    166–168
  traditional approach to, 164–166
Financial Management Rate of Return,
  128
Financial public relations, 426–427
Financials, pro-forma, 31, 35
Financial Statements
  tax statements versus, 68–73
  types of, 68–70, 71
  verifying, in LBO, 356–357
  who should prepare, 73
  write-offs on, 70–72
  See also Balance Sheet; Cash Flow
    Statement; Income Statement

Financial summary
  discussion of start-up money needed,
    30–35
  pro-forma financials in, 35
  sales and profit forecast in, 26–30
Financing
  equipment, 265–267
  government sources of short-term,
    273–274
  growth, 8
  inventory, 263–265
  mezzanine, 393–394
  piggy-back, 225–226
  rounds of, 28
  running out of, 34–35
  second-stage, 34, 37–38
  self-, 13
  sequencing of, 31–34
  start-up. See Start-up financing
  with venture capital, 36–41
Financing Statement, 253
Finnerty, John D., 232
Firm commitment, best offering versus,
  196–197
First call date, 208
First mover, 13, 44
Fitch, 212, 309
Fixed cost, 60
Float, Federal Reserve, 305–306
Floating rate notes, 232, 311
Floor price, 362
  calculating, 363–364
    in Able Case, 388–389
    accounting book value, 363
    liquidation value, 364
    market value, 363–364
    replacement value, 364
  negotiating between ceiling and,
    368–369
FloTech, 32
Followers, 131
Ford, Henry, 57
Ford Motor Company, 57, 261
Forecast
  profit, 26–30
  sales, 24, 26–30
Forecasting
  cash flow components, 99–108
    ratio approach and regression com-
      pared, 107–108, 110
    ratio approach to, 102–104
    with regression analysis, 104–107
Fraudulent conveyance, 373–374
Free Cash Flow, 82
Free money market securities, 306
Full Disclosure, 185
Functional management, 5
Funded reserve, 209
Funny money, 215
Future value, 133

GAAP. See Generally Accepted Accounting Practice
Garage Technology Ventures, 34

Garment industry, factoring in,
  269–270
Gates, Bill, 200
Gateway, 12
General and Administrative Expense,
  forecasting, 103, 105–106
General Creditor Ratio, 65–66
General Creditors, 64
General Electric Capital, 268
Generally Accepted Accounting Practice
  (GAAP), 58–59, 68–69, 70
  S-X accounting versus, 190
General obligation, 313
General Subordination, 67
GeoCities, 418
Going-in costs, 146, 152
Goodwill, 3, 71, 72, 368, 371, 397
Go public, 13, 184
  via back door, 198–201
  See also Initial public offering; Public
    offerings
Government Accounts Receivable,
  260–261
Government sources of short-term
  financing, 273–274
Graham, 165
Graphic image of company, 423–425
Greening, Daniel W., 117
Grinder, Brian, 227
Gross Profit, 6, 7, 56–58
  negative, 7
Growing a firm, 117
  by improvisation, 132
  purpose of, 117–118
  Technology Adoption Life Cycle
    method of, 131
Growth
  cash flow during, 88–92
  debt servicing capacity during,
    170–171
  desired versus expected, 118–120
  external, 117
  internal, 117
  meaning of, 116–117
  "more of the same," 118–119
  in "net-centric" environment, 315
  shifting for, 18
Guaranteed bonds, 206
Guarantees, insistance on, 272
Gumpert, David E., 37

Hammond, Mike, 12
Hard money, 229
Harvesting, 47, 431
Hertz, David B., 158
Heterogeneity of debt, 168–170
Hidden assets, 342
Highly elastic demand, 319
Highly leveraged transactions (HLTs),
  220, 236, 240
High-tech startup. See New Economy
  startup
HLTs (highly leveraged transactions),
  220, 236, 240

Hockable assets, 340–341
H & R Block, 119

Idea for start-up, 3
  criteria for, 4–15
  explaining, 14–15
  implementing, 16
Idealab, 27
Illegal Redemption, 373
Image of company
  annual report and, 424–425
  corporate uniqueness and, 427
  financial analysts meetings and,
    425–426
  financial public relations and,
    426–427
  graphic, 423–425
  logo and, 423–424
  name and, 421–423
  stationery and, 424
Income
  elasticity of cash discount versus pre-
    tax, 320–321
  Other, forecasting, 102
Income bond, 206–207
Income notes, 207
Income Statement, 50
  Balance Sheet versus, 61
  Cost of Goods Sold in, 56–58
  Depreciation Expense in, 59–61
  example of, 52
  Gross Profit in, 56–58
  Inventory valuation in, 58–59
  managing, 54–61
  revenue reporting in, 59
  Sales in, 54–56
  sample, 54
Indenture, 223–224
Index of Diffusion, 149–151
  estimating, 152
Industrial commercial paper, 308
Industry classification, effect of, on
  firm's multiplier, 411–412
Inelastic demand, 319
Information intensity of firm, 236
Ingram Group, 75
Initial public offering (IPO), 13, 28, 33,
  47, 187
  selling preparations for, 197–198
  See also Go public; Public offerings
Initial start-up financing, 8
Innovators, 131
Inquiry Form, 253–254
Insider information, 187
Insistance on guarantees, 272
Inspection certificate, 281
Installment Method of reporting sales,
  55–56
Integration, vertical, 117
Intel, 132
Intellectual property, 34
Interest
  compound, 133, 135
  compound versus simple, 129

Interest rate, of bonds, 213–214
Interest rate swap, 311
Intermediary, role of, 39–41
Intermediate-term lending, 235
  firm size and, 236–237
Internal growth, 117
Internal Rate of Return (IRR), 125,
    127–128, 129
  calculating, 129, 137–138
    in entrepreneurial model, 143
  in CAPM, 161
  deriving, in entrepreneurial model,
    144
  in Hertz model, 159
  mean, 144
  modal, 144
  with abandonment value, 156
  without abandonment value, 155
International Letters of Credit, 279
Internet Age, growth in, 315
Introduction, of Private Placement
    Memorandum, 22
Inventory, 9
  forecasting, 103–104, 106
  as hockable asset, 340–341
  obsolete, 56–57
  pledging
    in Able Case, 392, 393
    to banks, 263–264
    to finance companies, 271
  sensitivity to, 90–92
  turnover ratio of, in LBO, 365
  "writing down," 58
Inventory financing, 263–265
  criteria for, 264
  other than pledging, 265
Inventory valuation, 56–58
  financing and, 264
  in Leveraged Buy Out, 365–366
  unethical aspects of, 58–59
Investment
  capital, 10
  getting out of, 12–13
  Return on, 51, 52, 53–54
Investment banker. *See* Underwriter
Investment banking industry,
    organization of, 193–195
Investment hurdle rates, in CAPM, 162
Investor confidence scale, 38–39
Investors
  accredited, 189
  sophisticated, 189
IPO. *See* Initial public offering
Irreversibility problem, 105
Irrevocable Letters of Credit, revocable
    versus, 281–282

IRR. *See* Internal Rate of Return
Job shop products, 384
John Paul Mitchell Systems Inc., 9,
    32–33, 431
Joint bond, 206
Junk bond funds, 236, 238
Junk bonds, 185, 241

Kenney, George, 14
Key person, 3
  discussion of, in Private Placement
    Memorandum, 24–26
  evaluating, 15–19
King makers, 131
Kinko's Graphics, 13
Knockdown quick sale value, 266
Kurtzig, Sandra, 16, 40, 200

Late Majority, 131
LBO. *See* Leveraged Buy Out
L/C. *See* Letters of Credit
LEAPS, 211
Lease-buy decision, 155
Lenks, Toby, 8
Lettered stock, 186, 339
Letter of Commitment, 196
Letters of Credit (L/C), 278
  acceptance of, 287
  advantages of, 291–295
  application for, 283–287
  Back-to-Back, 291–292
  costs of, 289
  deferred payment of, 287, 290
  features of, 287–289
  meaning of, 279
  negotiation of, 287
  payment at sight of, 280, 287
  revolving, 290, 292–293
  transferrable, 292
  types of, 279–283
    actual, 282
    clean, 282, 293–295
    confirmed, 282–283
    documentary, 282
    Domestic, 279, 289–291
    International, 279
    irrevocable, 281–282
    nonconfirmed, 282–283
    revocable, 281–282
    standby, 282, 290–291
  use of, 280–281
Leverage, 32–33
  financial, 163, 164–172
    cash flow approach to, 168–172
    Debt/Equity Ratio and Modigliani
      and Miller approach to, 166–168
    traditional approach to, 164–166
  meaning of, 163–164
  operating, 164, 172–180
    cash flow and, 177–178
    certain sales versus probabilistic
      sales, 174–177
    Cost-Volume-Profit Analysis,
      172–174
Leveraged buildup, 337
Leveraged Buy Out (LBO), 336
  Able case study of. *See* Able Case
  adjusting book value for, 365–367
    inventory and equipment, 365–366
    liabilities, 366–367
  Alcar model for valuing acquisitions,
    380–381

approach letter in, 355–356
  calculating ceiling price for, 367–368
  calculating floor price for, 363–364
    accounting book value, 363
    liquidation value, 364
    market value, 363–364
    replacement value, 364
  criteria for, 339–348
    cash flow, 342–343
    compelling reason to sell, 344–345
    hockable assets, 340–341
    long-term debt, 341
    long-term future, 346–347
    pollution problems, 345–346
    quiet deal, 347–348
    size, 343–344
    status as old firm, 341–342
    type of company, 344
  due diligence process in, 356–359
    asset verification and appraisal,
      357–358
    "cook books," 358–359
    customer satisfaction, 358
    summary of, 359
    verifying financial statements,
      356–357
  finding a target for, 348–354
    ads in publications, 349
    banks and major accounting firms,
      351
    business brokers, 349–351
    manufacturers' directory, 352–354
    personal knowledge, 348–349
    trust companies, 351–352
  forms of transaction for, 369–375
    fraudulent conveyance, 373–374
    purchase/sale of assets, 370–373
    purchase/sale of stock, 374–375
    right of offset clause, 373
  negotiating between floor and ceiling,
    368–369
  soft dollars in, 375–377
Liabilities
  contingent, 372–373, 374, 399, 401,
    403
  in Leveraged Buy Out, 366–367
LIBOR (London Bank Offering Rate), 228
Life insurance companies, credit market
    and, 239–241
LIFO (Last-In, First-Out) Method of
    valuing inventory, 56, 264, 365
Limited Liability Company, 15
Line of credit, revolving, 292–293
Liquidating dividend, 370
Liquidation, Current Ratio and, 63–65
Liquidation preference, 229
Liquidation value, 265, 340
  of acquisition, 364
Liquidators, 266
Liquid Yield Option Notes (LYONs), 218
Loan(s)
  asset-based, 260
  bank, 237–239, 254–258
    psychology of obtaining, 254–258
    signature, 258

cash flow, 238
classify the, 167
evergreen, 258
intermediate-term, 235
revolver, 247
term, 235
Loan committee, 256
Loan covenants. *See* Covenants, loan
Loan from Stockholder, 366
Loan officer, 256
Loan rates, prime, 308
Lock box, 304–305
Logo, corporate, and image, 423–424
London Bank Offering Rate (LIBOR), 228
Long-term Debt
current portion of, 63–65
in Leveraged Buy Out, 341
Long-term option, 211
LYONs (Liquid Yield Option Notes), 218

MACRS (Modified Accelerated Cost Recovery System), 59–60
Macy, Granger, 117
Magnification of change in earnings, 164, 172
Management
effect of, on multiplier, 417
functional, 5
Management team, 3, 19
discussion of, in Private Placement Memorandum, 24–26
Manufacturer's Bank, 255
Manufacturers' directory, finding LBO target in, 352–354
Manufacturing company
cash flow of
under growth scenario, 88–92
under recession scenario, 96–99
under steady sales scenario, 84, 85
Margin accounts, 312
Margin requirements, 207
Marimba, 294
Marketable Securities Account, in Cash Flow Statement, 81
Marketing, discussion of, in Private Placement Memorandum, 24
Marketing research, 8, 24
Market maker, 200–201, 419
Market openers, 131
Market Out Clause, 196
Market price appraisal, 266
Market share, 7, 44
growth and, 116–117
Market size, 7–9
Market value
of acquisition, 363–364
of business, 116
of real estate, 340
Markowitz, Harry, 142, 149, 154
Marshall and Stevens, 266
Master Limited Partnership, 14
Maximum negative cash balance, 30
McNealy, Scott, 315

Mean difference test, 147, 148–149
Mean earnings, 148–149
Mean IRR, 144
Meister, William Von, 16, 200
Merger, 339
Merger and acquisition brokers, 350–351
Merrill Lynch, 218
Mezzanine financing, 393–394
Microsoft, 132, 315
Milken, Michael, 236
Miller, Gene, 45–46
Miller, Merton, 166–168
Minnie Pearl's Chicken, 55
Minus positive change (minus delta sign), 79
Mitchell, Paul, 32–33
Modal IRR, 144
Modified Accelerated Cost Recovery System (MACRS), 59–60
Modigliani, Franco, 166–168
Modigliani and Miller approach to financial leverage, 166–168
Mom-and-pop organization, 4–5
Money market funds, 307
Money market preferred stock, 228, 314
Money market securities, 63, 306–307
appropriate for M_o and M_c account, 307–314
bank deposit notes, 311
banker's acceptances, 311–312
CDs, 311
commercial paper, 308–310
money market preferreds, 314
repurchase agreements, 312–313
short-term municipal notes, 313
free, 306
where to procure, 314–315
Monte Carlo Simulation, 159
Moody's, 212, 309
Moore, Geoffrey, 131
Morris, John, 14, 230
Mortgage bonds, 206
Mortgage obligations
collateral, 206
collateralized, 232, 238
Multiple roots, 127
Multiplier, 27, 410
factors determining
absolute earnings per share, 416–417
corporate uniqueness, 427
Debt/Equity Ratio, 420–421
dividends, 420
financial analysts meetings, 425–426
financial public relations, 426–427
graphic image, 423–425
industry classification, 411–412
management, 417
name of company, 421–423
pattern of earnings, 412–416
stock market, 417–419
Municipal notes, short-term, 313
Murray, Roger, 165

Murrin, Jack, 380
Mutual California Bank, 255
Myers, Stewart C., 168, 172

Name of company, effect of, on multiplier, 421–423
NASDAQ, listing on, 185, 418–419
National Appraisers Association, 267
NcNally, Scott, 200
Nec Discretionary, 82, 169
Negative cash balance, maximum, 30
Negative covenants, 244–248
asset preservation in, 246–247
balance sheet preservation in, 245–246
cash flow control in, 244–245
strategy control in, 245
trigger in, 244, 247–248
Negative gross profit, 7
Negative pledge clause, 246
Negotiable Time Certificates of Deposit (CDs), 311
Negotiation of Letter of Credit, 287
Net Change in Cash and Money Market Securities Accounts, 81
Net Income, 29
collection effort versus, 328
elasticity of credit period versus, 325
Net Income Plus Depreciation (NIPD), 76, 82, 83, 166
Net Operating Cash Flow. *See* NOCF; NOCF'; NOCF"
Net Present Value (NPV), 126–129
Netscape, 75, 132, 249
Net Worth, 5
New Economy, 2, 431
New Economy start-up
acquisition versus, 2
business plan for, 22
getting investment out of, 12
investor confidence and, 39
profitability of, 6
selling, 5
sequencing of financing in, 32–34
See also Dot.com bubble; Dot.com companies
New York Stock Exchange, listing on, 185, 418–419
NIFO (Next-In-First-Out) inventory valuation, 365
NIPD. *See* Net Income Plus Depreciation
NOCF, 76, 80, 169
elasticity of, versus cash discount, 321, 322
NOCF', 81, 120–121
NOCF", 76, 168, 169–172, 177–178
defined, 82
in growth scenario, 88–92
probability density function and, 178–180
in recession scenario, 96–99
in steady sales scenario, 84–88
Noncallable preferred stock, 228

Noncompete agreement, 376, 396, 398
Nonconfirmed Letters of Credit, confirmed versus, 282–283
Nonconvertible preferred stock, 228
Noncumulative preferred stock, 227
Nondetachable warrants, 211
Notes
    bank, 311
    bonds versus, 231
    deposit, 311
    floating rate, 232
    income, 207
    Liquid Yield Option, 218
    short-term municipal, 313
    subordinated, 375, 398–399,
        400, 403
    zero coupon, 218
Notification, factoring with or without,
    270
NPV (Net Present Value), 126–129

Obsolete inventory, 56–57
Offer letter, 401–404
Old Economy, 3
Omidyar, Pierre, 18
One-product firm, 11
Open book credit, 289
Operating cash inflows, 79
Operating cash outflows, 79–80
Operating efficiency, 53
Operating leverage, 164, 172–180
    cash flow and, 177–178
    certain sales versus probabilistic sales,
        174–177
    Cost-Volume-Profit Analysis, 172–174
Operations, 80
Opportunity cost, 10, 123, 146, 299, 344
    of funds, 318, 330
Optimization process, 54
Option
    long-term, 211
    put, 314
Oracle, 315
Order-driven market, 419
Orderly resale value, 266, 267, 340
Organization
    form of, 4–5
    functional management, 5
    mom-and-pop, 4–5
Other Income, forecasting, 102
Outline, of Private Placement Memorandum, 22–26
Outstanding stock, 29

Package, 3. See also Private Placement
    Memorandum
Palm Springs Golf Co., 197
Partnership, Master Limited, 14
Par value, 224
Patents
    pros and cons of, 23–24
    royalty on, 377, 396–397, 398
Payback, 124–125, 129
    Relative, 124

Payment at sight of Letter of Credit, 280,
    287
Payment in kind (PIK) securities,
    231–232
Percentage of Completion Method of reporting sales, 54–55
Period-to-period change, 79
Perpetuity, 133
Personalty, 64, 252
Piggy-back financing, 225–226
PIK (payment in kind) securities,
    231–232
Pledging, 259
    accounts receivable
        to banks, 259–263
        to finance companies, 268–269
    factoring versus, 269
    inventory
        to banks, 263–264
        to finance companies, 271
Polese, Kim, 294
Pollution, by LBO target, 345–346
Pooling of interest, 339
Pop in earnings, 336, 337–338
Portfolio, 154
Portfolio Effect, 153, 155, 160, 162
Pounce value, 63
PR decision rule, 26
Preemptive right, 224
Preferred stock, 226–231
    callable, 228
    convertible, 228
    cumulative, 227
    dichotomizing, 227–228
    money market, 228, 314
    noncallable, 228
    nonconvertible, 228
    noncumulative, 227
    puttable, 228
Prepaid Expense, forecasting, 104, 107
Present Value, solving problems in,
    133–140
Present Worth (Value) of an Annuity
    table, 140
Present Worth (Value) table, 139
Pretax income, elasticity of cash discount versus, 320–321
Price
    ceiling. See Ceiling price
    floor. See Floor price
Pricing, 6–7
Prime loan rates, 308
Priorities of assets, 64
Priority Claims, 64
Priority outflows, 80
Private placement market, 235–236
Private Placement Memorandum, 3,
    21–35
    outline of, 22–26
    pro-forma financials in, 35
    sales and profit forecast in, 26–30
    start-up money needed in, 30–35
Private placements, 187–188
    characteristics of, 237, 238–239

gross issuance of, 240
    by nonfinancial issuers, 241
    non-insurance-company sources of,
        241–242
    public versus, 184
    registration of, 189–190
Probability density function, 174–177
    NOCF" and, 178–180
Probability distribution, cumulative,
    159
Prodigy, 249
Product
    demand-driven, 6
    discussion of, in Private Placement
        Memorandum, 22–24
    job shop, 384
    one, firm relying on, 11
    out-of-vogue, 14
    proprietary, 384
    too simple, 13–14
Profit
    concept of, 50–54
    DuPont formula for, 53–54
    Gross, 6, 7, 56–58
    managing, 50
        "cooked books" versus, 51
    market share versus, 116–117
    negative gross, 7
Profitability
    Basic, 6–7
    as capital budgeting criteria, 122, 129
    measures of, 51–53
Profitability Index, 127
Profitability statement, implications of,
    26–28
Profit and Loss Statement. See Income
    Statement
Profit forecast, in Private Placement
    Memorandum, 26–30
Pro-forma financials, 31, 35
Promotional stock, 229
Proprietary parts, 384
Prospectus, 185
    Red Herring, 198
Prowse, Stephen, 236, 237, 239, 240
Public bonds, characteristics of, 237,
    238
Public offerings, 188–189
    private versus, 184
Public relations, financial, 426–427
Public warehouses, 265
Purchase/sale of assets, 370–374
Purchase/sale of stock, 374–375
Purchase transactions, 339
    in Leveraged Buy Out, 369–377
Put option, 314
Puttable preferred stock, 228

Quick sale value, 265, 266, 267, 340
    knockdown (at auction), 266
Quote-driven market, 419

Rappaport, Alfred, 380–381
Rappaport's Alcar model, 380–381

Rate of return, 28
Average, 125–126, 129
ex ante, 128
Expected. *See* Expected Rate of Return
ex post, 128
Financial Management, 128
Internal. *See* Internal Rate of Return
Ratio approach to forecasting cash flow, 102–104
regression analysis compared to, 107–108, 110
Real bills doctrine, 263
Real estate
borrowing on, in Able Case, 392–393
as hockable asset, 340
Real Estate Investment Trust (REIT), 212, 271
Realty, 252
Receivables-backed bonds, 232
Recession
cash flow during, 92, 94, 96–99, 100–101
debt servicing capacity during, 170–171
Recourse, factoring with or without, 270
Red Herring prospectus, 198
Registration
of private placements, 189–190
public, of securities, 190–192
S-1, 190–191
S-18, 191–192
Regression analysis for forecasting cash flow, 104–107
ratio approach compared to, 107–108, 110
Regulation D of Securities and Exchange Commission, 189, 204
Reinvestment rate, 128
REIT (Real Estate Investment Trust), 212, 271
Relative Payback, 124
Relative priority in bankruptcy, 64
Repeat orders, single sale versus, 11
Replacement value, of acquisition, 364
Repos, 312–313
Representations, in loan covenants, 243
Repurchase, share, 119
Repurchase Agreements, 312–313
Required Rate of Return (RRR), 161–162
Resale value
inventory, 264
orderly, 266, 267, 340
Research, marketing, 8, 24
Reserve, 366
funded, 209
Reserve for Deferred Tax Liability, 108, 366
Reserve for Depreciation, 108
Retail banks, 254–255
Retained Earnings, 108
Return
Average Rate of, 125–126, 129
ex ante rate of, 128

Expected Rate of. *See* Expected Rate of Return
ex post rate of, 128
Financial Management Rate of, 128
Internal Rate of. *See* Internal Rate of Return
rate of, 28
Return on Assets (ROA), 51, 52
collection effort versus, 328–329
elasticity of, versus increase in credit period, 325–326
Return on Equity, 51, 52
Return on Investment (ROI), 51, 52
DuPont formula for, 53–54
Return on Sales, 51, 52
collection effort versus, 328–329
Revenue enhancement, practices of, 59
Revenue recognition, 59
Reverse, 313
Reviewed Statement, 69, 71
Revocable Letters of Credit, irrevocable versus, 281–282
Revolver loan, 247
Right of offset, 64, 373, 399, 403
ROA. *See* Return on Assets
Robinson Patman Act (1936), 247, 269
ROI. *See* Return on Investment
Roll, Richard, 167
Ross, Stephen, 168
Rounds of financing, 28
Royalty on patents, 377, 396–397, 398
RRR (Required Rate of Return), 161–162
Rule of 16, 14
Rule of 78, 272–273
Rural Business-Cooperative Service, 274

S-1 registration, 190–191
S-18 registration, 191–192
Sales
certain versus probabilistic, 174–177
collection effort versus, 327–328
elasticity of cash discount with respect to, 319
elasticity of credit period versus, 325
repeat, 11
reporting, 54–56
Return on, 51, 52
collection effort versus, 328–329
steady
cash flow and, 83–88
debt servicing capacity and, 170–171
Sales forecast, 24
in Private Placement Memorandum, 26–30
Sarbanes-Oxley law, 73
SBICs (Small Business Investment Companies), 274
Scripophily.com, 199
Search Fund Model, 75, 354
Second-stage financing, 34, 37–38
Secured Creditors' Claims, 64
Secured interest, 63–64
Securities
debt. *See* Bonds; Debentures; Notes

innovation in, 222–225
money market, 63
preparations for selling, 197–198
public registration of, 190–192
regulations on selling, 184–192
sweetened, 205
historical perspective on, 205–208
Securities Act (1933), Rule 144 of, 186, 339
Securities and Exchange Commission, 184
earnings estimates and, 426
public registration of securities with, 190–192
registration of private placements with, 189–190
Regulation D of, 189, 204
state corporations commission versus, 185–186
Security Agreement, 253
Seed money, 37
Self-financing, 13
Selling expense, 11
forecasting, 103, 106
Service company
cash flow of
under growth scenario, 92, 95
under recession scenario, 99, 101
under steady sales scenario, 84, 87–88
pledging receivables of, 260
Sexism, 294
Shadow warrants, 219–220
calculating number of, 220–221
Share repurchase, 119
Shell corporation, 198
Sherman Antitrust Act, 247
Shippers, 268
Short-term municipal notes, 313
Signature loans, 258
Silicone Valley Bank, 34
Silicon Graphics, 75
Simple interest, 129
Sinking fund, 165, 168, 209
Small Business Administration, financing from, 273–274
Small Business Investment Companies (SBICs), 274
Smith, Adam, 263
Soft dollars, 374, 375–377
in Able Case, 396–398
Sophisticated investor, 189
Sotheby's, 132
Sources and Applications of Funds Statement, 77
SOYD (Sum-of-the-Years-Digits), 61
Specific Subordination, 67
Staging financing, 31–34
Stakeholders, 68
Standard and Poors, 212, 223, 309
Standby Letters of Credit, 290–291
actual versus, 282

Start-up
  basic idea for, 3, 4–15, 16
  ingredients for doing, 3
  New Economy. *See* New Economy
    start-up
  order of ingredients in, 3–4
  reasons for doing, 2–4
Start-up financing
  amount needed for, 30–35
  initial, 8
  strategies for finding, 38–41
State corporations commission, Securities and Exchange Commission versus, 185–186
Stationery, corporate, and image, 424
Stewart, G. Bennett, 380
Stigum, Marcia, 307, 311
Stock
  classified, 228–231
  common. *See* Common stock
  dividing (example), 28–30
  lettered, 186, 339
  outstanding, 29
  preferred. *See* Preferred stock
  promotional, 229
  purchase/sale of, in LBO, 374–375
Stock market, effect of, on multiplier, 417–419
Straight line depreciation, 59–60, 371
Strategy
  control of, in negative covenants, 245
  for dealing with covenants, 248–250
Subordinated Creditors, 64
Subordinated Debt, 66, 214
  types of, 67
Subordinated note, 375
  in Able Case, 398–399, 400, 403
Summary, of Private Placement Memorandum, 22
Sum-of-the-Years-Digits (SOYD), 61
Sunk capital, 9–11
Sun Microsystems, 315
Surplus
  Appraisal, 67
  capitalizing earned, 416
Sweep accounts, 62, 81, 299–300
Sweetened securities, 205
  historical perspective on, 205–208
Sweeteners, in perspective, 221–222
S-X accounting, 190, 191
Syndicate, 198
Syndication, 394–395
Synthetic convertible, 210

TALC (Technology Adoption Life Cycle), 131
Tauber Aarons, 266
Taxes
  in Able Case, 399
  depreciation recapture, 370–371
  forecasting, 103

Leveraged Buy Outs and, 372
  selling firm and, 413–414
Tax Liability, Reserve for Deferred, 108, 366
Tax Reform Act (1986), 39, 55
Tax Statements, 68
  Financial Statements versus, 68–73
T-bills, 307
Tech Coast Angels, 33–34
Techies, 131
Technological obsolescence and development, 156
Technology Adoption Life Cycle (TALC), 131
Tender offer, 208
Term loan, 235
Texas Instruments, 12
Times Burden Earned, 165
Time shape of cash flow
  as capital budgeting criteria, 123–124, 129
  in entrepreneurial capital budgeting model, 146–148, 153, 154
Times Interest Earned, 164, 166
  in Able Case, 405
Time value of money, as capital budgeting criteria, 122–123, 129
Time Warner, 132, 249, 315
Timmons, Jeffrey A., 37
Title to goods in Letters of Credit, 289
Tombstone ad, 194
Toys 'R' Us, 132
Track record, 19
Trading on equity. *See* Financial leverage
Transshipment, 285–286
Trigger, pulling, 244, 247–248
Trust companies, finding LBO target through, 351–352
Turnaround state, 60–61
Turnover, 324
  inventory, in LBO, 365

UCC 1, 253
UCC 2, 253
UCC 3, 253–254
Udell, Gregory, 237
Underwriter
  classified by size, 193–194
  importance of quality of, 195
  selecting, 192–198
  structure of, 194–195
Uniform Commercial Code, 252–254
  forms related to, 253–254
Unit depreciation, 60–61
Unsecured bonds. *See* Debentures
Used equipment dealers, 266
Usury laws, 324

Valuation, 28–30, 34
  of acquisition. *See* Leveraged Buy Out
  of closely held company, 362–363

dot.com bust and, 430–432
  illustrative model of, 48–49
  inventory, 56–58
  See also Multiplier
VanHorne, James, 149
Variable cost, 60
Venture capital, 3
  financing with, 36–41
  strategies for finding, 38–41
  types of, 37–38
Venture capitalist confidence scale, 38–39
Venture capitalists, entry of, 33, 34
Vertical integration, 117

Waitt, Ted, 12
Walker, John, 18
Wall Street Arithmetic, 70, 71
Wall Street Journal, ads for businesses for sale in, 349
Warehousing, 265
Warranties, in loan covenants, 243
Warrants, 208
  bonds with, 210–214
    Diluted Earnings Per Share for, 215–216
    interest rate on, 213–214
    "in the money," 211–212
    number of warrants with, 212–213
    variations in, 216–221
  detachable, 210–211
  exchangeable, 217
  meaning of, 210–211
  nondetachable, 211
  shadow, 219–220
    calculating number of, 220–221
Weighting Expected Rates of Return, 145
Wells Fargo, 256
Westerfield, Randolph, 168
Weston, J. Fred, 161–162
Weston's CAPM model, 161–162
White Knight, 209
White paper, 70, 191
Wholesale company
  cash flow of
    under growth scenario, 92, 93, 94
    under recession scenario, 99, 100
    under steady sales scenario, 84, 86
Wholesale-oriented banks, 255
Women entrepreneurs, 294
Working capital, 9
Work In Process, 55
Worshow, 266
Write-offs, 70–72

Yahoo!, 418, 422
Yazdipour, Rassoul, 12, 16

Zero coupon bonds, 217–218
Zero coupon convertibles, 217–218
Zero coupon note, 218